N 0098088 9

THE VICTORIA HISTORY
OF THE
COUNTIES OF ENGLAND

A HISTORY OF
LEICESTERSHIRE

VOLUME III

Old Factories on the Grand Union Canal at Leicester

From a water-colour by G. M. Henton

THE VICTORIA HISTORY OF THE COUNTIES OF ENGLAND

EDITED BY R. B. PUGH, M.A., F.S.A.

PUBLISHED FOR
THE UNIVERSITY OF LONDON
INSTITUTE OF HISTORICAL RESEARCH
REPRINTED FROM THE ORIGINAL EDITION OF 1955
BY
DAWSONS OF PALL MALL
LONDON
1969

Published by the
Oxford University Press
in 1955

Reprinted for the University of London
Institute of Historical Research
by
Dawsons of Pall Mall
16 *Pall Mall, London, S.W.* 1

SBN: 7129 0369 0

Reprinted by Stephen Austin and Sons Ltd., Caxton Hill, Hertford

A HISTORY OF THE COUNTY OF LEICESTER

EDITED BY W. G. HOSKINS, M.A., PH.D.
AND R. A. McKINLEY, M.A.

VOLUME III

PUBLISHED FOR
THE UNIVERSITY OF LONDON
INSTITUTE OF HISTORICAL RESEARCH
REPRINTED BY
DAWSONS OF PALL MALL
LONDON

INSCRIBED TO THE

MEMORY OF HER LATE MAJESTY

QUEEN VICTORIA

WHO GRACIOUSLY GAVE THE TITLE TO

AND ACCEPTED THE DEDICATION

OF THIS HISTORY

CONTENTS OF VOLUME THREE

CONTENTS OF VOLUME THREE

LIST OF ILLUSTRATIONS

The frontispiece, the plate facing page 241 and the photographs facing page 111 are reproduced by courtesy of the Leicester Museums and Art Gallery Committee. The originals of the first two are in the Leicester Art Gallery. The photographs facing pages 14 and 110 are reproduced by courtesy of the *Leicester Mercury* and the *Leicester Evening Mail* respectively. The photographs facing pages 30, 31 and 58 were taken by Mr. F. L. Attenborough, and are reproduced by his permission. The plates facing page 240 are reproduced by courtesy of Mr. V. R. Pochin, the owner of the originals now at Barkby Hall.

LIST OF MAPS

The maps illustrating the chapter on Population were drawn by Mr. C. T. Smith. That on page 128 is based upon the published maps of the Geological Survey of Great Britain by permission of the Director and of the Controller of H.M. Stationery Office, Crown copyright reserved. All the other maps were drawn by Mr. T. Garfield.

EDITORIAL NOTE

THE system on which this volume has been compiled and edited is the same as that described in the editorial note to the second volume of the *Victoria History of Leicestershire*. The same group of Leicestershire patrons, under the distinguished chairmanship of Sir Robert Martin, have continued their generous grants for the support of a local editor, and the University of London has watched over the whole enterprise and published the results. Thus the merits of a partnership between the University and a local committee are further demonstrated.

The volume, like its predecessor, was planned by Dr. W. G. Hoskins, while still Reader in English Local History at University College, Leicester, and he was able to edit parts of it before his departure for Oxford. His work was completed by Mr. R. A. McKinley. Dr. Hoskins and Mr. McKinley may thus be looked upon in their several ways as joint local editors, though the inception of the scheme is the entire responsibility of the former.

Like those in Volume II the present set of articles mainly ignores the City of Leicester which will form the subject of a separate volume; where they do not, the fact is mentioned in text or footnote. The group of articles on education does not extend to the history of secondary schools, which, like primary schools, are reserved for treatment in the topographical volumes. This is a departure from the normal scheme of the *History*.

Once again sincere thanks are due to Professor Jack Simmons, to Dr. L. A. Parker, the Leicestershire County Archivist, and to Mrs. A. M. Woodcock, formerly Archivist to Leicester City, for services of many different kinds. Mention must also be made of the kindness of Mr. A. Wright, keeper of the Leicestershire history collection in the Leicester City Reference Library. Finally, tribute must be paid to a number of Leicestershire business houses and the members of their staffs, who most courteously supplied information which has been incorporated in the articles on industries and communications.

R. B. PUGH

LEICESTERSHIRE
VICTORIA COUNTY HISTORY
COMMITTEE

Where not otherwise stated members have served on the Committee from 1948 until the present time.

ALDERMAN LT.-COL. SIR ROBERT E. MARTIN, C.M.G., T.D., D.L. (Chairman) ALDERMAN MAJOR T. G. F. PAGET, D.L. (died 1952) COUNCILLOR MRS. M. E. KEAY, B.E.M. (from 1952) COUNCILLOR CAPTAIN W. G. COATES THE REVD. D. A. ADAMS	*Representing Leicester County Council*
ALDERMAN C. R. KEENE, C.B.E. COUNCILLOR P. G. HUGHES (resigned 1949) COUNCILLOR A. H. W. KIMBERLIN (1949–54) COUNCILLOR N. L. JACKSON (from 1954)	*Representing the City of Leicester*
C. D. B. ELLIS, ESQ., C.B.E., M.C.	*Representing the Leicestershire Archaeological Society*
J. MILNE, ESQ.	*Representing the Leicester Literary and Philosophical Society*
S. H. RUSSELL, ESQ.	*Representing Leicester and County Chamber of Commerce*
DR. ANNE K. B. EVANS (from 1950) PROFESSOR J. SIMMONS	*Representing University College, Leicester*
B. ELLIOTT, ESQ. (resigned 1952) P. A. STEVENS, ESQ.	*Representing the Leicester Branch of the Historical Association*
THE RT. REVD. DR. G. VERNON SMITH, M.C., *formerly* Bishop of Leicester (resigned 1953) THE RT. REVD. DR. R. R. WILLIAMS, D.D., Bishop of Leicester	*Representing the Diocese of Leicester*
A. TAYLOR MILNE, ESQ. (resigned 1950) R. B. PUGH, ESQ. (from 1950)	*Representing the Central Committee of the Victoria County History*

Co-opted Members

SIR WILLIAM BROCKINGTON, C.B.E.

L. H. IRVINE, ESQ., M.B.E.

PROFESSOR A. HAMILTON THOMPSON, C.B.E., F.B.A. (died 1952)

DR. J. H. PLUMB

H. P. R. FINBERG, ESQ. (Co-opted 1952)

DR. W. G. HOSKINS (Co-opted 1953)

DR. C. H. THOMPSON (resigned 1951) DR. L. A. PARKER	Honorary Secretary
S. B. BORDOLI, ESQ.	Honorary Treasurer

LIST OF CLASSES OF THE PUBLIC RECORDS

USED IN THIS VOLUME, WITH THEIR CLASS NUMBERS

Chancery
- C. 2 Proceedings, Series I
- C. 211 Petty Bag Office, Commissions and Inquisitions of Lunacy

Exchequer
- E. 134 Depositions taken by Commission
- E. 179 Subsidy Rolls, &c.
- E. 317 Parliamentary Surveys.

Home Office
- H.O. 41 Disturbances, Entry Books
- H.O. 52 Correspondence, Counties

State Paper Office
- S.P. 14 State Papers, Domestic, Jas. I

NOTE ON ABBREVIATIONS

Among the abbreviations and short titles used the following may require elucidation

Arch. Jnl.	*Archaeological Journal.*
Assoc. Arch. Soc. *Rep. and Papers*	Associated Archaeological and Architectural Societies' *Reports and Papers.*
C.J.	*Commons Journals.*
Curtis, *Topog. Hist. Leics.*	J. Curtis, *Topographical History of the County of Leicester.*
Farnham, *Leics. Notes*	G. F. Farnham, *Leicestershire Medieval Village Notes* (6 vols., 1929–33, priv. print., Leicester).
Fox-Strangways, *Geol. Leics. S. Derbys. Coalfield*	C. Fox-Strangways, *The Geology of the Leicestershire and South Derbyshire Coalfield* (Geological Survey of Great Britain, H.M.S.O., 1907).
Gent. Mag.	*Gentleman's Magazine.*
L.R.O.	Leicestershire Record Office.
Leic. and Nott. Jnl.	*Leicester and Nottingham Journal.*
Leic. Boro. Rec.	*Records of the Borough of Leicester* (ed. Mary Bateson and Helen Stocks, 4 vols., 1899–1923).
Leic. Chron.	*Leicester Chronicle.*
Leic. City Mun. Room	Leicester City Muniment Room, in Leicester Museum.
Leic. City Ref. Libr.	Leicester City Reference Library, Bishop Street, the local collection.
Leic. Jnl.	*Leicester Journal.*
Leic. Town Hall Rec.	Leicester City Records, in the Town Hall.
Leic. and Rut. Mag.	*Leicester and Rutland Magazine.*
Leland, *Itin.*	J. Leland, *Itinerary* (ed. L. Toulmin Smith, 11 parts in 5 vols., 1906–10).
Nichols, *Leics.*	J. Nichols, *The History and Antiquities of the County of Leicester* (4 vols. in 8, 1795–1811).
Rlwy. Mag.	*Railway Magazine.*
T.L.A.S.	*Transactions of the Leicestershire Archaeological Society.*
White, *Dir. Leics.* (1846)	W. White, *History, Gazetteer and Directory of Leicestershire, with Rutland* (1846, &c.).

INDUSTRIES

INTRODUCTION

THE greatest concentration of industry in Leicestershire is in the city of Leicester, which is by far the largest town in the county.[1] Leicester itself, however, will be dealt with in a later volume, and its industries will not in general be considered here, or in the articles on the hosiery and footwear industries which follow.[2] Apart from Leicester the county does not contain any large industrial town, and its industries have always been scattered amongst villages and small towns.

The earliest industries to develop in Leicestershire were mining and quarrying. Coal-mining was already being carried on in the west of the county in the late 13th century, and quarrying, which was practised to some extent in the Roman period, had been revived by 1300. Coal-mining in Leicestershire is confined to a relatively small area; the Leicestershire coalfield has never been one of the largest in Britain, and although there is one town of some size[3] which owes its existence entirely to coal-mining, and which did not exist before the 19th century, no large industrial towns have grown up in the mining area. Quarrying, too, has been largely confined to the part of Leicestershire lying west of the Soar valley, though in the last 80 years the ironstone workings in the north-east of the county have become important.

The other chief industries of Leicestershire are of much more recent growth than mining and quarrying. The hosiery industry was not established in the county until the 17th century, and did not become important until the 18th. Until after 1850 the industry was conducted on the domestic system, and was carried on in many scattered villages, mostly in the western half of the county. While the growth of mining and quarrying in certain areas was directly due to the existence there of minerals, it is not easy to explain why Leicestershire became the chief centre of hosiery manufacture in England. The progress of inclosure during the 18th century may, by depriving some agricultural workers of their normal employment, have helped to make labour available locally for industry, but Leicestershire does not seem to have possessed any natural advantages which make it especially suitable as the home of the hosiery industry. Nevertheless for many years hosiery manufacture in England has been chiefly carried on in Leicestershire, and to a less extent in the adjacent counties of Nottingham and Derby. When in the middle of the 19th century hosiery manufacture was beginning to be concentrated in factories, it was to some extent replaced as a domestic industry in west Leicestershire by the making of boots and shoes. The growth of the footwear industry in the county's villages was due to the need for the footwear factories, established in Leicester itself, to find additional labour for the carrying out of certain processes.

[1] Where no references are given in the introduction, see articles on individual industries for the facts on which statements are based.

[2] That is, Leicestershire must in the present context be considered as the county less the city of Leicester.

[3] Coalville.

By the end of the 19th century the manufacture of hosiery and footwear was very largely conducted in factories. The disappearance of the domestic system left many Leicestershire villages without any industry at all. The hosiery and footwear factories were mostly built in the towns of Loughborough and Hinckley, and in certain of the larger villages, such as, for example, Earl Shilton and Shepshed.[4] As other industries developed, their factories tended to be built in the small towns of the county rather than in the villages. The growth of the engineering industry at Loughborough is a notable example.

The general result of these developments has been that most Leicestershire villages are today without industries. The situation which is to be found in, for example, much of the West Riding of Yorkshire, where many villages contain a few small factories, does not exist in Leicestershire; most of the villages, especially in the east of the county, are purely agricultural and have consequently remained small. Some villages do possess important industrial plants; in the eastern half of the county, for example, there is a large iron-works at Asfordby, while in the west there are a number of larger villages each possessing several factories. But such cases are exceptional. On the other hand the towns of the county, though none of them is very large,[5] have acquired a variety of industries. Hinckley and Loughborough, which have for long been manufacturing towns, have become increasingly important in recent years, and factories have been established in the old-established market-towns of Melton Mowbray, Market Harborough, and Lutterworth. It may be said in general terms that Leicestershire's industries, with the important exceptions of mining and quarrying, are to be found chiefly in the towns, and that the western half of the county is still more important industrially than the eastern, as has been the case for many years.[6]

[4] Earl Shilton and Shepshed both possess hosiery and footwear factories: *Kelly's Dir. of Leics. and Rut.* (1936), 78, 937.

[5] In 1931 the population of Loughborough, the largest town in Leics. after Leic. itself, was 27,777: ibid. 862.

[6] On the distribution of population in Leics., see below, p. 153; and see map showing distribution of human settlements in R. M. Auty, 'Leics.' in *Land of Britain* (pt. 57), ed. L. D. Stamp, 259.

HOSIERY

The making of knitted-wear or hosiery is a post-medieval industry. It takes its origin from the invention of the stocking- or knitting-frame by William Lee of Calverton (Notts.) in 1589. After failing to obtain a patent for his invention from Elizabeth I, Lee tried his fortunes in France but he died in Paris in 1610 without attaining much success. His brother, James Lee, brought back eight frames to England and set them up in London, which became the first centre of the trade of framework-knitting in the country. James Lee soon sold up his London frames, and, having returned to his native county, introduced the trade to Nottingham with the help of Aston, a former apprentice of his brother William. From Nottingham the trade spread to Derbyshire and Leicestershire and henceforth the midlands became and still remain the principal seat of the hosiery industry.[1]

Knitting-frames were first set up in Leicestershire by William Iliffe at Hinckley about 1640.[2] From time to time attempts have been made to

[1] For the invention of the stocking-frame by Wm. Lee and the attempts by him and his brother James to establish the trade in Engl. and France, see W. Felkin, *Hist. Machine-Wrought Hosiery and Lace Manufactures* (1867), 23–58, and F. A. Wells, *Brit. Hosiery Trade: Hist. and Organization*, 22–27.

[2] This is the traditional date for the introduction of the stocking-frame into Leics. See Nichols, *Leics.* iv, 679; A. J. Pickering, *Cradle and Home of the Hosiery Trade*, 1. The inv. filed with the early Probate Rec. for the Archdeaconry of Leic. have been sampled for various years between 1649–94 for evidence of stocking-frames. The earliest ref. to a stocking-frame which has been found occurs in the inv. of Geo. Hogsonn of Dixley (Dishley) Mill, dated 4 Feb. 1660. Hogsonn, a silk-stocking weaver, possessed a frame and 'implement thereto belonging' which were valued at £25.

calculate the number of frames in the country. In 1669 there were about 50 frames in Leicestershire compared with 100 in Nottinghamshire and 400 in London.[3] Almost a century later, in 1753, Leicester possessed 1,000 frames, Nottingham 1,500, Derby 200, London 1,000, and scattered among the villages in the midland counties there were 7,300. The total number for England was now 13,200 compared with 650 in 1669.[4] Calculations made in the first half of the 19th century are more informative, for they give us evidence of the villages concerned as well as the principal towns. According to Blackner there were in 1812 4,700 frames in Derby and Derbyshire, 9,285 in Nottingham and Nottinghamshire, and 11,183 in Leicester and Leicestershire, of which 1,600 were within the borough (which is treated in a subsequent volume) and 9,583 scattered amongst 99 different villages in the county.[5] At London there were at this time under 150 frames. Thirty years later Felkin calculated that there were 6,447 frames in Derbyshire, 16,382 in Nottinghamshire, and 20,311 in Leicestershire, of which 4,140 were in Leicester borough and 1,750 in Hinckley.[6]

From the above figures it is clear that not only had London ceased to be an important centre of the industry by the middle of the 19th century but that even at the end of the 18th century it was eclipsed by the midland counties, amongst which Leicestershire (including Leicester) held the first place.

These statistics, however, do not give a complete picture of the extent to which the industry had spread in Leicestershire. Felkin took his census of the knitting-frames in 1844, listing 86 places outside the borough of Leicester as possessing frames. Next year evidence was taken before Richard M. Muggeridge, who had been appointed commissioner to report on the state of the framework-knitters. Yet in Muggeridge's report figures are given for the number of frames in six villages which are omitted from Felkin's return and five of those villages were considerable seats of the manufacture.[7] Blackner quotes 95 villages in the county as possessing frames in 1812 but he omits six places, which appear not only in Felkin's census but are also known to have possessed framework-knitters in the 18th century and, therefore, it may reasonably be inferred, were engaged in the industry when Blackner's list was compiled.[8] Finally, there were framework-knitters in the 18th century in at least twenty-three other villages or hamlets not mentioned by Blackner.[9]

In all, evidence has been found for framework-knitting in 118 villages and hamlets of the county at the turn of the 18th century compared with ninety-three village centres in the middle of the 19th. Allowing for any defects in the statistics this fall reflects a contraction in the rural industry. Its peak was reached at the close of the Napoleonic Wars. By the middle of the 19th century, as we shall see later, the withdrawal of the industry from the village centres had already begun; a process which continued slowly over the succeeding 50 or 60 years.

The industry was largely confined to that area of the county which lies west of a line drawn from Market Harborough through Leicester to Loughborough (see Map). In the eastern half of the county framework-knitting on a small scale was carried on in only a few scattered villages; even in a market-centre like Melton Mowbray the industry was negligible, but of the 93 known centres of the trade in the mid-19th century, for which we have the numbers of the frames engaged, 6 possessed over 500. Of these, Broughton Astley, Hinckley, and Shepshed had over 1,000; whilst at Loughborough, Earl Shilton, and Wigston Magna there were between 500 and 1,000. In 37 other villages the number of frames varied between 100 and 500 but 50 had under 100 frames apiece.

Geographically the rural centres fall into fairly well-defined groups. The Soar valley especially was thickly studded with such centres, dominated by Loughborough, Barrow upon Soar, Sileby, Mountsorrel, and Thurmaston. In the north-west there was a belt of framework-knitting villages extending from Shepshed through Hathern and Long Whatton to Castle Donington. The concentration of frames was not quite so heavy in the area between Whitwick and Ashby de la Zouch; nor in the area occupied by Anstey, Glenfield, Ratby, and Desford. South-west of Leicester there were two principal groups; first, Enderby, Narborough, Whetstone, Cosby, Blaby, Countesthorpe, and Broughton Astley, and secondly, Hinckley, Stoke Golding, Earl Shilton, Barwell, Sapcote, and Burbage. South-east of Leicester, Wigston Magna and Oadby were both large centres of the industry and beyond these there was the area covered by the villages of Kibworth, Smeeton Westerby, Fleckney, Arnesby, and Shearsby.

Although the making of stockings was the motive for the invention of the stocking-frame, the knitted fabric which it produced could be

[3] *Rep. on Condition of Framework Knitters*, [609] p. 15, H.C. (1845), xv.

[4] Ibid. 15.

[5] J. Blackner, *Hist. Nott.* 239–40. The statistics used by Blackner were assembled in 1812 by an unnamed person who spent several years collecting them. The frames were counted by people going from house to house.

[6] Felkin, *Hosiery and Lace Mftures.* 465–6.

[7] *1st Appendix to Rep. Cond. Framework Knitters*, [618] p. 349, H.C. (1845) xv, Broughton Astley (with Primethorpe and Sutton), 11,000 frames; ibid. p. 193, Thurmaston, 400 frames; p. 308, Long Whatton, 250 frames; p. 308, Kegworth, 176 frames; p. 198, Great Glen, 100 frames; p. 386, Ibstock, 47 frames.

[8] Arnesby, Barlestone, Barsby, Huncote, Smeeton Westerby, Shearsby.

[9] See below pp. 20–22.

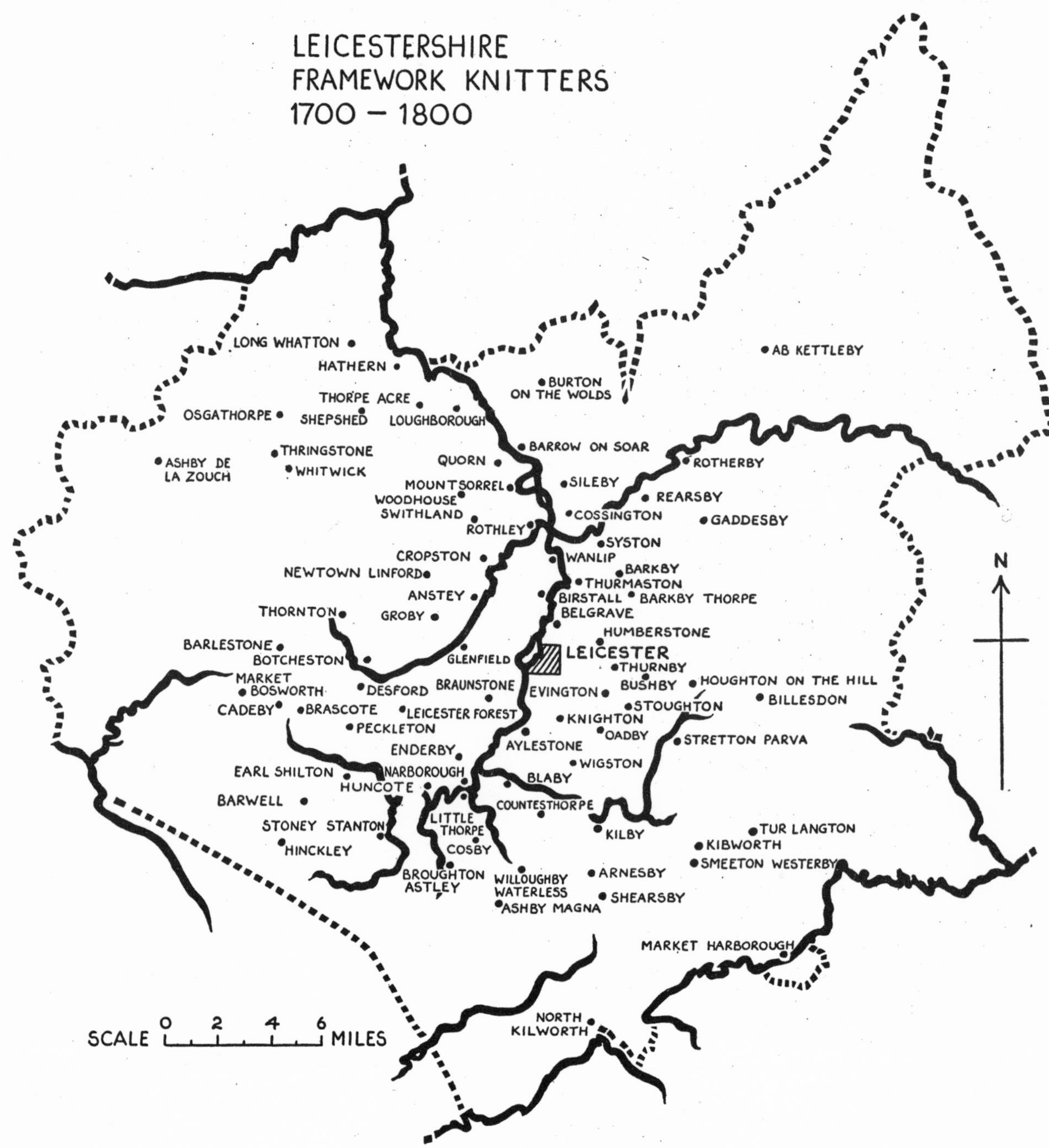
LEICESTERSHIRE
FRAMEWORK KNITTERS
1700 – 1800
LONG WHATTON
HATHERN
THORPE ACRE
OSGATHORPE
SHEPSHED
LOUGHBOROUGH
BURTON ON THE WOLDS
AB KETTLEBY
ASHBY DE LA ZOUCH
THRINGSTONE
WHITWICK
QUORN
BARROW ON SOAR
ROTHERBY
MOUNTSORREL
WOODHOUSE
SWITHLAND
SILEBY
REARSBY
COSSINGTON
GADDESBY
ROTHLEY
SYSTON
CROPSTON
WANLIP
NEWTOWN LINFORD
BARKBY
THURMASTON
ANSTEY
BIRSTALL
BARKBY THORPE
THORNTON
GROBY
BELGRAVE
HUMBERSTONE
BARLESTONE
BOTCHESTON
GLENFIELD
LEICESTER
THURNBY
MARKET BOSWORTH
DESFORD
BRAUNSTONE
EVINGTON
BUSHBY
HOUGHTON ON THE HILL
BILLESDON
CADEBY
BRASCOTE
LEICESTER FOREST
STOUGHTON
KNIGHTON
PECKLETON
OADBY
STRETTON PARVA
ENDERBY
AYLESTONE
EARL SHILTON
NARBOROUGH
WIGSTON
HUNCOTE
BLABY
BARWELL
COUNTESTHORPE
STONEY STANTON
LITTLE THORPE
KILBY
TUR LANGTON
KIBWORTH
HINCKLEY
COSBY
SMEETON WESTERBY
BROUGHTON ASTLEY
WILLOUGHBY WATERLESS
ARNESBY
ASHBY MAGNA
SHEARSBY
MARKET HARBOROUGH
N
NORTH KILWORTH
SCALE 0 2 4 6 MILES

used for many purposes,[10] so that we find that there are within the hosiery trade several diverse branches of which the manufacture of stockings is only one. By the end of the 18th century shirts, gloves, cravats, braces, together with a varied range of stockings and socks were all produced on the stocking-frame as well as a new type of manufacture, lace.[11] John Heathcoat of Loughborough was a pioneer in the manufacture of lace, but after the destruction of his lace-machines at Loughborough during the Luddite riots in 1816 he moved to Tiverton (Devon) and Leicestershire ceased to play a part in the making of lace, the main centre for which was Nottinghamshire.[12]

In general, worsted hosiery was made in Leicestershire, whilst cotton hosiery was largely concentrated in Nottinghamshire and silk hosiery in Derbyshire. The making of cotton hosiery was not, however, unknown in the county; it was in fact the staple article for Hinckley and the neighbouring villages of Barwell and Earl Shilton. The shirt trade was introduced into the borough of Leicester about 1796;[13] in the county Loughborough was the only centre for this branch. Glove-making, a more skilled and a more highly paid branch of the trade, employed in 1845 about 1,200 frames in Leicester.[14] Berlin gloves spread to Loughborough, Mountsorrel, Quorndon, South Croxton, and Barsby, but the fancy branch (French mitts) was confined almost entirely to the borough, employing only a few odd frames in the county.[15] Sock-making introduced into the county in *c.* 1810,[16] became an extensive branch in the second quarter of the 19th century and was to be found in Belgrave, Thurmaston, Syston, Sileby, Humberstone, Wigston, Great Glen, Whetstone, Rothley, Queniborough, Rearsby, and Keyham.[17] Cosby specialized in children's socks and Oadby in tuck socks.[18] Most of the county frames, however, were engaged in making the traditional wrought-hose or fully fashioned stockings and they continued to do so, even when the borough with its superior number of frames had turned almost entirely to the more cheaply produced straight-down hose and 'cut-ups' introduced at the beginning of the 19th century.[19]

The larger centres of the trade, as might be expected, tended to draw within their orbit the framework-knitters of the surrounding villages. Joshua Clarke, a manufacturer of Hinckley in the mid-19th century, employed 300 frames which were situated in Hinckley and in four or five neighbouring villages.[20] Warner, Cartwright & Warner of Loughborough employed several hundred frames, many of which were in the adjoining villages,[21] and the hands working for John Watson of Loughborough in 1845 lived and worked in Loughborough, Thringstone, Whitwick, Belton, Long Whatton, Shepshed, Osgathorpe, Diseworth, and Sutton Bonington (Notts.).[22] The manufacturers of Leicester, too, had many frames working in the villages which were within 5 or 6 miles of the borough.[23]

Yet the economic links between village and village did not follow so simple a pattern as geography might suggest. John Biggs & Sons of Leicester, in addition to frames in Huncote, Narborough, Little Thorpe, and Cosby, also had them in Hinckley.[24] One witness before the Commission of 1845 went so far as to suggest that the Hinckley manufacturers had become little more than agents of the Leicester manufacturers.[25] Of the 217 frames in Stoke Golding ten worked to Leicester, even though the remainder worked for the bag-hosiers or middlemen of Hinckley, which was barely 3 miles away.[26] At Newton Burgoland, 17 miles west of Leicester, there were nine frames. One or two worked for a middleman of Market Bosworth but the remainder worked direct to a manufacturer of Leicester.[27] Likewise, the framework-knitters of Ibstock turned not to Whitwick, a nearby centre of some dimensions, but to Leicester.[28] At Woodhouse some of the framework-knitters worked to Loughborough, others to Leicester.[29] In the north-west of the county Loughborough and Shepshed had no monopoly. The villages in this area were drawn economically towards Nottingham as well as to Loughborough.[30] Even at the end of the 19th century the framework-knitters of Hathern still looked towards Nottingham rather than to Loughborough, which was only 2 miles away.[31]

To bring the raw material to the more distant frames and to collect in return the finished article, carriers were employed. As will be seen later, the carriers were often small employers in the trade

[10] *Rep. Cond. Framework Knitters*, 21–24 lists 128 inventions between 1589 and 1843 designed to modify and improve the stocking-frame, yet there were no fundamental changes in it until the construction of the rotary frames and the application of power from the mid-19th cent. onwards.

[11] Lace was produced by various modifications to the stocking-frame. From about 1760 it became a separate industry from hosiery: Felkin, *Hosiery and Lace Mftures.* 121.

[12] Ibid. 237–42.

[13] *Rep. Cond. Framework Knitters*, 99.

[14] *1st App. to Rep. Cond. Framework Knitters*, 8.

[15] Ibid. 29, 128.

[16] *Rep. Cond. Framework Knitters*, 99.

[17] *1st App. to Rep. Cond. Framework Knitters*, 80.

[18] Ibid. 360 (Cosby), 115 (Oadby).

[19] See below, p. 12.

[20] *1st App. to Rep. Cond. Framework Knitters*, 199.

[21] Ibid. 421.

[22] Ibid. 423.

[23] Ibid. 160. Stokes & Nephews of Leic. owned 400–500 frames and employed 'many hundreds more in different parts of the county'. The framework-knitters of Anstey looked to Leic.: ibid. 180. So too at Thurcaston: ibid. 196, and Blaby: ibid. 357.

[24] Ibid. 51–52.

[25] Ibid. 246–7.

[26] Ibid. 274.

[27] Ibid. 389.

[28] Ibid. 384.

[29] Ibid. 435.

[30] The framework-knitters of Kegworth were employed by bagmen who worked for Nott. firms: ibid. 330.

[31] Ex inf. Fuller & Hambly, Ltd., Hathern.

LEICESTERSHIRE
FRAMEWORK KNITTERS
1801 – 1851
BOTTESFORD
HEMINGTON
CASTLE DONINGTON
KEGWORTH
DISEWORTH
LONG WHATTON
DALBY ON THE WOLDS
HATHERN
WYMESWOLD
BELTON
THORPE ACRE
WALTON ON THE WOLDS
SAXELBY
OSGATHORPE
SHEPSHED
LOUGHBOROUGH
ASFORDBY
MELTON MOWBRAY
COLEORTON
SEAGRAVE
THRINGSTONE
BARROW ON SOAR
ASHBY DE LA ZOUCH
SWANNINGTON
WHITWICK
QUORN
MOUNT SORREL
SILEBY
WOODHOUSE
REARSBY
RAVENSTONE
ROTHLEY
COSSINGTON
GADDESBY
HUGGLESCOTE
QUENIBOROUGH
CROPSTON
SYSTON
THORPE SATCHVILLE
HEATHER
STANTON UNDER BARDON
THURCASTON
BARSBY
IBSTOCK
MARKFIELD
BARKBY
SOUTH CROXTON
NEWTON BURGOLAND
ANSTEY
THURMASTON
BAGWORTH
BIRSTALL
BARKBY THORPE
NAILSTONE
THORNTON
GROBY
BELGRAVE
BARLESTONE
RATBY
HUMBERSTONE
CARLTON
GLENFIELD
LEICESTER
NEWBOLD VERDON
MARKET BOSWORTH
CADEBY
DESFORD
KNIGHTON
PECKLETON
SUTTON CHENEY
ENDERBY
OADBY
AYLESTONE
THURLASTON
STAPLETON
WIGSTON
DADLINGTON
EARL SHILTON
NARBOROUGH
BLABY
BURTON OVERY
STOKE GOLDING
WHETSTONE
GREAT GLEN
HUNCOTE
BARWELL
CROFT
LITTLE THORPE
COUNTESTHORPE
NEWTON HARCOURT
WYKIN
STONEY STANTON
KILBY
FOSTON
HINCKLEY
COSBY
SAPCOTE
PEATLING MAGNA
FLECKNEY
BURBAGE
BROUGHTON ASTLEY
ARNESBY
SMEETON WESTERBY
SHARNFORD
WILLOUGHBY WATERLESS
SADDINGTON
FROLESWORTH
DUNTON BASSETT
SHEARSBY
LEIRE
BRUNTINGTHORPE
CLAYBROOKE
ASHBY PARVA
LUTTERWORTH
WALCOTE
SCALE 0 2 4 6 MILES
N

themselves. The degree to which the carrier system had developed by the middle of the 19th century is vividly illustrated by John Palmer of Market Bosworth.[32] He tells us that the framework-knitters of Cadeby worked for a Leicester hosier. On Friday night they took their work to Market Bosworth, a distance of a mile and a half, whence it was taken to Leicester by a Bosworth carrier on Saturday morning. The carrier returned to Bosworth on Saturday night bringing in bags the raw materials for the next week's work. The Cadeby knitters collected materials on Sunday but no money. For their wages they went on Monday morning to Hinckley, where the hosier kept a grocery shop—a distance of 6 miles.

Until about the second decade of the 19th century the relationship between the framework-knitter and the manufacturer, or hosier, was, generally speaking, direct and simple. The manufacturer was an entrepreneur responsible for marketing the finished goods and for obtaining the raw materials with which the framework-knitter was supplied. He operated from his warehouse to which the framework-knitter came to collect his yarn and to return the finished article. The head of the household, owning his own frame or frames, and assisted, perhaps, by apprentices, paid journeymen, or by members of his own family, was the unit of production.

In rural districts framework-knitting was originally only an additional occupation combined with agriculture. Nathaniel Corah, the founder of the Leicester firm of N. Corah & Sons Ltd., was the son of William Corah (1747–1817), who was a farmer at Bagworth and who owned a number of frames, some of which at the time of his death stood in his own house; the remainder were let out.[33] Edward Cheney of Narborough was a yeoman who died at the close of 1740. He was a freeholder and farmed lands to the extent of 'half a quartern'[34] in the open fields of Narborough. His personal estate was valued on 5 January 1741 at £41 18*s*., half of which was accounted for by his household goods and the rest by his crops (in the fields and in the barn), by his hay, straw, pigs, and a stocking-frame valued at £5.[35] Jenings Berrington, a framework-knitter of Hathern, died in the summer of 1740, possessed of a yardland in the open fields of Hathern and 4 cow pastures, 2 of which together with a frame he had purchased from one Anthony Cock some time before the autumn of 1725.[36] In the neighbouring village of Long Whatton the Middletons were farmers as well as framework-knitters in the 18th century. Robert Middleton (d. 1768) and his brother Joseph (d. 1785) are both described in the probate records as framework-knitters. They inherited landed estate in Leicestershire and Derbyshire and in the 1740's we find them buying and exchanging land in the open fields of Long Whatton. In one transaction, which took place in 1747, Joseph Middleton is described as a yeoman.[37] Not all the farmer-framework-knitters owned freehold land. Thomas Gunton (d. 1747), a framework-knitter of Earl Shilton, possessed a copyhold estate in Earl Shilton manor.[38]

The Probate records furnish evidence of the independent status of the framework-knitter apart from those for whom hosiery-making was only an additional occupation.[39] Daniel Vann, a framework-knitter of Wigston Magna, died in 1680. His personal estate, which amounted to £60 19*s*., consisted of furniture and household goods to the value of 10 guineas, three cows and a pig worth £5. 9*s*., clothes and cash to the value of £5, and four stocking-frames each worth £10. John Bates of Hinckley (d. 1692) was not so wealthy; although his personal estate was only £29 7*s*., he nevertheless possessed three stocking-frames valued at £18. Thomas Fallows was a very humble framework-knitter in Little Thorpe. When he died in the early summer of 1725, his wealth amounted to just under £16 but he possessed his own working frame and two cows which accounted for 60 per cent. of his worldly wealth. Joseph Canner of Ashby de la Zouch was found at the time of his death (1740) to possess a shop of frames, comprising four and a half old stocking-frames, worth £15. 10*s*. and in another room he had one stocking-frame worth £3. 10*s*. In the same year died Thomas Lord, a framework-knitter of Countesthorpe; he owned his own house and at least two frames, one worked by his son, Joseph, and the other by a relative. William Wood of Knighton also possessed a shop of frames: two frames worth £7 each and one frame 'quite wore down' worth £4. But when he died in the spring of 1751 he was hopelessly in debt. Thomas Elkington (d. 1770), a framework-knitter of Newton Harcourt, owned his house and a few frames, and Thomas Gurford (d. between 1810 and 1812), a framework-knitter of Primethorpe in Broughton Astley parish, owned his own cottage together with a workshop, pigsty, and a small garden. One stocking-frame he bequeathed to his wife and the remainder he put in trust to be let out; the rents thereof were to go to his wife during her lifetime, after deducting the expenses incurred in repairing and maintaining the frames.

In the 17th and 18th centuries entry into the trade was normally by apprenticeship, usually for

[32] *1st App. to Rep. Cond. Framework Knitters*, 390.

[33] C. W. Webb, *Hist. Rec. of N. Corah & Sons, Ltd.* 13; Wm. Corah's Will in L.R.O. Probate Rec.

[34] i.e. ¼ of a yardland or virgate; the acreage is uncertain.

[35] L.R.O. Probate Rec.

[36] Ibid.

[37] The above details are extracted from a collection of MSS. rel. to the Middletons of Long Whatton in L.R.O.

[38] L.R.O. Probate Rec.

[39] This paragraph is based on the Wills and inv. among the L.R.O. Probate Rec. except for the will of Thos. Gurford of Primethorpe in Broughton Astley par., which is among the 'Moulton MSS.', ibid.

7 years, as in the case of the older industries which came within the scope of the Statute of Artificers of 1563.[40] By a charter granted by Charles II in 1663 the London framework-knitters became an incorporated company and, as such, they attempted to enforce their by-laws upon the framework-knitters of the midlands. Those efforts proved fruitless and we find that the midland framework-knitters in no way regarded themselves as restricted in the number of apprentices they might wish to employ.[41] Under the old Poor Law the overseers took advantage of the expansion of the industry in the 18th century to apprentice to the master framework-knitters the growing number of paupers left in their charge,[42] and, to meet the heavy demands made of the trade during the French Wars, large numbers of apprentices were brought into the county and borough from the neighbouring counties of Northampton and Warwick.[43] In Hinckley, it was said, some masters employed as many as a dozen apprentices.[44]

Apprenticing on such a scale had its nemesis. With the peace that followed Waterloo and the discharge of large numbers of framework-knitters from the armies, labour in the trade became redundant. As wages fell and the standard of living of the stockinger was reduced, so apprenticeship declined. In order to put a few more shillings into the family purse, the stockingers began to teach their own children how to work the frames. It had long been customary for children even from a very tender age to be employed in the subsidiary tasks of winding and seaming. When evidence was given before the Commission of 1845 it was reported that such practices had become almost the sole means of recruitment. One witness estimated that the 600 or more apprentices who used to be seen in Hinckley had dwindled to 20.[45]

The successful master also employed journeymen in addition to his apprentices. Some of the journeymen lived in with their employer and became known as indoor journeymen. It was not, however, so common in rural districts as in the borough for the journeymen to live in.[46]

To accommodate the frames worked by the apprentices and journeymen, buildings known as 'shops' were erected at the rear of the master stockinger's house. In some parts of the county framework-knitters' shops may still be seen and they are distinguished by the narrow windows, placed just under the eaves, which ran the whole length of the building.[47] It was the upper floor which was generally used to house the frames and it was approached by a ladder pushed through a trap-door in the floor.[48] As an alternative, a shop might be built over the top of several adjacent cottages. Not all the frames, however, were kept in shops; many remained in the stockinger's own rooms and the operatives sat back to back.[49]

Early in the 19th century, however, the independence of the framework-knitter was undermined by two factors; the widespread development of frame-letting and the emergence of middlemen who came between the knitter and the manufacturer.[50]

By 1800 the hiring of a frame at a rent instead of purchasing one was rapidly becoming the general practice of the framework-knitter.[51] The expansion of the trade and especially the practice of master stockingers in taking large numbers of apprentices at the end of the 18th century no doubt facilitated this development. Thomas Briers, a framework-knitter of Shepshed, who had known the trade for over 50 years, declared before the Commissioner of 1845 that 'the hosiers were principally the possessors of the frames in [his] time' and it was only partly true that 50 years before the frames had been largely the stockingers' own.[52] By the middle of the 19th century the personal frame of the operative had almost disappeared. There is abundant evidence that even those who owned their own frames had by that

[40] As the invention of the stocking-frame post-dated the Stat. of Artificers it was ruled in 1655 that the provisions of that Act respecting apprenticeship did not apply to framework-knitters. See E. Lipson, *Econ. Hist. Engl.* (3rd edn.), iii, 282.

[41] The Framework Knitters Co. lost a test case in 1728 brought against Cartwright of Nottingham, and again in 1745 further attempts to enforce their by-laws failed. This time protests from Nott. and Godalming (Surr.) resulted in an inquiry by a Select Cttee. of the Ho. of Commons, the outcome of which proved unfavourable to the Co.: Felkin, *Hosiery and Lace Mftures.* 74–81.

[42] Among the Desford Civil Par. Rec. (L.R.O.) there are 167 apprenticeship indentures, ranging from 1721 to 1831. Of these, 88 relate to paupers apprenticed to framework-knitting.

[43] *1st App. to Rep. Cond. Framework Knitters,* 10, 396.

[44] Ibid. 108, 396.

[45] Ibid. 17, 108, 226, 302.

[46] Ibid. 48. Chas. Pritchett of Woodhouse Eaves had 8 frames, 4 of which were worked by indoor journeymen living in his house: ibid. 437. Thos. Heafield, Sec. of the Whitwick Branch of the Framework Knitters' Union, also worked as an indoor journeyman in Whitwick: ibid. 339.

[47] e.g. in Hathern and Long Whatton.

[48] Ex inf. Mrs. Lister of Long Whatton, who came from an old stockinger family.

[49] Ex inf. Mrs. Lister.

[50] *1st App. to Rep. Cond. Framework Knitters,* 79–80. Joseph Swift of Eaton St., Leic., considered that the middleman system 'began to be prevalent about the year 1819 or 1820; but it was first introduced, I think, partially about 1812'. Edw. Allen of Leic. deposed that it 'commenced after the year 1816': ibid. 36, and Thomas Nevil of Leic. put the date about 1825: ibid. 45.

[51] Frame-letting was an established practice in the early 18th cent. By 1745 the letting of frames by those connected with the trade was causing some trouble to the Framework Knitters Co., which made a by-law that no member should 'hire frames but of such as are members': Felkin, *Hosiery and Lace Mftures.* 77.

[52] *1st App. to Rep. Cond. Framework Knitters,* 311.

time either sold them or put them aside in favour of renting a frame in order to make sure of receiving work.[53]

Not all frames hired were hosiers'. There was a large number of what were called 'independent' frames; that is to say, frames owned by people not in the trade but let out solely for the purpose of enjoying the profits of their rents. There were also the frames owned by the middlemen. Of this latter development we have already caught a glimpse in the will of Thomas Gurford of Primethorpe, who put his frames in trust to be let out on hire. Richard Wileman of Earl Shilton, who passed through the ranks from framework-knitter to manufacturer, possessed in 1845 between two and three hundred frames which he let out to the hands he employed.[54] The development of frame-letting cannot, indeed, be entirely separated from the growth of the middleman; the one reacted upon the other, and, as the knitter came more and more to depend upon the middleman for his supply of work, so the middleman made it a condition (implicit if not explicit) that he hire a frame. Frames not hired were the first to remain idle when trade became slack.[55]

Three types of middlemen may be distinguished: the putter-out, the undertaker or master, and the bagman or bag-hosier. It is, nevertheless, difficult at times to say when a bagman becomes an undertaker and some of the witnesses before the Commission of 1845 regarded the two latter terms as synonymous.[56] The putter-out took out to the villages the hosiers' yarn and brought back to the warehouse the made-up goods. He was in fact simply the channel through which the hosier distributed his raw materials. The putter-out did not contract with the hosier for any particular orders; he did not employ the knitters. They, on the contrary, were paid the warehouse rates and for the services of the putter-out they paid what were called 'taking-in' charges. Despite its apparent advantages, some framework-knitters preferred to walk miles to the hosier's warehouse in order to collect their raw materials and to take in their made-up goods.[57] In the mid-19th century some firms had several hundred separate accounts with framework-knitters, which were all dealt with on a Saturday by the personal visit of the knitter.[58]

The framework-knitter's suspicion that the putter-out might develop into an obstacle in the way of his direct relation with the manufacturer was not unjustified. It was but an easy step for the putter-out to become a middleman properly so called: that is, the actual employer of the operatives who were to make up the goods for which the middleman had contracted with the hosier.[59] Such was the undertaker, who, nevertheless, did not issue to the knitters his own yarn but the yarn supplied to him by the hosier.

The bag-hosier, on the other hand, was originally distinguished from the undertaker by the fact that he had his own yarn made up by the knitters and he marketed the finished goods himself. It was all on a small scale. His market was limited; he sold to hawkers or carried the hose in a bag—hence the name, given at first in contempt—to shops or to the Leicester hosiers.[60] The bag-hosiers bought their yarn from any source available; a large part of it was embezzled from the hosiers by the framework-knitters themselves, who then sent it to Leicester to be purchased by the bag-hosiers.[61]

But when the bag-hosier extended the limits of his market and also undertook to work for the larger manufacturers,[62] the distinction between himself and the larger-scale undertaker became increasingly more difficult to draw.

The undertaker and the bag-hosier sprang up from among the more enterprising framework-knitters, who gradually acquired a stock of frames. Some had an extraordinarily rapid success like the framework-knitter of Earl Shilton, who within a space of four years bought up thirty frames.[63] Not all their frames were purchased; they also rented independent frames which they then sub-let.[64] It seems that, generally speaking, by 1845 the county trade was not so extensively organized through middlemen as the borough trade.[65] A census of middlemen is not possible. There is no uniformity; some villages are dominated by the middleman; others are free of them. For example, among the villages within a short distance of the borough, Anstey, Thurcaston, and Blaby had no

[53] e.g. Storals Wise of Anstey who had possessed a frame of his own for 30 years was compelled 'through the badness of employment' to put it aside and take 2 hosiers' frames: *1st App. to Rep. Cond. Framework Knitters*, 178. Likewise Wm. Sheen of Little Thorpe was forced to sell his own frame: ibid. 186. Wm. Biggs, the Leic. hosier, declared that it was true that many sold their own frames for the purpose of renting one from the hosier in order to ensure regular employment: ibid. 65.

[54] Ibid. 295.

[55] Ibid. 65, 204.

[56] Ibid. 1, 21, 199, 327.

[57] e.g. the framework-knitters of Blaby walked the 4½ miles to Leic. each Sat. morning, for they were 'not possessed of that evil so much in Blaby as in other places—the evil of truck masters and undertakers' (ibid. 357). So, too, the framework-knitters of Narborough (ibid. 190), Thurcaston (ibid. 196), and Huncote (ibid. 353).

[58] Ibid. 421. Messrs. Warner, Cartwright, & Warner employing several hundred frames kept separate accounts with all their hands.

[59] *2nd App. to Rep. Cond. Framework Knitters* [641] p. 63, H.C. (1845), xv.

[60] *1st App. to Rep. Cond. Framework Knitters*, 182, 295.

[61] Ibid. 182–3.

[62] Ibid. 16. Observe, also, Wm. Sheen of Little Thorpe working for an undertaker named Mr. Colston, who worked in turn for several manufacturers in Leics.: ibid. 185.

[63] Ibid. 49.

[64] Ibid. 16–17.

[65] Ibid. 44, 416. John Cooke, a manufacturer of Loughborough, all of whose hands were directly employed from his warehouse, seldom had to deal with a hand who failed to make up his accounts. Such a failing was, he believed, 'one reason why there are so many middlemen now in being, especially in the Leic. trade'.

middlemen, but in Wigston the trade was in the hands of several undertakers and at Cosby the framework-knitters worked for two undertakers.[66] In Hinckley and Loughborough they did not possess an influence comparable to that held by the middlemen in Leicester,[67] though some of the villages which fell within their economic orbits were under middlemen. Such were Belton, Kegworth, and Long Whatton in the Loughborough area and Stoke Golding, Earl Shilton, and Barwell in the Hinckley district.[68] The knitters of Woodhouse Eaves, however, worked directly for the Loughborough warehouses.[69] Of the seventy frames operating in Market Bosworth at this time, twenty-three worked for a local bag-hosier and the remainder for two other bag-hosiers—one in 'Saddleton' (?Dadlington) and the other in Stoke Golding.[70] In Barrow upon Soar and Mountsorrel there was roughly the same number of frames. In the former there were no middlemen but the majority of the frames in Mountsorrel were employed by a bag-hosier of Sileby.[71]

The middlemen obtained their economic ascendancy over the rank and file by various practices, the foremost of which were truck, stinting, and price-cutting. Truck was a particularly powerful weapon in the hands of the middlemen. Abundant evidence was given before the Commission of 1845 which shows how the truck system operated and the grievous burden it imposed upon the framework-knitter. It appears that those who were engaged in grocery or general dealing were quick to exploit the practice of frame letting. Their example was followed by the incipient middlemen among the framework-knitters, who used the profits derived from selling foodstuffs to acquire frames.[72] They then let out their frames to the knitters, who were forced to accept truck as payment out of fear of losing work, so that the framework-knitter not only paid the middleman rent for the hire of his tools, i.e. his frame, but, in addition, contributed to the profits which he derived from his grocery trade.

Despite the Truck Act of 1831 and vigorous attempts to enforce its provisions, truck was still being practised in Leicestershire in the 19th century. It was more prevalent in the county than in the borough, probably, because in the borough moves to stop truck had the support of the manufacturers, who were able to give alternative employment to those hands who lost work through giving information against their truck masters. Prosecutions under the Truck Act had some effect in the county; though frequently the middlemen, and occasionally a larger manufacturer who was trucking turned only to indirect methods which put them outside the scope of the law.[73]

In Earl Shilton most of the small grocers held frames and acted as middlemen. In the words of Isaac Abbott, a framework-knitter of the village, 'they give out their work the same as the other hosiers, and they take it in the same. They do not, perhaps, take it in in the grocery shop, but they have a room above-stairs where they take in the work, and pay the hands their money in that room, and the hands have to pass through the shop in coming out of that room, and there they lay out their money, or pay off the bill for the goods they have had the previous week.'[74] At Cosby a bagman, employing 40 to 50 frames, did not keep his grocery shop and warehouse separate but made his 'shop of the warehouse, and the warehouse of the shop'.[75] A slightly different practice obtained at Ibstock where the truck master not only sold grocery but was a farmer, hosier, butcher, and draper.[76] He paid his hands in cash but they, then, paid it back to his wife for goods previously obtained on credit. At Whitwick the employers all kept shops; and, though they did not pay in goods, they forced their hands to buy foodstuffs from them under pain of losing work.[77] Similarly, at Huncote a very successful undertaker, who became a considerable manufacturer employing about 300 frames, retained his grocery and drapery shop to which his hands resorted lest they 'be deficient in work' when trade became flat.[78] Wigston, too, was a centre of small masters or middlemen, most of whom kept shops.[79] And at Oadby, which had almost a monopoly of the tuck-sock branch of the trade, the knitters themselves openly opposed the efforts to suppress truck for fear of the consequences, should they lay information against the two or three middlemen in whose hands that section of the trade was concentrated.[80]

Even when trucking was eliminated, the close connexion between the bag-hosiers and the retail trades was not severed. It still persisted at the end of the 19th century. Trade directories for the years 1888 and 1894 reveal that the licensee of the 'Sir Robert Peel' at Countesthorpe was a bag-

[66] *1st App. to Rep. Cond. Framework Knitters*, 180, 182 (Anstey), 196 (Thurcaston), 357 (Blaby), 366 (Wigston), 360–2 (Cosby).

[67] Ibid. 221 (Hinckley). 'There are a few bagmen, but comparatively speaking few', but observe the evidence of Wm. Wykes of Hinckley, ibid. 244: 'Many [bagmen] have set up, or there would not have been any employment in the town.' See for Loughborough, ibid. 416, 421, 423.

[68] Ibid. 327 (Belton), 330 (Kegworth), 331 (Long Whatton), 275 (Stoke Golding), 284, 287 (Earl Shilton), 276 (Barwell).

[69] Ibid. 437.

[70] Ibid. 389.

[71] Ibid. 430, 432.

[72] Ibid. 49.

[73] Ibid. 21. At Hinckley Edw. Kem Jarvis, a solicitor and former hosiery manufacturer, played a leading role in the attempt to suppress truck: ibid. 206–8. See also ibid. 225.

[74] Ibid. 284.

[75] Ibid. 362.

[76] Ibid. 385.

[77] Ibid. 335, 339.

[78] Ibid. 353.

[79] Ibid. 15, 366.

[80] Ibid 80, 114–15, 120. Other villages where truck was reported to the Commissioner were Belgrave, Broughton Astley (Primethorpe), Little Thorpe, Long Whatton, Kibworth, Smeeton Westerby, Saddington, Market Bosworth, Narborough, Rothley, Sileby, Stoke Golding, Syston, Thurmaston.

hosier.[81] So, too, was the licensee of the 'Blue Lion' at Thrussington.[82] At Oadby S. Matthews and S. Burnham were bag-hosiers and beer retailers.[83] G. Loveday of Smeeton Westerby was a general dealer, chimney-sweep, and bag-hosier.[84] The sub-postmaster of Hathern was also a bag-hosier and shopkeeper.[85] At Sharnford Joseph Sanders carried on the business of shopkeeper and carrier to Hinckley in addition to that of bag-hosier[86] and at Rothley Joseph Underwood, a shoe manufacturer, also acted as bag-hosier.[87] Lastly, Henry Johnson of Syston combined hosiery with brickmaking and grocery.[88]

Stinting was the practice whereby the weekly work of a frame was restricted. It seems to have been practised particularly when trade was slack. Among the middlemen it also took another form; namely, the spreading of the work received from the manufacturer over the middleman's independent frames as well as over the manufacturer's frames which he held and for which the work was issued.[89] 'They [the middlemen] take 20 frames from a certain manufacturer, and they divide that 20 frames' work into 30, and instead of the framework-knitter having what is allowed from the warehouse, he has but what we may call two-thirds of it.'[90] This practice was particularly odious to the framework-knitter. For he was thereby prevented from working his frames to their full weekly capacity, even though trade was good; and yet he was required to pay more frame-rents, standing- and taking-in charges than the amount of work warranted in respect of the extra frames put into operation. As for the undertaker or bag-hosier, it turned his independent frames into a profitable investment.

Price-cutting by the middlemen was a grievance which weighed heavily upon both framework-knitter and manufacturer. By relying upon the extra frame rents from their independent frames, and, if they were in addition truck masters, also upon the profits from their grocery, drapery, or general stores, the middlemen were able to sell the hosiery made up on their own account at cost or under cost price.[91] The Leicester manufacturers were particularly affected by such practices, for the middlemen came to Leicester and there contracted orders to be executed by the country hands at a reduced rate.[92] In Hinckley, the larger manufacturers had by 1845 almost become swamped by the middlemen, so that Hinckley, according to one witness as we have already observed, was well on the way to becoming the workshop of Leicester. In retaliation the manufacturers cut their costs by reducing wages. This was a serious imposition upon the framework-knitters. For their dread of the union workhouse rendered resistance to reductions ineffectual, since, under the Poor Law Act of 1834, out-door relief was reduced to a minimum and the framework-knitter, jealous of his independence, would rather take lower wages than enter the 'new Bastilles'.[93]

This fear played into the hands of the middlemen and in times of distress they even became a boon to the framework-knitter. During times of slack trade they would have small quantities made up at low rates, which the framework-knitters in those circumstances were only too pleased to accept. According to William Wykes, a middleman of Hinckley, if the bagmen had not set up in Hinckley, 'there would not have been any employment in the town. Those people used to go to Leicester, and fetch work and they the hosiers of Hinckley got them [i.e. the bagmen] to work for them at certain times.'[94]

Among the manufacturers opinion was likewise divided over the usefulness of the middleman. Some looked favourably upon his place within the structure of the trade and deemed him necessary because he took over the work of distributing the raw materials and of collecting the made-up goods from perhaps two or three hundred hands.[95] Other manufacturers, on the contrary, still kept separate accounts with large numbers of hands and one Hinckley firm which used to work through undertakers had returned to the practice of dealing directly with the framework-knitters.[96]

The first half of the 19th century was a period of prolonged depression for the framework-knitter. The nature of the trade itself made it somewhat seasonal and its prosperity was particularly sensitive to changes of fashion. As Felkin observed, fancy hosiery, which was at its zenith about 1800, began to decline and continued to do so for the next 40 years as a result of a change in fashion.[97] A witness before the Commission of 1845 attributed the shrinking of the home market to a 'change of fashion—to trousers, boots, gaiters, and long petticoats being worn'.[98] At Hinckley there was what was called the Hinckley season, which began

[81] C. N. Wright, *Dir. Leic.* (1888), 386; Wright, *Dir. Leic.* (1894), 367.
[82] Wright, *Dir. Leic.* (1888), 575.
[83] Ibid. 531.
[84] Ibid. 558; Wright, *Dir. Leic.* (1894), 585.
[85] Wright, *Dir. Leic.* (1888), 413; Wright, *Dir. Leic.* (1894), 464.
[86] Wright, *Dir. Leic.* (1888), 551; Wright, *Dir. Leic.* (1894), 578.
[87] Wright, *Dir. Leic.* (1888), 545.
[88] Ibid. 571.
[89] *1st App. to Rep. Cond. Framework Knitters* [618] pp. 3–4, 15–16, 160, H.C. (1845), xv.
[90] Ibid. 203.
[91] Ibid. 49, 183, 204, 208.
[92] Ibid. 21, 45.
[93] Ibid. 108–9, 183, 354–5.
[94] Ibid. 244.
[95] Ibid. 63.
[96] Ibid. 254. G. Woodcock of Hinckley employed over 300 hands directly from his warehouse and only 150 through bagmen. Warner, Cartwright, & Warner of Loughborough employed several hundred frames and kept separate accounts with the framework-knitters: ibid. 421. Joshua Clarke, a manufacturer of Hinckley, reverted to the practice of direct relations with the hands: ibid. 202.
[97] Felkin, *Hosiery and Lace Mftures.* (1867), 434.
[98] *1st App. to Rep. Cond. Framework Knitters*, 322.

at the end of November and lasted until the beginning of May. For the remainder of the year trade in wrought brown cotton hose, the staple trade of the area, was very flat.[99]

By the middle of the 19th century Leicestershire hosiery seems to have been largely eclipsed in the foreign markets, particularly in the American market, by the German manufacturers of Saxony.[1] According to William Biggs of the firm of John Biggs & Sons, Leicester, 90 per cent. of the Leicestershire trade in 1845 was for the home market; whereas twenty years earlier the export trade was three times as great as it was at that time.[2] Benjamin Knight, a smaller manufacturer of Primethorpe, by Broughton Astley, who employed about 170 hands, sold to the factors of London, Bristol and Manchester. Formerly, he worked a third of the year making foreign orders for the Leicester houses, but when he gave evidence in 1845 he declared that his shipping trade had gone.[3]

The decline in foreign trade, as regards the county, was not, indeed, entirely due to foreign competition. The distinction between the county and the borough trade must be borne in mind. The county was still engaged in making wrought hose when the borough had adopted the new technique of 'cut-ups' or 'spurious goods' and it was by exporting the latter that the borough was able to keep a place in the foreign markets.

For this reason most of the witnesses before the Commission of 1845 did not regard the competition of the Saxon framework-knitters as the sole, nor even the principal, cause of the depression which afflicted the trade at that time. They laid great stress upon the new type of hose—the 'cut-up' or the unfashioned stocking, which made its appearance at the close of the Napoleonic Wars.[4]

The 'cut-up', as its name implies, was made by cutting the stocking to shape from the fabric and sewing the pieces together. As the stocking had no narrowings to shape it to the leg, it was then laid upon a leg-board and shaped by applying heat and steam. Wider frames were built to make the fabric, so that, in effect, several stockings could be knitted at the same time compared with only one fashioned stocking produced on the narrow frame.[5] Since they could, therefore, be produced more cheaply and in greater quantities than the wrought hose, they found a ready market among the labouring classes as well as providing an export commodity which was able to compete with foreign hosiery.

The wide frames dealt a heavy blow at the rural industry. The older country stockingers, jealous of their skill, were strongly opposed to the wide frames and the 'spurious' hose they produced. The increased production from the wide frames, however, reacted unfavourably upon the country areas. The younger men drifted from the villages either to other industries or to Leicester to work on the wide frames or in the more highly paid glove branch.[6] The wide frames were, indeed, almost entirely restricted to Leicester borough.[7] At Broughton Astley and Hinckley, the larger centres in the south and south-west of the county, they made little progress.[8] In the north-west at Shepshed there were in 1845 only thirty-three wide frames compared with 1,051 narrow ones.[9] Wide frames were introduced at Kegworth but were later withdrawn, as the stockingers could not work them.[10] At Barrow upon Soar only one frame out of 250 appears to have been a wide one and all the 339 frames at Whitwick were reported to be engaged on wrought hose.[11] But at Loughborough they were being more extensively used[12] and at least one manufacturer there,

99 *1st App. to Rep. Cond. Framework Knitters*, 200, 205.

1 For the growth of the German hosiery industry, and its effects upon Brit. overseas markets, see the evidence of (*a*) Wm. Biggs: ibid. 53–54; (*b*) Joshua Clarke, manufacturer of Hinckley: ibid. 200; (*c*) E. K. Jarvis: ibid. 208; (*d*) Wm. Sills, a principal manufacturer in Hinckley: ibid. 253; (*e*) Wm. Cotton, a manufacturer of Shepshed: ibid. 322. Biggs said: 'Hinckley goods are now beaten out of the United States market by the manufacturers of the continent. The articles in which we have been superseded by the Germans are men's and women's brown and coloured hose and half-hose.' Clarke said: 'It is very seldom we can get any orders for shipping for wrought-hose—very seldom indeed. They cannot go the price we charge for them.'

2 Ibid. 64.

3 Ibid. 351.

4 Cf. Geo. Woodcock, a manufacturer of Hinckley: 'where perhaps, 7 years ago, a London house would buy their brown cotton hose in Hinckley, they now go to Leicester for the great bulk of them, because they can get a greater proportion of straight-downs made there. . . . I think we shall be obliged to get wide frames made here to compete with our neighbours at Leicester': ibid. 257.

5 Ibid. 33. 'The wide frames have been the ruin of the wrought-hose. They can make four and five at once. They have run us out. They can make many more than we can. We have to narrow them all through, and throw in between the needles to shape the leg and the feet the same, and the toes the same. The wide ones work through carriers.'

6 Ibid. 176.

7 Ibid. 63. 'Are there many wide frames in the country?—Very few. They are mainly confined to Leicester.'

8 Ibid. 351. The framework-knitters of Primethorpe (Broughton Astley par.) left to enter the 'cut-up' branch and glove branch at Leic. In Hinckley note: (*a*) ibid. 99: Joshua Clarke employed 300 frames, all on wrought cotton hose. (*b*) Geo. Woodcock employed about 400 frames (ibid. 254) all on wrought hose 'with the exception of a few wide frames'. (ibid. 257). (*c*) Wm. Sills employed about 800 frames (ibid. 252) but only recently had introduced a few wide frames (ibid. 253).

9 Ibid. 308.

10 Ibid. 329.

11 Ibid. 428 (Barrow upon Soar), 341 (Whitwick).

12 Ibid. 394, where stated that there were 100–150 wide frames in Loughborough.

John Cooke, fitted to his wide frames a newly invented piece of machinery, which mechanically narrowed or fashioned the stockings.[13]

There seems no doubt that during this period the industry was suffering from a surplus of labour.[14] It has already been stated that at the close of the 18th century the practice was to employ larger numbers of apprentices drawn especially from among the pauper children left on the hands of the overseers of the poor. The French Wars made heavy demands on the industry and, as the armies took away the younger framework-knitters, so their places were filled by semi-skilled hands.[15] After the peace the erstwhile soldiers returned to their frames;[16] wages dropped, declining by as much as 30 to 40 per cent.[17] Frame rents, moreover, began to rise as a result of the exploitation of the independent frame and the services of the newly risen class of middlemen—the undertakers and bag-hosiers—were charged upon the framework-knitter in the form of larger deductions from his weekly wage.[18] The framework-knitters, therefore, took on more and more frames in an effort to increase their earnings as well as to ensure a minimum of work from the manufacturers and middlemen whose frames they rented. These extra frames were worked not by apprentices but by their own children who grew up with no other knowledge than framework-knitting. The effect of these factors was cumulative. The total numbers in the trade increased out of all proportion to demand, especially for the wrought hose, the staple product of the rural trade.

Various methods were tried to arrest the deterioration in the status of the framework-knitter and to alleviate his distress. Frame-breaking, the natural reaction of the stockinger who saw his livelihood threatened by improved machinery, does not appear to have been very widespread in Leicestershire. This form of protest against new inventions was not unknown in the county in the 18th century[19] but during the period of distress 1811–12 when frame-breaking was serious in Nottinghamshire few frames were broken in Leicestershire.[20] The most serious outbreak was in 1816 at Loughborough where the lace frames of Messrs. Heathcoat, Lacy & Boden were destroyed.[21] As already observed Heathcoat left Loughborough and removed the lace trade from Leicestershire to Devonshire. Disturbances threatened in Hinckley and Loughborough in 1830, and, although the Home Office was petitioned for military aid as a precaution, it does not seem that anything serious developed.[22]

Trade unionism did not make much progress in the hosiery trade in Leicestershire during the first half of the 19th century. Associations were formed after the peace of 1815 to deal with the problem caused by the spread of 'cut-ups'.[23] Repeatedly appeal was made to observe the Statement, the agreed prices for work in the various branches of the trade,[24] but the rural stockingers were ready to take work from the middlemen at almost any price and especially when trade was flat.[25] Those who gave evidence before the Commission of 1845 complained of the lack of spirit

[13] *1st App. to Rep. Cond. Framework Knitters*, 416.

[14] Ibid. 122. Thomas Wood, a partner in the Leic. firm of Ann Wood & Sons, working mainly for the Scots market, declared that surplus labour had existed 'at all events certainly since 1836'. Robert Spencer of Loughborough had no doubt that excessive numbers of apprentices had caused an undue proportion of labourers in the market: ibid. 396.

[15] Cf. Thomas Wood: ibid. 122.

[16] Ibid. 108–9.

[17] *Rep. Cond. Framework Knitters*, [609] pp. 38, 39, H.C. (1845), xv; *1st App. to Rep. Cond. Framework Knitters*, 55. Wm. Biggs quotes the gross rate for the staple article made on the narrow frames—women's 24-gauge worsted stockings, 104 leads wide—as having fallen from 7*s*. 6*d*. a dozen in 1815 to 4*s*. 6*d*. a dozen in 1841. See *1st App. to Rep. Cond. Framework Knitters*, 499–500, for a tabular analysis of the evidence given in relation to wages.

[18] Until *c*. 1825 frame rent for the wrought-hose narrow frames was about 9*d*. a week but in 1844 it had risen to 1*s*. or even 1*s*. 3*d*. a week: *1st App. to Rep. Cond. Framework Knitters*, 191, 238. In addition to the frame rent there were deductions from the gross weekly wages for frame-standing, for carriage or taking-in, as well as for winding and seaming. For a tabular analysis of these 'shop-charges' given in the evidence see ibid. 488–90.

[19] Felkin, *Hosiery and Lace Mftures*. 229. In 1773 a mob at Leic. destroyed a newly-invented stocking-machine, and in 1788 the invention of Brookhouse for spinning worsted yarn, which had been adopted by Coltman & Whetstone, worsted-yarn makers of Leic., was destroyed together with the houses of Coltman and Whetstone.

[20] Felkin, op. cit. 236.

[21] Ibid. 237–42.

[22] H.O. 52/8. Letter 1 Feb. 1830 from Hinckley Justices; letter 4 June 1830 from J. Dyke, J.P., in Hinckley, asking for the military, because 'there is not much chance of the Hosiers and the Stocking makers coming to an understanding it might be advisable for you to station soldiers here for a few weeks or until things are settled—special Constables are but a poor protection at best owing to their connexion with the inhabitants'. Letters 30 Nov. 1830 from N. Heyrick—400 or 500 stocking-makers at Loughborough went to the houses of two manufacturers to demand higher wages.

[23] References to the formation of Framework Knitters Assocs. are to be found in the local newspapers. In 1794 there was such an assoc. to deal with the problem of absconded apprentices (*Leic. Jnl.* 25 July 1794) but after 1815 the chief problem concerned 'cut-ups' and the 'Statement' price for work done.

[24] e.g. *Leic. Jnl.* 19 April 1816, Meeting of framework-knitters of Leic. and Leics. Also, ibid. 3 Sept. 1819, General Meeting of the Loughborough District of Framework-knitters. It was resolved (*inter alia*) that it was 'the imperious duty of every Framework knitter immediately to enrol himself and become a member of the United Framework Knitters Union Soc. of the Town and County of Leic.' Other resolutions concerned the taking out of work under the Statement price.

[25] Cf. *1st App. to Rep. Cond. Framework Knitters*, 21.

among the country framework-knitters, who, it was alleged, considered themselves fortunate that work should even be given to them by the masters.[26] Thomas Upton of Thurmaston, who was in the sock branch, toured eighteen villages with the object of forming a union but found that the hands were unwilling to incur further expense.[27] Only among the framework-knitters in the glove branch centred on Leicester did trade unionism attain much strength. In order to overcome the opposition of this union the manufacturers in Leicester were forced to move their frames to Loughborough where there was no union.[28]

To guard against illness the framework-knitters associated themselves into voluntary sick clubs and friendly societies. At Little Thorpe such a club counted amongst its members most of the framework-knitters of the locality. Their age-limit for admission was over 16 years but under 35 and each member irrespective of age paid a monthly subscription of 1*s.* 2*d.* Sick benefit amounted to 6*s.* a week.[29] The sick clubs, however, were the first to feel the effects of a recession in trade. During the depression (1839–41) 13 of the 15 sick clubs in Hinckley, which numbered about 1,000 members, were closed owing to the inability of the members to pay their subscriptions.[30] The Anstey framework-knitters had a sick club of about a hundred members but members were continually being admitted and then rejected for failing to pay their contributions.[31] For the same reason there was a decline in the membership of the sick clubs of Ibstock and Thurcaston.[32]

At times of severe distress appeal was made to the generosity of the public at large and public subscriptions were raised to relieve the worst cases of poverty.[33] The cotton famine of 1862 caused the most acute distress in Hinckley and district. The Hinckley and District Relief Committee formed to deal with the problem disbursed more than £6,000 received from public and private donations.[34]

Another experiment, which appears to have been tried on a fairly extensive scale at the time of the Commission of 1845, was the provision of allotments for the framework-knitters on the principle that they would not only provide food for a framework-knitter's family when unemployment was rife, but they would also sustain the morale of the stockinger by furnishing an alternative occupation against enforced idleness. Associations were formed with the object of leasing land on favourable terms. At Great Glen the allotment society was incorporated and undertook to manage the allotments and guarantee the rents. In 1845 64 members held a total of 16 acres.[35] At Barwell an allotment system was first begun as early as 1820 but it was not generally introduced in the village until about 1843 when 9 acres were turned over to allotments for 130 members.[36] About the same time 250 members in Earl Shilton held 50 acres and at Hinckley 170 members 35 acres.[37] At Loughborough 160 members cropped 20 acres and at Cosby 23 acres were divided amongst 92 members.[38] Over the county as a whole the allotment system in 1845 was operating in about 60 different parishes.[39]

We have already noted how the making of 'cut-ups' and the glove trade in Leicester borough attracted the framework-knitters away from the villages. In the mining area of the county the exodus from the trade into the collieries became even more pronounced. In Ibstock there used to be 150 frames but in 1845 there were only 47.[40] At Bagworth there were 34 compared with 100–200 frames 25 years earlier[41] and in Newbold Verdon the frames were reduced to but a quarter of what they formerly were.[42] At Great Glen the move was largely back to agriculture, reducing the frames in the village by as much as 37 per cent. in the course of 15 years.[43] This drift from the rural centres was not halted until the last two decades of the century when the borough manufacturers once again enlisted rural labour for the factories that they began to build in the old village centres.

The middle years of the 19th century saw the emergence of two new factors which in the course of the succeeding 60 years destroyed the domestic character of the industry and brought it under the factory system. They were the employment of women in increasing numbers and the application of mechanical power to the stocking-frame.

It was the common practice for women and children to be employed in the ancillary tasks of winding, seaming, and footing. In the middle decades of the 19th century it was no longer the exception for women to work the frames themselves. John Geary of Anstey told the Commissioner of 1845 that whereas in 1810 few women were to be found working frames in Anstey it was lately the tendency for them to do so. He attributed the growing practice to the invention of the spinning-jenny which drove out the spinning-

[26] *1st App. to Rep. Cond. Framework Knitters*, 395.
[27] Ibid. 193–4. [28] Ibid. 159. [29] Ibid. 186.
[30] Ibid. 54, 233. [31] Ibid. 181, 185.
[32] Ibid. 385 (Ibstock) and 198 (Thurcaston).
[33] G. Mettam and J. Dyke in 1816 petitioned the H.O. regarding 'the present distressed state of the stocking manufactories at Hinckley', whether 'there would be any disposition on the part of the Government to advance some money to find employment for the poor until a favourable change takes place'. Lord Sidmouth replied 'Upon the best consideration, it is not deemed advisable on the part of the Government to issue Public Money for the purposes mentioned in your communication': H.O. 41/1.
[34] A. J. Pickering, *Cradle and Home of Hosiery Trade*, 110–11.
[35] *1st App. to Rep. Cond. Framework Knitters*, 372.
[36] Ibid. 278.
[37] *Rep. Cond. Framework Knitters*, 126.
[38] Ibid. [39] Ibid. 126–7.
[40] *1st App. to Rep. Cond. Framework Knitters*, 386, 388. [41] Ibid. 391. [42] Ibid. 393. [43] Ibid. 370.

Three Stocking Frames

Left: made by C. H. A. Reichel at Rothenthal, Saxony, *c.* 1790; one of a large number imported into Leicestershire *c.*1800. *Centre:* an early latch-needle machine, possibly made by Matthew Townsend of Leicester, the first maker of frames with the latch or self-acting needle which he invented in 1849. *Right:* a typical frame of *c.* 1830.

wheel and so deprived the women folk of the latter occupation.[44] Thomas Briers of Shepshed deposed that 50 years before he knew of only one woman in the parish to work in a frame but for a number of years there had been an increase in women framework-knitters.[45] Young single women as well as married women appear to have quite commonly worked the frames in the village of Woodhouse Eaves.[46] So it was at Barwell also,[47] but at Loughborough there were no great numbers working the frames, though experiments were being made at this time in withdrawing the seaming from the domestic hearth and assembling under one roof 40 to 50 girls to do this work under a supervisor.[48] In Leicester borough many frames were worked by women in most branches of the trade but more particularly in the glove branch.[49]

In the second half of the 19th century the number of women employees increased to such an extent that we find in the first quarter of the 20th century the ratio of women to men in the hosiery trade is 3 to 1. According to the Census Returns of 1931 of those engaged in the industry throughout England and Wales 73·66 per cent. were women and 26·34 per cent. men.[50] Thirty years earlier the proportion was much the same, there being in 1901 only 29·1 per cent. men to 70·9 per cent. women.[51] In Leicestershire the proportions were roughly the same as for the country at large. In county and borough in 1931 women numbered 71·8 per cent. and men 28·2 per cent.[52] Excluding the borough we find that over the county the proportion of men to women was only 1 to 2.[53] Eight years later the proportions were still roughly the same; for an analysis of the numbers of persons in insured employment in July 1939 reveals that for the county and city 74·2 per cent. were women and 25·8 per cent. men, or, excluding the city, women numbered 11,263 and men 5,513.[54]

Within the different hosiery areas in the county the ratios varied. In the Hinckley district men and women employees were more evenly balanced; 43 per cent. were men and 57 per cent. women. In Shepshed the proportion of women operatives was slightly larger, 58·4 per cent. women to 41·6 per cent. men; but in the Loughborough district the number of women employees was nearly three times as great as the men.[55]

This increase in the number of women employed in the trade seems to have been due largely to improvements to the frame, especially to the application of a rotary movement, first by means of a handle and later by mechanical power. Though there was no lack of inventive skill in modifying the stocking-frame,[56] the hosiery industry in the mid-19th century was barely touched by steam power which had revolutionized other industries. In 1816 Isambard Brunel invented a circular knitter which produced a seamless knitted tube, but experiments were not made with these machines until 30 years later.[57] These were doubtless the machines which Thomas Collins of Belgrave Gate, Leicester, had in his shop, where there were 34 rotary frames in 1845, 14 of which at least were worked by women. 'You have nothing to do but to turn the handle by the hand, and any boy or girl can turn those frames, if there is any one to look after them to see that they work rightly'.[58] The traditional frame was heavy and laborious for a woman to work but when William Cotton of the firm of Warner & Cartwright, Loughborough, successfully solved by 1864 the difficulties of applying power to the frame the burden was lightened.[59] In 1931 more than 75 per cent. of the 19,000 actually employed on the frames and machines in Leicester and Leicestershire were women.[60]

Cotton's patent frame and the circular knitter were the most important factors which turned the hosiery industry from the domestic system to the factory system. Nevertheless, experiments had been made in bringing the hand frames from the home into shops or 'factories', as contemporaries called them, during the years immediately preceding the Commission of Inquiry of 1845. According to Thomas Smith, a framework-knitter of 25 years' standing, who had moved from Hinckley into the glove branch at Leicester, a shop of 8 frames was considered large in his younger days but in recent years shops to house 40 or 50 frames had been built.[61] 'There is', says William Clarke

44 *1st App. to Rep. Cond. Framework Knitters*, 183.

45 Ibid. 311.

46 Ibid. 436.

47 Ibid. 395.

48 Ibid. 405.

49 Ibid. 17. In Barrow upon Soar, which possessed about 250 frames, there were very few females employed, but in nearby Sileby with about 500 frames there were many more: ibid. 430.

50 *Census, 1931: Industrial Tables*, p. 4.

51 Ibid. pp. 712–13.

52 Ibid. p. 76.

53 Ibid.

54 Ex inf. Min. Labour, N. Midlands Region.

55 These proportions are based on *Census, 1931: Industrial Tables*, pp. 233–5. A similar analysis cannot be made of the figures of persons insured against unemployment in the hosiery trade in July 1939, as these figures are subdivided according to exchanges which cannot be equated in all instances with the geographical areas on which the census returns are based.

56 See above, p. 5, n. 10.

57 Felkin, *Hosiery and Lace Mftures.* 496–7; J. H. Clapham, *Econ. Hist. Mod. Brit.* ii, 33.

58 *1st App. to Rep. Cond. Framework Knitters*, 138.

59 J. Deakin, *Loughborough in the 19th Cent.* 36.

60 *Census, 1931 Occupational Tables*, p. 254: 18,675 hosiery frame-tenters and machine-knitters. These 2 terms seem to comprehend all who work the various types of machines. In 1892 Jas. Holmes, President of the Midland Counties Hosiery Federation, giving evidence before the Royal Com. on Labour, stated that women worked the linking and stitching machines but not the frames, which were worked by men: [C. 6795–vi] questions 12687–8 H.C. (1892), xxxvi (2). This is hardly a complete picture in view of the evidence already quoted.

61 *1st App. to Rep. Cond. Framework Knitters*, [618] p. 5, H.C. (1845), xv.

of Leicester, 'a great deal more shopping now than there used to be when there was more wrought hose made. There used not to be one-quarter of the wide frames 20 or 30 years ago that there are now, and now they get into very large shops. Some 20 or 30 and more than that one man will hold. I never used to know a man to hold above 3 or 4 or 4 or 5 frames.'[62]

These larger shops were, however, limited to the borough of Leicester. At Hinckley Edward Kem Jarvis experimented with a large factory, in which neither frame rent nor standing charges were made, as was customary in the small shops, but his project failed owing to the opposition of the Hinckley framework-knitters to the regular routine which factory discipline required.[63] At Loughborough John Ward worked in the patent shirt branch; the frames for making these goods were not allowed into the workers' homes and Ward's employer had a factory of sixteen frames of this type.[64] But the hands employed by the Loughborough firm of Warner, Cartwright, & Warner worked mostly in their own homes or in small shops. None of the shops owned by this firm which were engaged in wrought hose contained more than 8 frames.[65] It seems that because the rural industry was almost exclusively engaged on the traditional wrought hose made on the narrow-frame experiments in large concentrations of frames were not made. The small shop with its modest number of frames was the rule in the country districts.[66]

It was in Loughborough about 1840 that Messrs. Cartwright & Warner opened the first power-driven factory in Leicestershire. They used steam power to drive the frames engaged in the shirt branch of the trade.[67] Five years later Paget of Loughborough turned the Zouch Mills into a hosiery factory by installing steam-driven rotary frames for making caps, shirts, and straight-down hose.[68] Steam power was not applied to the frames in the Hinckley district until 1855 when Thomas Payne built a factory in Wood Street, Hinckley.[69] The move into factories was, indeed, very slow. In 1871 there were only seventy-four hosiery factories in the county and borough.[70]

In the last quarter of the 19th century several factors assisted the change-over to the factory system. Frame rents, which had been so strong a vested interest in the rural areas for both manufacturers and middlemen in the first half of the 19th century, at first retarded the drift to the factories. But as more power-driven factories were opened speculation in the rents of hand frames became less attractive and frame rents were finally abolished by statute in 1874.[71] Even more crushing than the abolition of frame rents was the blow dealt by the Education Act of 1870, especially after 1876 when education between the ages of 5 and 14 was made compulsory. For now the hosiery trade was deprived of its child labour which had inevitably flourished when the industry was centred on the cottage home and which in consequence had proved a most powerful factor in sustaining the domestic system.[72] Lastly, there were the advantages of a stronger trade unionism which the factories had made possible and which resulted in better conditions for the factory hands than for the domestic framework-knitters.[73]

We now find factories appearing in the villages as well as in the larger centres such as Hinckley and Loughborough. By 1894 in the Hinckley district there were over twenty factories in Hinckley itself and one in the nearby village of Stoke Golding.[74] In the Loughborough area there were two hosiery factories in Kegworth, and the villages of Hathern and Rothley each possessed a factory erected in 1887.[75] In Loughborough itself Cartwright & Warner's factory at this time was employing over a thousand hands and, in addition, there were the large factories run by the Nottingham Manufacturing Company and Messrs. I. and R. Morley.[76] In the hosiery area south of Leicester power-driven frames had appeared alongside the hand frames in Blaby; and at Fleckney there were

62 *1st App. to Rep. Cond. Framework Knitters*, 33.

63 Ibid. 210.

64 Ibid. 400.

65 Ibid. 420.

66 Cf. Earl Shilton: John Homer, manufacturer there —the frames he employs are in the houses of the work-people; 'the factory system is not in operation here at all': ibid. 303. Mountsorrel: Ric. Jarratt, framework-knitter—frames 'generally speaking, in small shops': ibid. 432. Thornton: Nathaniel Mason, framework-knitter, formerly had a shop of 7 frames: ibid. 392. Shepshed: Thomas Briers, framework-knitter, had a shop of 7 or 8 frames: ibid. 311, and Wm. Thurman, framework-knitter, also possessed a shop of 7 frames: ibid. 313. Saddington: Thomas Bryant, framework-knitter, worked for Mr. Bailiff of Saddington in his shop of 7 frames: ibid. 376.

67 Ibid. 394.

68 Ibid. 404–5.

69 Pickering, *Cradle and Home of Hosiery Trade*, 49.

70 *Ret. of Manufacturing Establishments*, H.C. 440, p. 12 (1871), lxii.

71 Hosiery Manufacture (Wages) Act, 1874, 37 & 38 Vic. c. 48. When a Parl. Cttee. in 1854 recommended a Bill for the abolition of frame rents the Ho. rejected it. The gradual, though slow, change-over meant that the problem of frame rents solved itself. See F. A. Wells, *Brit. Hosiery Trade*, 147, 158–9.

72 In Hinckley attendance at the elementary schools doubled when girls were allowed to bring seaming to school in the afternoon: Wells, op. cit. 156.

73 We have already observed the slight progress which trade unionism made whilst the hosiery industry was located in the home. The task proved easier as the industry changed over to factory production, e.g. in the factories at Nott. the unions were able to obtain a 54-hour week: Wells, op. cit. 155.

74 Wright, *Dir. Leic.* (1894), 466 (Hinckley); ibid. (1888), 564 (Stoke Golding).

75 Ibid. (1894), 479 (Kegworth); 464 (Hathern), 383 (Rothley).

76 Ibid. 491.

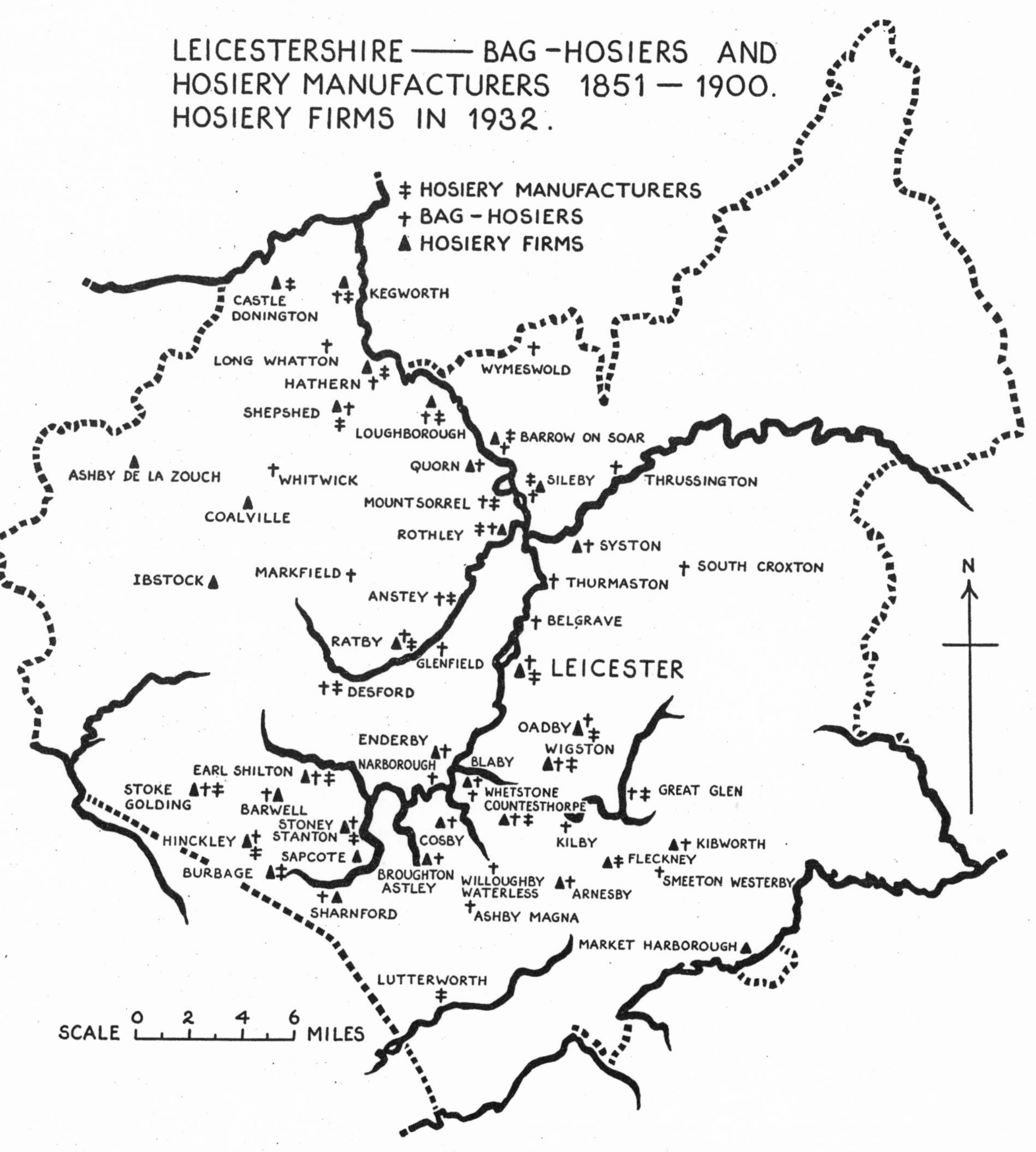
LEICESTERSHIRE —— BAG-HOSIERS AND HOSIERY MANUFACTURERS 1851 — 1900.
HOSIERY FIRMS IN 1932.
‡ HOSIERY MANUFACTURERS
† BAG-HOSIERS
▲ HOSIERY FIRMS
CASTLE DONINGTON
KEGWORTH
LONG WHATTON
HATHERN
WYMESWOLD
SHEPSHED
LOUGHBOROUGH
BARROW ON SOAR
ASHBY DE LA ZOUCH
WHITWICK
QUORN
SILEBY
THRUSSINGTON
MOUNTSORREL
COALVILLE
ROTHLEY
SYSTON
IBSTOCK
MARKFIELD
THURMASTON
SOUTH CROXTON
ANSTEY
BELGRAVE
RATBY
GLENFIELD
LEICESTER
DESFORD
OADBY
ENDERBY
WIGSTON
EARL SHILTON
NARBOROUGH
BLABY
STOKE GOLDING
BARWELL
WHETSTONE
COUNTESTHORPE
GREAT GLEN
STONEY STANTON
HINCKLEY
COSBY
KILBY
KIBWORTH
SAPCOTE
FLECKNEY
BURBAGE
BROUGHTON ASTLEY
WILLOUGHBY WATERLESS
ARNESBY
SMEETON WESTERBY
SHARNFORD
ASHBY MAGNA
MARKET HARBOROUGH
LUTTERWORTH
SCALE 0 2 4 6 MILES
N

at least three factories established by Leicester firms.[77]

Nevertheless, the hand frames persisted and they were still found early in the 20th century. Trade directories of the last decade of the 19th century reveal that hand frames continued to be used in the villages where factories had been set up.[78] The Hand Framework Knitters Federation in 1892 had a membership of about 1,440 and its Treasurer when giving evidence before the Royal Commission on Labour in that year estimated the number of hand framework-knitters in the midlands to be 5,000.[79] This survival of the hand framework-knitters in face of the progressive change-over to factory production was largely due to the conservatism of the War Office in still placing orders for the old style 'military pants', which could only be made on the hand frames.[80] It is, therefore, significant that in 1894 there were in Leicestershire about 180 bag-hosiers still operating in 44 villages in the county.[81]

But in the opening decades of the 20th century the old hand frames died out[82] and in 1932 the bag-hosier survived only in the village of Wigston.[83] There were in 1932 in the county, outside Leicester city, at least 177 hosiery firms. In Hinckley they numbered 59; in Wigston, 18; in Loughborough and in Earl Shilton, 12; and in Shepshed, 11.[84]

The expansion of the hosiery industry under the factory system is reflected in the number of people employed and in the production figures periodically returned to the Board of Trade. The growth in the number of women employees in the industry and their preponderance over men since the close of the 19th century has already been observed. In 1931 approximately 22,000 men and women were engaged in the hosiery trade in Leicestershire and 24,000 in Leicester city, making a total of 46,000 or almost half the total manpower in the trade over all England and Wales.[85] In July 1939 only 16,776 men and women in the county were insured against unemployment but in the city numbers had risen to 33,310.[86] Throughout the country the number of persons employed in the industry more than doubled itself between 1901 and 1931.[87] As about half the industry had been located in Leicester and Leicestershire since the mid-19th century, it may be assumed that during the first three decades of the 20th century the manpower of the county so employed expanded in proportion to the expansion of the industry as a whole.

With regard to production, precise figures for Leicestershire are not available and in view of the county's dominant position in the trade we can only infer that the output of the Leicestershire factories is fairly accurately reflected in the figures for the industry as a whole. The total value of stockings, socks, underwear, and fancy hosiery produced increased fivefold between 1907 and 1924 from just over £8 million to more than £40 million.[88] When the next production census was taken in 1930 output had declined by 15 per cent.; which is accounted for by the world depression of 1929–30.[89] In addition, there were knitted gloves, cravats, neckties, and other knitted articles not included in the above three main categories; these amounted in value to just over £2 million in 1924 and suffered a decline of about 7 per cent. in 1930.

Between 1907 and 1924 there was a greater increase in fancy hosiery than in either stockings and half-hose or underwear. Of the total value of output in these three groups fancy hosiery represented only 12 per cent. in 1907, but in 1924 it was approximately 24 per cent.; a proportion maintained in 1930. Throughout the period 1907–30 stockings and half hose accounted for roughly 50 per cent. in value of the total output in the three major branches of the trade.

[77] Wright, *Dir. Leic.* (1894), 364 (Blaby); 454 (Fleckney); but ibid. (1888), 400, it is stated that four Leic. firms had hosiery factories in Fleckney. Hosiery factories had also appeared by this time in Shepshed: ibid. (1894), 579, and in Thurmaston: ibid. 387.

[78] e.g. Blaby, Shepshed, Stoke Golding, Thurmaston.

[79] *Rep. Com. on Labour* [C. 6795–vi] Q. 13324, 13338, H.C. (1892), xxxvi (2). Cf. the number of members in the Midland Counties Hosiery Federation, membership of which was limited to workers on power-driven machinery. The President of the Federation estimated their numbers at 4,500 in Leics., Notts. and Derbys.: ibid. Q. 12683.

[80] Ibid. Q. 13358, 1360, 1362.

[81] Calculated from entries in Wright, *Dir. Leic.* (1894).

[82] The last hand frames disappeared in the Hinckley area (Barwell, Hinckley, Earl Shilton) in the early years of the First World War: Pickering, *Cradle and Home of Hosiery Trade*, 50. A. Bernard Clarke of the old Loughborough firm—Thomas Clarke & Sons—recalls that when he started work in 1903 his firm had tenants in an old factory who worked the hand frames but they were gone in a few years. The firm still received a few dozen hose or half-hose from bag-hosiers until the First World War (personal inf.). In 1951 hand-operated Griswold machines were still used by firms to make 'Argyle hose', a type which cannot be successfully manufactured by power-driven machinery. The firm of A. W. Dakin & Co. Ltd. of Kegworth still employ a number of outworkers in neighbouring villages on this type of work: Ex. inf. F. B. Mallinson of Rothley. So, too, the firm of Fuller & Hambly, Hathern, have both out-workers and employees in their factory working by hand the Griswold machine to produce this type of work: Ex. inf. Fuller & Hambly.

[83] *Kelly's Dir. Leics. and Rut.* (1932), 172, 800, records a bag-hosier at Leic., and another at Wigston Magna.

[84] Calculated from entries in *Kelly's Dir. Leics. and Rut.* (1932).

[85] *Census, 1931: Industrial Tables*, p. 76.

[86] Ex inf. Min. Labour, N. Midlands Region.

[87] *Census, 1931: Industrial Tables*, pp. 712–13.

[88] *Third Census of Production, 1924: Preliminary Rep. no. 9* (H.M.S.O.).

[89] *Fourth Census of Production, 1930* (H.M.S.O.).

As for quantities, there is only sufficient evidence for comparing the output at various years of stockings and half-hose. In 1844, when factory production was virtually non-existent, 4,018,000 dozen pairs were produced on the hand frames;[90] by 1907, when the change-over to the factory system was nearly complete, production had increased to 14 million dozen pairs[91] and in 1924 it reached just under 25 million dozen pairs,[92] dropping to 20 million dozen pairs in 1930.[93] Since the middle of the 19th century the most striking feature is the decline of cotton hose and the rise of silk and artificial silk hose. In 1844 silk accounted for only 2·05 per cent. of the total production but in 1924 hose made of silk or artificial silk thread rose to 20·8 per cent. of the total produced, and in 1930 reached 34·4 per cent., of which 5 per cent. was pure silk and 29·4 per cent. artificial silk. On the other hand, cotton hose declined from 53·9 per cent. of the total production in 1844 to 17·3 per cent. in 1924 and still further in 1930, when it sank to 12·7 per cent.

Although the increase in production which resulted from the factory system enlarged the export trade, the bulk of it still went into the home market. In 1843–4 exports in stockings and socks were only 11·9 per cent. of the total production[94] but in 1924 they rose to 21 per cent.[95] and since production had increased sixfold, exports were ten times larger. Nevertheless 79 per cent. of the output was still consumed at home, and, if we turn to the underwear and fancy branches of the trade, we find that exports were only 11 per cent. and 13 per cent. respectively.[96] We have already observed that in Leicestershire in the mid-19th century the hosiery frames had become almost entirely engaged for the home market. It is clear, therefore, that, despite the change-over to factory production, no fundamental change in the orientation of the trade had been effected by the second decade of the 20th century.

By reason of the late development of factory production in the hosiery trade, the hosiery hands were spared the grosser evils which had accompanied the pioneer experiments in factory organization in other industries during the early part of the 19th century. From the beginning the hosiery factories came under the Factory Acts and the supervision of the factory inspectors.[97] Trade unionism made greater progress in the trade with the growth of the factories[98] and the weekly wages of those working on Cotton's Patent frames averaged in 1892 between 25*s.* and 35*s.*, which was three to five times greater than the average rate throughout the trade in the county and borough in 1845.[99] Nevertheless, the continuance of domestic work, which was looked upon as a form of sweating, tended to lower wages[1] and a new problem arose with the growth of female employees in the factories, particularly married women, who were prepared to work at reduced rates[2]

Although on occasions as late as the last decade of the 19th century the hosiery workers in some parts of Leicestershire were still compelled to fight for the right to join a union,[3] a spirit of confidence between employer and employee developed in the second half of the 19th century. This showed itself in the establishment of a Board of Arbitration and Conciliation in Leicester in 1866, modelled on a similar body set up by A. J. Mundella in Nottingham 6 years earlier.[4] Even when this Board foundered in 1886 the spirit was not killed. For, as James Holmes, the President of the Midland Counties Hosiery Federation, declared to the Royal Commission on Labour in 1892, it was easy to get together to settle disputes, despite the break-up of the conciliation board.[5] The manufacturers developed their own associations[6] and in 1918 the earlier precedent for arbitration and conciliation was followed with the establishment of the National Joint Industrial Council of the Hosiery Trade.[7]

[90] *Rep. Cond. Framework Knitters*, [609] p. 19, H.C. (1845), xv.

[91] *Third Census of Production, 1924* (H.M.S.O.).

[92] Ibid.

[93] *Fourth Census of Production, 1930* (H.M.S.O.).

[94] Calculated from the export figures for 1843: *Rep. Cond. Framework Knitters*, 83, and the production figures for 1844: ibid. 19, since both sets of figures for the same year are not available.

[95] *Third Census of Production, 1924* (H.M.S.O.).

[96] In 1930 exports were as follows: only 16 per cent. for stockings and hose, 6 per cent. for underwear, and 11 per cent. for fancy hosiery, of the total production of each group: *Fourth Census of Production, 1930* (H.M.S.O.).

[97] Inspection of hosiery factories was well carried out, but more inspectors were needed: *Rep. Com. on Labour*, Q. 12830, 12833. Sanitary conds. in Leics. factories were generally good: ibid. Q. 12868.

[98] In 1885 the various district framework-knitters cttees. and unions amalgamated to form the Leic. and Leics. Amalgamated Hosiery Union. In 1895 the Hinckley workers broke away and formed their own union: Pickering, *Cradle and Home of Hosiery Trade*, 115.

[99] The average net weekly wage in 1845 for county and borough was about 7*s.* 6*d.*: *1st App. to Rep. Cond. Framework Knitters*, 499. For wages on Cotton's frames in 1892, see *Rep. Com. on Labour*, Q. 12698.

[1] Ibid. Q. 12774–5, 12785.

[2] Ibid. Q. 12806, 12808, 12811.

[3] At Earl Shilton, 8 men were locked out for forming a union: ibid. Q. 12789. At Fleckney 20 men were also locked out for the same reason: ibid. Q. 12840.

[4] See Pickering, *Cradle and Home of Hosiery Trade*, 120.

[5] *Rep. Com. on Labour*, Q. 12715–20, 12744.

[6] Pickering, op. cit. 118. The Hinckley manufacturers formed the Hinckley Hosiery Manufacturers' Assoc. in 1891. It changed its name in 1897 to the Hinckley & District Hosiery Manufacturers' Assoc.

[7] Pickering, op. cit. 203.

APPENDIX

EVIDENCE FOR FRAMEWORK-KNITTERS, STOCKING-FRAMES, BAG-HOSIERS AND MANUFACTURERS IN THE COUNTY OF LEICESTER

Columns 2 and 3 are based largely upon entries in the Register of Apprentices sworn before the mayors of Leicester printed in *Register of the Freemen of Leicester*, ed. H. Hartopp.

Column 4 is abstracted from J. Blackner, *History of Nottingham*, 239–40.

Details in column 5 are taken from W. Felkin, *History of the Machine-Wrought Hosiery and Lace Manufactures* (1867), 465–6.

Column 6 is based upon entries in the Minutes of Evidence of the *Report on the condition of the Framework Knitters*, 1845,[8] and column 7 upon details in the *Census, 1851*.

Column 8 has been compiled from entries in the various editions of *Wright's Directories of Leicester and Leicestershire* and column 9 from entries in *Kelly's Directory of Leicestershire and Rutland* (1932).

f.w.k.s. = framework-knitters.

1	*2*	*3*	*4*	*5*	*6*	*7*	*8*		*9*	
							1852–1900		*1932*	
Place	*1700–50 f.w.k.s.*	*1751–1800 f.w.k.s.*	*Blackner's return 1812 f.w.k.s.*	*Felkin's return 1844 frames*	*Report f.w.k. 1845 frames*	*Census returns 1851 f.w.k.s.*	*Bag-hosiers*	*Mfrs.*	*Bag-hosiers*	*Hosiery firms*
Ab Kettleby	Yes	...	...	...	...	...	...	...	...	...
Anstey	Yes	Yes	Yes	215	300	215	2	2	...	...
Arnesby	...	Yes	...	100	...	...	6	...	...	2
Asfordby	...	...	Yes	6	...	...	...	...	...	...
Ashby de la Zouch	Yes	Yes	Yes	14	...	...	...	...	...	1
Ashby Magna	...	Yes	...	...	...	...	2	...	...	...
Ashby Parva	...	...	...	20	...	...	...	...	...	...
Aston Flamville	...	...	Yes	...	...	...	...	...	...	...
Aylestone	Yes	Yes	Yes	76	...	...	...	...	...	...
Bagworth	...	...	Yes	34	34	...	...	...	...	...
Barkby	Yes	Yes	Yes	35	...	...	...	...	...	...
Barkby Thorpe	Yes	Yes	Yes	...	...	...	...	...	...	...
Barlestone	Yes	Yes	...	114	103	...	...	...	...	...
Barrow upon Soar	Yes	...	Yes	210	250	261	10	1	...	1
Barsby	...	...	...	29	...	...	...	...	...	...
Barwell	Yes	Yes	Yes	400	300	462	5	...	...	1
Bassett House	Yes	...	...	...	...	...	...	...	...	...
Belgrave	...	Yes	Yes	200	...	323	3	...	...	...
Belton	...	...	Yes	93	82–93	...	...	...	...	...
Billesdon	...	Yes	...	...	...	...	...	...	...	...
Birstall	Yes	Yes	Yes	...	...	...	...	...	...	...
Blaby	...	Yes	Yes	322	300	369	6	...	...	5
Bosworth, Market	...	Yes	Yes	80	70	...	...	...	...	...
Botcheston	...	Yes	...	...	...	...	...	...	...	...
Bottesford	...	...	Yes	...	...	...	...	...	...	...
Bowden, Great (Market Harborough)	...	Yes	...	...	...	...	...	...	...	1
Brascote	Yes	...	...	...	...	...	...	...	...	...
Braunstone	...	Yes	...	...	...	...	...	...	...	...
Broughton Astley (Primethorpe, Sutton)	...	Yes	Yes	...	1100	...	4	...	...	2
Bruntingthorpe	...	...	Yes	70	...	...	...	...	...	...
Burbage	...	...	Yes	450	500	572	...	1	...	7
Burton Overy	...	...	...	20	...	...	...	...	...	...
Bushby	...	Yes	...	...	...	...	...	...	...	...
Cadeby	...	Yes	Yes	...	...	...	...	...	...	...
Carlton	...	...	...	5	...	...	...	...	...	...
Claybrooke	...	...	...	44	...	...	...	...	...	...
Coalville	...	...	...	...	...	...	...	...	...	1

[8] [609] and [618], H.C. (1845), xv.

1	2	3	4	5	6	7	8		9	
							1852–1900		1932	
Place	1700–1750 f.w.k.s.	1751–1800 f.w.k.s.	Blackner's return 1812 f.w.k.s.	Felkin's return 1844 frames	Report f.w.k. 1845 frames	Census returns 1851 f.w.k.s.	Bag-hosiers	Mfrs.	Bag-hosiers	Hosiery firms
Coleorton (and Griffydam)	...	...	Yes	56	...	...	...	...	...	...
Cosby	...	Yes	Yes	250	161	291	2	...	...	1
Cossington	Yes	Yes	Yes	7	...	...	...	...	...	...
Countesthorpe	...	Yes	Yes	214	...	241	8	4	...	6
Croft	...	...	...	54	...	...	...	...	...	...
Cropston	...	Yes	...	...	...	...	...	...	...	...
Croxton, South	...	...	...	35	...	...	1	...	...	...
Dadlington	...	...	...	34	...	...	...	...	...	...
Dalby, Little	...	...	Yes	...	...	...	...	...	...	...
Dalby, Old	...	...	Yes	...	...	...	...	...	...	...
Desford	Yes	Yes	Yes	163	...	...	1	2	...	...
Diseworth	...	...	Yes	62	61–62	...	...	...	...	...
Donington, Castle	...	...	Yes	110	...	...	...	1	...	1
Dunton Bassett	...	...	Yes	120	...	...	...	...	...	...
Enderby	Yes	Yes	Yes	350	320	253	6	...	...	2
Evington	Yes	Yes	...	...	...	...	...	...	...	...
Fleckney	...	...	...	126	124	...	...	3	...	4
Foston	...	...	Yes	10	...	...	...	...	...	...
Frisby	...	...	Yes	...	...	...	...	...	...	...
Frolesworth	...	...	Yes	...	...	...	...	...	...	...
Gaddesby	Yes	...	Yes	...	...	...	...	...	...	...
Glen, Great	...	...	...	...	100	...	2	1	...	...
Glenfield	...	Yes	Yes	50	...	...	2	...	...	...
Groby	Yes	Yes	Yes	...	...	...	...	...	...	...
Hathern	...	Yes	Yes	367	...	270	6	1	...	2
Heather	...	...	Yes	23	...	...	...	...	...	...
Hemington	...	...	Yes	...	...	...	...	...	...	...
Hinckley	Yes	Yes	Yes	1750	1500	1531	1	21	...	59
Hoton	...	...	Yes	...	...	...	...	...	...	...
Houghton on the Hill	...	Yes	...	...	...	...	...	...	...	...
Hugglescote	...	...	Yes	...	...	...	...	...	...	...
Humberstone	Yes	Yes	Yes	22	...	...	...	...	...	...
Huncote	...	Yes	...	92	92	...	...	...	...	...
Ibstock	...	...	Yes	...	47	...	...	...	...	1
Kegworth	...	...	Yes	...	120–76	...	5	4	...	4
Kibworth	...	Yes	...	...	...	...	3	...	...	2
Kilby	...	Yes	Yes	...	...	...	1	...	...	...
Kilworth, North	Yes	...	...	...	...	...	...	...	...	...
Knighton	Yes	Yes	Yes	...	...	...	...	...	...	...
Langton, Tur	Yes	...	...	...	...	...	...	...	...	...
Leicester	Yes	Yes	Yes	4140	...	4147	Yes	Yes	1	[ ][9]
Leicester Forest	Yes	Yes	...	...	...	...	...	...	...	...
Leire	...	...	...	40	...	...	...	...	...	...
Little Thorpe	...	Yes	Yes	107	107	...	...	...	...	...
Loughborough	Yes	Yes	Yes	906	...	667	8	11	...	12
Lutterworth	...	...	Yes	90	...	...	...	2	...	...
Markfield	...	...	Yes	153	...	...	5	...	...	...
Melton Mowbray	...	...	Yes	...	...	...	...	...	...	...
Mountsorrel	...	Yes	Yes	258	190	203	1	1	...	...
Nailstone	...	...	Yes	...	...	...	...	...	...	...
Narborough	Yes	Yes	Yes	144	...	...	1	...	...	...
Newbold Verdon	...	...	Yes	60	20–25	...	...	...	...	...
Newton Harcourt	...	...	...	37	...	...	...	...	...	...

[9] No figure can be determined for the number of firms in Leic. in 1932 because the boundaries of the city were greatly enlarged between 1851 and 1932 and the statistics are not comparable.

1	2	3	4	5	6	7	8		9	
							1852–1900		*1932*	
Place	*1700–1750 f.w.k.s.*	*1751–1800 f.w.k.s.*	*Blackner's return 1812 f.w.k.s.*	*Felkin's return 1844 frames*	*Report f.w.k. 1845 frames*	*Census returns 1851 f.w.k.s.*	*Bag-hosiers*	*Mfrs.*	*Bag-hosiers*	*Hosiery firms*
Newton Burgoland and Newton Nethercote	...	...	...	10	9	...	...	...	...	...
Newtown Linford	Yes	Yes	Yes	...	...	...	...	...	...	...
Oadby	Yes	Yes	Yes	350	...	200	4	2	...	4
Osgathorpe	...	Yes	Yes	24	24	...	...	...	...	...
Peatling Magna	...	...	...	30	...	...	...	...	...	...
Peckleton	...	Yes	Yes	...	...	...	...	...	...	...
Primethorpe—See Broughton Astley										
Queniborough	...	...	Yes	110	...	...	...	...	...	...
Quorndon	...	Yes	Yes	188	...	...	1	[Elastic Web Mfrs.]	...	1
Ratby	...	...	Yes	120	...	...	7	2	...	2
Ravenstone	...	...	Yes	...	...	...	...	...	...	...
Rearsby	...	Yes	Yes	70	...	...	...	...	...	...
Rotherby	...	Yes	...	...	...	...	...	...	...	...
Rothley	Yes	Yes	Yes	159	...	...	1	1	...	1
Saddington	...	...	...	34	29	...	...	...	...	...
Sapcote	...	...	Yes	220	...	196	...	...	...	2
Saxelby	...	...	Yes	...	...	...	...	...	...	...
Seagrave	...	...	Yes	...	...	...	...	...	...	...
Sharnford	...	...	Yes	56	...	...	1	...	...	1
Shearsby	Yes	...	...	60	...	...	...	...	...	...
Shepshed	Yes	Yes	Yes	1209	1237	896	15	6	...	11
Shilton, Earl	Yes	Yes	Yes	650	...	733	5	2	...	12
Sileby	Yes	Yes	Yes	500	...	489	7	1	...	5
Smeeton Westerby	...	Yes	...	140	...	...	3	...	...	...
Stanton, Stoney	Yes	...	Yes	200	...	127	1	1	...	1
Stanton under Bardon	...	...	Yes	49	...	...	...	...	...	...
Stapleton	...	...	Yes	23	...	...	...	...	...	...
Stoke Golding	...	...	Yes	206	217	204	Yes	1	...	3
Stoughton	Yes	...	...	...	...	...	...	...	...	...
Stretton, Little	Yes	Yes	...	...	...	...	...	...	...	...
Sutton Cheney	...	...	Yes	...	...	...	...	...	...	...
Swannington	...	...	Yes	...	...	10	...	...	...	...
Swithland	...	Yes	...	...	...	...	...	...	...	...
Syston	...	Yes	Yes	280	...	221	2	...	...	1
Thornton	...	Yes	Yes	22	25	...	...	...	...	...
Thorpe Acre	Yes	...	Yes	47	...	...	...	...	...	...
Thorpe Satchville	...	...	Yes	...	...	...	...	...	...	...
Thringstone	...	Yes	Yes	160	155	71	...	...	...	...
Thrussington	...	...	...	...	...	...	1	...	...	...
Thurcaston	...	...	Yes	11	11	...	...	...	...	...
Thurlaston	...	...	...	85	...	...	...	...	...	...
Thurmaston	Yes	Yes	Yes	...	400	...	9	...	...	...
Thurnby	...	Yes	...	...	...	...	...	...	...	...
Walcote	...	...	...	70	...	...	...	...	...	...
Walton on the Wolds	...	...	Yes	...	...	...	...	...	...	...
Wanlip	Yes	Yes	...	...	...	...	...	...	...	...
Whatton, Long	Yes	Yes	Yes	...	250	...	2	...	...	...
Whetstone	...	...	Yes	297	...	295	7	...	...	...
Whitwick	Yes	Yes	Yes	423	339	240	4	...	...	...

1	2	3	4	5	6	7	8		9	
							1852–1900		*1932*	
Place	*1700–1750 f.w.k.s.*	*1751–1800 f.w.k.s.*	*Blackner's return 1812 f.w.k.s.*	*Felkin's return 1844 frames*	*Report f.w.k. 1845 frames*	*Census returns 1851 f.w.k.s.*	*Bag-hosiers*	*Mfrs.*	*Bag-hosier*	*Hosiery firms*
WIGSTON MAGNA (and WIGSTON, SOUTH)	Yes	Yes	Yes	550	550	523	16	8	1	18
WILLOUGHBY WATERLESS	...	Yes	Yes	80	...	...	2	...	...	...
WOODHOUSE (and WOODHOUSE EAVES)	Yes	Yes	Yes	158	150	...	...	...	...	...
WYKIN	...	...	...	10	...	...	...	...	...	...
WYMESWOLD	...	...	Yes	10	...	...	1	...	...	...

FOOTWEAR

Though Leicestershire is today one of the most important areas concerned with the English footwear industry, the industry is of comparatively recent origin in the county. In Leicester itself (which is treated in a subsequent volume) the industry began to take its rise after 1851. In the county there is little to record before 1870.

There is no sign of a footwear industry, in the sense of one producing for an external market, in White's *Directory of Leicestershire and Rutland* for 1846.[1] Boot- and shoe-makers are listed in considerable numbers—for example, 13 at Hinckley, 9 at Market Harborough, 7 at Earl Shilton, and 200 in Leicester—but these were no more that were necessary to supply the local population, roughly one to every two or three hundred people. They were bespoke boot- and shoe-makers.

In Leicester the transition to making for stock was just beginning to take place in the 1840's. Of the 200 boot- and shoe-makers listed in the 1846 directory, only Thomas Crick in Highcross Street is described as 'wholesale', and his name also appears among those of the curriers and leather cutters. As the scale of manufacture enlarged in the town, during the 1850's and 1860's, it became usual for the uppers to be cut and closed in the factory, and the making and finishing to be done by out-workers. At first the out-workers were found near the factories in the town itself, but as the industry grew—and the expanding hosiery industry also competed for labour—the Leicester manufacturers began to get the making and finishing done in the country districts, in the western part of the county, where there was a large class of depressed framework-knitters hopelessly competing with the new hosiery machinery and slowly going under. Thomas Crick is said to have been one of the first manufacturers to get work done outside the town, and notably in the decaying framework-knitting village of Earl Shilton. Sileby is also said to have been an early scene of this type of out-working.

This system was known as 'basket-work'. The closed uppers were taken from Leicester by cart, to be given out in the village to the workers who did the actual making and finishing in their own homes. The latter then returned the finished boots and shoes to the carter, who may or may not have been a true middleman. If he was a middleman, he paid the country workers and collected his own payment from the manufacturer when the completed footwear reached the warehouse. If he was not a middleman, he received payment as a carter from the Leicester manufacturer. In this way the manufacturer found cheaper labour than he could get in the town, and the depressed framework-knitters (or their children) secured a means of adding to the family income. It was probably not long before the country operatives turned over entirely from framework-knitting or agricultural labour to industrial employment on this domestic system. And it was no accident that the boot and shoe industry grew up in the west of the county, for it was here—chiefly in and around Hinckley—that framework-knitting developed in the second half of the 17th century and was decaying in the early 19th. The 17th-century inclosures in western Leicestershire had produced a considerable class of landless labourers, who attracted the attention of the early hosiers and renters of knitting-frames. In turn the mass of displaced or impoverished framework-knitters in the middle decades of the 19th century attracted the new Leicester boot and shoe manufacturers, on the look-out for cheap labour. The 1871 census showed that there were then nearly as many boot and shoe workers (male and female) in the county as in the town: 5,049 in the county, 5,103 in the town.

Enterprising men in the county were not con-

[1] There appears to be no evidence whatsoever for the statement in John Bland, *Bygone Days in Market Harborough*, 24, that 'in Queen Elizabeth's days the chief trade [at Market Harborough] was the making of shoes for export'.

tent, however, to see country labour used for the benefit of the town manufacturers. The first 'boot and shoe manufacturer' in the county was William Moore at Anstey. He is so described in White's *Directory* for 1863. In the 1861 directory he is called simply 'boot and shoe maker', like any other bespoke maker. By 1870 the directory lists four 'manufacturers' at Anstey, and the first 'shoe manufacturer' had made his appearance at Earl Shilton, now one of the largest of the shoe-manufacturing villages. This was the firm of Cotton & Son.[2] But the village was still described as composed chiefly of framework-knitters; the transition had only just begun. Neither at Hinckley nor at Barwell—both now considerable footwear centres—was there any trace of an industry in 1870, though at the former William Porter was described as 'leather-cutter and boot-top manufacturer'. He was possibly an embryo boot manufacturer, but nothing came of this start for he was not there 7 years later. The only other manufacturer in the county in 1870 appears to have been Joseph Clarke, 'shoe manufacturer and lime-burner' at Sileby.

Not only was the industry thinly distributed in the county in 1870—possibly six or seven manufacturers altogether—but the directories reveal, too, the rudimentary stage of its evolution at that point. At Sileby Joseph Clarke combined shoe manufacturing with lime-burning. At Earl Shilton in 1877 one of the Cottons combined boot manufacturing with farming; while the first manufacturer at Barwell (in 1877) was also a grocer and carrier. Possibly the capital for the early industry came partly from such established and older sources as this, and as the new venture prospered the parent occupation was dropped. It is in such ways as this that new industries are born.

The 'basket work' system remained the usual method of industrial organization in Leicestershire until the late 1880's. But in the early 90's it fell into disuse and from that time onwards boot and shoe manufacturers multiplied in the county and factories became the general rule.[3] What was probably one of the earliest factories in the county was started in three cottages on the main road at Earl Shilton. Four girls are said to have been sent from Leicester to teach local workers how to use the machines. Girls who learned the trade in this way got no wages for a month, and thereafter earned as little as 1*s*. 6*d*. a week at times. Child labour was also used.[4]

The 1881 census showed that there were 2,829 males and 828 females in the boot and shoe industry, a total of 3,657.[5] Ten years later, there were 4,930 males and 1,714 females, a total of 6,644 workers. In 1901, there were 6,206 males and 2,091 females, a total of 8,297, in the county. In the city at the same date there were 26,561 boot and shoe operatives, rather more than three times as many as in the county.

C. N. Wright's *Directory of Leicestershire* for 1896 lists about 90 wholesale and export boot and shoe manufacturers. Anstey was the largest centre with 17 manufacturers, Hinckley second (15), Earl Shilton third (12), and Barwell fourth (11). The only other centre of any size was Shepshed, in the north of the county, with 4 manufacturers, but a number of other villages and small towns had a factory or two.

The county industry grew slowly during the years before the First World War. The census of 1911 enumerates 9,832 operatives in the county, a rise of about 1,500 employees during the preceding 10 years. In 1913 there were 85 boot and shoe plants at work in the county, as against 165 in the city.[6] Roughly speaking, then, about two-thirds of the footwear industry was located within the city, and one-third in the county.

During the 1920's and 1930's, Leicestershire (county and city) remained the second largest footwear-producing region in Great Britain, specializing in women's shoes, for which it was easily the leading area. In 1924 Leicestershire produced 25 per cent. of the total output of footwear in Great Britain (by value), as against Northamptonshire's (town and county) figure of 32 per cent. In 1930 the respective figures were 26 and 34 per cent.; in 1935, 25 and 34 per cent.[7] In 1939 Leicestershire (city and county) supplied half the output of children's shoes in Great Britain, two-fifths of the women's shoes, and about one-twentieth of the men's.

Between 1924 and 1939 there was an increasing tendency in Leicestershire towards the up-grading of the quality of the product, the county producing footwear formerly a speciality of the city, and the city manufacturing types of footwear hitherto associated with Norwich. The smaller towns in Leicester county were also producing an increasing quantity of men's footwear.[8] There was also a marked tendency for the number of boot and shoe plants to fall, partly owing to the increasing size of the unit and to increasing mechanization. In Great Britain as a whole the number of plants fell between 1924 and 1939 from 1,073 to 673, a drop of 37 per cent. In Leicestershire (town and county) the number fell from 250 to 172 in the same period, a fall of 31 per cent. The county area showed a small fall (from 85 plants to 78), but in the city the number of plants nearly halved (165 to 94).[9] There was, too, a considerable fall in the number of boot and shoe operatives, amounting to 12·8 per cent. in the city between

[2] J. G. Harrod, *Dir. of Leics. and Rut.* (1870), 359, 602.

[3] Brit. United Shoe Machinery Co. *Hist. Surv. of Shoemaking* (1932).

[4] Ibid.

[5] The drop since 1871 is inexplicable, and is probably due to a change of classification in the census reports.

[6] H. A. Silverman, *Studies in Industrial Organization*, 205.

[7] Ibid. 206.

[8] Ibid. 204–5, 209.

[9] Ibid. 205.

1923 and 1937, but a much smaller fall in the county areas,[10] with the result that the city and county industries approached nearer each other in magnitude. It was estimated in 1939 that there were 107,000 insured workers in boot and shoe factories in Great Britain. Of these 31,900 were in Northamptonshire (town and county), and 27,700 in Leicestershire (city and county). Of the latter, about 16,000 were employed in the city, and 11,700 in the county.[11] The proportions between the city and county had changed very markedly since 1901.

The Second World War brought considerable changes, the magnitude of which cannot yet be fully assessed. Of the three major industries of city and county, hosiery and footwear were 'concentrated' under Board of Trade schemes in order to release factory space and manpower for the third industry of engineering, and there were fears that the two older industries would not fully recover the ground they had so lost. Certainly, in the city, engineering became the leading industry during the war, and has since remained so, and it seems likely that the county industry has crept much closer to the city in magnitude as a result of war-time changes. Thus in 1949 the city of Leicester produced 19 million pairs of footwear of all kinds and the county areas 17·2 million. The county's recovery from the war dislocations is illustrated in the following production figures:[12]

1946 (half year) . . . 7·8 million pairs
1947 . . . . . 15·9 million pairs
1948 . . . . . 16·9 " "
1949 . . . . . 17·2 " "

The county output in 1949 was made up as follows:

	Hundred thousand pairs	*Percentage of total pairage*
Men's	947	5·5
Women's . . .	5,838	33·9
Boys' and youths' . .	3,500	20·5
Girls' and maids' . .	3,000	17·2
Infants. . . .	1,900	10·9
Other types . . .	1,900	10·9

Of the total county production of 17 million pairs, the Hinckley–Barwell–Earl Shilton district accounted for 7 million pairs, including nearly 40 per cent. of the total output of boys' shoes. At the present time, the industry is scattered over some thirteen other towns and villages in the county, excluding the city of Leicester. Most of the firms are small in scale. A rough count made in 1950 showed that of 57 firms in the county, no fewer that 38 employed less than 100 workers. Twelve employed 100–249 workers, 6 employed 250 to 1,000 workers, and one employed over 1,000 workers. The last firm, operating in four factories, is one of the largest shoe-making concerns in Great Britain.[13]

ENGINEERING AND METAL WORKING

There is no evidence before 1778 that the making of tools or of machinery was practised in Leicestershire beyond the work of the ordinary blacksmith and the hosiery frame-smith. In that year the lower course of the River Soar was canalized up to Loughborough, and the transport of heavy materials was made practicable to that point. Coal from the Derbyshire collieries now reached Loughborough in more abundant quantities and sold at from 60 to 75 per cent. of its former price.[1] There was not, in any event, much local demand for the heavy products of the founders or the smiths in Leicestershire during the 18th century, except possibly in the coal-pits where pumping-engines of the Newcomen type were in use from some time before 1720 onwards.[2] The needs of the coal-pits may have been met in part by the forges which are known to have been set up at Whitwick by the great Birmingham iron-master, Humphrey Jennens, as early as 1673.[3] As for the 'machinery' for the growing hosiery industry, which had used knitting-frames from about 1640, it called for little in the way of iron-founding or engineering. The early frames were made of wood by the joiner. Such metal parts as there were came from the blacksmith. A specialized occupation of 'frame-smith' appears early in the 18th century, by which time frames were beginning to contain more metal. The first Leicester frame-smith seems to have been John Cartwright, who is so described in 1719.[4] He had, significantly, been trained as a joiner, his father's occupation before him. James Cartwright, the father, appears as a joiner between 1666 and 1693, and possibly made the early wooden frames.

The continuation of the Soar Navigation as far as Leicester in 1794 brought cheap coal and pig-iron to the town. Iron foundries and steam-plants

[10] M. P. Fogarty, *Prospects of the Industrial Areas of Gt. Brit.* (1945), 304.

[11] Silverman, op. cit. 205–6.

[12] These statistics of production are Board of Trade figures, now no longer collected.

[13] Much help has been received in the preparation of this article from Mr. E. E. Durie, Secretary of the Leics. County Boot Manufacturers' Federation, to whom the author's grateful thanks are due. Mr. Colin Ashworth, formerly of University College, Leic., also collected some material which has been used here.

[1] See p. 68.

[2] See p. 35; A. Raistrick, *Dynasty of Ironfounders*, 294.

[3] Nichols, *Leics.* iv, 856.

[4] *Reg. Freemen of Leic. 1196–1770*, ed. H. Hartopp, 384.

were set up in Leicester, all near the canal, within a few years of the completion of the Navigation. It is reasonable to assume a similar development at Loughborough, which by 1846 possessed an iron foundry, a bell foundry, and many manufactories of stocking-frames and other machinery.[4a]

An iron foundry at Belgrave Gate Wharf, Leicester, is mentioned in 1804,[5] as though it were no novelty. This was the Britannia Iron Works of James and Benjamin Cort, who may be truly regarded as the fathers of Leicester's great engineering industry today; for several of the early engineers like the Gimsons, the Peggs, and William Richards learnt their trade as apprentices with this firm.

The Corts were an old Leicestershire farming family. A John Cort held land in Great Bowden in the early 15th century,[6] and Corts continued there as substantial farmers up to the end of the 18th century at least. By the end of that century they had become graziers, like most Leicestershire farmers after inclosure, with one branch at Smeeton Westerby, near Kibworth, where they owned some land, and the other at Great Bowden. In 1784 James Cort, son of Benjamin Cort of Smeeton, grazier, was apprenticed to Alderman Price of Leicester, ironmonger,[7] also described as a cutler. There is no record of the apprenticeship of Benjamin Cort, who became a partner in the first Leicester foundry with this James, but presumably he was another son of the Smeeton grazier.

James Cort was admitted to the freedom of the borough by apprenticeship in 1792, and set up in business on his own account as an ironmonger and cutler. Benjamin Cort (probably his brother) first appears to be associated in 1799 when they are described as 'ironmongers'.[8] In 1801, however, they had taken one William Watts into partnership and they are then described as 'Jas. Cort, Benj. Cort and Wm. Watts, ironfounders and copartners'. They were taking on George Cooper 'to learn the art or trade of a whitesmith and fitter', and it is noted that 'Mr. Jas. Cort is a freeman, but the other two are not'. A few weeks later they took on a farmer's son 'to learn the art of a whitesmith in their foundry'.[9] The engineers were beginning to be born, though they had not yet acquired this name.

From this date onwards the Corts and Wattses took on a steady stream of apprentices—the sons of woolcombers, framework-knitters, schoolmasters, labourers, and many others—generally 'to learn the art of a moulder'. One of the most interesting apprentices was Francis Huntsman, the son of William Huntsman of Attercliffe, the great Sheffield steel manufacturer. Francis was apprenticed at Christmas 1801 for 5 years.[10] In these early years the company is usually described as iron-founders, or moulders, but in 1811 they appear as 'model-makers'.[11] By 1846 the firm had become Cort & Bell, when they are described as 'iron and brass founders and engineers'.[12] They ceased to carry on manufacturing early in the present century, but the retail ironmonger's business which James Cort had founded in 1792, and which James and Benjamin kept going as a separate concern from their foundry, was still in existence in 1951. The second oldest foundry business in Leicester seems to be Wilson & Co., who appear in the Leicester directory of 1815 in Charles Street. In Pigot & Co.'s *National Commercial Directory for 1828–9* they are described as 'Engineers and Millwrights'.

The castings from the Britannia Iron Works of the Corts were used for a wide variety of purposes, including the first gas-lamp standards (1821), windows, gratings, and mile-posts. Most important was the fact that metal parts could now be supplied for the great number of frames required by the hosiery trade, the makers of which had used the title of frame-smiths since George I's time. The Leicester directory of 1846 contains a long list of frame-smiths, who were distinct from the engineers.

By 1840 Leicester was connected by main line railways with Derby and the north, and with Rugby and London to the south. This brought many fresh trade contacts and increased the mobility of labour as well as that of industrial machinery, but the engineering trade in Leicester was still confined to the service of the staple hosiery trade and to the industrial needs of a growing town.

This subservience to purely local needs is illustrated by the establishment of the business of Samuel Pegg in Ruding Street some time before 1846. Pegg also had learned his trade with Corts,[13] but he and his successors in the business

[4] White, *Dir. Leic.* (1846), 272, 289.

[5] [Miss Watts] *A Walk through Leicester being a Guide to Strangers* (Leic., 1804), 11.

[6] 'The heirs of John Cort' held land in Great Bowden in 1439: J. E. Stocks and W. B. Bragg, *Market Harborough Records*, 172. The subsidy of 1524 shows John Cort as one of the most substantial farmers in the parish: Farnham, *Leics. Notes*, vi, 231). Numerous wills carry their history on through the 17th and 18th cents.

[7] *Reg. Freemen of Leic. 1770–1930*, ed. H. Hartopp, 465. For James Cort of Great Bowden, grazier, see ibid. 486 (1791). Henry Cort (1740–1800), the well-known iron-master, was born at Lancaster and appears not to be related to the Leicester family.

[8] *Reg. Freemen of Leic. 1770–1930*, 67, 493, 511.

[9] Ibid. 516–17. William Watts's origin cannot be traced.

[10] *Reg. Freemen of Leic. 1770–1930*, 518.

[11] The term 'model-maker' first appears to be used in connexion with the business in 1807: *Reg. Freemen of Leic. 1770–1930*, ed. Hartopp, 539.

[12] White, *Dir. Leic.* (1846), 133. Altogether there were 6 firms of iron and brass founders in Leicester in 1846. Gimsons are described as 'machine makers'.

[13] Samuel Pegg's apprenticeship cannot be traced but William Pegg (probably a brother) was apprenticed to Cort's in 1833: *Reg. Freemen of Leic. 1770–1930*, 610.

made it their concern to supply the local dye works with special plant. Pegg and Messrs. Mason Bros. also developed machinery and tools for the important granite quarries in the county. In this activity they were joined in 1871 by the firm now known as Goodwin Barsby & Co., St. Margaret's Iron Works, and later by Messrs. Parkers. These firms applied themselves so successfully to their task that their quarrying-plant is now to be found in all parts of the world.

Before Samuel Pegg's engineering business had acquired a more than local importance, William Richards had also left Corts and established an independent firm. 'William Richards & Co.' appears in the 1846 *Directory* as 'Phoenix Foundry' at the Public Wharf, near St. Mark's church. His speciality was the making of heavy castings required for bridge-building, which were in great demand by the railway contractors and can hardly be deemed a local trade. He and his descendants steadily developed this line of business, extending it when steel instead of iron became the dominant material, and again when steel was utilized in the construction of many types of buildings.

The 1840's were a time of great expansion for the infant Leicester engineering industry. It was in 1842 that Benjamin and Josiah Gimson, members of a family long settled in the town and county,[14] opened engineering works in Leicester at 36 Welford Road. They are described as 'millwrights' in the 1846 directory. Benjamin Gimson had been apprenticed, like so many embryo engineers, to Messrs. Cort in 1833 'to learn the art of a smith, fitter, and engineer'.[15] This seems to be the first specific reference in Leicester to the trade of 'engineer'. Benjamin's brother Josiah was apprenticed to the Corts in the following year.

The founding of Gimsons was an event of some importance in the history of the Leicester trade, for Josiah was a man of quite exceptional character and ability. Nothing was too big, and nothing too small, for him. He set out to supply Leicester factories with boilers and main engines, and when the boot and shoe trade came to the town he applied his mind to the production of the light machinery which that trade required. At one time a slump in trade made it necessary for him to compound with his creditors, but he surmounted his difficulties. Greatly to his honour, he ignored his legal immunity and paid off all the old debts in full. In 1878 he was able to build the first engineering works in the town with any pretensions to importance. His Vulcan Works covered 3 acres of ground. A contemporary said of the factory: 'To stand on the end platform of the great workshop and witness shafts and wheels revolving by invisible means, whilst skilled workmen use drill, lathe, and planing machine, is a wonderful sight.'[16] The term 'skilled workman' is indeed appropriate, for it was in the Gimson works that many master-men first learnt their craft, and the nucleus of a great army of trained mechanics was formed. Sidney Gimson, a son of Josiah, was the pioneer, too, in setting up the engineering school in the Leicester College of Technology, where many thousands of engineers have usefully supplemented their workshop experience.

It was in the 1870's that Leicestershire engineering began to lose its character of handmaiden to the hosiery, footwear, and elastic web industries. Not only did Leicester engineers find an important market in other areas of the United Kingdom, but engineers came into the town from outside to take advantage of the labour resources available, and began types of engineering which had no relation to the major industries of the town and county. The first of these new-comers was T. J. Gent, who was an electrical engineer of great ingenuity. He began to make telegraphic instruments in Leicester in 1872. From this an immense range of electrically controlled clocks and signals of all kinds was developed. Gent may be said to be the pioneer of 'light engineering' in Leicester, a trade very different from the ponderous work of the early iron-founders and turners. Work of even greater delicacy and precision was carried out from 1886 onwards by William Taylor, of Taylor, Taylor & Hobson, who manufactured engineering machines and lenses, an art in which the firm has since attained a world-wide eminence.

Local directories contain some evidence of the progress of the industry in the later 19th century. In White's *Directory* for 1877 27 'engineers and machinists' are listed, of whom 15 are located in Leicester and 6 in Loughborough. The other 6 firms were scattered about the country, 2 being at Melton. The rise of Loughborough as the second engineering centre to Leicester dates mainly from the late sixties and early seventies, for in the 1863 directory only one firm is listed in the engineering trade. Wright's *Directory* for 1900 shows a considerable expansion of the engineering industry in Leicester itself, but not much change in the county. Altogether 50 'mechanical engineers' are listed in the town, together with about 10 'hosiery machinists'. The county contained only 10 firms in mechanical engineering. Of these, 6 were at Loughborough, 2 of them being of outstanding importance.

In the last quarter of the 19th century the hosiery trade was emerging from the comparative simplicity of the stocking-frame and beginning to use machinery of great complexity and delicacy. One invention of primary importance was the long machine for the making of fully fashioned hose, patented by William Cotton of Loughborough in 1864. The initial difficulties of production were very considerable, and German and American firms were overwhelmingly successful in surmounting them. William Spiers and his

[14] Richard Gimson had been admitted to the freedom of the borough in 1559–60 as a butcher.

[15] *Reg. Freemen of Leic. 1770–1930*, 610.

[16] R. Read, *Modern Leic.* 271.

partner Thomas Grieve were amongst the pioneers in the making of circular hose machines, which held their own against strong foreign competition, but the hosiery machine trade in the eighties, and for long afterwards, presented a curious spectacle of divided purpose. The engineers were never quite clear whether they should concentrate on making machinery themselves or search for agencies for the best foreign machines and press their use upon the hosiery manufacturers. Nearly every firm seemed to consider that its own speciality should be used exclusively by the English hosiery trade, but that all the rest of a wide range of plant should be freely imported. Time and events have shown the unwisdom of relying too much on German machinery, and in the last 20 years great strides have been made to extend the range of English types, though it is only in the circular machines that striking successes have yet been achieved. By 1940 the machines patented by the firms of Mellor Bromley, Wildt & Co. and the Bentley Engineering Co. were supreme in the English market.

Whilst the future of hosiery-machine building in Leicester was doubtful and difficult to forecast, the development of the making of boot and shoe machinery followed a very different course, and the relation between home and foreign supplies of plant was definitely settled.

This was due to the activities of Charles Bennion (1857–1929). Bennion came from a Cheshire farming family, but never wanted to be anything but an engineer. After serving his apprenticeship in the railway works at Crewe he worked as a journeyman in marine engineering and took his engineer's certificate at sea. Back ashore, chance led him to acquire a partnership in a small firm in Nantwich which happened to make shoe machinery, and so he came to the trade with which he was to be so closely connected. The Nantwich partnership was not a happy one; and Bennion was glad to get out and make another venture in partnership with Merry of Erskine St., Leicester.

This brought him into touch with H. Pearson, who had for many years been making sewing and eyeletting machines in Leeds. Pearson had great confidence in Bennion's future and gave him every encouragement to push ahead. A partnership (Pearson & Bennion) was formed in 1886, taking up a strong position in the shoe-machinery trade in competition with Gimsons and others. As in the hosiery machinery trade, there was competition from machinery made by rival firms in the United States; but the course of events in the shoe-machinery industry proved different.

Bennion went out to the United States to sort out the tangle, and found that the leading American firms had been amalgamated under the style of the United Shoe Machinery Co. of America. The policy of the combine was to supply a complete range of machinery to the shoe manufacturers; and the heads of it persuaded Bennion that, with their agency and the resources of his own firm, he might usefully follow a similar policy in England. This he resolved to do, and in 1899, in association with the American concern and with the co-operation of one or two smaller English firms, Pearson and he converted their business into the British United Shoe Machinery Co.

They had recently moved to large new works in Belgrave Road, Leicester, which were to expand until by 1940 the company employed nearly 5,000 work-people and possessed a magnificent equipment of precision plant. The policy of the company was to rent plant to the manufacturers and not to sell it. This led to a bitter struggle with their rivals, who sold machinery outright, a struggle which was partly resolved in 1930 when the Gimson Shoe Machinery Co. came into the combine. Charles Bennion's works in the 20th century did what Josiah Gimson's had done in the 19th: they set a high standard in the industry and afforded a training ground for craftsmen of consummate skill. Without the Gimsons there would not have been a Leicester engineering industry of any size: without Bennion there would have been no later advance to the first place in the industries of the city.

It is proper to pause with the formation of the 'British United' in 1899, and to survey what other advances had been made at the close of the century. Apart from the hosiery, the boot and shoe, and the quarrying trades, one other great industry in the county called for the assistance of the engineers. This was coal-mining, carried out in the north-western part of the county, with its headquarters at the wholly modern township of Coalville. Here were situated Stableford's wagon works—for the making of railway and mining rolling-stock—and also heavy engineering works established in 1876 by the Wootton family, who had been prominent in Loughborough engineering for 50 years.

In Loughborough itself the excellent railway facilities appear to have encouraged the building of important works by two concerns who had no previous connexion with Leicestershire. The first to arrive was a London company, formed shortly before 1880, to develop the important electrical inventions of the American, Charles F. Brush. The old Falcon Works of T. G. Messenger were bought for this purpose in 1889, and much pioneering work was carried out in electric traction, in generating plants, and many other branches of electrical engineering. In some fields competition has been very fierce. Solid prosperity has been hard to maintain, but in the first part of this century the Brush was the largest engineering concern in the county.

To accelerate the rise of Loughborough as an important engineering centre another London company (Herbert Morris, Ltd., founded in 1884) moved there in 1900 to manufacture cranes and lifting-tackle. Their success has been great and their expansion constant. The works are believed to be the largest plant in the world solely devoted to the making of lifting and conveying machinery.

Closely allied with the engineering trade is the trade that provides its raw material, the production of iron from quarried stone. This was carried on at only one place in Leicestershire. The setting up of the works was due to the enthusiasm and energy of Richard Dalgleish, who first conceived the idea when surveying in 1874 for the construction of the railway from Melton to Nottingham. He took a lease of land near Holwell, and began by quarrying ironstone for dispatch to the Staffordshire furnaces; but he laid the foundations of his own furnace in 1878. This was 'blown in' on 1 December 1881 when an explosion in the gas flue killed two men and partially blinded Dalgleish. He survived this accident for 40 years, and lived to direct not only much iron-ore quarrying in the county, but the manufacture of cast-iron pipe and the utilization of slag for road material. Before Dalgleish died the Holwell Co. had been amalgamated with the rival pipe-makers, the Stanton Iron Co. During the 20 years between the two world wars great technical strides were made, and the 1890 output of 350 tons of iron a week had been multiplied by twelve.

The Census of 1901 is a convenient point at which to survey the growth of the Leicestershire engineering industry as a whole. That industry now employed (in town and county combined) 6,082 workers in 'engineering and machine-making', of whom all but eight were men. 'Iron and steel manufacture' employed another 205 workers, mostly in Leicester. At the same date the hosiery manufacture employed 25,858 workers in town and county, so that the engineering industry was about one-quarter the size of the hosiery industry at this date—still only a flourishing infant. Indeed, the *Guide to Leicester and Neighbourhood*, published for the visit of the British Association to the town in 1907, makes no mention whatever of the industry, except for a passing reference to the firm of Taylor, Taylor & Hobson.

In the early years of the 20th century, the coming of the motor-car, the introduction of electricity into private houses, and the development of automatic machinery for many manufactures, greatly stimulated the engineering trades, and any centre with an engineering tradition, such as Leicester, was certain to attract new enterprises. The most notable of these, perhaps, has been the machine-tool trade. Messrs. Jones & Shipman and Mr. Frederick Pollard introduced the manufacture of drilling-machines, and Messrs. Wadkin Ltd. expanded the works first started in 1897 to become the largest makers of woodworking machinery in the country.

To add to the diversity, the manufacture of typewriters was begun at Leicester by the Imperial Typewriter Co. in 1908, and after a difficult struggle against the virtual monopoly of American manufacturers, established itself solidly. The industry now employs over 2,000 work-people. A large part of these are women. The company may be regarded as the first of several to take advantage on a large scale of the technical skill acquired by generations of Leicester women through their participation in the hosiery trade. Until this date Leicester engineering had been entirely in the hands of men.

The strength of the Amalgamated Engineering Union encouraged a similar solidarity amongst the employers in their branch of the Federation of Engineering Trade Employers; and office-holding on the district committee has led to a strong bond of mutual respect and goodwill amongst the leaders of the industry in Leicestershire. This was admirably displayed in the First World War, when the district committee had the advantage of the services of Charles Bennion, Kingsley Gimson, Frederick Pollard, and other leading engineers, and also of the fierce drive and ability of Robert Dumas of the British-Thomson-Houston Co. of Rugby. The War Office tried hard to persuade the Leicester engineers to send away their skilled men to assist Vickers and other armament firms in the turning of shell bodies; but Dumas insisted that this was an unnecessary waste of resources. He suggested that the quantity of shells required justified the breakdown of the work to a number of semi-skilled processes, and asserted that the local firms, large and small, could make shells with their existing plant and, moreover, at a substantially lower cost. Skilled men could thus be retained for more complex work. Dumas had his way, and a committee of the local firms formed the Leicester Armament Group Ltd. This was a notable step in the conversion of peace-time engineering resources to armament production, and led to the further growth of the engineering industry in both Leicester and Loughborough.

At the close of the First World War, however, the engineering trade was still only third in importance in the city, and in the county as a whole. In Leicester itself there were rather more than 6,000 insured workers in engineering in 1923. The next sixteen years saw a remarkable advance in this figure. Whereas in Great Britain as a whole, the number of insured workers in general engineering fell between 1923 and 1937 by 4·2 per cent., the midlands showed a great increase, concentrated in Leicester and Coventry. By 1939 the number of insured engineering workers in Leicester had risen by 123 per cent. over the 1923 figure and stood at about 13,500.[17] Practically all sections of the trade had contributed to this growth, principally those making boot and shoe machinery, hosiery machinery, machine tools, typewriters, and other specialized works.

[17] These figures, and those that follow, are taken from H. A. Silverman, *Indust. Surv. Leics. Interim Rep.* (Nuffield Coll. Soc. Reconstruction Surv.).

Nearly two-thirds of Leicester's pre-war engineering was devoted to the manufacture of boot and shoe and hosiery machinery for factories all over the country.

The engineering industry of the county outside Leicester itself was concentrated mainly at Loughborough, and to a much smaller extent at Coalville. About 4,000 insured workers were engaged in engineering in the smaller towns, bringing the total for Leicester and Leicestershire up to about 17,500. In Leicestershire as a whole (city and county) there were 211,000 insured workers in 1939. Of these one-quarter were employed in hosiery, one-seventh in the footwear industry, and one-twelfth in engineering. There were about 140 engineering firms, of which a hundred were small, employing fewer than 100 workers. Only fifteen were large, each employing over 300 workers.

The authorities responsible for engineering supplies in the Second World War had learnt their lesson well, and the great bulk of the Leicester engineering resources were promptly directed to war purposes, the textile- and boot-machinery works being allotted contracts for components for guns, tanks, and aeroplanes. Moreover, the manufacturers of hosiery and of shoes were relentlessly deprived of many of their buildings and of most of their younger work-people, many of whom, particularly women, were required to enrol themselves at existing or new engineering works.

A considerable proportion of the advances thus made in output were retained by the Leicester engineers in the years following the termination of hostilities. The hosiery-machine builders took up vigorously the production of fully fashioned hose machinery, and the machine-tool makers and many new-comers in light engineering utilized the services of the greatly expanded labour force. In the Leicester employment exchange area engineering employed about 29,900 people in 1952, classified (in round numbers) as follows:[18]

General engineering . . .	22,000
Precision engineering . . .	1,100
Metal goods manufacture . . .	2,900
Metal manufacture . . .	800
Vehicle manufacture and maintenance (including garages) . . .	3,100
	29,900

Although the numbers of insured work-people employed in engineering in 1952 cannot be strictly compared with those for 1939, because of changes in industrial classification in the intervening period, it is roughly true to say that the numbers employed in the Leicester engineering industry have doubled between 1939 and 1952. The totals in 1952 for the hosiery industry were about 30,000 (excluding the auxiliary dyeing and finishing trades) and for footwear about 20,000. When it is borne in mind that the great majority of the hosiery workers are women, while nearly all the engineering hands are men, it is clear that the weekly wage bills of the engineering trade exceed those of any other trade in the county.

MINING

Of the minerals found in Leicestershire the most important, both in value and in quantity,[1] is coal. The coalfield is confined to the north-western part of the county; to the north-east it is bounded by the older rocks of Charnwood Forest, to the south and south-east, where the Coal Measures dip beneath a thick covering of Trias, the boundary of the coalfield runs from Desford, through Nailstone, to Snarestone, and to the west and north-west it extends into Derbyshire. The coalfield of Leicestershire and south Derbyshire forms a united whole, but only those parts of it which lie in Leicestershire will be treated here.[2] The coalfield is divided into two areas by an anticline, which runs southwards from Pistern Hill, in Derbyshire, through the districts of Ashby de la Zouch and Packington. In the zone occupied by the anticline the productive Coal Measures have been denuded, and as the lower measures which remain are of little value, no mining of importance has occurred. To the east of the anticline the Coal Measures reach the surface over an area stretching from the county boundary near Heath End south-eastwards roughly as far as an imaginary line from Whitwick to Alton Grange. To the south-east of this line the Coal Measures are covered by rock formations of more recent origin. To the west of the anticline the coalfield extends westward across the Derbyshire border, and southwards at least as far as Measham. The western section of the coalfield, unlike the section lying to the east of the central anticline, contains a number of important faults. Ironstone is found in the Coal Measures, but not in large quantities.[3]

There is no reliable evidence concerning mining

[18] Ex inf. Employment Exchange, Leic.

[1] In 1938 Leics. produced 2,867,494 tons of coal, with a net selling value of £2,177,819. The next most important mineral was ironstone, of which only 878,743 tons were produced in Leics. during the year: *18th Annual Rep. Sec. for Mines, and 31st Annual Rep. Chief Inspector of Mines* (H.M.S.O.), 140, 150.

[2] The boundary between Leics. and Derbys. was altered during the 19th cent. All districts, however, which have at any time been in Leics. are dealt with in this article.

[3] On the geology of the coalfield, see C. Fox-Strangways, *Memoirs of Geol. Surv., Geol. of Leics. and S. Derbys. Coalfield*, especially 18–55 and 78–100.

Steel Works at Asfordby

The South Leicestershire Colliery

A Fireclay Quarry at Croft

in Leicestershire for any period before the 13th century. The discovery at Measham of stone hammer-heads, wedge-shaped pieces of flint with hazel withes round them, and solid wooden wheels about 18 in. in diameter, has been taken as proof that coal was worked there in prehistoric times.[4] The age of the implements is, however, dubious,[5] and it is not clear whether they were found in coal workings.[6] In consequence the existence of prehistoric coal workings in Leicestershire cannot be considered as proved. Similarly there is no evidence that the ironstone of eastern Leicestershire was mined in prehistoric or Roman times, although in the adjacent parts of Lincolnshire and Northamptonshire iron-ore was worked under the Romans,[7] and a Roman iron-smelting furnace has been discovered near Woolsthorpe, just outside the county.[8] The first reliable references to coal-mining in Leicestershire relate to the area east of the Ashby anticline, where the Coal Measures form the surface, and where many outcrops of coal exist. A charter of 1204 shows that coal was then known to exist at Swannington,[9] and an interesting lawsuit of 1293 mentions a coal-mine dug in the waste of the same village; it was stated that the mine had been dug with the approval of the freemen of the vill, and that each freeman had the right to approve in the waste according to the size of his free tenement.[10] Another document of 1293, which mentions an annual rent of four cartloads of coal arising from land at Donington le Heath,[11] suggests that by the late 13th century coal was being mined there also. The scanty information available shows that in the late 13th and early 14th centuries both coal and iron were being worked in the parish of Breedon, to the north of Swannington. About 1270 Ralph Bozun and his wife granted to Garendon Abbey some lands at Worthington, in the southern part of Breedon parish, with appurtenances which included coal-mines.[12] In the judgement, delivered between 1295 and 1332, on an action concerning tithes, it was stated that Isabel de Hastings for at least 7 years before the action was brought had been working coal and iron at three named places within Breedon parish.[13] One of these places, Gelsmor, can be identified as a former common near Worthington.[14] It has not been possible to identify the other two places named, but both probably lay within Isabel's manor of Worthington.[15] A similar judgement, delivered between 1306 and 1336,[16] states that Sir William de Staunton had been working coal and iron within his manor of Staunton Harold.[17] In both of the preceding cases the workings are described as *quarrares sive putei*, so that it is uncertain whether they were merely open quarries, or short shafts. In the 19th century remains of old iron furnaces were still visible at South Wood and Heath End, near Staunton Harold.[18] Thus while at Staunton Harold and Worthington the exploitation of minerals in the waste was carried on in each case by the lord of the manor, to whom mineral rights would normally belong, at Swannington it was evidently possible for any freeman to dig for coal in the waste of the township. Bozun's grant shows that at Worthington it was possible for a freeholder to work coal on his own property, though unfortunately the nature of the land on which Bozun's coal-mines were situated is not clear. No doubt the way in which mining developed in each manor would depend on how far the lord enforced his rights over minerals.

The few remaining references to coal-mining in Leicestershire during the Middle Ages do not convey much additional information. Some property purchased by Henry Blodles of Worthington in 1321 included a coal-mine at Swannington,[19] and a document of 1369 also refers to coal-mines at the same place.[20] The first Leicestershire reference to coal-mining in the area west of the Ashby anticline occurs in a rental of Leicester Abbey, drawn up in 1477, which states that the abbey then possessed a coal-mine at Oakthorpe,[21] another area where there are outcrops of coal.[22]

4 P. Beaumont, *Hist. of the Moira Collieries*, 1; Fox-Strangways, op. cit. 5.

5 W. J. Harrison, *Sketch of Geology of Leics. and Rut.* 20.

6 Unfortunately adequate details of the discovery have not been recorded.

7 H. B. Hewlett, *The Quarries*, 12.

8 Ibid. 9, 12.

9 Fox-Strangways, *Geol. Leics. S. Derbys. Coalfield*, 5; no reference is given.

10 Farnham, *Leics. Notes*, iv, 192. Compare the customs of Burnley and Bolsover manors: J. U. Nef, *Rise of Brit. Coal Industry*, i, 315.

11 Hist. MSS. Com. *Hastings*, i, 41. This reference is derived from an unpublished essay by Dr. W. G. Hoskins on 'Early Coal Mining in Leics.'.

12 Nichols, *Leics.* iii, 791*. Bozun died in 1275–6: Farnham, *Leics. Notes*, ii, 27. These facts are also derived from Dr. Hoskins's essay (see n. 11 above).

13 John Rylands Libr. Manchester, Latin MS. 222, f. 61.

14 Nichols, *Leics.* iii, 731.

15 Isabel obtained the manor of Worthington in 1304: Farnham, *Leics. Notes*, ii, 30.

16 John Rylands Libr. Manchester, Latin MS. 222, f. 61*b*.

17 A number of coal outcrops occur near Staunton Harold: Fox-Strangways, *Geol. Leics. S. Derbys. Coalfield*, 26, 27.

18 Ibid. 112.

19 *Wyggeston Hosp. Rec.*, 436.

20 Ibid. 439.

21 Nichols, *Leics.* iii, 1031. As printed by Nichols, the passage in the rental describes the mine as 'minera carbonum marmorum', but 'marmorum' is probably an error for 'marinorum': it has not been possible to consult the original; Fox-Strangways, *Geol. Leics. S. Derbys. Coalfield*, 6, misleadingly states that the document in question was completed in 1502.

22 Fox-Strangways, op. cit. 45, 49.

Mining had probably begun at Coleorton by the late 15th century, for in 1498 two inhabitants of the village were described as 'collyers',[23] the first indication that professional miners existed in Leicestershire.

In the 16th century the evidence about mining in Leicestershire becomes more plentiful. A document of 1520 mentions five pits at Swannington,[24] while there are references to mines at Newbold in 1554,[25] and at Oakthorpe in 1570,[26] 1577–8,[27] and 1585.[28] At Coleorton, where the coal seams are said to have been on fire for many years under Henry VIII,[29] there was an important colliery about 1570.[30] Interesting evidence about the Leicestershire mining industry under Elizabeth I is provided by three manuscripts about the Coleorton pits.[31] The documents consist of two account books, entitled the 'Collpit Book' and the 'Synkinge Book', both relating to the last two months of 1572, and a statement of account dated November 1577. The 'Collpit Book' shows that the miners worked in gangs, from about 10 to 20 strong, who were paid collectively at the end of the week. Those employed on actual coal-getting seem generally to have been paid according to the output of the gang, at the rate of 1*s.* for each rook[32] of coal obtained, though one gang of 17 men paid a weekly rent of 25 rooks to the lessee of the mine, and then sold the coal obtained over that amount on their own behalf. For the week from 8 November to 14 November 1522 the earnings of 25 miners on piece rates averaged a little less than 2*s.* 5*d.*[33] There are entries which show that occasionally the coal-getters worked for day wages, but the rates of pay in such cases are not recorded. The 'Synkinge Book', which is chiefly concerned with expenditure involved in the extension of the workings, shows that men engaged in driving new headings were usually paid at the fixed rate of 6*d.* a day, although one case is recorded where 2 men were paid for driving a new heading at the rate of 1*s.* 4*d.* a yard for the pair of them.[34] At Coleorton the employer provided tools and candles, and paid for the sharpening of the tools.[35] The statement of 1577 shows that between November 1576 and November 1577 a total of 7,000 rooks of coal was obtained.[36] The 'Collpit Book' shows that in November and December 1572 the average weekly output was not quite 120 rooks. It would be unwise to calculate the year's output from this, as production may have varied at different times of the year, but the 1572 figures show that a yearly output of 7,000 rooks could have been achieved in the accounting year 1572–3. Considerable coal stocks were maintained, for in November 1577 there were 1,891 rooks of coal remaining unsold at Coleorton. It is unfortunately impossible to discover the weight of coal contained in a rook.[37] There was considerable activity at Coleorton in 1572, for several new headings were being driven, and two new shafts were being sunk. It is not clear how the miners engaged in sinking new shafts were paid though the 'Synkinge Book' mentions payments of earnest money.[38]

The surviving evidence provides little information about the technique of mining in 16th-century Leicestershire. The practice of draining mines by adits, or 'soughs',[39] was certainly known, for in 1554 it was stated that Nicholas Beaumont had licence to drive a 'sough' through Newbold Moor,[40] and one of the pits at Coleorton in 1572 was known as Sough Pit, presumably because it was drained by an adit. Considerable capital must have been required to operate pits where such costly arrangements for drainage were necessary. In the 1570's the Coleorton pits were being operated by Sir Francis Willoughby, a wealthy mine-owner who was interested in pits in Nottinghamshire, Derbyshire, and Warwickshire.[42] Willoughby was apparently leasing the Coleorton mines from Nicholas Beaumont, though the exact

[23] Farnham, *Leics. Notes*, ii, 77.

[24] Leic. City Mun. Room, Wyggeston Hosp. Terrier of Swannington, 1520. (This doc. has not been catalogued.)

[25] Fox-Strangways, *Geol.Leics. S. Derbys. Coalfield*, 6.

[26] Nef, *Brit. Coal Ind.* ii, 441.

[27] *Duc. Lanc.* pt. 4, *Cal. Pleadings* (Rec. Com.), 73.

[28] C. 2/O 1/40.

[29] W. Burton, *Description of Leics.* 198.

[30] Nott. Univ. Libr. Uncatalogued doc. in Middleton MSS.

[31] Nott. Univ. Libr. Middleton MSS. The 3 docs. have not yet been catalogued; 2 of them, the accounts of 1572, are mentioned in Hist. MSS. Com. *Middleton*, 495.

[32] The rook was a stack of coal of a fixed size. In the midlands it seems to have contained between 1 and 2 tons: Nef, *Brit. Coal Ind.* ii, 376–7.

[33] This is the only week for which it is possible to calculate the earnings per head.

[34] For wages in other coalfields at the same period, see Nef, *Brit. Coal Ind.* ii, 182. During the 16th cent. wage-rates in Leics. seem to have been similar to those prevailing elsewhere.

[35] This was not always the case: Nef, op. cit. i, 415.

[36] It seems to have been the practice at Coleorton to begin the financial year early in November, on a Saturday. Both the 'Collpit Book' and the 'Synkinge Book' begin on 8 Nov., a Saturday, and the account of 1577 runs from 10 Nov. 1576 to 2 Nov. 1577, both dates being Saturdays. The accounts in the 'Collpit Book' and the 'Synkinge Book' are weekly accounts.

[37] See n. 32 above.

[38] i.e. advance payments to the group of workers engaged in sinking.

[39] A 'sough' was an underground passage running from the workings to a valley which lay at a lower level than the workings, so that water could drain off through the 'sough' without the need of pumps. Such a method could obviously be used only where the coal-seams lay at a higher level than parts of the adjacent country.

[40] Fox-Strangways, *Geol. Leics. S. Derbys. Coalfield*, 6.

[41] Nott. Univ. Libr. Middleton MSS. 'Synkinge Book' of Coleorton, f. 1*a*.

[42] Hist. MSS. Com. *Middleton*, 307, 309, 314–16, 320; Nef, *Brit. Coal Ind.* ii, 12, 13, 155.

relationship between the two is not clear.[43] A payment of 2*d*. a rook, mentioned in 1577, was probably a royalty, though this is not specifically stated.[44] Willoughby's activities at Coleorton were apparently profitable, for the account of 1577 shows a net surplus of revenue over expenditure of £188. 16*s*. 2*d*. for the financial year. Camden's statement that the pits at Coleorton were being worked very profitably[45] is thus borne out.

That all mining enterprises of the period were not successful is shown by the results of Lord Beaumont's activities at Measham.[46] Lord Beaumont leased the mines in 1611 at the excessively high rent of £500 a year, and paid £169. 13*s*. 9*d*. for the stock of coal on the surface.[47] Between 1611 and 1623 losses totalling £4,890 were incurred at Measham. In some years the income obtained from coal sales can have barely sufficed to cover the expenses of mining, for in 1614 the profit, before payment of the £500 rent, was only £25. 4*s*. 6*d*., and in 1619 it was only £18. 17*s*. 6*d*. The fate of Beaumont's undertaking at Measham shows that mining on a relatively large scale was not without hazards in the 17th century. No doubt many Leicestershire pits remained very small, in contrast to such important pits as those at Coleorton and Measham. Under Elizabeth I, for example, two mines at Oakthorpe and Swadlincote were sold for £20,[48] and in 1652 the yearly value of the coal royalties arising from Newbold Moor, together with court profits, was estimated at only £2. 16*s*. 8*d*.[49]

Although it is impossible to estimate even approximately the yearly coal output of Leicestershire under the Tudors and Stuarts, by the 17th century the county's yearly production must have been considerably larger than has sometimes been estimated.[50] In the 1570's the yearly production of Coleorton Colliery must have been about 10,000 tons.[51] The rent of £500 paid for the colliery at Measham may have been excessive, but the fact that in 1617, for example, Beaumont made a profit, before paying rent, of over £400,[52] when the price of coal at the pit head was 1*s*. 6*d*. or 2*s*. a ton,[53] indicates that Measham could produce several thousand tons a year. The absence of any evidence about the output of the numerous small pits makes it impossible to estimate the county's yearly production of coal.

In the 16th century, collieries, so far as the evidence shows, were operated by lessees, rather than by the owners of coal-bearing land. The leasing of the mines at Coleorton and Measham has already been mentioned. On a much smaller scale was the lease for 21 years in 1570 of a mine at Oakthorpe by Thomas Henshaw for a yearly rent of £2.[54] Much of the capital provided for the mines in the 16th and 17th centuries seems to have been furnished by landowners. Both Lord Beaumont and Sir Francis Willoughby were important landlords in the midlands, and Sir Francis Anderson, who had operated the Measham colliery before it was leased by Beaumont,[55] was a man of the same class.[56] In the 17th century the Hastings family, who were also important landowners in Leicestershire, were interested in the coal industry, although the evidence is not sufficient to indicate the part they played. In 1621 Henry Hastings, Earl of Huntingdon, bought some coal-mines at Heather,[57] and in 1652 it was said that the Earl and his son had previously been taking profits from a pit at Oakthorpe.[58] Later in the 17th century Lord Loughborough, another member of the family,[59] was concerned in the operation of mines at either Oakthorpe or Measham.[60] The Hastings family, however, do not seem to have undertaken large-scale mining at this time. John Osbaston, who bought mines at Oakthorpe and Swadlincote about 1580, was a Londoner and a merchant of the Staple,[61] though his name suggests that he was connected with Leicestershire. Osbaston's case is the only indication that capital from trade was being invested in Leicestershire mines under the Tudors.

While evidence about the origins of the capital

43 The account of 1577 (see n. 31 above) is headed 'Account between Sir Francis Willoughby Knt. and Nicholas Beaumont', but does not indicate what the connexion between the two was. There are several references to Willoughby's connexion with Coleorton in the Middleton MSS. (Hist. MSS. Com. *Middleton*, 430, 434, 547). Willoughby, before 1576, proposed to buy Coleorton manor, but was unable to complete the purchase: *Proc. in Chan. in Reign of Eliz.* (Rec. Com.), iii, 271.

44 Account of 1577. (See n. 31.)

45 Camden, *Brit.* (1806), ii, 298.

46 S.P. 14/157/no. 51, cited by Nef, *Brit. Coal Ind.* i, 69.

47 The stock on the surface is stated as 2,405 'three quarters'. The 'three quarters' was evidently a unit of measurement: Nef, op. cit. ii, 377; Hist. MSS. Com. *Rutland*, iv, 484.

48 C. 2/O 1/40. Swadlincote is in Derbys.

49 E. 317/Leicester, 11.

50 Nef, *Brit. Coal Ind.* i, 69, estimated the county's yearly output as from 1,000 to 2,000 tons at the succession of Eliz. I, and as unlikely to be more than 10,000 tons by 1700. It should be said that Nef was unable to obtain access to the Middleton MSS. and his estimates were in any case tentative: ibid. ii, 337, 366.

51 See figures given above.

52 S.P. 14/157/no. 51.

53 Nef, *Brit. Coal Ind.* ii, 391–2.

54 Ibid. 441.

55 S.P. 14/157/no. 51.

56 Nef, *Brit. Coal Ind.* ii, 16; Nichols, *Leics.* iii, 1032.

57 Farnham, *Leics. Notes*, vi, 335–6. Although Heather lies in an area where the Coal Measures are in general covered by a considerable thickness of other strata, the village lies in a valley, where the coal is near the surface: Fox-Strangways, *Geol. Leics. S. Derbys. Coalfield*, 21, 26, 65.

58 E. 317/Derby 26.

59 Died 1667: *Complete Peerage.*

60 E. 134/5 W. and M./17, fs 3*b*.

61 C. 2/O 1/40.

employed in Leicestershire collieries during the 16th and 17th centuries is inadequate, information about the origins of the labour employed is almost entirely lacking. The fact that in the very few cases in which the names of miners can be discovered they are mostly the names of families which appear in Leicestershire during the Middle Ages suggests that the miners were in general recruited from the local population, and not brought in from other mining areas. In view of the scanty nature of the evidence it is impossible to come to any definite conclusion on this subject.

The development of the Leicestershire coalfield must have been hindered by the absence of adequate water transport in the area. A market for coal was found in Leicester, where by 1578 it had become usual for the town authorities to lay in stocks of coal for sale to the poor.[62] In 1603 it was ordered that coal for the town stock should be bought from Coleorton.[63] Early in the 17th century coal was brought to Leicester from pits in the north-west of the county by pack-horses,[64] which made use of the road then known as Coal Pit Lane.[65] The expense of transporting coal by land, even for a moderate distance,[66] can be seen from the fact that while coal was being sold at Leicester in 1603 for 10*s.* a ton,[67] the price at the pit head at Measham in 1611 was estimated at only 1*s.* 7*d.* a ton.[68] Only small quantities of coal can have been distributed from the pits by such methods. Leicester itself was supplied with coal during the 17th century from Warwickshire, Staffordshire, and Derbyshire,[69] while towards the end of the century it was observed that the inhabitants of south Leicestershire were forced to rely on cow-dung for fuel, though they obtained some coal from Warwickshire.[70] The fact that it was worth while to import coal from relatively distant areas to Leicester shows that the pits in the county were not able to meet even the local demand, either because of difficulties in distributing the coal, or because the total production was inadequate.

During the 17th and most of the 18th centuries, coal-mining in Leicestershire seems to have continued on a modest scale without spreading to new areas. In the middle of the 17th century the Civil War caused some interruption to the industry, for in 1652 it was stated that no coal had been raised at Oakthorpe since the beginning of the war,[71] and the skirmishing between the Parliamentarians at Coleorton and the Royalist garrison of Ashby de la Zouch must have disturbed the mining area.[72] The industry evidently recovered from any damage suffered, for later in the 17th century mining was being actively carried on at Swannington and at Coleorton, while coal production continued at Oakthorpe and Measham.[73] It is notable that the places at which mines are mentioned in the 16th and 17th centuries are all in areas where coal seams outcrop.[74] Valuable information concerning mining is provided by the evidence of a number of local men, including miners, in a lawsuit brought in 1694 by John Wilkins against Lord Beaumont over a lease of workings at Silver Hill, Swannington.[75] Lord Beaumont and his brother had, about 1684, themselves carried on mining at Silver Hill, which formed part of the waste of Swannington Manor, but had been forced to abandon the workings through flooding.[76] In 1685 Lord Beaumont leased Silver Hill to John Wilkins,[77] who was also the lessee of certain mines at Swannington belonging to Wyggeston Hospital,[78] and had earlier leased pits at Coleorton from Lord Beaumont.[79] It was claimed on Wilkins's behalf that he was highly skilled in mining operations,[80] and the number of pits leased by him shows that he must have had wide experience. He must also have possessed considerable capital, for a 'sough' built by him to drain the Silver Hill workings is said to have cost about £2,000,[81] and his pits at Silver Hill employed nearly 300 men.[82] Wilkins evidently wished to secure a monopoly of the local coal trade, for witnesses produced by him stated that his pits were capable of supplying the whole district with coal,[83] and that he had only leased Silver Hill on the understanding that no one should mine coal at Coleorton for the duration of the lease.[84] No figures are given for the output of the Silver Hill workings, but the pits earlier leased by Wilkins at Coleorton are said to have produced about twenty-four loads a day.[85]

[62] *Rec. Boro. of Leic. 1509–1603*, ed. Mary Bateson, 172–3.

[63] *Rec. Boro. of Leic. 1603–88*, ed. J. E. Stocks, 2.

[64] Ibid. 168.

[65] The modern Braunstone Lane: L. Fox and P. Russell, *Leic. Forest*, 62, 63.

[66] Coleorton is about 14 miles from Leicester.

[67] *Rec. Boro. of Leic. 1603–88*, 2, cited Nef, *Brit. Coal Ind.* ii, 408.

[68] S.P. 14/157/no. 51, cited Nef, op. cit. ii, 391.

[69] *V.C.H. Derbys.* ii, 353; *Rec. Boro. of Leic. 1603–88*, 241.

[70] *Journeys of Celia Fiennes*, ed. C. Morris, 162. The Warws. pits around Bedworth were nearer to south Leics. than were the mines of the Leics. coalfield.

[71] E. 317/Derby 26, m. 2.

[72] *Diary of Marches of Royal Army*, ed. C. E. Long (Camden Soc. 1st ser. lxxiv), 178, 183, 279; *Rec. Boro. of Leic. 1603–88*, ed. J. E. Stocks, 349, 350.

[73] Nichols, *Leics.* iii, 1123–4; E. 134/5 W. and M./17.

[74] Nef apparently believed that coal was being mined in east Leics. in the early 17th cent.: *Brit. Coal Ind.* i, 69. The mine at 'Sturley Park' (Hist. MSS. Com. *Rutland*, iv, 484) was, however, at Strelley Park (Notts.) and not in Leics.

[75] E. 134/5 W. and M./17.

[76] Ibid. mm. 2, 3.

[77] Ibid. m. 2.

[78] Ibid. m. 7.

[79] Ibid. mm. 6, 7, 7 d, 8.

[80] Ibid. m. 2.

[81] Ibid. mm. 2, 3.

[82] Ibid. m. 3 d.

[83] Ibid. m. 3.

[84] Ibid. m. 2.

[85] Ibid. m. 2. In 1694 the wainload, which is probably here meant, was fixed by statute at 17½ cwt. Both before and after this date it seems to have varied in practice: Nef, *Brit. Coal Ind.* ii, 376.

The price of coal was 6*s*. 6*d*. a load.[86] While the existence of such an undertaker as Wilkins[87] is of great interest, the evidence provided about the treatment of miners throws a great deal of light upon conditions in the mining industry. A number of witnesses hostile to Wilkins testified that he had repeatedly beaten and ill treated his employees,[88] and as the only reply made was that Wilkins had only struck his men under great provocation, and that the heavy drinking and 'other miscarriages' of the miners made strict discipline necessary,[89] the charges of ill treatment were probably well founded. One witness declared that he was evicted from his house because he refused to work for Wilkins.[90] The only evidence regarding wages is a statement by one miner that he was offered 1*s*. a day to work at Silver Hill.[91] If this was the usual pay, miners' wages had doubled between 1572 and 1694. Hours of work were evidently long in some cases, for a Swannington miner mentioned that he ended his day's work about 11 at night.[92] The evidence shows that it was then unusual to work both day and night shifts,[93] for while witnesses brought forward by Beaumont said that Wilkins was the only mining employer in the district who worked two shifts,[94] it was testified on Wilkins's behalf that two shifts were only worked in an emergency, or for sinking new shafts.[95] It may be noted that two shifts were sometimes worked at Coleorton a century earlier.[96] Injuries to miners were no doubt frequent, and the evidence given during the 1694 lawsuit contains several references to miners who were maimed or blinded at Silver Hill.[97] It was said that Wilkins provided food, blankets, and medical care for injured workers at his own expense, and sometimes paid them 4*s*. a week while unable to work,[98] but such treatment of miners was probably unusual. There is unfortunately no evidence about the depth or extent of the workings leased by Wilkins, but the number of his employees shows that his operations were on a considerably larger scale than those of Willoughby a century earlier.

It was probably early in the 18th century that the 'longwall' system of mining replaced the 'bord and pillar' method in Leicestershire. There is no definite evidence for this important change before 1852, when it was reported that nearly all mining in the midlands was carried on by 'longwall' working,[99] but it is known to have reached Warwickshire soon after 1720, and it was already in use in Derbyshire in the middle of the 18th century.[1] Early in the 18th century also steam power was introduced into the Leicestershire mines. The first recorded engine on the coalfield was in use at Swannington some time before 1720.[2] A second steam engine was being used by John Wilkins at Swannington about 1720.[3] These engines, like the 'waterwheel engine' which existed at Swannington about the same time,[4] were almost certainly used for pumping. A few years before 1760 another steam engine was set up at Swannington,[5] and a map based on a survey made in 1775–7 marks steam engines at Measham, Lount, and Newbold.[6] These steam engines must all have been of the Newcomen type, and were probably used for pumping only. Regulations enacted early in the 18th century by Swannington manor court, providing that all pits should be filled in or covered on pain of a small fine, indicate that there were then many small workings in the manor, probably on or near the coal outcrops.[7] It is evident, however, that mining on a large scale, such as had earlier been conducted by Wilkins, was continuing at Swannington. In 1752 a new colliery, drained by a brick 'sough', was established at Swannington for the working of the 'Stone Smut' seam, which is about 6 ft. thick at Swannington, and the 'Nether Coal', a seam 4½ ft. thick lying about 20 ft. below the 'Stone Smut'.[8] The 'Nether Coal', which was apparently considered as the lowest productive seam,[9] had been worked at Talbot Wood, Swannington, since about 1720, if not earlier.[10] In 1760 Gabriel Holland began the 'sinking' of two pits on Swannington Common, with the object of working, besides the 'Stone Smut' and

86 E. 134/5 W. and M./17, m. 6. Compare the price of 5*s*. a load in south Notts. in 1655, and 6*s*. 6*d*. in Derbys. in 1693: Nef, op. cit. ii, 393.

87 Wilkins must have had a long career in mining, for he was still owning or operating pits at Swannington in 1724: Leic. City Mun. Room, Swannington Ct. R. 1724. On his use of steam engines, see below.

88 E. 134/5 W. and M./17, mm. 6, 6 d.

89 Ibid. mm. 3, 3 d.

90 Ibid. m. 6 d.

91 Ibid. m. 6 d.

92 Ibid. m. 6.

93 Described as 'double turn'.

94 E. 134/5 W. and M./17, m. 6.

95 Ibid. mm. 3, 4, 6 d.

96 Nott. Univ. Libr. Middleton MSS. 'Synkinge Book' of Coleorton, f. 1*a*.

97 E. 134/5 W. and M./17, mm. 2 d, 3 d.

98 Ibid. mm. 2 d, 3 d.

99 *Rep. Inspectors of Coal Mines*, [1845] p. 88, H.C. (1854), xix.

1 T. S. Ashton and J. Sykes, *The Coal Industry of the 18th Century*, 30. See also *Rep. from the Sel. Cttee. on Coal*, H.C. 313, p. 39 (1873), x.

2 Nichols, *Leics.* iii, 1125*.

3 Ibid. Steam engine cylinders were supplied to Sir Geo. Beaumont of Coleorton in 1727, 1730, and 1734, but it is not known where the engines were situated: A. Raistrick, *Dynasty of Ironfounders*, 294.

4 Nichols, *Leics.* iii, 1125*.

5 Ibid.

6 L.R.O. J. Prior, Map of Leics. 1779.

7 Leic. City Mun. Room, Wyggeston Hosp. Doc., Swannington Ct. R., 1714, m. 1; 1719, m. 2; 1724, m. 2. The fine for failing to fill in or cover pits was fixed at 3*s*. 4*d*. in 1714, 6*s*. 8*d*. in 1719, and 3*s*. 4*d*. again in 1724.

8 Nichols, *Leics.* iii, 1125*; Fox-Strangways, *Geol. Leics. & Derbys. Coalfield*, 31.

9 Fox-Strangways, op. cit. 31. The 'Nether Coal' is the seam later known as the 'Swannington Coal'.

10 Nichols, *Leics.* iii, 1125*. The 'Stone Smut Rider', a thin seam lying about 30 ft. above the 'Stone Smut', was also worked at Swannington in the 18th cent.: ibid.; Fox-Strangways, op. cit. 22, 32.

the 'Nether Coal', a new and deeper seam, which he claimed to be the first to utilize.[11] It is not clear what this seam was,[12] but Holland's claim shows that until about 1760 the 'Nether Coal' was the deepest seam worked. A shaft sunk by Holland at Swannington about 1760 was elliptical in form, and lined with brick. The shaft was roofed over, and provided with a 'gin wheel' and pulleys for hoisting purposes,[13] power being presumably supplied by horses.[14] Holland's pits on Swannington Common were drained by a fire engine.[15] Holland, like Wilkins at an earlier date, was a lessee of the mines, some being leased from Wyggeston Hospital for three lives, and others from Elizabeth Brainbridge for a term of years.[16]

Until the closing years of the 18th century the most active part of the coalfield seems to have been the district around Coleorton and Swannington. A map based on a survey taken in 1775–7 marks 15 pits near Coleorton and a further 5 near Swannington. In addition, 5 pits are marked around Newbold, and 3 at Lount. In the western part of the coalfield only 7 pits are marked, all lying between the villages of Oakthorpe and Measham; in this district the chief seam was exhausted in the area then worked before 1800.[17] By 1775 a lead mine was being worked at Heath End, near Staunton Harold.[18] The amount of lead ore available was small, though of good quality.[19] Lead mining in this area continued for most of the 19th century, but never became important.[20]

The coalfield must have suffered considerably from the lack of water transport before the building of canals. Gabriel Holland, in a printed circular issued in 1760, stressed the advantages which Swannington possessed as a road centre,[21] but land transport was very costly.[22] Gabriel Holland, though he obtained financial assistance from Isaac Dawson, an Ashby lawyer, was in serious difficulties in 1760, and shortly afterwards went bankrupt.[23] The lack of means for cheaply transporting coal must have limited the possibilities of expanding the coalfield's production. It had been proposed to construct a number of tramways to serve Leicestershire collieries in the late 18th century,[24] but the time had not yet arrived when railways could provide adequate transport for the coalfield. As early as 1786 a Bill was introduced to provide for the construction of a canal from Whitwick to the Soar at Barrow, for carrying stone, coal, and lime,[25] but the measure was defeated,[26] and it was not until 1791 that an Act granted powers to render the Soar navigable from Loughborough to Leicester, and to construct a canal from Loughborough to Thringstone in the eastern part of the coalfield.[27] As completed in 1794 the communication between Loughborough and the collieries through the difficult country of Charnwood Forest consisted of a canal for part of the way, and of two short lengths of railway, so that between the pits and the Soar bulk had to be broken three times.[28] Despite this disadvantage the new system of canals and railways enabled Leicestershire coal to compete at Leicester with Nottinghamshire coal, which could be brought in by means of the Erewash canal and the Soar.[29] The prospect of improved communications appears to have stimulated development in the coalfield, for about 1790 two new collieries were established at Coleorton, and when the canal was planned it was proposed to sink new shafts at

[11] Nichols, *Leics.* iii, 1125*.

[12] The seam lying next below the 'Nether Coal' is the 'Soft Coal', which is over 40 ft. below the 'Nether Coal' at Swannington: Fox-Strangways, op. cit. 22.

[13] Nichols, *Leics.* iii, 1125*.

[14] In 1760 Holland stated that he had built stables for 40 horses, though the purpose for which they were employed is not mentioned: ibid.

[15] Nichols, *Leics.* iii, 1125*. In 1791 pits at Measham were drained by steam engines: A. Young, *Tours in Engl. and Wales* (London School of Econ. 1932), 287.

[16] Northants. Rec. Off. (Lamport Hall): Box 1289; Contract between Thos. Hall and Ric. Holland, 27 May 1762.

[17] L.R.O. J. Prior, Map of Leics. 1779; W. J. Harrison, *Sketch Geol. of Leics. and Rut.* 21. At Measham the main seam lay at a depth of 50 to 70 ft.: Fox-Strangways, *Geol. Leics. S. Derbys. Coalfield*, 244. Prior's map is not a complete guide to the coal workings, as coal-mines at Hugglescote were mentioned in 1774 (Nichols, *Leics.* iv, 748) though not shown on the map. Prior probably marked all collieries of any importance.

[18] L.R.O. J. Prior, Map of Leics. 1779.

[19] Nichols, *Leics.* iii, 718; W. Pitt, *General View of Agriculture in the County of Leic.* 8.

[20] J. Curtis, *Topog. Hist. Leics.* 164; Harrison, *Sketch Geol. of Leics. and Rut.* 16.

[21] Nichols, *Leics.* iii, 1126*. A copy of the circular is in the custody of the Northants. Rec. Off. at Lamport Hall, Box 1289.

[22] Ashton and Sykes, *Coal Ind. of 18th Cent.* 230, 231.

[23] Nichols, *Leics.* iii, 1125*; Northants. Rec. Off. (Lamport Hall) Box 1289, contract between Thos. Hall and Ric. Holland, 27 May 1762.

[24] A petition of 1786 advocated the building of tramways at Swannington, Coleorton, and Staunton Harold: *C.J.* xli, 270.

[25] Ibid. xli, 270, 303, 547.

[26] Ibid. xli, 770.

[27] Ibid. xlvi, 562; 31 Geo. III, c. 65 (Local Acts).

[28] Fox-Strangways, *Geol. Leics. S. Derbys. Coalfield*, 7; C. E. Stretton, *Hist. Midland Rlwy.* 3. See the contemporary map at the beginning of Nichols, *Leics.* ii, (1). The Act which gave powers for the construction of the canal provided that the coal should be carried by railway from the pits at Coleorton and Swannington to the canal at Thringstone, where the loaded railway wagons were to be run on to floats or barges. The barges were then to carry the coal to the far end of the canal at Nanpantan, where the wagons were to be run off the barges and placed on a second railway, along which they were to travel to the Soar navigation, near Loughborough: Nichols, *Leics.* i, pp. clxi, clxii. This arrangement, if actually adopted, must have reduced the disadvantages of the complicated system of canals and railways.

[29] Stretton, op. cit. 4.

Coleorton and Swannington.[30] In 1799 the banks of the canal through Charnwood Forest burst, and were not repaired.[31] This disaster must have been a severe blow to the Leicestershire coal industry, for it enabled the Nottinghamshire and Derbyshire pits to monopolize the coal trade at Leicester.[32]

The western district of the coalfield was more fortunate in the matter of canals. In 1794 an Act was passed for the building of a canal from the Coventry Canal at Marston Bridge to Ashby de la Zouch.[33] By 1805 the canal was completed as far as Ashby Woulds, and tramways connected it with collieries at Heather, Normanton le Heath, Lount, and Staunton Harold.[34] A rapid development of the mining areas connected with the new canal followed, for the improvement in communications made it profitable to work deeper, but better-quality seams.[35] In 1799 a pit was sunk at Donisthorpe.[36] About 1805 it was said that the coal-mines at Staunton Harold, described early in the 18th century as little used,[37] had recently become very extensive, and that the price of coal from the pits there leased from Earl Ferrers had risen from 6*s.* to 18*s.* or £1 a ton.[38] At Measham, where the canal passed close by the village, the existing pits were extended by the opening up in 1799 of a new district, where the important seam known as the 'Main Coal' was worked at a depth of 450 ft.[39] On Ashby Woulds a large colliery was established by the Earl of Moira, who had been one of the supporters of the canal.[40] In 1804 the earl began the sinking of the Double Pits on the Woulds,[41] and about 1806 he sank the adjacent Furnace Pits, where by 1812 the 'Main Coal' was being worked at a depth of 603 ft.[42] One of the mines on Ashby Woulds, probably that known as the Double Pits, was equipped with a steam engine for hoisting coals,[43] the first recorded case of steam power being used for such a purpose in Leicestershire. Short tramways connected the new shafts with the canal.[44] In 1809, coal from the Moira colliery was being sold for 10*s.* a ton at the pit head, a considerable increase over the 1800 figure.[45] In 1813 the Bath Pits were sunk by Lord Moira, close to the canal,[46] and in 1821 the Rawdon Pit farther north was sunk, reaching the 'Main Coal' at a depth of about 740 ft.[47] At all these pits of the Moira collieries the only seam worked was the upper part[4] of the 'Main Coal'.[49] To accommodate the miners from the new pits the village of Moira was built in 1811.[50] The new canal, by its link with the Coventry Canal, opened the London market to Leicestershire coal, and in 1815 coal from the pits on Ashby Woulds was first brought to the capital. Leicestershire coal was sold in London at a slightly higher price than coal from north-east England, but its quality was superior.[51]

While the western part of the coalfield was thus expanding, the eastern area seems to have been in a rather depressed state during the early years of the 19th century. Apart from the mines around Lount and Staunton Harold, which were connected with the Ashby canal by a tramway, none of the pits to the east of the Ashby anticline was provided with adequate means of distributing its coal. An important mine, equipped with a steam engine, near Coleorton, was closed about 1800.[52] Despite difficulties, however, mining continued on a considerable scale in this district, after the failure of the Charnwood Forest Canal.[53] Shortly after 1800 a large mine, furnished with a new steam engine capable of pumping 760 gallons of water a minute, was being worked by William Burslem at Coleorton, where the inhabitants were said to be mostly miners,[54] and a list drawn up in 1810 mentions collieries at both Coleorton and Alton Grange.[55] The Swannington collieries are not included in the list of 1810, and may have ceased production. Soon after

30 L.R.O. A Plan of the Intended Navigation from Loughborough to Leic.

31 Stretton, *Hist. Midland Rlwy.* 4; Curtis, *Topog. Hist. Leics.* p. xxx.

32 Stretton, op. cit. 4.

33 *C.J.* xlix, 469.

34 Nichols, *Leics.* i, p. clxxi; Stretton, *Hist. Midland Rlwy.* 99, 100; P. Beaumont, *Hist. Moira Collieries*, 2.

35 *Rep. Cttee. of H.C. on Coal Trade, 1800* (Reps. from Cttees. of H.C. First Series, x), p. 565, evidence of Joseph Wilkes.

36 Fox-Strangways, *Geol. Leics. S. Derbys. Coalfield*, 228.

37 Nichols, *Leics.* iii, 715.

38 Ibid. iii, 718. Earl Ferrers was amongst the supporters of the canal: *C.J.* xlix, 238. In 1800 the price of coal at Measham and Oakthorpe was from 4*s.* to 7*s.* a ton: *Rep. Cttee. of H.C. on Coal Trade, 1800* (Reps. from Cttees. of H.C. First Series, x) p. 565, evidence of Joseph Wilkes.

39 Harrison, *Sketch Geol. of Leics. and Rut.* 21.

40 *C.J.* xlix, 239. Trial borings were made on the Woulds in 1796. Leic. City Mun. Room, 13 D 40/13, ff. 69, 70.

41 Beaumont, *Hist. Moira Collieries*, 2.

42 Ibid.

43 Nichols, *Leics.* iii, 638*.

44 L.R.O. Ashby Woulds Inclosure Award, m. 4.

45 Pitt, *Gen. View of Agric. of County of Leic.* 7. See n. 38.

46 Beaumont, *Hist. Moira Collieries*, 2.

47 Ibid. 8.

48 Known as 'over coal'.

49 Beaumont, *Hist. Moira Collieries*, 8.

50 Ibid. 2. Beaumont prints (p. 115) a photograph of miners' cottages built in 1811.

51 Ibid. 2. In 1815 the price at London for coal from the Earl of Moira's pits was 47*s.* a ton.

52 Nichols, *Leics.* iii, 740.

53 Fox-Strangways states that the Swannington and Coleorton pits were 'practically closed', but this seems to be an exaggeration: *Geol. Leics. S. Derbys. Coalfield*, 7.

54 Nichols, *Leics.* iii, 739, 740.

55 Fox-Strangways, op. cit. 8. The Alton mine was apparently not in use in 1810.

1820, however, coal-mining began to spread from the established mining districts southwards and eastwards into the area where the Coal Measures lie hidden beneath a thick covering of other rock formations. In 1824 Whitwick Colliery was opened, near the present town of Coalville, and for some years a seam was worked there at a depth of 347 ft.[56] In 1825 a farmer named Thurlby sank a shaft about 200 ft. deep at Ibstock, reaching a seam of coal 3½ ft. thick,[57] and about a year later Viscount Maynard established a large colliery on his manor of Bagworth.[58] By 1830 there was much activity in the eastern portion of the coalfield, despite the lack of railways and canals. It was already being planned to enlarge Whitwick Colliery[59] by deepening the shaft and working two new and deeper seams.[60] In 1830 a new mine was begun at Peggs Green, near Coleorton, and a shaft sunk to a depth of about 360 ft. apparently reached the seam now known as the 'Main Coal'.[61] Meanwhile mining continued in the old districts of Coleorton and Swannington. In 1830 coal was being worked at Coleorton at a depth of 600 ft.,[62] while the numerous pits at Swannington varied in depth from 150 to 450 ft.[63] At the same time progress continued in the western part of the coalfield, and at the Moira collieries on Ashby Woulds new shafts were sunk in 1830 and 1832.[64] Despite these developments, mining in Leicestershire was still on a much smaller scale than it was in later times. A good impression of the size of collieries as they were just before the introduction of railways can be gained from the number of miners enumerated in the 1831 census.[65] The figures, while not altogether trustworthy, do show in general terms the scale on which the Leicestershire mines were then being operated. In the parish of Whitwick, which included the collieries at Long Lane and Swannington, there were only 72 men employed in mining and quarrying. In the parish of Breedon, which included the mines at Lount and Newbold, there were only 54 men working in the pits; at Coleorton, 41 men were employed in the collieries. At Heather, the very small size of the coal-workings is indicated by the fact that they employed 13 men, while at Ibstock the recently opened mine employed only 12. The total for Leicestershire of 261 miners mentioned in the 1831 census cannot be complete, as no miners are recorded at Oakthorpe, Measham,[66] Ashby Woulds, or Bagworth, where mines are known to have been in operation. The numbers employed in such relatively important districts as Coleorton and Whitwick do, however, serve to show the general size of the mining industry.

The difficulties of transporting the growing output of the eastern part of the coalfield must have been serious. In 1828 William Stenson, the active member of the partnership which operated Whitwick Colliery,[67] decided after a visit to the Stockton & Darlington Railway to promote a railway between Leicester and the mining area around Swannington.[68] In 1830 powers were granted by Act to construct a railway between Leicester and the north end of Swannington village, with branches to the collieries at Bagworth and Ibstock and to the Whitwick Colliery at Long Lane.[69] In 1831 the railway between Leicester and Bagworth was completed, and in 1833 the line was ready as far as Swannington.[70] In 1832 Sir George Beaumont began the construction of a railway from the Swannington terminus of the line from Leicester, to the old tramway between the Ashby Canal and Breedon.[71] As a result of the building of the Leicester & Swannington Railway coal from the Leicestershire pits was being sold for 10*s.* a ton at Leicester in 1832, and the trade in Nottinghamshire coal, which had previously been brought in along the River Soar, was ruined.[72]

The building of the railway naturally led to a great expansion of coal-mining in the areas near the new line. In 1831 the famous railway engineer George Stephenson, who had been consulted about the building of the railway,[73] established a colliery at Snibston, with the support of two Liverpool acquaintances,[74] and in 1832 a branch line was built from the Leicester & Swannington Railway to Stephenson's No. 2 pit at Snibston.[75] By 1846 four shafts had been sunk at Snibston, to a depth of about 700 ft., and coal of a very high quality was being produced. The village of Snibston was largely built by Stephenson and his partners.[76] Farther east the town of Coalville grew up around Whitwick Colliery at Long Lane. When the Leicester & Swannington Railway was built it was not considered

[56] Curtis, *Topog. Hist. Leics.* 184; White, *Dir. Leics.* (1846), 365.

[57] Curtis, op. cit. 80.

[58] Ibid. 9; White, *Dir. Leics.* (1846), 595. At Bagworth the highest seam lies about 325 ft. below the surface: Fox-Strangways, *Geol. Leics. & Derbys. Coalfield*, 303.

[59] Whitwick Colliery was not at the village of Whitwick, but at Long Lane, the modern Coalville.

[60] Curtis, *Topog. Hist. Leics.* 184; White, *Dir. Leics.* (1846), 365.

[61] Curtis, op. cit. 174; Fox-Strangways, *Geol. Leics. & Derbys. Coalfield*, 325.

[62] Curtis, op. cit. 44.

[63] Ibid. 168.

[64] Beaumont, *Hist. Moira Collieries*, 8.

[65] The figures only relate to men over 20: boys were also employed: *Census, 1831*.

[66] Oakthorpe and Measham were in Derbys. in 1831, and are therefore listed under that county.

[67] Leic. City Mun. Room, Deed of Partnership between Wm. Stenson, Jas. Whetstone, and Samuel Smith Harris, 1828.

[68] Stretton, *Hist. Midland Rlwy.* 4.

[69] Ibid. 12. The 3 branches were built at the expense of the colliery owners.

[70] Ibid. 20, 27.

[71] Ibid. 25.

[72] Ibid. 32.

[73] Ibid. 4, 5.

[74] Ibid. 12.

[75] Ibid. 25.

[76] White, *Dir. Leics.* (1846), 24.

necessary to have a station at Long Lane,[77] but by 1846 Coalville had a population of 1,200.[78] Nevertheless, even after the growth which followed the introduction of railways, the Leicestershire coal industry was still in the middle years of the 19th century on a small scale compared both with activities in other coalfields at the same period, and with the size of the Leicestershire mining industry in the 20th century. The census of 1851 gives the number of miners in the county as only 1,147.[79] The 1861 census only records 2,455 miners in Leicestershire, against more than 13,000 employed in 1920, and against a total of 246,613 coal-miners in England and Wales in 1861.[80] In 1854 439,000 tons of coal were produced in the county,[81] compared with 2,867,494 in 1938.[82]

In 1856 it was reported that mining in the area which included Leicestershire was mostly carried on by the 'longwall' method. The pits were ventilated by rather primitive methods.[83]

A minor activity of the Leicestershire coal-mines was the mining of fireclay, which is often found in conjunction with coal seams.[84] As early as 1800 the Earl of Moira was evidently aware of the value of the fireclay obtainable on Ashby Woulds, for the Act by which the Woulds were inclosed contained provisions protecting his interests in clay useful for manufacturing pot and porcelain.[85] By 1830 firebricks and earthenware were being manufactured from the clay obtained on the Woulds.[86] Whitwick Colliery, established at Long Lane in 1824,[87] seems to have been intended almost from the start to produce clay as well as coal. A lease of mineral rights made in 1827 empowered the partnership operating the colliery to obtain clay, as well as coal, while by an agreement of 1828 the partners agreed to participate in the manufacture of bricks and tiles.[88] Subsequently the production of bricks and tiles was carried on by the Whitwick Colliery Co., while William Whetstone, who had obtained an interest in the colliery, manufactured ornamental tiles on his own account.[89]

The important expansion of the Leicestershire mining industry in the first half of the 19th century seems to a considerable extent to have been carried out by the owners of the coal-bearing lands. The Moira collieries, which were perhaps the most important group of pits in the coalfield, were begun by the Earl of Moira,[90] an important landowner who had inherited the extensive properties of the Hastings family in Leicestershire and Derbyshire.[91] Lord Maynard, who established a colliery on his manor of Bagworth, was also a landowner in Leicestershire, though on a smaller scale.[92] William Thurlby, the founder of Ibstock Colliery, seems to have provided the capital for his venture himself. He was the owner of a modest farm, on which the original pit was sunk.[93] By 1846 the Ibstock pit was already being worked by a company,[94] which suggests that Thurlby's capital was not adequate for the development of a colliery. It may be noted that there were landed families who, though they had earlier taken an active part in the mining industry, preferred in the 19th century to lease their mineral rights. The Beaumonts of Coleorton do not seem to have played an active part in mining after the 17th century, though during the 19th century, coal was being worked on their lands by lessees.[95] Similarly the Boultbees of Thringstone, though actively engaged in the operation of Leicestershire collieries in the 18th century,[96] were content to allow the important Peggs Green Colliery to be established by lessees.[97] Besides the local landowners who developed the mineral resources of their own

[77] Stretton, *Hist. Midland Rlwy.* 28.

[78] White, *Dir. Leics.* (1846), 565.

[79] Ibid. (1863), 20. This figure cannot be considered as altogether reliable. On the growth of population in the mining area generally, see below, p. 150.

[80] *Census*, 1861; *Rep. of Chief Inspector of Mines, for 1938* (H.M.S.O.), 160. The statistics for 1861 and 1938 are not strictly comparable, as the 1938 figure includes clerical and administrative personnel employed at collieries, unlike the 1861 figure.

[81] *Ret. of Coal, &c., Raised, for 1854 and 1855*, H.C. 328, p. 2 (1856), lv.

[82] *Rep. of Chief Inspector of Mines, for 1938* (H.M.S.O.), 140.

[83] *Rep. of Inspectors of Coal Mines*, [1845] pp. 88, 112, H.C. (1854), xix.

[84] Fox-Strangways, *Geol. Leics. S. Derbys. Coalfield*, 27, 28, 39, 41, 44–48.

[85] Nichols, *Leics.* iii, 614; L.R.O. Ashby Woulds Inclosure Award, m. 4.

[86] Curtis, *Topog. Hist. Leics.* 4.

[87] Ibid. 184; White, *Dir. Leics.* (1846), 365.

[88] Leic. City Mun. Room, 1/D 43/19; Lease by Thos. Stenson to Wm. Stenson, 11 Oct. 1827; Deed of Partnership between Wm. Stenson, Jas. Whetstone, and Samuel Smith Harris, 1828.

[89] White, *Dir. Leics.* (1877), 190; Leic. City Mun. Room, 1/D 43/19, Indenture between Wm. Whetstone and Thos. Tertius Paget, 1871.

[90] Created Marquess of Hastings in 1817: *Complete Peerage*.

[91] Beaumont, *Hist. Moira Collieries*, 9; H. G. Bell, *Huntingdon Peerage*, 165.

[92] At his death in 1865 Maynard was worth less than £50,000: *Complete Peerage*, viii, 604.

[93] Curtis, *Topog. Hist. Leics.* 80; L.R.O. Ibstock Land Tax Assessments, 1825.

[94] White, *Dir. Leics.* (1846), 564.

[95] Leic. City Mun. Room, 1/D 43/19; Indenture between the Whitwick Colliery Co., Ltd., and Wm. Whetstone; L.R.O. Charnwood Forest Railway (extension to Lichfield), Bk. of reference.

[96] Northants. Rec. Off. (at Lamport Hall), Box 1289, contract between Thos. Hall and Ric. Holland; L.R.O. Plan of the Intended Navigation between Leic. and Loughborough.

[97] L.R.O. Plan of Intended Extension of the Leic. & Swannington Railway to the Ashby de la Zouch Railway, 1832.

property, other men with strong local connexions played important parts in the growth of the Leicestershire mines. William Stenson, for example, one of the partners in the Whitwick Colliery,[98] belonged to a family who had been yeomen and tradesmen at Whitwick,[99] though he himself was apparently a professional engineer.[1] Some leases of mineral rights for Whitwick Colliery were obtained by him from a relative.[2] James Whetstone, another partner in the Whitwick Colliery, came from a family which was prominent in textile manufacture at Leicester.[3] Of the new collieries established in Leicestershire during the first half of the 19th century, the only one financed by men without previous connexion with the county seems to have been the Snibston Colliery, which belonged to George Stephenson and his two Liverpool associates, Sir Joshua Walmersley and Joseph Saunders.[4]

The expansion of the Leicestershire collieries was accompanied by a gradual improvement in the miners' lot, although during the 19th century the conditions of work in the pits remained in many respects unsatisfactory by the standards of more recent years. In 1791 it was said that the colliers around Measham were earning from 2*s.* to 3*s.* 6*d.* a day, a high wage for the period.[5] The practice of allowing miners free coal was already established, and near Measham each miner received at that time 3½ cwt. of coal free a week in summer, and 4½ cwt. in winter.[6] A charge of 4*d.* a week for carriage was made.[7] The increase in the safety of the miners' occupation during the course of the 19th century does not seem to have presented any distinctive features in Leicestershire. The system of 'butties',[8] which gave rise to serious abuses in the midlands coalfields, still persisted in Leicestershire in the middle of the 19th century. In the western portion of the coalfield it was the practice, about 1840, for a group of hewers to contract to work a pit, and to hire the other workers needed to operate it.[9] The butties of the Moira collieries are mentioned in 1852,[10] but by 1873 the butty system was apparently confined to south Staffordshire.[11] The truck system does not seem to have been employed at the Leicestershire collieries.[12] There is no evidence that women were ever employed underground in the county, and while it might be dangerous to deduce from the absence of evidence that women never worked in the Leicestershire pits, it seems unlikely that they can have done so at any time during the 19th century.[13] About 1840, however, boys and youths were much employed in the Leicestershire mines, though they formed a smaller proportion of the labour force than was the case in some other coalfields.[14] The Children's Employment Commission of 1842 found no children under 7 working underground in the county,[15] though in some other areas children of 5 or 6 did so.[16] The Snibston and Whitwick Collieries were not employing children under 10 in 1842, and the Moira collieries do not seem to have employed children at all.[17] Young children at the Leicestershire pits were being paid 8*d.* daily in 1842. Older children, employed to lead horses underground, received 1*s.* 5*d.* to 1*s.* 8*d.* a day, while those over 16 were paid 2*s.*, rising in time to 3*s.*[18] Generally, the conditions of the miners seem to have been better in Leicestershire than in many other mining districts.[19] It was remarked in 1842 that the Leicestershire colliers generally appeared healthy,[20] and that more care was taken to prevent pit accidents in Leicestershire than in most mining areas.[21]

In 1856 it was reported that the Leicestershire mine-owners, unlike those of Warwickshire, had made efforts to improve the education of the inhabitants of the mining villages.[22] Hours of work, however, were long. In 1842 it was said that

98 Established 1824: Curtis, *Topog. Hist. Leics.* 184; White, *Dir. Leics.* (1846), 385.

99 Leic. Univ. Coll. Libr. *The Poll at the Electing of Two Knights of the Shire, to Represent the County of Leics. 1830* (printed Thos. Combe), 66; Leic. City Mun. Room, 1/D 43/19, Deed of Partnership between Wm. Stenson, Jas. Whetstone, and Samuel Smith Harris, 1828; L.R.O. Whitwick, Thringstone, and Peggs Green Inclosure Award.

1 Stenson is described as engineer in a deed of 1828, and in a poll book of 1830 (cited in n. 99). It is plain from the terms of the partnership deed of 1828 that he was to be the active director of the pit.

2 Leic. City Mun. Room, 1/D 43/19; Lease by Thos. Stenson to Will. Stenson of coal-mines under a farm called the Wastes, Whitwick, 1827.

3 *Reg. Freemen of Leic. 1196–1770*, ed. H. Hartopp, 301, 353, 358, 453, 532; White, *Dir. Leics.* (1846), 166; A. Fielding Johnson, *Glimpses of Ancient Leic.* (1906), 296–7.

4 Stretton, *Hist. Midland Rlwy.* 12.

5 A. Young, *Tours in Engl. and Wales* (edn. London School of Econ. 1932), 287.

6 Ibid.

7 Ibid.

8 A 'butty' was a contractor who agreed with the owner or lessee of a mine to raise coal at a given price. The 'butty' was thus a middleman intervening between the working miners and the owner or lessee of the pit. On the origin of the system, see T. S. Ashton and J. Sykes, *Coal Ind. of the 18th Century*, 113.

9 *Children's Employment Com. 1st Rep.: Mines*, [380] p. 39, H.C. (1842), xv.

10 Beaumont, *Hist. Moira Collieries*, 42.

11 *Rep. Sel. Cttee. on Coal*, H.C. 313, p. 225 (1873), x.

12 *Children's Employment Com. 1st Rep.: Mines* (1842), pp. 159–61.

13 Ibid. 36.

14 Ibid. 11, 38.

15 Ibid. 10.

16 Ibid. 9, 11.

17 Ibid. 11.

18 Ibid. 154.

19 F. Engels, *Condition of the Working Classes in Engl.* (trans. F. K. Wischnewetzky), 246–7.

20 *Children's Employment Com. 1st Rep.: Mines* (1842), pp. 11, 162.

21 Ibid. 138.

22 *Rep. Commissioner on Population in Mining Districts*, [2275] pp. 6–7, H.C. (1857, Sess. 2), xvi.

miners in the midlands usually worked from 6 in the morning until 6 at night.[23] The time allowed for meals varied; at some Leicestershire pits such as that at Ibstock, half an hour was allowed for breakfast, and an hour for dinner, while at others, such as Whitwick and Snibston Collieries, only half an hour for dinner was permitted; at other Leicestershire pits there were no fixed meal times.[24] Most Leicestershire miners continued to work from 6 in the morning until 6 at night, with about an hour and a half for meals,[25] until after 1870, though in one part of Leicestershire it was usual, about 1870, for the hewers to start work about 2 a.m., and continue until 10 a.m. or noon.[26] After 1870 the hours of work were reduced, perhaps because the heavy demand for coal placed the mine-workers in a stronger position. The normal working day was reduced by 2 hours, and about the same time the practice was introduced of stopping work at 10 a.m. on Saturdays, in place of working six full days a week.[27] In 1873 it was stated that double-shift working underground was unknown in the county.[28] About 1870 the hewers in one district of Leicestershire were being paid in accordance with their output, at the rate of 3*s.* 6*d.* for every ton of coal cut. A hewer's daily wage under these conditions was 4*s.* 6*d.* or 5*s.* The pay of loaders at the same period was 4*s.* or 4*s.* 6*d.* a day, while boys employed to lead horses underground received 2*s.* 6*d.* a day.[29]

The increased demand for coal after 1870 led to a new period of expansion for the Leicestershire mining industry. The county's annual coal output, which had fallen from over 1 million tons in 1867 to less than 600,000 tons in 1870, rose to over 700,000 tons in 1871, and reached over 1 million tons again in 1874.[30] In the following years existing mines were deepened to enable new seams to be worked, and mining was extended to fresh areas by the sinking of new pits. The most important development was the establishment of new collieries to the south of the old mining areas around Swannington and Coleorton. New pits were sunk at Hugglescote in 1876, and at Ellistown and Nailstone about the same time.[31] Progress also continued in the older districts; a new pit was sunk on Coleorton Moor in 1875, and about 1877 Whitwick Colliery was deepened to 915 ft., to enable a seam of high quality, known as the 'Roaster', to be worked.[32] Rather earlier, in 1868, the Rawdon Pit, near Moira, was deepened to a total of over 1,000 ft.[33] During the 1870's also, many of the dwellings which still exist in the mining villages were erected. Typical examples of the long terraces of stone houses built during this period can be seen stretching for a considerable distance along the main road from Bagworth to Hugglescote.[34] Between 1880 and 1939 the only important extension of the area of mining was the sinking in 1900 of the Desford Colliery,[35] which in 1939 marked the farthest limit of the mining district to the south-east.

Most of the existing collieries in Leicestershire were already established before the outbreak of the First World War. In 1913 there were just over 10,000 persons employed in the Leicestershire mines, producing in the year 3,175,000 tons of coal,[36] or more than double the amount produced in 1891.[37] The proportion by which Leicestershire's coal output increased between 1891 and 1913 was considerably greater than the proportionate increase for the coalfields of Britain as a whole, so that the relative importance of the county as a coal producer increased during this period.[38] The average production per man of 307·3 tons of coal from the Leicestershire pits during 1913 was considerably greater than the average production of 260 tons per man for the whole United Kingdom in that year.[39] Despite the recruitment of many miners into the forces during the war, and the consequent reduction of man-power and influx of inexperienced labour into the pits,[40] output was increased. In 1917 the highest level of production was reached with an output of 3,595,669 tons of coal from the Leicestershire mines.[41] In the early stages of the war a small quantity of coal was produced from open-cast workings in the county, the highest production being reached in 1916, when 870 tons were obtained.[42] The large output of the war years was only obtained by neglecting both maintenance work and the further development of the coalfield, and after 1918 it proved difficult

[23] *Children's Employment Com. 1st Rep.: Mines* (1842), p. 106.
[24] Ibid. 119.
[25] *Rep. Sel. Cttee. on Coal* (1873), p. 133.
[26] Ibid.
[27] Ibid. 133–4.
[28] Ibid. 133.
[29] Ibid.
[30] Ibid.; Harrison, *Geol. of Leics. and Rut.* 27.
[31] Harrison, op. cit. 25, 55; Fox-Strangways, *Geol. Leics. S. Derbys. Coalfield*, 282.
[32] Harrison, op. cit. 24; Fox-Strangways, op. cit. 330; White, *Dir. Leic.* (1877), 192.
[33] Beaumont, *Hist. Moira Collieries*, 8; Fox-Strangways, op. cit. 218.
[34] For date of erection, see inscriptions on houses.
[35] Fox-Strangways, *Geol. Leics. S. Derbys. Coalfield*, 307.
[36] *Rep. on the Brit. Coal Industry* (Political and Econ. Planning), 56.
[37] Anon. 'General Notes on the Yorks., Leics., and Warws. Coalfields', *Colliery Guardian*, 1892. This reference comes from Mr. P. W. Glover, of St. Edmund Hall, Oxford, who has allowed the notes prepared by him for a thesis on the economics of the Leics. and S. Derbys. coalfield to be used in the compilation of this article.
[38] *Coal Ind. Com. Rep.*, [Cmd. 361] App. 5, H.C. (1919), xiii.
[39] *Statistical Abstract for U.K. for 1913 and 1918–31*, [Cmd. 4489] Table 184, H.C. (1933–4), xxvi.
[40] *Gen. Rep. Chief Inspector of Mines, 1916*, pt. 1, [Cd. 8732] p. 33, H.C. (1917–18), xxxvii; ibid. *1918*, pt. 1, [Cmd. 339] p. 81, H.C. (1919), li.
[41] Ibid. *1917*, pt. 3, [Cmd. 4] p. 114, H.C. (1919), li.
[42] Ibid. 15.

to find employment for demobilized miners, whose places during the war had been filled by new-comers to the industry.[43] The end of hostilities was followed by a decline in output, and in 1919 the Leicestershire mines produced 3,171,398 tons of coal.[44] In Leicestershire, as in other parts of Great Britain, the post-war period was marked by labour troubles, though in general relations between employers and employed were better in the midlands than in many coalfields elsewhere in the country.[45] In May 1926 the coal-mines in Leicestershire were closed as a result of the General Strike, and the Leicestershire Miners' Council decided on strike pay at the rate of £1 a week to each adult member, with 2*s*. a week for every child under 14.[46] Towards the end of August some mines were reopened, and a working day of 8 hours was established in Leicestershire, compared with a 7½-hour day in the adjacent counties of Nottingham and Derby. By early October all the mines were open, though they were not fully manned.[47] As a result of the stoppage less than 2 million tons of coal were produced from the Leicestershire pits during 1926.[48] During the years which followed the General Strike there was much unemployment, though as the Leicestershire coalfield chiefly supplied coal for consumption in Great Britain the pits in the county were less affected than those in many other areas.[49] The county's output of coal declined from just over 3 million tons in 1927[50] to less than 2¼ millions in 1933.[51] Output of fireclay, which continued to be a secondary product of several Leicestershire pits,[52] fell similarly from more than 95,000 tons in 1927, to less than 27,000 tons in 1933.[53] In this situation the policy was adopted of closing parts of the pits, and concentrating on the most economic seams.[54] Under the Coal Mines Act of 1930 the Leicestershire pits were included in the Midland (Amalgamated) District, and their output was controlled.[55] An improvement in the coal trade began in 1934,[56] and by 1938 output had increased again to nearly 3 million tons.[57] The quota allotted to Leicestershire under the Act of 1930 seems to have been too small, for from 1936 onwards Quota Tonnage was acquired, chiefly from south and west Yorkshire.[58] The mines were still far from producing to their full capacity, and in 1938 the average number of days weekly on which coal was wound in the Leicestershire pits was only 4·19.[59] Only 19 mines were operating in the county during 1938,[60] compared with 30 in 1919.[61] The general depression of the coal-mining industry in the period between the two wars naturally caused a fall in the number of men employed at the Leicestershire pits. During 1927 the average number employed in the county's mines was a little under 12,000,[62] but in the following years the figure fell steadily, until during 1937 only just over 9,000 were employed.[63] In 1938 there was a slight rise in the number of miners at work.[64]

During the period between the two wars the Leicestershire coal-mining industry did not spread into new areas, although a new colliery was established at Lount in 1924.[65] In 1928 Ibstock Colliery was closed.[66] The individual collieries remained of small or moderate size; in 1924 no Leicestershire colliery employed more than 2,000 people, and only six employed more than 1,000.[67] The period between the wars was, however, notable for the increased use made of machinery in the pits, and the degree of mechanization attained in Leicestershire was greater than that reached in most British coalfields. By 1938, for example, 71 per cent. of the output of Leicestershire mines was mechanically conveyed and 84 per cent. mechanically cut, compared with averages of 54 and 56 per cent. for England and Wales.[68] During 1935 the East Midland Division, of which Leicestershire formed a part, had the highest output per head of any division in

43 *Gen. Rep. Chief Inspector of Mines, 1918*, pp. 81, 82.

44 Ibid. *1919*, pt. 1, [Cmd. 925] p. 180, H.C. (1920), l.

45 *Coal Mining; Rep. Technical Advisory Cttee.* [Cmd. 6610] p. 36, H.C. (1945), iv.

46 *Leic. Mercury*, 5 May 1926, p. 8.

47 *Rep. Inspector of Mines, 1926: No. 4, N. Midland Div.* (H.M.S.O.), 3.

48 Ibid. 8.

49 *Rep. Inspector of Mines, 1927: No. 4, N. Midland Div.* (H.M.S.O.) 3; ibid. *1928*, 3; ibid. *1932*, 5; *Rep. on the Brit. Coal Ind.* (Political and Econ. Planning), 56.

50 *Rep. Inspector of Mines, 1927: No. 4, N. Midland Div.* (H.M.S.O.), 7.

51 Ibid. *1933*, 7.

52 In 1924, 7 collieries in Leics. produced fireclay. In addition, 2 small mines at Ashby Woulds, and 3 at Woodville, produced fireclay only: *List of Mines in Gt. Brit. and the Isle of Man, 1924* (H.M.S.O.), 168–70.

53 *Rep. Inspector of Mines, 1927: No. 4, N. Midland Div.* (H.M.S.O.), 7; ibid. *1933*, 7.

54 Ibid. *1931*, 4.

55 W. H. B. Court, *Hist. Second World War; Coal*, 18.

56 *Rep. Inspector of Mines, 1934: No. 4, N. Midland Div.* (H.M.S.O.), 5.

57 *18th Annual Rep. Sec. for Mines, and 31st Annual Rep. Chief Inspector of Mines* (H.M.S.O.), 140.

58 Central Valuation Board; Coal Industry Nationalization Act, 1946. Stage II, Proc. Leics. Districts' Claim to Compensation. Summaries of Statistics, Table T.J.S. 8. (Ex inf. Mr. P. W. Glover.)

59 *18th Annual Rep. Sec. for Mines, and 31st Annual Rep. Chief Inspector of Mines* (H.M.S.O.), 166–7.

60 Ibid. 203.

61 *Gen. Rep. Chief Inspector of Mines, 1919*, [Cmd. 925] p. 179, H.C. (1920), l.

62 *18th Annual Rep. Sec. for Mines, and 31st Annual Rep. Chief Inspector of Mines* (H.M.S.O.), 160.

63 Ibid.

64 Ibid.

65 *Rep. Inspector of Mines, 1924: No. 4, N. Midland Div.* (H.M.S.O.), 5.

66 Anon. 'The Hist. of the Ibstock Private Railway', *Coalville Times*, 26 Jan. 1951.

67 *List of Mines in Gt. Brit. and the Isle of Man, 1924* (H.M.S.O.), 168–70.

68 *18th Annual Rep. Sec. for Mines, and 31st Annual Rep. Chief Inspector of Mines* (H.M.S.O.), 140.

Great Britain,[69] and the costs for producing each ton of coal were considerably lower than the average for the country as a whole.[70] The efficiency and comparative prosperity of the Leicestershire pits were reflected in the miners' earnings, which in 1938 were rather above the general level prevailing in the British mining industry.[71]

QUARRYING

The quarrying of stone in Leicestershire began at a very early date. At Buddon Wood, near Quorndon,[1] granite mill-stones were quarried in the early Iron Age.[2] Under the Romans, stone from the Charnwood Forest area was used for building in Leicester, though brick was also employed.[3] Some of the buildings of Roman Leicester were roofed with slate quarried at Swithland, about 6 miles away.[4] Swithland slate has also been found among Roman remains at Norton Disney (Lincs.),[5] so that this material, which became well known in the 17th century, was probably worked to a considerable extent in the Roman period. Between the end of the Roman occupation of Britain and the 13th century there is no evidence about the state of the quarrying industry in Leicestershire. It is unlikely that during the intervening period stone can have been used at all extensively for building, though the fact that Leicester possessed town walls of masonry by 1282[6] shows that stone could then be used on a scale which was considerable by the standards of the time. There is evidence that by the end of the 13th century stone was being worked at a number of places within the county. The use of slates at Beaumanor in 1277[7] suggests that by that date slate was again being worked at Swithland, although the first reference to a slate quarry there is not found until 1343.[8] In the 14th century Swithland slates, costing 3*s.* 1*d.* a thousand, were used to roof Leicester castle,[9] and references to slaters occur amongst the records of Leicester borough from about 1260 onwards.[10] The stone of the Charnwood Forest area was sometimes used for building in the 13th century[11] though the hardness of the material must have made it difficult to use. In the 14th century stone from quarries at Swannington and Ibstock was used for building at Leicester,[12] while during the same period Garendon Abbey possessed a quarry at Swannington.[13] In 1481 stone for the new castle at Kirby Muxloe was obtained from quarries at Alton Grange, near Ravenstone, Stewards Hey, near Ratby, and from Barrons Park, near Kirby Muxloe itself.[14] Some idea of the cost of transporting building material at this time can be obtained from the fact that the charge for carrying a cart-load of freestone from Alton to Kirby, a distance of just over 10 miles, was 1*s.* 4*d.*[15] Stone for the rebuilding of Ashby de la Zouch castle, at about the same time, was obtained from a quarry close to the castle site.[16] Apart from the quarrying of building material, marl was being worked near Breedon early in the 13th century, presumably for use as fertilizer.[17] The quarrying of lime at Barrow upon Soar is first mentioned in 1396.[18] An account of the late 15th century mentions fifty-five lime-pits at Barrow,[19] and in 1481 Barrow lime was being used in the building of Kirby Muxloe castle.[20] The evidence about the quarrying of building-stone during the Middle Ages is very incomplete, and it is probable that in eastern Leicestershire, where the abundant ironstone makes good building material, there existed many small quarries of which no record remains.

Even for a later period, it is impossible to come to any general conclusion about the amount of quarrying carried on in the county. Such evidence as is available mostly concerns the production of lime, rather than of building-stone. The lime-pits at Barrow upon Soar continued to be worked in the 16th and 17th centuries,[21] and by 1673 the lime produced there was already well known for its binding qualities.[22] A map based on a

[69] *Rep. Inspector of Mines, 1935: No. 4, E. Midland Div.* (H.M.S.O.), 7.

[70] *Statistical Digest, from 1938*, [Cmd. 6538] p. 54, H.C. (1943–4), viii. In 1938 the average cost in Leics. was 13*s.* 8·47*d.*, against 16*s.* 0·34*d.* for the whole of Gt. Brit.

[71] Ibid. 65–66.

[1] i.e. Quern Hill: E. Eckwall, *Oxf. Dict. Engl. Place Names*, 131, 358, 360.

[2] W. G. Hoskins, *Leics. Heritage*, 20.

[3] F. J. Haverfield, *Roman Leic.* 32, 33, 38.

[4] Ibid. 37; A. Herbert, *Swithland Slate Headstones*, 6.

[5] Ex inf. Mr. M. W. Barley, F.S.A.

[6] *Leic. Boro. Rec. 1103–1327*, 197–8.

[7] *Quorndon Rec.* ed. G. F. Farnham, 49.

[8] Farnham, *Leics. Notes*, vi, 363.

[9] Herbert, *Swithland Slate Headstones*, 6; L. Fox, 'Leicester Castle', *T.L.A.S.* xxii (2), 143. The cost includes a charge for transport between Swithland and Leicester, a distance of about 6 miles.

[10] *Leic. Boro. Rec. 1103–1327*, 112, 121, 132–3, 208–9, 390.

[11] Hoskins, *Leics. Heritage*, 80.

[12] *Leic. Boro. Rec. 1327–1509*, 8, 78.

[13] Nichols, *Leics.* iii, 792*.

[14] A. H. Thompson, 'Building Accts. of Kirby Muxloe Castle', *T.L.A.S.* xi, 218, 225–6, 229, 247, 260.

[15] Ibid. xi, 229.

[16] T. H. Fosbrooke, *Ashby de la Zouch Castle*, 27.

[17] John Rylands Libr. Manchester, Latin MS. 222, f. 37*b*.

[18] *Quorndon Rec.* 115.

[19] Farnham, *Leics. Notes*, vi, 376.

[20] *T.L.A.S.* xi, 231–2.

[21] G. F. Farnham, *Charnwood Forest and Its Historians*, 64, 67; Camden, *Brit.* (1806), ii, 299.

[22] R. Blome, *Brit.* (1673), 139.

survey made between 1775 and 1777 marks four lime-works at Barrow, and four more near Worthington, in Breedon parish.[23] In 1784 it was said that there were several lime quarries at Breedon, 30 to 40 ft. deep. The carboniferous limestone obtained there was burnt in kilns built against the side of Breedon Hill, close to the quarries. The kilns were filled with alternate layers of lime, 18 in. thick, and coal, 6 in. thick, and burning was continuous. The lime produced was used as fertilizer, 5 or 6 qr. making a good dressing for an acre.[24] At the end of the 18th century there were lime-works at Grace Dieu, Barrow Hill, and Cloud Hill, all in north-west Leicestershire, besides those at Breedon and Barrow upon Soar,[25] and one of the reasons for the construction of the Charnwood Forest canal at that time was to provide transport for lime from the quarries around Breedon and Grace Dieu.[26] About 1807 lime from the Earl of Stamford's quarries at Breedon and Cloud Hill was being sold for 10*s.* a ton.[27] Breedon lime was considered rather strong for use as manure, but it was valued by builders for use in making mortar.[28] The production of lime at Breedon, and at Staunton Harold nearby, seems to have increased considerably after the construction of the Ashby canal, to which the lime-works around Breedon and Staunton were connected by a tramway.[29] At the beginning of the 19th century the limestone quarries at Barrow upon Soar were owned and worked by a number of farmers. The limestone was estimated to cost 3*d.* a cubic foot to quarry, and it was not economic to work the deeper layers. The lime was carried out of the pits, piled up in cones, and burnt.[30] In 1807 lime from Barrow upon Soar was being sold at about 12*s.* 6*d.* a ton; it had a high reputation, both as manure and as a material for mortar.[31]

It is clear that by 1800 the quarrying of lime was being conducted on a considerable scale in the areas around Breedon and Barrow upon Soar, while the production of slate at Swithland was also a well-established industry. The beginning of the 19th century saw an attempt to establish open-cast iron workings on Ashby Woulds. Iron-ore was found at a depth of from 5 to 8 yds. on land belonging to the Earl of Moira, who set up a foundry beside the Ashby canal, but it was not considered profitable to continue working the ironstone deposit.[32] During the early 19th century clay for the manufacture of pottery and porcelain was also dug on Lord Moira's land on Ashby Woulds.[33] A more important development during the first half of the 19th century was the growing use of the hard, igneous rocks from Mountsorrel and the Charnwood Forest district. It was shortly before 1800 that attempts to use broken granite macadam for road surfacing began in Leicestershire. The first person in the county to employ it is said to have been the overseer of a section of the turnpike between Harborough and Loughborough.[34] The material for the roads was obtained from quarries at Mountsorrel, where granite was being worked by 1787.[35] The records of the trustees of the turnpike from Harborough to Loughborough show that from 1818 onwards, and probably earlier,[36] the trustees were obtaining large quantities of broken granite from Mountsorrel. Some of the material was obtained from the trustees' own quarry there, but from about 1820 they were purchasing in addition some 2,000 tons of granite a year from other quarries at the same place. The turnpike records provide useful evidence about the cost of granite for road repairs. In 1818 a price of 2*s.* 3*d.* a ton for Mountsorrel stone 'broke to size' was quoted to the trustees when they invited tenders for the supply of 1,000 tons of granite. In 1822 the turnpike trustees laid down that the maximum price to be paid for Mountsorrel stone, broken and ready for use, was to be 5*s.* 9*d.* a ton, including cost of transport[37] between the quarries and Leicester. At the same time the maximum price for similar stone when delivered at Debdale, near Harborough, was 8*s.* 2*d.*[38] The hardness of the Mountsorrel stone made it very difficult to dress for building purposes. Shortly before 1830, however, one Jackson brought in workmen from Scotland, and made the local granite available for building.[39] In 1844 Jackson gave up the working of the quarries, and his lease of them was taken over by John Martin, who had previously been quarrying at Buddon Wood, near Quorndon.[40]

[23] L.R.O. J. Prior, Map of Leics. 1779.

[24] Marshall, *Rural Econ. of the Midland Counties,* (1790), ii, 2, 3.

[25] L.R.O. Plan of Intended Navigation from Loughborough to Leicester.

[26] *C.J.* xli, 270, 302, 633.

[27] W. Pitt, *General View of Agric. of County of Leic.* 8.

[28] Ibid.; Nichols, *Leics.* iii, 687.

[29] Nichols, *Leics.* iii, 718; C. E. Stretton, *Hist. Midland Rlwy.* 99, 100.

[30] Nichols, *Leics.* iii, 69.

[31] Pitt, *Gen. View of Agric. of County of Leic.* 8.

[32] Ibid. 8, 9.

[33] Nichols, *Leics.* iii, 614; Curtis, *Topog. Hist. Leics.* 4; L.R.O. Ashby Woulds Inclosure Award (1807), m. 4.

[34] Curtis, op. cit. p. xxxii.

[35] Ibid. 128; Nichols, *Leics.* iii, 90.

[36] In May 1803, and often subsequently, the turnpike trustees bought stone from a certain Adderley: L.R.O. Orders and Proc. of Trustees Market Harborough to Loughborough Turnpike 1803–25, esp. ff. 6*b*, 8*a*, 28*a*. It is not stated where the stone came from, but Adderley was one of the pioneers in the working of Mountsorrel granite: E. W. Hensman, 'Mountsorrel', in *Mem. of Old Leics.* ed. Alice Dryden, 131.

[37] Apparently the material was transported along the navigable R. Soar, though this is not expressly stated.

[38] L.R.O. Orders and Proc. of Trustees Market Harborough to Loughborough Turnpike, 1803–25, esp. entries for 5 Oct. 1818, and 18 Nov. 1822.

[39] Curtis, *Topog. Hist. Leics.* 128.

[40] *Mem. of Old Leics.* 131; and personal inf. from Mr. C. H. Martin.

Martin's operation of the quarries proved successful, and in 1954 his family still retained an interest in them.[41] The census of 1831 records the number of workers employed at the quarries in Barrow parish, which included Mountsorrel, as only 92, but by 1849 200 men were employed in the Mountsorrel quarries.[42]

The working of the igneous rocks of the Charnwood Forest region thus began at Mountsorrel, spread during the early and middle years of the 19th century to other places in Leicestershire where similar stone could be obtained. By 1830 syenite was being worked at Markfield and Groby, on the southern edge of Charnwood.[43] In 1857 Breedon Everard, who had for some years been working a small quarry at Billa Barrow, in Charnwood Forest, opened a quarry at Bardon Hill, where the extensive workings of the firm of Ellis & Everard Ltd., later became one of the most important sources of road metal in Britain.[44] The exploitation of the outlying deposits of syenite and similar rocks situated to the south of the Charnwood region began during the same period. By 1830 the diorite of Stoney Stanton was being worked,[45] and by 1846 syenite was also being quarried at Sapcote.[46] By 1877 syenite was also being obtained from large quarries at Enderby, Croft, and Huncote.[47] As the hard stone found in the western half of Leicestershire occurs in a region where the rock formations mostly consist of softer material, the Leicestershire quarries were well placed for supplying the east midlands.[48] During the later years of the 19th century Leicestershire became the most important area in England for the production of hard stone.[49] Out of a little more than 2,500,000 tons of igneous rock produced in England during 1900, over 1,100,000 tons were obtained from Leicestershire.[50]

The expansion of the quarries of igneous rock in west Leicestershire was paralleled during the later 19th century by the rapid growth of ironstone workings in the north-east of the county. The ironstone deposits of this region, though extensive, for long remained unworked, because the proportion of metal in the ore was considered to be too low to make the exploitation of the deposits profitable.[51] In 1874, however, workable ore was discovered north of Melton Mowbray. Quarrying of the ironstone was started soon afterwards at Holwell, near Melton, and in 1878 further quarries were opened at Wartnaby. The ironstone around Tilton was first exploited after the building of the railway between Melton and Market Harborough in 1879, and in 1894 a beginning was made of working the ore in an area on the eastern border of Leicestershire, around Buckminster.[52] By the end of the 19th century north-east Leicestershire had become an important source of ironstone, and in 1900 over 300,000 tons were produced from the county's quarries, while a further 400,000 tons were obtained from shallow workings.[53] In all, Leicestershire furnished more than 5 per cent. of the total iron-ore produced in England.[54]

While the new industry of ironstone quarrying was growing up, the famous old slate-pits at Swithland were suffering severely from the competition of cheap Welsh slate, and in 1887 the last of the Swithland pits was forced to close.[55] Small quantities of rough slate stone continued to be produced in the county,[56] but as a large-scale industry slate quarrying in Leicestershire came to an end. The production of lime and clay continued in Leicestershire during the second half of the 19th century, though not on a scale comparable with the quarrying of igneous rocks. In 1900 the Leicestershire quarries produced not quite 150,000 tons of limestone,[57] and about 470,000 tons of clay.[58]

41 *Mem. of Old Leics.* 131; and personal inf. from Mr. C. H. Martin.

42 *Mem. of Old Leics.* 131; *Census*, 1831.

43 Curtis, *Topog. Hist. Leics.* p. xxxii.

44 W. J. Harrison, *Geol. of Leics. and Rut.* (1877), 12; C. D. B. Ellis, *Centenary Bk. of Ellis & Everard, Ltd.* 7.

45 Curtis, *Topog. Hist. Leics.* p. xxxii.

46 White, *Dir. Leics.* (1846), 589.

47 Harrison, *Geol. of Leics. and Rut.* (1877), plates facing pp. 28, 32, 68.

48 W. W. Watts, *Geol. of Ancient Rocks of Charnwood Forest*, 78.

49 *Gen. Rep. Mines and Quarries, 1899*, [Cd. 387] p. 199, H.C. (1900), cii.

50 *Gen. Rep. Mines and Quarries, 1900*, [Cd. 818] pp. 152–3, H.C. (1902), cxvi (2).

51 Harrison, *Geol. of Leics. and Rut.* (1877), 39. The percentage of metal obtainable from a ton of iron-ore has been lower in Leics. than in most Engl. counties. See *Gen. Rep. Mines and Quarries, 1915*, [Cd. 8444] p. 127, H.C. (1917–18), xxxvii; *Gen. Rep. Mines and Quarries, 1918*, [Cmd. 531] p. 162, H.C. (1920), l; and equivalent reps. for other years.

52 H. B. Hewlett, *Quarries*, 17, 23, 25. In another place (ibid. 14) the same writer gives 1892 as the date when the Buckminster workings were begun. This, however, appears to be only a passing reference, so the date 1894, given in the main account of the Buckminster quarries (ibid. 25), has been preferred.

53 Less than 20 ft. deep.

54 *Gen. Rep. Mines and Quarries, 1900*, pp. 152–3, 158–9, 219.

55 Herbert, *Swithland Slate Headstones*, 3.

56 In 1901, Leics. produced 900 tons of slate, valued at £58; this was probably obtained from spoil tips: *Gen. Rep. Mines and Quarries, 1901*, [Cd. 1307] pp. 140–1, 260, H.C. (1902), cxvi (2). For some years after 1888 some work was done at an old slate quarry at Groby, mainly for the production of roofing-slate.

57 *Gen. Rep. Mines and Quarries, 1900*, pp. 152–3; a further 13,000 tons were obtained from mines in the county: ibid. pp. 148–9.

58 Ibid. pp. 152–3. This figure does not include clay obtained from mines (for which see above p. 42) or the considerable quantity obtained from workings too shallow to be included in returns made under the Quarries Act: ibid. p. 177.

By the end of the 19th century the Leicestershire quarrying industry had become important for its production of both igneous rock and ironstone. The number of men employed in the industry in 1900 was, however, only 4,000.[59] Between 1900 and 1939 the production of igneous rock continued generally at the level reached at the end of the 19th century. In 1938 1,280,000 tons of igneous rock were obtained from Leicestershire quarries, or about 170,000 tons more than had been obtained in 1900. This was the largest tonnage produced by any English county.[60] In the intervening years considerable fluctuations had been caused by war and economic depression, but in general the west Leicestershire quarries remained a very important source of hard stone. Most of the material quarried was used for road metalling, but during the hundred years ending about 1930 very substantial tonnages of paving setts were produced in the quarries where the stone was suitable. The industry probably started at Mountsorrel about 1830, when a few workmen were introduced from the granite-quarrying areas of Scotland. The trade quickly spread to the other areas where suitable stone was being quarried, and when at its maximum, early in the 20th century, something over 600 men and boys were employed at Mountsorrel, Markfield, Cliffe Hill, Croft, Narborough, Enderby, Huncote, Stoney Stanton, Sapcote, and Earl Shilton. A few setts were also made at Groby and the Charnwood quarry near Shepshed. The total tonnage produced at that period was between 90,000 and 100,000 tons per annum. The setts from Leicestershire were used very widely in the manufacturing towns of the midlands and the West Riding of Yorkshire, and in the middle of the 19th century in London.

The craft of sett-making and the allied craft of blocking involved a high degree of skill and judgement, and success in it depended upon identifying accurately what was known as the 'cut' of the stone—better known to geologists as the cleavage planes. The industry was purely manual, no machine having ever been devised to take the place of hand-work. Blocks of stone weighing a ton or more were reduced to manageable size by the use of 'bursting hammers' weighing up to 28 lb. and shod with high carbon steel: a nick would be cut across the top surface of the stone from side to side, and when 'drawn' by blows from the flat end of the hammer at the end of the stone it would split across as straight as if it had been sawn. The two halves were then similarly reduced to blocks some 18 in. square by 9 in. deep and these were in turn split and dressed by the sett-makers: they used smaller hammers with a sharpened end for 'nicking' and a flat end for 'knapping', the stone being turned upside-down between these two processes, into pieces roughly of the size required for the trade at the time. These rough pieces were then dressed with smaller solid steel hammers into the straight-sided rectangular blocks known as setts.

The faculty of sett-making ran often in families, and there were many instances of it being followed by three successive generations. Many of the sett-makers built their own houses: they were the aristocrats of the quarrying industry and often had their own territories in the public house.

The Leicestershire-born sett-makers were to be found in all the quarrying districts of England and Wales, where there was rock suitable for the trade, and in every state in the United States of America where granite was quarried. The small colony of Mountsorrel sett-makers who had emigrated to Clee Hill (Salop), always took a holiday at the time of Mountsorrel Fair, in the middle of July.

Throughout the same period large quantities of dressed granite kerb were produced in the same quarries. The 'rough kerb' was made at the quarry face, often by the use of small wedges known as plugs and feathers, and was transported to the sheds where the kerb dressers reduced it to the required size by the use of hammers, chisels, and picks.

A limited quantity of dressed masonry was also produced in Leicestershire, notably for the village war memorials which were erected after the First World War; good instances of these may be seen at Croft, Anstey, Rothley, Woodhouse Eaves, and on the Castle Hill at Mountsorrel. The last four are made of Mountsorrel stone, the first three being of the grey variety, with Swithland slate panels. That on the Castle Hill—one of the finest sites in the whole county—is of red Mountsorrel, the names being on bronze plaques.[61]

Closely connected with these developments has been the manufacture of various types of artificial stone, largely composed of small broken material from quarries of igneous rock, combined with Portland cement.[62] Quarrying of ironstone has also continued on an increasing scale in eastern Leicestershire, though the exhaustion of certain areas has necessitated the opening of new workings, and in one case, at Holwell, the increasing depth of the overburden above the ironstone has made it necessary to resort to mining.[63] In 1938

[59] *Gen. Rep. Mines and Quarries, 1900*, pp. 152–3. This figure only includes those employed in quarries over 20 ft. deep. There were some shallower clay and ironstone workings, for which there are no official returns of employees.

[60] *18th Annual Rep. Sec. for Mines, and 31st Annual Rep. Chief Inspector of Mines* (H.M.S.O.), 140.

[61] The information contained in the preceding seven paragraphs has been supplied by Sir Robert Martin, who has also contributed very largely to this article in other ways.

[62] F. J. North, *Limestones* (1930), 399; Watts, *Geol. of Ancient Rocks of Charnwood Forest*, 79. And personal inf. from Sir Robert Martin.

[63] Hewlett, *Quarries*, 16, 17, 22, 26, 28.

the output of ironstone from the quarries in Leicestershire reached 878,000 tons.[64] Similarly, by 1938 the amounts of clay and limestone quarried in the county exceeded the figures for 1900, although at the end of the First World War there had been a sharp fall in the quantity of clay obtained.[65] On the other hand, there has been during the same period a very marked increase in the output of sand and gravel from Leicestershire workings. In 1900 a total of only 17,000 tons of these two materials was obtained, and in 1919 the amount produced was only 11,000 tons.[66] By 1926 the figure had risen sharply to 88,000 tons,[67] and in 1938 output reached 138,000 tons.[68]

BELL-FOUNDING

In early times the itinerant bell-founder played no small part in equipping churches with bells. Wandering from place to place and building his furnace in some convenient spot, he would cast bells when and where required, sometimes in the churchyard, or even in the church itself. In Leicestershire an example of such methods is known, for a furnace or mould for the casting of church bells has been discovered in Scalford churchyard, together with a mass of bell-metal in a state of fusion. Similarly in 1610 the Leicester bell-founder William Newcombe, with Henry Oldfield of Nottingham, cast the celebrated bell 'Great Tom' in the Minster yard at Lincoln.[1]

The bells of one of the churches in Leicester are mentioned as early as 1306.[2] The earliest known bell-founder at Leicester is Roger le Belleyetere, who is first mentioned in 1307 and who occurs until 1318.[3] Roger was followed by Stephen le Bellyeter, who was a member of the Merchant Guild at Leicester in 1328–9, and who appears in deeds until 1348.[4] John Hose, whose cottage near All Saints' church, Leicester, is mentioned in 1352, was another 14th-century bell-founder. He was admitted to the Merchant Guild at Leicester in 1366–7.[5] To one of these three founders H. B. Walters attributes a group of bells which bear no founder's name.[6] John of Stafford, who was admitted to the Merchant Guild at Leicester in 1338–9, is the earliest Leicestershire bell-founder whose work can be definitely identified. A number of bells bearing his name still exists, inside and outside Leicestershire. Stafford was three times mayor of Leicester.[7] Another 14th-century bell-founder was Thomas of Melton, who is first mentioned in 1368–9 at Leicester, and who occurs until 1392.[8] Three bell-founders occur at Leicester in the 15th century, Thomas Hose, who is mentioned in 1406–7,[9] William Noble, mentioned 1417–27,[10] and Thomas Innocent, mentioned 1458–95.[11] Innocent is known to have cast a bell for the church of St. Mary de Castro at Leicester in 1491.[12] William Millers or Mellors, who was described as a bell-founder when admitted to the Leicester Merchant Guild in 1499–1500,[13] was probably connected with the famous Nottingham bell-founders of the same name. He was a chamberlain of the borough of Leicester in 1504–8, and probably died soon afterwards.[14] No bells made by him exist, so far as is known.

During the 16th century the Newcombe family became prominent as bell-founders at Leicester. The first of the family known to have been connected with the industry was Thomas Newcombe, admitted to the Merchant Guild in 1507–8,[15] whose tomb-stone in All Saints' church, Leicester, shows he was a bell-founder.[16] Thomas Newcombe's son, Robert,[17] was also a bell-founder. Robert married the daughter of another bell-founder, Thomas Bett,[18] and even-

[64] *18th Annual Rep. Sec. for Mines, and 31st Annual Rep. Chief Inspector of Mines* (H.M.S.O.), 140.

[65] *Gen. Rep. Mines and Quarries, 1900*, pp. 152–3; ibid. *1919* [Cmd. 925] p. 195, H.C. (1920), l; *18th Annual Rep. Sec. for Mines, and 31st Annual Rep. Chief Inspector of Mines* (H.M.S.O.), 140.

[66] *Gen. Rep. Mines and Quarries, 1900*, pp. 152–3; ibid. *1919*, p. 195; the production in 1900 was higher than in the years immediately preceding and following: ibid. *1899*, pp 136–7; ibid. *1901*, [Cd. 1307] pp. 140–1, H.C. (1902), cxvi (2).

[67] *Rep. Inspector of Mines, 1926: No. 4, N. Midland Div.* (H.M.S.O.), 37.

[68] *18th Annual Rep. Sec. for Mines, and 31st Annual Rep. Chief Inspector of Mines* (H.M.S.O.), 140.

[1] T. North, *Ch. Bells of Leics.* 55.

[2] J. Thompson, *Hist. of Leic.* i, 108.

[3] *Leic. Boro. Rec. 1103–1327*, 256, 311; *Reg. Freemen of Leic. 1196–1770*, ed. H. Hartopp, 27. Roger was not a native of Leic.: *Leic. Boro. Rec. 1103–1327*, 355.

[4] *Leic. Boro. Rec. 1327–1509*, 4, 391–2; *Reg. Freemen of Leic. 1196–1770*, 33.

[5] *Reg. Freemen of Leic. 1196–1770*, 45; *Leic. Boro. Rec. 1327–1509*, 396.

[6] H. B. Walters, *Ch. Bells of Warws.* 13.

[7] *Reg. Freemen of Leic. 1196–1770*, 37; H. Hartopp, *R. of Mayors of Leic.* 20–22; North, *Ch. Bells of Leics.* 37–39.

[8] *Leic. Boro. Rec. 1327–1509*, 143, 409.

[9] Hist. MSS. Com. *Hastings*, i, 63. A Thomas Hose is mentioned in 1392, and may be the same person: *Leic. Boro. Rec. 1327–1509*, 408.

[10] *Leic. Boro. Rec. 1327–1509*, 415, 417.

[11] Ibid. 266, 347.

[12] 'Accts. of the Ch. Wardens of St. Mary, Leic.' *T.L.A.S.* vii, 155.

[13] *Reg. Freemen of Leic. 1196–1770*, 59.

[14] *Leic. Boro. Rec. 1327–1509*, 365. His will is dated Nov. 1508: L.R.O. Probate Rec. Wills, 1508.

[15] *Reg. Freemen of Leic. 1196–1770*, 61.

[16] He died in 1520: Nichols, *Leics.* i, 552. He described himself in his will as *fusor campanarius*: North, *Ch. Bells of Leics.* 41–42.

[17] North, op. cit. 42.

[18] Hartopp, *R. of Mayors of Leic.* 63.

tually inherited Bett's foundry near All Saints' church.[19] Robert Newcombe was a prominent citizen of Leicester, and after holding several civic offices became mayor in 1550.[20] His descendants continued for many years to carry on the business of bell-founding, and many bells cast by members of the Newcombe family still exist.[21] Several members of the Newcombe family were tanners as well as bell-founders,[22] and it may be noted that about 1600 members of the Norris family were also practising the two trades of tanning and bell-founding.[23] The Watts family also became well known as bell-founders in Leicester during the 16th century. The first member of the family known to have been connected with the industry is Francis Watts, who in 1564–5 bought the bell-wheels from the Leicester church of St. Peter, which was then being demolished.[24] Francis was closely connected with the Newcombe family in business, and his daughter Helen married one of the Newcombes.[25] Hugh Watts, son of Francis,[26] was also a bell-founder; nearly 200 bells made by him still exist in Leicestershire.[27] Hugh Watts became mayor of Leicester in 1633[28] and died in 1643.[29] He bequeathed his tools and implements to his son,[30] but after the middle of the 17th century there apparently ceased to be bell-founders at Leicester for some time, for in 1655–6 the crier's bell was sent to Nottingham for casting, instead of being dealt with at Leicester.[31] Thomas Clay, of Leicester, was the maker of two bells, dated 1711, still existing in the county,[32] but very little is known about Clay's operations. Towards the end of the 18th century a foundry was opened at Leicester by Edward Arnold, who first cast bells at Leicester in 1784. Many bells cast by Arnold still exist in the county.[33]

Before coming to Leicester, Edward Arnold had worked at St. Neots (Hunts.), where he continued to maintain a foundry for some time after moving to Leicester. Towards the end of the 18th century the business at St. Neots passed into the hands of Robert Taylor, who had been apprenticed there. The concern was carried on by Robert Taylor and by his sons, first at St. Neots, and later at Oxford and elsewhere. In 1840 a member of the firm, John Taylor, came with his son to Loughborough to recast the bells, and decided to set up a foundry in the town.[34] The firm thus established rapidly became well known,[35] and supplied bells to many parts of the world. Among the bells cast at Loughborough may be mentioned 'Great Paul' of St. Paul's cathedral. This bell, weighing $16\frac{3}{4}$ tons, was too large to be carried by rail, and had to be transported from Loughborough to London on a specially constructed vehicle.[36] The firm of John Taylor & Co. built a new foundry at Loughborough in 1859, and enlarged it in 1875.[37] The firm still continues[38] to be one of the principal bell-founding concerns in the country.

APPENDIX I

LEICESTER BELL-FOUNDERS[39]

1.	Robert le Belleyetre	1307–18.[40]
2.	Stephen le Bellyeter	1328–48.[41]
3.	John Hose	1352–66.[42]
4.	John of Stafford	2nd half of 14th cent.[43]
5.	Thomas of Melton	1368–92.[44]
6.	William Noble	1417–27.[45]
7.	Thomas Innocent	1458–69.[46]
8.	William Millers	1497–1506.[47]
9.	Thomas Newcombe I	1507–20.[48]
10.	Thomas Bett	d. 1538.[49]
11.	Robert Newcombe I	(Son of no. 9) d. 1557.[50]
12.	Matthew Norris	1571/2–1575/6.[51]

[19] Hartopp, *R. of Mayors of Leic.* 57–58; North, *Ch. Bells of Leics.* 45–46.

[20] Hartopp, *R. of Mayors of Leic.* 62–63; *Leic. Boro. Rec. 1509–1603*, 458–9, 463, 467.

[21] *Reg. Freemen of Leic. 1196–1770*, 78, 85, 97; North, *Ch. Bells of Leics.* 48–51, 53–58, *Ch. Bells of Lincs.* 89–90.

[22] *Reg. Freemen of Leic. 1196–1770*, 78, 85, 97.

[23] Ibid. 81, 93, 101.

[24] North, *Ch. Bells of Leics.* 59.

[25] Ibid. 60–61.

[26] *Reg. Freemen of Leic. 1196–1770*, 106.

[27] North, *Ch. Bells of Leics.* 62.

[28] Hartopp, *R. of Mayors of Leic.* 92.

[29] Ibid. [30] North, *Ch. Bells of Leics.* 70.

[31] *Leic. Boro. Rec. 1603–1688*, 440. In 1656–7 Hugh Watts's equipment was in the hands of his widow: ibid. 437. [32] North, *Ch. Bells of Leics.* 72, 171.

[33] Ibid. 73, 267. [34] Ibid. 73–74.

[35] White, *Dir. Leics.* (1846), 273.

[36] See *Chambers's Encyclopaedia* (1950) under 'bell'.

[37] White, *Dir. Leics.* (1877), 498. [38] In 1952.

[39] Unless otherwise stated, dates in this list are those at which the name of bell-founder concerned is mentioned. [40] *Leic. Boro. Rec. 1103–1327*, 256, 311.

[41] Ibid. *1327–1509*, 4, 392.

[42] Ibid. 396; *Reg. Freemen of Leic. 1196–1770*, 45.

[43] *Reg. Freemen of Leic. 1196–1770*, 37; H. Hartopp, *R. of Mayors of Leic.* 20–22.

[44] *Leic. Boro. Rec. 1327–1509*, 143, 409.

[45] Ibid. 415, 417.

[46] Ibid. 266, 347; *T.L.A.S.* vii, 155.

[47] *Reg. Freemen of Leic. 1196–1770*, 59; *Leic. Boro. Rec. 1327–1509*, 352, 375, 466; North, *Ch. Bells of Leics.* 40.

[48] Nichols, *Leics.* i, 552; *Reg. Freemen of Leic. 1196–1770*, 61.

[49] Hartopp, *R. of Mayors of Leic.* 57; Wm. Millers, Thos. Newcombe I, and Thos. Bett were all in turn husbands of the same woman: North, *Ch. Bells of Leics.* 41–44.

[50] Hartopp, *R. of Mayors of Leic.* 63; *Leic. Boro. Rec. 1509–1603*, 96. He was a son-in-law of no. 10; Hartopp, op. cit. 63.

[51] *Leic. Boro. Rec. 1509–1603*, 137; *Reg. Freemen of Leic. 1196–1770*, 81.

13. Thomas Newcombe II d. 1580.[52]
14. Robert Newcombe II d. *c.* 1598.[53]
15. Edward Newcombe I d. 1629.[54]
16. Robert Newcombe IV baptized 1576.[55]
17. Thomas Newcombe III „ 1584.[56]
18. Edward Newcombe II „ 1585.[57]
19. William Newcombe „ 1590.[58]

Nos. 16, 17, 18, 19 were all sons of no. 15. All seem to have worked at Leicester until about 1612.[59]

20. Hew Wat *c.* 1563.[60]
21. Francis Watts I *c.* 1564.[61] d. 1600.[62]
22. Hugh Watts II (Son of no. 21) born *c.* 1582.[63] d. 1643.[64]
23. Hugh Watts III (Son of no. 22) d. 26 Aug. 1656.[65]
24. Francis Watts II (Son of no. 22) apprenticed 1636.[66]
25. George Curtis (Foreman of no. 22) d. 1650.[67]

APPENDIX II
LEICESTERSHIRE BELLS

The 1,319 church bells in Leicestershire are thus dated:

Pre-1500	25
1500–1600	88
1600–1700	304
1700–1800	228
1800–1900	348
1900–52	326
Total	1,319

They may be subdivided and allotted to their various periods and founders thus:

Period	*Name of founder*	*Place of manufacture*	*No. of bells manufactured*
	Ancient undated bells		58
	Ancient blank bells		12
1506–1642	Newcombe & Watts	Leicester	233
1584–1787	Oldfield & Hedderley	Nottingham	131
1714–23	Hedderley & Halton	Nottingham	6
1707–13	A. Rudhall	Gloucester	4
1602–99	T. Norris	Stamford	13
1702–6	A. Rigby	Stamford	3
1706–26	H. Penn	Peterborough	2
1739	W. Brooke	Bromsgrove (Worcs.)	1
1795	T. Osborn	Downham Market (Norf.)	6
1675–84	H. & M. Bagley	Chacomb (Northants.)	7
1656	B. Eldridge	Chertsey (Surr.)	2
1720–71	Eayre	Kettering (Northants.) & St. Neots	84
1773–98	Arnold	St. Neots & Leicester	32
1796–1822	J. Briant	Hertford	26
1701–32	J. Smith	Edgbaston, Birmingham	1
1769–78	Lester, Pack & Chapman	Whitechapel	9
1807–40	T. Mears & Son	Whitechapel	42
1850	C. & G. Mears	Whitechapel	1
1873–1903	Mears & Stainbank	Whitechapel	3
1872–1911	J. Barwell	Birmingham	8
1896–1906	C. Carr Ltd.	Smethwick	3
1919	Alfred Bowell	Ipswich	2
1873–87	J. Warner & Son	London	5
1801–12	R. Taylor	St. Neots	6
1841–1952	J. Taylor & Co.	Loughborough	510
c. 19th and 20th cents.	Modern undated bells		51
1908–52	Gillett & Johnston	Croydon	28
1595–1877	Dated but founders unknown		30
TOTAL .	. . . . . .	. . . . . .	1,319

[52] North, *Ch. Bells of Leics.* 59, and see 47–52. Son of no. 11.
[53] Ibid. 53–54; son of no. 11.
[54] Hartopp, *R. of Mayors of Leic.* 86.
[55] North, *Ch. Bells of Leics.* 54.
[56] Ibid. 58.
[57] Ibid.
[58] Ibid.
[59] Ibid. 57–58.
[60] Ibid. 59.
[61] Ibid.
[62] Ibid. 60.
[63] Ibid. 61.
[64] *Leic. Boro. Rec. 1603–88,* 17, 145, 602, 604; Hartopp, *R. of Mayors of Leic.* 92.
[65] Nichols, *Leics.* i, 316; North, *Ch. Bells of Leics.* 70.
[66] *Reg. Freemen of Leic. 1196–1770,* 122; North, *Ch. Bells of Leics.* 66.
[67] North, *Ch. Bells of Leics.* 71.

BANKING

Until the middle of the 18th century Leicestershire was without banks, although some banking business is said to have been carried on under Elizabeth I by Robert Herrick, an ironmonger who became mayor of Leicester in 1584–5.[1] The first person in the county who is definitely known to have acted as a banker is William Bentley, who became a freeman of Leicester in 1721,[2] and at first carried on business as a mercer, a trade which his family had pursued at Leicester for many years previously.[3] The development of Bentley's banking activities cannot be traced in detail. As late as 1768 he was still described as a mercer,[4] but before his death in 1784 he had built up a prosperous banking firm, and a contemporary described him as 'an eminent banker'.[5] After William Bentley's death the bank was carried on by his son and by his nephew, Thomas Buxton, who was the active partner.[6] The firm continued to conduct a prosperous banking business for the rest of the 18th century. A branch was opened at Melton Mowbray.[7] Besides the firm founded by William Bentley, only one other bank of any importance existed at Leicester before 1800. This was the business established by John Mansfield, a mercer like Bentley,[8] and Peter Oliver, a wine merchant.[9] In 1776 Mansfield and Oliver were appointed by the Treasury to receive and exchange deficient gold coin, so that by that date they were presumably in business as bankers.[10] In 1783 Oliver left the firm, and was replaced by Joseph Boultbee.[11] After John Mansfield's death in 1798 several changes took place in the names of the partners, but Mansfield's second son, John, remained the leading member of the firm until he died in 1839.[12] Besides the two firms connected with the families of Bentley and Mansfield, Leicester had for a time in the 18th century a third bank, the partners in which were William Hodges, Edmund Carr, and Edward Hodges. This firm was in existence by 1776, when it was appointed to receive and exchange deficient gold coin, but in 1783 it was forced to close.[13]

Towards the end of the 18th century small private banks were established at a number of lesser places in Leicestershire. The earliest bank to be established in the county outside Leicester itself seems to have been that founded by Joseph Wilkes at Ashby de la Zouch in 1780.[14] Ten years later another bank, known as Farnell's & Co., was set up at Ashby, but it ceased to exist in 1804.[15] The bank of Thorp & Middleton was established at Loughborough in 1790.[16] By 1793 the banks of Inkersole & Goddard, at Market Harborough, and Wainer & Co., at Melton Mowbray, were also in existence.[17] The Melton bank was a short-lived concern, for it ceased operation in 1808,[18] and after that date Melton Mowbray had no bank of its own, though several Leicester banks established branches there. Even at so small a place as Lutterworth the bank of Goodacre & Buzzard was established in 1803.[19] At Hinckley, the Hinckley Commercial Bank[20] was established in 1808,[21] while another Hinckley bank, that of Sansome & Blakesley, was in existence at about the same time.[22] These firms must all have been very small, and it is remarkable that such small places as Lutterworth and Melton were ever able to support banks of their own.

Although by the beginning of the 19th century there were eight banks in Leicestershire, including two in Leicester itself, five new banks came into existence at Leicester between 1800 and the passage of the Country Bankers Act in 1826. In 1800 a new bank was established at Leicester by four partners, Thomas and John Pares, Thomas Paget, and James Heygate.[23] As early as 1763 the father of Thomas Pares, together with Joseph Bunney, was proposing to accept deposits and pay interest on them,[24] but no bank was actually established.[25] The bank founded in 1800 was named the Leicestershire Bank, but seems to have been generally known as 'Pares & Heygate'. By 1824 the firm had branches at Melton Mowbray, Loughborough, and Lutterworth,[26] and by 1831 a branch had also been established at Hinckley.[27] The branches, however, were only open on market days,[28] and

[1] C. J. Billson, *Leic. Memoirs*, 2; H. Hartopp, *R. of the Mayors of Leic.* 76.

[2] *Reg. Freemen of Leic. 1196–1770*, ed. H. Hartopp, 231.

[3] Ibid. 143, 231; Billson, *Leic. Memoirs*, 3, 4.

[4] *Reg. Freemen of Leic. 1196–1770*, 359.

[5] J. Throsby, *Leics. Views*, ii, 262; Billson, *Leic. Memoirs*, 4.

[6] Throsby, op. cit. ii, 267; Billson, op. cit. 5.

[7] Billson, op. cit. 5.

[8] Hartopp, *R. of the Mayors of Leic.* 175.

[9] Billson, *Leic. Memoirs*, 6.

[10] Ibid. 6.

[11] Ibid. 7.

[12] Ibid. 8, 9, 10.

[13] Ibid. 13–15.

[14] W. F. Crick and J. E. Wadsworth, *Hundred Years of Joint Stock Banking*, 244, 447; *Bankers' Almanac and Year Bk.* (1950–1), 1698.

[15] Ibid. 1651.

[16] Ibid. 1693.

[17] Ibid. 1662, 1695.

[18] Ibid. 1695.

[19] Ibid. 1654; A. H. Dyson, *Lutterworth* (ed. H. Goodacre), 136.

[20] Otherwise known as Goodacre & Co.; later, after 1818, as Jervis & Co.

[21] *Bankers' Almanac* (1950–1), 1654, 1660.

[22] H. J. Francis, *Hist. Hinckley*, 137.

[23] Billson, *Leic. Memoirs*, 22; *Rep. Sel. Cttee. on Joint Stock Banks*, H.C. 591, App. p. 201 (1836), ix.

[24] J. Thompson, *Hist. of Leic.* ii, 120.

[25] Billson, *Leic. Memoirs*, 16, 17.

[26] Ibid. 25.

[27] Pigot & Co. *Comm. Dir. Derby, Leic., Nott., and Rut.* (1831), 70.

[28] *Rep. Sel. Cttee. on Joint Stock Banks*, H.C. 591, App. p. 201 (1836), ix; Pigot & Co. *Nat. and Commercial Dir. of Leics. and Rut.* (1835), 142, 158.

this long continued to be the case.[29] The firm of Pares & Heygate seems to have enjoyed considerable prosperity.[30] Another bank, with the name of 'Pares & Heygate', and the same partners as the Leicester firm, existed until 1830 in Aldermanbury, and acted as the London agency of the Leicester bank.[31] Some time before 1805 another bank was established at Leicester by A. W. Bellairs, his son George, and C. C. E. Welby. A. W. Bellairs had been a banker since at least 1783, and was a partner in banks at Stamford and Derby. His Leicester bank was, however, a separate concern, and not a mere branch of Bellairs' older bank at Stamford.[32] The establishment of two new banks at Leicester was balanced by the failure, in 1803, of Bentley & Buxton, the oldest bank in the town. A commission in bankruptcy was issued against the partners, but eventually all creditors were paid in full.[33] The financial crisis of 1814 caused the failure of Bellairs, Son, & Welby. The partners were declared bankrupt, but again all the creditors appear to have been paid in full.[34] In 1818 John Clarke and Joseph Philips established another bank at Leicester.[35] In 1821 Thomas Miller, who had earlier been a partner in Mansfield's bank, set up a bank of his own at Leicester, in partnership with his son,[36] and in 1825 Thomas Paget, formerly a partner in the bank of Pares & Heygate, similarly set up a banking business of his own, in partnership with his relatives, Joseph and William Paget, and with Samuel Kirby, who had been chief cashier at Pares & Heygate.[37]

The early Leicestershire bankers derived their capital from a number of different sources. Some were originally retail tradesmen; William Bentley and John Mansfield were both mercers at Leicester,[38] while Inkersole and Goddard, the Harborough bankers, both came from families of local ironmongers, and still carried on an ironmongery business until the failure of the bank.[39] In such cases it seems reasonable to assume that the capital of the early banks originated in the profits of retail trade. Joseph Wilkes, the founder of the Ashby bank, was an industrialist of some importance, for he began his career as a partner in a spinning firm at Tamworth, and later he erected two cotton mills at Measham.[40] Wilkes was a partner in banks at London and Measham, besides his bank at Ashby, and he was an active experimenter with new methods in agriculture.[41] In other cases the capital employed in the early banks was derived from land. Thomas and John Pares inherited considerable property from their father, a successful lawyer who was much concerned with the management of local estates, and both enlarged their lands by purchases.[42] John Pares was also a hosiery manufacturer, like his partner, James Heygate.[43] Thomas Paget came from a family well known for their farming activities,[44] and Thomas Babbington was the lord of the manor and soke of Rothley, and a member of an ancient land-owning family.[45] Finally, it may be noted that several men rose to be partners in Leicestershire banking firms who had begun their careers as bank clerks. Examples are John Dalby, who became a partner in Mansfield's bank after having been a clerk there,[46] Thomas Smith, who similarly rose from being an employee in the bank of Clark & Philips to be a partner,[47] and Samuel Kirby, who became a partner in Paget's bank after having been a cashier for Pares & Heygate.[48]

The early years of the 19th century saw, besides the establishment of a number of private banks, the beginnings of savings banks in Leicestershire. The first savings bank in the county was opened at Loughborough in 1816.[49] Other savings banks were established at Leicester in 1817, Ashby de la Zouch in 1818, Lutterworth in 1822, and at Hinckley in 1823.[50] Five Leicestershire towns had thus acquired savings banks at a time when the spread of such institutions throughout the country had only just begun, but after 1823 no further savings banks were established in the county until 1838, when Market Harborough and Melton Mowbray each acquired one.[51] In 1841 the amount deposited in Leicestershire savings banks was very small in proportion to the county's population, compared with the

29 E. S. Drake & Co. *Comm. Dir. Leics.* (1861), 238, 312.

30 Billson, *Leic. Memoirs*, 25.

31 Ibid. 22.

32 Ibid. 27; *Bankers' Almanac* (1950–1), 1632.

33 Billson, *Leic. Memoirs*, 28, 29; *Bankers' Almanac* (1950–1), 1632.

34 Billson, op. cit. 28, 29; *Bankers' Almanac* (1950–1), 1632.

35 Billson, op. cit. 29.

36 Ibid. 31; *Bankers' Almanac* (1950–1), 1674. Crick and Wadsworth in *Hundred Years*, 449, give 1814 as the date when Miller's bank was established. But see the other references cited.

37 Billson, op. cit. 32; *Bankers' Almanac* (1950–1), 1679.

38 *Reg. Freemen of Leic. 1196–1770*, 231, 263, 271, 278; Hartopp, *R. of the Mayors of Leic.* 175.

39 *Market Harborough Par. Rec. 1531–1837*, ed. J. E. Stocks, 231, 233, 236; Crick and Wadsworth, *Hundred Years*, 256.

40 A. Young, *Tours in England and Wales* (edn. London School of Econ. 1932), 272, 274, 275, 278, 286.

41 Ibid. 274–6, 282–8; Crick and Wadsworth, *Hundred Years*, 244.

42 Billson, *Leic. Memoirs*, 18–20; Nichols, *Leics.* i, 299; iv, 213, 218, 323, 517, 611, 815.

43 Billson, op. cit. 21; Nichols, *Leics.* i, 349.

44 Billson, op. cit. 22; A. Young, *Tours in England and Wales* (edn. London School of Econ. 1932), 297.

45 Nichols, *Leics.* iii, 596.

46 Billson, op. cit. 11.

47 Ibid. 29.

48 Ibid. 32.

49 H. O. Horne, *Hist. Savings Banks*, 379.

50 Ibid. 81, 380, 382; White, *Dir. Leics.* (1846), 408.

51 Horne, *Hist. of Savings Banks*, 383.

corresponding figures either for the adjacent counties, or for the whole of England and Wales,[52] and in 1842 the total number of depositors at the seven savings banks in Leicestershire was only 5,237.[53] The most important banks were at Leicester, where there were a little over 2,000 depositors in 1842, and Loughborough, where there were just over 1,000.[54] In 1842 all the Leicestershire savings banks were paying interest at the rate of £3. 6*s*. 8*d*. per cent.,[55] but by 1846 the Loughborough bank had reduced the interest rate to £2. 17*s*. 1*d*.[56] For the rest of the 19th century the savings banks made little progress in the county. No further savings banks were opened. The existing bank at Harborough was closed in 1867, that at Hinckley in 1870, and that at Ashby de la Zouch in 1900.[57]

The financial crisis of 1825, which forced many country bankers to suspend payment,[58] was survived by all the Leicestershire banks, although the credit of both Clarke & Philips, and Miller & Son, was shaken.[59] The crisis was followed in 1826 by the enactment of certain legislation concerning banks, including the Country Bankers Act[60] which allowed the establishment of banks with more than six partners at any place over 65 miles from London. Although the whole of Leicestershire lay outside the prohibited area around the capital, it was not until 1829 that advantage was taken of the Act of 1826 by the foundation of the Leicestershire Banking Co., the first joint-stock bank in the county. The formation of the new firm was greeted with much opposition, and in particular it was insinuated that the founders of the concern would derive improper advantages from knowing the financial position of their clients.[61] The Leicestershire Banking Co. had a nominal capital of half a million pounds, divided into 5,000 shares, but up to July 1837 only 3,296 shares had been issued. A call of £5 per share was made in 1829, and further calls of the same amount were made in 1830 and 1835. In 1837 the paid-up capital was only £49,440.[62] This was not a very large sum by the standards of the time, and in 1832 the firm was described as having been established on a limited scale.[63] Despite the opposition with which the foundation of the bank had been greeted, the new joint-stock firm made rapid progress. Deposits, which stood at just under £15,000 in June 1830,[64] had risen to over £27,000 six months later,[65] and by the end of 1835 the total of deposits was more than £118,000.[66] A separate reserve fund had been set up by June 1831, when it stood at the modest figure of £142.[67] Branches were soon opened at Hinckley, Harborough, and Melton,[68] and in 1836 the bank's note circulation was over £36,000,[69] as against only £13,000 at the beginning of 1831.[70] By the middle of 1830 the bank had already made a number of advances to farmers, hosiery and shoe manufacturers, and retailers.[71] The connexion with several different types of economic activity, thus begun, was to be a feature of the bank's history. The new joint-stock bank absorbed in 1835 the small private bank of Miller & Son at Leicester.[72] In the same year the firm of Fisher, Simmonds, & Mammatt, which had succeeded the bank established by Wilkes, at Ashby, was forced to suspend payment on the death of one of the partners. The Leicestershire Banking Co. promptly opened a branch at Ashby, and soon afterwards bought out the local bank.[73] The absorption of these two private banks did much to strengthen the Leicestershire Banking Co., and in 1838 its position was further improved by the purchase of the branch and business of the Northamptonshire Banking Co. at Market Harborough.[74] In 1831, despite the fact that the bank's business was still quite small,[75] a dividend of 4 per cent. was paid.[76] In succeeding years the figure was repeatedly increased, and in 1837 the bank was able to pay a dividend of 8 per cent.[77] The policy pursued by the directors of declining to issue the shares that had not been already taken up to anyone who was unable to bring a substantial amount of business to the bank,[78] may have been

[52] B.M. Add. MSS. No. 40583, f. 115*b*.

[53] *Return of Interest Paid to Depositors in Savings Banks*, H.C. 281, pp. 2–9 (1843), xxx.

[54] Ibid. p. 8.

[55] Ibid. pp. 2–9.

[56] White, *Dir. Leics.* (1846), 285.

[57] Horne, *Hist. of Savings Banks*, 380, 382.

[58] J. W. Gilbart, *Hist. and Principles of Banking* (1866), 53.

[59] Billson, *Leic. Memoirs*, 29, 31.

[60] 7 Geo. IV, c. 46.

[61] Crick and Wadsworth, *Hundred Years*, 249–50.

[62] *Rep. Sel. Cttee. on Joint Stock Banks*, H.C. 531, App. p. 72 (1837), xiv.

[63] *Rep. Cttee. of Secrecy on Bank of Engl. Charter*, H.C. 722, Question 4258 (1831–2), vi.

[64] First Balance Sheet of the Leics. Banking Co. (June 1830), now in the custody of the Midland Bank. The original records of the Leics. Banking Co. have been examined by courtesy of the Midland Bank, and of its Information Officer, Mr. J. E. Wadsworth.

[65] Second Balance Sheet of the Leics. Banking Co. (Dec. 1830) now in custody of the Midland Bank.

[66] Based on a table drawn up by Mr. J. E. Wadsworth, from the balance sheets of the Leics. Banking Co.

[67] Ibid.

[68] *Rep. Sel. Cttee. on Joint Stock Banks* (1837), App. pp. 72–73.

[69] *Second Rep. Sel. Cttee. on Banks of Issue*, H.C. 410, Minutes of Evidence, p. 92 (1841), v.

[70] Crick and Wadsworth, *Hundred Years*, 251.

[71] Leics. Banking Co., Minutes of Directors' Proc. 1829–37, ff. 1–23. (In custody of the Midland Bank.)

[72] Billson, *Leic. Memoirs*, 31, 33; Crick and Wadsworth, *Hundred Years*, 251, 449.

[73] Ibid. 251–2, 447.

[74] Ibid. 251–2.

[75] Ibid. 251.

[76] *Rep. Sel. Cttee. on Joint Stock Banks* (1837), App. pp. 72–73.

[77] Ibid.

[78] Leics. Banking Co., Minutes of Directors' Proc. 1829–37, *passim*. (Kept as above.)

one cause of the high level of prosperity which the new joint-stock enterprise attained in a few years, despite the initial opposition.

In March 1836 a second joint-stock bank was formed at Leicester by the conversion of the private firm of Pares & Heygate into a joint-stock company, under the name of Pares' Leicestershire Banking Co. As first constituted, the new company had a nominal capital of £100,000, divided into 8,000 shares, but only 6,540 shares were issued, and at first only £16,350 of the capital was called up. A further £16,350 was called up in February 1837. As a company the bank continued to enjoy its old prosperity, and in 1837 a dividend of 10 per cent. was paid. The bank's note circulation in the last quarter of 1836 was £30,138.[79]

Some information is available about the business methods of the two Leicestershire joint-stock banks. Both of them, like many other country banks,[80] paid interest on deposits. Before 1830 Pares & Heygate, then still a private bank, paid an interest of 3 per cent. on deposits. In 1830 the rate was reduced to 2 per cent., but it was raised to 2½ in 1832.[81] The Leicestershire Banking Co., when first established, paid 3 per cent. interest on deposit accounts, after 2 months. Current accounts were allowed 3 per cent. when in credit, and charged 5 per cent. interest when overdrawn. In March 1830 it was found necessary to reduce the interest on credit balances to 2½ per cent.[82] Pares & Heygate's Bank did not issue post bills, but the Leicestershire Banking Co. issued post bills payable not exceeding 21 days' date, or 7 days' sight.[83] The early records of the Leicestershire Banking Co. show that the conduct of business was closely supervised by the directors, who personally authorized all advances and overdrafts.[84] In 1829 the bank granted its general manager a salary of £300 a year, and at the same date the pay of one of the clerks was £50 a year.[85]

After 1836 no joint-stock bank of permanent importance was established in Leicestershire. In 1836 an attempt to transform the Market Harborough bank of Goddard & Co.[86] into a joint-stock company was unsuccessful.[87] In 1840 the Leicestershire and Warwickshire Joint Stock Banking Co. was established, with twelve partners, and with branches at Hinckley, Ashby de la Zouch, and Market Bosworth, but although the firm still existed in 1842 it seems to have ceased operations at the end of 1840.[88] In 1835 the private bank of Hemming & Needham was established at Hinckley, with Needham as the active partner.[89] In 1840 the partners decided to convert their firm into a joint-stock bank, and for this purpose requested their London agents, the London & Westminster Bank, to advance them £6,000. The London bank refused, and requested that the Hinckley bank's overdraft of £3,000 should be settled at once. As a result of this, Hemming & Needham ended their connexion with the London & Westminster Bank. Shortly afterwards Hemming & Needham failed, so that the caution of the London & Westminster Bank's committee was evidently justified.[90] Several banks from outside Leicestershire were, however, successful in establishing branches within the county. The first London bank to set up a branch at Leicester was the National Provincial Bank.[91] In accordance with the original plan on which this bank was formed, it was at first proposed to establish at Leicester a local bank, with local shareholders and directors, connected with the main National Provincial Bank, and amongst the solicitors appointed to receive applications for shares was a Leicester firm.[92] But at a general meeting of the National Provincial Bank's shareholders in May 1835 the plan of forming local banks was given up,[93] and in April 1836 a branch of the usual type was opened at Leicester.[94] The Stamford, Spalding & Boston Banking Co., established in 1831, set up branches at Melton and Harborough, and the Nottingham & Nottinghamshire Banking Co., soon after its establishment in 1834, opened a branch at Loughborough.[95] Finally, in 1844, the Bank of England set up a branch at Leicester.[96]

While joint-stock banks from outside Leicestershire were thus establishing branches within the county, the number of purely local banks there was being reduced. In 1831 the small Lutterworth

79 *Rep. Sel. Cttee. on Joint Stock Banks* (1837), App. pp. 65, 166.

80 J. H. Clapham, *Econ. Hist. of Modern Brit.* (1939), i, 266.

81 *Rep. Sel. Cttee. Joint Stock Banks* (1837), App. p. 65.

82 Crick and Wadsworth, *Hundred Years*, 250. Leics. Banking Co., Minutes of Directors' Proc. 1829–37, ff. 6*b*, 7*a*, 20*b*. (Kept as above.)

83 *Rep. Sel. Cttee. on Joint Stock Banks* (1837), App. pp. 72–73.

84 Leics. Banking Co., Minutes of Directors' Proc. 1829–37, *passim*. (Kept as above.)

85 Ibid. ff. 3*b*, 6*b*.

86 Earlier known as Inkersole & Goddard.

87 Billson, *Leic. Memoirs*, 34.

88 *Return of All Joint Stock Banks, 1840–2*, H.C. 85, p. 5 (1843), lii; *Return of Joint Stock Banks established under 7 Geo. IV, c. 46*, H.C. 423, p. 2 (1844), xxxii; *Bankers' Almanac* (1950–1), 1666.

89 B.M. Add. MSS. No. 40583, f. 165; *Bankers' Almanac* (1950–1), 1659.

90 T. E. Gregory, *Westminster Bank through a Century*, i, 242; *Bankers' Almanac* (1950–1), 1659. The pass-book of a client of Hemming and Needham is now in the custody of the Midland Bank.

91 The National Provincial Bank had its head office at London, and may be considered a metropolitan bank, though it did not conduct banking business in London before 1866: H. Withers, *Nat. Provincial Bank, 1833–1933*, 38, 45, 66.

92 Withers, op. cit. 38, 40, 48.

93 Ibid. 49.

94 Billson, *Leic. Memoirs*, 34.

95 *Ret. of Joint Stock Banks* (1844), pp. 3, 4; Gregory, *Westminster Bank*, ii, 132.

96 Crick and Wadsworth, *Hundred Years*, 256.

bank of Goodacre & Buzzard was absorbed by Clarke & Philips' Bank, and in 1839 the same firm took over the business of Mansfield's Bank, the oldest bank then existing at Leicester.[97] At the same time Clarke & Philips admitted two new partners, Richard Mitchell and Thomas Smith.[98] The sharp financial crisis of 1843, however, caused the failure of Clarke, Mitchell, Philips, and Smith, with debts of £540,000.[99] An attempt to form a joint-stock company to carry on the bank's business was a failure.[1] As the firm had branches at Lutterworth, Melton, Oakham, and Uppingham, and possessed a large connexion both with the local agricultural interest and with the Leicester manufacturers, its collapse caused considerable distress.[2] At the same time the Market Harborough bank of Inkersole, Goddard, & Goddard failed, with debts of £190,000.[3]

After 1843 the only surviving Leicestershire banks were the two joint-stock firms at Leicester, Pares' Bank and the Leicestershire Banking Co., and two private banks, Paget's at Leicester and Middleton & Craddock[4] at Loughborough. The Loughborough bank was a very small concern, its maximum note issue as authorized under the Act of 1844 being only £7,000, while about 1850 its capital was only some £5,000.[5] Paget's, which had branches at Loughborough and Melton,[6] was a larger concern, and in 1844 its permissible note circulation was fixed at £32,222.[7] The maximum note issue of £86,060 authorized for the Leicestershire Banking Co. at the same time gives a rather exaggerated idea of the firm's relative importance, for it happened that during the period, early in 1844, which was used as a basis for calculating the note issues to be authorized, the bank's circulation was unusually large.[8] It is, however, evident that the joint-stock Leicestershire Banking Co. was much larger than either of the two surviving private banks in the county. In 1845 the capital of the joint-stock firm was raised to £90,400 by transferring £22,600 from the reserve fund to pay up £5 on each share, while at the same date deposits at the bank totalled nearly half a million pounds.[9] Pares' Bank was allotted a maximum note issue of £59,300 in 1844,[10] so that the two joint-stock banks in Leicestershire had a total authorized note circulation of £145,360, against only £39,322 for the two private banks.

The local banks in the county survived the crises of 1856 and 1866 without disaster, and the three Leicester banks continued to enjoy a prosperous independence until the closing years of the 19th century. The Loughborough firm, on the other hand, came to an unexpected end in 1878. Middleton's bank, though its capital was very small in comparison with the extent of its business, was not by any means in a desperate position, and its collapse was due to the precipitate action of the inexperienced junior partner, who, left in charge through the death of the senior partner, suddenly suspended payment without any adequate cause. It was subsequently found that the bank's assets exceeded its liabilities, and there seems to have been no reason why the bank could not have remained solvent. An attempt to form a limited company to take over the business failed, and the premises and goodwill were sold to the Leicestershire Banking Co. for £6,000.[11] The oldest existing Leicestershire bank thus came to an unsatisfactory end. The sole remaining private bank in the county, Paget's, survived as an independent concern until 1895. The two Leicestershire joint-stock banks had little to fear from the competition of similar institutions from outside the county. The National Provincial Bank continued to maintain a branch at Leicester,[12] but the Leicester branch of the Bank of England was closed in 1872.[13] By 1882 the Stamford, Spalding & Boston Banking Co., which had long been operating in the east of the county, had established a branch at Leicester, and the short-lived Cheque Bank[14] also had a branch there.[15] By 1889 a branch of the Birmingham & Midland Bank had been added to the number of banks at Leicester.[16] The establishment of branches of outside banks at Leicester reflected the growing industrial importance of the town, and the amount of business remaining to the local banks was as much as they could handle. The history of the two Leicester joint-stock banks during the second half of the 19th century resembles in general that of similar institutions elsewhere. Both banks found that their note issues fell steadily, so that the imposition of a maximum figure for their circulation under the Act of 1844 cannot have had any serious effect upon their business. The Leicestershire Banking Co., with an authorized maximum issue of over £86,000,

97 *Bankers' Almanac* (1950–1), 1671. The Leics. Banking Co. had considered purchasing Mansfield's in 1837. (Memorandum now in the custody of the Midland Bank.)

98 Billson, *Leic. Memoirs*, 29.

99 White, *Dir. Leics.* (1846), 69.

1 Billson, *Leic. Memoirs*, 30.

2 Ibid. 30; Pigot, *Dir. Leics. and Rut.* (1841), 38, 48.

3 White, *Dir. Leics.* (1846), 479.

4 Formerly Thorp & Middleton.

5 Crick and Wadsworth, *Hundred Years*, 258, 266.

6 White, *Dir. Leics.* (1846), 249, 285.

7 *Return of Every Bank trading in the United Kingdom*, H.C. 296, p. 6 (1880, Sess. 2), lxvii.

8 Crick and Wadsworth, *Hundred Years*, 258.

9 Ibid.

10 *Ret. of Banks trading in U.K.* (1880), p. 3.

11 Crick and Wadsworth, *Hundred Years*, 266–8.

12 Billson, *Leic. Memoirs*, 34.

13 Crick and Wadsworth, *Hundred Years*, 256.

14 Established 1873; liquidated 1901: *Bankers' Almanac* (1950–1), 1641.

15 C. N. Wright, *Comm. and Gen. Dir. Leic. and Six Miles Around* (1882), 202.

16 Crick and Wadsworth, *Hundred Years*, 95; Wright, *Dir. Leic. and Twelve Miles Around* (1889), 233.

had in 1850 a note circulation of £65,000, which had fallen by 1890 to £49,000.[17] Similarly Pares' Bank, with a permitted issue of nearly £60,000, had in 1880 an average note circulation of just over £43,000.[18] The business of the two banks, however, increased in volume, and in the later years of the 19th century, when agriculture in Britain was much depressed, it was no doubt to the advantage of the Leicester banks that they were operating in an area where industry was expanding. In the middle years of the century the Leicestershire Banking Co. made use of its profits to increase the amount of its paid-up capital by a total of 10 guineas a share, thus raising its capital to £150,000 by 1858.[19] Two calls, each of £5 per share, further increased the bank's capital to £225,000,[20] and by 1879 the paid-up capital was £300,000.[21] The growing extent of the bank's activities was also shown in the rapid increase of deposits, which more than doubled between 1850 and 1880.[22] During the same period the Leicestershire Banking Co. began to set up branches outside its own county. Branches were set up at Kettering (Northants.) in 1856, at Swadlincote (Derbys.) in 1865, and at Nuneaton (Warws.) in 1874.[23] Later, between 1880 and 1890 branches were opened at Grantham, Peterborough, Northampton, Wellingborough, and Burton on Trent.[24] In 1878 and 1879 the general trade depression caused some losses to the Leicestershire Banking Co., and in 1880 the firm, like so many other banks about the same time, became a limited-liability company, with a paid-up capital of £400,000.[25] Pares' Bank had a very similar history during the same period, and its operations were on a very similar scale. By 1880 its paid-up capital had reached £330,000, and deposits totalled £1,130,000.[26] In 1880 Pares' Bank also became a limited-liability company, and at the same time the nominal capital was increased from £500,000 to £1,000,000. It was provided that none of the additional capital should be called up, unless the company should be wound up,[27] so that in effect a reserve liability was created, in the way provided for by Act[28] in 1879. After their conversion into limited-liability companies the two Leicestershire joint-stock banks continued to expand. Pares' Bank experienced some bad years during the period 1885–90, but by 1901 the total of deposits was over £2,000,000, while the reserve fund had been increased from £110,000 in 1863, to £185,000 in 1901.[29] Similarly, by 1890 the Leicestershire Banking Co.'s deposits totalled nearly £2,000,000.[30] In 1895 the firm's business was considerably extended by the purchase of a private bank, Hardy & Co. of Grantham.[31]

Paget's Bank outlived all the other private banks of the county, surviving as a separate institution almost until the end of the 19th century. The maximum note circulation of £32,222 authorized for the bank in 1844 does not ever seem to have been reached, and in 1880 the average note issue was under £20,000.[32] There were branches, open on market days only, at Loughborough and Melton.[33] The concern enjoyed continuous prosperity, and one of the partners, Thomas Tertius Paget, was a millionaire when he died in 1892.[34] Although, however, Paget's Bank was able to play a considerable part in the industrial development of Leicester,[35] the resources of a private bank were inadequate to meet the town's growing needs. This fact, together perhaps with other, more general, circumstances adverse to private banks,[36] brought the firm's existence to a close. In 1894 one of the partners, Thomas Guy Paget, met with a fatal accident, and shortly afterwards one of the two remaining partners expressed a desire to retire from business.[37] Early in 1895 it was announced that Lloyds Bank had arranged to acquire the concern. In order to minimize the effects of the change it was provided that E. F. Cooper, who had for long been employed by Paget's, should become the local manager of Lloyds, while the two surviving partners of Paget's were to attend the bank daily for several months,[38] an arrangement which shows the personal nature of the relations between the private bankers and their clients. The absorption of the last of Leicester's private banks was followed a few years later by the amalgamation of the town's two joint-stock banks with larger firms. The Leicestershire Banking Co. had for some time been finding that its resources were inadequate to provide the necessary facilities for the continuing expansion of local industry. The acquisition of Hardy & Co. in 1895 had increased the paid-up capital of the bank to £440,000 with deposits totalling £2,617,000, but the relief brought by this increase in the bank's funds was only temporary.[39] For some years before 1900 the directors of the Leicestershire Banking Co. had been aware of the need for

[17] Crick and Wadsworth, *Hundred Years*, 275.
[18] *Ret. of Banks trading in U.K.* (1880), p. 3.
[19] Crick and Wadsworth, *Hundred Years*, 260.
[20] Ibid. 261.
[21] *Return rel. Joint Stock Banking*, H.C. 246 (1878–9), lxv.
[22] Crick and Wadsworth, *Hundred Years*, 275.
[23] Ibid. 260–1, 266.
[24] Ibid. 268.
[25] Ibid. 268.
[26] Gregory, *Westminster Bank*, ii, 78–79.
[27] Ibid. ii, 77.
[28] 42 and 43 Vict., c. 76.
[29] Gregory, *Westminster Bank*, ii, 80.
[30] Crick and Wadsworth, *Hundred Years*, 275.
[31] Ibid. 270–1.
[32] *Return of Banks trading in U.K.* (1880), p. 6.
[33] E. S. Drake & Co., *Comm. Dir. Leics.* (1861), 238, 312.
[34] *Leic. Daily Post*, 14 Jan. 1895.
[35] Ibid.
[36] J. H. Clapham, *Econ. Hist. Mod. Brit.* (1939), iii, 280–2.
[37] *Leic. Daily Post*, 14 Jan. 1895.
[38] Circular issued by Paget's Bank, 14 Jan. 1895.
[39] Crick and Wadsworth, *Hundred Years*, 271.

amalgamation with a larger concern, and they had increased the bank's dividends from 10 per cent. to 12½ per cent. to obtain good terms for their firm.[40] At an Extraordinary General Meeting of the shareholders held at Leicester in July 1900 the amalgamation of the Leicestershire Banking Co. with the London, City, & Midland Bank was agreed to without opposition. The chairman of the Leicestershire bank, Simpson Gee, had for some years been a shareholder in the London, City, & Midland Bank, and this personal link had facilitated the amalgamation. Gee now became a director of the London bank.[41] James Lawford, who had been for 30 years the manager of the Leicestershire Banking Co., became the local manager of the London, City, & Midland Bank.[42] At the time of the amalgamation the Leicestershire Banking Co. had 27 branches, and a paid-up capital of £440,000. Deposits amounted to £3,285,000, while bills and loans totalled £3,243,627.[43]

The absorption of Pares' Bank into a larger institution took place 2 years later. The small size of Pares' Bank had, as the chairman of the directors told the shareholders, led to difficulties that were not experienced by larger concerns, and for some years past other banks had been making offers of amalgamation.[44] The firm which eventually absorbed the local business was Parr's Bank, which after beginning in south Lancashire had become a large national firm. The amalgamation was accepted by the shareholders of Pares' Bank in May 1902,[45] and duly carried through.[46]

The three surviving Leicestershire banks were thus merged in larger concerns, and after 1902 the history of Leicestershire banking is bound up with institutions centred on London. The period between the beginning of the absorption of the local banks and the outbreak of the First World War saw a great extension of branch banking in Leicestershire. In 1895 there were in all 38 banking offices in the county,[47] while by 1916 the number had risen to 71.[48] The important series of banking amalgamations which took place in 1918 caused little real change in Leicestershire, though the London County & Westminster Bank amalgamated with Parr's.[49] Of the 5 great banks which emerged from the unions of 1918, the Westminster, the Midland, and Lloyds had directly or indirectly absorbed the 3 Leicester banks. The Stamford, Spalding & Boston Banking Co. became part of Barclay's Bank in 1911, and the United Counties Bank did the same in 1916, so that by the latter year Barclay's had 14 branches in Leicestershire.[50] The National Provincial Bank, though it had long had a branch at Leicester, failed to obtain any considerable number of branches in Leicestershire through amalgamation,[51] but by 1936 it had 15 branches in the county.[52] All the 5 great English banks participated in the further expansion of branch banking which took place between the two wars. By 1936 the number of branches and agencies of banks in Leicestershire had risen to 109, with the 35 branches of the Midland Bank forming the most numerous group.[53]

[40] *Leic. Daily Post*, 28 July 1900.

[41] Ibid.; Crick and Wadsworth, *Hundred Years*, 271–2.

[42] W. Scarff, *Leics. and Rut. at the opening of the 20th Century*, 176.

[43] Crick and Wadsworth, *Hundred Years*, 271–2; *Leic. Daily Post*, 28 July 1900.

[44] Crick and Wadsworth, *Hundred Years*, 272.

[45] *Leic. Daily Post*, 28 May 1902.

[46] Ibid.; *Bankers' Almanac* (1950–1), 1679; Gregory, *Westminster Bank*, ii, 81.

[47] *Kelly's Dir. Leics. and Rut.* (1895), 441.

[48] Ibid. (1916), 726–7.

[49] Gregory, *Westminster Bank*, ii, 14.

[50] *Bankers' Almanac* (1950–1), 1690, 1695; *Kelly's Dir. Leics. and Rut.* (1916), 726–7.

[51] In 1920 the Nat. Provincial absorbed the Northants. Union Bank, which had branches at Leicester, Anstey, and Harborough. *Bankers' Almanac* (1950–1), 1677; *Kelly's Dir. of Leics. and Rut.* (1916), 726–7.

[52] *Kelly's Dir. Leics. and Rut.* (1936), 1061.

[53] Ibid. 1060–1.

ROADS

I. Prehistoric Tracks. II. Roman Roads. III. Anglo-Saxon Influences. IV. Medieval Roads. V. Turnpike Roads.

I. PREHISTORIC TRACKS

IN Leicestershire two considerable masses of high land rose above the thick forest which covered the clay soils of most of the county in prehistoric times, and it is on these highlands that traces must be sought of the most ancient trackways. These two tracts were the waste of heath and rock to the west of the Soar known as Charnwood Forest, and the marlstone escarpment which runs in a general north-easterly direction from the neighbourhood of Husbands Bosworth in the southern tip of the county to that of Belvoir in the extreme north-east and which forms 'High Leicestershire'.

The open country of 'High Leicestershire' extends through Northamptonshire and beyond to the south-west (where on Salisbury plain many ridges converge); in the north, the Lincoln ridge—the highway to the Humber estuary—can be closely approached.

The great trackway that extends from the populous downlands of Wiltshire to the Yorkshire wolds is commonly known as 'The Jurassic Way' because the ridges and swells of the uplands along which it runs are due to formations of that age. This great track enters Leicestershire by the narrow gap between the east-flowing Welland and the west-flowing Avon. From this point high ground runs north-east towards the Kibworth saddle, which separates the Soar (or Trent) basin from that of the Welland.

From Kibworth north-eastward to Tilton—a distance of 8 miles—there still is a line of lanes which is almost coincident with that of the watershed as marked out by the Trent and Welland Catchment Boards. It runs by Carlton Grange, Three Gates, Rolleston New Inn, and Rolleston Grange. By use over many centuries the surface had become so broken that the line of the road was unmistakable, and served as a convenient boundary for fully 6 miles when the limits of the parishes were settled before and after the Norman Conquest.

Beyond Tilton the watershed no longer trends north-east; and to follow it a considerable diversion to the right was necessary through Halstead, Withcote, and Langham to reach the Sewstern Lane or 'Drift Road' which took a clear ridge line from Stamford (the stone ford on the Welland) for no less than 22 miles to Harston. At some point along the 'Drift Road' a crossing must have been made to the parallel ridge beyond the Witham which ran north to Lincoln and then northward to the Humber and so over to the Yorkshire Wolds. Where the crossing of the Witham was made is uncertain, but the 'Drift Road' marks the eastern limit of Leicestershire, so that the further course of the 'great Jurassic trail' need not here be traced.

In later times a quicker way may have been found from Tilton to the Lincoln Edge by cutting across the valley of the Eye, instead of round its head, though it is doubtful whether such a course could have been adopted before the tools of the Iron Age were available. The approach to the Eye could be made from Tilton (700 ft. above sea level) along high ground to Somerby (589 ft.). From there one track may have crossed the Eye at Stapleford (the ford marked by a stapol or large post); or, still by high ground, to the great Iron Age fort at Burrough Camp, from which 5 miles of deserted bridle road leads straight to a crossing of the stream by Melton on its gravel knoll. Incidentally, this deserted road affords a clear impression of what a road might be before the introduction by Macadam of good metalling over a restricted width.

Once across the Eye (or Wreak as the lower course of the stream is called) the ancient roads would seek the Leicestershire Wolds ridge and turn along it eastwards to join the Sewstern Lane ridge at Three Queens, above Croxton Kerrial. Pushing northwards up a ridge past Great Framlands and then by 3 miles of deserted lane (a parish boundary) to Brock Hill, the track along the Wolds would be reached.

The once all-important trail lost its importance as a long-distance road when the valleys were cleared and inhabited. Apart from its intrinsic interest, the trail is notable because it carried the traffic between Yorkshire and the south-west, and this traffic has often been a principal element in the history of Leicestershire roads.

Sewstern Lane is the central part of a prehistoric ridge road which must have been used from very early times as a cross-country link between the navigable Welland and the Trent, and the whole course of it is more clearly marked than most of the prehistoric trails. The track crosses the Welland at the stone ford (Stamford) on the edge of the Fens and may be followed along the Roman Ermine Street for several miles. A little beyond Stretton, however, the ancient road bears left, and passing just west of Thistleton, climbs to its summit of 500 ft. near Buckminster. Thence it goes on over Saltby Heath, past King Lud's entrenchments, past Three Queens (where the Wold ridgeway links up), and the Iron Age village of Harston, where the ridge ends above the Vale of Belvoir.

How far Sewstern Lane was used in the Bronze Age is uncertain, for the Jurassic Trail, as has been explained, may have only come in near the northern end of the 20-mile march from Stamford. It served until the railway age for a considerable amount of traffic from Nottingham and the Vale of Belvoir to Stamford and beyond. For 9 miles from Harston to nearby Thistleton it served as a boundary when the districts of Lincoln and Leicester were formed as shires, and the road took the name of 'shire street' as early as 1258.[1]

The road along the Leicestershire Wolds from the Three Queens on the Sewstern Lane (near Croxton Kerrial) to Barrow upon Soar has all the characteristics of a prehistoric ridge road. From Barrow upon Soar the course is clearly marked by the line of the present road past Pawdy Farm and Six Hills. Immediately above Old Dalby wood the edge of the escarpment of the wolds is reached (511 ft.) and the road continues along this for several miles to Holwell Mouth, being followed by parish boundaries for a great part of the way. From Holwell Mouth the course of these boundaries strongly suggests that the ancient track took a semicircular sweep along the highest ground by Brock Hill rather than face the crossing of a shallow valley which breaks the direct line. This direct

[1] Nichols, *Leics.* ii, App. 81.

Sewstern Lane (The Drift)

The Gartree Road near Shangton

crossing is made by the present road, and may well have been constructed by the Romans when they learnt to use the Wolds road as a handy line between the Fosse Way and the Ermine Street. A little farther on the main ridge of the wolds (followed by the parish boundaries) swings away to the right (that is east rather than north-east) south of Goadby Marwood to skirt the deep valley of the Devon, and again there is evidence that the Roman engineers took a direct line north of Goadby to rejoin the earlier way at Ling Hill. The whole length of this Wolds road from Barrow to the Sewstern Lane is 18 miles, and approximately 14 miles were subsequently used as parish boundaries. It is a vexed question whether this well-marked east–west route to Barrow upon Soar was used in the Bronze Age as a means of approach to the western side of the river and the high ground of Charnwood Forest. Beacon Hill camp is generally regarded as a Bronze Age site,[2] and from Barrow the road through the villages of Quorndon and of Woodhouse is a direct line to it.

The wolds form the northern rim of the valley of the Wreak. South of that stream there are four roughly parallel ridges coming westwards from the high gravel plateau round Tilton, and each of these is followed by a road which has parish boundaries over part of its length as indications of ancient origin. Of these 'four fingers' the most northerly leaves Lowesby on the left and reaches the flood plain of the Wreak at Queniborough. A second ridge runs by Cold Newton to Syston, the old name for the road upon it being Ridgemere. At both Queniborough and Syston evidences of Bronze Age occupation have been found.[3] The third and fourth of the tracks running west from the Tilton plateau are more important, as they appear to have carried east–west traffic (coming to Tilton by the Withcote–Halstead road) not merely to settlements overlooking the Soar valley, but to crossings of that river near to Leicester, and on to the high ground of Charnwood. The Withcote–Halstead approach to Tilton, as has already been argued, may have been part of the great Jurassic Trail, but has connexion with the important stone ford of the Welland at Stamford by a ridge-way running above the River Gwash on the one hand and the Chater on the other.

The two tracks from Tilton to the Soar crossings lead along the high plateau to its abrupt end at Billesdon Coplow, from which one (our third trail) takes a line north of the brook (which reaches the Soar as the Willow Brook) whilst the other (or fourth trail) takes the ridge to the south. The third or northern track is indicated by bridle roads and paths as far as Old Ingarsby but becomes clearer on reaching Scraptoft, where the existing lane is continued by Gipsy Lane to Checketts Road,[4] and the crossing of the Soar at or near Belgrave Old Bridge.[5] The track is continued up the steep Mowmacre Hill, where the hollow way near the summit is the result of long-continued traffic and not of the labours of the road engineer. From Billesdon Coplow the fourth track may be traced by footpath to Palace Hill on the present main Uppingham road and thence by that road or near to it until the Crown Hill ridge afforded a view of the low gravel plateau on which the town of Leicester was subsequently built. One branch of the track appears to have approached the present centre of the town by what is known as Green Lane Road, whilst the other crossed the (Willow)

[2] V.C.H. *Leics.* i, 169–70.

[3] Ibid. 171; W. G. Hoskins, *Heritage of Leics.* 23.

[4] In Leicester.

[5] John Leland rode from the Charnwood area to Uppingham through Belgrave, Ingarsby, and Withcote. *Leland Itin.* ed. Toulmin Smith, i, 20–22.

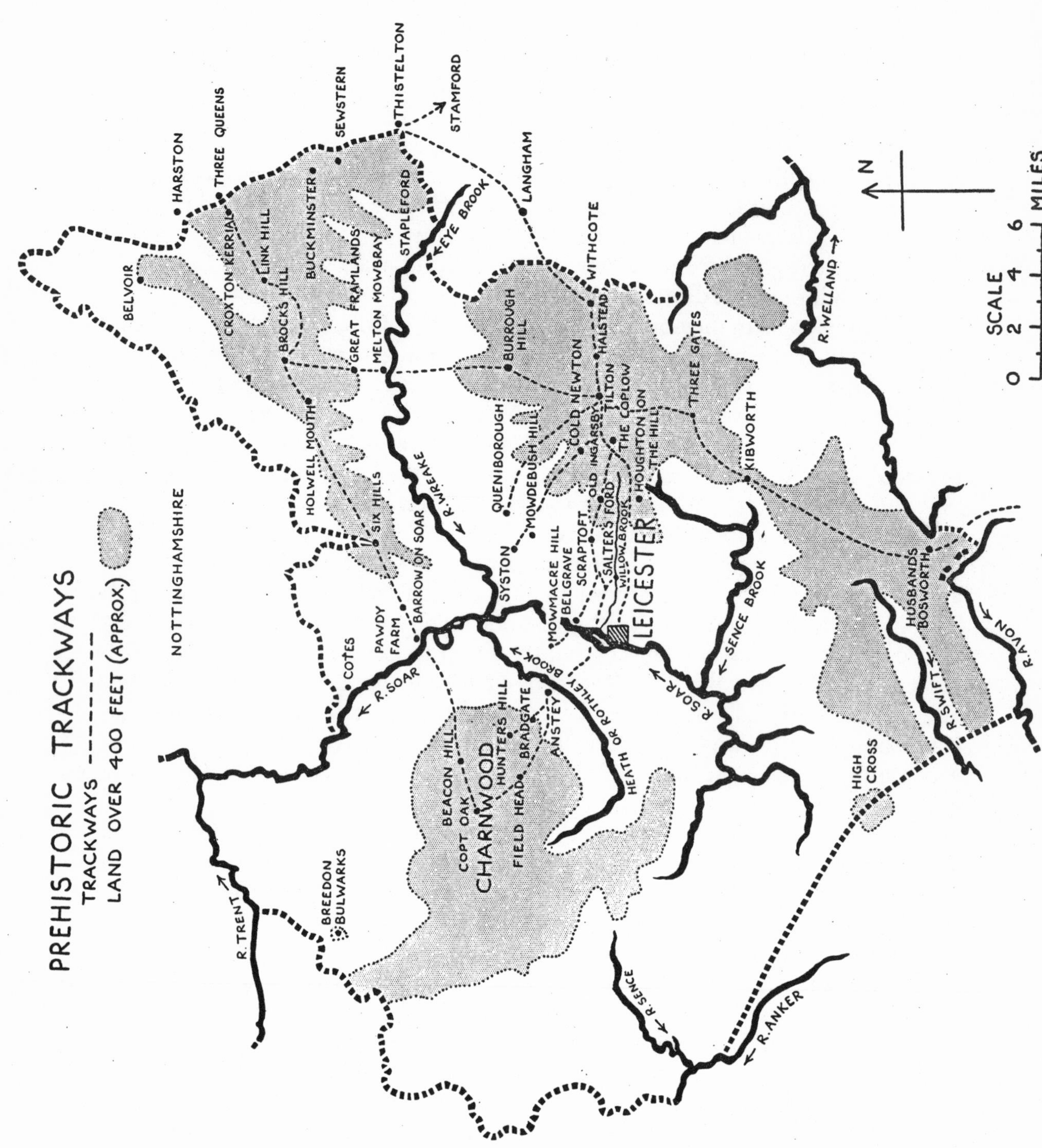
PREHISTORIC TRACKWAYS
TRACKWAYS
LAND OVER 400 FEET (APPROX.)
NOTTINGHAMSHIRE
BELVOIR
HARSTON
THREE QUEENS
CROXTON KERRIAL
LINK HILL
BROCKS HILL
BUCKMINSTER
SEWSTERN
THISTELTON
STAMFORD
GREAT FRAMLANDS
MELTON MOWBRAY
STAPLEFORD
LANGHAM
EYE BROOK
WITHCOTE
BURROUGH HILL
HALSTEAD
COLD NEWTON
TILTON
THE COPLOW
THREE GATES
HOLWELL MOUTH
SIX HILLS
BARROW ON SOAR
R. WREAKE
QUENIBOROUGH
MOWDEBUSH HILL
OLD INGARSBY
SALTER'S FORD
HOUGHTON ON THE HILL
KIBWORTH
SYSTON
MOWMACRE HILL
BELGRAVE
SCRAPTOFT
WILLOW BROOK
LEICESTER
SENCE BROOK
COTES
PAWDY FARM
R. SOAR
HEATH OR ROTHLEY BROOK
ANSTEY
BRADGATE
HUNTERS HILL
BEACON HILL
COPT OAK
CHARNWOOD
FIELD HEAD
BREEDON BULWARKS
R. TRENT
HIGH CROSS
HUSBANDS BOSWORTH
R. SWIFT
R. AVON
R. WELLAND
R. SENCE
R. ANKER
N
SCALE
0 2 4 6 MILES

Brook at Salter's Ford, and in common again with traffic from the Scraptoft direction approached the Soar in the neighbourhood of the abbey. There has been too much work on the meadows and on the bed of the river itself to fix the position of a ford with any precision, but on the opposite or western bank the track is continued by another road of undoubtedly ancient origin. This is the track or Gorse leading to Anstey. It escaped the attention of the turnpike engineers, and within living memory was a very wide but irregular track of uneven surface between overgrown hedges. It was thus a good example of a road developed by use throughout long periods of time instead of by any conscious piece of engineering.

The road was carried across the marshy valley of the Heath (now Rothley) Brook by a long causeway at both approaches to the actual ford (or, later, narrow bridge) and there are many traces of the road as it advances a little to the east of the present road on its way to Newtown Linford and Fieldhead. The name Anstey itself signified 'a pathway' and therefore indicates the existence of the track before any settlement was made. At Fieldhead we are not far from Copt Oak, where the road, which has already been discussed, comes in from the direction of Barrow by Beacon Hill.

Near Fieldhead stood the 'Auterstone' which is mentioned in an early but undated deed describing the manor boundaries of Shepshed and Whitwick, and the road beyond (towards Copt Oak) is described in the same deed as 'Westermansway'.[6]

The passage of the Heath Brook having been secured at Anstey, several ancient tracks are known to have penetrated the uplands of Charnwood from that point, in addition to that already described. Of these the most important appears to have been that which climbed by Bradgate (the broad way) up the hill of Old John and passed on to Shepshed—perhaps 'la Heyway' mentioned in a fine of 1240.[7] On this track, beyond the boundary wall of Bradgate Park, is Hunt's Hill, apparently a meeting-point of great antiquity, for wide unmetalled tracks come up to it from Hall Gates and from Newtown (Smithy), the latter affording an excellent example of a hollow way formed by the repeated scramble of hooved animals up the steep slope.

Between Charnwood and the Trent lies a belt of country about 7 miles wide. The existence of Bronze Age tracks here is very doubtful, but when the lower ground came to be partially cleared there must have been trails radiating from the important Bulwarks on Breedon Hill and from the heights of Charnwood. In 1316 the track coming from Copt Oak and Beacon Hill by Nanpantan to Loughborough was in part[8] 'the highway' and very much earlier than that it may have served as a passage towards the great east–west line of the Wolds, which could easily be reached if the Soar were crossed at Cotes (opposite Loughborough).

Before closing this admittedly tentative account of the prehistoric trackways of Charnwood it should be said that maps drawn before the inclosure of the forest, and particularly the maps of Prior[9] and of King,[10] indicate that the modern metalled roads were nearly all preceded by ancient tracks following the same general line. The surveyors preparing the inclosure map itself, however,

[6] Farnham, *Leics. Notes*, vi, 347.
[7] Ibid. vi, 349.
[8] Ibid. vi, 360.
[9] J. Prior, *Map of Leics.* (1779).
[10] W. King, *Map of the Tract of Country surrounding Belvoir Castle* (1806).

concentrated on the delineation of the numerous existing inclosures rather than on the marking of the trackways—which, after all, were merely part of the open common land now to be portioned out and inclosed.[11]

With one or two exceptions, notably the Sewstern Lane and the Wolds road, the ancient tracks were largely abandoned when the people of the county were able to make use of iron tools and begin to clear and drain the lower lands in the valleys of the brooks and rivers. In place of hill-top camps the centres of population sprang up at important navigational points or crossings of the rivers and the roads were either constructed by the Romans to connect such focal points or developed out of the traffic between the thousands of settlements. If there was sufficient traffic along any one stretch of land that stretch became a road—which was essentially a right of passage established by custom—and might be, in fact usually was, a track of earth of indeterminate width, beaten and disturbed by the passage of horses and cattle, and occasionally by that of some lumbering wagon. Such surfaces were indeed those of the prehistoric ridgeways, but the continuance of the lowland agricultural settlement has resulted in much metalling and levelling during the last 200 years, whilst the whole stretch of the ridgeways lost its function 2,000 years ago, and can only be traced, even in part, by the closest examination of the evidence afforded by modern detailed maps, supported by observation and by finds in the field.

II. THE ROADS DURING THE ROMAN OCCUPATION

Before the arrival of the Romans in England the county of Leicester had already taken something like its modern shape by the settlement of the Belgic tribe known as the Coritani round a centre known as Ratae.[12] This was the site at which such a 'capital' might be expected to develop; for it afforded fairly easy access to and from a much larger area of cultivable land than any other. The Soar itself, often marshy, was a considerable barrier to movement and so were the valleys of the Wreak and the Sence. Between the two streams was the place to look for a main passage from east to west.

The gravel height ending in a bluff immediately above the stream (at St. Nicholas) afforded a safe starting-point whilst the sandstone escarpment of the Dane Hills on the opposite bank was at least approachable when the waters were low. In winter the floods would at least abate more quickly than on the higher and lower stretches of the valley, as they still do. The ancient approaches to Leicester already described were of course available and it is possible that some of the lines straightened and metalled by the Romans were tracks which had already been cleared, for the Romans in their advance must have found some sort of access to the tribal capital other than the ancient east–west tracks from the Tilton plateau to Charnwood.

The roads constructed by the Romans have been described and mapped in an earlier volume of this history, but it is necessary to recall them briefly, as they were, and indeed to a considerable extent are, used by all subsequent dwellers in the county, from the Saxons to ourselves.

The Watling Street which connected London and the ports of entry from Europe with the legionary fortress of Chester, was laid out, possibly along a

[11] L.R.O. Charnwood Forest Inclosure Award. The Act for inclosing Charnwood Forest was passed in 1808: T. R. Potter, *Charnwood Forest*, 30.

[12] Now Leicester.

course already in use by the British tribes, not as a ridge road, but as one that passed over the headwaters of the rivers only, leaving the main rivers of the Bristol Channel to one side and those falling into the Humber on the other.

The nearest point on the Watling Street to Leicester, High Cross, is distant fully 12 miles and the through traffic from London to Chester can have had little influence on the life and trade of the people of Ratae. When the English midlands were divided into counties, the high banking of the metalled road made a first-class boundary mark, and a boundary of Leicestershire it became.

The Fosse (a name recorded first in a charter of 956),[13] however, ran through the town of Ratae, crossed the Soar under its gravel knoll, and was essentially the great road of the district or canton. Along it came soldiers and merchants from the great camps in Yorkshire and the colony of Lincoln, *en route* for Bath and the rich villas and estates of the Cotswolds and south-west. A widely accepted theory[14] is that the Fosse Way was constructed as a military work to strengthen a temporary frontier in the early stages of the Roman conquest, that is, in or about A.D. 46, but it has been pointed out[15] that at Lincoln, Margidunum, Leicester, Cirencester, and Bath, the line of the Fosse strongly suggests that it was constructed after the towns had been developed, and that the road may well have been made in the time of Hadrian. 'Like much of the contemporary town planning, it may have been too grandiose for the economy of the country to support and have fallen rapidly out of repair, thus accounting for its omission from the Antonine Itineraries.' The absence of anything but a small posting-station at High Cross, where the Fosse Way intercepted the great Watling Street, also fits in with the view that the Fosse Way was built at a relatively late date.[15a]

As a through road the Wolds road from Six Hills to the eastern limit of the county at the Sewstern Lane was perhaps third in importance of those used by the Romans in Leicestershire, for it afforded a link between the Fosse Way and the Ermine Street. The nature of the ground surface high above the deep soft clays would make unnecessary any elaborate construction such as marked the Watling Street and Fosse; and as has already been said, the principal changes in the prehistoric track appear to have been two or three short cuts where the old track wound round the heads of valleys. The antiquity of this road is proved by the fact that parish boundaries follow it for 14 miles. Its long, straight stretches suggest Roman influence.

A spurious importance was long attached to the Roman road which runs from Leicester through Medbourne, owing to the lectures in the 1750's of Dr. Charles Mason, Woodwardian professor. Mason claimed it as part of a great Roman road from Colchester to Chester, for which he invented the name of *Via Devana*. No satisfactory evidence has ever been adduced for the existence of the road north-west of Leicester, but it appears reasonable to think that it was carried across the Welland and on to Godmanchester, although the course of the road between Medbourne and the county boundary on the Welland is one of the stretches which cannot be traced. In considering the history of the road in medieval times and later the road will be dealt with as Road Six. There can be no doubt that this road, although not paved so thoroughly as the main Roman

13 *Cart. Sax.* ed. Birch, iii, 92, cited E. Ekwall, *Oxf. Dict. of Eng. Place Names*, 176.

14 R. G. Collingwood, 'The Fosse', *Jnl. of Roman Studies*, xvi, 252–6.

15 K. M. Kenyon, *Excavations at Jewry Wall Site, Leic.* (Soc. Antiq. Res. Cttee. *Reports*, 15), 38–40.

15a For the later history of the Fosse see below, p. 70.

roads, was regularly formed of good material brought from a distance, and was very different from the straggling beaten earth tracks with brushwood and loose stone in some of the worst of the holes which served all but the Romans throughout the centuries until modern times.

Thomas Leman, the student of Roman antiquities, left a record, quoted by Nichols,[16] that 'in Slawston lordship . . . it [the road] is formed of a strong whitish gravel, such as is not found within a mile of the places where I discovered the ancient stratum'. In the open field of Cranoe 'it is very discoverable in the same manner, across several furlongs of arable land, where its course is marked by a coarse gravelly soil intermixed with brown pebbles'.

The fifth and last of the Leicestershire roads now considered to have been constructed or reconstructed by the Romans is that which runs from the small Roman station of Mancetter towards Leicester, the distance between the two towns being 17 miles. Mancetter stands on the Watling Street where that road crosses the River Anker. When Mancetter was examined in 1927 the conclusion was reached that it had been occupied from about A.D. 100 and for some 20 or 30 years the occupation was continued and vigorous.[17] This is the only clue available to the date of the construction of the road. A straight run of roads (the Fen Lanes) survives for 5 miles from Mancetter, and although destroyed in the park of Kirkby Mallory the same line is continued by the existing road through that village and on through Peckleton and—by bridle road and footpath—for some distance beyond. The course of the Roman road for the last 6 miles into Leicester has been the subject of much speculation but remains uncertain.[18] Some writers have claimed that the road was used by one or both of the armies in their march to the battle of Bosworth; but there is no evidence that the road has been used as a through route by any traffic since the Roman occupation.

The whole length of these five Roman roads as they pass through Leicestershire (including 19 miles of the Watling Street along the border) is 95 miles, which is no great proportion of a total length of over 5,000 miles of Roman roads in Great Britain. The clearing of the tangle of forest cannot have proceeded very far, and it was only the central watershed position of the Leicestershire area that made it of much importance in Roman times. There are no great military works and but one humble town and half a dozen villas.

III. ANGLO-SAXON INFLUENCES

After the departure of the Romans the Watling Street in Leicestershire lost nearly all its importance, and there were considerable deviations from the straight line of the old Roman Fosse. Hence it is true to say that the destruction of the Roman work was more or less continuous—the stone and gravel being taken for farm and village use—though much survived until the late 18th century, when demand for road material became rapidly keener and the means of transporting it on a large scale much more effective.

So far as there was any through traffic in Anglo-Saxon times it continued to centre mainly on Leicester; but the number of people living there was a very small proportion of the population of the county, and the great mass of the countrymen had their own places of assembly for the purposes of war, of counsel and of justice. At an early date, probably in the 10th century, Leicestershire

[16] Nichols, *Leics.* ii, 797.

[17] *Trans. Birmingham Arch. Soc.* liii, 173–95.

[18] Hoskins, *Heritage of Leics.* 25; L. Fox and P. Russell, *Leic. Forest*, 56.

was divided into wapentakes, which were originally four in number. The wapentake of Gartree, occupying the south-east part of the county, is believed to take its name from a site on the Roman road from Leicester to Medbourne. At this place, 9 miles from Leicester, there is a triangle of ways formed by the Roman road itself, by the road from Kibworth to Three Gates, and by a short connecting road. The triangular area or gore, covering about 150 acres, enclosed by these three roads may have been the meeting-place for the wapentake. At this point there was in the 18th century an old thorn tree, known as the Gartree bush.[19]

It is reasonable to suppose that the places where the men of the wapentake met together, and where wapentake courts were held, were for the sake of convenience often placed at points on existing roads. The place now known as Great Framlands, on the track running north from Burrough Hill through Melton Mowbray to Brock Hill, and only 3 miles from the great track along the wolds, may have been the original meeting-place of Framland Wapentake, in north-east Leicestershire. Croft Hill, near the Fosse Way, may have been the meeting-point for the wapentake of Guthlaxton; it was certainly a place of assembly before the Norman Conquest.[20] The meeting-place for Goscote Wapentake was almost certainly on Mowdebush Hill (near Syston), where the wapentake court was held in the 18th century.[21] The hill is near the ancient road, called Ridgemere Lane, along which runs the boundary between the parishes of Queniborough and Barkby.

During the period before the Conquest the town of Leicester must have become a fairly important centre of communications. The Fosse (North and South), the Gartree road, and the old east–west tracks from Tilton and from Anstey could usefully be employed; but the Saxons and the Danes founded many villages which were remote from these routes, particularly in the Soar valley and on the wide lands between the Gartree road and the southern Fosse. It is to be expected that in the absence of special outside circumstances, small groups of men, or individuals, would find their way to the shire town by using first one village lane and then another, the whole string eventually forming a customary route or road. Therefore, it seems reasonable to fix in Saxon times the origin of many straggling roads which have nothing of the character of earlier times.

The early settlements of the Saxons are believed to have been fixed by men arriving from the Welland valley,[22] and it is safe to say that the route through Lutterworth, Gilmorton, the Peatlings, Countesthorpe, Port Hill, Glen Parva, and down the Saffron Lane to Leicester is an early line. Another such line is through Bowden, Gumley (down the hollow way), Fleckney, across the Sence at Wain Bridge, and on through Wigston Magna to the South Gate of Leicester. The road through Kibworth, Glen, Oadby, and on to join the Gartree road on the brow of the hill above Leicester must be the origin of the great through route developed later.[23] More important proved to be the development of the lanes

[19] Nichols, *Leics.* ii, 431, where it is stated that courts were held at this spot until the early 18th cent.

[20] W. G. Hoskins, 'Croft Hill', *T.L.A.S.* xxvi, 85–86.

[21] Nichols, *Leics.* iii, 2, 453. In the 18th cent. the wapentake court used to meet formally at Mowdebush Hill, before adjourning to an inn at Mountsorrel, and this practice certainly shows that the court had been held on the hill at an early period.

[22] *T.L.A.S.* xviii, 119.

[23] P. Russell, *Leics. Road*, 1–15; W. G. Hoskins, 'Origin and Rise of Market Harborough', *T.L.A.S.* xxv, 56–68.

through Loughborough, Quorndon, Mountsorrel, Rothley, Wanlip, Birstall, and along the Soar bank to a ford or wooden bridge by Frog Island to the North Gate[24] of Leicester.

As need arose for through traffic to places outside the county these approaches were frequently modified by choosing a line over more open country; for neither military commanders, nor drovers, nor merchants with their pack-trains would be inclined to favour frequent entanglement in the narrow lanes through the built-up area and the closes of the villagers; and in many cases the villagers would be well content to see the strangers pass clear of their dwellings. Whilst there are actually no 'here-paths' in Leicestershire there can be little doubt that the straightening of the Loughborough road to pass above Rothley and Wanlip can be attributed to the passage of 'armies' between Derby and Leicester. The barrier of the Trent had been overcome by the establishing of Willen ferry, and the route from Derby to Leicester was to become more and more used until it became one of the great roads of England—from Carlisle (and Manchester) to London. Incidentally, the importance of this north–south traffic would account for the rise of Loughborough on the west bank of the Soar and the decline of Cotes, though both stood on the same cross-traffic line. It is notable that Loughborough is laid out on an east–west axis. Apart from Derby and Leicester the Danish confederacy of the Five Boroughs consisted of Nottingham, Lincoln, and Stamford. The men of Nottingham may have approached Cotes through Rempstone—as they did throughout the coaching days—or they may have used the Fosse, as they do now that this road has been reconstructed.

Until the whole country was united under one government the traffic to London would not be of great importance, but before it developed, the line later taken by that traffic had certainly been established by considerable movements between Leicester and Northampton. Northampton was not a Roman town, but when the Saxons (and later the Danes) used the eastern rivers to push up into the heart of the country, its position at the head of the navigable waters of the Nene became one of great importance. A road to Towcester on the Watling Street was soon established and in 917 the Danish armies of Leicester and Northampton combined to make a surprise assault upon a Saxon force stationed at Towcester.[25] The road developed to Leicester, crossed the Avon at Welford (the water passage) but may first have come on through Kilworth and Gilmorton to Saffron Lane. Eventually a much more open route was adopted by Wigston, Arnesby, and Shearsby—all good well-drained ground; and this must have been sufficiently well established to justify the building of a stone bridge over the Sence (Kilby Bridge) in the 13th century.[26]

The development of the high open road from Lutterworth to Leicester, passing clear of all villages except for the fringes of Blaby affords a difficult problem; for the Sence floods very badly where the road crosses it and must have often been impassable. South and west of Lutterworth the road loses its open character and passes through the villages by abrupt and difficult turns. Leland mentions no villages on his ride from Leicester to Lutterworth.[27] No parish boundaries attest the antiquity of this road, and the date of its origin must remain an open question.

[24] Russell, op. cit. 20–32.

[25] *Angl. Sax. Chron.* (Rolls Ser.), i, 194 and ii, 82; F. M. Stenton, *Anglo-Saxon Engl.* (2nd edn.), 323.

[26] *T.L.A.S.* xix, 194.

[27] *Leland Itin.* ed. Toulmin Smith, i, 19.

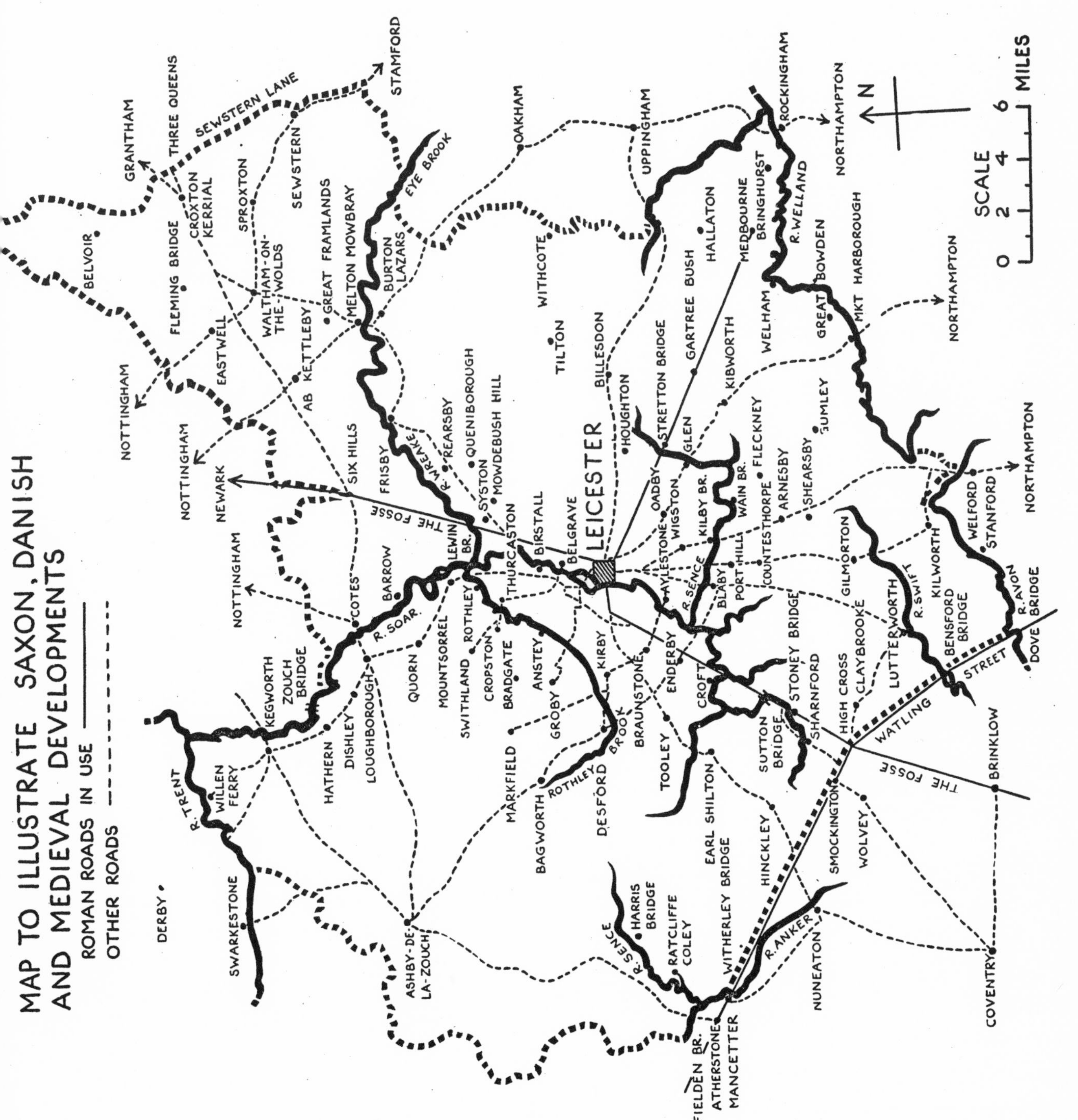
MAP TO ILLUSTRATE SAXON, DANISH
AND MEDIEVAL DEVELOPMENTS
ROMAN ROADS IN USE
OTHER ROADS
SCALE
0 2 4 6 MILES
N
LEICESTER
THE FOSSE
WATLING STREET
SEWSTERN LANE
R. TRENT
R. SOAR
R. WREAKE
R. SENCE
R. SWIFT
R. AVON
R. WELLAND
R. ANKER
EYE BROOK
ROTHLEY BROOK
DERBY
SWARKESTONE
WILLEN FERRY
KEGWORTH
ZOUCH BRIDGE
HATHERN
DISHLEY
LOUGHBOROUGH
COTES
NOTTINGHAM
NEWARK
SIX HILLS
FRISBY
BARROW
QUORN
MOUNTSORREL
ROTHLEY
SWITHLAND
CROPSTON
BRADGATE
ANSTEY
GROBY
MARKFIELD
BAGWORTH
DESFORD
KIRBY
BRAUNSTONE
ENDERBY
CROFT
TOOLEY
EARL SHILTON
HINCKLEY
ASHBY-DE-LA-ZOUCH
HARRIS BRIDGE
RATCLIFFE COLEY
WITHERLEY BRIDGE
FIELDEN BR.
ATHERSTONE
MANCETTER
NUNEATON
SMOCKINGTON
WOLVEY
COVENTRY
BRINKLOW
HIGH CROSS
CLAYBROOKE
SUTTON BRIDGE
SHARNFORD
STONEY BRIDGE
LUTTERWORTH
BENSFORD BRIDGE
DOVE BRIDGE
KILWORTH
WELFORD
STANFORD
NORTHAMPTON
GILMORTON
COUNTESTHORPE
PORT HILL
BLABY
AYLESTONE
WIGSTON
OADBY
KILBY BR.
WAIN BR.
ARNESBY
SHEARSBY
FLECKNEY
GUMLEY
KIBWORTH
GLEN
STRETTON BRIDGE
GARTREE BUSH
HOUGHTON
BILLESDON
TILTON
WITHCOTE
UPPINGHAM
OAKHAM
STAMFORD
HALLATON
MEDBOURNE
BRINGHURST
ROCKINGHAM
WELHAM
GREAT BOWDEN
MKT HARBOROUGH
BELGRAVE
BIRSTALL
THURCASTON
LEWIN BR.
SYSTON
MOWDEBUSH HILL
QUENIBOROUGH
REARSBY
MELTON MOWBRAY
BURTON LAZARS
GREAT FRAMLANDS
AB KETTLEBY
WALTHAM-ON-THE-WOLDS
EASTWELL
FLEMING BRIDGE
CROXTON KERRIAL
SPROXTON
SEWSTERN
BELVOIR
GRANTHAM
THREE QUEENS

On the western side of the county the Fosse no doubt continued to carry such through traffic as there was. It was a good line of communication with Warwick before the fixing of the Danish frontier along the Watling Street, and when the country was reunited the Fosse would still serve, and could carry the traffic from the town of Hinckley which was cut off from Leicester by a considerable belt of forest.

Although some of the present main roads of the county were thus beginning to take shape before the Norman Conquest, the great contribution of the Saxons and the Danes was the enormous number of tracks which joined village to village and hamlet to hamlet. Although some villages were still to be founded by far the greater number were established by 1066, and the present network of roads is substantially that laid down before the Norman Conquest.

One distinctive mark of the Saxon occupation is the making of long artificial boundaries for the avoidance of dispute between neighbouring settlements as to land rights and as to burdens of tax and legal responsibilities. Frequently, as has been seen, an old road, its course well worn and obvious, made a good ready-formed boundary, and streams too were useful for many a devious mile. Failing that, it was necessary to mark out boundaries by lines of stones; or, better still (since more permanent) creating a wide neutral belt with a ditch on either side, some 20 ft. wide. A single ditch might be filled up and re-dug, but such a belt was as permanent a thing as could be desired. These green belts between ditches (and later between hedges) look like roads, and sometimes were found to be useful as such—for example, Mere Road, Leicester; but they were originally the boundaries or meres, and may still be observed. One of the best known is the 2 miles of boundary between Oadby parish in Guthlaxton hundred and Great Glen in Gartree hundred. Known in Wigston records as the Old Mere, it runs right across the main road between the villages from near Wigston almost to the Gartree road at Stretton, and is less clearly continued by other boundaries towards Houghton.[28] Another such green 'mere' runs for a considerable distance south of Countesthorpe between the parishes of Willoughby Waterless and Peatling Magna.

IV. MEDIEVAL ROADS

When the Normans occupied Leicester many manors were allotted by King William to form the honour of Leicester and to sustain a military household at the newly-built castle.[29] The movement of supplies from the manors and of members of the great household to and from these estates must have had a considerable effect on the development of the roads as 'customary lines of travel'. Many manors were held in the county itself, but valuable lands were held both in Warwickshire and in Northamptonshire. It was not until the death of John of Gaunt in 1399 and the dispersal of the great establishment at the castle that this 'feudal' influence gradually ceased to be felt.[30]

From the middle of the 12th century the growth of trade, both internal and external, and the establishment of great fairs with their attendant trains of pack-horses led to the demand for safer travel, particularly over the rivers. Increasing prosperity allowed the building of stone bridges, which in turn affected the relative importance of particular roads and sometimes caused a con-

[28] *T.L.A.S.* xix, 192.   [29] *E.H.R.* liv, 386.   [30] *T.L.A.S.* xxii, 153.

siderable diversion of traffic. When all the medieval references to Leicestershire bridges are collated we get an overwhelming impression of the vigorous developments which took place during the reign of Edward I. By the 14th century the records refer most frequently to measures necessary to repair bridges already existing; in the 15th and 16th centuries there is little record of anything being done at all.

There are no really large rivers in Leicestershire, and no attempt was made to build a bridge over the Trent where it forms a northern boundary of the county. The Soar below its junction with the Wreak is a fairly considerable stream, and requires high-built stone bridges for safe passage as far up as Leicester. The Wreak and the Sence, and on the western borders the Avon and the Anker, also called for something better than pack-horse bridges and a ford—which served very well over many minor streams.

At the close of this article is a list of the principal road bridges in the county other than those made necessary by canal and railway construction. A study of the available evidence shows that 29 of these were built in stone in medieval times, and only 23 were added later. More remarkable is the fact that out of 16 bridges of primary importance,[31] certainly 9, and probably 12[32] seem to have been built between 1272 and 1327.

Before leaving the subject, however, it seems proper to review the division of responsibility between the Corporation of Leicester and the county authorities for the maintenance of bridges in the immediate neighbourhood of the town. In 1392 a mortmain licence was granted to the mayor and commonalty of Leicester to hold properties in the town for charitable uses including 'repairing and bettering of the six bridges'.[33] There is no list extant of the six bridges, but there is amongst the borough records a map of 1600 showing bridges from which C. J. Billson concluded that the six bridges were the North (St. Sunday's), the Little North (Frogmire), the West, the Bow, and the Braunstone Gate Bridges, and one in the Cow Pasture (South Fields).[34] The 17th-century accounts make it clear that the Corporation always insisted that Braunstone Gate Bridge lay outside the borough;[35] and it is possible that the sixth of the town bridges was the Spital Bridge over the Willow Brook. It is curious that the town authorities were able to evade liability for the upkeep of the North Bridge, especially as the parish of St. Leonard's was at one time part of the borough; but it is clear that by 1795 it was agreed that the County Justices had the chief responsibility and that the borough was only chargeable with about one-seventh, presumably representing the one arch nearest the town.[36]

A few pack-horse bridges survive which appear to be 15th-century work. Two of these (Aylestone and Enderby) were for the use of a growing coal trade[37] and another (Anstey) was probably erected by the Grey family to facilitate movement from their new mansion at Bradgate. After the great spate of energy in Edwardian times no new carriage bridge was built, so far as is known, until that at Glen in 1751.[38]

[31] Bridges over the Soar at Kegworth, Zouch Bridge, Cotes, Cossington, Belgrave, and two bridges at Leicester; Melton Bridge and Lewin Bridge over the Wreak; Blaby and Kilby Bridges over the Sence; and Harborough Bridge, Dove Bridge (on Watling Street), Witherley Bridge, Fieldon Bridge, and Farnham Bridge (near Rothley).

[32] See list of bridges, below, App. I.

[33] *Leic. Boro. Rec. 1327–1509*, 205–6.

[34] C. J. Billson, *Medieval Leic.* 100–4.

[35] *Leic. Boro. Rec. 1603–88*, 151, 249.

[36] L.R.O. Q. Sess. Rec. 1795.

[37] Fox and Russell, *Leic. Forest*, 62–63.

[38] On this date, see inscription on Glen Bridge.

In some counties (e.g. Gloucestershire) the development of the larger religious houses was a powerful factor in determining the course of roads in the 12th and 13th centuries, and something will be said of road diversions in the neighbourhood of the town of Leicester consequent on the activities of the abbots of St. Mary of the Meadows, founded 1143. By the end of the 14th century, if not earlier, all these factors—feudal, regal, mercantile, technical, and monastic—had affected the patterns and proportions of the road system of Leicestershire, and in the 15th century there was little to cause any further change, unless a slow deterioration in the volume of traffic and in the maintenance of bridges and so forth is to be considered a change.[39] In fact there were no changes of great importance until the development of wagons and coaches in the 17th century led to the activities of professional surveyors appointed by turnpike trustees in the eighteenth.

The combined influence of these factors—in their varying ways—was, however, so important and so lasting that it seems desirable to describe the principal roads of the county as they had developed in medieval times. For this purpose the roads radiating from Leicester will be described in turn, beginning at the north and going east; the marginal roads will then be reviewed; and finally any other through routes which did not reach the county town.

1. The Loughborough Road

The Derby–Loughborough road to Leicester did not attain its full importance until the construction of the Cavendish Bridge (Derbys.) in 1758, and it is not shown on the 14th-century road map (the Gough map) now in the Bodleian Library. By the time of John Ogilby (1675), however, it was part of one of the great roads of the country, from London to Manchester and Carlisle, a position which it has retained.[40]

South of Loughborough the pass of Mountsorrel was of great importance in the 12th and 13th centuries. Though masked by the line of houses the distance between the banks of the Soar and the great bluff on which the castle stood is less than 100 yds. and the narrow gap is certainly the most striking natural feature of any main road in the county. From the height the garrison dominated all the traffic. The king seized it from the Earl of Leicester in 1174, and in the struggle between Henry III and the nobles allied to Louis the Dauphin in 1217 the castle played an important part. After the royal victory at Lincoln in 1217, the castle was razed to the ground.[41]

2. The Nottingham Road

The second road is that which comes from Nottingham through Rempstone and Hoton to cross Cotes Bridge. The long causeway approach to Cotes Bridge may well be older than the bridge itself, which was built well before 1333.[42] King John probably came this way in 1209.[43]

3. The Fosse Way

In Danish times the Fosse Way may have provided the link between Leicester and Nottingham as it certainly did between Leicester and Lincoln,

39 Sidney and Beatrice Webb, *King's Highway* (1913), 8–9.

40 J. Ogilby, *Britannia* (1675).

41 E. W. Hensman, 'Mountsorrel', in *Memorials of Old Leics.* 115–21; *V.C.H. Leics.* ii, 82, 84–85.

42 See list of bridges, below, App. I.

43 *Rot. Litt. Pat.* (Rec. Com.), Itin. of King John, Nov. 1209.

Approaches to Leicester from the North and East.

(1) Roman Fosse Way. (2) Early medieval road from Loughborough. (3) Road from Leicester Abbey to Stoughton Grange. (4) Road known as the 'Fosse' in the Middle Ages. (5) 17th-century road from Loughborough, by-passing the walled town. (6) New road and bridge of 1835. (7) Prehistoric track from Tilton (via Gipsy Lane, Checketts Road, the ford at Belgrave, and Mowmacre Hill). (8) Prehistoric track from Tilton to Leicester (via Uppingham Road and Green Lane). (9) Presumed prehistoric trail to cross the Soar and proceed by Anstey Gorse.

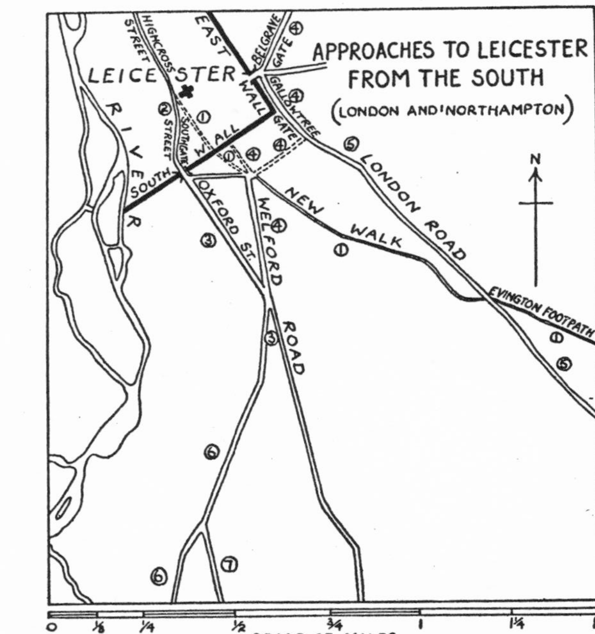

Approaches to Leicester from the South.

(1) Conjectural Roman line of approach (Gartree Road). (2) Diversion of line towards the altered South Gate (Saxon or early Norman). (3) Line of medieval road. (4) 'By-pass' to avoid town gates, tolls, &c. (15th or 16th century). (5) Road from Harborough adopted as main road in the 16th or 17th century. (6) Medieval road from Lutterworth, over Blaby Bridge, and from Aylestone (Coal Pit Lane). (7) Conjectural Saxon line of approach by Port Hill, Glen Parva, and Saffron Lane.

yet another of the Five Boroughs. When in 1078 Leicestershire came under the control of a bishop with his seat at Lincoln intercourse with the cathedral city must have been frequent, but there can be no doubt that much traffic from the counties north of the Trent passed this way to reach Coventry and the Severn valley. The principal evidence is that at a very early date enough traffic was turning aside from the straight approach to the east gate of Leicester to transfer the name of Fosse to a string of lanes which by-passed the town.[44] This by-pass ran along Checketts Road to Belgrave village where it crossed the Soar by the old bridge, and after a short length along the Loughborough road moved on ground above the meadows of the Soar by Blackbird Lane and what is now known as Fosse Road North, Central, and South. At what is now Imperial Avenue it swung back into the Roman line on its way to Narborough and High Cross. It has now been straightened and 'tamed' into a suburban highway, but within living memory it was largely a country lane. It is still used as a by-pass by modern traffic.

The origin of Belgrave Old Bridge is obscure. A passage in Knighton's Chronicle about a riot in 1357 describes the road over it as the Fosse Way but also mentions the interference with the wagons bringing the usual provisions to Leicester Abbey.[45] Possibly the abbots built the bridge to allow passage from their great demesne farm at Stoughton without coming through the town of Leicester; certainly the through traffic Yorkshire–Warwickshire often passed this way. As for some distance north of Leicester the Fosse Way passes through no villages, there can have been little accommodation for travellers over a stretch of road of well over a dozen miles, and all the evidence is that from the 14th century onwards the Fosse fell into disuse, though there were two or three cavalry movements along it in the 17th century, when Newark played so prominent a part in the campaigns.

The continuing importance of the traffic from north-east to south-west through Leicester is brought out by the 1939 Road Act, in which the road from Leicester to Worcester, and the road to London, through Leicester, from Yorkshire, are two out of eight great highways to be constructed.

4. The Melton Road

This road ran above the eastern bank of the Wreak from Melton to Leicester. Although it has some of the character of an open market road it really falls into the class of the village link-road, for its original course lay through Frisby, Rotherby, Brooksby, and Rearsby though it passed just outside the villages of Kirby and Syston. It seems reasonable to put it down as a through road from the 14th century, when Grantham and Melton were prospering and the traffic between the Humber and Severn areas increasingly deserted Newark and the Fosse.[46]

5. The Stamford Road

Stamford, whose fair was of great international repute in the 13th century, remained a place of considerable wealth until the early 16th century. The old lane leading from Leicester through Tilton and Withcote was still called 'the

[44] Hen. Knighton, *Chron.* (Rolls Ser.), ii, 96–97.

[45] Ibid.; *Public Works in Medieval Law* (Selden Soc.), ed. C. T. Flower, i, 214–17.

[46] A road linking Leicester, Melton, and Grantham is marked on the Gough Map, now in Bodl. Libr.

Stamford road' on a map drawn for All Souls College, Oxford, in 1620, but the modern Uppingham road running clear of villages between Billesdon and Leicester may finally have been adopted to comply with the code laid down in the Statute of Winchester.[47] The road led to the main or eastern gate of Leicester, outside which the bulk of the carts, horses, and burdens were halted on market-days. The widest of all the spaces reserved for markets was that along the Humberstone (or Stamford) road, where the great trading fairs were held twice a year—a circumstance which has eventually been of immense value in handling the traffic of modern times.

6. The Gartree Road

It is difficult to assess the volume of traffic which continued to use this route, the ancient Roman road from Medbourne, in medieval times. The name Port Hill occurs north of Medbourne and in 1220 Henry III travelled from Leicester to Rockingham;[48] but the traffic which might have been expected to seek the midlands from the rich districts of East Anglia was largely centred on Northampton and the two roads to Leicester from that town would appear to have accommodated most of it. None the less Leland chose to come this way.[49] The improvements in the Harborough–Leicester road from 1726 onwards no doubt hastened the decline of the Gartree road, and before the end of the 18th century whole lengths of it had been ploughed over, and as a through route it had ceased to exist.[50]

A feature of interest is the course of the Roman way near Leicester. As a continuous roadway it is lost in suburban development after skirting the southern side of the lands now forming the Leicestershire Golf Club links, but some lengths of it survive as a foot passage, including that which emerges at the crest of Gallows Hill opposite the gates of the present Victoria Park. Thus far would come the wagons and the flocks from Stoughton Grange bound for Leicester Abbey before turning down the hill to pass by the eastern gate of Leicester.[51] The old way itself continued as a boundary between the parish fields of St. Mary and St. Margaret, and was ultimately relaid and remade as the Queen's Walk[52] in 1785. A continuation of this line would have carried the road to the south wall of the town near Wycliffe Street; but the old Roman street pattern was lost, and when the town area was reoccupied the new South Gate lay closer to the river. The last stretch of the Roman way was therefore superseded by the new track and parish boundary of Hangman's Lane (now Newarke Street).[53]

7. The Welford Road

The Harborough road now shares with the road from Loughborough the distinction of being part of one of the great through roads of England, A6 from London to Carlisle, but in the Middle Ages its story can only be understood in relation to the road from London and Northampton through Welford to Leicester.

As has been said in discussing the roads of the county in Saxon times, the road via Welford was certainly of the first importance before the Conquest and the

[47] The map of Whatborough is printed by R. H. Tawney in *Agrarian Problem in the 16th Cent.* 223.

[48] *Pat. R.* 1216–25, 238–9; *Rot. Litt. Claus.* (Rec. Com.), i, 421–2. But the king seems to have travelled via Northampton.

[49] *Leland Itin.* ed. Toulmin Smith, i, 16.

[50] Nichols, *Leics.* ii, 431.

[51] See above, p. 72.

[52] Now the New Walk.

[53] Russell, *Leics. Road,* 8, 9.

stone bridge (Kilby Bridge) over the Sence must have made it much more serviceable. The Wyggeston Hospital records show this to have been in existence in the late 13th century.[54] In 1307 Edward II must have used this road, for he lodged at Guilsborough; as also Queen Isabel, who broke her journey at Sulby Abbey.[55] None the less it is the Harborough road and not the Welford one which is shown on the Gough map.[56] However, Sir George Vernon chose the Welford road on his journey to London in 1552 and on Speed's map of 1610 the Welford road is still 'the London waye'.[57] By the time that map was drawn the ancient approach of the road to the South Gate of Leicester had been superseded by a short cut (the present Welford road) towards the new centre of the town of Leicester at the East Gate.[58]

This account of the road through Welford towards Northampton and London clears the way for a study of the present London road leading to Northampton through Market Harborough. Much later this became more important as a through route than the road through Welford.

8. The Harborough Road

The oldest part of the road appears to be the stretch from the Gallows Hill (the present Victoria Park gate) to Oadby and as far as Kibworth, for a hundred boundary runs along it for 2 miles. Beyond that it passed (before the modern by-pass) through the villages of Oadby, Glen, and Kibworth. It would thus form the link by which the villagers reached the fortress and market of Leicester. The mile of road between the summit of Gallows Hill and the east gate of the town with its title of Gallowtree Gate may be assumed to be medieval, for it was used to reach the trading centre already discussed and by the abbey people passing from Stoughton Grange. The extension across 6 miles of open country to Harborough probably came into use in the late 12th century when that market-town appears to have been built.[59] Before that time the manor of Great Bowden, in which Harborough lies, might be reached from Leicester through Fleckney and Gumley.[60]

It seems reasonable to suggest that the accommodation available at the numerous villages between Leicester and Harborough and familiarity with the route as a road to eastern Northamptonshire induced travellers to take this way to Northampton in preference to the high and lonely thoroughfare over the Mowsley Hills to Welford. It was only in 1675 that Ogilby spoke of the road through Harborough as 'in general a bad deep way but very much recompensed by the reiterated good Towns and Places of Accommodation you pass through',[61] but the observation might have been made with accuracy long before his time.

9. The Lutterworth Road

As noted above it is very difficult to date this road, but the years following the Statute of Winchester appear likely. Before it was rebuilt in 1935 there was a narrow stone bridge (probably medieval) carrying the road over the Sence,

[54] *T.L.A.S.* xix, 194.

[55] Kelly, *Royal Progresses and Visits to Leic.* 132; *Cal. Pat.* 1307–13, 8; *Cal. Close*, 1307–13, 3.

[56] Now in Bodl. Libr.

[57] Hist. MSS. Com. *Rutland*, iv, 571; J. Speed, *Theatre of the Empire of Gt. Brit.* (1611).

[58] Russell, *Leics. Road*, 11.

[59] *T.L.A.S.* xxv, 56–68.

[60] Ibid.

[61] Ogilby, *Brit.* (1675), pl. 40.

widened by brickwork on both sides—which may fairly be attributed to the Turnpike Trustees.

10. Fosse Way (Southern Portion)

We have seen that communication with other towns of the Danelaw has had a strong influence on the road-making of north and east Leicestershire, and that on the south communication with London was the dominant factor. West of the Soar it is Coventry that has been the road focus, and that has led to the abandonment of old routes and to the adoption of new. This can readily be appreciated by superimposing the lines of the midlands roads of 1675, as described by Ogilby,[62] on a map showing the Roman road system. The most striking diversion of roads to serve the rising city is that of the great road from London to Chester and north Wales—the Watling Street. From early medieval times this road turned away from the Roman line at Weedon to approach Coventry, whence one branch led away to Birmingham, Shrewsbury, and Chester, whilst the other took the north-bound traveller back to the Watling Street near Lichfield, the stretch of 50 miles from Weedon being neglected and largely abandoned.[63]

The Fosse Way, which passed about 4 miles east of the site of Coventry, was similarly neglected, little use being made of it south of Stoney Bridge near Sapcote, whilst fresh traffic created new highways such as that from Coventry to Derby and Nottingham through Atherstone and Ashby de la Zouch.

With the rise of Coventry in mind we return to the consideration of the Roman Fosse Way. The Roman bridge over the Soar at Leicester cannot be sited with certainty and may have been a little north of the Leicester West Bridge. A minor bridge over the second arm of the stream would always be necessary, and it may be that Bow Bridge, at Leicester, was earlier than Braunstone Bridge. In any case, the present Narborough road, which passed just east of the manor house of Westcotes must be the line of the Roman road. At what is now Imperial Avenue the important by-pass lane which has usurped the name of Fosse came in from the north, and all the traffic was carried forward along a line comfortably above the flood meadows of the Soar.[64] There were no villages on the track, for Narborough was left to the south until the turnpike alterations of 1753. Beyond Narborough the winter flooding of which Ogilby complained became very difficult to avoid. The Romans probably constructed the long causeway over the Soar known as Langham Bridge (perhaps the long holm bridge).[65] It is a pity that a careful examination was not made when it was entirely reconstructed in 1935. This cleared the western arm of the Soar, but the determination of the Roman engineers to push straight for the elevated ground at High Cross involved them in considerable difficulties from the flooding of the other arm. A first crossing was necessary at Sutton Mill (where the arch of the bridge shows three periods of construction) and the second at Stoney Bridge, where the main road now leaves the Roman line. Stoney Bridge is obviously of ancient date, as it lies at the junction of three parishes, and in the 18th century the maintenance of the bridge was a joint charge on all three,[66] which complication probably explains its neglect. Beyond the bridge the Roman Fosse is now merely a lane and presently a bridle road through fields, and as it

[62] Ibid.
[63] T. Codrington, *Roman Roads in Brit.* 65.
[64] See above, p. 72.
[65] *V.C.H. Leics.* i, 208.
[66] Nichols, *Leics.* iv, 971.

approaches High Cross (to leave the county) it is nothing but a line of field gates, for the gravel bed of the old road appears to have been carted away wholesale by turnpike surveyors. It was probably at one of the periods when Stoney Bridge was in disrepair that the custom of passing on to Coventry through Sharnford, Smockington, and Wolvey developed. The old Fosse ran on to Brinklow, where there is a Norman castle, and Coventry could then be reached by a road which ran by Coombe Abbey or by a turn along the great road from Weedon at Dunsmore Heath. The ford at Sharnford must occasionally have been troublesome, but the line through the villages was shorter and afforded accommodation and shelter to the traveller. The Roman Fosse was definitely superseded; but the Sharnford road sometimes held first and sometimes second place in carrying traffic to Coventry and to the wealthy towns of the Avon and Severn valleys.

11. The Hinckley Road

It was, however, the administrative needs of the honour of Leicester that accounted for the development as a customary route of the rival road to Coventry and Warwick through Earl Shilton, Hinckley, and Nuneaton. At the first two places the earls of Leicester possessed manors[67] whilst they held another manor at Nuneaton. These holdings would enable shelter and refreshment to be obtained by all the earl's people on their journeys to Warwick and the south-west, and by persons travelling under the earl's protection.

The course of the road is of great interest. The first 5 miles out of Leicester may very possibly obscure the Roman trackway from Mancetter, for the straight lengths through Kirkby Mallory and Peckleton may well have continued by the long straight bridle road and footpath which leaves Desford Hall on the north and reaches the present main road at Oaks Farm Gate. Beyond that point the main road bears away for the high ground above Tooley Park, and then slants down the hill for 3 miles towards the steep ridge of Shilton. The road crossed the stripling Soar and then took the firm ground in a direct line for Shilton Castle, which was situated to the east of the church. Beyond the castle the road followed the crown of the ridge until it could swing away across a shallow valley to Brick-kiln Hill and the castle of Hinckley. The castle at Earl Shilton was little used after the 13th century and the steep pack-horse lane up the ridge was superseded by the present road, with its double right-angled corners. The later road is nearly as steep as the lane and is still a very awkward piece for a main road. Beyond Hinckley the road followed or formed the boundary between the common fields of the town, used a short length of the Watling Street to cross some marshy ground, and then turned along the low ridgeway known as the Long Shoot to cross the Anker to the market-place outside the convent gate at Nuneaton. Until 1628 7 miles of the Hinckley road out of a total length of 12 lay within the boundaries of the Forest of Leicester, where rights of vert and venison were reserved for the owners of Leicester Castle. The outer limit was the Soar brook below Shilton hill and the fields of Leicester and Westcotes stretched over the brow of the Shoulder of Mutton Hill to the Doveland Gate across the highway just west of Braunstone Park.[68]

[67] L. Fox, *Administration of the Honour of Leic.* 18–19; *E.H.R.* liv, 390; Hist. MSS. Com. *Hastings*, i, 339–40.

[68] Fox and Russell, *Leic. Forest*, map facing p. 120.

12. The Groby Road

The Groby road is also a forest and a feudal road, for the castle at Groby belonged to the earls of Leicester.[69] The road leaves Leicester by the North Bridge along the Wood (i.e. forest) Gate, and soon crosses the Fosse by-pass. The double right-angled bend at the foot of the hill, just outside Leicester, was only eliminated in 1939. These angles, together with those along Blackbird Road, Leicester, are almost certainly the result of changes caused by the foundation of Leicester Abbey, which lay to the north of this road.[70] At the foot of the short steep climb to the plateau above the Soar valley stood the Holin (or hollow) Gate of Leicester Forest, and until the 19th century the road to the west of the gate consisted of a ride about 100 yds. broad with the main forest dyke on the southern side and the fences and ditches of three early inclosures (Gilroes, Leicester Frith, and Gynsills) to the northern. The forest stretched for 2 miles and was left by a gate at what is now called Anstey Grange.[71]

Beyond this stretch the road crosses the Rothley brook and reaches Groby. Groby stands on the outskirts of the lofty and craggy forest of Charnwood, too inhospitable a ground to invite any systematic cultivation until the 19th century, and the through road to Ashby was very little used until it was taken over by a Turnpike Trust in 1753.[72] In an 18th-century map printed by Nichols the length near Markfield is described as 'Slough Lane'.[73] The road attains the considerable height for Leicestershire of 683 ft. and is always the most exposed of the main roads of the county to frost and snow.

13. The Anstey Gorse

On the map the next road is the Anstey Gorse. In medieval times there seems to have been no great call for the use of this broad and ancient way. In 1314 it was apparently regarded as an inclosed parcel of the forest for the herbage rights were being let at 3 shillings.[74] From 1508 onwards the powerful family of Grey had their residence at Bradgate and deserted Groby. This may have led to a greater use of the Gorse, but the quarrel with the Hastings family over the possession of Birds' Nest Lodge in 1525 suggests that the route by the Gynsills lane and the Groby road was still the most important.[75]

14. Mowmacre Hill Road

There is reason to think that the Mowmacre Hill road, ascending steeply to the north of Leicester, was a very ancient track continuing the Scraptoft–Green Lane–Checketts Road line to the high lands of Charnwood. In medieval times it communicated with Thurcaston, and on by the Sandham bridge to Cropston and to Swithland. Along this road would come the heavy roofing slates from Swithland.

15. Cross Roads

The importance of the road through Loughborough across Cotes Bridge to the Wolds has already been emphasized, and the very continuance of the through passage for the full length of 18 miles makes it clear that it can never have fallen

[69] Benedict Abbas, *Gesta Regis Henrici Secundi* (Rolls Ser.), i, 48; *V.C.H. Leics.* ii.

[70] *V.C.H. Leics.* ii.

[71] Fox and Russell, *Leic. Forest*, 24, 60; *Leic. Boro. Rec. 1103–1327*, 6.

[72] *C.J.* xxvi, 773.

[73] Nichols, *Leics.* iii, 131.

[74] Fox and Russell, *Leic. Forest*, 127.

[75] Ibid. 81; *T.L.A.S.* xii, 133–58.

into disuse. At the 'Three Queens' it joined that other ancient ridge road, 'Sewstern Lane', but north of Ab Kettleby it crossed the great road from Nottingham to London, which had been taken up for through traffic in Norman times. This highway crossed the Wreak at Melton and went on through Rutland to traverse the Welland at Rockingham. At Eastwell another Nottingham road was encountered—this time carrying what must have been a considerable weight of traffic to Stamford by Sproxton and the southern part of the Sewstern Lane.

The prehistoric ridgeway of Sewstern Lane had been settled as the boundary between Leicestershire and Lincolnshire, running along the lane from Harston to the 'Three Queens' (3 miles). Another 12 miles of this ancient road brought the traveller to the junction with the Ermine Street, 7 miles north of Stamford. In the Middle Ages the central part of Sewstern Lane was the 'Shire Street'.[76] Although the North Road from Newark to Grantham and Stamford was much more important than the 'Shire Street', it is likely that in medieval times the road was already used for a considerable amount of the droving which gave it the name of 'the Drift' by the 17th century. The relative importance of the condition of the surface soil and of the natural drainage compared with any attempt at metalling on a highway is shown by the fact that the earls of Rutland were quite content to move their great retinue along the whole length of the Sewstern Lane in the 17th century, instead of seeking the shortest connexion with the conventional main route of the North Road.[77]

The western half of the Leicestershire border is of more interest. There is a road from Harborough to Lutterworth within the county, and from Lutterworth there was Coventry-bound traffic through Claybrooke to High Cross. Watling Street, except for the short links used for the radial roads, had little interest, but the Coventry traffic to Derby, Nottingham, and other places in the valley of the Trent was of importance. In north-western Leicestershire this traffic depended on the road from Atherstone to Ashby de la Zouch. This entered the county at the River Anker by what is called the Fieldon Bridge. Beyond Ashby four roads radiated through rich farming lands in the angle between the courses of the Trent and the Lower Soar. The most northerly was the Derby road by Melbourne and Swarkeston Bridge. The second was also important as leading by Kegworth Bridge to Nottingham. The third and fourth were of less importance. One reached the Soar below Hathern at Zouch mills, to gain touch across the river with the line along the wolds, whilst the fourth followed the northern foothills of the forest of Charnwood to reach the market-town of Loughborough.

One other pair of roads carried something more than village traffic in medieval times, and these are the two coal roads to Leicester. Coal was being dug in the neighbourhood of Swannington as early as 1293,[78] and shallow pits and drift mines became more and more common. The pannier ponies came over Bagworth Heath to Kirby and thence along the forest lane (the coal-pit dike) to Braunstone and across the Soar by the causeway and bridge near Aylestone, where their hollow tracks up the river bank may be observed.[79] This passage enabled them to move on dry ground to Leicester. The second coal road passed through Desford and took a line by the Forest court house at Heathley to

[76] Nichols, *Leics.* ii, App. 81.

[77] Hist. MSS. Com. *Rutland*, iv, 290–2.

[78] Farnham, *Leics. Notes*, iv, 192–3; cf. above, p. 31.

[79] *Leic. Boro. Rec. 1603–88*, 168; Fox and Russell, *Leic. Forest*, 62–63; and see above, p. 34.

Enderby and again across the Soar by a narrow bridge, deserted since the Desford Coal Road Turnpike Trust about 1788 built a bridge 100 yds. lower down the stream.[80]

The score of radial and other important roads described would have a total length of about 350 miles, but except for the decaying gravel pavements of the Roman tracks there was little metalling or made-up surface.

In addition to the main roads reviewed there were thousands of miles of open tracks and enclosed lanes between the villages and outlying hamlets. The evidence of the side road indications on John Ogilby's strip maps[81] and of John Prior's county map of 1779[82] is that the network of roads before the parish inclosures was very much as it is now. Inclosure awards mention allotments for road-making as if these were to be new lines, but comparison with Prior's map will show that improvements, not innovations, were intended. As the 1-in. Ordnance map witnesses, the new farms built after the inclosures were either sited on existing roads or connected with them by narrow private tracks. There have, of course, been diversions and additions consequent on the construction of canals and of railways, but broadly speaking the roads of Leicestershire follow lines fully determined by the end of the 13th century. It is, however, true to say that when properly trained surveyors became available for inclosure work, opportunity was taken to realign the old roads on a standard width and to arrange for their proper drainage. For example, the inclosure map of Barsby and South Croxton (1798)[83] shows the regular alignment of 2 miles of the old through track from Queniborough to Twyford, the divergence from the old line being as much as 300 yds. in places.

V. TURNPIKE ROADS

Under Tudor legislation the roads in the county of Leicester were maintained by the parishes until the middle of the 19th century, practically the only improvements being a certain straightening and a good deal of ditching when common fields were inclosed and, more important, the care of particular roads by the turnpike trustees under specific Acts of Parliament.

It was the growing volume of long-distance, and particularly of wheeled, traffic that made it essential for greater resources to be deployed than could be provided by the parishes. Until the 18th century Foxton, for example, had to maintain nearly 2 miles of the principal road from London. It was partly because of such anomalies that the system of turnpike trusts grew up. In the year 1726 the leading men of the county and the borough of Leicester obtained an Act to collect tolls for a period of 21 years to be devoted to the repair of the principal road from London, from its entry to the county at Harborough through Leicester to Loughborough.[84] This was the first turnpike trust to be set up in Leicestershire. What was done in the first 20 years amounted to this. Carts and men were hired by the Trustees' Surveyor to remove unriddled gravel from pits lying near the road and were spread to form a track about 14 ft. wide, four or five loads being used for each yard forward. A dozen labourers were each allotted 2 miles of road, and their duties were to 'let the

[80] Fox and Russell, op. cit. 63–64; *C.J.* xliii, 189.
[81] Ogilby, *Brit.* (1675), plates 40, 48, 72.
[82] J. Prior, *Map of Leics.* (1779).
[83] L.R.O. Barsby and South Croxton Inclosure Award.
[84] *C.J.* xx, 567, 680.

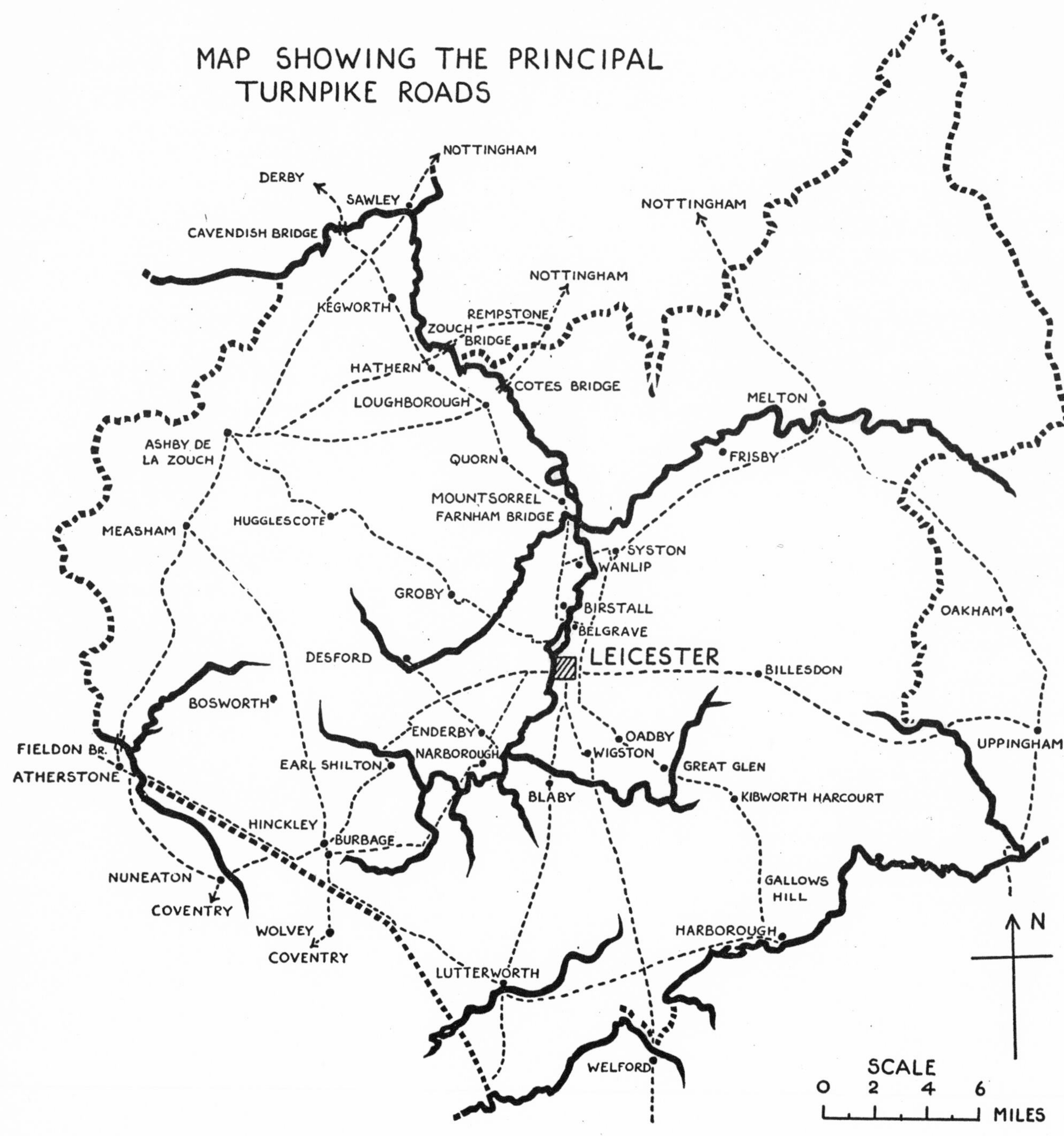
MAP SHOWING THE PRINCIPAL TURNPIKE ROADS
NOTTINGHAM
DERBY
SAWLEY
CAVENDISH BRIDGE
NOTTINGHAM
NOTTINGHAM
KEGWORTH
REMPSTONE
ZOUCH BRIDGE
HATHERN
COTES BRIDGE
LOUGHBOROUGH
MELTON
ASHBY DE LA ZOUCH
QUORN
FRISBY
MOUNTSORREL
FARNHAM BRIDGE
MEASHAM
HUGGLESCOTE
SYSTON
WANLIP
GROBY
BIRSTALL
OAKHAM
BELGRAVE
DESFORD
LEICESTER
BILLESDON
BOSWORTH
ENDERBY
OADBY
FIELDON BR.
NARBOROUGH
WIGSTON
UPPINGHAM
ATHERSTONE
EARL SHILTON
GREAT GLEN
BLABY
KIBWORTH HARCOURT
HINCKLEY
BURBAGE
NUNEATON
GALLOWS HILL
COVENTRY
WOLVEY
HARBOROUGH
N
COVENTRY
LUTTERWORTH
WELFORD
SCALE
0 2 4 6
MILES

water off the road' and to prepare gravel and other material for the parish teams to cart and lay when the time for statute work came round.[85]

In 1753 and 1754 the town and county authorities again combined to obtain statutory powers for trustees to collect tolls and repair the roads leading from Hinckley, Coventry, Uppingham, Narborough, and Ashby de la Zouch to the borough of Leicester. This brought under the turnpike system the second great traffic route of Leicestershire—that is, from north-east to south-west.[86] In 1764 the road from Leicester to Melton Mowbray and Grantham was also put under the control of the turnpike trust.[87] Besides the routes mentioned, a number of lesser roads in Leicestershire became turnpikes during the 18th century, especially during the years 1750–66.[88]

Road surfacing was still crude when the new trusts set to work. In 1767 the Melton Trust gave orders that the road in Queniborough parish should be ploughed up and flung out on both sides to a width of 18 ft.[89] Gravel was extensively used by the trustees of the various roads but became scarcer, and it was the use of granite which made real improvement possible. In Leicestershire the use of granite was fostered by Sir John Danvers, owner of the quarries at Mountsorrel. In the year 1758 he offered £200 over a period of 4 years to the trustees of the Harborough to Loughborough road if they would lay a granite causeway 18 ft. wide through the town of Mountsorrel. In 1774 a similar causeway was constructed through the town of Leicester, but it was only in 1787 that Alderman John Nichols persuaded his fellow trustees to reconstruct the road through the town as a flat causeway built of the famous granite 'setts', that is of squared stones laid in even rows. The making of such setts at the quarries led to the accumulation there of large quantities of small pieces and chips of granite. In the closing years of the century these were much used by Thomas Bown, surveyor to several of the trusts, and the material was doubtless superior to gravel for sustaining heavy traffic. There is no evidence, however, that Bown imposed the tests for use of stone of uniform size which was the principal reform introduced by Macadam in 1816, when he took charge of 148 miles of roads in the neighbourhood of Bristol.[90]

The first of the 18th-century bridges to be built was that on the Harborough road over the Sence brook near Great Glen. Edward Gooddess, bricklayer, was then surveyor to the trust, and it was he who supervised the making of the five brick arches in 1751. The width of the roadway was 16 ft.[91] Several of the old narrow bridges on the road were widened about the same time. The Hinckley road minutes show that when the trust took over in 1754 one of their first acts was to eliminate the fords and to build small bridges below Dane Hills and below Earl Shilton.[92] Although the records have been lost it seems likely that the Blaby and Kilby bridges were widened for carriage use when the roads to Lutterworth and to Welford were taken over by the trustees in 1764 and 1765 respectively. Strictly speaking, the widening of bridges, and certainly the building of new ones, was work outside any definition of 'repair', but the liberal use of their powers by the then turnpike trustees encouraged the County Justices to follow

85 L.R.O. Order Bks. of Harborough to Loughborough Turnpike, 15–D34/1–7.

86 *C.J.* xxvi, 773, 903, 911, 978, 1018.

87 Ibid. xxix, 1057.

88 Ibid. xxiii, 203; xxvi, 516, 821, 1018; xxvii, 247, 782, 828; xxviii, 535, 863, 927; xxix, 258, 350; xxx, 426, 348; xliii, 459; xlix, 417.

89 L.R.O. 15–D34/16–20.

90 Russell, *Leics. Road*, 86–89; L.R.O. 15–D34/1–7.

91 L.R.O. 15–D34/1–7; and see inscription on bridge.

92 L.R.O. 15–D34/11–13.

their example. The same individuals, often with the same professional advisers, were concerned both with the turnpike roads and with the road and bridge business transacted at Quarter Sessions.[93]

In bridge building the spur to activity was supplied by the example of northern neighbours, for in 1758 the Nottinghamshire Justices took the leading part in rebuilding the big five arched bridge over the Soar at Kegworth.[94] In the same year Sir Matthew Lambe obtained a special Act of Parliament and constructed the great Cavendish Bridge over the Trent to carry the main road from Manchester to Leicester and London, previously dependent on Willen Ferry.[95] This bridge, 48 yds. long and 19 ft. wide, was destroyed by floods following the heavy snows of February 1947. The county advanced from repair to improvement in 1786 when they employed John Cheshire, of Whitacre in Warwickshire, to rebuild in stone and brick the Fieldon Bridge over the River Anker.[96] Happily this survives as an example of Cheshire's work, since his Zouch Bridge of 1790 as well as his new Leicester North Bridge of 1795 and his Braunstone Gate Bridge have been demolished.[97] Joseph Vinrace of Ashby de la Zouch did much bridge-building for the county early in the 19th century. A neat brick bridge at Ratcliffe Culey (1811) as well as a good stone-faced bridge over the Welland (near Medbourne) still survive, but the finest example of his work is the beautiful stone bridge at Melton, constructed by him in 1822 to the plans of William Kirk, senior.[98] Vinrace's work extended into the classic period of road improvement, for this lasted from the peace of 1815 to the triumph of the railways 25 years later.

Apart from the growing wealth of the country the improvements had been made practicable by the construction of the canals during the previous forty years. The reaction of canal construction on the science of road-making was a double one. In the first place it allowed the transport over wide areas of good road and building material, which the inferior roads could never have carried. In the second place it bred a whole host of civil engineers, skilled artisans, and lusty 'navigators' who could make light work of the hill lowering and the marsh embanking, which so vastly bettered the conditions for rapid and comfortable travel on the turnpike roads in Regency times. To these resources England was able to add the engineering powers of Thomas Telford and the practical ability of Thomas Macadam.

Some examples of the new science had been given in Leicestershire, even in the war-time. In 1802 Edward Parsons, surveyor for most of the county roads, co-operated with Lord Moira as landowner in the great improvement of the southern exit from the town of Loughborough. Two right-angled turns were cut out and a direct run from the main street into the turnpike was thus allowed.[99] In 1810 Parsons constructed the 'New Road' at Kibworth Harcourt, which passes in an even sweep west of the castle enclosure, instead of burrowing into the village and out again.[1] His next big undertaking was to build for the Melton road trust nearly 2 miles of new road from the hill above Rotherby

[93] L.R.O. 15–D34 *passim*, and Leics. Q. Sess. Rec. *passim*.

[94] L.R.O. Beaumont Smith's Reg. of Bridges.

[95] *C.J.* xxviii, 290.

[96] L.R.O. Leics. Q. Sess. Rec.

[97] C. J. Billson, *Medieval Leics.* 101, 103; L.R.O. Q. Sess. Rec. Contracts with J. Cheshire for repair of Leic. North Bridge, Braunstone Gate Bridge, and Zouch Bridge.

[98] L.R.O. Q. Sess. Rec. Ord. Bk. 1809–30 (under 1822); Contracts with J. Vinrace for repairing bridges at Ratcliffe Culey and Medbourne.

[99] Russell, *Leics. Road*, 21.

[1] Ibid. 120–1.

towards Kirby Bellars, so cutting out the steep and tortuous lane through Frisby-on-the-Wreak.[2]

After 1815 Edward Parsons was succeeded by his son William; who was surveyor to the county and most of the Leicestershire Trusts from 1819.[3] He was just at an age to take full advantage of opportunities before road revenues fell away after 1836. In the lowering of hills his first and one of his most successful efforts was the cutting to carry the road up the 100-ft. bluff of Brick Kiln hill near Hinckley; and amongst other tasks he followed this with the making of a low 'new and even' slope up Red Hill at Birstall, cutting out the narrow and awkward lane which climbed the hill nearer the village. Another big undertaking was the lowering of the hill and raising of a 20-ft.-high embankment to improve the gradient between Mountsorrel and Farnham Bridge. His principal achievement in regrading, however, was the building of 1,200 yds. of new road south of the Bowden Inn to carry the main London road up the marlstone escarpment at Gallows Hill. The old track largely survives as an accommodation road, and demonstrates how great were the technical advances being made by Parsons and his contemporaries. All these new lengths of road, and indeed the surfaces generally, were laid on Macadam's principle of small granite stones 'broken to size'.[4]

Parsons was a man of great versatility—he built the Theatre Royal in Leicester[5]—and, in addition to his general regrading and resurfacing, he it was who, in 1834, cut out the awkward turn of the main road through Belgrave village and across the medieval bridge. He designed and supervised the building of the new and direct road to the foot of Red Hill, crossing the Soar by a bridge of five brick arches (with cast-iron ribs to span the central one). This bridge is still in service.[6]

It was the opening of the railway from London to Birmingham (with its imminent extension to Manchester) that warned the Leicestershire bankers and administrators that the expansion of debts by turnpike trusts ought now to cease—and with it any further improvements of importance. This opening occurred in 1836, which was a peak year for toll revenues in Leicestershire, though the general increase of population and of short-distance travel prevented any catastrophic decline.[7] On the Harborough–Loughborough road the general abandonment of the Manchester–London coach business involved a fall of about £2,000 in a total toll revenue of £6,000; but such a loss was exceptional in the county.[8] The rapid extension of the railway system, however, turned the minds of men from road improvements. The administration was largely left to the professional surveyors and to the lawyer clerks, and whilst fairly competent, it was unimaginative. From 1850 onwards, however, a growing number of Members of Parliament favoured the closing down of the trusts and the transfer of the turnpike roads to the new highway boards. Trustees applying for the usual extension of their acts were informed that the new lease was final, and that the debts must be reduced as rapidly as possible, so that the tolls might be discontinued and the roads repaired out of rates collected by the Highway boards. This policy resulted in the closing of the Leicestershire trusts between 1871 and 1878.[9]

[2] L.R.O. 15–D34/16–20.
[3] L.R.O. 15–D34/1–24; Russell, *Leics. Road*, 125.
[4] Ibid. 125–7, 129; L.R.O. 15–D34/1–7, 11–13.
[5] R. Leacroft, *Theatre Royal*, 20.
[6] Russell, *Leics. Road*, 139–41.
[7] Ibid. 141.
[8] Ibid. 144.
[9] Ibid. 151–2, 158.

An appendix[10] lists the principal turnpike roads in the county, with figures of revenue and of debt in 1836. It will be seen that on the average the debts were less than four times the amount of the annual tolls so that the trustees were not in the awkward predicament of many of the western trusts, where the building of mountain roads and ravine bridges had left a debt out of all proportion to the tolls which could be gathered when the railways took the cream of the traffic. There were a few failures in Leicestershire, including a number of roads taken in hand to serve some of the collieries and quarries. The Wanlip toll figures are almost laughable, and the Desford Coal Road figures interesting as showing the transfer of the distribution of coal to the railways. Particular interest attaches to the Narborough–Burbage road, as the results of making it a turnpike were quite different from those anticipated by the principal promoter, John Frewen Turner. From 1754 to 1814 the Coventry and south-western traffic had passed almost entirely along the Hinckley–Nuneaton line. The Hinckley Road trustees repaired the road from Leicester to Narborough but no farther. It was this arrangement which led to the abandonment of the Fosse Way itself beyond the Enderby turn, the turnpike road branching off to the centre of Narborough village. In 1814 Turner and his friends obtained an act to collect tolls and 'repair' the road from Narborough along the Fosse to Sapcote and thence to Burbage.[11] This (they hoped) would allow the development of the quarries at Stoney Stanton and at Croft. They widened the ancient arches at Langham Bridge and at Sutton Mill and generally put the road in such good order that it became a fair alternative route to Hinckley, but their tolls never exceeded £266 and in the first 5 years the capital outlay had exceeded £5,000. They had, however, repaired the Fosse itself to within 4 miles of Smockington on the Watling Street, and thus opened up again the old road from Leicester to Coventry.[12] With the great growth of Coventry and Birmingham in the present century the route became one of first-class importance, but this was hardly what Turner had intended.

In 1888 Parliament set up County Councils ranking in authority with the larger cities and towns known as County Boroughs. The new County Councils were instructed to take over the principal roads, under the style of 'main roads' and the great mass of secondary roads was to be maintained by Urban and Rural District Councils. Substantially the 'main roads' were the old turnpike roads, or at least those of them which were worth taking over. As the County Council also took over responsibility for the 'County' bridges, their surveyor had now in charge practically all the bridges of any importance in the county, except those which were sited within the county borough of Leicester.

The introduction of motor vehicles has made great changes to the roads essential. With the aid of the central Road Board (1910) and later of the Ministry of Transport the County Council has spent vast sums on rebuilding and widening bridges to a standard width of 40 ft. and regrading and widening the carriageways from the turnpike trust 18 ft. to 30 and 40 ft. pushing beyond that to the construction of many miles of dual carriageways on the old Harborough, Melton, and Ashby turnpikes. On the great road of the county, the Harborough–Loughborough road (A6) an entirely new road has by-passed the long village of Oadby (1930) whilst the county borough of Leicester has con-

[10] App. II, below.
[11] *C.J.* lxix, 233.
[12] L.R.O. 15–D34/11–13.

structed (1931), at a cost of over £1 million, a by-pass (Charles Street) to avoid the old centre of traffic at the East Gates.[13]

From an historical point of view the most interesting feature of the work of the Road Board and its successors has been the revival as a first-class highway of the old Fosse Way, from where it crosses the Nottingham–Melton road to where it joins the Melton–Leicester road at Syston. More and more of the Leicester–Nottingham traffic uses this route every year. Of similar interest is the designation of the old Watling Street as a great through road (A5). Although it had never, like the Fosse, sunk to a bridle road, many stretches of it had long been neglected, and others developed in a very limited way by turnpike trusts of narrow resources. A great deal of work has been done, such as the rebuilding of Dove and Witherley bridges, but much more remains to be done before the road can be described as fit for the traffic for which it is intended.

APPENDIX I

THE PRINCIPAL ROAD BRIDGES OF LEICESTERSHIRE[14]

Over the River Soar

Name of Bridge	*Road*	
Kegworth	Coventry to Nottingham	First mentioned in 1316, when a grant of pontage for 5 years was made for its repair.[15] Rebuilt as a bridge of 5 arches by Nottinghamshire and Leicestershire jointly in 1758.[16] Iron foot-paths were added at the sides in 1757.[17] In 1937 the ironwork was removed, and the bridge widened.
Zouch	Ashby to Rempstone	In 1358 it was said that Zouch Bridge was built under Edward I, and that no community was legally chargeable for its repair.[18] The bridge is perhaps that mentioned in 1318.[19] It was rebuilt in 1790 by John Cheshire, for Leicestershire and Nottinghamshire,[20] and again rebuilt in 1931 by the two counties.[21]
Cotes	Loughborough to Nottingham	Said to be mentioned in 1333, but this is uncertain.[22] Marked on a map of 1576,[23] and mentioned in 1644.[24] A bridge of 13 arches, shown in an illustration of about 1800 may be Cotes Bridge.[25] The present bridge is one of 6 arches, constructed at an unknown date.
Barrow	Quorndon to Barrow	Already existed in 1274,[26] and it is mentioned in 1396–7.[27] Rebuilt 1845–6 by the county authorities.[28]
Mountsorrel	Sileby to Mountsorrel	Already existed in 1274.[29] In 1852 the old bridge of rubble stone was replaced by one of wrought iron.[30]

[13] The spot now generally known as the 'Clock Tower'. On cost of Charles Street, see *City of Leic. Abstract of Acts. 1931–2*, 486.

[14] Bridges built in connexion with railways or canals have been omitted.

[15] *Cal. Pat.* 1313–17, 394, 511.

[16] L.R.O. Beaumont Smith's Reg. of Bridges.

[17] Ibid.

[18] *Cal. Inq. Misc.* iii, 104.

[19] *Chron. Edw. I and Edw. II* (Rolls Ser.), ii, lxxxii; Hen. Knighton, *Chron.* (Rolls Ser.), i, 412.

[20] L.R.O. Q. Sess. Rec. Bridge Contracts; Nichols, *Leics.* iii, 779.

[21] L.R.O. Beaumont Smith's Reg. of Bridges.

[22] E. Jervoise, *Ancient Bridges of Mid. and Eastern Engl.* 51, states that an inquisition about Cotes Bridge was held in 1333, but cites no authority.

[23] C. Saxton, *Map of Warws. and Leics.* (1576) reproduced in B. L. Gimson and P. Russell, *Leics. Maps*, 3.

[24] *C.J.* iii, 435.

[25] Nichols, *Leics.* iii, 779. The easternmost of the stone arches of the old 13-arched bridge still exists. The arch was originally 12 ft. wide, but it has been widened to 18 ft.

[26] *Rot. Hund.* (Rec. Com.), i. 238.

[27] *Quorndon Rec.* ed. G. F. Farnham, 117.

[28] L.R.O. Beaumont Smith's Reg. of Bridges.

[29] *Rot. Hund.* (Rec. Com.), i, 238.

[30] L.R.O. Beaumont Smith's Reg. of Bridges.

Name of Bridge	*Road*	
Cossington	Rothley to Cossington	Probably existed in 1325, when 'Briggefurlong' at Cossington is mentioned.[31] Certainly existed in 1331.[32] Rebuilt by the county in 1822.[33]
Belgrave Old Bridge	Leicester to Loughborough	Mentioned in 1357.[34] An ancient stone bridge of 7 arches still exists. In 1762 the trustees of the Harborough to Leicester turnpike assumed responsibility for the bridge, on the parish of Belgrave paying them £100.[35]
North Bridge, Leicester (or Saint Sunday's Bridge)	Leicester to Ashby de la Zouch	Probably one of the Leicester bridges mentioned in 1260,[36] but the first specific reference occurs in 1305.[37] Repaired at the expense of the borough of Leicester in 1306–7.[38] In the 16th century described as having 7 or 8 arches.[39] Largely destroyed by a flood in 1795, and replaced by a new bridge of 3 arches, built at the joint expense of the county and of Leicester borough.[40] In 1867–8 a new iron bridge was built by the borough.[41]
West Bridge, Leicester	Fosse Way	Probably existed in the first half of the 12th century.[42] In 1325 a new stone bridge was built at the expense of Leicester borough.[43] This bridge, which had 4 arches,[44] and by 1365 had a chapel at its east end,[45] lasted until 1842–3, when a new bridge was built.[46] A new iron bridge was built in 1890.
Bow Bridge,[47] Leicester	Leicester to Glenfield	May have been one of the 6 bridges at Leicester mentioned in 1392.[48] Marked on a map drawn about 1600.[49] An old stone bridge[50] was replaced by the existing iron bridge in 1863.[51]
Braunstone Gate Bridge, Leicester	Fosse Way	Perhaps the bridge leading to Bromkinsthorpe, mentioned in 1317.[52] The bridge certainly existed in 1600,[53] and in 1613–14 it was established that it was to be maintained at the expense of St. Mary's parish, Leicester.[54] Largely rebuilt at the county's expense in 1792.[55] Again rebuilt after damage by floods in 1795.[56] The existing bridge was erected in 1884.[57]
Aylestone Old Bridge	Aylestone to Braunstone	Date of erection unknown. Is of rubble stone, only 4 ft. wide, and approached by causeways on either side.[58]
Enderby New Bridge	Barlestone to Blaby road	First bridge on this site was built by a turnpike trust in 1792.[59] A new bridge was built by the same trust in 1846.[60]

31 Farnham, *Leics. Notes*, ii, 116.

32 *Cal. Pat.* 1330–4, 115.

33 L.R.O. Q. Sess. Ord. Bk. 1809–30, under 1822.

34 Hen. Knighton, *Chron.* (Rolls Ser.) ii, 97.

35 L.R.O. Acts and Ords. of the Trustees of the Harborough and Loughborough Road, 1726–64, 231.

36 *Leic. Boro. Rec. 1103–1327*, 92.

37 Ibid. 249.

38 Ibid. 249, 262. The cost of the new bridge was £28. 0*s.* 5¼*d.*; the chief mason was Peter of Bagworth.

39 *Leland Itin.* ed. Toulmin Smith, i, 16.

40 Nichols, *Leics.* i, 555; L.R.O. Q. Sess. Rec. Bridge Contracts. The bridge built after 1795 is depicted in Nichols, *Leics.* i, 549, pl. xxxviii.

41 J. Storey, *Boro. of Leic. Hist. Sketch, 1836–95*, 12.

42 *Leic. Boro. Rec. 1103–1327*, 43.

43 Ibid. 349–52.

44 Nichols, *Leics.* i, 301.

45 Ibid.; *Leic. Boro. Rec. 1327–1509*, 140; C. J. Billson, *Medieval Leic.* 102.

46 Storey, *Boro. of Leic.* 11–12.

47 Adjacent to the main Bow Bridge, there was in the 18th cent. a footbridge which was also known as Bow Bridge. The footbridge was demolished in 1791: Nichols, *Leics.* i, 301–2.

48 *Leic. Boro. Rec. 1327–1509*, 205–6.

49 Ibid. *1509–1603*, p. xvii.

50 Depicted Nichols, *Leics.* i, pls. xxii, xxiii, p. 301.

51 Storey, *Boro. of Leic.* 12.

52 *Leic. Boro. Rec. 1103–1327*, 375.

53 Ibid. *1509–1603*, p. xvii.

54 Ibid. *1603–88*, 151.

55 Nichols, *Leics.* i, 301; L.R.O. Q. Sess. Rec. Bridge contracts.

56 L.R.O. Q. Sess. Rec. Bridge Contracts.

57 Storey, *Boro. of Leic.* 86.

58 The causeway on the east side has been cut by the construction of a canal.

59 L.R.O. 15–D34/11–13.

60 Ibid.

Name of Bridge	*Road*	
Enderby Old Bridge	Enderby to Whetstone	An ancient stone bridge of 2 arches, 6 ft. wide and without parapets. Date unknown.
Langham Bridge	Fosse Way	Consists of a series of causeways and small arches on the Roman road. About 1790 described as being of very primitive construction.[61] At some unknown date widened by the construction on one side of several small brick arches. The whole was entirely reconstructed by the county in 1935.
Croft Bridge	Croft to the Fosse Way	Marked on a map published in 1779.[62] Rebuilt in 1857 by the county of Leicester.[63]
Sutton Bridge	Fosse Way	Originally a stone pack-horse bridge of 3 arches. Widened at an unknown date in brick. Again widened by the county about 1933.[64] Marked on a map of 1675.[65]
Stoney Bridge	Fosse Way	Marked on a map published in 1779.[66] It stands at the junction of Sapcote, Stoney Stanton, and Broughton Astley parishes, which in the 18th century were jointly responsible for its repair.[67]
Sharnford Bridge	Leicester to Coventry	Apparently there was only a ford at Sharnford until 1884, when a bridge was built by the Lutterworth Highway Board.[68] A new bridge was constructed by the county about 1933.
		OVER ROTHLEY BROOK
Farnham Bridge	Leicester to Loughborough	Marked on a map of 1576.[69] The old pack-horse bridge of 5 arches widened by the trustees of the Loughborough to Harborough turnpike in 1748 for carriages and largely rebuilt in 1798.[70]
Anstey Old Bridge	Anstey to Leicester	Ancient pack-horse bridge of 5 arches, made of rubble stone. Farther down stream is a ford, now spanned by a modern bridge.
		OVER THE RIVER WREAK
Lewin Bridge[71]	Fosse Way	Marked on a map of 1779.[72] About 1800 the bridge was very dilapidated and had to be repaired by the company which canalized the Wreak.[73] In 1819 the existing bridge was built by the county.[74]
Leicester Bridge, Melton Mowbray	Leicester to Melton	Marked on a map of 1576,[75] and bridge masters existed at Melton in 1582.[76] A small stone arch at one end of the bridge was built by the Earl of Harborough in 1775.[77] About 1800 the bridge was being maintained by the Melton town estate,[78] but in 1822 it was rebuilt by the county.[79] Widened in 1930.
Burton Bridge, Melton Mowbray		Must have existed before 1659, when it was repaired.[80] Again repaired in 1785, and about 1800 it was being maintained by the Melton town estate.[81]

[61] J. Throsby, *Leics. Excursions*, 519–20, where it is said 'The arches are built of forest stone, without much design but that of durability. They are narrow, without a fence or wall on either side.

[62] J. Prior, *Map of Leics.* (1779).

[63] L.R.O. Beaumont Smith's Reg. of Bridges.

[64] Ibid.

[65] Ogilby, *Brit.* (1675), pl. 72.

[66] J. Prior, *Map of Leics.* (1779).

[67] Nichols, *Leics.* iv, 971.

[68] L.R.O. Beaumont Smith's Reg. of Bridges.

[69] C. Saxton, *Map of Warws. and Leics.* (1576).

[70] Russell, *Leics. Road*, 27, 69, 119; and see inscription on bridge. The family of Farnham was already settled at Quorndon, near the bridge, by 1284; G. F. Farnham, *Leics. Medieval Pedigrees*, 70.

[71] A certain Lewin held land near the site of the bridge in the 11th cent. (*V.C.H. Leics.* i, 315, 330, 336) but there is no evidence that the bridge's name is derived from him.

[72] J. Prior, *Map of Leics.* (1779).

[73] Nichols, *Leics.* iii, 453.

[74] L.R.O. Q. Sess. Rec. Bridge Contracts.

[75] C. Saxton, *Map of Warws. and Leics.* (1576).

[76] J. Ward, *Melton Mowbray*, 119.

[77] Nichols, *Leics.* ii, 248.

[78] Ibid.

[79] L.R.O. Q. Sess. Order Bk. 1809–30, under 1822.

[80] Nichols, *Leics.* ii, 248.

[81] Ibid.

Name of Bridge	*Road*	
		OVER REARSBY BROOK[82]
Rearsby Bridge	Leicester to Melton	The Leicester to Melton road crossed Rearsby Brook by a ford until 1777, when the present bridge was built by the turnpike trustees.[83]
Rearsby Pack-horse Bridge		A pack-horse bridge of 7 semicircular arches, of unknown date, stands beside Rearsby church.
		OVER QUORN BROOK[84]
Quorn Bridge	Leicester to Loughborough	A bridge of 5 arches at Quorndon is marked on a map of 1675.[85] Not mentioned in the records of the turnpike trust which controlled the Leicester–Loughborough road.[86]
		OVER DISHLEY BROOK[87]
Dishley Bridge	Loughborough to Derby	In 1675 there was a bridge of two arches.[88] Extensively repaired by the county in 1889.[89]
		OVER QUENIBOROUGH BROOK[90]
Queniborough Bridge	Leicester to Melton	Marked on a map of 1779.[91] Rebuilt in 1824 by the trustees of the Leicester to Melton turnpike[92] and widened in 1874 by the county.[93] Was being reconstructed in 1952.
		OVER SYSTON BROOK[94]
Syston Bridge	Leicester to Melton	A bridge must have existed at Syston well before 1797, when the old bridge was rebuilt in 9 days.[95]
		OVER WILLOW BROOK[96]
Spital Bridge	Belgrave Rd., Leicester	First mentioned in 1569–70, when it was repaired.[97] Probably one of the 6 bridges at Leicester mentioned in 1392.[98] Repaired in 1610 by Leicester borough.[99]
Saltersford Bridge	Leicester to Uppingham	Marked on a map of 1779.[1] Probably built by the trustees of the Leicester to Uppingham road, whose records have been destroyed. Widened at the cost of the county in 1862.[2]
		OVER THE RIVER SENCE[3]
Kilby Bridge	Leicester to Welford	There was a stone bridge at Kilby in the late 13th century.[4] In the 19th century most of it was of stone, with 2 small pointed arches, widened on each side by brickwork.[5] Entirely rebuilt in 1937 by the county.
Great Glen Bridge	Leicester to Harborough	The bridge of 5 arches was built in 1751 by the trustees of the Harborough to Loughborough turnpike.[6] Has been widened later.
Wain Bridge	Wistow to Newton Harcourt	Mentioned in a will of 1525.[7] Rebuilt by the county in 1879.[8]
Stretton Bridge	Gartree Road	Mentioned in a will of 1541.[9] Widened by the county in 1860.[10]

82 A tributary of the Wreak.
83 L.R.O. 15–D34/16–20; J. Prior, Map of Leics. (1779).
84 A tributary of the Soar.
85 Ogilby, *Brit.* (1675), pl. 40.
86 L.R.O. 15–D34/1–7.
87 A tributary of the Soar.
88 Ogilby, *Brit.* (1675), pl. 40.
89 L.R.O. Beaumont Smith's Reg. of Bridges.
90 A tributary of the Wreak.
91 J. Prior, *Map of Leics.* (1779).
92 L.R.O. 15–D34/16–20.
93 Beaumont Smith's Reg. of Bridges.
94 A tributary of the Wreak.
95 Nichols, *Leics.* iii, 453.
96 A tributary of the Soar.
97 *Leic. Boro. Rec. 1509–1603*, 132.
98 Ibid. *1327–1509*, 205–6.
99 Ibid. *1603–88*, 107–8.
1 J. Prior, *Map of Leics.* (1779).
2 L.R.O. Beaumont Smith's Reg. of Bridges.
3 A tributary of the Soar.
4 *T.L.A.S.* xix, 194.
5 L.R.O. Beaumont Smith's Reg. of Bridges.
6 See inscription on bridge.
7 L.R.O. Reg. Bk. of Wills, 1515–26, f. 476, will of Wm. Chamberlayne.
8 L.R.O. Beaumont Smith's Reg. of Bridges.
9 L.R.O. Wills 1541, will of John Marshall.
10 L.R.O. Beaumont Smith's Reg. of Bridges.

ROADS

Over the River Trent

Name of Bridge	Road	
Cavendish Bridge	Loughborough to Derby	Built by Sir Matthew Lambe about the middle of the 18th century,[11] and consisted of 3 main arches and 2 small flood arches.[12] This important bridge replaced the crossing of the Trent at Willen Ferry. Repaired by the county in 1932.[13] Destroyed by floods in 1947.
		Over the River Devon
Fleming Bridge		Built by the Revd. Samuel Fleming (d. 1620).[14] It consists of 2 segmental arches.
		Over the River Welland
Bringhurst Bridge	Bringhurst to Cottingham	Marked on a map of 1779.[15] Rebuilt in 1842 by Leicestershire and Northamptonshire.[16]
Medbourne Bridge	Medbourne to Ashley	Marked on a map of 1779.[17] Rebuilt as a bridge of 4 arches by Leicestershire and Northamptonshire in 1820.[18]
Welham Bridge	Welham to Weston by Welland	A stone bridge, of 2 arches, which existed in the 18th century, was probably built in 1678.[19] Rebuilt by Leicestershire and Northamptonshire in 1810.[20] Again rebuilt by them in 1880 after being destroyed by floods.[21]
Great Bowden Bridge	Great Bowden to Little Bowden	Probably one of the 'briggs and causies' of Great Bowden mentioned in 1523.[22] Rebuilt in 1821.[23]
Chain Bridge, Harborough	Leicester to Northampton	First mentioned in 1228,[24] and there are grounds for believing that Market Harborough first became important in the late 12th century.[25] In 1439 the 'great bridge' at Harborough was mentioned.[26] In 1675 the bridge consisted of 6 arches,[27] and about 1800 the bridge had 3 stone arches, and 3 arches of timber with stone piers.[28] The name of the 'Chain Bridge' mentioned in 1721,[29] was derived from the practice of stretching a chain across the bridge to compel vehicles to use the adjacent ford at times when the Welland was fordable.[30] A new bridge of 3 arches was built by Leicestershire and Northamptonshire in 1814,[31] and in 1928 the bridge was again rebuilt.[32]
		Over the Eye Brook[33]
Finchley Bridge	Leicester to Uppingham	Marked on a map of 1779.[34] Rebuilt in 1832–3 by Leicestershire and Rutland.[35]
		Over the River Avon
Welford Bridge	Leicester to Welford	A stone bridge of 2 arches existed before 1800;[36] rebuilt in 1817.[37]

[11] Nichols, *Leics.* iii, 779.
[12] See ibid. iii, pl. cvii, opposite p. 779.
[13] L.R.O. Beaumont Smith's Reg. of Bridges.
[14] Nichols, *Leics.* ii, 91.
[15] J. Prior, *Map of Leics.* (1779).
[16] L.R.O. Beaumont Smith's Reg. of Bridges.
[17] J. Prior, *Map of Leics.* (1779).
[18] L.R.O. Q. Sess. Rec. Bridge Contracts.
[19] Nichols, *Leics.* ii, 865.
[20] L.R.O. Q. Sess. Rec. Bridge Contracts.
[21] L.R.O. Beaumont Smith's Reg. of Bridges.
[22] *Market Harborough Rec. to 1530*, ed. J. E. Stocks and W. B. Bragg, 222.
[23] L.R.O. Beaumont Smith's Reg. of Bridges.
[24] *Cal. Close*, 1227–31, 301.
[25] *T.L.A.S.* xxv, 56–68.
[26] *Market Harborough Rec. to 1530*, 172–3.
[27] Ogilby, *Brit.* (1675), pl. 40.
[28] Nichols, *Leics.* ii, 487.
[29] *C.J.* xix, 743.
[30] Nichols, *Leics.* ii, 487.
[31] L.R.O. Q. Sess. Rec. Bridge Contracts.
[32] L.R.O. Beaumont Smith's Reg. of Bridges.
[33] A tributary of the Welland.
[34] J. Prior, *Map of Leics.* (1779).
[35] L.R.O. Beaumont Smith's Reg. of Bridges.
[36] Nichols, *Leics.* ii, 463, pl. lxxx, where the bridge is depicted.
[37] L.R.O. Q. Sess. Rec. Bridge Contracts.

Name of Bridge	*Road*	
Stanford Bridge	Swinford to Yelvertoft	About 1800 there were two bridges over the Avon at Stanford, but neither appears to have carried the public road.[38] The present bridge, built in 1844 by Leicestershire and Northamptonshire,[39] was probably the first to carry the public road.
Dove Bridge	Watling Street	Said to have existed in 1329,[40] and is mentioned about 1600.[41] In the 17th and 18th centuries it was maintained jointly by Warwickshire, Leicestershire, and Northamptonshire.[42] About 1875 the bridge consisted of 6 arches, lying mostly in Northamptonshire.[43] This bridge still exists, but it has been superseded by a modern concrete bridge, wholly in Warwickshire.
		OVER THE RIVER SWIFT[44]
Lutterworth Bridge	Lutterworth to Harborough	Marked on a map of 1576.[45] Rebuilt by public subscription in 1778.[46]
Bensford Bridge[47]	Watling Street	Marked on a map of 1576.[48] In the 16th century the bridge collapsed, but was repaired.[49] In 1648–9 the bridge was again in decay, and was repaired shortly afterwards by Warwickshire and Leicestershire.[50] In 1808, however, the Leicestershire authorities decided that the bridge was not a county one, but should be maintained by the parishes of Lutterworth and Cotesbach.[51] Since 1934 the bridge has been wholly in Warwickshire.[52]
		OVER THE RIVER ANKER[53]
Witherley Bridge	Watling Street	Mentioned in 1666, when it was partly repaired by Warwickshire.[54] In the 18th century it was jointly maintained by Warwickshire and Leicestershire.[55] Rebuilt in 1920, but has been wholly in Warwickshire since 1934.[56]
Fieldon Bridge	Coventry to Derby	A pontage for repair of the bridge was granted to the abbot of Merevale in 1332.[57] From 1625 it was being partly maintained by Warwickshire,[58] with Leicestershire presumably meeting the rest of the cost. In 1786 it was rebuilt by the two counties.[59]
		OVER THE RIVER SENCE[60]
Ratcliffe Culey Bridge		Date of building unknown, but rebuilt in 1811 by the county, with 3 brick arches.[61]
Harris Bridge	Sibson to Twycross	From 1693 onwards the county helped to maintain the bridge.[62] Rebuilt by the county in 1809,[63] and again in 1939.

38 Nichols, *Leics.* iv, 350.
39 L.R.O. Beaumont Smith's Reg. of Bridges.
40 Nichols, *Leics.* iv, 74, 81.
41 W. Camden, *Brit.* (ed. R. Gough, 1806), ii, 297.
42 *Warws. County Rec.* ed. S. C. Ratcliff and H. S. Johnson, ii, 63–64; iii, 139, 189; vi, 30, 37; L.R.O. Q. Sess. Order Bks. *passim.*
43 L.R.O. Beaumont Smith's Reg. of Bridges.
44 A tributary of the Warws. Avon.
45 C. Saxton, *Map of Warws. and Leics.* (1576).
46 A. H. Dyson, *Lutterworth,* 100.
47 Or Bransford Bridge.
48 C. Saxton, *Map of Warws. and Leics.* (1576).
49 Camden, *Brit.* (1806), ii, 297.
50 *Warws. County Rec.* ii, 198, 225; iii, 43.
51 L.R.O. Q. Sess. Order Bk. 1802–9, under 1808.
52 L.R.O. Beaumont Smith's Reg. of Bridges.
53 A tributary of the Tame.
54 *Warws. County Rec.* v, 38; on subsequent repairs by Warws. see ibid. vii, 72, 237.
55 L.R.O. Q. Sess. Order Bks. *passim.*
56 L.R.O. Beaumont Smith's Reg. of Bridges.
57 *Cal. Pat.* 1330–4, 259.
58 *Warws. County Rec.* ii, 11; iii, 330–1; v, 61; vi, 60; vii, 237.
59 L.R.O. Q. Sess. Order Bk. 1782–9, under 1786.
60 A tributary of the Anker.
61 L.R.O. Q. Sess. Rec. Bridge Contracts.
62 L.R.O. Q. Sess. Order Bks. *passim.*
63 L.R.O. Q. Sess. Rec. Bridge Contracts.

APPENDIX II

A SCHEDULE OF TURNPIKE ROADS IN LEICESTERSHIRE[64]

(Some of those running on the fringes of the county are omitted)

Name of Road	Length in miles	Date of 1st Act	Tolls in 1836 £	Debt in 1836 £	Modern title
1. Loughborough to Leicester	12	1726	2,958	7,000	A6
2. Nottingham to Cotes Bridge[65]	14	1737	...	...	...
3. Melton to Leicester	16	1764	1,246	1,800	A607
4. Uppingham to Leicester	15	1754	1,284	5,027	A47
5. Harborough to Leicester	15	1726	3,862	7,044	A6
6. Welford to Leicester	16	1765	1,380	6,836	A50
7. Lutterworth to Leicester	16	1764	745	1,770	A426
8. Fosse Way (South Section, from Narborough)	12	1814	266	5,203[66]	A46
9. Hinckley to Leicester (including Narborough to Leicester Road)	17	1754	1,484	4,470	A47
10. Ashby de la Zouch to Leicester	17	1753	1,087	3,975	A50
11. Lutterworth to Hinckley	13	1761	776	3,146[67]	B577–8
12. Desford Coal Road	15	1788	251	2,660	B582
13. Wanlip Road	2	1771	50	1,066[68]	...
	...	...	15,389	49,997	...

[64] This schedule is based on figures obtained from the rec. of the turnpike trusts: L.R.O. 15–D34/1–24; and from *Rep. Sel. Cttee. Turnpike Trusts*, H.C. 547 (1836), xix.

[65] Figures for tolls and debt have been omitted, as this road was mainly in Notts.

[66] These are the Burbage to Narborough figures.

[67] Collected tolls from coaches to the north-west.

[68] No interest ever paid.

CANALS

BEFORE the middle of the 18th century, in an age when water-carriage played a very large—almost a dominant—part in the means of transport, the situation of Leicestershire, much of which bestrides the central watershed of England, was an appreciable handicap to its economic development. 'Had it a navigable river', wrote Burton of the town of Leicester in 1622, 'whereby it might have trading and commerce, it might compare with many of no mean rank.'[1] The trading and commerce did indeed grow with the coming of the hosiery industry, but the handicap remained. By 1750 the whole of eastern England between the Humber and the Thames was well served with waterways which were navigable or had been made so, and the western midlands were similarly provided for by the Severn and Mersey and their affluents. But in the centre of the country there was a large area which had no navigable waterways at all, and of this area Leicestershire formed a considerable part.

The first attempt to improve the Soar was made only a dozen years after Burton wrote. In 1634 Thomas Skipwith secured a grant of letters patent empowering him to make the river navigable from its junction with the Trent up to Leicester.[2] Several of the features characteristic of later attempts can already be seen in this. In particular, the transport of coal, which was afterwards to be 'a dominant factor in the canal movement',[3] was advanced as the principal argument in favour of the scheme. The work was carried out for 5 or 6 miles from the Trent, but afterwards abandoned for lack of money, and the river gradually relapsed into its former state.[4] A hundred years later, in 1737, the project was revived. By this time legislation had replaced letters patent from the Crown as the normal means by which river improvements were authorized. A petition was therefore presented to the House of Commons for leave to bring in a bill for a 'navigation', but the landowners who considered their interests threatened were able to secure its rejection.[5] After the lapse of another 40 years, a limited success was obtained, and the river made navigable as far up as Loughborough. First, by an Act of 1766, the 'navigation' was to extend to the point where the Hermitage Brook entered the Soar, and cuts were to be made thence to the Rushes and the Hermitage Pool at Loughborough. But it was found impracticable to carry the provisions of this Act into effect because of frequent floods, and a company was then incorporated which secured a second Act in 1776. By authority of this the Soar was improved and made navigable to Bishop's Meadow, whence a canal 1½ miles long was constructed through Knight Thorpe and Thorpe Acre to the Rushes, the whole being completed in 1778.[6]

[1] W. Burton, *Description of Leics.* 146.
[2] V. A. Forbes and W. H. R. Ashford, *Our Waterways*, 71.
[3] J. H. Clapham, *Econ. Hist. Mod. Brit.* i, 78.
[4] T. S. Willan, *River Navigation in Engl. 1600–1750*, 26.
[5] Ibid.
[6] J. Priestley, *Hist. Acc. of Navigable Rivers, Canals and Rlwys. throughout Gt. Brit.* (1831), 611–13; *Leic. and Nott. Jnl.* 17 Feb. 1776, 25 Jan. 1777, 22 Aug. 1778.

The Soar Navigation, however, represented only one-half of its projectors' intentions. The same combination of Derbyshire coal-owners and Loughborough business and professional men which had financed it also built the Erewash Canal a year later, from the collieries in that valley to the Trent opposite the infall of the Soar. Thus a continuous water-communication was created from these collieries to Loughborough, and the town's trade and prosperity were greatly increased in consequence. Cheaper and more abundant supplies of coal, the desire for which had been the chief stimulus of the whole undertaking, were now available. The Soar Navigation Co., like most of its kind, did not act as a carrier; but even the sum total of the charges of company, carriers, and wharfingers amounted to appreciably less than the previous cost of land-carriage, so that coal could now be sold in Loughborough at from 60 to 70 per cent. of its former price.[7] There was a corresponding increase in the availability and cheapness of other commodities, and since the leading carriers and traders, such as Cradock, Ella & Co., were also shareholders in the Soar Navigation, they prospered doubly. A barge-building industry appeared, 'large and extensive' wharves were constructed, and new houses and warehouses erected. The tolls taken at the Navigation Wharf were said to amount to £120 a month, and the company's shares stood at 30 above par.[8]

The Soar Navigation had now produced a state of affairs which led, not only to further river improvements of the same kind, but also by a natural and logical sequence to the first completely artificial waterways, or true canals, in Leicestershire. Rarely perhaps is the gradual character of the transition from the older 'navigation', or improved river, to the canal more clearly to be seen than here. In the first place the Soar Navigation resulted in a demand that the work should be continued up to Leicester. This in turn led to the corollary that the Wreak should also be made navigable up to Melton Mowbray. Out of the protracted struggle to achieve the Leicester and Wreak Navigations came the Charnwood Forest and, less directly, the Ashby de la Zouch Canals. And finally the Union, and so the Grand Union, Canals were the natural sequel to the Leicester Navigation, as the Oakham Canal was to the Wreak Navigation; thus completing the network of waterways by which all parts of the county were reached and quickened into commercial activity.

The central theme of all these developments was the long-contested Leicester Navigation; and again the primary stimulus, together with the spectacle of Loughborough's prosperity, was the desire for more and cheaper coal. Before the Soar Navigation had been made the Coleorton and other west Leicestershire mines had held the monopoly of supplying not only Leicester itself but all the south and east of the county, though the roads in the neighbourhood of the coalfield were so bad that as far as Leicester the coal had to be carried mainly on the backs of horses and mules.[9] Already, however, the navigation had enabled the Derbyshire mine-owners to enter into competition, even though from Loughborough onwards their coal had also still to be brought by road. In consequence, the west Leicestershire men had been compelled to lower their prices.[10] If the Soar Navigation were completed by a Leicester Navigation and a Wreak Navigation as well, argued the townsfolk of Leicester and Melton

[7] Ibid. 25 Jan. and 31 May 1777; 30 Jan., 1 Feb., 12 June, and 18 Dec. 1779.

[8] Ibid. 2 Jan. and 18 Dec. 1779, 22 Apr. 1780.

[9] *Leic. Jnl.* 6 Nov. 1789.

[10] *Leic. and Nott. Jnl.* 22 Apr. 1780.

Mowbray, the cost of coal would be still further reduced. In addition many other commodities could then be obtained more conveniently and cheaply. For Leicester, these would include not only the produce of the north of England but a large variety of heavy goods from London and dye-wares for the hosiery industry. This trade between Leicester and London, in view of the bad state of the roads throughout the country, was in those days conducted slowly and circuitously by sea and river. Coasting brigs brought merchandise from the capital to Gainsborough, where it was transferred to 'Trent boats' for carriage upstream, the final stage of the journey overland to Leicester being performed by wagon. As late as 1780 the grocers of Leicester were obliged to lay in a 6 months' stock in October, to ensure a supply against the chances of adverse winds, storms at sea, and floods or frosts on the Trent, all of which were incidental to this roundabout route.[11] But the making of the Soar Navigation had at least meant that the Trent boats could now come to Loughborough instead of unloading at Shardlow. Since water-carriage was so much cheaper than road-transport, this was, or rather, ought to have been, a marked advantage, which an extension to Leicester would increase.

The position was complicated in the 1780's, however, by another factor. The construction of the Soar Navigation had given Loughborough a 'waterhead' position on this route, of which it was not slow to take advantage. A number of traders of that town who were also shareholders in the navigation used their dual position to create for a few years something like a monopoly for themselves. As virtual controllers of the lower reaches of the Soar, they were able to delay the forwarding of goods consigned to Leicester merchants and shopkeepers as long as they had anything of the same kind left unsold in their own warehouses; and for these articles they charged prices at Leicester calculated to be just, but only just, below what their customers would have to pay if driven to resort to land-carriage from London. In the middle 1780's, as a matter of fact, these would-be monopolists partly overreached themselves, by pitching their prices so high that a considerable quantity of goods did after all come to Leicester from the metropolis by road. Nevertheless the situation which had been created largely prevented the Leicester merchants from reaping the benefit of the cheaper carriage between Shardlow and Loughborough, and intensified their desire for an extension of the Soar Navigation to Leicester. At the same time it gave the 'Loughborough ring' a motive for fighting tooth and nail to preserve the *status quo* which was so profitable for themselves.[12]

The project of a navigation to Leicester was first mooted in 1779, and in 1780 the engineer William Jessop was commissioned by 'a number of considerable persons' of that town to make a survey.[13] Nothing further was done for some years, probably because the supporters of the plan, who do not seem to have included any influential landowners, boggled at the prospect of an expensive contest with a powerful opposition. The real battle, therefore, did not begin until 1785. It was a typical example of the prolonged struggles between conflicting interests which in that period usually accompanied any application to Parliament for leave to bring in a canal Bill. In these contests promoters and their opponents would each hold meetings and issue statements and counter-

[11] Anon. *Hist. Leics.* (1834) in Leic. Ref. Libr. Pamphlets, i.
[12] *Leic. and Nott. Jnl.* 8 Apr. 1786.
[13] Ibid. 30 Jan. and 13 Feb. 1779, 20 and 27 May, and 17 June 1780.

statements of the advantages and disadvantages of the proposal which was in debate. Both would seek to influence the public opinion of their neighbourhood, aiming first to win the support of the majority, or at least of the most influential, of the great landowners, and then applying to the rest the traditional weapons of local politics—influence, coercion, and misrepresentation. Petitions for and against the Bill would be collected, and evidence marshalled before parliamentary committees. Even if the promoters were eventually successful, the expenses incurred in these preliminaries would form a large item in the total cost of the enterprise.

The Leicester merchants and bankers who had originally sponsored the project of a navigation to their town, being now well aware of the difficulties which would confront them, had taken the precaution of securing the benevolent and public-spirited Earl of Harborough as their patron and champion.[14] They then opened a campaign of industrious propaganda for their proposal in the *Leicester and Nottingham Journal.* The prospect was painted of an ever-increasing trade with Liverpool and the 'Western Seas' through the recently constructed Trent and Mersey Canal, and with Scandinavia, Russia, and the 'Eastern Seas' by way of Gainsborough and Hull. From near at hand, not only coal but also lead from the mines of Derbyshire, building timber, bark for tanners, and salt, coming from Cheshire by the Trent and Mersey Canal to Shardlow, would all be available more cheaply. Of the produce of more distant lands, iron, deal, wine, logwood, and other dye-stuffs, with much else, could be brought by way of the Soar into the centre of England. In return Leicestershire could export grain, malt, flour, cheese, Swithland slates, and Barrow lime, and great quantities of wool for the Yorkshire trade would be sent to Leeds, Wakefield, and Halifax.[15] Since Lord Harborough's estate at Stapleford Park gave him a close interest in the fortunes of Melton and the Wreak valley, a corollary proposal to make the Wreak navigable was also raised. Hard on the heels of this came a plan for carrying the proposed line of water-communication farther eastward by a canal from Melton to Oakham, and Lord Harborough joined a group of Rutland landowners in engaging Jessop to make a survey and find out whether this was practicable.[16]

In spite of propaganda and optimistic expectations, a formidable opposition had developed. The chief components of this were the west Leicestershire coal-owners and proprietors of lime-works (lime being then in growing demand as a fertilizer, in view of the progress of new and more modern methods of farming), the possessors of estates and mills on the banks of the two rivers, and the Soar Navigation Co. This last, of course, was concerned to preserve the advantages which Loughborough enjoyed under the existing circumstances. The owners of riparian lands believed that river improvement would mean the raising of the level of the water, with the result that the richest parts of their estates—the meadows which lay along the river-banks—would be rendered boggy and useless by flooding. They also feared that the constant passage of bargemen would destroy their peace and expose their gardens, hen-roosts, sheep, rabbits, and woods to perpetual plunder. As for the coal-owners of west Leicestershire, they protested loudly that their pits would be compelled to close and that their Derbyshire rivals, left in sole possession of the market, would promptly raise the

[14] *Leic. and Nott. Jnl.* 28 May and 5 Nov. 1785.
[15] Ibid. 17 and 24 Sept. 1785.
[16] Ibid. 29 Oct. and 5 Nov. 1785.

price of coal again. The ablest and most redoubtable opponent of the undertaking was Lord Rawdon (afterwards, as Marquess of Hastings, governor-general of India), who as son and heir of the Earl of Moira had a family interest both in the collieries of the west of the county and in its general prosperity. Earl Ferrers and the earls of Huntingdon and Stamford, who all owned mines or lime-works in west Leicestershire, Sir John Danvers of Swithland and many other landowners also aligned themselves with the opposition.[17]

Out of this situation arose a proposal for a compromise. In the hope of winning over the most dangerous section of their opponents, the coal-owners, the promoters of the Leicester Navigation scheme revived an idea which had been mooted in 1780, and offered to enlarge their plan to include the linking of Loughborough by canal and railway to the Coleorton pits. These would then be able to continue sharing the local market with the Derbyshire collieries. The mine-owners of the Coleorton district accepted this proposition after some haggling, and a plan for a 'Charnwood Forest Canal' was incorporated into the original draft.[18] Such a canal was of no value to the Moira and Oakthorpe mines, which lay well to the west of Coleorton. Lord Rawdon therefore persisted in his opposition, and in 1786 the bill for a Leicester Navigation was defeated at its second reading in the Commons. The Wreak Navigation Bill and the project of a Melton–Oakham canal, which had meanwhile been expanded into a plan for a waterway through Oakham to Stamford, were thereupon dropped.[19]

After a relative lull of two years the 'Leicester Interest' brought forward another Bill in the winter of 1788–9. This time Joseph Cradock, the cultured and philanthropic squire of Gumley, took a leading part in the attempt; and Charles Rozzell, a gifted, genial, but dissipated local poet, wrote topical verses on the beauties and blessings of navigations. Again the parliamentary opposition proved too strong, and an amendment putting the Bill off until the next session was carried.[20] By that time the end of the long struggle was at hand, however, thanks to the conversion of Rawdon, who in turn persuaded the other hostile landowners to withdraw their opposition. The proprietors of the Soar Navigation were won over by the Leicester Navigation Co.'s undertaking to make good any deficit by which their gross annual income might ever fall below £3,000. An equally potent argument may have been the reflection that the increased volume of trade, which would in future pay them tolls for passing through their part of the river, would more than compensate for any loss of present advantage. Bills for the Leicester and Charnwood Forest navigations, as well as for a Wreak and Eye Navigation which would form a branch to Melton, therefore passed smoothly through Parliament in 1791.[21] The plans for the Forest Canal differed somewhat from those of 1785–6. Starting near Thringstone Bridge, as previously suggested, it was to pass Shepshed and Garendon Park on the south instead of on the north, and not to be carried through to the Leicester Navigation, since the fall of the ground near Loughborough would call for locks and it was thought that the region would not furnish enough water to supply them. Instead, it was to end at Loughborough Lane, whence there was to be a railway[22]

[17] *Leic. and Nott. Jnl.* 10 and 24 Sept. and 15 and 29 Oct. 1785, 8 Apr. and 13 May 1786.

[18] Ibid. 27 May 1780, 24 Sept., and 26 Nov. 1785, 7 Jan. 1786.

[19] Ibid. 24 Sept., 26 Nov., and 24 Dec. 1785, 7 Jan. to 13 May 1786.

[20] *Leic. Jnl.* 25 Oct. 1788, 13 Feb., 6, 13, and 20 Mar., and 22 May 1789.

[21] Ibid. 2 Apr., 2, 16, and 30 July and 6 Aug. 1790, 20 and 27 May 1791.

[22] It is interesting to notice that the term used in the earliest suggestion of this plan was 'a Newcastle

for horse-drawn wagons to Loughborough Basin. At the other end, besides railways from the Coleorton and Swannington pits, there were to be others from the lime-works at Breedon and Grace Dieu, as well as a short branch or cut from the canal to Osgathorpe. Great expectations were formed on the strength of these arrangements. New mines were opened at Coleorton; and at Leicester the banks of the Soar 'already wore the appearance of improving commerce'. Wharves and factories were being built, and land or houses on or near the line of the intended navigation rose sharply in price. An anonymous local poet exhorted his fellow townsmen:

'Let Leicester's sons no more in party rage
Prosperity's fair dawning bounties lose.
Let friendly Commerce all her train unite;
While bounteous plenty leads her gen'rous bark
E'en to our favoured streets, let strife depart.'[23]

In fact, the whole of Leicestershire and the neighbouring counties, in common with most of the rest of the country, were seized in 1791–3 by the 'Canal Mania'. The revival of the Oakham Canal scheme followed naturally on the success of the Wreak and Eye Navigation. The Earl of Harborough again took a leading part, and in 1793 an Act was obtained for a canal to link this latter navigation with Oakham.[24] The plan for an extension to Stamford, however, was now abandoned (though it was apparently considered again in 1815 and 1828), and difficulties encountered during construction delayed the completion of the Oakham Canal until 1802. These difficulties included shortages of money and water, and the wish of some of the shareholders to suspend work until after the end of the war with France.[25] The Wreak Navigation also ran into obstacles and was not completed until the company, having overspent its authorized capital, had secured leave by a supplementary Act of 1800 to raise a further sum by subscription or mortgage.[26] Another project formed in 1791 which affected the interests of a part of Leicestershire was the proposal for a canal from Grantham to the Trent. In view of the scarcity and dearness of fuel in the north-east of the county, and especially in the Vale of Belvoir, these districts would benefit greatly from such an undertaking. But a vigorous opposition to the scheme came from Lincoln, where it was feared that water would be taken from the Witham or from streams flowing into it. Though clauses were inserted in the Grantham Canal Bill guaranteeing that nothing of the sort would occur, the hostility continued and the Bill failed twice. The promoters then obtained the support of the Duke of Beaufort, who was Lord Lieutenant of Leicestershire during the youth of his nephew the Duke of Rutland, and made some alterations in the proposed line of the canal, with the result that it gained parliamentary sanction in 1793.[27]

More important, potentially at least, than either the Oakham or Grantham canals was the project broached at Market Harborough early in 1792 to link that town with the Leicester Navigation by a canal. The prime movers in this enterprise, apart from one or two country gentlemen such as J. P. Hungerford,

road'. The best-known examples of such early railways were those linking the collieries near Newcastle upon Tyne with the river or the sea.

23 T. R. Potter, *Charnwood Forest*, 27–28; *Leic. Jnl.* 1 July and 28 Oct. 1791, 19 May and 23 June 1792.

24 Ibid. 27 Apr. 1792 and 11 May 1793; *Leic. Herald*, 10 Nov. 1792; Oakham Canal Act, 39 & 40 Geo. III, c. 56 (Local and Personal Acts).

25 *Leic. Herald*, 29 Mar. 1794; *Leic. Jnl.* 24 May 1799 and 11 June 1802.

26 Melton Navigation Act, 39 & 40 Geo. III, c. 55 (Local and Personal Acts).

27 *Leic. Herald*, 12 May and 18 Aug. 1792, 20 Apr. 1793, 29 Mar. 1794; *Leic. Jnl.* 26 Aug. and 28 Oct. 1791, 27 Apr. 1792, 24 May 1799, 11 June 1802.

were a strong body of leading citizens and merchants of Leicester. The presence among them of prominent 'Corporation men' such as Alderman Burbidge, together with notable members of the town 'opposition', suggests that in this matter at least Leicester's sons were taking their poet's recent advice to sink party strife in the pursuit of prosperity. The necessary aristocratic support and parliamentary influence, however, were provided by Beaufort, Earl Ferrers, Lord Rawdon, and several other landowners.[28] A further extension of the proposed 'Harborough Canal' to Northampton was soon afterwards arranged with representatives of that town and neighbourhood, who looked forward to the prospect of sending their grain and timber north, and receiving in exchange coal from Derbyshire, Nottinghamshire, and Leicestershire.[29]

The whole character of the undertaking soon changed. It had begun as a proposal to carry into the south of the county the network of inland waterways which was already being extended over the north, centre, and east. But it acquired a new and greater importance when it became known that a group of the leading canal projectors of the day was considering a plan for a waterway, later to be called the Grand Junction, from the Thames at Brentford to the Oxford Canal at Braunston (Northants.).[30] This would link the midlands to London by a much more direct and convenient route than the previous one along the whole length of the Oxford Canal and then down the Thames. Moreover it would mean a correspondingly more efficient connexion between Trent, Mersey, and Thames. Since the spring of 1791 these rivers had been linked by the completion of the Coventry Canal, which at its southern end branched from the Oxford Canal, so that it met the Trent and Mersey Canal on the north. The Grand Junction would improve this connexion to the same extent as it shortened that between the industrial midlands and London. The main line of communication would still pass to the west of Leicestershire, which would merely lie on a branch of the developing system, by way of the River Trent and the Soar and Leicester Navigations. But if the canal already planned to Harborough and Northampton were carried on to meet the Grand Junction, the trade between London on the one hand and the east midlands and the regions north of the Thames on the other would pass along this line and so through the heart of Leicestershire. Leicester, as the *Journal* exultantly foresaw, would become 'the centre of extensive navigable lines' and would have direct water-communication with the capital. With this prospect before them, the shareholders of the Harborough Canal Co. eagerly voted for the extension to the Grand Junction.

The proposed undertaking was now renamed the 'Leicestershire and Northamptonshire Union Canal', Jessop was appointed engineer, and the *Journal* waxed almost lyrical about 'the magnificence and utility of the design'. 'The Grand Junction Canal', it wrote, 'was offered to the public as a means of connecting the whole inland trade in manufactured and raw materials with London. . . .' But the object of the Grand Junction, continued the newspaper, would be incomplete without the Union Canal. Since the Oxford and Coventry canals, like several others among the first to be built, had been constructed with narrow locks to save expense, the subsequent volume of traffic not having been fully foreseen, vessels coming along the Grand Junction Canal from London

[28] *Leic. Jnl.* 9 Feb. 1792; *Leic. Herald*, 30 June 1792.

[29] Ibid. 2, 16, and 30 June 1792.

[30] *Leic. Jnl.* 3 Aug. 1792.

would have had to tranship their cargoes at Braunston into boats suitable for the narrow dimensions of these older waterways. 'They would then', proceeded the *Journal*, 'be carried pretty directly to Birmingham, Coventry, and Staffordshire, but the passage would be too circuitous for business in the counties to the east and north of the Trent.' Now, however, 'the Union Canal gives opportunities for the most direct trade between them and London. It is . . . to be executed on the same grand scale of dimension' as the Grand Junction. 'The whole may be justly considered as the line uniting Trent, Nene, and Thames—expediting goods from the interior counties to the ports of London, Lynn,[31] Hull, Liverpool and Bristol', and in return dispersing imports through the middle of England. Derbyshire coal would be exchanged for Northamptonshire corn, and Leicester would 'receive upon its quays the vessels from Thames and Trent . . . an inexhaustible source of commercial wealth'.[32]

Only the south-east and south-west of Leicestershire remained to be provided, on paper at least, with navigable waterways. Both gaps were filled, as far as exuberant planning could do it, before the end of 1792. A meeting at Uppingham led to a decision to promote a Bill for a canal to join the Union Canal at Smeeton Westerby.[33] At the same time a long-meditated notion of linking the mines near Ashby de la Zouch with the main line of water-communication between the midlands and the Thames also took definite shape. As early as 1782, while the Oxford and Coventry canals were still being built, notice had been given of an intended Bill for a canal from Ashby Woulds by way of Market Bosworth and Hinckley to join the Coventry Canal at Griff. In view of the probable cost and the opposition expected from the majority of the landowners on the proposed line this scheme had been dropped.[34] It was now resurrected and amplified by proposals for branches from the main canal to the lime-works at Ticknall, Staunton Harold, and Cloud Hill.[35] But although the Uppingham projectors prevailed on the Union Canal Co. to include a clause in their Bill permitting an extension to be made to Uppingham at any future time,[36] it was never built; and the history of the Ashby Canal was to be chequered.

The would-be investors of Leicester did not confine their outlook to their own neighbourhood, but ranged far afield in hopes of securing shares in promising canal enterprises elsewhere, descending upon Wisbech (Cambs.), Ellesmere (Salop), Newport (Salop), Sheffield, and anywhere else where there seemed to be a good prospect. In addition to those who genuinely wished to invest their money, there were others who hoped to make their fortunes by quicker and more dubious methods. The excitement and credulity engendered by the Canal Mania gave scope for much sharp practice. Engrossing and forestalling of canal shares became common. This was facilitated by the fact that a subscriber need at first pay only a fraction of the price of the shares for which he set down his name, as deposit, the remainder being required of him by successive 'calls' as the undertaking proceeded. A speculator or 'mushroom subscriber' starting with a few pounds could therefore make large sums by buying shares, selling them again at a profit, and repeating the process on a progressively greater scale.[37] To

31 i.e. by way of the R. Nene Navigation, with which the Union Canal was to be connected at or near Northampton.

32 *Leic. Jnl.* 14 Sept. 1792.

33 *Leic. Herald*, 22 Sept. and 3 Nov. 1792.

34 *Leic. and Nott. Jnl.* 26 Jan. and 7 Sept. 1781, 14 Sept. and 12 Oct. 1782.

35 *Leic. Jnl.* 14 Sept. 1792.

36 *Leic. Herald*, 5 and 26 Jan. 1793.

37 Ibid. 20 Oct. and 1 Dec. 1792.

avoid the presence of these gentry, the genuine promoters of canal schemes took to holding their subscription meetings as unobtrusively as possible. As a result of this again, both the 'mushroom men' and the undiscriminating enthusiasts who were panting to get shares in any canal undertaking, irrespective of its merits, were prone to suspect any gathering of being a subscription meeting in disguise. There were episodes which anticipated in miniature the gold-rushes of a later age. On one occasion a rumour that the Ashby Canal subscription was being quietly opened led to a stampede from Leicester in which 'everything in the town that had four legs and could amble' was pressed into service. Shortly afterwards at least seventy of the townsfolk travelled post-haste to an assembly of gentry and farmers at Six Hills, only to discover that it was a hunt dinner. Again, a meeting at Wellingborough of merchants and bargemen connected with the Nene Navigation drew a hundred or so interlopers from Leicestershire. Even when they had been convinced, with some difficulty, that it had merely been called to arrange for repairs to that navigation, the more enterprising of the visitors tried hard to persuade the natives to take the opportunity of opening a subscription for a canal to somewhere.[38]

The shock to commerce and credit consequent upon the outbreak of war with France in 1793 served to curb the wildest extravagances of the Canal Mania. Meanwhile the construction of the Leicester Navigation was meeting with increasing difficulties. The launching of the Union Canal project meant that the Leicester Navigation would at many points have to be made wider and deeper than had originally been intended, since it was now to be not merely a waterway to Leicester, Melton, and Rutland, but a main artery of trade.[39] Contractors proved wasteful and unsatisfactory, and the company itself had to take over the work of construction. Costs of materials rose, while shareholders fell into arrears with the instalments of their subscriptions, and money began to run short.[40] Even after communication between Loughborough and Leicester had been opened on 21 February 1794, some months passed before coal, the chief *raison d'être* of the whole undertaking, could be transported by it, since the Charnwood Forest Canal and its attendant railways were not yet finished and the Leicestershire coal-owners refused to release the company from its original promise that no Derbyshire coal would be conveyed along the navigation until they were in a position to compete.[41]

By October, though much remained to be done on the 'Forest Line', it had been made possible for a boat-load of Coleorton coal to reach Loughborough, and the whole navigation was formally declared open for the transport of coal.[42] But this single boat-load was an isolated achievement, and not the beginning of a continuous traffic from the Leicestershire pits. The reservoir which was to feed the Forest Canal still remained to be built, and the tolls charged on the 'River Line' between Loughborough and Leicester, having been fixed too low, were not sufficient by themselves to provide the company with an adequate revenue. Debts were piling up, which was probably the main reason why the company could not succeed in coming to terms with any contractor for the building of the reservoir, and had to undertake that also itself.[43] Hence it is

[38] *Leic. Herald*, 24 Nov. 1792; *Leic. Jnl.* 28 Sept. 1792.

[39] *Leic. Jnl.* 10 Jan. 1794.

[40] Leic. City Mun. Room, Leic. Navigation Co.'s Minute Bk. 1791–1800, 28–29, 35–36, 43–44, 47, 69, 74, 81, 90, 96, 134.

[41] Ibid. 101, 107, 115.

[42] Ibid. 167; *Leic. Jnl.* 31 Oct. 1794.

[43] Leic. City Mun. Room, Leic. Navigation Co.'s Statements of Acct. 1795–1818, 5 Jan. 1795; Minute Bk. 1791–1800, 178–81 and 210.

difficult to avoid the suspicion that the subsequent disaster was due at least partly to building on the cheap.

By June 1796 the reservoir was finished, but the whole Forest Line now threatened to become a white elephant. Originally, it seems to have been thought that trucks of coal from Swannington or Coleorton could be shipped bodily on to barges at Thringstone Bridge, transferred again to the railway at Loughborough Lane, and shipped once more at Loughborough Basin. But this now proved impossible, and the cost of three transhipments of their coal between trucks and barges *en route* meant that the Leicestershire pits were still unable to compete with the Derbyshire coal which was now selling in Leicester at 7*d.* and 8*d.* a hundredweight instead of its former price of 1*s.* The line, in consequence, remained practically unused.[44]

The company, however, began to emerge from its difficulties when in 1797 it secured a second Act of Parliament giving it power to increase its tolls and borrow more money on their security. The increase in its receipts, although these came almost entirely from the 'River Line' alone, was immediate and substantial, enabling it to set about bringing its finances into better order and to declare its first dividend, of 3 per cent., at the beginning of 1798.[45] It was even able to survive another serious blow, when the spring thaws and floods of 1799, following upon exceptionally severe frosts, burst the new reservoir at Blackbrook and did much damage to the Forest Canal. By suspending the payment of dividends, the company was able within less than 2 years to rebuild the reservoir, repair the other damage, and compensate the country-folk who had suffered loss.[46] For the Leicestershire coal-owners, however, this disaster was the last straw, since they had made little or no profit for some time previously. Disregarding the company's assurances that the Forest Line would soon be open again, and giving up any scanty hopes of competing with Derbyshire to which they might hitherto have clung, they closed down their pits.[47] Derbyshire coal retained the monopoly of the Leicester market until the coming of the railways, while the company was left with the restored reservoir and the Forest Canal on its hands. In 1804 the new reservoir was 'taken down in such manner as to preclude all apprehension of danger from floods injuring the adjacent lands'.[48] The canal remained 'an unsightly ditch' when Potter wrote his history of Charnwood Forest a generation or so later;[49] but the passage of time and the progress of cultivation have softened and broken down its lines, until now only fragments and vestiges of it remain.

Despite the failure of its Charnwood Forest enterprise the Leicester Navigation Co. now entered upon a long period of mild but steady prosperity, thanks to the traffic which flowed along its main 'River Line'. In the first 18 years of the new century its dividends rose slowly from 3 to 6 per cent., and then to 8 and 9 per cent. by 1830.[50]

The Union Canal project also encountered many difficulties, from which

[44] Minute Bk. 1791–1800, 234, 248, 251, and 256.

[45] Ibid. 281–90, 295–6, 306, 340–2, 361–2; Statements of Acct. 1795–1818, 2 July 1797, 1 Jan. and 2 July 1798, and 7 Jan. 1799.

[46] Statements of Acct. 1795–1818, 1 July 1799, 6 Jan. and 7 July 1800 and 5 Jan. 1801; Minute Bk. 1791–1800, 384–5, 391–2, 404–5, 410–11.

[47] *Leic. Jnl.* 4 Nov. 1796, 21 July and 29 Sept. 1797, 7 Dec. 1798, 22 Feb., 15 Mar., 24 May, and 15 Nov. 1799.

[48] Leic. Navigation Co.'s Statements of Acct. 1795–1818, 7 Jan. 1805.

[49] Potter, *Charnwood Forest*, 27–28.

[50] Leic. Navigation Co.'s Statements of Acct. 1795–1818; Minute Bk. 1824–32.

it was even longer in emerging. When war broke out in 1793 many shareholders urged that construction should be suspended for a time, and had to be over-persuaded or outvoted. Persistent opposition from landowners to the proposed route compelled a change of plan and an expensive tunnel was built near Saddington which must have cut deeply into the company's capital. By 1797 the canal had advanced as far as Debdale Wharf near Gumley. There it came to a halt for many years, in face of the obstacle presented by the long ridge of high ground which runs from Great Bowden to near Husbands Bosworth, though a branch was built from Gumley to Market Harborough between 1805 and 1809. In part, no doubt, the stoppage was due to the necessity of waiting for the completion of the Grand Junction Canal, which was not finished until 1805. After 1802, however, the Grand Junction was virtually complete except for the Blisworth Tunnel, and a large and increasing proportion of Leicestershire's trade with the south could now be conducted by the direct route, though still partly by road. Pickford's barges from London conveyed goods, with a brief transhipment to a temporary railway at Blisworth, to and from Brownsover Wharf on the Oxford Canal near Rugby; from there services of wagons ran to Leicester and the smaller towns of the county. After the Ashby de la Zouch Canal had been opened in 1804 this road-haul became shorter, since water-communication from London now extended as near Leicester as Hinckley.[51]

The main reason for suspension of work on the Union Canal was financial. Canals built later than 1790, and especially those built after the outbreak of the French Wars, suffered from the increased cost of labour and materials. The original estimates were thrown badly out, especially as they had generally been framed in a spirit of excited optimism. The Leicester Navigation, undertaken only shortly after 1790, had encountered this problem and solved it with some difficulty. The Union Canal, whose construction had begun later and had dragged out into the new century, had to be saved by outside help. In 1808 the proprietors, the most prominent of whom was now Thomas Paget of the Leicester banking firm of Pares, Paget, Pares & Heygate, were obliged to admit openly that they lacked funds to complete the original enterprise, and offered to hand over their plans and any relevant information they possessed to any persons who would form a company to carry on in their stead. Fortunately the nature of the enterprise was such as to attract London capital to the rescue of the local capital upon which this, like most of the earlier canal projects, had had to depend. The demand of the metropolis for midland coal had been growing, especially since the French Wars had exposed its seaborne traffic in Tyne coal to attacks by French privateers. Certain directors of the Grand Junction Co. therefore combined with one or two Leicester men to form the Grand Union Canal Co. The Grand Union, linking the Union Canal near Gumley to the Grand Junction at Long Buckby (Northants.), was opened in 1814.[52] Thus, 21 years after the start of the enterprise, was completed 'the great line of canals which extended from the Thames to the Humber, bringing the trade of Yorkshire, Lincolnshire, Derbyshire, Nottinghamshire, and Leicestershire by inland navigation to London'.[53] How large coal bulked in this trade is seen by a calculation of 1820 that the Leicester Navigation carried annually 56,000 tons of coal to be consumed

[51] *Leic. Jnl.* 1 and 15 Feb. and 18 Apr. 1794, 30 Oct. 1795, 21 Apr. 1797, 26 Feb. and 2 Apr. 1802, 3 Aug. 1804, 29 Mar. 1805.

[52] Ibid. 3 and 17 June 1808, 5 and 19 Aug. 1814.

[53] Prospectus of Grand Union Canal Co. in *Leic. Jnl.* 24 June 1808.

in Leicester and the neighbourhood, 59,000 tons to be forwarded to other canals, and 11,500 tons of other merchandise.[54] In return, the heavy goods from London which the coasting brigs used to convey so painfully by sea could now be brought to Leicester by Pickford's fly-boats within a few days of their being ordered by post. The raw materials of the hosiery manufacture could be obtained, and the finished goods distributed, more speedily and cheaply; and what had formerly been the waste-products of the industry were now carried north to Yorkshire and disposed of at a profit.[55] The rapid growth of new branches of the hosiery trade in Leicester during the first decade of the 19th century and its relative prosperity during those years were probably due in no small degree to the fact that from 1802 onwards this development of communications had been largely completed.

The formation of the Grand Union Canal Co. in 1808, and the consequent probability that 'the great line of canals' would after all be carried through Leicestershire, had led to some revival of interest in other local canal enterprises which had been abandoned or remained unrealized. In particular the idea of a water-communication with Stamford, which had slumbered since the dropping of the proposal to extend the Oakham Canal thither, was raised again in a new form. The suggestion now made in 1809 was for a canal to that town from Harborough, along the south side of the Welland. By extending this eastward towards the sea, it was hoped that a direct line of communication could be established between the Union and Grand Union on the one hand and the ports of Wisbech, King's Lynn, Spalding, and Boston on the other. In the first flush of enthusiasm the shares of the projected Harborough, Stamford, Spalding, and Peterborough Canal were in great demand, and notice was duly given of intention to apply for an Act of Parliament. But the proposal met with even more than the usual amount of opposition from a particularly powerful body of landowners, as well as from the town of Northampton and the Nene River Commissioners, who petitioned against the project on the ground that as the intended canal would run parallel to the Nene Navigation and compete with it their interests would be seriously injured. In face of this formidable resistance the undertaking was abandoned. Much later, in 1828, the old plan of continuing the Oakham Canal to Stamford was resurrected for the last time, but on the threshold of the railway age it proved impossible to attract sufficient subscribers.[56]

Meanwhile the Ashby de la Zouch Canal, projected in 1792, had become the subject of the usual battle between rival groups of local magnates. Its principal supporters were the Earl of Stamford, Earl Ferrers, Lords Wentworth and Maynard, Francis Burdett of Foremark (Derbys.), Edward Dawson of Long Whatton, Thomas Pares the prosperous Leicester attorney who had become the owner of Hopwell Hall, and Thomas Paget of Scraptoft, father of the banker of the same name who afterwards figured prominently in the Union Canal Co. The opposition was headed by the Hon. Penn Assheton Curzon of Gopsall House, a Member of Parliament for Leicestershire who possessed considerable influence in the county and was chiefly concerned lest the canal should interfere with the irrigation of his estates, and in particular with one spring on which the water-supply of his house depended. The decisive factor, as with the Leicester Navigation 3 years previously, was the attitude of Lord Rawdon, now the Earl

[54] S. Watts, *Walk through Leic.* (1810), 13.
[55] W. Gardiner, *Music and Friends*, iii, 821.
[56] *Leic. Jnl.* 6 and 27 Oct. 1809, 2 Mar. and 7 Sept. 1810, 5 Feb. and 8 Mar. 1811, 1 Aug. 1828.

of Moira. Although he obviously stood to profit, through his collieries, by the success of the plan, and was apparently willing to allow the canal to pass through his land, Moira had promised not to support actively any scheme by which his neighbour Curzon might suffer injury. When Curzon had at last been convinced that his water-supply would be in no danger, Moira felt free to give the project his backing, and the Bill passed peaceably in 1794.[57]

This was only the beginning of the Ashby Canal's troubles. The projectors in their optimism had dreamt of a subsequent extension to the Trent near Burton and of a considerable through traffic, and had therefore built the canal as broad as the Grand Junction.[58] The unnecessarily large expense this involved was intensified by the war-time rise in the cost of labour and materials. When the Canal Mania began to wane soon after 1794, the company found it increasingly difficult to get the shareholders to respond to its successive calls; and as construction limped along their loss of interest was shown by the fact that practically every general meeting had to be postponed from the original date and re-announced in the local press because the attendance did not amount to a quorum. Even the introduction of a system of fining those who did not attend in person or by proxy 5*s.* for every share they held proved only a temporary cure for this apathy.[59] When at last the canal was opened in 1804, some local trade in coal and Ticknall lime developed with Bosworth and Hinckley, but the larger hopes of the projectors were unrealized.[60] Indeed, the criticism advanced when the canal was first suggested in 1782, that the coal-mines which it served could not expect in competition with those of Warwickshire and Staffordshire to find sufficient markets to make it a profitable concern, seems to have been well founded.[61] The £100 shares fell until they reached £10, where for some years they remained, and the company never paid a dividend until 1828, by which time the opening of new pits in west Leicestershire had created a more favourable situation by enlarging the coal supplies for which at the moment the canal served as chief carrier.[62] Even this brief advantage was snatched away 4 years later by the opening of the Leicester & Swannington Railway, which connected these pits with Leicester and so with its whole system of communications.

If the Leicestershire waterways are considered as a whole, from the standpoint of their success or failure, it will be seen that they fall into two main groups. Those which lay to one or other side of the main north–south line of water-communication through the centre of the county were in varying degrees unsuccessful. The Charnwood Forest Canal ended in total failure; the Ashby Canal was for most of the time an unprofitable venture for its shareholders; and though the Oakham Canal appeared about 1815 to be emerging from the difficulties against which it had struggled for many years, it seems never to have become very prosperous. In each case there were special circumstances contributing to complete or relative failure: the unfavourable terrain of the Forest Canal and the disaster to its reservoir, the over-optimistic estimate of the trade to be expected along the Ashby Canal, and the fact that the Oakham Canal did not run through or to an area capable of such industrial development as would provide a large enough traffic to repay the original expenditure. It was, in fact, a typical example of the many waterways built at that time on a speculative basis

[57] *Leic. Herald*, 28 Oct. and 17 Nov. 1792, 9 Feb., 4 and 25 May, 28 Sept., 7 and 28 Dec. 1793, 17 May 1794.

[58] C. Hadfield, *Brit. Canals*, 51.

[59] *Leic. Jnl.* 11 Oct. 1799.

[60] Ibid. 3 Aug. 1804 and 19 Jan. 1821.

[61] *Leic. and Nott. Jnl.* 14 Sept. and 12 Oct. 1782.

[62] *Leic. Jnl.* 23 May 1828.

through agricultural areas in the hope of creating enough trade to make them profitable. But the success or failure of canals during this period also depended very much upon whether they were begun early enough or pushed forward fast enough to escape the worst of the war-time rise in costs. The difference in this respect between the earlier and later canals is apparent even within the great main line constituted by the Soar and Leicester Navigations and the Union and Grand Union canals. The Soar or, as it is later called, the Loughborough Navigation, which alone belonged completely to the pre-war period, was almost phenomenally prosperous. It was, of course, extremely fortunate in the fact that after having been built as a comparatively inexpensive project for making a river navigable over a distance of a few miles, it came subsequently to form a main link in a great arterial chain of waterways. Indeed, it was 'the outstanding example of a river that lived in plenty on the connexion it made with canals'.[63] In 1796 it had paid a dividend of 30 per cent. for 'several years past'; in 1805 it paid 96 per cent.; in 1824 its £100 shares stood at £4,600; and even in 1833 the growing threat of railway competition had brought them no lower than £1,240.[64] The Leicester navigation, too, though falling on the later and less happy side of 1790, was built early enough, especially since it served an area ripe for industrial advance, to arrive at a comfortable competence after a shaky start. The Union Canal, whose construction was begun a little later still and drawn out almost through the war period, got into difficulties from which it was rescued only by outside help which would not have been forthcoming but for its obvious economic importance. Taken as a whole this great chain of waterways, traversing Leicestershire from north to south and linking it with London and the major ports and productive areas of the country, ultimately satisfied almost all the expectations formed of it both as regards returns to shareholders and its effect upon the prosperity of the district. The network of canals of which it was an important part had removed the previous obstacles to the growth of manufactures and population in the central tract of England, and from the beginning of the 19th century Leicestershire, in common with the rest of the east midlands, began to grow rapidly in industries and population. This result is most clearly reflected in the population curve of the town of Leicester. The relatively improved roads of the later 18th century and the hosiery trade had produced an increase from an estimated 6,000 in 1700 to 16,933 at the census of 1801. It was still largely a country town, but in the next 20 years, when the canals were coming into operation, the population almost doubled, for it was over 30,000 in 1821. It then continued to rise at the rate of 10,000 every decade until 1850, after which the effect of the railways is seen in a further acceleration.

The relation between the canals and the growth of Leicester, especially in the first 20 years of the 19th century, becomes even more clearly apparent when one considers in what parts of the town that growth was most evident. The eastward drift across the line of Church Gate, Gallowtree Gate, and the London road, which had been going on since the 15th century and was natural in a town confined by a river on its westward side, still continued. The houses in Granby Street and its environs grew more numerous. But for about 25 years after 1791 or thereabouts it was probably at the north-eastern corner of the town that the

[63] Hadfield, *Brit. Canals*, 170.

[64] Ibid.; *Leic. Jnl.* 13 May 1796 and 27 Dec. 1805; F. Eyre and C. Hadfield, *Engl. Rivers and Canals*, 20.

thrust was most pronounced, thanks to the navigation and the Public Wharf. The areas on both sides of Belgrave Gate—Archdeacon Lane, Barkby Lane, Wharf Street, and presently the smaller streets branching from them—began to be filled up. This process of filling in open spaces, of which much of Leicester's growth during the first half of the century consisted, since it originally covered an unusually large area in proportion to its population, was also very much in evidence farther to the west, in the neighbourhood of the now commercialized river, where

'. . . ancient Soar, along his fertile bed,
Sacred to commerce, saw new structures spread.'[65]

Not only did the former Vauxhall or Bath Gardens give place to wharves and warehouses, but the appearance of houses and streets in the Black Friars dates from 1799 or 1800, and the Pingle began to be laid out for streets within a short time afterwards.[66]

Industrial Leicester, to adopt one summary of the situation,[67] did not owe its origin to canals; but without them, and without canal-borne coal, it must be added, comparatively little advance could have been made until the Railway Age. 'The fuel famine of the eighteenth century would have stopped the growth not solely of industry but of population . . . had not means been devised for overcoming it.'[68]

The failure of waterway interests to appreciate in time the full menace of the railways to them, or at least to make the most of such opportunities of effective opposition as they possessed, was also strikingly illustrated in Leicestershire. When the opening of the Leicester & Swannington Railway in 1832 seemed likely to restore to the west Leicestershire collieries the monopoly of supplying Leicester with coal, the mine-owners of Derbyshire and Nottinghamshire were naturally driven to consider counter-measures. Their first important move was an attempt to come to an agreement with the canal companies involved, whereby the latter should cut their charges and the coal-owners their prices, so that they would still be able to compete in the Leicester market. Since it would be necessary to bring down the 16*s.* a ton which was the former price of their coal at Leicester to 10*s.*, the colliery proprietors proposed that each of the three waterways concerned, namely the Erewash Canal, which received 2*s.* a ton for tolls and wharfage, the Loughborough Navigation, which received 3*s.*, and the Leicester Navigation, which received 1*s.* 8*d.*, should make a reduction of 1*s.* But the canal committees refused to go beyond a drawback of 6*d.* a ton each, and the colliery-owners turned to the plan of a railway of their own, which developed into the Midland Counties and then into the Midland Railway, and so increased progressively the weight of competition which the canals of the district had to meet.[69]

For a few years longer the principal Leicestershire waterways, like others elsewhere, were enabled to maintain a fair degree of prosperity by the extra traffic furnished by the carriage of the materials with which their new rivals the railways were being built. Even in the 1840's the wharves of Leicester could

[65] Extract from Prologue composed by Miss Susannah Watts, and spoken at the opening of the New Theatre in Leic. Market Place in 1800; *Leic. Jnl.* 28 Mar. 1800.

[66] The conclusions in this paragraph are based on a large number of advertisements of 'newly-erected houses' and of building land for sale, together with notices of intended streets laid out, in *Leic. Jnl.* 1786–1830, *passim.*

[67] P. Russell, *Leics. Road*, 113.

[68] Clapham, *Econ. Hist. of Mod. Brit.* i, 78.

[69] Hadfield, *Brit. Canals*, 179.

still be described, with perhaps some wishful exaggeration, as 'crowded with boats', and on Sundays as many as 30 or 40 could be seen moored to the Public Wharf or lying near the West Bridge.[70] But in 1846 the expanding Midland Railway bought up the Ashby Canal at the same time as it purchased the Leicester & Swannington line. Two years later it also bought up the Oakham Canal after a struggle with the Earl of Harborough, who was a leading shareholder, in order to substitute a branch railway to Stamford. The Wreak and Eye Navigation thereupon gradually decayed, and ended by going into voluntary liquidation in 1877. The main line of waterways survived, though with dwindling business and receipts, into the period beginning in the 1870's when fear of railway monopolies produced some talk of reviving the canals and several Acts of Parliament attempted without notable success to afford them some protection. The encouragement which these Acts also held out to canal amalgamation had one important sequel when in 1894 the Grand Junction Co., still relatively powerful, bought up both the Union and Grand Union canals and followed this by an agreement upon through tolls with the Leicester and Loughborough navigations, as well as the Erewash Canal Co., offering these concerns a guarantee of minimum receipts and receiving in return the option of purchasing them. The Grand Junction's object in this was to get control of the coal trade of the Erewash Valley and lower the rates for the carriage of coal to London. The attempt failed and the Grand Junction lost money through its guarantee of receipts and had to relinquish its options. In 1929, the year, incidentally, in which the Grantham Canal was closed, the Grand Junction amalgamated with several canal companies in the Birmingham and Warwick area to form a new organization which took the old name of the Grand Union Co. Three years later this in turn absorbed the Leicester and Loughborough Navigations. The last stage came when the surviving waterways of Leicestershire, thus brought under one control, passed by the Transport Act of 1947 to national ownership.

[70] J. T. Gent, *Robert Finch*, 50.

RAILWAYS

ALTHOUGH the recorded history of railways in Leicestershire does not begin until 1789, it is right to remember that the pioneer in the introduction of railways into England 200 years earlier was almost certainly a Leicestershire man. We have clear evidence that a wooden railway was in use at Wollaton (Notts.) in 1597; and the same device appears some 10 years later near Bedlington in Northumberland. Both railways had the same purpose: the conveyance of coal from the pits to a river. The direction of both collieries was in the hands of the same man—Huntingdon Beaumont, younger brother of Sir Henry Beaumont of Coleorton—and the introduction of the railway into Northumberland was expressly ascribed to him by a writer of the next generation.[1] It is quite possible that Huntingdon Beaumont's first experiments with railways had been conducted at home, on his brother's estates: that evidence may yet appear to establish the claim of Leicestershire, rather than Nottinghamshire, to be the scene of the first English railway.

In Leicestershire, as elsewhere in England, the earliest railways were all designed to convey heavy goods—above all coal—to navigable water; and here, as elsewhere, it was the development of canals in the later 18th century that led to a demand for railways, to act as feeders to them. The railway was particularly valuable in hilly country, where the construction of a canal was an expensive business, involving a long series of locks. It usually happened that the coal had to be hauled by railway *down* from the pit-head to the canal. This meant easy work for the horses, which had to pull only empty wagons up hill.

The earliest railways in Leicestershire of which we have certain knowledge almost all followed this general pattern. The first of them was the Loughborough and Nanpantan line, laid down by William Jessop in 1789 to provide a feeder to the Soar Navigation. The historic importance of this railway has long been recognized, but it has often been misunderstood. Robert Stevenson, the Scottish engineer, described it as 'the first public railway company'.[2] One cannot tell exactly what he meant by that phrase, but the statement is certainly inaccurate. Again, we can no longer accept the statement that it was for this line that Jessop designed and cast the first rails made entirely of iron. Such rails seem to have been in use in Coalbrookdale as early as 1768.[3]

It has often been supposed, however, that Jessop's Loughborough and Nanpantan line was of even greater importance in another way: that not only the material but the shape of the rails was new. 'Here', wrote Robert Stevenson, 'this eminent engineer introduced the edge-rail, the upper surface of which was of an elliptical figure, with flanges upon the wheels to guide them upon the tracks of the road; for hitherto the plate or broad rail, under various forms, is understood to have been solely in use.'[4] In other words, Stevenson asserted that

[1] See the evidence set out in C. E. Lee, *Evolution of Rlwys.* (2nd edn.), 21–23.

[2] *Prize Essays and Trans. Highland Soc. of Scot.* vi, 131.

[3] *Rlwy. Mag.* xcvii, 632–3; A. Raistrick, *Dynasty of Ironfounders*, 180.

[4] *Prize Essays and Trans. Highland Soc.* vi, 132.

it was on the Loughborough and Nanpantan line that the flange was for the first time transferred from the rail to the wheel itself. Mr. Charles E. Lee has conclusively refuted this tale.[5] The railway of the modern form, bearing wagons with flanged wheels, is much older. The L-shaped plateway was a local variant, found mainly in the north midlands, the Forest of Dean, and south Wales.[6] Jessop's 'innovation' on the Loughborough and Nanpantan line consisted solely in reverting to what had been a standard earlier practice, and one that had never been abandoned in other parts of England.

Jessop's policy in this matter differed from that of his partner Benjamin Outram, who constructed all his lines as plateways. His principle did not always prevail over Outram's, even in Leicestershire. Plateways were built by the Ashby de la Zouch Canal under its Act of 1794. The main line was about 8¼ miles long, running from Willesley Basin, a mile north of Measham, past Ashby to the lime-works at Ticknall in Derbyshire. At Old Park it ran through a tunnel for 450 yds., and just north of this point it threw off a branch, 3¾ miles long, to Cloud Hill lime-works. From Willesley Basin to the north end of the tunnel the track of the railway was double: elsewhere it was single.[7] The section from Ashby to Worthington was later converted into a railway of the modern type; but the Ticknall line remained a plateway, for horse traction only. All regular traffic on it had ceased for many years before it was closed in September 1915.[8]

Another early railway in Leicestershire was a private line built for the Duke of Rutland from Belvoir Castle to the Grantham Canal. On the authority of C. E. Stretton, this line has been ascribed to the year 1793, but Mr. Lee has proved from documents in the Belvoir Castle Estate Office that it in fact dates from 1815.[9] Sections of the track of the line are preserved at the Science Museum, South Kensington, and the Railway Museum, York.

The Leicester Navigation followed the example of the other canals in the county by embracing railways in its scheme of construction. They fell into two groups. First came the vital railway that linked the main navigation at Loughborough with the Charnwood Forest Canal. It was an edge-railway,[10] 2¾ miles long, and in that distance it rose 185 ft.—an average gradient of 1 in 78.[11] To build a canal up this incline would have meant a long and expensive series of locks: a railway was plainly cheaper and more efficient. It was completed in 1794.[12] From Forest Lane wharf at the summit, the canal ran westwards to Barrow Hill, whence a short railway penetrated the limestone quarries. 'A further extension of ⅞ of a mile of railway is provided for in the Act, to Cloud Hill limestone quarry; where, had this last extension been executed, junctions would very nearly have been effected with the Ashby de la Zouch railway branch, and also with the proposed Breedon railway [which was intended to run down to the Trent at King's Newton].'[13] Other railways were also projected to link the canal with the collieries at Coleorton and Swannington. But all these railways, actual and projected, disappeared when the Charnwood Forest Canal fell into disuse

[5] Lee, *Evolution of Rlwys.* 62; Simmons, *Par. and Empire*, 151–2.

[6] Lee, op. cit. 61–69.

[7] J. Farey, *Gen. View of Agric. of Derbys.* iii, 298–300.

[8] C. F. Dendy Marshall, *Hist. of Brit. Rlwys. down to the Year 1830*, 43–44; Lee, op. cit. 101; C. E. Stretton, *Hist. Midland Rlwy.* 101; *Rlwy. Mag.* lxxxv, 7–8.

[9] *Rlwy. Mag.* lxxxii, 391–4.

[10] Farey, *Gen. View of Agric. of Derbys.* iii, 298.

[11] These figures are given in a paper by Alexander Scott of Ormiston in *Prize Essays and Trans. Highland Soc.* vi, 13.

[12] Stretton, *Hist. Midland Rlwy.* 3.

[13] Farey, *Gen. View of Agric. of Derbys.* iii, 378.

after the bursting of its reservoir in 1799.[14] One interesting detail of their working has, however, been preserved: 'The bodies of the trams [i.e. the railway wagons] were made to lift off, or to be placed on their wheels, by means of cranes erected on the Forest Lane and Thringstone Bridge Wharfs, so that the bodies of the trams only, stowed close together, could be carried in the boats on the water-level.'[15]

The Charnwood Forest Canal was never rebuilt. Its collapse meant the end of an ambitious attempt to bring the coal and lime of Leicestershire to Loughborough and Leicester itself. For the next 30 years these towns drew their coal from Derbyshire and Nottinghamshire, whence it was brought cheaply by the Leicester Navigation: the Leicestershire coal was distributed by the Ashby Canal through the western part of the county and southwards into Warwickshire. But that did not satisfy the Leicestershire coal-owners. The clue to a solution of their problem was found by a Coleorton man, William Stenson, an engineer who had become a partner in a colliery at Whitwick. He was anxious to develop deep coal-mining in the Leicestershire field, but was deterred by the expense of carrying the coal to its market. In 1828 he paid a visit to the north-east of England and saw the Stockton & Darlington Railway in operation. On his return home he surveyed the ground between Whitwick and Leicester and found what he thought would be a practicable route for a railway like the Stockton & Darlington: one, that is, on which heavy loads could be handled by steam locomotives, something altogether bigger than the short lengths of railway for horse-drawn traffic, with their steep gradients, which were the only railways Leicestershire had yet seen. Stenson secured the backing of his partners and then of John Ellis of Beaumont Leys.[16] As soon as he was satisfied that the idea was a good one, Ellis went off to consult his friend George Stephenson, who was then engaged on the Liverpool & Manchester Railway. Stephenson allowed himself to be interested in the scheme and returned with Ellis to Leicester, taking his son Robert with him. After going over the ground with Stenson he concluded that the railway could be built for about £75,000; and considering the trade that the railway would open up—not only in coal and lime, but in granite and building-sand and bricks—he thought it would be a profitable speculation. When a company was formed to build the railway, he himself became the first subscriber, putting his name down for shares to the value of £2,500. About two-thirds of the money was found in Leicester, the remaining third in Liverpool. George Stephenson refused to become engineer to the new company, but recommended his son Robert instead. The recommendation was accepted. Robert Stephenson was twenty-five at the time, and it was his second appointment as a railway engineer.[17]

The company secured its powers by Act of Parliament (11 Geo. IV and 1 Will. IV, c. 58, priv. act) in May 1830.[18] It was authorized to build a railway from the West Bridge at Leicester to Swannington, together with branches to the collieries at Bagworth, Ibstock, and Whitwick, to be made at the expense of

[14] *T.L.A.S.* xxvii, 89.

[15] Farey, *Gen. View of Agric. of Derbys.* iii, 379.

[16] F. S. Williams, *Midland Rlwy: its Rise and Progress*, 597–9. The best account of the Leic. & Swannington Railway is that of C. R. Clinker, in *T.L.A.S.* xxx. This article corrects a number of mis-statements about the railway made by Stretton and others.

[17] Stretton, *Hist. Midland Rlwy.* 4–8; S. Smiles, *Lives of the Engineers: George and Robert Stephenson* (1904 ed.), 279–83; J. C. Jeaffreson, *Life of Robert Stephenson*, i, 154–5.

[18] The Corp. of Leic. gave its formal consent to the project on 2 Apr. 1830: Leic. Town Hall Rec., Common Hall Bk. 1825–35, 124.

Locks on the Grand Union Canal at Foxton

East Norton Viaduct under Construction

East Norton Tunnel under Construction

the collieries themselves. There was also to be a short branch—never in fact built—from the Fosse Road to the North Bridge. The system was to be completed by a line to Coleorton, which was to link up with the Ashby and Cloud Hill tramroad. This was to be built by a separate company, which secured its parliamentary powers in 1833.[19]

The main line of the Leicester & Swannington Railway was 16 miles 5 chains long. It included three important engineering works: the Glenfield tunnel and the Bagworth and Swannington inclines. The tunnel was the longest that had yet been built for a railway in this country (1 mile 36 yds.). It was dead straight, lined with brick throughout, and so narrow that in later years special coaches were used on the trains that worked through it: their doors were locked and their windows provided with bars to prevent passengers from putting their heads out.[20] The Bagworth incline was 43 chains long, with a gradient of 1 in 29. It was much too steep to be operated by a locomotive, and rope traction was used instead. It was self-acting: the wagons descended by force of gravity and hauled the ascending wagons up at the same time. The incline was most inconvenient in use, particularly to passengers, who were expected to leave their train at the beginning of the incline and to walk up or down it to join another. All that could be said for it was that it avoided a long detour and that the gradient was in favour of the loaded coal-trains. The Swannington incline, at the northern end of the railway, was steeper still—its gradient was 1 in 17—and it was always worked by a cable and stationary steam-engine. It continued in occasional use until 1948.[21]

The track of the Leicester & Swannington Railway presents one or two points of interest. In the Glenfield tunnel the rails are said to have been laid on longitudinal (instead of transverse) sleepers. This arrangement was extensively used by Brunel on the Great Western Railway, and it has sometimes been implied that he invented it.[22] But if this statement is correct, the Leicester & Swannington Railway anticipated the Great Western in the use of this device by two or three years.[23] Half the remainder of the line was laid on transverse timber sleepers, half on stone blocks. The stone blocks are said to have proved unsatisfactory in use, needing 'constant attention—lifting, packing, and keeping to gauge'; and the track laid on them was thought less comfortable to ride over than that resting on wooden sleepers. However this may be, some of the blocks remained in use on the main line for nearly 40 years; and George Stephenson was not deterred from adopting them on the Maryport & Carlisle Railway, which he began to build in 1837.[24]

In 1831, while the line was being made, the Snibston estate, south-west of Whitwick, came up for sale. Robert Stephenson was convinced that coal would be found on it and he persuaded his father to buy it, with two partners from Liverpool. The prediction was correct. After considerable initial difficulties, a rich seam of coal was found, and the colliery became one of the main props of the substantial fortune that the two Stephensons built up for themselves.[25] George Stephenson signalized his new interest in Leicestershire by buying Alton Grange,

[19] Stretton, *Hist. Midland Rlwy.* 25; H. G. Lewin, *Early Brit. Rlwys.* 31.

[20] There is a good photograph of the western portal of the tunnel, which remains unaltered, in *T.L.A.S.* xxx, 89.

[21] Ibid.

[22] Cf. F. S. Williams, *Our Iron Roads*, 201–2.

[23] Stretton, *Hist. Midland Rlwy.* 17; cf. E. T. MacDermot, *Hist. G.W.R.* i, 47–49.

[24] Stretton, op. cit. 17; J. Simmons, *Maryport and Carlisle Rlwy.* 30.

[25] Jeaffreson, *Robert Stephenson*, i, 164–5.

near Ashby de la Zouch, in 1833. That was his home until 1841, when he moved to Tapton House, near Chesterfield.[26]

The first locomotive to be used on the Leicester & Swannington Railway was a four-wheeled engine named *Comet*. It was built in Robert Stephenson's works at Newcastle and dispatched by sea to Hull and thence by the Trent and Soar to Leicester. It had its trial on the railway on 5 May 1832—the first locomotive to run in the midlands.

The section of the line from Leicester to the foot of the Bagworth incline was now nearly finished, and it was decided to bring it into use without waiting for the completion of the northern part. The date fixed was 17 July 1832. On that day, according to a notice in the Leicester newspapers of 14 July, 'the locomotive engine, with a train of carriages, will start from the Augustine Friars at 10 o'clock, and proceed to Bagworth; and the proprietors may be supplied with tickets on application at the Directors' room in the Friar Lane, between the hours of 10 and 12 this day'. All—or almost all—went according to plan. The train was an imposing procession. Next to the engine was a covered-in vehicle for the directors, who sat on chairs taken from the board-room for the purpose. Then came the one vehicle specifically designed for passenger traffic that the company yet possessed—a simple four-wheeled open truck. It was followed by ten coal-wagons, fitted up for the accommodation of passengers by the laying-down of planks of wood, which were covered in green cloth. In one of these wagons rode the band, and on the last a small cannon was mounted, which was fired when the train started from a station and when it arrived at the next one. The train was decorated with flags bearing such inscriptions as 'Cheap coal and granite', 'Warm hearths and good roads', and 'May the triumph of science prove the blessing of the people'.

George Stephenson himself drove the engine. As the train was running through the Glenfield tunnel, its chimney hit the roof and was knocked down, causing all the passengers to be covered with soot and the band to stop playing. No one, however, was injured, and the damage was largely repaired by a stop at the Glenfield Brook to enable the passengers to wash themselves. This was the only mishap that befell the train. At Bagworth a cold collation was waiting for the gentlemen, and cakes and wine for the ladies at the house of Mr. Pickard. 'Water', we are told, 'was almost the only liquid in request [i.e. lacking]—ale, porter, cider, sherry, bucellas,[27] and champagne being provided in the greatest profusion.' On the return journey four more wagons were added to the train, two loaded with coal and two with stone. When the train reached Leicester the company marched in procession, accompanied by the band and a cart of coal, from the station at the West Bridge to the Bell, where fifty gentlemen sat down to dinner. The only unfavourable comment came from the *Leicester Journal*, which primly censured 'several individuals [for] displaying flags and attempting to excite a party feeling in the celebration of an event fraught with so much interest to all parties'. The *Journal* was a Tory paper: it looks as if the Whigs and Radicals of Leicester used the occasion to drive home the defeat their enemies had suffered by the passing of the Reform Bill six weeks earlier.[28]

[26] Smiles, *Lives of the Engineers*, iii, 352.

[27] A Portuguese white wine.

[28] This account of the opening of the railway is based on that in the *Leic. Jnl.* 20 July 1832, and those given by Stretton in his lectures on the Leic. & Swannington Railway of 1885 and 1891 (printed reps. of which are in the Leic. City Ref. Libr.) and in his *Hist. Midland Rlwy.* 20–22. Stretton's work has here a special authority, for his father and grandfather both travelled on the first train, but as Mr. Clinker has shown, his account

It was proper that that triumphant procession should have included a coal-cart, for it was in the transport of coal that the real importance of the railway consisted. The effect of its opening on the price of coal in Leicester was immediate. Derbyshire coal, brought up by the Leicester Navigation, had cost 18*s.* a ton in the town: coal of the same quality from the Leicestershire pits was now sold at 11*s.* The Coleorton colliery, which had been shut down for 30 years, was reopened.[29] Other people profited besides the coal-owners, too. Lord Stamford built a branch line from his granite quarries at Groby to the railway near Glenfield, which was in operation when the line opened: it was noted at once that the freight brought into Leicester included 'small stones for macadamising'.[30] Another branch was also built to the lime-kilns at Breedon.[31]

Though much was made of the passengers on the opening day, and though, when the railway was new, 'numbers of respectable parties . . . availed themselves of the opportunity to visit Bagworth and its neighbourhood',[32] the Leicester & Swannington Railway was always primarily interested in freight traffic. Stations were provided at Glenfield, Ratby, Desford, Merry Lees,[33] Thornton, and Bagworth, and passengers were conveyed on three trains a day in each direction. The line was extended from the top of the Bagworth incline to Ashby Road station (later Bardon Hill) about 1 February 1833; thence to Long Lane (Coalville) on 22 April 1833 for coal traffic and five days later for passengers; and in November 1833 to Swannington. On this section the company did not think it was worth while to build stations of its own, but at Ashby Road and Long Lane the passengers booked their tickets at the railway inns and waited for the trains there. This arrangement explains the curious layout of Bardon Hill station today. In 1838, when the line had been in operation for five years, it was conveying fewer passengers than any other comparable railway in England—an average of 443 a week, against 11,718 on the Liverpool & Manchester, for example, and 26,697 on the London & Greenwich. In the first half of 1843, 94·9 per cent. of its receipts were from goods traffic, 5·1 per cent. from passengers.[34]

The Leicester & Swannington Railway claims to have been a pioneer in two technical developments. 'The first steam-operated warning appliance used on a locomotive'[35] was made for it in Leicester in 1833. A train had run into a horse and cart at the level-crossing on the Bagworth–Thornton road, the engine-driver being unable to give sufficient warning of the train's approach, even though he 'blew the horn' and made all the noise with steam he could. The manager of the company then went over to Alton Grange to consult George Stephenson on the possible means of overcoming this difficulty; and as a result

of the Leic. & Swannington Railway is open to much criticism. A delightful oil painting, said to represent the arrival of the first train at Bagworth, was acquired by the City of Leic. Mus. in 1946.

It should be noted that where in this article a precise date is given for the opening of a line, it is the date of opening for public passenger traffic.

29 W. Gardiner, *Music and Friends*, i, 93; Smiles, *Lives of the Engineers*, iii, 353, says that the price was reduced to 8*s.* a ton.

30 *Leic. Jnl.* 27 July 1832.

31 Ibid. 20 July 1832.

32 Stretton, *Hist. Midland Rlwy.* 23, quoting *Leic. Chron.*

33 Merry Lees Station was closed on 28 Feb. 1871. The original stopping place at Thornton was the Stag and Castle Inn. This was closed on 31 Dec. 1841. A new station on the same site, 'Thornton Lane', was opened in 1850 and closed on 1 Oct. 1865. See *T.L.A.S.* xxx, 81.

34 H. G. Lewin, *Early Brit. Rlwys.* 59; *Jnl. Statistical Soc.* viii, 225; *Second Rep. Sel. Cttee. Rlwys.* H.C. 517, p. 393 (1839), x; *Fifth Rep. Sel. Cttee. Rlwys.* H.C. 474, pp. 364–8 (1840), xiii.

35 The phrase is Charles E. Lee's, used in a paper on 'Adrian Stephens: Inventor of the Steam Whistle' read to the Newcomen Soc. 14 Feb. 1951.

of their conference a musical instrument-maker in King Street, Leicester, was asked to design a 'steam trumpet', which could be sounded by the steam of the engine. This 'trumpet' was tried out before the board of directors, approved, and fitted to all the company's locomotives: one was then exported to the Liverpool & Manchester Railway.[36] The stationary engine designed by Robert Stephenson to haul wagons up the Swannington incline was one of the first engines to be equipped with the piston slide-valve.[37] It remained in use from 1833 to 1951 and is now preserved, in part, in York Railway Museum.

With the exception of a short branch in Leicester itself, thrown across the river to Soar Lane in 1834,[38] the Leicester & Swannington Railway made no attempt to expand. It had a purely local objective, with which it remained content. But it takes, nevertheless, the foremost place in the history of the railways of Leicestershire. Not only was it the first Leicestershire railway of the modern kind. It was the only railway of any importance whose limits lay wholly within the county. And it bore an intensely local character. A considerable part of the capital was subscribed, it is true, in Liverpool. But the first board of directors was constituted entirely from Leicestershire: one notices the familiar names, Ellis, Goddard, Martin, Packe, and Pares. Above all, it was the Leicester & Swannington Railway that contributed most to the revival of the Leicestershire coalfield after the eclipse it had suffered during the previous 40 years.

The success of the Leicester & Swannington Railway meant serious loss to the coal-owners of Derbyshire and Nottinghamshire. Two of their representatives had attended the opening of the line. Their report on its success led the coal-owners first to try to reach an arrangement with the Soar and Leicester navigations for a reduction of rates. This attempt having failed, a meeting was called to discuss the whole matter. It took place at Eastwood (Notts.) on 16 August 1832, when a resolution was unanimously passed that 'there remains no other plan for our adoption than to attempt to lay a railway from these collieries to the town of Leicester'.

The first project was for a line from the Mansfield & Pinxton Railway (which had been built under an Act of 1817) at Pinxton to Leicester, and a subscription for it was set on foot. When local support proved insufficient, the promoters turned, as the Leicestershire men had turned two years earlier, to Liverpool. The Liverpool men were not much interested in the woes of the north midland coal-owners: what they cared about was the development of railways as a good investment. The Liverpool & Manchester Railway was in satisfactory operation; plans were far advanced for a railway from London to Birmingham; for another, the Grand Junction, to link it with the Liverpool and Manchester; and for a third to run from Derby to Leeds. Here was a chance to fill an important gap in the new system. If a railway were built from Rugby, on the London & Birmingham line, through Leicester to Derby, with a branch to Nottingham and another from the Derby–Leeds line to Pinxton, both the coal-owners and the railway projectors could be satisfied. On these terms, and on no others, the Liverpool men were prepared to give their support.

[36] Stretton, *Hist. Midland Rlwy.* 26–27, with drawing of trumpet. Mr. Clinker has shown good grounds for doubting this whole story: *T.L.A.S.* xxx, 71–72. It must be regarded with suspicion, but we are not entitled to dismiss it as a myth.

[37] *Rlwy. Gazette*, xcvi, 64.

[38] This line crossed the river by an unusual drawbridge, operated by pulleys; a drawing of it is in the Stretton collection in the Leic. City Mus. The branch was opened for traffic on 4 Oct. 1834: *T.L.A.S.* xxx, 74.

The result was the formation of the Midland Counties Railway, which was set on foot in the autumn of 1833. When the company finally secured its parliamentary powers, after much negotiation and hard bargaining, in 1836, the Pinxton branch was eliminated.[39] In other respects the original plan was retained, in spite of a spirited attempt by the people of Northampton to get the southern portion of the route altered, so as to run from Leicester through Market Harborough and Northampton to Blisworth, effecting its junction with the London & Birmingham Railway there instead of at Rugby. But as this would have saved only 4 miles in the distance between Leicester and London, while adding £500,000 to the cost, the attempt was unsuccessful.[40]

The attitude of the Corporation of Leicester to the Midland Counties scheme is interesting. Though there was a good deal of support for the railway in the town, and a ratepayers' meeting, held on 11 February 1836 at the instance of the town council, passed a resolution 'that a railway passing through Leicester communicating with the London and Birmingham Railway would be highly advantageous to the town',[41] the Corporation itself opposed the project. It pointed out that the railway would interfere with the Town Conduit (which stood near the junction of Conduit Street and the London Road, on the site of the present station) and that by crossing the South Fields it would depreciate their potential value as building land. Much discussion took place with the Midland Counties officials, but no solution satisfactory to the Corporation could be found.[42] The Bill was therefore passed without its support.

Though the Midland Counties Railway was not a purely Leicestershire concern, as the Leicester & Swannington was, we meet well-known local names on its board of directors, and T. E. Dicey of Claybrooke was its chairman; it held its first annual general meeting, on 30 June 1837, at Loughborough; and its secretary, John Fox Bell, had his headquarters at Leicester.

The line presented no great engineering difficulties, and its first section, from Nottingham to Derby, was opened on 4 June 1839. The section from Trent junction to Leicester was opened privately on 4 May 1840, and the public service began to run the next day. 'About 12 o'clock on Monday last [4 May]', the *Leicester Chronicle* records, 'four first-class and six second-class carriages reached the station in this town from Nottingham, preceded by the *Leopard* steam engine.' An hour after its arrival the train returned. On 5 May, though the morning was cold, a large crowd assembled to see the first train leave Leicester at 7.30; and at Loughborough, where the train arrived at 8 o'clock, 'judging from the crowds of people who thronged the bridge and banks of the line, the whole population appeared in waiting to receive it'.[43] This excitement was not merely a temporary thing, which disappeared when the novelty had worn off. The railway remained a picturesque object in the landscape for a long time. As Potter remarked in his *Charnwood Forest* in 1842, from Long Cliff 'the trains of the Midland Counties Railway may be observed, almost uninterruptedly from Sileby to Derby, and form a pleasing object darting across the grand panorama'.[44]

[39] For the reasons see Stretton, *Hist. Midland Rlwy.* 36.

[40] Williams, *Midland Rlwy.* 15–18. A Bill for a 'South Midland Counties Railway' from the London and Birmingham at Collingtree (Northants.) to Wigston was actually framed: F. Whishaw, *Analysis of Rlwys.* (1837), 220–5.

[41] Leic. Town Hall Rec., Minutes of Finance Cttee. 1836, f. 102.

[42] Ibid. ff. 89–102; Leic. Town Hall Rec., Common Hall Bk. 1835–9, ff. 12–15, 63. This matter will be discussed further in *V.C.H. Leics.* iv.

[43] *Leic. Chron.* 9 May 1840.

[44] T. R. Potter, *Charnwood Forest*, 187.

At Leicester a 'central and superb'[45] station was built, in the classical style with a noble portico. It stood in Campbell Street, a little to the north of the present London Road station, and it contained, on the first floor, the offices of the Company.[46]

Meanwhile, work was progressing on the third section of the line, from Leicester to Rugby. 'In the deep cutting at the New Walk', we are told in May, 'workmen appear so numerous as to remind the looker-on of a hive of industrious bees. Close to the tunnel, under Knighton hill, the same sight presents itself.' The line was opened on 30 June 1840.[47]

Through the completion of the Midland Counties Railway, Leicester was brought into rail communication with London, with Birmingham, Liverpool, and Manchester, with Leeds and York.[48] Already its position on the railway system gave it greater advantages in cross-country communication than it had enjoyed in coaching days. The time taken to London was little more than half that of the fastest coach.[49]

The coach proprietors met the new competition in various ways. Two of them can be neatly illustrated from a single page of the *Leicester Chronicle*. C. S. Pettifor of the 'Stag and Pheasant' announces that after running coaches for 25 years, 'in consequence of the adoption of railway conveyance he has been compelled to abandon those roads on which coaches have been superseded by the new and rapid mode of travelling by steam. It is also, he trusts, with feelings of honest pride that he announces himself as the AGENT to the Midland Counties Railway Company, for the collecting and delivery of goods and parcels at the Leicester and Syston stations, *specially appointed by the Directors*'. Immediately below Pettifor's advertisement stands another, headed 'Under the immediate and especial patronage of the PUBLIC ONLY'. J. G. Briggs of the 'George' here announces that he and his father have been coach proprietors in Leicester for 40 years past, and now, 'without the adoption of railway conveyance, he has not been compelled to forsake his old friends the Public, by abandoning those roads on which his coaches have usually run, but that the same will be continued, in defiance of the monopoly of steam and rails, at the usual cheap and expeditious rate'.[50]

But if Briggs was prepared to fight gallantly, it was in a losing cause.[51] The railway had so many advantages. Not only was it quicker than its rivals. It could transport heavy freight—above all, coal—far more economically: on the opening of the Midland Counties Railway, Derbyshire coal was retailed in Leicester at 12*s*. a ton, a price that could once again compete with that of coal from the Leicestershire field. Railway travel, too, was cheap. The ordinary fares were lower than those by coach. But the Midland Counties Railway was prepared, on extraordinary occasions, to make them cheaper still. It can claim

[45] *Guide or Companion to the Midland Counties Rlwy.* (1840, publ. R. Tebbutt), 86.

[46] For an engraving of this station, see ibid. 73.

[47] *Leic. Chron.* 23 May and 3 July 1840.

[48] It had been intended to add a branch to the granite quarries at Mountsorrel, and an Act was secured for that purpose in 1837. But though the chairman of the Midland Counties Railway reiterated the company's intention of building it in 1838 (Williams, *Midland Rlwy.* 27), the powers were allowed to lapse. They were revived under a fresh Act of 1859, which authorized the Earl of Lanesborough to carry out the work. A typescript of this Act is in the L.R.O.

[49] In Jan. 1841 the connexion from the 8.30 p.m. mail train from Euston arrived at Leic. at 1.44 a.m. (*Leic. Chron.* 25 Jan. 1851): the fastest mail coach took 10 hours.

[50] *Leic. Chron.* 9 May 1840.

[51] The 'George' was to let in March 1849 owing to the 'ill-health' of Briggs; ibid. 16 March 1849.

to have been a pioneer in the use of excursion trains. The Nottingham Mechanics' Institution hired a special train to enable its members to visit an industrial exhibition in Leicester at a low fare on 20 July 1840.[52] The visit was returned, on similar terms, by the Leicester Mechanics' Institute a week later; and in August the Midland Counties Railway began to run excursion trains on its own account. The first, from Nottingham to Leicester on 24 August 1840, is said by eye-witnesses to have consisted of nearly seventy coaches, containing more than 2,000 people.[53] Its success was undoubted, and the plan was soon adopted by other railway companies. Nor was this all. It was a wood-turner and temperance-preacher of Market Harborough, Thomas Cook, who first saw the full possibilities of the new idea that had appeared in this somewhat haphazard way. He ran an excursion train—at his own risk, though the secretary of the Midland Counties Railway contributed towards the preliminary expenses[54]—from Leicester to Loughborough on 5 July 1841 at a return fare of one shilling. 'To Mr. Thomas Cook belongs the honour of being the first person to hire a special train at his own risk, sell railway tickets to the public, and personally travel with the train to look after the comfort of his passengers.'[55] From this small beginning sprang the great business that has spread from Leicestershire all over the world.[56]

We have seen that the Midland Counties Railway had originally been planned as one of three lines centring upon Derby. The other two had also been incorporated in 1836, as the North Midland and the Birmingham & Derby Junction companies. Though the three railways shared a common station at Derby and though much traffic passed over each to and from the others, their interests were by no means identical. The true solution to their difficulties lay in combining together, not in fighting one another; and at length, in 1843, they determined to adopt it. An Act of Parliament was necessary to authorize the combination, and it was passed in 1844. By it the three companies were merged to form a single 'Midland Railway'. It was the first important amalgamation in English railway history, and it brought under a single direction a system of 179 route miles, stretching from Rugby and Birmingham to Leeds.

The immediate effects of the amalgamation on Leicestershire were slight. The chief offices of the new company were naturally established at Derby, so that Leicester station ceased to be a railway headquarters. Mr. Dicey, the chairman of the old Midland Counties Co., was not included in the new board; but John Ellis became deputy-chairman to George Hudson, the 'Railway King', and he was supported by three other Leicester directors in a board of fifteen.

Hudson's policy for the new Midland Railway was one of immediate expansion, particularly to the east in order to establish an entry into Lincolnshire and the country round Peterborough before the direct London and York line, which had been planned, could be established. Accordingly, the Midland Co. applied for powers to build a branch from Syston, passing through Melton Mowbray, Oakham, and Stamford, and terminating at Peterborough in a junction with a

52 *Leic. Chron.* 25 July 1840.

53 See the accounts ibid. 15 and 29 Aug. 1840.

54 W. F. Rae, *Business of Travel*, 21. It should be noted that these were not the first excursion trains, as has often been supposed: one or two companies in the north of England had already begun to run them. See *Rlwy. Mag.* c, 426.

55 Stretton, *Hist. Midland Rlwy.* 46.

56 For the development of the firm of Thomas Cook & Son, see Rae, *Business of Travel*, and J. Pudney, *The Thomas Cook Story*.

projected line of the Eastern Counties Railway, which Hudson also controlled. The scheme, however, came up against the vehement opposition of the Earl of Harborough, who disliked the idea of a railway running through his park at Stapleford and feared, with justification, that when the railway was opened it would injure the trade of the Oakham Canal, of which he was one of the chief proprietors. He flatly refused to allow the line through his park to be surveyed, and in November 1844 there was a series of free fights between his servants and the railway's. He then took legal action, as a result of which some of the railway's men received short sentences of imprisonment for riot and trespass. While the Bill was passing through Parliament in the following spring, the Midland Railway agreed to buy up the Oakham Canal at a good price.[57] But Lord Harborough remained unappeased.

By the Syston & Peterborough Railway Act of 1845 it was laid down that there should be a tunnel under the Cuckoo Plantation in Stapleford Park. It proved impracticable to build this tunnel, and the railway proceeded to make an open cutting instead. Lord Harborough then succeeded in getting an injunction to prevent the railway from proceeding farther with their works at this point. A deviation was accordingly decided on, to avoid the Cuckoo Plantation, but Lord Harborough again impeded the surveyors in their work in November 1845, and again there was an uproar. This time it was the company that brought the action, but after a 5-hours' trial in July 1846 Lord Harborough and his servants were found not guilty of assault. Meanwhile the second Act, authorizing the deviation, had passed through Parliament, and Lord Harborough at length showed himself willing to come to terms. His obstruction, however, had two consequences, one temporary, the other more lasting. The Syston–Melton section of the line was ready and was opened on 1 September 1846, the Peterborough–Stamford section on 2 October following: but the middle section, from Melton to Stamford, was now so far behind that it could not be brought into use until 1 May 1848. The deviation was always known as 'Lord Harborough's curve', and it was on much too short a radius. This did not matter greatly at first, for no fast trains ran by the Midland line to Peterborough. But in 1880 this section of the line began to form part of the new Kettering–Oakham–Nottingham express route, and then the inconvenience caused by the sharp curve became serious. It was eliminated 12 years later, by agreement with Mr. James Hornsby, Lord Harborough's successor. The new curve was brought into use on 28 February 1892. But the line of 'Lord Harborough's curve' can still be seen quite plainly on the ground today.[58]

In the railway mania of 1845–6, many schemes were put forward for railways crossing Leicestershire.[59] Two of them directly threatened the vital interests of the new Midland Co. A railway was projected from Atherstone (on the Trent Valley line) to Burton-on-Trent, passing Ashby de la Zouch and throwing out

[57] See the discussion of this purchase given in the evidence by G. H. Betts, on behalf of the Oakham Canal, before the Sel. Cttee. on Railways and Canals Amalgamation: *Second Rep.* H.C. 275, pp. 54–56 (1846), xiii; and the objections put forward to it by Wm. Latham, clerk to the Melton Canal Navigation: ibid. pp. 76–78.

[58] For the Battle of Saxby, see Stretton's paper in *Rut. Mag.* v, 213–19.

[59] To give a few examples: the Gt. Eastern and Western Railway (Yarmouth–Swansea), the London and Manchester Direct Independent Railway, the Gt. Leeds and London Direct Railway, the Nott., Birmingham, and Coventry Junction Railway, the Coventry and Leic. Junction Railway. Prospectuses of all these companies are to be found in the B.M. collection of company prospectuses; pressmark 1881 b. 23. In 1846 the Estate Cttee. of the Leic. Boro. Council considered and reported on five schemes. See Leic. Town Hall Rec., Common Hall Bk. 1844–47, ff. 203, 221–2, 253.

branches to Moira, Ticknall, and Breedon. The Midland dealt with this threat by buying up the Ashby Canal, at the price of £110,000, in 1846. The Bill for the Atherstone and Burton line failed to pass. The other threat was more alarming. In 1845 a Leicester and Bedford Railway Co. was formed, designed to link the London and York Railway (afterwards the Great Northern) with the Leicester & Swannington—which had as yet no physical connexion with any other railway. It was to run from Leicester to Hitchin by way of Wigston, Market Harborough, Kettering, and Bedford, and it would enable Leicestershire coal to be taken direct to London. The Midland met this challenge in two ways: first by opening negotiations for the purchase of the Leicester & Swannington Co., and second by promoting a Leicester–Hitchin line of its own.

The Midland Co. secured parliamentary permission to absorb the Leicester & Swannington in 1846[60] and to make certain consequent extensions and alterations in the existing line. Acts of Parliament of 1846 and 1847 authorized the Midland to extend the line from Coalville to Burton-on-Trent, where it was to form a junction with the Midland line from Birmingham to Derby; to build a deviation, on a gradient suitable for locomotives, to cut out the Bagworth incline; to make a railway (which was not in fact built) from Desford to Broughton Astley on the Leicester–Rugby section; and to link up the two railways at the Leicester end by a line from Desford to Knighton. It may appear strange that this last link should have had to be so long. But this route avoided the building of a line through the heart of Leicester (from the West Bridge station to the Midland main line) and the widening of the one-track Glenfield tunnel, which would have been a most expensive operation. The new Bagworth incline was brought into use on 27 March 1848 and the whole line from Knighton junction to Burton on 1 August 1849. West Bridge station continued to be used, both for passengers and for goods. A new building was opened on 13 March 1893. The station was closed to passengers on 24 September 1928.[61]

The rival Leicester and Bedford schemes both came to grief in the session of 1846. The Midland then opened negotiations with its opponent, and the two came to terms. They united to back a new Leicester and Hitchin plan, which was authorized in 1847. It was George Hudson's wish that the line should not stop at Hitchin but should run on thence to Hertford, where it could make a junction with the Eastern Counties Railway and so take the Leicester traffic to Shoreditch instead of King's Cross. Parliament, however, expressly refused to sanction this part of the plan. It was specially provided in the Act that the Leicester and Hitchin line was to terminate in a junction with the Great Northern, which it was not to cross, and that its trains were to be timed in connexion with the Great Northern's.

But the powers thus secured with so much difficulty were allowed to lapse. The real motive for the Midland's anxiety to promote the scheme had been defensive—to prevent a rival from securing access to its own territory. Having come to terms with that rival it could afford to ignore the interests of south Leicestershire and the towns down to Bedford that would have been served by the railway. Its interest in the idea revived only in 1852, when its relations with the London & North Western Railway (the successor company of the London

60 This was opposed by Sir Francis Head on behalf of the Grand Junction Canal Co.: *Second Rep. Sel. Cttee. Rlwys. Canals Amalg.* H.C. 275, p. 47 (1846), xiii.

61 Stretton, *Hist. Midland Rlwy.* 102–4; H. G. Lewin, *Rlwy. Mania and its Aftermath*, 320; *T.L.A.S.* xxx, 78.

& Birmingham) had become strained by the interchange of traffic at Rugby, so as to make the Midland wish to secure an alternative route to London. In 1853, therefore, the Midland promoted a new Bill for a railway from Leicester to Hitchin, by the same route as before. Again the application was successful, and this time the line was built.

Unhappily it was built on the cheap. Labour was dear, and the workmen on the line were highly paid.[62] Economies in construction were adopted. Instead of securing an independent entrance into Market Harborough from the north, the Midland contented itself with running powers over 66 chains of the Stamford and Rugby line of the London & North Western Railway[63] from Great Bowden junction to Market Harborough station, of which it became a tenant. It was an uncomfortable arrangement, causing frequent delays to traffic, and it was ended only by the building of separate sets of lines for the two companies and a new joint station. The station was brought into use on 14 September 1884 and the additional lines on 28 June following.[64] The site of the old line is occupied today by the Market Harborough carriage sidings.

But this was not the only unsatisfactory feature of the new railway. Its alignment is open to a good deal of criticism. Two very sharp curves are to be found on the Leicestershire section of the line alone, at Wigston north junction and Market Harborough, and there is a third at Wellingborough: though this might almost be called a Midland Railway practice, for such curves abound over the whole system.[65] Even worse, in order to avoid the expense of tunnelling, the gradients of the line were made most severe, and the noise that is still emitted by the struggling engines of coal-trains climbing the Kibworth, Desborough, and Sharnbrook banks is a continuing reminder of the short-sighted policy adopted by the builders of the railway in the fifties.[66]

The line was opened on 8 May 1857. Through passenger trains from Leicester to King's Cross, via Hitchin, began to run on 1 February 1858. The arrangement between the Midland and the Great Northern Railways, however —like most others of its kind—proved unsatisfactory in working, and the Midland soon began to consider undertaking an independent line to London on its own account. The result was the extension from Bedford to St. Pancras, which came into use on 1 October 1868.

With the opening of the line from Leicester to Market Harborough in 1857, it could be said that the whole of the central part of the county was fairly well served with railways. But the western and eastern districts were less well provided for. A Coventry, Nuneaton, Birmingham, and Leicester Railway had been projected in 1846, under the chairmanship of John Biggs of Leicester,[67] and had actually secured parliamentary powers to build a line from Nuneaton to Wigston; but they had not been used.[68] They were revived, partially in 1859 in the form of a line from Nuneaton to Hinckley, and wholly in 1860, when the South Leicestershire Railway was permitted to extend that line to Wigston

[62] A. Helps, *Life and Labours of Mr. Brassey*, 370.

[63] Opened from Rugby to Market Harborough 1 May 1850, from Market Harborough to Rockingham 1 June 1850, and from Rockingham to Luffenham Junction 2 June 1851.

[64] Stretton, *Hist. Midland Rlwy.* 156.

[65] Cf. Ambergate, Manton, and Bedford.

[66] Cf. the comments of Sir William Acworth, *Rlwys. of Engl.* 155.

[67] Biggs became Liberal candidate for the borough, together with John Ellis, the deputy chairman of the Midland Railway. The two were the subject of a paragraph headed 'More Railway M.P.s' in the *Staffs. Advertiser*, 26 Aug. 1848.

[68] Lewin, *Rlwy. Mania*, 176–7.

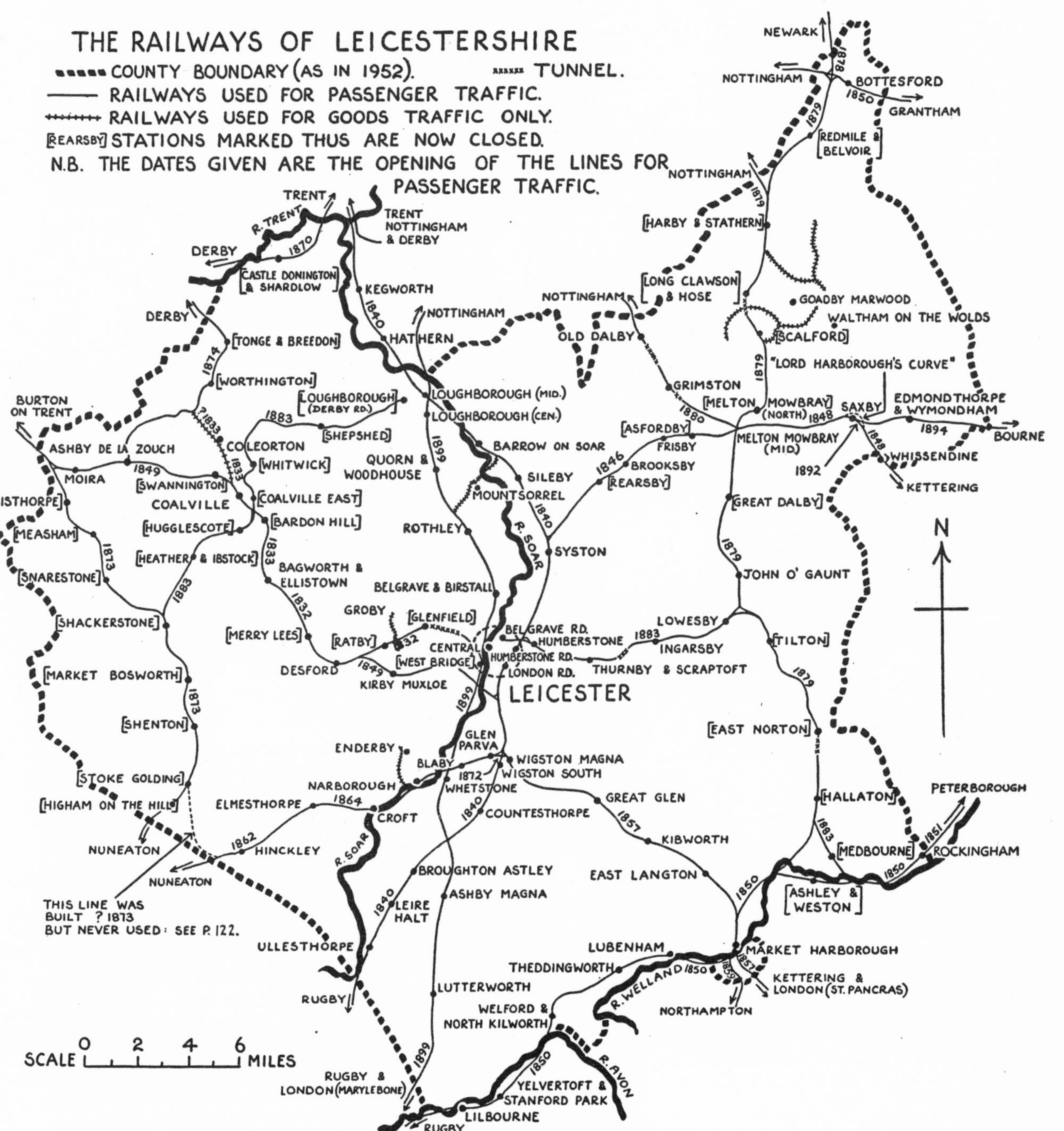
THE RAILWAYS OF LEICESTERSHIRE
COUNTY BOUNDARY (AS IN 1952).
TUNNEL.
RAILWAYS USED FOR PASSENGER TRAFFIC.
RAILWAYS USED FOR GOODS TRAFFIC ONLY.
[REARSBY] STATIONS MARKED THUS ARE NOW CLOSED.
N.B. THE DATES GIVEN ARE THE OPENING OF THE LINES FOR PASSENGER TRAFFIC.
THIS LINE WAS BUILT ? 1873 BUT NEVER USED: SEE P. 122.
SCALE 0 2 4 6 MILES
LEICESTER
N

and to exercise running powers thence over the Midland into Leicester.[69] The South Leicestershire Railway was a protégé of the London & North Western (which formally absorbed it in 1867), and this meant that the London & North Western had obtained access to Leicester. But the Midland secured compensating advantages: running powers over the South Leicestershire line and on to Coventry (1860) and authority to build a railway from Nuneaton to Whitacre on its Birmingham and Derby line (1861). This was important for Leicestershire, for it linked Leicester with Birmingham by a direct route, where previously all traffic had had to go by way of Rugby, Burton, or Derby. These lines were opened as follows: Nuneaton (Trent Valley station) to Hinckley, 1 January 1862; Hinckley to Wigston, 1 January 1864;[70] Nuneaton to Whitacre, 1 November 1864. The system was completed by the Wigston south curve (authorized 1869, opened 1872),[71] which enabled traffic from London and the south to pass direct on to the South Leicestershire line without running on to Leicester station to reverse,[72] and the branch to the granite quarries at Enderby, built under the Midland Railway (Additional Powers) Act, 1890.

But the successful promotion of the South Leicestershire Railway did not satisfy the ambitions of the London & North Western. That company was anxious not only to reach Leicester itself but also to tap the Leicestershire coalfield. Accordingly, in 1866 it sponsored the 'London & North Western and Midland Counties Coalfields Railway', to run from Nuneaton to Ashby, by way of Market Bosworth. The Midland Railway had secured powers to make a similar line in 1846, but they had lapsed. It now took the simple course of asking Parliament's permission to revive them. This permission being granted, the two companies came to terms and agreed to build the line jointly.[73] The main line was originally intended to run from Hinckley to Ashby, with a connecting spur to Nuneaton. But though the whole system was built, the Hinckley to Stoke Golding section was never used, and trains ran only to Nuneaton. The Ashby and Nuneaton line was opened on 1 September 1873.[74] The Charnwood Forest Railway, worked by the London & North Western, later built a branch from Shackerstone, through Coalville, to Loughborough (Derby Road), opened on 16 April 1883.[75] The railway communications of this part of the county were further improved by the conversion of part of the old tramroad, from Ashby to Worthington, into a railway, and its extension, by way of Breedon, to Weston junction. This made direct traffic possible between Ashby and Derby, from 1 January 1874.

The railway system was now complete in the western part of the county: but east Leicestershire was still very badly served. The Grantham–Nottingham branch of the Great Northern Railway (opened 15 July 1850)[76] crossed its northern tip at Bottesford; the London & North Western line from Rugby

[69] *Bradshaw's Rlwy. Shareholders' Manual* (1861), 251.

[70] G. P. Neele, *Rlwy. Reminiscences*, 71, 132.

[71] *Bradshaw's Rlwy. Shareholders' Manual* (1876), 245; Stretton, *Hist. Midland Rlwy.* 196.

[72] For about 10 years (1872–82) the Midland Railway ran a service of through trains between St. Pancras and Birmingham (E. L. Ahrons, *Locomotive and Train Working in the latter part of the 19th Cent.* ii, 122); but this attempt to compete with the London and North Western was unsuccessful, which is hardly surprising, since the distance by this route was 132 miles, against 113 by the main London and North Western route from Euston. The curve is still used occasionally for special passenger trains: in the summer of 1953 it was used regularly by a Birmingham–Clacton train on Saturdays.

[73] Williams, *Midland Rlwy.* 190, 220–2.

[74] Neele, *Rlwy. Reminiscences*, 192.

[75] *Leic. Chron.* 21 Apr. 1883. Neele (279) mistakenly gives the date as 14 Apr.

[76] Lewin, *Rlwy. Mania*, 396.

to Stamford skirted its southern edge; the Syston–Peterborough line alone ran through it, providing also, at the stations between Whissendine and Manton, some service for the villages on the Leicestershire–Rutland border. East Leicestershire was opened up by railways only very late, in the last quarter of the 19th century: an important fact in the economic and social history of that part of the county.

The opening-up, when it came, was due less to the railway companies' positive desire to serve east Leicestershire than to their rivalry among themselves. The Great Northern Co. had a twofold interest in the district. It wished to take a share in the development of the unworked ironstone that was known to exist there, particularly round Waltham on the Wolds. And it was influenced by the woollen manufacturers of the West Riding, who obtained some of their raw wool from Leicestershire and sent back much spun wool to Leicester to be made into hosiery. In 1871 the Great Northern therefore promoted a Bill for a line from Newark to Leicester, by way of Bottesford, Melton Mowbray, and Tilton.[77] The Midland determined at once to resist this invasion of its territory and put forward a scheme in the same session for lines from Nottingham to Saxby and Manton to Rushton, just north of Kettering. As the Syston–Peterborough line already covered the intermediate section from Saxby to Manton, this amounted to a plan for a new main line from Nottingham through east Leicestershire to Kettering, and so to London. The Midland Railway's Bill was successful in 1872. The Great Northern's was rejected by the House of Lords, largely through the vehement opposition of landowners who feared the railway would interfere with hunting. (This added to the unpopularity of the House of Lords among the Radicals of Leicester, and an 'indignation meeting' was held in the town in 1872 to protest against the House's decision.)[78]

The Great Northern did not take this defeat as final. In 1873 the old plan reappeared, with important additions. A line was to be built from Tilton, on the proposed Newark–Leicester line, to Market Harborough, where it was to join the Rugby–Stamford branch of the London & North Western Railway. The expense of constructing the new line was to be shared between the Great Northern and the London & North Western companies, and a spur was to be built from Stathern to a point between Bingham and Radcliffe-on-Trent (later named Saxondale junction), whence the London & North Western was to be granted running powers over the Great Northern into Nottingham.

Faced with this formidable combination of its two greatest rivals, the Midland sought the alliance of the Manchester, Sheffield, & Lincolnshire Railway, and a scheme far more grandiose than the Rushton–Nottingham plan of the previous year was brought forward by the two companies. It was for a line from Rushton to Askern, near Doncaster, designed to give the Midland convenient access to the North Eastern Railway (much impeded since the building of the Great Northern) and the Manchester, Sheffield, & Lincolnshire a route to London.

Neither of these Bills was successful. In 1874 the Midland abandoned its joint scheme with the Manchester, Sheffield, & Lincolnshire Co. and reverted to its original plan of 1872; and the Great Northern and London & North Western at length secured the powers they sought, though the section from Tilton to Leicester had to be built by the Great Northern alone, and not by the two companies jointly. The new Midland line was opened in two stages:

77 C. H. Grinling, *Hist. Gt. Northern Rlwy.* 266–70.

78 Ibid. 274–5.

Nottingham–Melton Mowbray on 2 February 1880, and Manton–Kettering on the following 1 March.

The Newark and Market Harborough line went forward much more slowly. It was opened as follows: Newark–Bottesford, 1 July 1878; Bottesford–Market Harborough, 15 December 1879. The Tilton–Leicester branch was opened for goods traffic in May 1882, for passengers on 1 January 1883.[79] For its Belgrave Road station in Leicester the Great Northern acquired a site of no less than 36 acres. In doing so, the company acted, in the double-edged phrase of its historian, 'with a foresight which may yet prove to have been enlightened'.[80] Fifty years later, we are in a position to pass a less ambiguous judgement. The great station is little used, and for 9 months in the year the passenger service over the line from Leicester to John o' Gaunt[81] consists of a single train a day in each direction: in the summer two or three additional trains are run on Saturdays to Skegness and Mablethorpe.

The Leicestershire railway system was completed by three more lines. The first was the Medbourne curve, built by the London & North Western and Great Northern companies jointly. It was opened, with a station at Medbourne, on 2 July 1883, enabling the Great Northern Railway to run a through passenger service between Leicester and Peterborough, over a route 4 miles shorter than the Midland line via Syston and Stamford. This service was maintained until 1914, but the Medbourne curve is now derelict. The second line, authorized in 1889, linked Saxby with Bourne and the Eastern & Midlands (later Midland & Great Northern Joint) Railway and so provided a new cross-country route from Leicester to the resorts on the Norfolk coast. It was opened for goods on 5 June 1893 and for passengers on 1 May 1894. The third line was a very much bigger affair.

We have seen that in 1873 the Manchester, Sheffield, & Lincolnshire Co. was willing to go into partnership with the Midland in undertaking an ambitious new railway, in order to provide itself with access to London. Despite the failure of that scheme, the company never lost sight of its objective; and 20 years later it was attained. In 1893 the Manchester, Sheffield, & Lincolnshire Railway secured powers to build an entirely new line, quite independently, from Annesley (Notts.) to Quainton Road (Bucks.), whence it was to exercise running powers over the Metropolitan Railway as far as West Hampstead and then to proceed to its own terminus in London on the Marylebone Road. The new line was to enter Leicestershire a little north of Loughborough and, passing through Leicester, to leave it in the parish of Shawell. It could not be said to open up any part of north Leicestershire that was not already served by the Midland line. But it was more useful in the southern part of the county, especially in giving the town of Lutterworth a station of its own on a main line, instead of the old Ullesthorpe, 4 miles away on the Leicester–Rugby branch.

It was a costly, indeed extravagant, line to build. The mistakes made during the construction of the Leicester and Bedford railway—through a similar, though rather more difficult terrain—were not repeated. The new line had no

[79] Grinling, op. cit. 333, 336, 338, 360–1. It is to be presumed that the mineral line from Scalford to Waltham on the Wolds was brought into use at the same time as the Bottesford–Market Harborough section. This line was occasionally used to convey passengers to the race-meeting at Croxton Park: *Rlwy. Mag.* c, 204.

[80] Grinling, op. cit. 360.

[81] The junction station between the joint line to Market Harborough and the Leic. branch. It is in the par. of Burrough on the Hill. Its name was taken from a fox covert 1¼ miles to the south, close to the actual point of divergence of the lines, which is known as 'Marefield junction'.

sharp curves whatever; and where the Midland had found it necessary to cross the top of the Northamptonshire uplands at Desborough, the Manchester, Sheffield, & Lincolnshire extension pierced them by the Catesby tunnel, nearly 2 miles long. It ran through Leicester on a great viaduct, traversing the western part of the old town: a Roman pavement lay on the site of its new station, which the company was obliged, by a clause in its Act, to preserve in a chamber specially built for the purpose.[82]

The opening of the new Great Central Railway (into which the Manchester, Sheffield, & Lincolnshire had transformed itself) on 15 March 1899[83] broke the Midland Co.'s virtual monopoly in Leicester, giving the town a new route to London, to Manchester and Liverpool, and to the West Riding of Yorkshire. The distance from Leicester to Marylebone was 4 miles greater than that to St. Pancras (103 miles, as against 99), but that disadvantage was offset by the superior alignment of the Great Central route. The new company and the old at once entered into hot competition, and for the next 40 years Leicester enjoyed, in consequence, a better express train service to and from London than any other comparable town.[84]

No new railways have been opened in Leicestershire during the 20th century. Rather, the story is one of the closing of lines and stations that have proved economically unjustified. The following lines were closed to passengers, on the dates given: Ashby–Nuneaton and Shackerstone–Loughborough, 13 April 1931; Ashby–Chellaston East junction, 22 September 1930; Leicester (West Bridge) to Desford junction, 24 September 1928.[84a] The Bottesford–Market Harborough line was similarly closed on 7 December 1953, though one passenger train a day is still advertised between Leicester (Belgrave Road) and John o' Gaunt. British Railways have shut down a number of stations considered superfluous. Rearsby and Asfordby were closed on 2 April 1951, Swannington and Great Glen on 18 June 1951, Redmile on 9 September 1951, and Bardon Hill on 12 May 1952.

Only two serious railway accidents have ever occurred in Leicestershire: one at Desford on 22 October 1881, causing five deaths,[85] the other on the joint line at Melton Mowbray on 25 July 1892, when three people were killed.[86] Among minor accidents may be mentioned two on the Leicester–Rugby line: the fire in the Countess of Zetland's carriage in 1847[87] and the collapse of the Crow Mills viaduct in the floods of the autumn of 1852, when disaster was averted through a warning given by a miller who lived nearby.[88]

The student of railway antiquities will find a good deal to interest him in the county today. In addition to those already mentioned—such as the Glenfield tunnel, the Swannington incline, and 'Lord Harborough's curve'—the most interesting objects are perhaps the stations themselves. Taken together, they form a conspectus of the history of railway architecture. Two excellent buildings

[82] The preservation of this pavement was largely due to the persistent action of the Leics. Arch. Soc. See *T.L.A.S.* viii, 375; ix, 6, 15, 68, 114, 152, 154.

[83] See the accounts in *The Times*, 10 and 16 Mar. 1899. The line had been open to coal traffic since 25 July 1898.

[84] In the summer of 1939, 12 trains a day by the Midland route were booked to cover the distance between Leic. and St. Pancras in 99 mins., at an average speed of exactly 60 m.p.h.; the best train on the Marylebone line took 108 minutes.

[84a] Ex. inf. British Railways.

[85] *The Times*, 24 Oct. 1881; *Return of Accidents* [c. 3209], pp. 205 sqq. H.C. (1882), lx.

[86] *The Times*, 26 July 1892; *Return of Accidents* [c. 6944], pp. 58 sqq. H.C. (1893–4), lxxviii.

[87] See the account in D. Lardner, *Rlwy. Econ.* (1850), 345–56.

[88] Williams, *Midland Rlwy.* 138.

in the classical style survive on the Syston–Peterborough line, Brooksby and Melton Mowbray (Midland).[89] Kibworth offers a good example of the polychrome Gothic of the fifties. The Great Northern and joint-line stations of the eighties, though commodious (absurdly commodious for the traffic they handle today), are harsh buildings, wholly without style, in staring red brick.[90] At Market Harborough the façade of the joint station of 1885 shows a surprising return to the classical manner. London Road station, Leicester, opened in 1892, was designed by the Midland Co.'s architect, C. Trubshaw.[91] It is a large building, sensibly planned, and still adequate after 50 years for all ordinary demands that are made upon it. The decorations are insipid, but if the façade were disencumbered of the crude advertisements by which it is now defaced, the station could be ranked among the more satisfactory buildings of the city. The Central station at Leicester (1899) has a less opulent appearance. Its architectural style throughout is distinctly Jacobean—an interesting reflection of the changing taste of the nineties. Its dining-room is of great interest, since it preserved all its original fittings, except the lights, to the moment of its closing (29 December 1951): many of the chairs and much of the cutlery and plate still in use then bore the arms of the Great Central Railway or its initials. Finally, it may be mentioned that the station at Blaby is a building of the cheapest wooden construction, rebuilt by the London & North Western Railway after the original had been burnt down by suffragettes; and that the polygonal locomotive depot just north of London Road station, Leicester, is a characteristic example, on a large scale, of the unpleasing ferro-concrete architecture favoured by the London, Midland, & Scottish Railway in the 1930's.

The place of Leicestershire in English railway history should now be clear. It made its own contribution to the pre-locomotive railway in the lines at Loughborough, Belvoir, and Ashby. The Leicester & Swannington Co. introduced the locomotive, and with it the modern railway, into the midlands. It was in Leicestershire that some of the earliest excursion trains ran; in Leicestershire that one of the last great battles between landowners and railway projectors took place, in the seventies. But perhaps the greatest service rendered to railways by the county lay in the steady and powerful assistance it gave to the making of the Midland Railway. Three of its chairmen were Leicester men. John Ellis, a founder of the Leicester & Swannington, succeeded George Hudson in the chair of the Midland Co. in 1849. That he should have been elected to the office was itself a high tribute to his integrity and sound sense. He had been Hudson's deputy throughout the Mania and so in a measure associated, however innocently, with some of Hudson's mistakes and misdemeanours. Yet it was to him that the Midland shareholders turned on Hudson's fall. He could not have succeeded at a more difficult time. The company's dividend had to be halved. It fell still farther, to its lowest point, 2 per cent., in 1850; but thereafter it gradually rose again, until in 1858, when Ellis resigned the chair, it stood at $4\frac{7}{8}$ per cent. That is a true reflection of the shrewd and successful policy pursued by the great company under his leadership. He was followed by a Birmingham man, Samuel Beale, but on Beale's retirement in 1864 another Leicester man was chosen, W. E. Hutchinson. Like Ellis, he was a Quaker. He had been

[89] The north side of the station only. The building was much enlarged in the late 19th cent.

[90] It may perhaps be mentioned that a 'Second Class Waiting Room' is still to be seen at Melton Mowbray (joint) station, though all 2nd-class facilities were withdrawn on this line in 1911. Redmile, as the station for Belvoir, has a few ornamental flourishes.

[91] Stretton, *Hist. Midland Rlwy.* 330, 337.

a chemist in Gallowtree Gate, but he threw up his business in 1839 to become superintendent of the Midland Counties Railway. He was one of the members of the original Midland board of 1844. He served as chairman from 1864 to 1870 and continued as a director until his death in 1882: a continuous period of service of 38 years. From 1873 to 1879 the company's chairman was E. S. Ellis, John Ellis's son. He has been described as 'a man of one great idea, and that was all treasured up in the Midland Railway'.[92] When he died, in December 1879, he was buried by his father in Leicester cemetery. Three years later Hutchinson was also buried there, and in 1892 Thomas Cook.[93] The graves of all four lie close to one another; and rightly, for the work of each of these men was closely related to that of the rest. Taken together, they symbolize and sum up much of the contribution that Leicestershire has made to the development of railways in England.

[92] Stretton, *Hist. Midland Rlwy.* 273.

[93] For John Ellis, see *Leic. Jnl.* 31 Oct. 1872: for E. S. Ellis, see *The Times*, 4 Dec. 1879: for Thomas Cook, see *D.N.B.*; Rae, *Business of Travel*; and Pudney, *The Thomas Cook Story*.

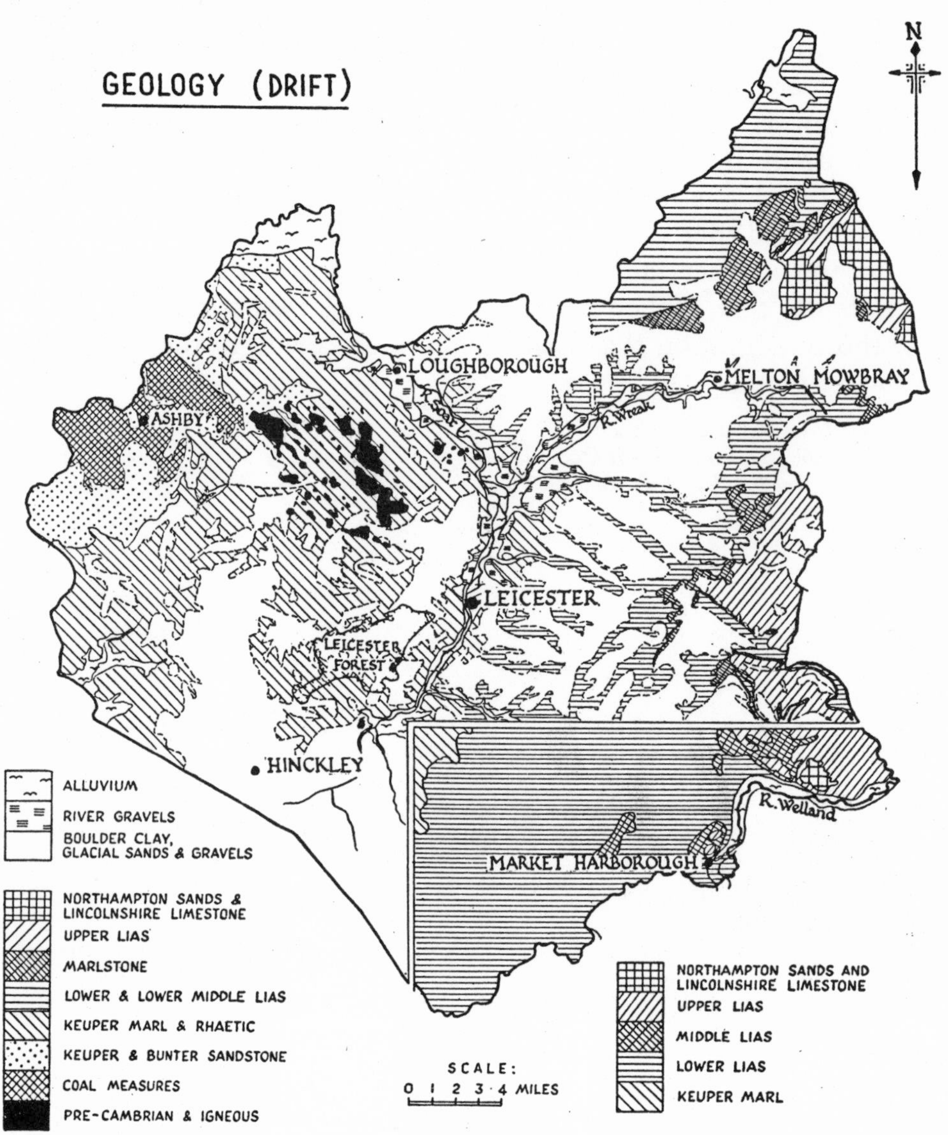

Fig. 1. No drift edition of the geology is available for the south-east corner of the county and the solid edition has therefore been used.

POPULATION

I. The Areas of Settlement. II. Domesday Population. III. The 13th and 14th Centuries. IV. The 15th and 16th Centuries. V. 1603–1801. VI. 1801 to the Present Day.

I. THE AREAS OF SETTLEMENT

THE history of population must be viewed against a geographical background which is richer in variety and bolder in contrast than would be expected from a superficial acquaintance with Leicestershire[1] (see Fig. 1). The River Soar divides the county into two roughly equal areas. To the south-west lies a low plateau where the underlying Keuper Marl gives rise to clay loams, except where a patchy cover of boulder clay and glacial sands and gravels, best developed in the south, has tended to lighten the soil. To the north-west old, hard rocks are exposed in Charnwood Forest, and soils derived from them are poor and stony, though the short, parallel valleys of Charnwood, often filled with Keuper Marl, are sometimes surprisingly fertile.[2] Farther to the north-west, soils derived from the Coal Measures are on the whole poor. They are often sandy, and nearly always acid.[3] Nor are the Keuper and Bunter Sandstones productive of a soil which would attract the medieval farmer. The very names of some of the villages where they appear suggest a poor natural vegetation quite unlike the damp oakwood forests which must have covered most of Leicestershire—Normanton le Heath, Heather, Donington le Heath, Packington on the Heath are examples.

East of the River Soar the ground rises from the alluvial flood plain and the gravel benches of the Soar through the mostly boulder-clay-covered Lower Lias to the discontinuous escarpment produced by the Marlstone—a rich, golden-brown ironstone prominent in all the older building of east Leicestershire. Above the Marlstone, which weathers to a friable, loamy soil, often calcareous, are the cold stiff clays of the Upper Lias, rarely relieved by patches of boulder clay. In the north-east of the county light, calcareous loams are characteristic on the Northampton Sands and Lincolnshire Limestone, which outcrop in a group of four or five parishes. In the east of the county the heavy clays are lightened little by boulder clays and by the patches of glacial sands and gravels which are so important in the siting of settlements. The boulder clays produce variable soils, but loams and marls are prominent among them, especially where the superficial drift is derived mainly from the chalk and Lincolnshire Limestone.

II. THE DOMESDAY RETURNS

Excluding the borough of Leicester and the holders of land, 6,406 people were recorded in the Leicestershire Domesday, composed as follows: 2,594

[1] This chapter does not deal with the population of Leicester, which is to be treated in a later volume.

[2] D. M. Auty, 'Leics.' in *Land of Britain*, ed. D. L. Stamp, pt. 57, 253. See also *V.C.H. Leics.* ii, 145–6.

[3] Ibid.

villeins, 1,892 sokemen, 1,365 bordars, 418 *servi* and bondwomen, 8 men (*homines*), 44 priests, 54 *Francigenae*, 25 knights, and 6 freemen. This is a figure slightly different from Stenton's total of 6,400[4] or the 6,662 used by Russell.[5]

It is impossible to say what relationship the figure of 6,406 bears to total population.[6] There were omissions and duplications. The arrangement of the information by feudal holdings may have resulted in the mention of some land-occupiers more than once, and some not at all. Neither borough populations nor the clergy receive adequate treatment. Only 44 priests are mentioned in the whole county, though many more may have been included under some other heading. The omission of detailed accounts of borough populations matters little outside Leicester itself. Most of those who were concerned with industry or trade may have held land and may have been included, though there is an interesting mention of *mercatores* in the entry for Melton Mowbray. Finally, it may be that each recorded *servus* was the head of a family, but it is also possible, since bondwomen are sometimes separately recorded, that each entry represents an individual.[7] Even if the assumption is made, however, that the numbers recorded in Domesday represent the number of households, there still remains the insuperable difficulty of finding a reliable figure for the average number of people in a household. Maitland suggested 5,[8] Russell 3·5,[9] though the latter figure is reached on the basis of later evidence.

One other problem of Domesday interpretation presents itself—that of identifying Domesday place-names. Only 5 of the 277 populated settlements recorded in the Leicestershire Domesday are unidentified. Few places that exist now were not mentioned: Market Harborough, founded in the 12th century, and Coalville, founded in the 19th, are the most notable omissions. A number of places in the south-west and in Charnwood are likewise not recorded and may not then have existed, but the silence of Domesday in the case of any particular settlement can never be taken as conclusive evidence that it did not exist. Bringhurst, for example, in the Welland valley was probably one of the first settlements made in Leicestershire by the Angles, yet it is not mentioned in the Survey. There is little doubt that the information concerning it is included under the entry for Great Easton.[10]

With its 6,406 recorded people, then, possibly representing as many households, Leicestershire had an average density of 12·7 persons recorded per 1,000 acres, a figure which stands moderately high among Domesday populations. The county lay as a transitional zone between the relatively dense populations of eastern and southern England and the sparsely settled north and west. Lincolnshire and Northamptonshire had average densities of 14·7 and 13·1 recorded people per 1,000 acres; the comparable figures for Derbyshire and Staffordshire were 4·6 and 4·2.[11] The distribution of recorded population within Leicestershire reflects very strongly the transitional position of the county (Fig. 2). The

[4] *V.C.H. Leics.* i, 305.

[5] J. C. Russell, *Brit. Medieval Population*, 53.

[6] See F. W. Maitland, *Dom. Bk. and Beyond*, 17.

[7] See D. Holly, 'Domesday Geog. of Leics.' *T.L.A.S.* xx, 168–202, for a comparison of maps of recorded population including and excluding the *servi*.

[8] Maitland, *Dom. Bk.* 408, 436.

[9] Russell, *Brit. Med. Population*, 50, 52.

[10] W. G. Hoskins, 'Origins and Rise of Market Harborough', *T.L.A.S.* xxv, 56.

[11] Densities in counties other than Leics. recalculated from the figures in Maitland, *Dom. Bk.* 400.

most striking feature of the map of the distribution is the contrast between east and west Leicestershire. Of the recorded adults in the county, over two-thirds lived east of the Soar and only one-fifth to the west of it. The remainder were concentrated in the Soar valley. The average density of recorded population

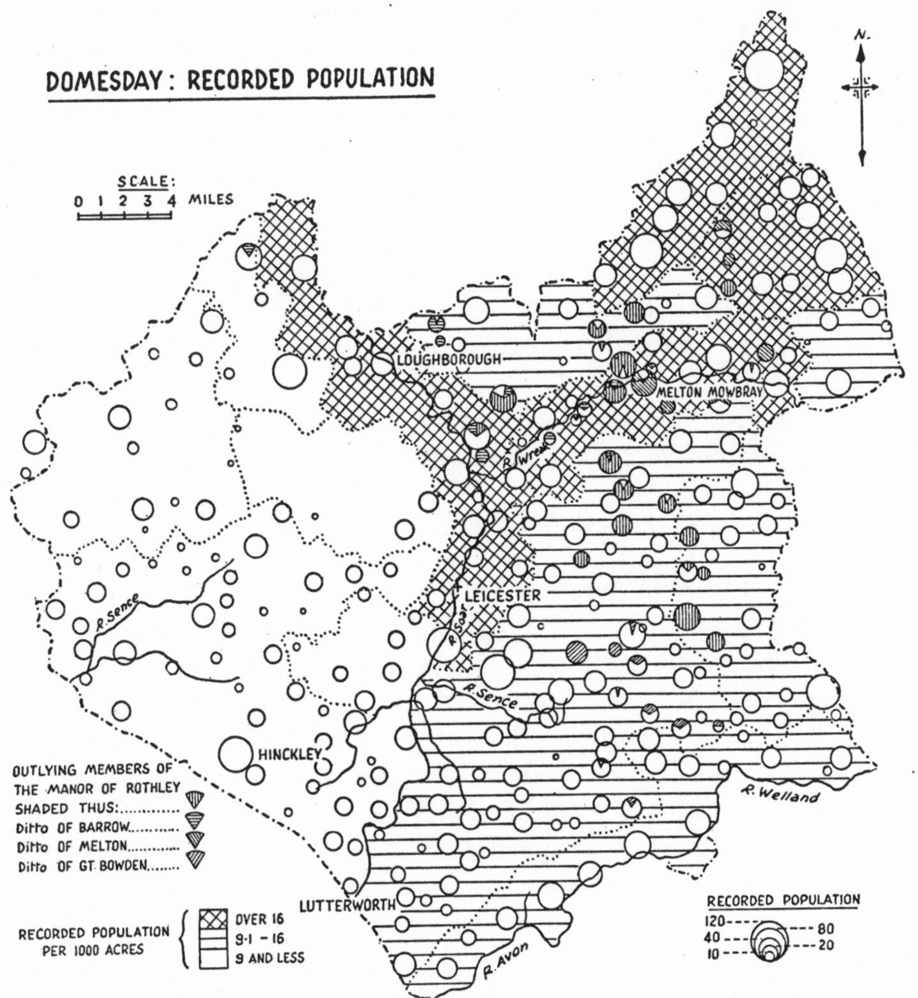

FIG. 2. Landholders are excluded. Totals of recorded population but no figures for individual places are given for the outlying members of the manors of Rothley, Great Bowden, Barrow, and Melton. The total populations have therefore been divided in proportion to the number of plough-teams, which are recorded in detail.

in the east, 13·9 per 1,000 acres, was twice as high as the density in the west. Five areas stand out as being densely peopled, and they contained all but a few of the vills with over 40 recorded people. Three of these areas are the valleys of the Soar, with 18 recorded people per 1,000 acres, the Welland, with 16, and the Wreak with 19·2. All of these areas had the resources to support a fairly dense population. The broad flood plains produced hay as well as summer pasture,[12] and it was often the supply of winter fodder that limited stock-rearing. The gravel terraces provided excellent settlement sites with a reliable water-supply as well as good, well-drained loams for arable farming. Around Leicester a high proportion of the population in such large vills as Whetstone (42), Wigston Magna (86), and Oadby (59) were the sokemen who represented the descendants of Danish armies which had once swelled the village populations,[13] and the same is, in general, true of the north-east of the county. The

[12] *T.L.A.S.* xx, figs. 6, 9.

[13] W. G. Hoskins, 'Further Notes on Anglian and Scandinavian Settlement of Leics.' *T.L.A.S.* xix, 108.

two remaining regions of dense recorded population in Domesday were both in this area of the north-east. Of the four vills which lay predominantly on the light, easily tilled soils developed on the Lincolnshire Limestone or the Northampton Sands, three were very large and the other was above the average for the county (Saltby: 77 recorded adults; Sproxton: 41; Croxton Kerrial: 59; Stonesby: 26). The average density here was the highest in the county (19·5). The deep, grey loams of the Vale of Belvoir supported a comparable density of 19·2.

West of the Soar the paucity of settlement is the most emphatic feature of the population map. The Triassic Sandstones and the acid soils of the Coal Measures supported heath and thin forest better than men. The average density was only 7·1 recorded people per 1,000 acres here, and it was not very much more (8·2) over the whole of the south-west, though Hinckley was already a substantial place of 69 recorded people and the density of population around it was moderately high. Charnwood still remained the largely untouched waste of the four great manors of Groby, Barrow upon Soar, Shepshed, and Loughborough which were scattered round its margins.[14]

III. THE 13TH AND 14TH CENTURIES

The returns to an inquisition of 1279[15] throw a little indirect light on population in the west of the county, though the nature of the return precludes any attempt to derive accurate population figures. In many of the entries, the numbers of villeins and free tenants are given, but they cannot be regarded as complete lists. Sub-tenancies, the complications of tenure in villages containing more than one manor, and the possibility of an individual being listed under different headings as a result of his holding land in different capacities make it impossible to use the statistics as an accurate indication even of the land-occupying population. No precise conclusions can therefore be drawn from the 1279 inquisition, certainly in the east of the county, for which few returns survive. But in the west there is unmistakable evidence of an increase in numbers since Domesday. In 29 places in the west of the county where the manor coincided with the village in 1279, 657 tenants are recorded, as against a recorded population of 309 in Domesday. Evidence of increase since the 11th century is most striking in Charnwood.

Charnwood Forest was never a forest in the legal sense of the term.[16] It must always have been a region in which gorse, bracken, and heather crowned the gaunt ridges above the thick woodlands of the clay-covered valleys. The thin, stony soils had been unattractive to the Domesday farmer, and there were no more than 187 recorded adults in the four manors which shared it and part of the surrounding lowlands. Between Domesday and 1279 new settlements had been established in the heart of Charnwood. Monastic orders had been prominent in the 12th-century colonization: Ulverscroft Priory was founded about the middle of the 12th century;[17] Charley Priory existed by 1190;[18] Alderman's Haw is mentioned in a charter of the reign of Henry I.[19] The lay

[14] The only settlement in the heart of Charnwood to be mentioned in Domesday is Charley (*Cernelega*), where there were 4 carucates of land which was waste: *V.C.H. Leics.* i, 336.

[15] Bodl. Libr. Rawlinson MS. 135; partly printed in Nichols, *Leics.* i, p. cx.

[16] G. F. Farnham, *Charnwood Forest and its Historians*, 1 sqq.; *V.C.H. Leics.* ii, 268.

[17] *V.C.H. Leics.* ii, 19–20.

[18] Ibid. 23.

[19] Ibid. 1.

settlement of Swithland was first mentioned in 1209–19 and Woodhouse in 1209–35.[20] By 1279, Markfield, Botcheston, Ratby, and Groby on the southern flanks of Charnwood had 131 tenants, nearly a fourfold increase on the 35 recorded persons of Domesday. Barrow, to the east, had a recorded population of 27 in 1086, but an extent of the manor of Barrow records a total of 144 free and customary tenants in 1273, including 14 tenants at Woodhouse.[21] In the west of Charnwood only one villein was recorded in 1086 at Whitwick, but in 1340 an inquisition post mortem on Henry (Beaumont) Earl of Buchan mentioned 40 villeins and an unstated number of free and customary tenants.[22]

The 1279 returns are too fragmentary to permit the distribution of population to be examined, and there is little else of value before the Black Death other than the 1334 assessments for the tenths and fifteenths. These survive for the whole county.[23] Since the assessments were collectively agreed by officials and the resident heads of religious houses in consultation with representatives of the townships themselves,[24] it is likely that they represent fairly accurately the general distribution of wealth (Fig. 3) and may indirectly reflect the distribution of population. Charnwood was poor in 1334, in spite of new settlement and the increase of numbers between 1086 and 1279. Possibly the pressure of population had driven farmers of the late 13th and early 14th centuries to till soils that were too thin and poor to provide anything but a scanty living. The area around Leicester Forest, too, was poor, but the tax assessments seem to confirm the suggestion in the 1279 inquisition that the remainder of west Leicestershire was more populous, in relation to the rest of the county, than it had been in Domesday. In east Leicestershire, villages on the stiff Upper Lias clays of the eastern uplands between the Wreak and the Welland were poor compared with the rest of the county, and Croxton Kerrial, Sproxton, Saltby, and Stonesby on the light soils of the north-east are also much less prominent on the distribution map of assessed values in 1334 than they are on the map of recorded population in Domesday.

It is not until after four visitations of the plague that the 1377 poll tax returns provide further material. They survive in a number of different forms. For the whole county, excluding Leicester, the enrolled accounts yield a total of 31,730 adults who paid a tax of 4*d.* each.[25] A considerable number of detailed assessments also exist, though they do not survive for the whole county. The receipts for the tax of 4*d.* a head from all adults give the total amount paid and the total number who paid,[26] and another set of records lists the names of those who paid 4*d.*, but in this version a man and wife counted as one person and only paid 4*d.*[27] These latter records survive for Goscote hundred and for most of Sparkenhoe, both in the west, and for a few parishes in Gartree.[28] The former survive for Framland Hundred and a number of places in the rest of the county. For 37 out of 51 villages where both the receipts and the returns survive, the totals agree fairly well if the number of wives is added in the

[20] E. Ekwall, *Oxf. Dict. Engl. Place Names*, 436; Farnham, *Charnwood Forest*, 37.

[21] Ibid. 49–50.

[22] Ibid. 136.

[23] Nichols, *Leics.* i, p. lxxxix.

[24] J. F. Willard, *Parl. Taxes on Personal Property, 1290–1334*, 5, 12.

[25] Two versions of the enrolled accounts survive. These were published by J. Topham, 'Subsidy Roll of 51 Edw. III', *Archaeologia*, vii, 337 sqq., and by C. Oman, *Great Revolt of 1381*, 163–5. See also J. C. Russell, *Brit. Med. Population*, 131. Both versions agree on the number taxed in Leics.

[26] E 179/133/17–24.

[27] E 179/133/26.

[28] Most of them were transcribed by Farnham in *Leics. Notes* and in MS. in Leics. Mus. Farnham MSS. 5 D/33/43.

second version to the total paying tax; it is obvious in some of the cases where there is no agreement that not all of the wives had been recorded. Thus at Barwell 176 paid according to the receipts, but only 2 wives are recorded for the 84 adults whose names appear in the lists of the second version.

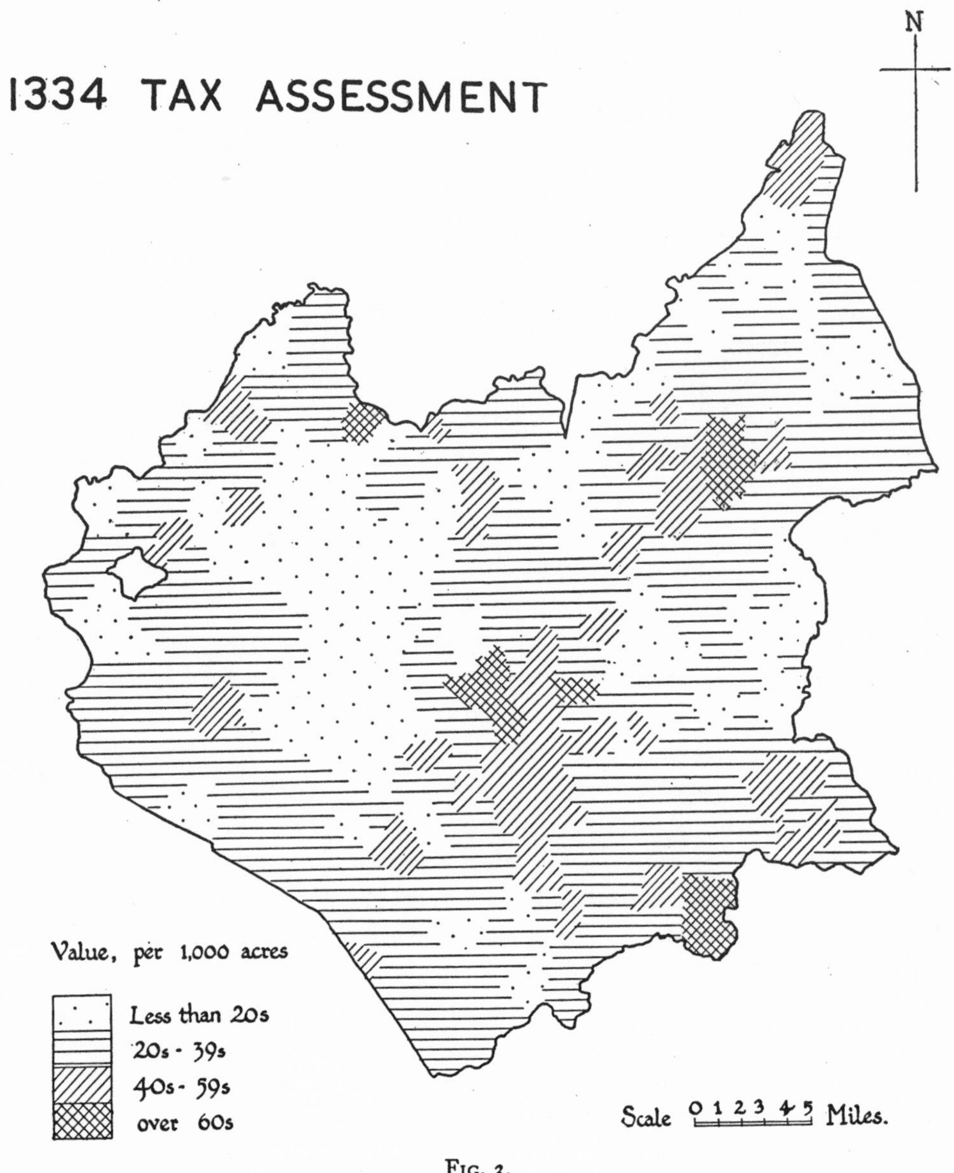

FIG. 3.

The 1377 poll tax returns are the best medieval material from which to make an estimate of total numbers, though there are two outstanding difficulties: the degree of evasion, and the relationship between tax-paying and total population. There is no means of assessing the amount of evasion, though J. C. Russell considers it to have been of little importance.[29] The tax was levied on adults of over 14 years of age, which should include two-thirds of the total population according to Russell's calculations of life-expectancy in the 14th century.[30] If these assumptions are valid, the total population in Leicestershire in 1377, excluding Leicester itself, may have been 47,595, a figure which appears to represent a very considerable increase since Domesday. With a density of 58 people to the square mile, Leicestershire was the sixth most

[29] Russell, *Brit. Med. Population*, 143–4.

[30] Ibid. 23–24, ch. viii, 173–93.

densely peopled county in England, closely following Norfolk, Bedfordshire, Northamptonshire, Suffolk, and Rutland.[31] The west of Leicestershire was much more densely peopled than it had been at Domesday (Fig. 4) and its share in the total population of the county had risen from a fifth to a third. The average size of the western village (89·8 taxpayers) was very little below the average of 95·6 for all parts of the county for which detailed records survive,

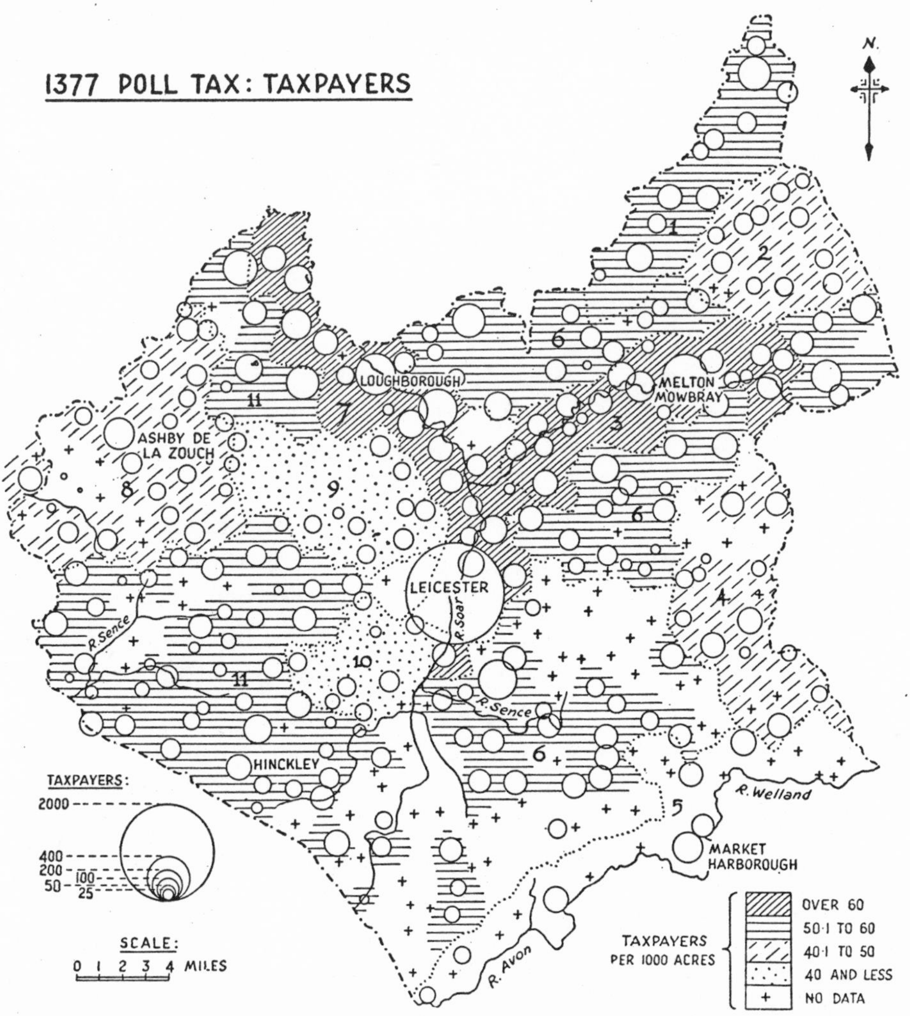

FIG. 4. Densities shown are averages for groups of parishes with broadly similar geographical characteristics, as follows: 1. The Vale of Belvoir. 2. Area of light soils in N.E. Leics. 3. Wreak valley. 4. Eastern uplands. 5. Welland valley. 6. Remainder of east Leics. 7. Soar valley 8. Coal Measures, Keuper and Bunter Sandstones. 9. Charnwood. 10. Leicester Forest. 11. Remainder of west Leics.

though the density in Charnwood was still well below the average. The large villages of the Soar, Welland, and Wreak valleys stood out in 1377 as they did in Domesday and as they continued to do until the end of the 18th century, but there had been changes in the distribution of population in the east of the county. The villages on the light soils of the north-east and those on the heavy clays of the eastern uplands were poor in 1334 and they were sparsely populated in 1377. In Domesday the former group of villages had been among the largest in the county, and the 203 persons then recorded may represent a larger population than the 323 adults who paid poll tax in 1377. The eastern uplands had been an area with well above the average density for the county in 1086,

[31] R. A. Pelham, '14th Cent. Engl.' in *Hist. Geog. of Engl. before 1800*, ed. H. C. Darby, 235.

but they fell far short of the average in 1377, and it is possible that numbers may have fallen here too.

A few villages had emerged well above the average in numbers and wealth by 1377 and had begun to take on the character of market-towns as a result of the expansion of trade and good geographical position. The largest places in 1086 had drawn their strength primarily from their wealth in land, but by 1377 they had ceded first place to rivals for whom trade was important. Melton Mowbray contained 440 taxpayers in 1377, Loughborough 360, and there were 200 at Market Harborough, which had probably been founded in the decade 1160–70, had acquired a market in or before 1203,[32] and was well placed in relation to both the Leicester–Northampton road and the wealthy and populous Welland valley. These were the largest places in the county, together with Wigston Magna, Castle Donington, Bottesford, Wymeswold, Shepshed, Sileby, and Ashby de la Zouch. No other place apparently had over 200 taxpayers, though the figures are incomplete and there is no evidence, for example, for Lutterworth, which had counted 25 burgesses among its recorded population of 67 in 1279. All of the places mentioned above, except Shepshed, Sileby, Bottesford, and Wigston Magna, had fair or market rights, though many other places which also had them in 1377 were no more than purely agricultural villages.[33]

It is impossible to assess accurately the effect of the Black Death and subsequent plagues on population in the second half of the 14th century. The register of Garendon Abbey in the north of the county enumerates five outbreaks in 1348–9, 1369–70, 1375–6, and 1390.[34] The last was regarded as the 'Great Pestilence' and suggests, perhaps, that in 1377 the worst of the plague had yet to come. Estimates of losses of population rest mainly on clerical evidence, and attention has always been concentrated on the first great outbreak. Coulton suggested that a third of the population was cut down by the Black Death;[35] Russell has reduced this figure to 26 per cent.[36] For Leicestershire, the registers of the Bishop of Lincoln for 1349–50 list 84 institutions to benefices as a result of the deaths of incumbents.[37] Eight of these were vacated twice, so that out of those men who held the 208 benefices of Leicestershire in 1348, no fewer than 76 died in the summer and autumn of 1349[38]—a mortality rate of 36·5 per cent. A year later and a year earlier, the average death-rate among the clergy was 6 per cent., so that the loss to be attributed directly to the plague was about 30 per cent., a figure which might approximate to, or be slightly higher than, the general fall in numbers.[39] How great losses were between the end of the first great plague and 1377 or the end of the century, it is impossible to say. Russell concludes that the fall in population

32 *T.L.A.S.* xxv, 56–68; *Pipe R. 1203* (P.R.S. N.S. xvi), 34. 33 See *V.C.H. Leics.* ii, 175 n. 13, 176.

34 Nichols, *Leics.* iii, 830; B.M. Lansdowne MS. 415, f. 39*a*. The register misdates by one year the first outbreak of the plague and also the battle of Agincourt. The error has therefore been corrected for the other dates mentioned: W. G. Hoskins, 'Midland Peasant' (unpublished hist. of Wigston Magna in Dr. Hoskins's possession).

35 G. C. Coulton, *Black Death*, 64–66.

36 Russell, *Brit. Med. Population*, 214–32. The figure of 26 per cent. is derived from life-tables based on Inquisitions post mortem.

37 A. H. Thompson, 'Reg. of John Gynewell, Bp. of Linc.', *Arch. Jnl.* lxviii, 301–60.

38 Nine institutions were made in Apr. and May, 16 in June, 16 in July, 13 in Aug., 12 in Sept., 6 in Oct., 10 in Nov. and Dec. and 2 in Jan., Feb., and Mar.

39 Coulton, *Black Death*, 64–66, calls attention to the fact that the lower clergy were more likely to come into contact with the disease in the course of their duties than most men.

in the four plagues from 1349 to 1377 was about 40 per cent. in the whole country, followed by a further drop of 5 per cent. by the end of the century,[40] but there is little valuable information in Leicestershire to show what happened there.

IV. THE 15TH AND 16TH CENTURIES

There is no record in the 15th century which can be used to estimate population, but in 1445 there was a substantial reduction of the 1334 tax assessment, which was distributed over the county according to the needs of each separate village. The tax reduction reveals little of the trend of population, but the distribution of the tax cuts hints at possible changes in the distribution of population since 1334, and may indicate some of the places that had been worst hit by the plague. The reduction for Leicestershire was £118 16*s.* 6*d.* on a total assessment of £756 10*s.* 11½*d.*, or 15·7 per cent.[41] Some of the larger settlements in the county appear to have suffered a decline in wealth or numbers that was well above the average: the tax assessment of Melton Mowbray was cut by 38 per cent., that of Wigston Magna by 40 per cent., and that of Barrow upon Soar by 47 per cent., though the highest reduction of all was one of 60 per cent. at Humberstone. The distribution of the cuts is uneven, though the south-west suffered most—the assessment of Sparkenhoe hundred was cut by 17·3 per cent.—and the Vale of Belvoir least, with an average cut of only 5·3 per cent.

The lay subsidies of 1524 and 1525,[42] followed by an ecclesiastical census made in 1563, are the earliest valuable evidence with a direct bearing on population after the poll tax returns of 1377. The lay subsidies should have included everyone who earned £1 a year or more, or whose goods or land were valued at £1 or more. This must have included the greater part of the labouring classes, and probably all the landholders except the clergy were included.[43] They were, of course, a tax and not a census, but they may indicate roughly the number of households. There was certainly evasion. For example, in 14 places out of 106 in Leicestershire, none at all paid on wages or land worth £1 to £2, though the normal proportion paying on this amount was as high as a third,[44] and whereas 35 paid tax in Lutterworth in 1524, for example, 42 paid in the following year. If one attempts to eliminate the crudest deficiencies of the subsidy returns, there were some 3,817 taxpayers (representing, perhaps, roughly as many households) in 184 places, or an average of 22 in each village.

In 1563 a general inquiry into the ecclesiastical organization of the county was made by diocesans at the request of the Privy Council. Among other matters the diocesans were asked to state how many households there were in each parish and chapelry. Several of them, including the Bishop of Lincoln, seem to have taken pains to found their answers upon a systematic investigation.[45] The returns for Leicestershire[46] appear to be conscientious estimates and cover

[40] Russell, *Brit. Med. Pop.* 263, 269.

[41] Nichols, *Leics.* i, pp. lxxxix–xci, from B.M. Harl. MS. 543, f. 175.

[42] Lay subsidy of 1524: E 179/133/104, 114 (Goscote), /108 (Framland), /121, 122. Lay subsidy of 1525: E 179/133/109, 115, 124 (Gartree), /110, 116, 117 (Goscote). Not all the county is included in the surviving returns. Part of Goscote hundred is missing, and almost all of Sparkenhoe.

[43] S. H. A. Hervey, *Suffolk in 1524* (Suff. Green Books, x), p. xvi.

[44] This argument need not apply in villages which had been inclosed and depopulated; e.g. at Withcote only one wealthy family was recorded in 1524, and 40 years later there was still only one.

[45] B.M. Harl. MS. 595, f. 77.

[46] B.M. Harl. MS. 618 (a return of population in the Archdeaconry of Leic.).

all but one or two minor places. Naturally the relationship between numbers and population is hard to determine. Nevertheless the 1563 return must be regarded as providing the most accurate available estimate of population for the 16th century.

Excluding the 591 families of Leicester, 8,573 families are recorded. If adjustment is made for a few parishes which were not included, there were

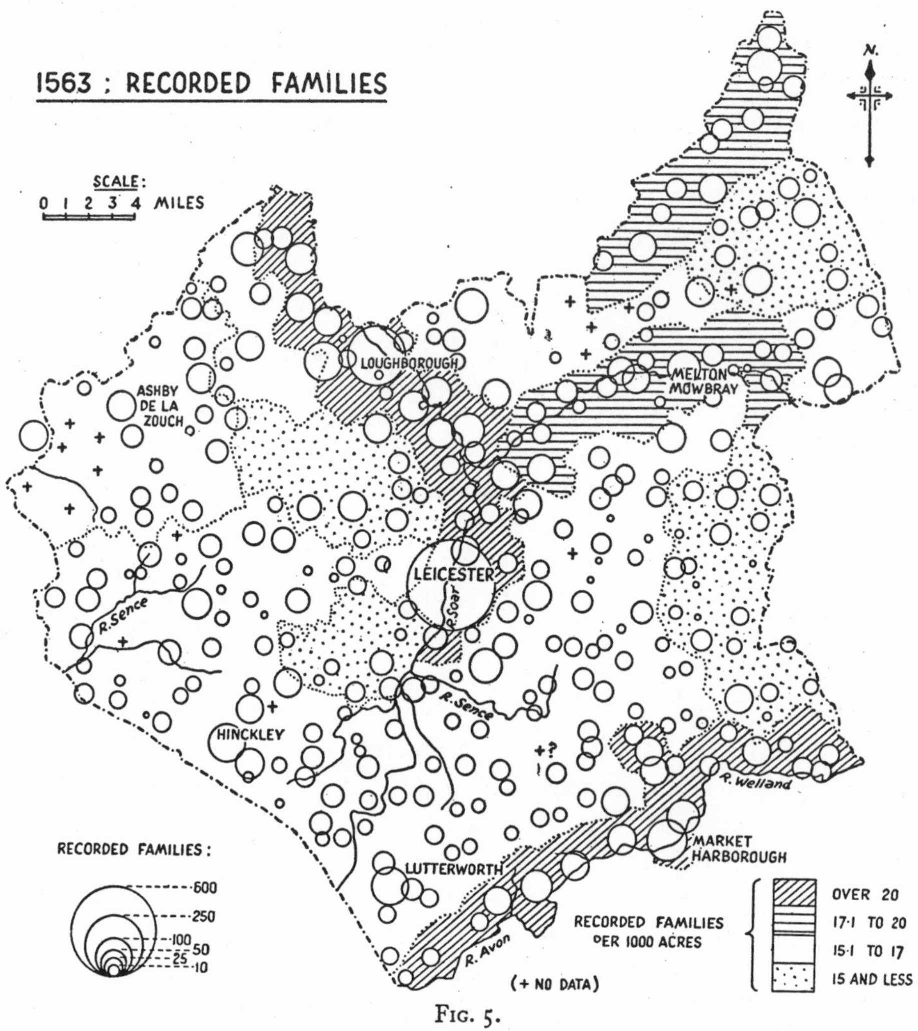

Fig. 5.

approximately 8,750 families altogether.[47] It is difficult to make comparisons, but it seems certain that the population of the county in 1563 was still far below the level it had reached before the Black Death and was substantially smaller than it had been in 1377. Numbers appear to have been increasing, however. In the 184 places for which the lay subsidies of 1524 and 1525 are usable, 5,014 households are recorded in 1563, representing an increase of 31 per cent. over the number of taxpayers recorded in the subsidies. The figures are not strictly comparable and the real increase may have been less, but it is also clear that population must have been at a very low level in the 15th and early 16th centuries.

By 1563, the west of the county was still below the east in terms of population density, with an average of 14·4 households per 1,000 acres against the

[47] Ratby, Swithland, Cropston, Anstey, Thurcaston, Stanton, and Newtown Linford are entered twice. Stonesby, Grimston, Keyham, Wartnaby, Wycomb and Chadwell, and Swinford are missing, and the total of 8,750 is reached on the assumption that each of these places contained 20 families or thereabouts.

average of 16 in the east. Charnwood and Leicester Forest still had few people, and so had the light-soil region of the north-east, with a low average density of 13·4 per 1,000 acres. Coal-mining was beginning to add to the population of the north-west. Coleorton, for example, had 16 households in 1377 and was assessed at only 29 shillings in 1334, but by 1563 it was one of the larger villages in the county with its 62 households. The most prosperous and densely peopled parts of the county were still the river valleys. The Welland and the Wreak had densities of 21·4 and 17·7 households per 1,000 acres respectively, but it was along the Soar that the largest villages in the county were to be found. Barrow, Sileby, Syston, and Belgrave, and particularly Mountsorrel appear to have benefited from growing trade as well as from wealth in meadow, pasture, and good arable land. The parishes of the Soar valley, excluding Loughborough and Leicester, had a density half as great again as the average for the whole county of 16·1 households per 1,000 acres. Among the towns, Loughborough had replaced Melton Mowbray as the largest place in the county outside Leicester, and Lutterworth and Hinckley had reached equality with Melton. All, except Melton, were larger than they had been in 1377. Market Harborough had 78 households, but its population as a town should probably include some of the 110 households recorded at Great Bowden. With the exception of Shepshed no other place had over 100 households. The gap between the size of market-towns and the largest of the purely agricultural settlements had widened considerably since the 14th century.

The 16th-century population figures occasionally give an indication of the depopulation which had followed inclosure for sheep farming and which was leading to the desertion of whole villages.[48] Some had already been so

Place	*1279 Tenants*	*1334 Assessment*	*1377 Poll tax recorded adults*	*1381 Poll tax recorded adults*	*1445 Tax cut (per cent.)*	*1524/5 Lay subsidies taxpayers*	*1563 Households*
		£ s. d.					
Baggrave	..	1 12 0	..	38	20	..	2
Bittesby	25	1 14 6	21	..	3	3	..
Brascote	..	with Newbold Verdon	..	..	..	..	2
Brooksby	..	1 1 0	41	..	36	10	..
Elmesthorpe	39	1 19 0	..	..	44	..	..
Eye Kettleby	..	1 5 0	40	..	35	..	..
Frisby (in Galby)	..	13 0	..	39	nil	10	8
Gopsall	6	18 0	20	..	28	..	..
Ingarsby	..	9 0	..	25	nil	..	1
Keythorpe	..	15 0	..	18	nil	..	2
Knaptoft	..	2 12 0	..	..	12	7	13
Lindley	19	1 18 0	..	..	30	..	1
Lowesby	..	1 15 0	25	..	24	18	4
Lubbesthorpe	18	1 1 0	26	..	41	7	10
Marston, Potters	..	17 6	26	..	26	..	..
Poultney	24	15 4	..	..	13	..	..
Quenby	..	18 6	27	..	13	4	1
Shoby	..	19 0	18	..	10	12	..
Stormsworth	35	1 11 0	63	..	11	..	..
Stretton, Great	..	1 9 0	..	21	31	4	15
Wellsborough	12	1 3 0	..	..	39	..	..
Whatborough	..	5 6	22	..	45	..	1
Whittington	..	10 0	21	..	20	..	..
Withcote	..	17 0	45	..	20	1	1

[48] W. G. Hoskins, 'The Deserted Villages of Leics.', *T.L.A.S.* xxii, 242–62; *V.C.H. Leics.* ii, 200–6.

completely depopulated that they are not mentioned; others show no more than a few taxpayers or households, and five had only one family in 1563 (see Table below). The villages already depopulated in 1563 had little in common in their previous demographic history. Many had undoubtedly been small, poor places in the 13th and 14th centuries, and their insignificance may have been one of the factors making for easy inclosure, though this was not always the case. Some, but by no means the majority, may have been severely reduced by the Black Death and subsequent plagues in the second half of the 14th century or by some obscure local disaster of the early 15th century, and already show high reductions of their tax assessments in 1445. But it is impossible to generalize, as the examples in the Table (p. 139) illustrate.

Numbers were increasing in 1563, but the next forty years saw the culmination of this upward trend in a period of even more rapid increase. The *Liber Cleri* of 1603[49] records the number of communicants in each parish, and yields a total for the county, excluding Leicester, of 38,710. Evidently total population had reached and passed the level of 1377 by 1603. But to some extent the return is suspect, since too many of the figures for individual places are suspiciously like rough guesses, and rather less than half of the parish totals are rounded off to the nearest ten. Moreover, the statistics offer no enlightenment as to the proportion of communicants to the total population or to a family. It is dangerous to use a multiplier and even more dangerous to use a multiplier for a period for which it is not designed, but, failing any more suitable figure, it may be of some value to apply to the 1603 census the ratio of 2·8 communicants to a household which is applicable for 1670–6.[50] This would make the *Liber Cleri* total equivalent to 13,825 households, representing an increase of 58 per cent. on the household census of 1563. This may approximate to reality, but whatever reasonable figure is adopted for the unknown ratios, the total certainly points to a remarkable increase since 1563. The increase of population was fairly equally distributed over the county, though the market-towns continued to grow at a considerably faster rate than the rural population, as one would expect from the increasing trade of the period. It was the smaller market centres which grew most: Hallaton and Billesdon, for example, which had been no larger than many a purely agricultural village in the first half of the 16th century, began to supplement Uppingham, Market Harborough, and Leicester as market centres in the south-east of the county.

Parish	*1524 Taxpayers*	*1563 Families*	*1603*	
			Communicants	*Households*
Loughborough	..	256	1,800	430
Market Harborough	..	78	} 1,320	315
Gt. Bowden	..	110		
Melton Mowbray (with chapelries)	..	149	1,280	300
Lutterworth	..	106	850	200
Hinckley	..	100	650	150
Hallaton	31	47	405	145
Billesdon	21	38	} 432	154
Goadby and Rolleston	17	24		

From the late 16th century to 1801 it is possible to supplement occasional estimates of population by the evidence of the parish registers, though they

49 *State of the Church*, ed. C. W. Foster (Lincs. Rec. Soc. xiii), 286–99.
50 See below, p. 143.

provide no accurate information of total numbers or precise trends and the records used by no means cover the whole county. In general, the evidence of the parish registers confirms the startling increase suggested by the ecclesiastical returns in the second half of the 16th century. The table below gives the average annual baptisms and burials in those parishes for which fairly complete figures are available:

Average Annual Baptisms

Parish	*1561–70*	*1571–80*	*1581–90*	*1591–1600*	*1601–10*	*1611–20*	*1621–30*
Claybrooke . . .	13·8*	16·6*	16·8*	16·3*	21·5	20·4	20·7
South Kilworth . .	5·7	4·7	4·4	6·4	6·0	4·0	5·1
Stoney Stanton . .	6·1	7·5	5·3	5·5	6·6	7·5	5·8
Rotherby . . .	1·0*	1·9	3·6	3·6	4·4	3·5*	4·9
Peatling Parva . .	2·8*	3·6	4·2	1·4	3·4	4·5	2·2
Muston . . .	8·6	5·6	7·6	7·9	8·7	6·9	8·7
Wigston Magna . .	..	14·4	22·9	19·5	20·9	22·8	19·7
Birstall	..	3·4*	4·2	6·7	7·9	5·6	6·5
Peckleton . . .	..	4·5	3·4	4·0*	3·3	4·5	3·2
Totals . . .	..	62·2	72·2	71·2	82·7	79·7	76·8

Average Annual Burials

Parish	*1561–70*	*1571–80*	*1581–90*	*1591–1600*	*1601–10*	*1611–20*	*1621–30*
Claybrooke . . .	6·8*	7·0*	6·6*	9·0*	10·4	17·7	16·7
South Kilworth . .	1·8	2·5	2·0	3·0	3·0	3·5	5·1
Stoney Stanton . .	3·7	4·2	2·6	2·7	3·4	5·2	3·3
Rotherby . . .	0·8*	1·2	1·8	2·3	2·5	2·4*	2·7
Peatling Parva . .	1·2*	1·4	2·2	1·4	2·1	1·8	2·8
Muston . . .	4·9	4·9	5·6	6·9	6·1	4·3	5·3
Wigston Magna . .	..	5·4	13·3	14·9	19·2	14·1	16·9
Birstall	..	2·4*	3·7	2·4	5·0	5·0	5·5
Peckleton . . .	..	2·3	3·1	2·1*	1·8	3·9	3·1
Totals . . .	..	31·3	40·9	44·7	53·5	57·9	61·4

*Records incomplete: not less than 7 years' records available for the decade.

Average Annual Excess of Baptisms over Burials

Parish	*1561–70*	*1571–80*	*1581–90*	*1591–1600*	*1601–10*	*1611–20*	*1621–30*
Claybrooke . . .	7·0	9·6	10·2	7·3	11·1	2·7	4·0
South Kilworth . .	3·9	2·2	2·4	3·4	3·0	0·5	0
Stoney Stanton . .	2·4	3·3	2·7	2·8	3·2	2·3	2·5
Rotherby . . .	0·2	0·6	1·8	1·2	1·9	1·1	2·2
Peatling Parva . .	1·6	1·6	2·8	0	2·0	2·4	0·4
Muston . . .	3·7	0·7	2·0	1·0	2·6	2·6	3·4
Wigston Magna . .	..	9·0	9·6	4·6	1·7	8·7	2·8
Birstall	..	1·0	0·5	4·3	2·9	0·6	1·0
Peckleton . . .	..	2·2	0·3	1·9	1·5	0·6	0·1
Totals . . .	...	30·2	32·3	25·7	29·9	21·5	16·4

In all except two of the parishes above, there was a marked increase in the number of baptisms in the first part of the period (33 per cent. from 1571 to 1610), but after reaching a maximum in the decade 1601–10 the number of baptisms declined slightly. The number of burials increased less rapidly than the number of baptisms, and probably less rapidly than the total population, from 1571 to 1600. Contemporary wills from Wigston Magna tell of surprisingly large families whose members had survived the hazards of childhood.[51] The rise of the yeoman farmer had been accompanied by an improvement in housing conditions, in furnishings, and in the standard of living generally, which was bound to have its effect on the death-rate.[52]

[51] Hoskins, 'Midland Peasant'.

[52] W. G. Hoskins, 'Leics. Farmer in 16th Cent.' *T.L.A.S.* xx, 48–94.

V. 1603—1801

From about 1590 to 1600 the number of deaths rose rapidly to a much higher level. Visitations of plague occurred and infant mortality increased rapidly. In Wigston Magna there were attacks of the plague in 1592, 1598, 1602, and in 1609 when 34 people were buried in the eleven weeks between 1 August and 18 October. Less violent outbreaks continued to the 1660's. At Claybrooke the average burial-rate rose sharply in the 1590's, and there was plague again in 1613 and 1614. South Kilworth was attacked in 1604, 1611, and in 1621 when 21 out of 27 burials took place in April and May. Elsewhere in the county the parish registers point to high mortality rates in the first 60 years of the 17th century as the tables below indicate.

Average Annual Baptisms

Place	*1611–20*	*1621–30*	*1631–40*	*1641–50*	*1651–60*	*1661–70*
Muston	6·9	8·7	9·2	8·3	6·0	6·7
Hoby	7·9	5·5	5·6	10·0*	9·1*	5·4*
Aston Flamville	1·4	2·6	1·6	3·0	2·4	2·7
Croft	4·0	4·3	4·6	4·5	4·2	3·5
Stoney Stanton	7·5	5·8	6·0	6·7	6·2	5·5
Wigston Magna	22·8	19·7	21·1	21·0*	20·5	20·6
Totals	50·5	46·6	48·1	53·5	48·4	44·4

Average Annual Burials

Place	*1611–20*	*1621–30*	*1631–40*	*1641–50*	*1651–60*	*1661–70*
Muston	4·3	5·3	5·4	6·5	6·4	6·9
Hoby	4·0	4·4	6·2	5·9*	7·7*	3·0*
Aston Flamville	1·7	1·6	3·1	0·9*	2·9*	1·8*
Croft	2·3	2·1	4·5	3·2	4·5	3·5
Stoney Stanton	5·2	3·3	3·8	4·3	5·4	4·1
Wigston Magna	14·1	16·9	18·8	14·0*	16·4	17·0
Totals	31·6	33·6	41·8	34·8	43·3	36·3

* Records incomplete: not less than 7 years' records available for the decade.

Average Annual Excess of Baptisms Over Burials

Place	*1611–20*	*1621–30*	*1631–40*	*1641–50*	*1651–60*	*1661–70*
Muston	2·6	3·4	3·8	1·8	−0·4	−0·2
Hoby	3·9	1·1	−0·6	4·1	1·5	2·4
Aston Flamville	−0·3	1·0	−1·5	2·1	−0·5	0·9
Croft	1·7	2·2	0·1	1·3	−0·3	0
Stoney Stanton	2·3	2·5	2·2	2·4	0·8	1·4
Wigston Magna	8·7	2·8	2·3	7·0	4·1	3·6
Totals	18·9	13·0	6·3	18·7	5·1	8·1

The failure of the number of baptisms to rise after the period 1600 to 1610 suggests that the increase of population may have come to an end then or possibly a little later. From 1630 to 1660 village populations were scarcely replacing themselves. The proportion of burials to baptisms reached an average of 96 per cent. in 14 parishes in the decade 1631–40, and 98 per cent. in 7 parishes in 1651–60, whereas it had been as low as 57 per cent. from 1561 to 1590.

The hearth tax returns for Leicestershire for Michaelmas 1670[53] and a return of the population made in 1676 for the Bishop of Lincoln provide further opportunities for an estimate of total population, though the former, of course, gives only households[54] and the latter lists of Anglican communicants,

[53] E 179/240/279.

[54] Households in the hearth tax returns are to be identified with families rather than with separate houses: see P. E. Jones and A. V. Judges, 'London Population in the late 17th Century', *E.H.R.* vi, 45–58.

papists, and Protestant non-conformists.[55] The average ratio between communicants and households worked out parish by parish is 2·8, and the fact that this ratio is fairly consistently maintained suggests that the returns can give moderately accurate estimates. Out of 170 places where both returns appear to cover the same area, two-thirds give a ratio of communicants to households which falls within 20 per cent. of the mean of 2·8. In Framland hundred, the

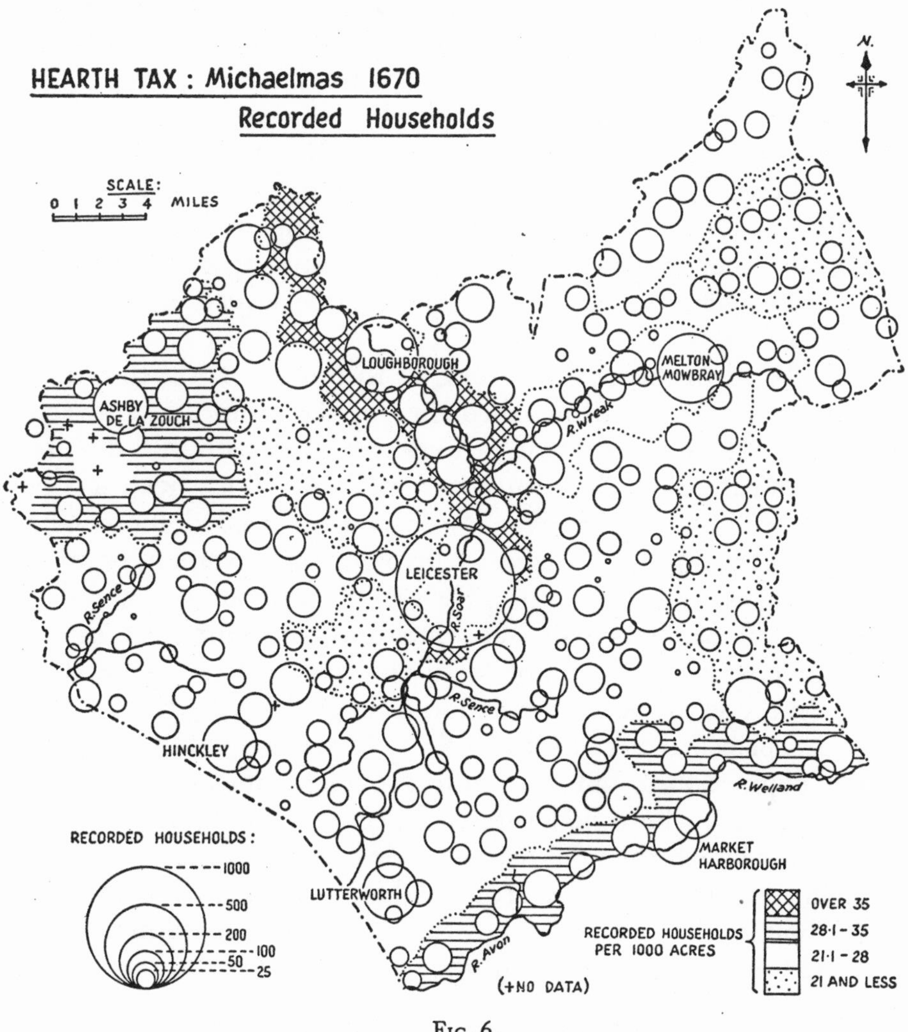

Fig. 6.

average ratio of communicants to households is higher, but examination of the hearth tax returns shows that the average proportion of hearths exempt from taxation was lower by 9 per cent. than the county average of 30 per cent. The hearth tax returns, then, give a total of 14,486 households (excluding Leicester), representing a population two-thirds greater than that of 1563, and perhaps 5 per cent. greater than that of 1603. The ecclesiastical census gives a total, again excluding Leicester, of 39,013 Anglican communicants, papists, and Protestant non-conformists, a figure 1 per cent. above the total of 1603.[56]

[55] W. G. D. Fletcher, 'Religious Census of Leics. in 1676', *T.L.A.S.* vi, 296–306.

[56] To estimate total population from these figures is hazardous. An assumption that communicants represented ⅔ of the total population would give a multiplier of 4·2 for households to population. This is rather higher than the revised multiplier of 4·04 for villages and hamlets reached by D. V. Glass on the basis of Gregory King's estimates for 1695, but slightly lower than the multiplier of 4·4 for cities and market towns outside London: 'Gregory King's estimate of the Population of Engl. and Wales', *Population Studies*, iii (4), 338–74. The hearth tax would give estimates of 59,411 or 61,181 persons, according to the multiplier used.

The discrepancy is one of no more than a few per cent. Certain it is that the rapid increase of population which characterized the second half of the 16th century came to an end in the early 17th century and was followed by very slow growth or even slight decline.

In the distribution of population (see Fig. 6) the market towns show little change since 1603. Melton Mowbray and Hinckley had grown substantially, but it was Mountsorrel, strung out along the main road from Leicester to Derby, that had grown most. West Leicestershire had reached equality, in its density of 25 households per 1,000 acres, with the east of the county. The inclosure of Leicester Forest was making itself felt in the size of the surrounding villages. There had been substantial growth in the coal-mining villages of the north-west, where Worthington had grown from 34 households in 1563 to 113 in 1670, and Coleorton from 160 communicants in 1603 to 291 in 1676. There were no other general changes in the distribution of population, but locally inclosure seems to have had considerable effect on the fortunes of individual villages.

It was believed in the 17th century, as in the late 16th, that the contemporary inclosure movement diminished the population in places affected by it, but no simple correlation can always be expected. Inclosure still usually implied conversion to pasture, though pasture for cattle as well as sheep was becoming more common.[57] Dairying or even cattle-rearing needed more labour than extensive sheep-rearing, but if inclosure involved improvement or continuation of arable farming or even more intensive use of common land, the demand for labour might well be increased. The inclosure movement of the late 16th century in Leicestershire does not seem to have affected general trends of population. In the so-called depopulation returns of 1607, 40 people were said to have been displaced at Scraptoft and 80 at Cotesbach,[58] but no tendency can be found for population to fall or even to grow less rapidly between 1563 and 1603 in those places where inclosure had occurred between 1587 and 1607. In 48 villages for which the final date of inclosure lay between 1603 and 1676 and for which comparable figures are available, it is again possible to seek some connexion, though the available statistics are crude instruments for precise measurement.[59] In no less than 35 of the 48 villages the number of communi-

Population Trends in Parishes inclosed in the 17th century[60]

	1563 Households	*1603 Communicants*	*1670 Households*	*1676 Communicants*	*1705 Families*	*No. of places*	*Per cent. change 1563–1670*	*Per cent. change 1603–76*
Eastern uplands	419	1,886	451	1,306	410	16	+8	−31
Wreak valley	83	341	104	300	97	6	+25	−12
Rest of east Leicestershire	381	1,896	545	1,439	541	13	+43	−24
West Leicestershire	362	1,555	564	1,596	615	10	+55	+3
Totals	1,336	6,023	1,778	4,977	1,758	48	+32	−17

cants was smaller in 1676 than in 1603. The average fall in numbers was 17½ per cent. At Foston, Goadby Marwood, Thorpe Arnold, Pickwell, and

57 See *V.C.H. Leics.* ii, 220–1.

58 L. A. Parker, 'Depopulation Returns for Leics. in 1607', *T.L.A.S.* 229–92.

59 For dates of inclosure, see M. W. Beresford, 'Glebe Terriers in Open Field Leics.' in *Studies in Leics. Agrarian Hist.*, ed. W. G. Hoskins, 81, 102–14, 119–23; *V.C.H. Leics.* ii, 254–9; *T.L.A.S.* xxii, 242–64.

60 See B.M. Harl. MS. 618 (1563); *State of the Church*, ed. C. W. Foster, 286–99 (1603); E 179/240/279 (1670); *T.L.A.S.* vi, 296–306 (1676); Assoc. Arch. Soc. *Rep. and Papers*, xxii, 227–365 (1705).

Shangton, for example, households were fewer in 1670 than in 1563. There had been a distinct fall in numbers between 1603 and 1676 in inclosed parishes in the eastern uplands, the Wreak valley, and the eastern lowlands, all regions predominantly of clay-loams or heavy clays. The decline was most marked on the heavy clays of the eastern uplands. There had been a slight increase in the inclosed parishes of the west and south-west where soils were lighter and better suited to arable farming.

Between 1705 and 1718, further estimates of population were made for the bishops of Lincoln,[61] in terms of families and including papists and dissenters. The estimates are rough and often rounded off to the nearest ten, and give a total of 15,340 for the county, excluding Leicester—a slight increase on the 1670 figure. Parish registers of the period 1660 to 1710, however, point to a considerable increase in the number of baptisms and to a fairly low burial rate while the average number of marriages in a sample of 27 places increased by 14 per cent. between the decades 1671–80 and 1701–10. The market towns, with the exception, perhaps, of Lutterworth and Melton and some of the smaller market centres, were growing more rapidly than they had been for a century (see Table below).[62] The drift to towns and the larger

Place	*1563* *Households*	*1603* *Communicants*	*1670* *Households*	*1676* *Communicants*	*1705* *Families*	*1801* *Families*	*1801* *Population*
Market Harborough	78 }	881	136	363 }	420	365	1,716
Great Bowden	110 }		159	471 }		173	783
Loughborough	256	1,200*	413	1,123*	530	1,000	4,603
Lutterworth	106	564	225	644	*c.* 300	401	1,652
Hinckley	100	435*	204	522	*c.* 300	966	5,070
Melton Mowbray	80	910*	340	826	*c.* 300	351	1,957
Ashby de la Zouch	64	700*	216	677*	300	635	2,674
Billesdon	38 }	432	134 }	339	150	127	695
Goadby and Rolleston	.. }		.. }		..	..	..
Hallaton	47	405	165	407	140	135	548

* Including chapelries

villages, and above all to Leicester, may well have absorbed much of the natural increase in the generation that was alive about the turn of the century. The Leicester Register of Apprentices reveals a constant flow of young men to Leicester from the countryside for 10 miles around. Families thrown off the land by inclosure became established in the towns or in the hosiery villages. New families were to be seen in Wigston Magna, for example, in the closing years of the 17th century, many of them dependent on the hosiery trade.[63]

Summaries of parish register statistics for one year in every ten and including all except 30 parishes in the county are the main source of information for population trends of the 18th century,[64] unsatisfactory though these are. Rickman's estimates of 18th-century population, like his estimates of earlier population, are based on them, with the assumption that baptismal, burial, and marriage rates were similar to those of the years about 1801.[65] In addition the decennial averages of marriages in some 27 places have been worked out. High mortality is clearly evident in the first half of the century. The number of

61 Assoc. Arch. Soc. *Rep. and Papers*, xxii, 227–365.

62 See sources cited in n. 60, and *Census*, 1801.

63 Hoskins, 'Midland Peasant'.

64 *Census*, 1801.

65 See Tables VII and VIII.

burials increased rapidly between 1710 and 1730, exceeding in that year the number of baptisms, but falling until 1740. The number of baptisms fell after 1700, regaining the level of that year only in 1740. From 1740 to the end of the century, however, the parallel increase of baptisms, burials, and marriages suggests a growing population, particularly from *c.* 1780, when the increase in the burial rate lagged behind that of baptisms. By 1801 the population was 130,000, or 114,000 excluding Leicester.

The economic changes of the 18th century in mining, industry, agriculture, trade, and transport were accompanied by very different consequences for the contrasting geographical regions of the county (see Fig. 7). The Leicestershire coalfield was hampered in its competition with the Derbyshire and Nottinghamshire fields even for the Leicester market by its poor facilities for water transport.[66] The expansion of the mining parishes in the 18th century was therefore much less rapid than it became when the railway solved problems of transport, though it was nevertheless substantial. Framework-knitting, though concentrated in Leicester, Derby, Nottingham, and to a smaller extent in Hinckley, was also a rural industry which helped to swell the population of many of the villages in the west of the county. Charnwood Forest, for example, almost doubled its population in the 18th century as a result of the expansion of framework-knitting in such villages as Anstey, Markfield, or Whitwick, and many of the villages and small towns in the Soar valley below Leicester added still further to their population through framework-knitting as well as through the increasing trade passing between Leicester and Derby on the newly navigable Soar or the turnpiked road. In the villages where framework-knitting became well established population doubled from 1705 to 1801. It is impossible to state exactly when this expansion took place, but the records of baptisms for Sparkenhoe hundred, which contained a fairly high proportion of framework-knitting villages, suggest that much of the increase came in the last few decades of the 18th century, and particularly in the 1790's, when the hosiery industry reached a peak of prosperity.[67]

The west of the county was committed to an industrial future by the end of the 18th century, and the rapidity of its population growth reflected this fact. The east of the county was still almost wholly dependent on agriculture, and the patterns of population growth were therefore very closely linked with the labour requirements of a changing agriculture. The Norfolk rotation, the cultivation of turnips, and other new methods of arable farming seem to have been of most significance for population on the light, calcareous soils of the north-east, where the increase of population between 1705 and 1801 was about 25 per cent., to be compared with an increase of only about 4 per cent. in the rest of east Leicestershire. Similarly in the first half of the 19th century, numbers increased between 1801 and 1841 by 65 per cent. in the north-east, but by only 25 per cent. in the rest of east Leicestershire. The heavy clays and clay loams of the east were, however, eminently suitable for experiments in the new methods of pastoral farming with its relatively lower labour requirements. According to William Pitt's report to the Board of Agriculture,[68] there was very little arable in the east of the county, and the process of conversion to grass which had begun in the 15th century seems to have been carried as far as the

[66] See pp. 34, 36. [67] For the places concerned and the industry in general, see pp. 3, 20–22.
[68] W. Pitt, *General View of Agric. of Leics.*

need for winter fodder permitted. The eastern uplands, with their cold, stiff clays and steep slopes which made arable farming difficult, lost population in the 18th century. In 1670 863 households were enumerated there and 759 families in 1705, but there were only 707 families in 1801. There was no more than a slight increase on the clays and clay-loams of the boulder clays and Lower Lias to the east of Leicester, but the Vale of Belvoir was still as populous as its reputation in the agriculture of the county implied it to be, and numbers had increased by about 17 per cent. in the 18th century.

Among the market towns, the smaller market centres of east Leicestershire, Billesdon, and Hallaton, seem to have reached the peak of their importance in the late 17th and early 18th centuries. They had been well placed to gather in the produce of the countryside within a radius of three or four miles, but the improvement of the roads in the 18th century seems to have diverted much of their trade to larger places. In 1801 there were fewer families in Billesdon and Hallaton than there were a hundred years earlier, though the average family had probably increased in size. In the first half of the 19th century both places grew at a rate no faster than that of the surrounding villages. The relatively slow growth of Melton, Market Harborough, and Lutterworth between 1705 and 1801 reflected the fate of the surrounding agricultural areas, just as the rapid growth in the west of Loughborough and particularly of Hinckley reflected closely the strength of their interest in the hosiery trade. Ashby de la Zouch gathered in some of the trade of the coal-mining villages and seemed to be sharing fully in their growth.

VI. 1801 TO THE PRESENT DAY

The regularity of the census returns from 1801 permit a closer analysis of the relationship between inclosure and population than is possible for the 17th century. Pitt considered that inclosure had been followed by depopulation in some parts of the county,[69] but if the population trends of those places which were inclosed after 1780 in Leicestershire are examined it becomes clear that no simple relationship exists. Excluding the villages and towns in which non-agricultural pursuits played a significant part, twelve villages were wholly or partly inclosed by Act of Parliament between 1781 and 1790. Six of them showed a drop in numbers between 1801 and 1811,[70] which could, perhaps, be attributed to the effects of inclosure. Of the 18 inclosed in the next decade,[71] five actually lost population between 1801 and 1811,[72] though only two (the Langtons and Slawston) suffered anything like a serious fall in numbers (10 per cent. and 24 per cent. respectively), and all five increased by more than 10 per cent. in the next decade. Between 1801 and 1811 two out of four parishes showed a decline in that decade—Sibson (inclosed 1803) and Bringhurst, with Easton and Drayton, in which 3,500 acres were inclosed in 1804. The effect of inclosure on population trends depended on factors such as the social structure of the village and the distribution of landholders as well as on changes in land use, as, for example, on the Duke of Rutland's estates,[73] and the changes in

[69] Ibid. 70, 81. See also *V.C.H. Leics.* ii, 228, 233.

[70] Cropston (1781), Orton on the Hill (1782), Osgathorpe (1785), Bitteswell (1787), Humberstone (1788), Mowsley (1788): see *V.C.H. Leics.* ii, 260–4; *Census*, 1801; *Census*, 1811.

[71] See *V.C.H. Leics.* ii, 260–4.

[72] The Langtons (1791), Stathern (1792), Walton on the Wolds (1792), Slawston (1793), Swithland (1798)

[73] J. D. Chambers, 'Enclosure and Labour Supply in the Industrial Revolution', *E.H.R.* lxviii, 319–43.

land use were not invariably in one direction. The inclosure of Charnwood from 1808 was followed by an increase of 35 per cent. in the population between 1801 and 1821, though expansion of the hosiery industry may have been partly responsible as well as cultivation of new land. Over much of Leicestershire inclosure had no apparent effect on population at the end of the 18th and

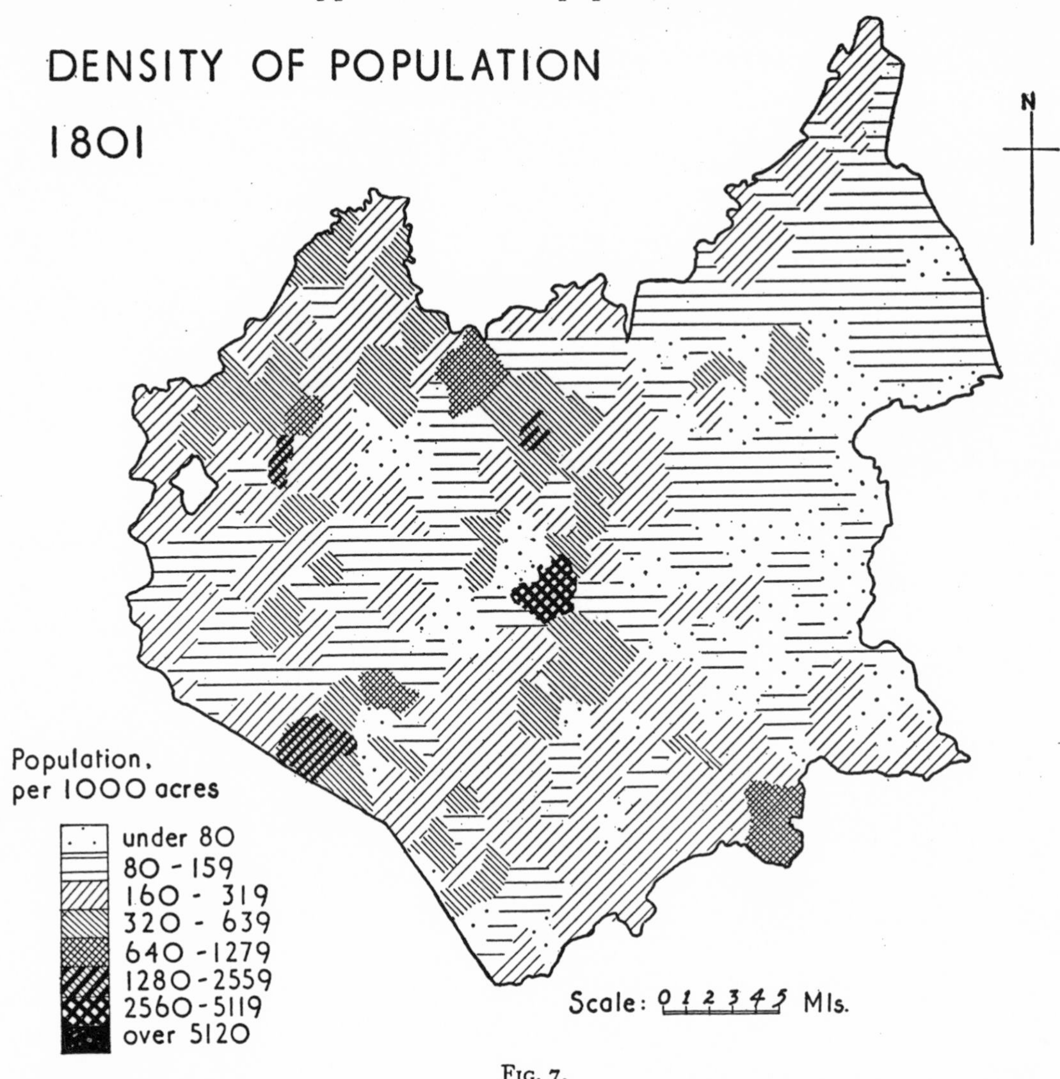

FIG. 7.

in the early 19th century. Places recently inclosed by 1801 in the Vale of Belvoir showed a general trend very similar to that in other, previously inclosed, parishes. The parishes in which numbers did fall after inclosure were those on the heavy clays of the eastern uplands, but much of this region had already undergone depopulation much earlier as a result of inclosure and conversion to pasture between the 15th and 18th centuries, Withcote and Leesthorpe in the Tudor period, for example, or Pickwell, Shangton, or Blaston in the 17th century. Horninghold, inclosed by Act of Parliament in 1730 had contained 36 households in 1670 but only 76 people in 1801.[74] Depopulation following parliamentary inclosure at the end of the 18th or in the early 19th century was thus merely the last episode in a long history of the adjustment of farming methods to soils and relief which were essentially unfavourable for arable cultivation.

[74] See p. 189; E 179/240/279; *V.C.H. Leics.* ii, 261.

Regional demographic trend in the first half of the 19th century in relation to inclosure

Area	Percentage change on 1801					Number of places	Average size of population in 1801
	1811	1821	1831	1841	1851		
1. Eastern uplands:							
A. Places inclosed in 17th century or earlier .	+5	−18	+21	+27	+21	13	106
B. Places inclosed in 18th century before 1780	0	+14	+24	+26	+36	4	399
C. Places inclosed after 1780 . . .	−15	−10	−7	+6	+30	2	203
2. Welland and Avon valleys:							
A	+6	+12	+23	+18	+15	4	124
B	+12	+10	+15	+24	+27	5	448
C	−6	+2	+3	+8	+11	7	435
3. Lincolnshire Limestone and Northampton sands: All enclosed by 1781	+17	+37	+48	+64	+62	5	291
4. Eastern lowlands:							
A	+1	+11	+19	+23	+30	19	155
B	+8	+20	+28	+35	+36	15	379
C	+10	+22	+32	+38	+41	5	382
5. Marlstone uplands and Boulder Clay wolds:							
A	+15	+33	+56	+63	+68	11	170
B	+13	+31	+41	+49	+49	9	323
C	+1	+17	+22	+27	+27	3	216
6. Vale of Belvoir:							
A	..	..	..	..	..	..	..
B	+9	+26	+45	+52	+54	3	577
C	+3	+22	+31	+55	+65	5	361

The growth of population in Leicestershire as a whole from 1801 to 1831 kept pace with the national average, but from then until the sixties the rate of growth slackened considerably. From 1831 to 1841 it was only 10 per cent. compared with the average of 14 per cent. for all of England and Wales; in the next decade it dropped to 7 per cent., and in the fifties to 3 per cent. Rural Leicestershire shared the experience of whole counties in the south-east of England in its decline of population. The notes to the *Census Reports* bear witness to the growing difficulties of the agricultural labourer and the small farmer, confronted with the need for greater capital in farming and the increasing use of machinery. A note referring to the Poor Law Union of Market Harborough stated in 1851: 'Decreases in the population of some of the parishes in this district arise from fewer hands being employed in agriculture, the unemployed having gone to the manufacturing towns.' Similar notes report migration from such widely scattered places as Thorpe Acre and Dalby on the Wolds in 1851, and Thurlaston, Stoney Stanton, Sapcote, Dishley, Walton on the Wolds, and Thurmaston in 1861.[75] Framework-knitting offered little hope of relief for those who failed to find work on the farms, since the depression of the hosiery industry in the thirties and forties had reduced wages below those to be had in agriculture, and the coal-mining of the north-west of the county was in difficulties until the opening of the Leicester–Swannington railway in 1832 enabled Leicestershire coal to compete in Leicester with the Nottinghamshire and Derbyshire product.[76]

It is not surprising, therefore, that many Leicestershire-born men chose

[75] See pp. 205–6.

[76] See pp. 12–13, 37–38.

to leave the county. By 1861 26 per cent. of those born in Leicestershire had migrated to other parts of England, but only 17 per cent. of the population of Leicestershire in that year had been born outside the county, as compared with 15 per cent. in 1841.[77] The currents of population movement are always complex, but certain trends appear to have been constant in Leicestershire in the mid-19th century: a small but significant net movement from Rutland and Northamptonshire; a much greater shift to the neighbouring counties to the north and west; and a substantial net movement to London, the West Riding and Lancashire. In 1861 there were as many Leicestershire-born persons in London as there were in both the neighbouring counties of Northamptonshire and Lincolnshire, and more in Yorkshire than in Lincolnshire.

On a much more local scale, the original returns of the 1851 census make possible a detailed study of the composition of the population in a few representative places (see Table opposite). Loughborough had more than doubled its population since 1801, and it had drawn most of its migrants from a wide area between Nottingham and Leicester, but particularly from the depressed hosiery villages of west Leicestershire. Kegworth and Shepshed had each contributed more than 100 persons to the growth of Loughborough, and as many as 40 had come from Hinckley. The strength of the Nottingham contingent suggests Loughborough's interest in lace as well as hosiery manufacture. The population of the coal-mining villages was drawn mainly from outside their own boundaries, especially in the case of Coalville. The total population in these villages had more than doubled since 1801 and Coalville had not then existed. Coleorton sent a particularly large contingent, but it was a village which had been losing population since 1801. Much of the Derbyshire element derived from the coalfield around Swadlincote on the southern flank of the Ashby anticline. The figures for the hosiery villages and Hinckley express the effects of long-continued depression in the industry. Hinckley had scarcely grown at all since 1811; Earl Shilton's population had slowly reached a peak of 2,364 and Barwell's population had been stationary since 1841. Low wages and chronic under-employment seem to have deterred immigrants and the high percentage of non-native population at Anstey and Narborough probably reflected the relatively small size of the places rather than attractiveness to migrants. Among the agricultural villages Market Bosworth and Bottesford did not grow appreciably from 1831 nor did Somerby from 1841. All of them had grown only moderately since 1801, yet they show a high rate of migration. Obviously, the numbers coming into these places must have been counterbalanced by those going out. The immigrants from surrounding villages were relatively fewer than in the hosiery or coal-mining places, and more came from adjacent counties or beyond. It seems possible, then, that the figures for migration in rural Leicestershire are symptomatic of a short-range movement of agricultural labour from village to village, with a generally northward and westward drift towards the higher agricultural wages prevailing near the industrial regions.

The growth of population and its changing distribution since 1851 are perhaps best viewed against a regional background (Figs. 8 and 9). In east Leicestershire the characteristic trend has been a steady decline from 1851 to 1939, broken by a short-lived recovery in the seventies. At first it was the lower labour requirements of more highly capitalized farming that threw population

[77] *Census*, 1841; *Census*, 1861.

MIGRATION TO SELECTED PLACES IN LEICESTERSHIRE, 1851

Column *A* of each section represents the number of persons born in the area concerned, column *B* the same number as a percentage of the total population, and column *C* the number as a percentage of the non-native population

Place	Total population	Non-native population		Birthplaces of non-native population																								
		Number	Percentage of total population	Surrounding villages			West Leics.			East Leics.			Leicester			Nearest neighbouring county				Other neighbouring counties			The rest of England and Wales			Ireland		
				A	B	C	A	B	C	A	B	C	A	B	C	County	A	B	C	A	B	C	A	B	C	A	B	C
Agricultural Villages																												
Market Bosworth	996	426	43	78	7	18	160	16	38	25	2	6	10	1	2	Warws.	45	4	11	39	4	10	54	5	11	..	..	..
Husbands Bosworth	1,002	464	46	85	8	19	22	2	5	134	13	30	15	1	3	Northants.	93	9	20	49	5	10	58	6	13	..	..	..
Bottesford	1,374	564	41	63	5	11	7	1	1	78	6	12	4	..	..	Lincs.	177	13	31	18	1	3	39	3	6	2	..	..
																Notts.	164	12	30									
Somerby	503	278	56	52	10	19	4	1	1	74	15	27	9	2	3	Rut.	73	15	26	224	4	8	31	6	10	..	..	..
Hosiery Villages																												
Barwell	1,362	306	23	106	8	35	78	6	26	24	2	8	12	1	4	Warws.	40	3	13	20	2	7	15	1	5	5	..	2
Earl Shilton	2,364	666	27	119	5	15	213	9	28	74	3	10	58	2	8	,,	53	2	7	61	3	8	36	2	4	6	..	..
Wigston Magna	2,430	703	29	136	6	19	129	6	18	178	7	25	59	2	8	Northants.	57	2	8	59	2	8	49	2	7	9	..	1
Anstey	826	302	37	58	7	19	120	15	40	38	5	13	40	5	13	Notts.	19	2	6	11	1	4	11	1	4	5	..	1
Narborough	782	353	45	89	12	25	72	9	21	77	10	22	39	5	11	Northants.	16	2	4	21	3	6	36	4	10	2	..	..
Coal-mining Villages																												
Whitwick	2,145	1,078	54	273	13	25	316	15	29	33	1	3	27	1	2	Derbys.	108	5	10	69	3	6	60	3	5	89	4	8
																Notts.	71	3	6									
Swannington	822	501	61	225	27	45	110	14	22	11	1	2	5	1	1	Derbys.	56	7	11	56	7	11	17	2	3	10	1	2
Thringstone	1,298	674	52	330	25	48	141	12	21	13	1	2	3	..	..	,,	68	5	10	71	5	10	23	2	3	9	1	1
Hugglescote and Donington	1,014	521	51	171	17	34	187	19	37	21	2	4	15	1	3	,,	55	5	10	51	5	10	17	2	3	..	..	..
Coalville	620	507	83	147	24	29	103	16	20	10	2	2	6	1	1	,,	128	20	25	69	11	13	12	2	2	1	..	..
Towns																												
Hinckley	5,974	1,753	29	343	6	20	399	7	23	93	2	5	122	2	7	Warws.	342	6	20	193	3	11	157	3	8	57	1	3
Loughborough	10,977	4,317	46	667	6	13	1,520	13	30	439	4	9	256	2	5	Derbys.	301	3	6	303	3	6	454	4	9	166	1	3
																Notts.	489	4	10									
																Nottingham (town)	280	3	6									

off the land, and later the competition of cheap overseas wheat which added to the difficulties of arable farming. There were, however, two significant exceptions to this trend. On the one hand, an almost exclusively pastoral economy had already been adopted in the eastern uplands by the middle of the 19th century and the population of the area, already fairly sparse, was therefore little

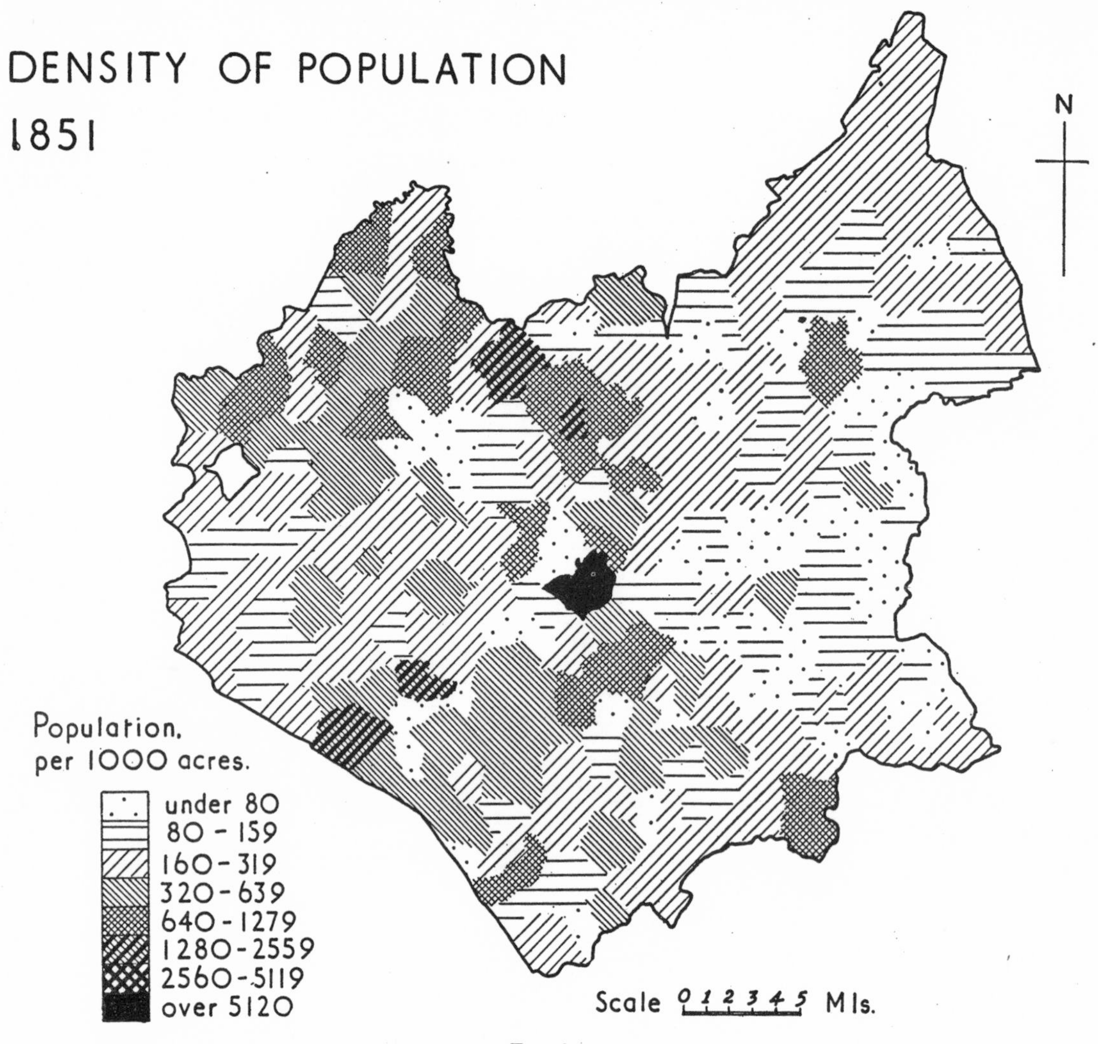

FIG. 8.

affected by the collapse of grain prices in the sixties and continued to grow until 1881. On the other hand, the limestone region of the north-east, with its lighter soils, was more definitely committed to arable farming than the Lias clays, and conversion to a pastoral economy was less easy, so that population continued to decline from 1841 to 1939:

	1841	*1851*	*1861*	*1871*	*1881*	*1891*	*1900*	*1939*
Eastern uplands . .	4,537	4,719	4,973	5,147	5,297	4,883	4,576	4,099
Limestone region .	2,394	2,361	2,284	2,175	1,966	1,703	1,569	1,516
Eastern lowlands .	3,266	3,408	3,528	3,398	3,500	3,028	3,029	2,781

(Figures for the eastern lowlands consist of a random selection of 10 parishes in the area.)

In the west of the county it was industry that mattered most and it was the coal-bearing region where changes were most marked. The growth of population in this region had been sporadic during the 18th century when the expansion of mining had been limited by the difficulties of transport. It was not until the construction of the Leicester–Swannington railway that coal-mining in Leicestershire received the stimulus which led to the haphazard but rapid growth of the new, drab town of Coalville.[78] With a population of a few hundred in 1851 Coalville had grown to a town of 25,744 people in 1951. Other changes in the population of the coalfield were characteristic of the fate of

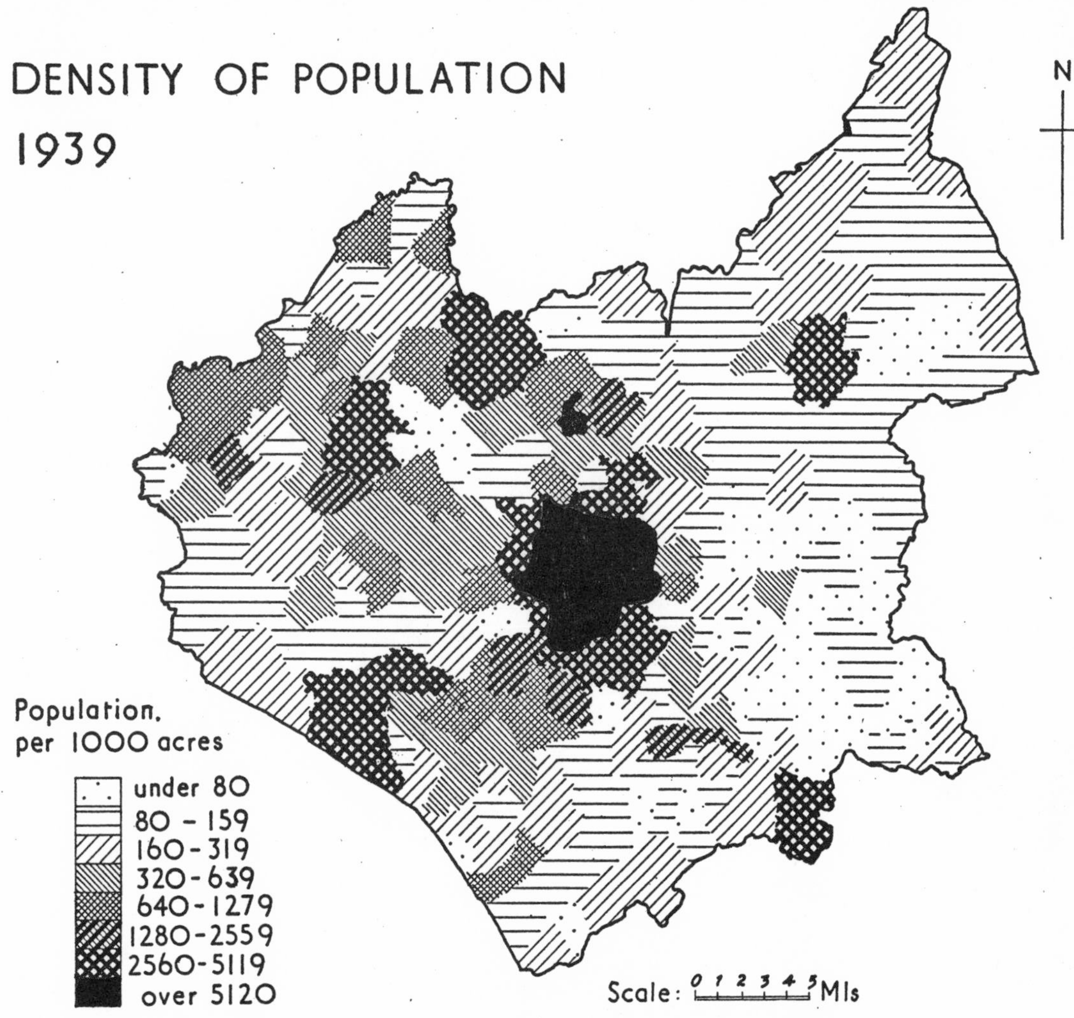

FIG. 9. Based on the Registrar-General's estimate of population.

coal-mining villages throughout the country. As the scale of working grew and as old pits were worked out and new ones created, the centres of population shifted, usually eastward to the deeper coal underlying the Keuper Marl.

Growth over much of the south-west of the county was dependent mainly on the fortunes of the hosiery industry. Apart from Loughborough, Leicester, and Hinckley, 22 villages which were engaged in the industry in 1831 had contained some 22,800 people in 1801, and numbers increased to a maximum of 32,800 in 1841. But depression, low wages, and under-employment had become almost endemic in the trade since the end of the Napoleonic Wars, and there was a gradual exodus to the towns, which is mentioned for several places in the notes to the *Census Reports*. From 1841 numbers stagnated. In the fifties and sixties, however, the factory system brought better wages and

[78] See p. 38.

conditions and a significant withdrawal of the industry from the smaller places.[79]

It was, of course, the drift to the towns that dominated the demographic history of Leicestershire in the 19th century. Hinckley, Loughborough, and Coalville eventually emerged in 1951 as the three largest towns after Leicester. In the east of the county Market Harborough and Melton shared a much slower rate of growth until the expansion of light industry in them in the 20th century.[80]

Though Leicester City is here excluded, it is impossible to consider the population of the county in the 19th and 20th centuries without some mention of it. The city increasingly dominates the pattern of population, drawing into it, partly as a result of its central position, many of the people who sought work or wealth which was not to be had in the more rural parts of the county. Even by 1851, the city had nearly a quarter of the whole population of the county; by 1901 it had 36 per cent., and in 1951 its 285,181 people constituted no less than 45 per cent. of all the people in the county—and over a half if one includes the whole sprawl of the city beyond its administrative boundaries. If in the 19th century Leicester came to dominate the county economically, in the 20th it has come to dominate it physically (compare Figs. 8 and 9). Even in 1881, Leicester had spread beyond its boundaries to swell the populations of Aylestone, Humberstone, Evington, and Knighton. In 1871 these parishes contained some 4,600 people; in 1881, 14,720. Since 1901 a second ring of parishes has been involved in the urban spread and in these population has grown from 10,000 in 1901 to 38,500 in 1939.[81]

SUMMARY AND CONCLUSION

No more than tentative conclusions may be drawn from the medieval evidence for population changes. Domesday records a population of 6,406, which might represent roughly that number of households. Between 1086 and 1279 there is no evidence for population changes: although the evidence found in 1279 is poor it points to a substantial increase in the west of the county since 1086. In 1377 the poll tax of 4*d.* was paid by 31,730 adults, representing, perhaps, 47,595 people. This is the most reliable estimate that can be made of the population during the Middle Ages. It suggests a substantial increase since Domesday, particularly if it has been rightly assumed that there was a fall of 30 to 40 per cent. between 1348 and 1377. By 1377 Leicestershire was among the most densely peopled counties of England, situated on the fringe of a zone of high density which extended to the south and east to East Anglia. In 1563, when more reliable data are available, the population of 8,750 households, or thereabouts, had not yet regained the level of 1377. In the second half of the 16th century and again in the last quarter of the 17th, ecclesiastical estimates of population, the hearth tax returns and the parish registers indicate periods of rising numbers coinciding with economic prosperity and followed by periods of high mortality and slow population growth or even slight decline. Numbers rose again from *c.* 1740, but the rapid growth characteristic of the 19th century to 1831 appears to have been set in motion only in the last decades of the 18th

[79] See pp. 16, 18.

[80] See Population Table, pp. 183, 188, 193.

[81] Birstall, Thurmaston, Scraptoft, Thurnby, Oadby, Braunstone, Glenfields, Kirby Muxloe, and Blaby.

century. In the 19th century the rate of growth slackened from 1831 and reached a minimum of 3 per cent. in the decade 1851–61, after which the rate of growth recovered in the sixties and seventies. In 1951 the total population of the county was 631,077 but 45 per cent. of this number were concentrated in the city of Leicester.

There have been fundamental changes in the distribution of population. In Domesday the most striking feature is the contrast between east and west Leicestershire, and the distinction between them has continued to the present. In the 14th century the west was much more densely peopled than in 1086, in spite of the poverty of Charnwood and the existence of Leicester Forest. It was not until the end of the 17th century that the densities of population in east and west Leicestershire were equal, but in the 18th and 19th centuries it was the expansion of coal-mining and rural industry in the west that enabled its population to exceed that of the east, where there was no alternative occupation to farming which was increasingly concerned with stock-raising, dairying, and fattening. In east Leicestershire differences of soil and relief influenced population distribution, but not always in the same way. The ease with which the light soils of the north-east could be cultivated may have been a factor in the high density of its population in Domesday, but it is clear that this was an area which was less prosperous or less populous than most of the county in the 14th century and in 1563. Again, in the late 18th and 19th centuries the revolution in methods of farming seems to have produced population trends on the light soils of this area which were different from those on the clays and clay loams. The eastern uplands, with their heavy soils and difficult relief, best suited to permanent pasture, were an area of low population density from the 14th century onwards, and it was here that inclosure, from the 15th to the early 19th century, was usually attended by loss of population. The Soar valley has always attracted population, at first because of its agricultural wealth and its accessibility from the Trent, and later because of the spread of industry along a much-frequented route from London to the north. The Welland valley, on the other hand, was densely populated as long as agriculture was the predominant source of wealth, but since it connected no industrial towns with one another and carried little traffic the valley lost its importance as an area of settlement in the late 18th and 19th centuries.

The growth of the towns, foreshadowed in the 14th century, becomes important in the distribution of population in the 16th and 17th centuries, which also saw the rise of smaller market centres between Leicester and the towns near the boundaries of the county. By 1563 Melton had given way to Loughborough as the largest place outside Leicester, but it was not until the 18th century that Hinckley and Ashby de la Zouch in the industrial west began to draw ahead of the eastern towns. Ashby itself was overtaken and surpassed by the mushroom growth of Coalville. By 1951 more than 70 per cent. of the total population of the county was concentrated in Leicester, Loughborough, and the urban districts.

Table I

DOMESDAY: RECORDED POPULATION, EXCLUDING LANDHOLDERS

In this table chapelries, hamlets, &c., are grouped under the parishes of which they formed part.

Parish	*Sokemen*	*Villeins*	*Bordars*	*'Servi'*	*Priests*	*Knights*	*'Francigenae'*	*Freemen*	*Men*	*Total*
Framland Hundred										
Ab Kettleby	6	7	4	..	1	..	..	..	..	18
Holwell	..	3	2	..	1	..	..	..	..	5
Barkestone	25	17	2	7	1	..	..	..	..	52
Belvoir	..	..	..	..	..	..	..	..	..	..
Bescaby	..	..	..	..	1	..	10	..	..	..
Bottesford	67	14	18	10	..	..	..	..	..	120
Normanton	..	..	..	..	..	..	..	..	..	..
Easthorpe	..	..	..	..	..	..	..	..	..	..
Branston	6	10	1	4	..	..	..	..	..	21
Broughton, Nether	24	9	4	..	..	..	..	..	..	37
Buckminster	20	8	3	..	..	..	..	..	..	31
Sewstern	1	6	..	..	..	..	..	..	..	7
Burton Lazars	..	6	4	..	..	..	..	..	..	10†
Clawson, Long	33	19	5	13	..	..	..	..	..	70
Coston	12	10	1	2	..	..	..	..	..	25
Croxton Kerrial	30	22	2	5	1	..	..	..	..	59
Dalby, Little	23	5	1	..	..	..	..	..	..	30
Eastwell	..	7	3	..	..	..	..	..	..	10†
Eaton	..	..	..	..	..	..	..	..	..	..
Edmondthorpe	4	33	6	4	1 includes Wymondham				..	48
Garthorpe	..	..	2	..	..	..	..	..	..	2
Goadby Marwood	..	..	..	..	..	..	..	..	..	..†
Harby	26	7	6	8	..	..	..	..	..	47
Harston	20	5	1	..	..	..	..	..	..	26
Hose	8	23	6	11	..	..	1	..	..	49
Kirby Bellars	..	6	4	..	..	..	..	..	..	10†
Knipton	15	10	4	4	..	..	..	..	..	33
Melton Mowbray	..	20	14	4	2+*mercatores*		..	..	..	40
Freeby	..	..	..	..	..	..	..	..	..	..†
Welby	18	7	3	..	..	..	..	..	..	28
Eye Kettleby	..	..	..	..	..	..	..	..	..	..†
Muston	..	..	..	..	..	..	..	..	..	..
Overton, Cold	4	8	4	..	1	..	..	..	..	17
Plungar	..	..	..	..	..	..	..	..	..	..
Redmile	2	..	2	..	..	..	..	..	..	4
Saltby	23	24	14	16	..	..	..	..	..	77
Saxby	6	11	..	..	..	..	..	..	..	17
Scalford	17	5	14	..	..	..	..	..	..	36
Somerby	..	11	5	..	1	..	..	..	..	17*
Sproxton	30	7	1	2	1	..	..	..	..	41
Stapleford	23	23	4	4	..	..	..	..	..	54
Stathern	28	2	3	..	..	..	..	..	..	33
Stonesby	11	4	5	7	..	..	..	..	..	27
Sysonby	3	4	..	..	..	..	..	..	..	7†
Thorpe Arnold	11	24	11	2 includes Brentingby			..	..	..	48
Waltham on the Wolds	24	1	8	4	..	1	..	..	..	38
Withcote	..	1	..	..	..	..	..	..	..	1
Wyfordby	..	12	8	7	..	..	..	..	..	27†
Brentingby	See Thorpe Arnold			..	..	..	..	..	..	..
Wymondham	See Edmondthorpe			..	..	..	..	..	..	..
Outlying parts of manor of Melton(†)	100	10	13	..	..		..	..	..	123

POPULATION

Parish	*Soke-men*	*Vil-leins*	*Bor-dars*	*'Servi'*	*Priests*	*Knights*	*'Franci-genae'*	*Free-men*	*Men*	*Total*
Gartree Hundred										
Billesdon . . .	..	15	5	2	..	..	..	..	..	22
Goadby . . .	..	4	2	1	..	..	..	..	..	7
Rolleston . . .	..	7	1	..	..	1	..	..	..	9
Blaston . . .	15	1	..	..	..	..	..	..	..	16
Bosworth, Husbands .	20	10	13	3	..	..	..	..	..	46
Bowden, Great . .	13	12	24	..	..	..	..	..	..	49
Market Harborough .	..	..	..	..	..	..	..	..	..	..
Bringhurst . . .	..	..	..	..	..	..	..	..	..	..
Drayton . . .	..	..	..	..	..	..	..	..	..	..
Prestgrave . .	..	4	2	..	..	..	..	..	..	6
Great Easton . .	12	20	5	..	..	2	..	..	..	39
Burrough on the Hill .	1	5	7	4	..	..	..	..	..	17
Burton Overy . .	6	15	5	8	..	..	..	..	..	34
Carlton Curlieu . .	..	9	8	5	1	..	1	..	..	24*
Cranoe . . .	..	4	..	..	..	..	..	..	..	4*
Evington . . .	..	29	2	6	..	..	..	..	..	37
Fleckney . . .	..	2	1	..	..	..	..	..	..	3
Foxton . . .	3	18	3	6	1	..	..	..	..	31*
Galby. . . .	11	14	2	7	..	2	1	..	..	37*
Frisby . . .	1	2	3	1	..	..	..	..	..	7
Glen, Great . .	20	14	6	5	..	..	..	..	..	45
Stretton, Great . .	..	..	..	..	..	..	..	..	..	..*
Glooston . . .	..	6	2	..	..	..	..	..	..	8
Gumley.. . . .	3	6	5	4	1	..	..	1	..	20
Hallaton . . .	1	19	3	2	..	..	..	1	..	26
Horninghold . .	3	8	2	..	..	..	..	..	..	13
Houghton on the Hill .	..	5	3	2	..	..	..	..	..	10
[Hungarton (part)] .	..	..	..	..	..	..	..	..	..	..
Baggrave . . .	..	..	..	..	..	..	3	..	..	..‡
Ingarsby . . .	..	16	7	5	..	..	..	..	..	32
Illston on the Hill .	15	3	4	..	1	..	1	..	..	22*
Kibworth Beauchamp .	..	17	8	3	..	..	..	..	..	28
Kibworth Harcourt .	6	10	5	6	..	..	1	..	..	28
Knossington. . .	21	2	8	..	..	..	..	..	..	31
Langton, Church . .	1	21	7	3	1	1	..	..	..	34
Langton, East . .	..	..	..	..	..	..	..	..	..	..
Langton, Thorpe . .	..	11	11	7	..	..	..	..	2	31
Langton, Tur . .	2	25	6	6	..	..	..	..	..	39
Langton, West . .	..	..	..	..	..	..	..	..	..	..
Laughton . . .	..	3	2	2	..	..	..	..	..	7
Lubenham . . .	..	25	10	7	..	1	2	..	..	45
Medbourne . .	..	13	6	3	..	..	..	..	..	22*
Holt, Neville . .	..	..	..	..	..	..	..	..	..	..
Mowsley . . .	..	5	2	1	..	..	..	..	..	8
Norton, King's . .	..	..	..	..	..	..	..	..	..	..*
Noseley . . .	..	16	8	3	1	..	..	..	..	28
Owston and Newbold .	..	15	6	..	..	..	1	..	..	22
Pickwell and Leesthorpe	26	7	9	14	1	..	..	..	..	57
Saddington . . .	11	17	5	..	..	..	..	..	..	33
Scraptoft . . .	6	6	3	4	..	..	..	..	..	19
Shangton . . .	2	4	4	3	..	..	..	..	..	13*
Slawston . . .	..	4	4	..	..	..	..	..	..	8
Othorpe . . .	2	8	4	..	..	..	..	..	..	14
Smeeton Westerby .	9	3	4	..	..	..	..	..	..	16*
Stockerston . . .	34	21	5	4	..	..	..	..	..	64
Holyoaks . . .	..	4	2	1	..	..	..	..	..	7
Stonton Wyville . .	..	15	2	2	1	..	..	..	..	20
Stretton, Little . .	..	..	..	..	..	..	..	..	..	..
Theddingworth . .	9	13	14	..	..	..	..	..	2	38
Thurnby . . .	..	..	..	..	..	..	..	..	..	..
Bushby . . .	..	..	..	..	..	..	..	..	..	..
Stoughton . . .	..	..	..	..	..	..	..	..	..	..

Parish	*Soke-men*	*Vil-leins*	*Bor-dars*	*'Servi'*	*Priests*	*Knights*	*'Franci-genae'*	*Free-men*	*Men*	*Total*
[Tilton (part)]	..	..	..	..	..	..	..	..	..	..
N. and S. Marefield	..	..	..	..	..	..	..	..	..	..‡
[Tugby (part)]	..	..	..	..	..	..	..	..	..	..
Keythorpe	1	4	3	1	..	..	1	..	..	10
Welham	..	11	1	3	1	..	..	..	..	16
Wistow	9	5	5	1	..	..	2	..	..	22
Newton Harcourt	8	11	5	6	1	1	..	..	..	32
Outlying parts of the manor of Gt. Bowden(*)	60	2	16	..	..	..	..	..	..	78
East Goscote Hundred										
Allexton	..	4	4	..	..	..	..	..	..	8‡
Asfordby	..	2	..	..	..	..	..	..	..	2‡
Ashby Folville	..	27	3	2	1	..	..	..	..	33
Newbold Folville	..	5	4	..	..	..	..	..	..	9
Barsby	..	3	..	..	..	..	..	..	..	3‡
Barkby	10	7	3	3	..	..	4	..	..	27
Barkby Thorpe	..	6	5	1	..	..	4	..	..	12
Thurmaston (part)	See Belgrave		..	..	..	..	..	..	..	..
Hamilton	..	..	..	..	..	..	..	..	..	..
Barrow upon Soar	..	11	13	3	..	..	..	..	..	27
Beeby	5	21	3	2	..	..	..	..	..	31
Belgrave	7	11	5	3	..	..	..	..	..	26
Thurmaston (part)	2	18	7	5	..	..	..	..	..	32
Brooksby	..	..	2	..	..	..	..	..	..	2°
Cossington	..	..	..	..	..	..	..	..	..	..°
Croxton, South (with Quenby)	..	11	6	5	..	..	1	..	..	22
Dalby, Great	16	13	1	2	..	1	..	..	..	33
Dalby, Old	2	13	8	..	..	1	..	..	..	24
Frisby on the Wreak	..	..	..	..	..	..	..	..	..	..‡°
Gaddesby	..	..	1	..	..	..	..	..	..	1‡°
Grimston	2	5	..	..	..	..	..	..	..	7‡
Hoby	..	8	4	..	..	..	..	..	..	12
Humberstone	14	..	6	..	..	..	..	..	..	20
Hungarton (part)	7	..	..	2	..	..	..	..	..	9
Quenby	See S. Croxton		..	..	..	..	..	..	..	..
Launde	..	..	..	..	..	..	..	..	..	..
Loddington	9	7	7	..	..	..	..	..	..	23
Lowesby	7	6	5	..	1	..	..	..	..	19
Newton, Cold	5	4	2	..	..	..	..	..	..	11
Norton, East	3	9	4	..	..	..	..	..	..	16
Prestwold	1	..	..	..	..	..	..	..	..	1°
Burton on the Wolds	11	?6	?3	..	..	..	..	..	..	?20
Cotes	..	..	..	..	..	..	..	..	..	..
Hoton	..	2	..	..	..	..	..	..	..	2°
Queniborough	..	28	7	..	..	..	..	..	..	35
Ragdale	4	..	..	..	..	..	..	..	..	4
Willowes	..	..	..	..	..	..	..	..	..	..
Ratcliffe on the Wreake	..	3	2	..	..	..	..	..	..	5
Rearsby	..	1	3	..	1	..	..	..	..	5°
Rotherby	..	..	..	..	..	..	..	..	..	..°
[Rothley (part)]	..	..	..	..	..	..	..	..	..	..
Keyham	..	..	..	..	..	..	..	..	..	..‡
Wartnaby	..	..	..	..	..	..	..	..	..	..‡
Saxelby	..	..	..	..	..	..	..	..	..	..‡
Seagrave	..	4	4	..	..	..	..	..	..	8‡°
Shoby	8	4	2	..	..	..	..	..	..	14
Sileby	4	18	4	4	..	..	..	..	..	30‡°
Skeffington	..	..	..	..	..	..	..	..	..	..‡
Syston	11	17	1	..	1	..	..	..	..	30
Thrussington	30	4	3	..	..	..	..	..	..	37

Parish	*Sokemen*	*Villeins*	*Bordars*	*'Servi'*	*Priests*	*Knights*	*'Francigenae'*	*Freemen*	*Men*	*Total*
Tilton (part)	..	17	3	..	1	..	..	..	..	21‡
Halstead	..	..	..	..	..	..	..	..	..	..‡
Whatborough	1	3	11	..	..	..	..	..	..	15
Tugby (part)	..	..	..	..	..	..	..	..	..	..‡
Twyford	..	..	3	..	..	..	..	..	..	3‡
Thorpe Satchville	..	..	..	..	..	..	..	..	..	..
Walton on the Wolds	7	2	1	..	..	..	..	..	..	10
Wycomb and Chadwell	..	..	..	..	..	..	..	..	..	..‡
Wymeswold	4	18	5	1	..	..	11	..	..	39
Outlying parts of the manor of Rothley (‡)	204	157	94	..	..	..	..	..	..	455
West Goscote Hundred										
Ashby de la Zouch	6	8	4	2	1	..	..	..	..	21
Alton Grange	..	15	4	4	..	1	..	..	..	24
Blackfordby	..	..	..	..	..	..	..	..	..	..
Boothorpe	..	1	..	..	..	..	..	..	..	1
Woodcote	..	..	..	..	..	..	..	..	..	..
[Barrow upon Soar (part)]	..	..	..	..	..	..	..	..	..	..
Beaumanor	..	..	..	..	..	..	..	..	..	..
Maplewell	..	..	..	..	..	..	..	..	..	..
Mountsorrel	..	..	..	..	..	..	..	..	..	..
Quorndon	..	..	..	..	..	..	..	..	..	..
Woodhouse	..	..	..	..	..	..	..	..	..	..
Beaumont Leys	..	..	..	..	..	..	..	..	..	..
[Belgrave (part)]	..	..	..	..	..	..	..	..	..	..
Birstall	9	11	15	3	..	..	..	..	..	38
Belton and Grace Dieu	..	..	..	..	..	..	..	..	..	..
Bradgate	..	..	..	..	..	..	..	..	..	..
Breedon	..	..	..	..	..	..	..	..	..	..
Tonge	2	27	8	..	..	..	..	..	..	37
Wilson	..	..	..	..	..	..	..	..	..	..
Andreschurch	..	..	..	..	..	..	..	..	..	..
Staunton Harold	..	6	1	..	..	..	..	..	..	7
Worthington	4	6	2	..	..	..	..	..	..	12
Newbold	..	..	..	..	..	..	..	..	..	..
Charley	..	..	..	..	..	..	..	..	..	..°
Coleorton	..	?3	?3	..	..	..	..	..	..	?6
Diseworth	..	6	6	..	..	..	..	..	..	12
Donington, Castle	5	30	11	..	1	..	..	..	..	47°
Wartoft	..	..	..	..	..	..	..	..	..	..
Garendon	..	..	..	..	..	..	..	..	..	..
Hathern	..	..	..	..	..	..	..	..	..	..
Kegworth	..	25	13	3	..	..	..	..	..	41
Isley Walton	..	..	..	..	..	..	..	..	..	..
Langley	..	..	..	..	..	..	..	..	..	..
Leicester Abbey	..	..	..	..	..	..	..	..	..	..
Lockington	..	..	..	..	..	..	..	..	..	..
Hemington	..	..	..	..	..	..	..	..	..	..
Loughborough	15	9	18	..	..	..	..	..	..	42
Knight Thorpe	..	..	..	..	..	..	..	..	..	..
Woodthorpe	..	..	..	..	..	..	..	..	..	..
Newtown Linford	..	..	..	..	..	..	..	..	..	..
Osgathorpe	..	3	5	..	..	..	..	..	..	8
Packington	5	3	1	..	1	..	..	..	..	10
Snibston	..	..	..	..	..	..	..	..	..	..
Ravenstone	..	..	..	..	..	..	..	..	..	..
Rothley	..	..	..	..	..	..	..	..	..	..
Seal, Nether	4	2	..	..	..	..	..	..	..	6
Seal, Over	..	21	12	..	..	..	..	..	..	33
Donisthorpe	..	..	..	..	..	..	..	..	..	..
Oakthorpe	..	..	..	..	..	..	..	..	..	..
Stretton en le Field	..	..	..	..	..	..	..	..	..	..
Shepshed	20	36	16	2	..	2	..	..	..	76

Parish	*Soke-men*	*Vil-leins*	*Bor-dars*	*'Servi'*	*Priests*	*Knights*	*'Franci-genae'*	*Free-men*	*Men*	*Total*
Swepstone	..	15	8	..	1	..	..	..	..	24
Newton Burgoland	..	1	..	..	..	..	..	..	..	1
Swithland	..	..	..	..	..	..	..	..	..	..
Thorpe Acre	3	16	8	..	..	..	..	..	..	27
Dishley	16	16	1	..	..	..	..	..	..	33
Thurcaston	..	22	4	4	..	..	..	..	..	30
Anstey	..	13	4	4	..	..	..	..	..	21
Cropston	..	..	..	..	..	..	..	..	..	..
Ulverscroft	..	..	..	..	..	..	..	..	..	..
Wanlip	..	..	..	..	..	..	..	..	..	..
Whatton, Long	..	..	..	..	..	..	..	..	..	..
Whitwick	..	1	..	..	..	..	..	..	..	1
Swannington	..	..	..	..	..	..	..	..	..	..
Thringstone	..	..	..	..	..	..	..	..	..	..
Outlying parts of the manor of Barrow (°)	31	37	15	1	..	4	..	..	..	88
Guthlaxton Hundred										
Arnesby	..	17	5	1	..	..	..	..	..	23
Ashby Magna	13	1	13	2	..	..	..	..	..	29
Ashby Parva	..	6	1	..	..	..	..	..	..	7
Aylestone	6	45	18	2	..	..	..	..	..	71
Glen Parva	..	..	..	..	..	..	..	..	..	..
Bitteswell	..	2	15	..	1	..	..	..	..	18
Blaby	28	4	4	1	..	..	..	..	..	37
Countesthorpe	..	..	..	..	..	..	..	..	..	..
Broughton Astley	8	6	4	..	..	..	..	..	..	18
Primethorpe	..	3	3	..	..	..	..	..	..	6
Sutton	2	..	2	..	..	..	..	..	..	4
Bruntingthorpe	9	3	6	2	..	..	..	..	..	20
Catthorpe	..	..	..	..	..	..	..	..	..	..
Claybrooke	9	9	6	2	..	2	..	..	..	28
Bittesby	..	10	4	..	..	..	..	..	..	14
Wibtoft	..	..	..	..	..	..	..	..	..	..
Ullesthorpe	..	9	4	4	..	..	..	..	..	17
Wigston Parva	..	..	5	..	..	..	..	..	..	5
Cosby	26	3	5	1	..	..	3	..	..	38
Little Thorpe	..	2	1	..	..	..	..	..	..	3
Cotesbach	..	10	2	..	..	..	..	..	2	14
Dunton Bassett	9	7	4	..	..	..	..	..	..	20
Foston	11	8	4	3	..	..	..	..	..	26
Frolesworth	16	..	3	..	..	..	..	..	..	19
Gilmorton	24	..	..	1	..	..	4	..	..	29
Kilby	10	9	7	2	..	..	..	..	..	28
Kilworth, North } Kilworth, South }	8	7	14	4	..	..	..	..	..	33
Kimcote	6	6	7	..	..	..	..	..	..	19
Cotes-de-Val	4	..	..	..	..	..	..	..	..	4
Walton	10	..	..	..	..	..	..	..	..	10
Knaptoft	2	10	6	3	1	..	..	..	..	22
Shearsby	2	4	3	..	..	1	..	..	..	10
Knighton	4	20	..	..	..	..	..	..	..	24
Leire	2	12	4	..	1	..	..	..	..	19
Lutterworth	12	6	7	3	..	..	..	..	..	28
Misterton	3	6	1	..	..	..	..	..	..	10
Walcote	2	3	1	1	..	..	..	..	..	7
Poultney	..	9	5	5 (+9 burgesses in the city)				..	..	19
Oadby	45	..	11	4	..	..	..	..	..	60
Peatling Magna	7	1	2	..	..	..	..	..	..	10
Peatling Parva	6	17	9	..	1	..	..	..	..	33
Shawell	..	23	11	6	..	..	..	..	..	40
Stormsworth	12	2	1	..	..	..	..	..	..	15
Swinford	10	11	1	1	..	..	..	..	2	25

POPULATION

Parish	*Soke-men*	*Vil-leins*	*Bor-dars*	'Servi'	*Priests*	*Knights*	*'Franci-genae'*	*Free-men*	*Men*	*Total*
Whetstone	24	11	5	2	..	1	..	..	..	43
Wigston Magna	31	32	12	3	{ 1 1 clerk }	2	4	..	..	86
Willoughby Waterless	16	1	4	1	..	..	..	..	..	22
Sparkenhoe Hundred										
Appleby	4	8	6	..	..	..	..	..	..	18
Aston Flamville	..	..	..	..	..	..	..	..	..	..
Burbage	..	20	2	2	..	..	..	..	..	24
Sketchley	..	..	..	..	..	..	..	..	..	..
Smockington	..	6	2	1	..	..	..	..	..	9
[Aylestone (part)]	..	..	..	..	..	..	..	..	..	..
Lubbesthorpe	..	10	6	..	..	..	..	..	..	16
Barwell	8	14	3	..	1	..	..	..	..	26
Potter's Marston	3	..	5	..	..	..	..	..	..	8
Stapleton	..	2	3	..	..	..	..	..	..	5
Bosworth, Market	7	10	11	4	{ 1 1 deacon }	..	..	..	..	34
Barlestone	..	8	7	..	..	..	..	..	..	15
Carlton	..	..	..	..	..	..	..	..	..	..
Shenton	..	8	6	..	..	..	..	..	..	14
Sutton Cheney	..	6	2	..	..	..	..	..	..	8
Coton	..	..	..	..	..	..	..	..	..	..
Naneby	..	..	..	..	..	..	..	..	..	..
Bromkinsthorpe	..	6	3	3	..	..	..	..	..	12
Cadeby	..	7	3	..	1	..	..	..	..	11
Osbaston	..	10	..	2	..	..	..	..	..	12
Congerstone	..	11	7	..	..	..	..	..	..	18
Croft	4	12	8	3	..	..	3	..	..	30
Desford	..	1	..	..	..	..	..	..	..	1
Drayton, Fenny	..	14	8	..	..	..	..	..	..	22
Elmesthorpe	..	..	..	..	..	..	..	..	..	..
Enderby	..	10	1	1	..	..	..	..	..	12
Glenfield	4	3	2	2	1	..	..	..	..	12
Braunstone	2	4	1	4	..	..	..	..	..	11
Kirby Muxloe	..	6	2	..	..	..	..	..	..	8
Heather	..	4	..	..	..	..	..	..	..	4
Higham	..	..	..	..	..	..	..	..	..	..
Lindley	..	..	..	..	..	..	..	..	..	..
Hinckley	3	42	16	8	..	..	..	..	..	69
Wykin	..	..	..	..	..	..	..	..	..	..
Stoke Golding	..	..	..	..	..	..	..	..	..	..
Dadlington	..	..	..	..	..	..	..	..	..	..
Ibstock	10	..	11	..	..	..	..	..	..	21
Hugglescote	..	..	..	..	..	..	..	..	..	..
Donington le Heath	..	1	..	..	..	..	..	..	..	1
Kirkby Mallory	8	3	6	..	..	..	..	..	..	17
Earl Shilton	4	10	5	1	1	..	..	..	..	21
Markfield	..	..	2	..	..	..	..	..	..	2
Nailstone	..	3	..	..	..	..	..	..	..	3
Barton in the Beans	..	1	2	..	..	..	..	..	..	3
Normanton le Heath	..	..	..	..	..	..	..	..	..	..
Narborough	..	..	..	..	..	..	..	..	..	..
Huncote	2	20	8	3	1	..	..	..	..	34
Newbold Verdon	..	3	2	..	..	..	..	..	..	5
Brascote	..	..	..	..	..	..	..	..	..	..
Norton juxta Twycross	..	1	2	..	1	..	..	..	..	4
Bilstone	3	..	..	..	..	..	..	..	..	3
Orton on the Hill	..	15	13	1	..	..	..	..	..	29
Gopsall	..	8	5	..	..	..	..	..	..	13
Peckleton	..	..	3	1	..	..	..	..	..	4

Parish	*Soke-men*	*Vil-leins*	*Bor-dars*	*'Servi'*	*Priests*	*Knights*	*'Franci-genae'*	*Free-men*	*Men*	*Total*
Ratby	..	10	5	1	1	..	..	..	..	17
Groby . . .	1	10	5	..	..	..	..	..	..	16
Whittington . .	..	..	..	..	..	..	..	..	..	..
Newtown Unthank .	..	..	..	..	..	..	..	..	..	..
Botcheston . .	..	..	..	..	..	..	..	..	..	..
Sapcote . . .	7	5	6	..	..	..	..	..	..	18
Shackerstone . .	..	5	..	..	..	..	..	..	..	5
Odstone . . .	3	..	..	..	..	..	..	..	..	3
Sharnford . . .	1	..	8	..	..	..	..	..	..	9
Sheepy Magna . .	..	11	8	..	..	..	..	..	..	19
Ratcliffe Culey . .	..	6	2	2	..	..	..	..	..	10
Sheepy Parva . .	..	..	..	..	..	..	..	..	..	..
Sibson . . .	..	30	17	1	..	..	..	..	..	48
Wellsborough . .	..	..	..	..	..	..	..	..	..	..
Upton . . .	..	..	..	..	..	..	..	..	..	..
Snarestone . . .	..	..	..	..	..	..	..	..	..	..
Stanton, Stoney . .	..	7	3	..	..	..	..	4	..	14
Thornton . . .	..	..	..	..	..	..	..	..	..	..
Bagworth . .	3	24	7	1	..	..	..	..	..	35
Stanton under Bardon	..	13	5	..	..	..	..	..	..	18
Thurlaston . . .	..	9	7	2	..	..	..	..	..	18
Normanton Turville .	..	..	..	..	..	..	..	..	..	..
Twycross . . .	..	11	6	1	..	..	..	..	..	18
Weston . . .	1	12	..	4	..	..	..	..	..	17
Witherley . . .	..	..	..	..	..	..	..	..	..	..
Atterton . . .	..	..	..	..	..	..	..	..	..	..
Unidentified										
Elvelege . . .	..	2	..	2	..	..	..	..	..	4
Lilinge . . .	..	9	3	2	..	..	..	..	..	14
Netone . . .	..	9	1	..	..	..	..	..	..	10
Plotelei . . .	..	4	1	2	..	..	..	..	..	7
Ricoltorp . . .	..	3	1	..	..	..	..	..	..	4
	1,892	2,594	1,365	418	44	25	54	6	8	6,406

POPULATION

Table II

1377 POLL TAX

Place	Returns E 179/133/26 Total recorded population	Receipts E 179/133/17–24 Total taxpayers
Framland Hundred		
Ab Kettleby	..	52
Barkestone	..	89
Bottesford	..	258
Branston	..	84
Brentingby	..	53
Broughton, Nether	..	29
Buckminster (?with Sewstern)	..	178
Burton Lazars	..	158
Clawson, Long	..	178
Coston	..	82
Croxton Kerrial	..	91
Dalby, Little	..	142
Eastwell	..	60
Eaton	..	99
Edmondthorpe	..	86
Eye Kettleby	..	40
Freeby	..	96
Garthorpe	..	121
Goadby Marwood	..	86
Harby	..	126
Harston	..	48
Holwell	..	55
Hose	..	87
Kirby Bellars	..	191
Knipton	..	82
Melton Mowbray	..	440
Muston	..	96
Normanton	..	70
Overton, Cold	..	103
Plungar	..	59
Redmile	..	85
Saltby	..	72
Saxby	..	96
Scalford	..	130
Somerby	..	118
Sproxton	..	87
Stapleford	..	152
Stathern	..	115
Stonesby	..	73
Thorpe Arnold	..	102
Waltham on the Wolds	..	62
Welby	..	42
Withcote	..	45
Wyfordby	..	44
Wymondham	..	220
Gartree Hundred		
Blaston	..	129
Bosworth, Husbands	157	..
Bowden, Gt.	107	..
Burton Overy	72	..
Bushby	46	..
Carlton Curlieu	75	..
Harborough, Market	..	200
Kibworth Beauchamp	..	134
Kibworth Harcourt	..	122
Langton, Thorpe	..	125
Mowsley	..	72
Newton Harcourt	..	63
Rolleston	..	133
Saddington	..	135
Shangton	..	73
Slawston	..	138
Smeeton Westerby	..	122
Stockerston	53	..
Stonton Wyville	103	..
Wistow	..	130
East Goscote Hundred		
Allexton	49	..
Asfordby	158	139
Ashby Folville	83	87
Barkby	132	..
Barrow upon Soar	..	337
Barsby	64	69
Beeby	96	..
Belgrave	74 (?incomplete)	136
Brooksby	41	39
Cossington	85	..
Cotes	81	..
Croxton, South	67	..
Dalby, Great	103	..
Dalby, Old	70	..
Frisby on the Wreak	105	129
Gaddesby	176	177
Grimston	78	83
Halstead	41	..
Hoby	53	118
Hoton	56	53
Humberstone	101	124
Hungarton	77	72
Keyham	55	..
Loddington	120	143
Lowesby	25	..
Newton, Cold	38	38
Norton, East	30	..
Prestwold	..	59
Quenby	27	..
Queniborough	136	..
Ragdale	52	84
Ratcliffe on the Wreake	89	78
Rearsby	77	82
Rotherby	28	..
Saxelby	93	..
Seagrave	163	..
Shoby	18	12
Skeffington	45	51
Syston	..	32
Thorpe Satchville	33	..
Thrussington	94	..
Thurmaston	178	179

Place	*Returns* E 179/133/26 *Total recorded population*	*Receipts* E 179/133/17–24 *Total taxpayers*
Tilton	77	..
Tugby	75	136
Twyford	98	..
Walton on the Wolds	65	28
Wartnaby	55	..
Whatborough	22	..
Wymeswold	..	250
West Goscote Hundred		
Anstey	88	..
Ashby de la Zouch	..	223
Belton	..	170
Birstall	73	..
Blackfordby	63	50
Bradgate	29	41
Breedon	..	107
Coleorton	..	47
Cropston	54	..
Diseworth	..	120
Donington, Castle	224	280
Donisthorpe	5	..
Hathern	128	153
Kegworth	119	181
Lockington	110	156
Loughborough	352	360
Mountsorrel	156	..
Newbold	..	64
Newtown Linford	62	62
Oakthorpe	2	..
Osgathorpe	..	30
Packington	..	87
Quorndon	..	179
Ravenstone	..	72
Rothley	131	..
Seal	120	121
Shepshed	..	250
Snibston	..	6
Staunton Harold	..	69
Stretton en le Field	21	..
Swithland	62	..
Thorpe Acre	..	68
Thringstone	67	79
Thurcaston	85	92
Tonge	53	88
Wanlip	83	..
Whatton, Long	161	200
Whitwick	64	69
Wilson	..	45
Woodhouse	85	79
Woodthorpe	..	25
Worthington	..	94
Guthlaxton Hundred		
Arnesby	..	117
Ashby Parva	..	78
Aylestone	111	126
Bittesby	21	..
Blaby	100	..
Catthorpe	..	55
Claybrooke	155	..
Countesthorpe	..	71
Foston	..	99
Gilmorton	132	..
Glen Parva	54	..
Leire	..	65
Oadby	..	123
Peatling Magna	99 (incomplete)	111
Poultney	54	..
Stormsworth	..	63
Sutton in the Elms	..	81
Walcote	52	..
Wigston Magna	314	..
Sparkenhoe Hundred		
Appleby	93	94
Aston Flamville	49	55
Bagworth	..	88
Barlestone	..	..
Barwell	86 (incomplete)	176
Bosworth, Market	107	125
Botcheston	..	66
Braunstone	79	..
Burbage	64	..
Cadeby	..	51
Coton	29	..
Croft	42	..
Dadlington	37	..
Desford	120	120
Donington le Heath	53	51
Drayton, Fenny	92	98
Enderby	..	88
Gopsall	20	..
Groby	75	66
Heather	..	60
Higham	..	88
Hinckley	60 (incomplete)	136
Hugglescote	..	42
Huncote	..	56
Ibstock	86	83
Kirby Muxloe	..	68
Kirkby Mallory	69	93
Lubbesthorpe	26	..
Markfield	..	62
Marston, Potters	26	..
Nailstone	109	..
Newbold Verdon	..	69
Normanton le Heath	58	?66
Normanton Turville	49	..
Norton juxta Twycross	75	119
Odstone	71	..
Orton on the Hill	125	..
Osbaston	51	..
Peckleton	62	72
Ratby	..	85
Ratcliffe Culey	36 (incomplete)	..
Sapcote	..	81
Shackerstone	54	55
Sharnford	..	132

Place	*Returns* E 179/133/26 *Total recorded population*	*Receipts* E 179/133/17–24 *Total taxpayers*
Sheepy Magna .	82	..
Sheepy Parva . .	20	..
Shenton . . .	107	..
Shilton, Earl . .	..	144
Sibson . . .	24 (incomplete)	..
Sketchley. . .	25	..
Snarestone . .	86	49
Stanton, Stoney .	51	..
Stanton under Bardon	..	44
Stapleton. . .	58	..
Stoke Golding . .	58	..
Sutton Cheney. .	41	..
Thornton . .	123	126
Thurlaston . .	72	72
Twycross . .	79	..
Upton . . .	50	..
Whittington . .	..	21
Witherley . .	104	123

Table III

DIOCESAN POPULATION RETURN, 1563

Place	Households
Deanery of Akeley	
Ashby de la Zouch	64
Blackfordby	13
Barrow upon Soar	64
Mountsorrel	40
Quorndon	60
Woodhouse	44
Belton	50
Breedon	32
Tonge	24
Wilson	10
Staunton Harold	9
Worthington	34
Coleorton	62
Diseworth	33
Donington, Castle	70
Hathern	42
Kegworth	68
Isley Walton	17
Lockington	38
Hemington	27
Loughborough	256
Knight Thorpe	6
Woodthorpe	13
Loughborough Park	1
Burleigh Park	1
Markfield	39
Osgathorpe	12
Packington	38
Snibston	7
Seal	62
Shepshed	103
Swepstone	24
Snarestone	15
Newton Burgoland	18
Swithland	29
Thorpe Acre	18
Dishley	4
Thurcaston	25
Anstey	35
Cropston	14
Wanlip	12
Whatton, Long	40
Whitwick	36
Swannington	25
	1,634
Deanery of Framland	
Ab Kettleby	20
Holwell	14
Barkestone and Plungar	31
Plungar	26
Bottesford	70
Normanton	16
Easthorpe	35
Branston	27
Broughton, Nether	24
Buckminster	35
Sewstern	25
Burrough on the Hill	23
Clawson, Long	57
Coston	26
Croxton Kerrial	50
Dalby, Little	29
Eastwell	15
Eaton	31
Edmondthorpe	44
Garthorpe	24
Goadby Marwood	33
Harby	33
Harston	11
Hose	24
Kirby Bellars	57
Knipton	30
Melton Mowbray	80
Freeby, Burton Lazars, Sysonby, Eye Kettleby	86
Muston	34
Overton, Cold	31
Redmile	33
Saltby	22
Saxby	18 3
Scalford	46
Somerby	38
Sproxton	30
Stapleford	11 24
Stathern	53
Stonesby	..
Thorpe Arnold	31
Waltham on the Wolds	44
Withcote	1
Wyfordby	4
Brentingby	8
Wymondham	43
	1,450
Deanery of Gartree	
Allexton	17
Billesdon	38
Goadby, Rolleston	24
Blaston	7
Bosworth, Husbands	72
Bringhurst	70
Easton, Great	21
Burton Overy	32
Carlton Curlieu	25
Illston on the Hill	19
Cranoe	8
Foxton	48
Frisby by Galby	8
Galby	14
Glen, Great	20
Glooston	9
Gumley	20
Hallaton	47
Horninghold	20
Houghton on the Hill	32
Kibworth	82
Knossington	22
Langton, Church	50
Langton, Thorpe, Langton, Tur	55
Langton, East, Langton, West	56
Laughton	13
Lubenham	60
Medbourne	42
Holt, Nevill	14
Norton, King's	12
Stretton, Little	19
Noseley	8
Owston	31
Pickwell	26
Saddington	23
Scraptoft	22
Shangton	17
Slawston	21
Stockerston	16
Stonton Wyville	15
Stretton, Great	15
Theddingworth	40
Thurnby	40
Stoughton	7
Welham	23
Wistow	16
Newton Harcourt, Kilby, Fleckney	12
	1,308
Deanery of Goscote	
Asfordby	48
Ashby Folville	27
Barsby	28
Barkby	44
Barkby Thorpe	12
Beeby	19
Belgrave	42
Birstall	26
Thurmaston	25
Cossington	30
Croxton, South	32
Dalby, Great	48
Frisby on the Wreak	32
Gaddesby	28
Hoby	37

POPULATION

Place	House-holds
Humberstone	24
Hungarton	27
Baggrave	2
Ingarsby	1
Quenby	1
Loddington	22
Lowesby	4
Cold Newton	15
Norton, East	15
Prestwold	14
Burton	33
Cotes	23
Hoton	9
Queniborough	48
Ragdale	8
Ratcliffe on the Wreake	14
Rearsby	25
Rotherby	13
Saxelby	15
Seagrave	46
Sileby	78
Skeffington	13
Syston	55
Thrussington	26
Tilton	28
Halstead	16
Marefield	6
Whatborough	1
Tugby	28
Keythorpe	2
Twyford	26
Thorpe Satchville	15
Walton on the Wolds	17
Wymeswold	79
	1,227
Deanery of Guthlaxton	
Arnesby	30
Ashby Magna	30
Ashby Parva	14
Aston Flamville	17
Burbage	57
Sketchley	6
Aylestone	40
Glen Parva	10
Lubbesthorpe	10
Bitteswell	38
Blaby	20
Countesthorpe	18
Broughton Astley	34
Primethorpe	10
Sutton	6
Bruntingthorpe	14
Catthorpe	15
Claybrooke	36
Ullesthorpe	21
Wibtoft	12
Wigston Parva	4
Cosby	24
Cotesbach	19
Croft	13
Desford	40
Dunton Bassett	24
Enderby and Whetstone	82
Foston	21
Frolesworth	33
Gilmorton	26
Glenfield	15
Braunstone	24
Kirby Muxloe	27
Kilworth, North	46
Kilworth, South	23
Kimcote	13
Walton	17
Knaptoft	13
Shearsby	18
Leire	23
Lutterworth	106
Misterton	30
Walcote	27
Mowsley	20
Narborough	38
Huncote, Little Thorpe and Cosby	28
Oadby	40
Peatling Magna	32
Peatling Parva	14
Ratby	66
Sapcote	34
Sharnford	32
Shawell	20
Stanton, Stoney	27
Swinford	27
Thurlaston	17
Normanton Turville	6
Wigston Magna	80
Willoughby Waterless	18
	1,605
Deanery of Sparkenhoe	
Barwell	48
Stapleton	15
Bosworth, Market	59
Shenton, Osbaston, Coton, Naneby	41
Barlestone	16
Carlton	13
Sutton Cheney	25
Cadeby	12
Osbaston	5
Congerstone	11
Drayton, Fenny	21
Heather	20
Higham	29
Lindley	1
Hinckley	100
Dadlington, Stoke Golding	33
Ibstock	29
Hugglescote, Donington	35
Kirkby Mallory	25
Earl Shilton	50
Nailstone	33
Barton in the Beans	8
Normanton le Heath	12
Newbold Verdon	16
Brascote	2
Norton juxta Twycross	16
Bilstone	5
Orton on the Hill	31
Peckleton	16
Shackerstone	41
Sheepy Magna	40
Ratcliffe Culey	16
Sibson	40
Thornton	42
Bagworth	34
Stanton	15
Twycross	28
Witherley	30
Atterton	7
	1,020
Knighton	17
Leicester	
All Saints	66
St. Leonard	32
St. Margaret	164
St. Martin	160
St. Mary	120
St. Nicholas	22
St. Peter	27
	591
Exempt and Extra-Parochial Places	
Bowden, Great	80
Little Bowden and Market Harborough (St. Mary's)	30
Evington	31
Groby	21
Harborough, Market	78
Newtown Linford (in Groby Manor)	47
*Ratby	27
*Botcheston	5
*Newtown Unthank	4
*Newtown Linford	27
Rothley	26
*Swithland	30
Thurcaston	
*Anstey	24
*Cropston	13
*Stanton	14
	457
Totals:	
Deanery of Akeley	1,634
,, Framland	1,450
,, Gartree	1,308
,, Goscote	1,227
,, Guthlaxton	1,605
,, Sparkenhoe	1,020
Knighton	17
Exempt and Extra-Parochial Places	457
	8,718
Leicester	591
Total	9,309
Total, excluding duplicated places	9,164

* It is likely that these estimates are duplicated elsewhere.

Table IV

LIBER CLERI, 1603: COMMUNICANTS AND RECUSANTS

Parish	*Communicants*
Deanery of Akeley	
Ashby de la Zouch	700
Barrow upon Soar, Quorndon, Woodhouse, part of Mountsorrel	600
Belton	227
Breedon	522
+3 recusants	
Coleorton	160
Diseworth	133
Dishley	132
Donington, Castle	380
Hathern	183
Kegworth	335
+4 recusants	
Lockington	311
Loughborough	1,200
Osgathorpe	70
Packington	230
Seal, Nether	240
+1 recusant	
Shepshed	392
Swepstone and Snarestone	250
+1 recusant	
Thurcaston	216
Wanlip	54
Whatton, Long	204
Whitwick	317
	6,865
Deanery of Framland	
Ab Kettleby	133
Barkestone	123
Bottesford	477
Branston	160
Broughton, Nether	124
Buckminster	232
Burrough on the Hill	80
Clawson, Long	335
Coston	95
Croxton Kerrial	160
Dalby, Little	120
Eastwell	70
Eaton	140
Edmondthorpe	212
Garthorpe	94
Goadby Marwood	100
Harby	230
Harston	54
Hose	164
Kirby Bellars	200
Knipton	126
Melton	910
Muston	123
Overton, Cold	124
Plungar	99
Redmile	170
Saltby	88
Saxby	76
Scalford	160
Somerby	146
Sproxton	122
Stapleford	240
Stathern	230
Thorpe Arnold	162
+3 recusants	
Waltham on the Wolds	167
Wyfordby	24
Wymondham	160
	6,433
Deanery of Gartree	
Billesdon, Goadby, Rolleston	431
+1 recusant	
Bosworth, Husbands	320
Bowden, Great, and Market Harborough	881
Bringhurst, with Gt. Easton and Drayton	403
Burton Overy	217
Carlton Curlieu and part of Illston	76
Cranoe	56
Foxton	200
Galby	173
Glen, Great	238
Glooston	64
Gumley	110
Hallaton	405
Horninghold	96
Houghton on the Hill	189
Kibworth Beauchamp	444
Knossington	113
Langton	670
Laughton	118
Lubenham	261
Medbourne	243
Norton, King's	154
Noseley and part of Illston	41
Owston	152
Pickwell	120
Saddington	110
Scraptoft	106
Shangton	69
Slawston	129
Stockerston	70
Stonton Wyville	78
Theddingworth	205
Thurnby with Bushby and Stoughton	249
Welham	86
Wistow with Newton Harcourt, Kilby, and Fleckney	335
	7,613
Deanery of Goscote	
Allexton	47
Asfordby	200
Ashby Folville	226
+7 recusants	
Barkby	260
Beeby	112
Belgrave, Birstall, Thurmaston	483
Brooksby	10
Cossington	121
Croxton, South	130
Dalby, Great	126
Frisby on the Wreak	140
Hoby	140
Humberstone	120
Hungarton	196
Loddington	160
+1 recusant	
Lowesby	70
Prestwold	320
Queniborough	225
Ragdale	40
Ratcliffe on the Wreake	55
Rearsby	146
Rotherby	80
Saxelby	100
+2 recusants	
Seagrave	178
Sileby	341
Skeffington	59
Syston	274
Thrussington	140
Tilton	230
Tugby	106
Twyford	245
Walton on the Wolds	122
Wymeswold	351
	5,563
Deanery of Guthlaxton	
Arnesby	90
Ashby Magna	110
Ashby Parva	80
Aston Flamville with Burbage	240
Aylestone	250
Bitteswell	80
Blaby	300
Broughton Astley	240
Bruntingthorpe	115
Catthorpe	77
Claybrooke	437
Cosby	212

POPULATION

Parish	Communicants
Cotesbach	72
Croft	100
Desford	215
Dunton Bassett	110
Elmesthorpe	10
Enderby and Whetstone	350
Foston	90
Frolesworth	147
Gilmorton	180
Glenfield }	
Kirby Muxloe }	178
Braunstone }	
+4 recusants	
Kilworth, North	120
Kilworth, South	75
Kimcote	210
Knaptoft	300
Leire	70
Lutterworth	564
Misterton	143
Narborough }	204
Huncote }	
Oadby	350
Peatling Magna	130
Peatling Parva	60
Sapcote	162
Sharnford	151
Shawell	122
Stanton, Stoney	140
Swinford	80
Thurlaston	120
Wigston Magna	380
Willoughby Waterless	106
	7,174
Deanery of Sparkenhoe	
Appleby	225
Barwell }	284
Stapleton }	
Bosworth, Market	704
+2 recusants	
Cadeby	72
Congerstone	60
Drayton, Fenny	90
Heather	94
Higham	130
Hinckley }	
Stoke Golding }	435
Wykin }	
Dadlington }	
Kirkby Mallory	70
Markfield	170
Nailstone	150
Newbold Verdon	100
Norton juxta Twycross	200
Orton on the Hill	103
Peckleton	66
Shackerstone	200
Sheepy Magna }	98
Ratcliffe Culey }	
Shilton, Earl	340
Sibson	145
Thornton }	382
Bagworth }	
Twycross	106
Witherley	132
	4,358
Exempt	
Ratby	200
Rothley	500
+4 recusants	
Total excluding Leicester	38,710
Leicester	
St. Mary	300
St. Martin	150
Total	39,160

Table V

HEARTH TAX, MICHAELMAS, 1670

Place	Households		
	Paying	*Exempt*	*Total*
Framland Hundred			
Ab Kettleby (?)	26	4	30
Barkestone	29	9	38
Bottesford	52	15	67
Branston	27	10	37
Broughton, Nether	47	8	55
Buckminster	25	10	35
Burton Lazars	30	10	40
Clawson, Long	75	11	86
Coston	22	9	31
Croxton Kerrial	37	12	49
Dalby, Little (?)	18	9	27
Easthorpe	31	6	37
Eastwell	22	..	22
Eaton	28	10	38
Edmondthorpe	15	9	24
Freeby	26	2	28
Garthorpe	23	6	29
Goadby Marwood	20	3	23
Harby	49	5	54
Harston	18	7	25
Holwell	16	4	20
Hose	42	20	62
Kirby Bellars	25	2	27
Knipton	22	15	37
Melton Mowbray	284	56	340
Muston	35	14	49
Normanton	14	1	15
Overton, Cold	20	6	26
Plungar	19	8	27
Redmile	43	6	49
Saltby	25	8	33
Saxby	18	3	21
Scalford	41	26	67
Sewstern	30	6	36
Somerby	39	11	50
Sproxton	36	5	41
Stapleford	29	..	29
Stathern	50	12	62
Stonesby	27	4	31
Sysonby	7	..	7
Thorpe Arnold	24	..	24
Waltham on the Wolds	50	21	71
Welby	7	..	7
Wyfordby and Brentingby	16	..	16
Wymondham	40	24	64
Total			1,986
Gartree Hundred			
Billesdon	71	63	134
Blaston	14	13	27
Bosworth, Husbands	73	25	98
Bowden, Great	96	40	136
Bringhurst	15	7	22
Burrough on the Hill	23	4	27
Burton Overy	44	18	62
Bushby	11	7	18
Carlton Curlieu	8	5	13
Cranoe	11	12	23
Drayton	15	10	25
Easton, Great	64	42	106
Evington	28	18	46
Fleckney	26	15	41
Foxton	60	21	81
Frisby	10	5	15
Galby	16	7	23
Glen, Great	46	17	63
Glooston	20	3	23
Goadby	11	..	11
Gumley	28	11	39
Hallaton	73	92	165
Harborough, Market	124	35	159
Holt, Nevill	6	11	17
Horninghold	21	15	36
Houghton on the Hill	60	7	67
Illston on the Hill	19	13	32
Ingarsby	2	..	2
Kibworth Beauchamp	50	16	66
Kibworth Harcourt	41	22	63
Knossington	25	10	35
Langton, East	35	18	53
" West	19	13	32
" Thorpe	37	11	48
" Tur	26	23	49
Laughton	18	12	30
Leesthorpe	3	..	3
Lubenham	58	31	89
Marefield, South	6	3	9
Medbourne	36	25	61
Mowsley	25	5	30
Newbold	9	..	9
Newton Harcourt	16	6	22
Norton, King's	12	5	17
Noseley	1	..	1
Owston	27	11	38
Pickwell	12	4	16
Rolleston	6	4	10
Saddington	33	14	47
Scraptoft	16	10	26
Shangton	11	..	11
Slawston	24	16	40
Smeeton Westerby	50	19	69
Stockerston	17	8	25
Stonton Wyville	14	..	14
Stoughton	23	7	30
Stretton, Great	5	..	5
Stretton, Little	26	6	32
Theddingworth	40	9	49
Thurnby	14	8	22
Welham	18	3	21
Wistow	3	4	7
			2,590

POPULATION

Place	Households: Paying	Exempt	Total
East Goscote Hundred			
Allexton	12	5	17
Asfordby	58	25	83
Ashby Folville	21	8	29
Barkby(?)	40	15	55
Barkby Thorpe	8	6	14
Barrow upon Soar	72	29	101
Barsby	43	7	50
Beeby	26	7	33
Belgrave	37	19	56
Brooksby	1	..	1
Burton on the Wolds	25	29	54
Cossington	24	10	34
Cotes	9	..	9
Croxton, South	48	12	60
Dalby, Great	44	16	60
Dalby, Old	29	12	41
Frisby on the Wreak	42	17	59
Gaddesby	31	35	66
Grimston	24	15	39
Halstead	17	7	24
Hamilton	1	..	1
Hoby	34	13	47
Hoton	16	7	23
Humberstone	28	23	51
Hungarton	27	8	35
Keyham(?)	28	23	51
Launde	1	..	1
Loddington	29	11	40
Lowesby	5	..	5
Newton, Cold	8	7	15
Norton, East	23	4	27
Prestwold	10	1	11
Quenby	1	..	1
Queniborough	45	39	84
Ragdale	11	..	11
Ratcliffe on the Wreake	13	4	17
Rearsby	35	32	67
Rotherby	12	10	22
Saxelby	21	15	36
Shoby	1	..	1
Seagrave	43	15	58
Sileby	67	52	119
Skeffington	27	..	27
Syston	90	48	138
Thorpe Satchville	18	22	40
Thrussington	40	20	60
Thurmaston	38	41	79
Tilton	22	20	42
Tugby	34	5	39
Twyford	32	15	47
Walton on the Wolds	22	13	35
Wartnaby	14	11	25
Withcote	3	..	3
Wycomb	9 }	11	31
Chadwell	11 }		
Wymeswold	81	15	96
			2,271
West Goscote Hundred			
Abbey Gate	13	17	30
Anstey	46	20	66
Ashby de la Zouch	167	49	216
Beaumont Leys	5	..	5
Belton	47	21	68
Birstall	25	11	36
Blackfordby	16 }	11	33
Boothorpe	6 }		
Bradgate	1	..	1
Breedon	29	24	53
Charley	8	4	12
Coleorton	38	39	77
Cropston	18	10	28
Diseworth	57	26	83
Donington, Castle	99	51	150
Donisthorpe	12	..	12
Grace Dieu	3	..	3
Hathern	61?	11	72?
Hemington	23	13	36
Kegworth	63	50	113
Langley Priory	1	..	1
Lockington	20	21	41
Loughborough	235	178	413
Maplewell	4	..	4
Mountsorrel	84	84	168
Newtown Linford (?)	42	6	48
Osgathorpe	21	9	30
Packington	40	13	53
Quorndon	61	50	111
Ravenstone	15	8	23
Rothley	60	48	108
Seal	21	..	21
Shepshed	120	33	153
Snibston	4	..	4
Staunton Harold	26	20	46
Stretton en le Field	10	6	16
Swannington	19	15	34
Swepstone and Newton Burgoland	36	23	59
Swithland	33	9	42
Thorpe Acre and Dishley	15	6	21
Thorpe, Knight	8	3	11
Thringstone	27	45	72
Thurcaston	24	12	36
Tonge	18	10	28
Ulverscroft	7	..	7
Walton, Isley	8	..	8
Wanlip	12	4	16
Whatton, Long	44	31	75
Whitwick	42	17	59
Wilson	12	15	27
Woodhouse and Beaumanor	32	41	73
Woodthorpe	14	2	16
Worthington and Newbold	46	67	113
			3,030
Guthlaxton Hundred			
Arnesby	34	7	41
Ashby Magna	26	5	31
Ashby Parva	31	11	42
Aylestone	45	5	50
Bitteswell	43	15	58

Place	Households Paying	Households Exempt	Households Total
Blaby	40	16	56
Broughton Astley, Primethorpe, and Sutton	64	11	75
Bruntingthorpe	37	..	37
Catthorpe	18	9	27
Claybrooke	39	17	56
Cosby and Thorpe	46	46	92
Cotesbach	11	7	18
Countesthorpe	30	19	49
Dunton Bassett	31	9	40
Foston	8	..	8
Frolesworth	26	7	33
Gilmorton	47	16	63
Kilby	26	6	32
Kilworth, North	43	19	62
Kilworth, South	27	14	41
Kimcote	13	10	23
Walton	49	10	59
Knaptoft	6	..	6
Leire	34	17	51
Lutterworth	142	83	225
Misterton and Walcote	30	19	49
Oadby	55	16	71
Peatling Magna	23	16	39
Peatling Parva	13	3	16
Shawell	23	5	28
Shearsby	33	8	41
Swinford	48	20	68
Ullesthorpe	42	10	52
Whetstone	50	40	90
Wigston Magna	112	47	159
Wigston Parva	5	..	5
Willoughby Waterless	34	3	37
The Newarke and Castle of Leicester	17	..	17
			1,954
Sparkenhoe Hundred			
Appleby	30	17	47
Aston Flamville	12	5	17
Bagworth	36	24	60
Barlestone	36	7	43
Barton in the Beans	13	6	19
Barwell	58	27	85
Bilstone	19	5	24
Bosworth, Market, and	70		
Coton	27	7	104
Botcheston and Newton Unthank	14	..	14
Braunstone	17	11	28
Braunstone Gate	9	3	12
Burbage and	58		
Sketchley	7	34	99
Cadeby	12	3	15
Carlton	13	2	15
Congerstone	29	11	40
Croft	21	..	21
Dadlington	14	5	19
Desford	53	25	78
Drayton, Fenny	21	2	23
Enderby	48	29	77
Glenfield	22	13	35
'Foresters'	5	..	5

Place	Households Paying	Households Exempt	Households Total
Gopsall	1	..	1
Groby	26	33	59
Heather	36	27	63
Higham and Lindley	39	12	51
Hinckley	59		
Hinckley Bond	83	54	204
Wykin	8		
Hugglescote and Donington le Heath	31	4	35
Huncote	17	11	28
Ibstock	42	23	67
Kirby Muxloe	13	8	21
Kirkby Mallory	26	4	30
Lubbesthorpe	6	..	6
Markfield	41	27	68
Nailstone	29	11	40
Narborough	26	31	57
Newbold Verdon	34	5	39
Newhall Park	2	..	2
Normanton Turville and Bassett House	1	..	1
Normanton le Heath	17	6	23
Norton juxta Twycross	29	11	40
Odstone	10	4	14
Orton on the Hill	22	14	36
Osbaston	19	4	23
Peckleton	21	6	27
Ratby	29	26	55
Ratcliffe Culey	24	14	38
Sapcote	35	14	49
Shackerstone	18	14	32
Sharnford	40	13	53
Sheepy Magna	38	10	48
Sheepy Parva	9	4	13
Mythe	1	..	1
Newhouse	2	..	2
Moor Barns	1	..	1
Temple Hall	3	..	3
Shenton	18	3	21
Shilton, Earl	94	25	119
Sibson and Upton	14	2	16
Snarestone	23	6	29
Stanton, Stoney	28	14	42
Stanton under Bardon	21	10	31
Stapleton	15	7	22
Stoke Golding	25	14	39
Sutton Cheney	25	12	37
Thornton	37	34	71
Thurlaston	21	15	36
Twycross	32	9	41
Wellsborough	2	..	2
Witherley and Atterton	46	23	69
			2,714
Total excluding Leicester	..	..	14,486
Borough of Leicester	700	268	968
Bishop's Fee	34	..	34
Leicester, total, including Abbey Gate, Braunstone Gate, Newarke, and Castle	..	..	1,061
Total	..	..	15,547

POPULATION

Table VI

ECCLESIASTICAL CENSUS, 1676

The figures shown here represent the sums of Anglican communicants, papists and Protestant nonconformists, into which the population was divided in the census.

Parish	*Population*
Deanery of Akeley	
Ashby de la Zouch	678
Barrow upon Soar	1,109
Belton	222
Birstall	114
Breedon	910
Coleorton	291
Diseworth	138
Dishley	91
Hathern	163
Kegworth	327
Lockington	231
Loughborough	1,123
Osgathorpe	90
Packington	209
Seal	308
Shepshed	376
Swepstone	68
Swithland	138
Thurcaston	91
Anstey	140
Cropston	53
Wanlip	49
Whatton, Long	187
Whitwick	483
	7,589
Deanery of Framland	
Ab Kettleby	156
Barkestone	122
Bottesford	581
Branston	121
Broughton, Nether	160
Buckminster	251
Clawson, Long	235
Coston	68
Croxton Kerrial	173
Dalby, Little	68
Eastwell	75
Eaton	128
Edmondthorpe	118
Garthorpe	97
Goadby Marwood	61
Harby	185
Harston	76
Hose	131
Kirby Bellars	104
Knipton	117
Melton Mowbray	1,078
Muston	120
Overton, Cold	84
Plungar	94
Redmile	131
Saltby	103
Saxby	73
Scalford	175
Somerby	216
Sproxton	129
Stapleford	181
Stathern	192
Stonesby	102
Thorpe Arnold	90
Waltham on the Wolds	210
Wyfordby	50
Wymondham	122
	6,177
Deanery of Gartree	
Billesdon	247
Rolleston	35
Blaston	54
Bosworth, Husbands	360
Bowden, Great	363
Bringhurst	449
Burrough on the Hill	60
Burton Overy	122
Bushby	61
Carlton Curlieu	64
Cranoe	69
Evington	121
Fleckney	114
Foxton	296
Galby	94
Glen, Great	249
Glooston	62
Goadby	57
Gumley	113
Hallaton	387
Harborough, Market	471
Holt, Nevill	57
Horninghold	102
Houghton on the Hill	160
Illston	93
Kibworth	551
Kilby	114
Knossington	72
Langton, East and West	309
Langton, Thorpe	116
Langton, Tur	138
Laughton	65
Lubenham	193
Medbourne	195
Mowsley	127
Newton Harcourt	95
Norton, King's	38
Noseley	20
Othorpe	52
Owston	131
Pickwell	30
Saddington	144
Scraptoft	60
Shangton	26
Slawston	146
Stockerston	80
Stonton Wyville	42
Stoughton	54
Stretton, Great	14
Stretton, Little	96
Theddingworth	102
Thurnby	28
Tugby	151
Welham	44
Wistow	30
	7,523
Deanery of Goscote	
Allexton	51
Asfordby	221
Ashby Folville	264
Barkby	274
Beeby	86
Belgrave	131
Thurmaston	116
Brooksby	17
Cossington	76
Croxton, South	139
Dalby, Great	178
Frisby on the Wreak	136
Hoby	90
Hoton	81
Humberstone	131
Hungarton	290
Loddington	118
Lowesby	49
Norton, East	62
Prestwold	158
Queniborough	226
Ragdale	36
Ratcliffe on the Wreake	56
Rearsby	180
Rotherby	65
Saxelby	84
Sileby	301
Skeffington	104
Syston	367
Thrussington	195
Tilton	211
Tugby	151
Twyford	80
Walton on the Wolds	96
Wymeswold	182
	5,002
Deanery of Guthlaxton	
Arnesby	226
Ashby Magna	68
Ashby Parva	54
Aston Flamville	51
Burbage	258
Aylestone	189
Bitteswell	183

Parish	Population
Blaby	285
Braunstone	66
Broughton Astley	209
Bruntingthorpe	133
Catthorpe	70
Claybrooke	362
Cosby	195
Cotesbach	55
Countesthorpe	180
Croft	83
Desford	168
Dunton Bassett	119
Enderby	195
Foston	21
Frolesworth	108
Gilmorton	213
Glenfield	101
Kilworth, North	183
Kilworth, South	100
Kimcote	150
Kirby Muxloe	76
Leire	144
Lutterworth	644
Misterton	131
Narborough	208
Oadby	192
Peatling Magna	94
Peatling Parva	53
Sapcote	167
Sharnford	130
Shawell	78
Shearsby	143
Stanton, Stoney	131
Swinford	140
Thurlaston	124
Whetstone	247
Wigston Magna	455
Willoughby Waterless	91
	7,273
Deanery of Sparkenhoe	
Appleby	240
Barlestone	107
Barwell	231
Stapleton	49
Bosworth, Market	715
Cadeby	53
Carlton	48
Congerstone	77
Dadlington	62
Drayton, Fenny	73
Heather	112
Higham on the Hill	129
Hinckley	522
Hugglescote and Donington	95
Ibstock	190
Kirkby Mallory	119
Markfield	143
Nailstone	234
Newbold Verdon	115
Norton juxta Twycross	168
Orton on the Hill	128
Peckleton	91
Shackerstone	142
Sheepy, North	143
Sheepy, South	174
Shenton	92
Shilton, Earl	234
Sibson	164
Stoke Golding	78
Sutton Cheney	125
Thornton and Bagworth	328
Twycross	95
Witherley	173
	5,449
Total excluding Leicester	39,013
Leicester	
All Saints	346
St. Leonard	105
St. Martin	927
St. Mary	398
St. Nicholas	186
Trinity Hospital	109
	2,071
Total	41,084

POPULATION

Table VII

PARISH REGISTER STATISTICS, 1700–1800

Baptisms

Hundred	*1700*	*1710*	*1720*	*1730*	*1740*	*1750*	*1760*	*1770*	*1780*	*1790*	*1800*
Framland . .	350	279	230	295	285	321	315	336	288	315	300
Gartree . .	392	315	376	374	358	407	446	443	483	494	541
East Goscote .	291	179	298	268	245	275	259	279	429	460	404
West Goscote .	414	365	434	428	474	601	544	683	747	799	676
Guthlaxton .	256	237	294	255	251	320	333	366	378	378	426
Sparkenhoe .	348	320	368	321	373	487	495	472	531	593	929
Total including Leicester .	2,215	1,819	2,057	1,962	2,173	2,620	2,582	2,871	3,034	3,347	3,610

Burials

Hundred	*1700*	*1710*	*1720*	*1730*	*1740*	*1750*	*1760*	*1770*	*1780*	*1790*	*1800*
Framland . .	195	208	368	275	213	232	209	225	258	174	219
Gartree . .	263	288	350	361	316	324	375	468	493	402	395
East Goscote .	181	126	197	212	158	139	167	169	280	300	234
West Goscote .	341	236	344	398	352	395	361	462	483	531	556
Guthlaxton .	192	230	262	231	169	293	243	248	304	285	303
Sparkenhoe .	245	263	258	407	375	333	284	406	378	413	700
Total including Leicester .	1,537	1,430	1,919	2,068	1,768	1,933	1,947	2,249	2,452	2,412	2,705

Marriages

Hundred	*1700*	*1710*	*1720*	*1730*	*1740*	*1750*	*1760*	*1770*	*1780*	*1790*	*1800*
Framland . .	..	..	..	..	..	..	81	71	83	75	88
Gartree . .	..	..	..	..	..	..	148	146	150	159	153
East Goscote .	..	..	..	..	..	..	120	106	107	104	99
West Goscote .	..	..	..	..	..	..	202	189	163	211	190
Guthlaxton .	..	..	..	..	..	..	87	109	120	95	102
Sparkenhoe .	..	..	..	..	..	..	160	175	139	176	178
Total including Leicester .	..	..	..	..	..	..	881	892	844	934	926

Table VIII

RICKMAN'S ESTIMATES OF POPULATION

(*Census*, 1841, p. 34)

The same proportion of baptisms, burials, and marriages to total population are assumed as in 1800 and 1801. The average for three years, e.g. 1569, 1570, 1571 is taken.

	1570	*1600*	*1630*	*1670*	*1700*	*1750*
Estimate according to total of baptisms .	73,895	80,428	79,564	74,246	86,410	104,224
Estimate according to total of burials .	60,975	59,771	79,400	91,708	78,435	92,352
Estimate according to total of marriages .	67,800	68,160	67,698	53,604	75,784	98,889
Average of above	67,557	69,453	75,554	73,186	80,210	98,448

TABLE OF POPULATION
1801–1951

The population table printed below differs from any formerly published in the *History* in several respects. Hitherto the population areas appearing in such tables have been those of the 'ancient' parishes, chapelries, and townships as constituted in 1831. The population of 'ancient' parishes was excluded from the *Census Reports* after 1881, and that of chapelries and townships, not being civil parishes, after 1861. Consequently in compiling the earlier tables it was necessary, wherever a boundary change had occurred, to calculate with the aid of maps and the enumerators' schedules the number of persons presumed to have been living in the area affected by the change. There are the following objections to perpetuating this system. First, some 'ancient' parishes, chapelries, and townships have in course of time become absorbed into other areas. Some of these existed in 1831 and some did not. To strike a total in respect of absorbed areas or to ignore areas created since 1831 makes the population table unrealistic. Secondly, it is suspected that in certain instances the calculations hitherto made have been only approximate. Thirdly, the original Census Returns for 1931 no longer exist, so that it would never be possible to apply the previous system to places where boundaries were changed between 1921 and 1951.

In distinction from its predecessors the present table shows the population of every area mentioned as a parish or as a distinct part of a parish for civil administrative purposes in any *Census Report* between 1801 and 1951 and of the more important of the other local government areas for which totals have been struck at the censuses since 1801.[1] The administrative areas chosen for inclusion are ancient counties (1801–1901) and administrative counties (1891–1951); hundreds (1801–71) and urban and rural districts (1881–1951); boroughs (1801–41), municipal boroughs (1851–1951), and county boroughs (1891–1951); ancient parishes (1801–71), townships, chapelries, &c. (1801–71), and civil parishes (1881–1951). The population is always expressed for the area as constituted at the date of the census concerned, except in certain cases where, however, the fact is always noted.

The choice of these areas, and of the particular dates for each of them, has depended upon a series of alterations made in the 19th century in the conduct and areas of local government.[2]

Counties. The boundaries of some ancient counties, not including Leicestershire, were altered in 1844[3] when detached parts of counties were joined to those counties by which they were surrounded or with which they had the longest common boundary. This had already been done for parliamentary purposes in 1832. The Local Government Act of 1888 created administrative counties, which were in many cases identical with ancient counties. Where an urban sanitary district extended into two counties, it was taken to be in that administrative county which had contained most of its population in 1881. Leicestershire was thus enlarged by the addition of part of the urban districts of Market Harborough and Hinckley which were formerly in Northamptonshire and Warwickshire respectively. County boroughs were also created which had a separate administration from the rest of the administrative county. Under the Divided Parishes Acts, 1876–82, some changes were made in parish boundaries which also affected county boundaries. Several of these changes were made in Leicestershire between 1881 and 1891[4] but the *Census Report* of 1891 completely ignored them. Differences between ancient and administrative counties were increased by the Local Government Act of 1894 which made possible adjustments of county boundaries to conform with those of civil parishes and rural districts, similar to those made for urban districts under the former Act. This enlarged the administrative county of Leicester by a further 3,802 acres. Further changes in the areas of administrative counties were made under the Local Government Act of 1929. Leicestershire was not affected by these until 1935 when 634 acres of the county were transferred to Warwickshire and 240 acres were transferred from Warwickshire to Leicestershire. An exchange of territory also took place in 1935 and 1936 between the administrative county and the county borough.

Hundreds were included in all the *Census Reports* until 1881, except that of 1851. They are included in the population table whenever they occur in the *Census Reports*, but no attempt has been made to calculate their population in 1851. The constituent 'ancient' parishes of hundreds are shown on pp. 209–11. The Act of 1844, which altered certain county boundaries (see above), also altered the

[1] e.g. no figures are given for ecclesiastical, parliamentary, petty-sessional, or registration areas, for poor law unions, or for wards of boroughs and urban districts.

[2] For a full explanation of changes in the areas treated in the *Census Reports* see Interdepartmental Cttee. on Soc. and Econ. Research, *Guides to Official Sources, No. 2: Census Reports, 1801–1931* (H.M.S.O. 1951), 95–104.

[3] Detached Parts of Counties Act, 7 & 8 Vic. c. 61.

[4] The part of Packington which had been in Derbyshire was transferred to Leicestershire in 1884 and the whole of Ravenstone with Snibston was ordered to be in Leicestershire on its formation in 1884. The part of Oakthorpe and Donisthorpe in Leicestershire was apparently transferred to Derbyshire in the inter-censal period but the Local Government Board Order effecting the change has not been found.

boundaries of hundreds to make them conform with the changed county boundaries. This did not affect Leicestershire.

Urban and rural districts. These appeared first as urban and rural sanitary districts under the Public Health Act of 1872. Their boundaries underwent considerable change and new districts were created from time to time. In particular, the number and areas of the rural districts of Leicestershire were considerably changed under the Local Government Act of 1894.

The constituent civil parishes of urban districts are grouped in the population table under the urban districts, since these form compact and administratively unified areas: in many cases the civil parishes have been united to form one parish coextensive with the urban district. Where changes in boundaries of urban districts are mentioned in the *Census Reports*, they have been shown in the notes to the population table. Where the date of the district's formation is not mentioned, then it may be assumed to have been formed under the Act of 1872.

The constituent civil parishes of rural districts are shown on pp. 211–17, where a brief history of each district as an area is also given. Changes in the boundaries of rural districts have been so frequent and complex that it has not been possible to express them in the notes to the population table, and apparently large changes in the population of rural districts must be considered with caution. Since changes which involved the transference or amalgamation of whole parishes are shown in the list on pp. 211–17, reference to this list makes possible a rough comparison of population at different dates, but for exact comparison the figures and notes for each constituent parish should be consulted.

Boroughs, municipal boroughs, and county boroughs. The subdivision of boroughs into municipal and parliamentary was made necessary by the Reform Act of 1832, which took away parliamentary representation from some boroughs, created boroughs with parliamentary status, and altered the parliamentary limits of others. Municipal boroughs have also been created at various dates. Under the Representation of the People Act of 1918 parliamentary counties and boroughs were once more made coextensive with the corresponding local government areas. Sixty-one large boroughs were made into county boroughs by the Local Government Act of 1888.

Parishes. The bulk of the figures in the population table relate to parishes or parts of parishes, and the alteration in the boundaries and status of parishes are the most important factors influencing the form of the table.[5] Where ancient parishes were subdivided into chapelries, hamlets, or townships with recognizable boundaries, their population was often expressed in the early *Census Reports*, though these areas were not regularly returned. The *Census* of 1841 was much the fullest in this respect.

An 'ancient' parish divided between two or more hundreds is entered only once in the table, with the total population of all its parts together. The distribution of the parts, however, is shown in the table of hundreds (see pp. 209–11).

In 1871 areas which levied their own poor rates, whether 'ancient' parishes or not, were renamed 'civil parishes', but the grouping under 'ancient' parishes was retained in the *Reports* until 1881, although 'ancient' parishes as such had no civil significance by then. For the purpose of this table it has been found best to make the change between 1871 and 1881. The *Census Reports*, hampered by the complicated administrative and historical background, make no clear division between the old and new systems, and this date is convenient since the urban and rural districts appear in 1881 and the new grouping under urban districts can, where necessary, follow upon grouping under 'ancient' parishes. Therefore the component parts of 'ancient' parishes are grouped in the table under the 'ancient' parishes until 1871, while from 1881 each civil parish has a separate entry unless it was part of an urban district. Cross-references and notes make it possible to trace these changes in each case.

The boundaries of parishes have undergone changes at many times. In 1857[6] extra-parochial places were made into parishes for poor relief purposes, unless they were very small, in which case, if the owners and occupiers of two-thirds of the land consented, they were annexed to an adjoining parish. In 1868[7] any extra-parochial place which had by chance evaded the provisions of this Act was joined to the civil parish with which it had the longest common boundary. The Divided Parishes Acts of 1876, 1879, and 1882 provided for the annexation to one or more surrounding civil parishes of detached or nearly detached parts of civil parishes. The Local Government Act of 1888 permitted the alteration of civil parish boundaries and the amalgamation of civil parishes by Local Government Board orders. Under the Local Government Act of 1894 a civil parish divided between two urban districts or between an urban and a rural district became two separate civil parishes. Before this the overlapping of local government boundaries was such that it has been found necessary to make duplicate entries in some cases to show the population of entire civil parishes as well as of their component parts in various districts.

[5] The *Census Report* of 1801 is particularly unreliable in its general description of nearly every place as a 'parish'. This was admitted in the Introduction to the *Census Report* of 1811 and the descriptions of status of places given in the *Census Report* of 1801 have therefore been ignored.

[6] Act for the Relief of the Poor in Extra-parochial Places, 20 Vic. c. 19.

[7] Poor Law Amendment Act, 31 & 32 Vic. c. 122.

Place-Names. The spelling of place-names follows that in the Ordnance Survey maps. The names of obsolete areas are given in the form they took in their last occurrence under the relevant status in the *Census Reports.* Occasional variants are not mentioned unless they reflect boundary changes.

Census Reports. The population table is based almost solely on the information given in the *Reports.* From 1801 to 1831 the returns were made chiefly by the parish overseers, more than one day was allowed for enumeration, and the army (including the militia), navy, seamen in registered shipping, and convicts in the hulks were omitted. From 1841 the conduct of the Census passed to the General Register Office, the enumeration was more strictly completed on the fixed day, and members of the classes formerly excluded from the returns were included in the parishes in which they happened to pass the night of the census. The dates of the censuses were:[8]

10 March	1801	30 March	1851	31 March	1901
27 May	1811	7 April	1861	2 April	1911
28 May	1821	2 April	1871	19 June	1921
30 May	1831	3 April	1881	26 April	1931
6 June	1841	5 April	1891	8 April	1951

The notes and commentary. Changes in boundaries and comments on extraordinary changes in administrative status are shown in the *Notes* on each page of the table. These notes do not purport to supply a complete list of such changes: all changes recorded in the *Census Reports* are included in the notes but the *Census Reports* do not apparently give particulars of every change. It is improbable that any changes of importance are omitted. The explanations in the *Census Reports* of the reasons for particular changes in population, excluding boundary changes, and the comments on the occupations or condition of persons have been formed into a separate *Commentary* (pp. 203–9), where their chronological arrangement makes it more possible to trace social and economic tendencies in the county as a whole. An asterisk (*) placed by the relevant figure in the table indicates the existence of such a note.

Acreages. The acreages of parishes, though included in population tables in earlier volumes of the *History*, have been excluded from the present table. Acreages were first expressed in the *Census Reports* in 1831, when they were calculated on a system devised by John Rickman. Some were corrected in 1851 from information derived from Tithe Commission records and Ordnance Survey Maps.[9] Later, at dates varying from one parish to another, these figures were again amended from information received from the Ordnance Survey Department. After 1881 changes in boundaries which made any important difference to areas were explained in the *Census Reports* and the explanations have been copied in the notes to this table. Small changes were apparently not always notified and the assessment of areas seems sometimes to have varied slightly. It would therefore be difficult to choose a date for which areas could be given with equal certainty for all parishes. To supply all the different assessments given in the *Census Reports* would add greatly to the complexity of the table.

[8] *Guides to Official Sources, No. 2*, p. 2.

[9] Ibid. 14, 20.

POPULATION

POPULATION TABLE, 1801–1951

Abbreviations

A.P.	Ancient parish	E.P.P.	Extra-parochial place	pop.	Population
chap.	Chapelry	ham.	Hamlet	R.D.	Rural district
C.B.	County borough	lib.	Liberty	tnp.	Township
C.P.	Civil parish	M.B.	Municipal borough	U.D.	Urban district

	1801	*1811*	*1821*	*1831*	*1841*	*1851*	*1861*	*1871*	*1881*	*1891*	*1901*	*1911*	*1921*	*1931*	*1951*
LEICESTERSHIRE: Ancient County	130,081[a]	150,419[a]*	174,571	197,003	215,867	230,308	237,412	269,311	321,258	373,584	434,019	..	..	..	..
Administrative County with the County Borough of Leicester	..	..	..	..	..	..	..	..	..	375,092[b]	437,490[c]	476,553	494,469	541,861	631,077[d]

	1801	*1811*	*1821*	*1831*	*1841*	*1851*	*1861*	*1871*	*1881*	*1891*	*1901*	*1911*	*1921*	*1931*	*1951*
LEICESTER C.B.;[e] from 1896 C.B. and C.P.[f]	..	..	..	..	..	..	..	..	..	174,624	211,579	227,222	234,143	239,169*	285,181[g]
LEICESTER borough[h]	16,953	23,146	30,125	39,904	48,167	60,584	68,056	95,220*	122,376	..	..	..	..	..	..
ALL SAINTS A.P. and C.P.	2,838	3,362	3,440	3,284	4,608*	5,131*	5,945	6,458	6,371	6,867[i]	..	..	..	..	..
AUGUSTINE FRIARS E.P.P. and C.P.[j]	128	..[k]	207	180	245*	243	119	149	94	81	..	..	..	..	..
AUGUSTINE FRIARS	..	..	..	..	198[l]	..	..	..	..	..	..	..	..	..	..
FREAKS GROUND[l]	..	..	..	..	13	See Freaks Ground E.P.P., outside Leicester[l]						..	..	..	..
NEW PARKS[l]	..	..	..	..	34	See New Parks E.P.P., outside Leicester[l]					..	..	..	..	..
BLACKFRIARS E.P.P. and C.P.	..[k]	..[k]	597	1,152*	992	1,095	1,173	1,175	2,108	2,512	..	..	..	..	..
CASTLE VIEW E.P.P. and C.P.	See Castle View E.P.P., outside Leicester[m]					124	139	153	153	136	..	..	..	..	..
NEWARKE lib. and C.P.	219	281	219*	194	842	1,178	1,341	1,666	1,688	1,776	..	..	..	..	..
ST. LEONARD A.P. and C.P.	390	423	490	444	466	458	441	1,028	3,046	3,409	..	..	..	..	..
ST. MARGARET part of A.P.; C.P.[n]	5,809	10,158	15,026*	23,954*	30,784*	36,699*	41,194	59,062	78,805	92,929[o]	..	..	..	..	..
ST. MARTIN A.P. and C.P.	3,167	3,254	3,200	3,034	2,889	2,863	2,778	2,507	2,171	1,862	..	..	..	..	..

(a) When the figures given in the earlier Censuses were revised in 1851, those for 1801 and 1811 were corrected to 130,082 and 150,559 respectively.

(b) Comprised the ancient county together with part of Little Bowden C.P. (Northants. ancient county) (pop. 948 in 1891) in Market Harborough U.D., and Hydes Pastures (Warws. ancient county) (pop. 22 in 1891) in Hinckley U.D. and C.P. There had been other changes in the county boundary in the inter-censal period which were not accounted for in the *Census Report*, see p. 176.

(c) Comprised the administrative county as constituted in 1891, together with part of Appleby Magna (pop. 376 in 1901), and the whole of Chilcote, Measham, Oakthorpe and Donisthorpe, Stretton en le Field, and Willesley (all in Derbys. ancient county), but without parts of Ashby Woulds U.D. and Blackfordby C.P. (pop. respectively 1,201, 441 in 1901) and the whole of Nether and Over Seal C.P. (pop. 1,856 in 1901) which had all been transferred to Derbys. administrative county.

(d) Comprised the administrative county as constituted in 1931, together with part of the administrative county of Warws. viz. part of Nuneaton M.B. (pop. nil in 1931), part of Stretton Baskerville C.P. (pop. nil in 1931), and part of Wolvey C.P. (pop. 24 in 1931) added to Hinckley U.D.; part of Copston Magna C.P. (pop. 15 in 1931) added to Sharnford and Wigston Parva; part of Monks Kirby C.P. (pop. 7 in 1931) added to Lutterworth; parts of Wibtoft C.P. (pop. respectively nil, 26, nil in 1931) added to Bittesby, Claybrooke Parva, and Ullesthorpe; and parts of Willey C.P. (pop. respectively nil, 3 in 1931) added to Bittesby and Lutterworth; but without part of Hinckley U.D. (pop. 13 in 1931) and parts of Catthorpe, Cotesbach, Fenny Drayton, Higham on the Hill, Lutterworth, Shawell, and Witherley (pop. respectively 5, nil, 18, 175, nil, 12, 78 in 1931) all of which had been transferred to Warws. administrative county.

(e) Leicester was made a county borough under the Local Government Act 1888. Its area was not altered until the Leicester Extension Act 1891 came into force on 1 Jan. 1892, but the population shown for it and its constituent civil parishes in 1891 is that of the areas as constituted after the Act came into force, both in the *Census Report* and in this table. The C.B. as constituted at the date of the Census in fact contained only 142,045 persons. For the areas added, see notes to the individual civil parishes affected, viz. notes a, d, e, f, g, h, i, and j on p. 180.

(f) In 1896 all the C.P.s in Leicester C.B. were constituted Leicester C.P.; the C.B. and C.P. of Leicester were thereafter coextensive.

(g) The following changes took place in 1935 and 1936: part of Leicester C.B. (pop. 16 in 1931) was transferred to Oadby U.D. Parts of Oadby U.D., Thurmaston U.D., and Wigston U.D. (pop. respectively nil, 1,127, 648 in 1931), parts of Anstey, Beaumont Leys, Birstall, Braunstone, Evington, Kirby Muxloe, Leicester Frith, Lubbesthorpe, New Parks, and Thurnby C.P.s (pop. respectively nil, 169, 741, 4,753, 1,791, nil, 381, 4,513, 700, 88 in 1931) and the whole of Braunstone Frith, Gilroes, and Humberstone C.P.s were transferred to Leicester C.B. In 1939 a further part of Wigston U.D (pop. nil in 1931) was transferred to Leicester C.B., and part of Leicester C.B. (pop. nil in 1931) was transferred to Wigston.

(h) The municipal and parliamentary limits of the borough were the same.

(i) Part of St. Margaret (pop. 498 in 1891) was transferred to All Saints in 1885.

(j) Augustine Friars was formerly known generally as Whitefriars.

(k) No return was apparently made for Augustine Friars in 1811, or for Blackfriars in 1801–11.

(l) No returns were apparently made for Freaks Ground, New Parks, or New Found Pool until 1841 when they were said to be part of Augustine Friars. The population of New Found Pool was included in that of Augustine Friars itself in that year. They may all have been included in it in previous returns, but in 1851 and later they were all said to be outside Leicester, and were not connected with Augustine Friars.

(m) Castle View was returned as outside the borough until 1851, when it was said to be in Leicester.

(n) Part of St. Margaret A.P., viz. Knighton chapelry, lay outside the borough and was returned separately. It became a separate C.P. Another part of the parish, Bishop's Fee, was also said in 1831 to be outside the borough, but it was never returned separately and was later assumed to be in Leicester.

(o) In 1882 part of Abbey Park and Pasture (pop. nil in 1891) were transferred from Knighton C.P. to St. Margaret, and in 1885 part of St. Margaret (pop. 498 in 1891) was transferred to All Saints.

POPULATION TABLE, 1801–1951 (*continued*)

	1801	1811	1821	1831	1841	1851	1861	1871	1881	1891	1901	1911	1921	1931	1951
ST. MARY A.P. and C.P.	..	..	..	..	..	10,942*	13,264	21,097	26,110	30,828[a]	..	..	..	..	..
ST. MARY	3,454	4,079	5,406	5,168	5,840*	8,141	..	..	..	..	..	..	..	..	..
SOUTH FIELDS lib.	See St. Mary A.P., outside Leicester[b]					2,801	..	..	..	..	..	..	..	..	..
ST. NICHOLAS A.P. and C.P.	947	1,589	1,540	1,494	1,501	1,851	1,662	1,925	1,830	1,670	..	..	..	..	..
Civil Parishes added 1892[c]															
AYLESTONE C.P.[d]	..	..	..	..	..	..	..	..	..	5,381	..	..	..	..	..
BELGRAVE C.P.[e]	..	..	..	..	..	..	..	..	..	11,405	..	..	..	..	..
EVINGTON, NORTH C.P.[f]	..	..	..	..	..	..	..	..	..	4,173	..	..	..	..	..
HUMBERSTONE, WEST C.P.[g]	..	..	..	..	..	..	..	..	..	3,284*	..	..	..	..	..
KNIGHTON C.P.[h]	..	..	..	..	..	..	..	..	..	6,075	..	..	..	..	..
LEICESTER ABBEY C.P.[i]	..	..	..	..	..	..	..	..	..	76*	..	..	..	..	..
NEW FOUND POOL C.P.[j]	..	..	..	..	..	..	..	..	..	2,160	..	..	..	..	..

	1801	1811	1821	1831	1841	1851	1861	1871	1881	1891	1901	1911	1921	1931	1951
AB KETTLEBY A.P. and C.P.	See Kettleby, Ab. ..			..	..	..	..	..	..	..	..	..	..	..	..
ALDERMAN'S HAW	See Barrow upon Soar A.P.				..	..	..	..	..	..	..	..	..	..	..
ALLEXTON A.P. and C.P.	88	84	74	68	81	78	67	69	48	64	66	46	56	45	58
ALL SAINTS A.P. and C.P.	See Leicester		..	..	..	..	..	..	..	..	..	..	..	..	..
ANSTEY C.P.	Chapelry of Thurcaston A.P., q.v.								1,279	1,759[k]	2,544*	2,976	3,010	3,174	3,685[l]
ANSTEY PASTURES E.P.P. and C.P.	..[m]	..[m]	11	19	15	25	34	41	43	28	36	48	30	28	..[n]
APPLEBY A.P. and C.P. (Derbys. and Leics.)	935	1,123	1,185*	1,150	1,075	1,181	1,070	885	757	..	..	..	..	..	..
the part in Leics.	478	..[o]	..[o]	610*	496*	571	494*	393*	319	See Appleby C.P.[p]			..	..	..
APPLEBY C.P.[p]	..	..	..	..	..	..	..	..	..	285	See Appleby Magna C.P.[q]				..
APPLEBY MAGNA C.P.[q]	..	..	..	..	..	..	..	..	..	..	649	675	752	763	829
ARNESBY A.P. and C.P.	321	400	459	442	505	567	573	478*	421	399	402	354	273	282	304
ASFORDBY A.P. and C.P.	364	367	424	467	482	527	485	513	539	717	1,062*	1,336*	1,409	2,003*	2,332[r]
ASHBY DE LA ZOUCH R.D.	..	..	..	..	..	..	..	..	22,188	24,055	14,447	16,255	17,064	17,462	13,781
ASHBY DE LA ZOUCH A.P.	2,917	3,403	4,227	4,727	5,652*	6,230*	6,958	8,028	..	..	..	..	..	..	..
ASHBY DE LA ZOUCH	2,674	3,141	3,973	4,400	5,208	5,691	6,337	7,302*	See Ashby de la Zouch C.P.				..	..	..
BLACKFORDBY chap., part of[s]	243	262	290	327	444	539	621	726	See Blackfordby C.P.			..	..	..	..
ASHBY DE LA ZOUCH C.P.[t]	Part of Ashby de la Zouch A.P., q.v.								7,465	7,710	..	..	..	..	..
the part in Ashby de la Zouch U.D., q.v.	..	..	..	..	..	..	..	..	4,536	4,496[u]	See Ashby de la Zouch U.D. and C.P.[t]				
the part in Ashby Woulds U.D., q.v.	..	..	..	..	..	..	..	..	2,929	3,214	See Ashby Woulds U.D. and C.P.[t]				
ASHBY DE LA ZOUCH U.D.; from 1894 U.D. and C.P.[v]	..	..	..	..	..	..	..	..	4,536	4,535	4,726	4,927	4,983	5,091	6,405[w]

(a) Part of Braunstone (pop. 25 in 1891) was transferred to Leicester C.B. and to St. Mary C.P. in 1892. See note (e) on previous page.

(b) Part of St. Mary A.P., viz. South Fields liberty, was said to lie outside the borough and was returned separately until 1851, when it was said to be inside the borough. From 1861 it was apparently regarded as an integral part of the parish and included in the main return.

(c) See note (e) on previous page.

(d) Part of Aylestone C.P. was transferred to Leicester C.B. as Aylestone C.P. in 1892. See note (e) on previous page.

(e) Belgrave U.D. was dissolved, and part of its constituent C.P. was transferred to Leicester C.B. as Belgrave C.P. in 1892. See note (e) on previous page.

(f) Part of Evington was transferred to Leicester C.B. as North Evington C.P. in 1892. See note (e) on previous page.

(g) Part of Humberstone was transferred to Leicester C.B. as West Humberstone C.P. in 1892. See note (e) on previous page.

(h) Part of Knighton C.P. was transferred to Leicester C.B. as Knighton C.P. in 1892. See note (e) on previous page.

(i) Part of Leicester Abbey (pop. 20 in 1891) and the whole of Freaks Ground (pop. 56 in 1891) were transferred to Leicester C.B. as Leicester Abbey C.P. in 1892. See note (e) on previous page.

(j) New Found Pool was transferred to Leicester C.B. in 1892. See note (e) on previous page.

(k) Part of Bradgate Park (pop. nil in 1891) was transferred to Anstey in 1884.

(l) In 1935 part of Anstey (pop. nil in 1931) was transferred to Leicester C.B. and part (pop. 6 in 1931) to Glenfield C.P. In 1936 part of Anstey (pop. 3 in 1931) was transferred to the new Glenfields C.P. and parts of Anstey Pastures, Beaumont Leys, and Newtown Linford (pop. respectively 11, nil, 132 in 1931) were transferred to Anstey.

(m) No separate return made: included in Anstey chapelry in Thurcaston A.P.

(n) Anstey Pastures C.P. was dissolved in 1936. Part (pop. 11 in 1931) was transferred to Anstey and part (pop. 17 in 1931) to Glenfields.

(o) No separate return made of the part in Leics.

(p) Until 1891, the two parts of Appleby were returned as one civil parish. In 1891 they were treated as separate civil parishes with the same name. The order effecting this change has not been found.

(q) In 1897 Appleby (Derbys.) (pop. 376 in 1901) was transferred to Leics. administrative county and renamed Appleby Magna North, while Appleby (Leics.) (pop. 273 in 1901) was renamed Appleby Magna South. The two parishes were united as Appleby Magna in 1898.

(r) In 1935 part of Melton Mowbray U.D. (pop. nil in 1931) and in 1936 part of Welby C.P. (pop. 87 in 1931) were transferred to Asfordby.

(s) From 1841 to 1871 Blackfordby chapelry was said to extend into Seal A.P., and separate returns were made for each part.

(t) In 1894 the part of Ashby de la Zouch C.P. in Ashby de la Zouch U.D. was created Ashby de la Zouch C.P., and the part in Ashby Woulds U.D. was created Ashby Woulds C.P. The two U.D.s therefore became coextensive with their constituent C.P.s.

(u) Alton Grange (pop. 39 in 1891) in the part of Ashby de la Zouch C.P. which was in Ashby de la Zouch U.D. was transferred to Ravenstone with Snibston C.P. in 1884.

(v) Ashby de la Zouch U.D. first consisted of part of Ashby de la Zouch C.P. only. Alton Grange in this part of the C.P. was transferred to Ravenstone with Snibston C.P. in 1884, but the boundaries of the U.D. remained unchanged until 1894 when this part of Ravenstone with Snibston was transferred from the U.D. to Ashby de la Zouch R.D. In 1894 the part of Ashby de la Zouch C.P. outside the U.D. (i.e. in Ashby Woulds U.D.) was created Ashby Woulds C.P., so that Ashby de la Zouch U.D. and C.P. became coextensive.

(w) In 1936 part of Ashby de la Zouch U.D. (pop. nil in 1931) was transferred to Ashby Woulds U.D. and parts of Ashby Woulds U.D., Blackfordby, Packington, and Willesley (pop. respectively 75, 493, 87, 80 in 1931) were transferred to Ashby de la Zouch.

POPULATION TABLE, 1801–1951 (*continued*)

	1801	1811	1821	1831	1841	1851	1861	1871	1881	1891	1901	1911	1921	1931	1951
ASHBY DE LA ZOUCH C.P., part of	..	..	..	..	..	..	..	..	4,536	4,496	..[a]	..	..	..	..
RAVENSTONE WITH SNIBSTON C.P., part of	..	..	..	..	..	..	..	..	..	39	See Ravenstone with Snibston C.P.[a]				
ASHBY FOLVILLE A.P.	337	384	405	391	437	495	450	447	..	..	..	..	..	..	..
ASHBY FOLVILLE	135	145	163	161	146	189	160	174	See Ashby Folville C.P.				..	..	..
BARSBY chap.	202	239	242	230	291	306	290	273	See Barsby C.P.			..	..	..	..
ASHBY FOLVILLE C.P.	Part of Ashby Folville A.P., q.v.								131	115[b]	111	139	119	123	See Gaddesby C.P.[c]
ASHBY MAGNA A.P. and C.P.	283	260	280	330	337	323	315	275	253[d]	279	292	262	261	257	217
ASHBY PARVA A.P. and C.P.	135	150	176	169	179	173	160	141	148[d]	137	111	126	130	147	135
ASHBY WOULDS U.D.; from 1894 U.D. and C.P.[e]	..	..	..	..	..	..	..	..	2,929	3,214	2,799[f]	2,783	3,199	3,351	3,418[g]
ASHBY DE LA ZOUCH C.P., part of	..	..	..	..	..	..	..	..	2,929	3,214	..[e]	..	..	..	..
ASTON FLAMVILLE A.P.	1,162	1,419	1,584	1,703	1,909	2,028	1,946	1,833	..	..	..	..	..	..	..
ASTON FLAMVILLE	63	71	80	85	82	77	81	108	See Aston Flamville C.P.				..	..	..
BURBAGE chap.	} 1,099	1,348	1,504	1,618	1,780	1,894	1,801	} 1,725	See Burbage C.P.			..	..	..	..
SKETCHLEY ham.					47	57	64								
ASTON FLAMVILLE C.P.	Part of Aston Flamville A.P., q.v.								113	100	77	78	84	107	125
ATTERTON C.P.	Hamlet of Witherley A.P., q.v.								58	35[h]	29	34	47	43	See Witherley C.P.[i]
AUGUSTINE FRIARS E.P.P. and C.P.	See Leicester		..	..	..	..	..	..	..	..	..	..	..	..	..
AYLESTONE A.P.	649	703	749	758	757	668	575*	675	..	..	..	..	..	..	..
AYLESTONE	440	500	540	528	526	444*	392	450	See Aylestone C.P.			..	..	..	..
GLEN PARVA tnp.	128	126	128	160	148	150	119	152	See Glen Parva C.P.			..	..	..	..
LUBBESTHORPE chap.	81	77	81	70	83	74	64	73	See Lubbesthorpe C.P.			..	..	..	..
AYLESTONE C.P.	Part of Aylestone A.P., q.v.								2,546	See Leicester C.B.[j]			..	..	..
BAGGRAVE lib.	See Hungarton A.P.			..	..	..	..	..	..	..	..	..	..	..	..
BAGWORTH C.P.	Chapelry of Thornton A.P., q.v.								604	642[k]	631	1,419*	1,481	1,568	2,103[l]
BAGWORTH PARK lib.	See Thornton A.P.			..	..	..	..	..	..	..	..	..	..	..	..
BARDON E.P.P. and C.P.	65	52	69	65	63	56	63	59	74	69	567[m]	554	511	463	38[n]
BARKBY A.P.	576	684	719	806	849	857	791	758	..	..	..	..	..	..	..
BARKBY	389	} 454	457	550	521	} 525	504	440	See Barkby C.P.			..	..	..	
HAMILTON ham.	4				7										
BARKBY THORPE chap.	72	62	70	72	70	62	78	66	See Barkby Thorpe C.P.				..	..	..
THURMASTON, NORTH chap.	111	168	192	184	251	270	209*	252	See Thurmaston U.D.			..	..	..	..
BARKBY C.P.	Part of Barkby A.P., q.v.								579	631	682[o]	670	730[p]	955	405[q]
BARKBY THORPE C.P.	Chapelry of Barkby A.P., q.v.								47	59	68[o]	58	72	73	72
BARKESTONE A.P. and C.P.	238	305	341	297*	403	448	411	330*	302	329	270	253	255	238	See Redmile C.P.[r]
BARLESTONE C.P.	Chapelry of Bosworth, Market A.P., q.v.								708	805[s]	829	1,042	1,137	1,134	1,229[t]

(a) See note (v) on previous page.
(b) The 'Cheney Arms', &c. (pop. 7 in 1891) was transferred from Ashby Folville to Gaddesby in 1882, and Ashby Newbould (pop. nil in 1891) was transferred from Ashby Folville to Barsby in 1884.
(c) The whole of Ashby Folville was transferred to Gaddesby in 1936.
(d) In 1877 detached parts of Ashby Magna, Kimcote, and Leire (pop. respectively 8, nil, 27 in 1881) were transferred to Ashby Parva.
(e) The part of Ashby de la Zouch C.P. in Ashby Woulds C.P. was created Ashby Woulds C.P. in 1894, so that the U.D. and C.P. became co-extensive.
(f) In 1897 part of Ashby Woulds U.D. and C.P. (pop. 1,201 in 1901) was transferred to Derbys. administrative county as part of the new C.P. of Woodville.
(g) In 1936 part of Ashby Woulds U.D. (pop. 75 in 1931) was transferred to Ashby de la Zouch U.D., and parts of Ashby de la Zouch U.D., and Blackfordby (pop. respectively nil, 137 in 1931) were transferred to Ashby Woulds.
(h) Part of Atterton (pop. nil in 1891) was transferred to Witherley in 1885.
(i) The whole of Atterton was transferred to Witherley in 1935.
(j) The greater part of Aylestone (pop. 5,381 in 1891) was transferred to Leicester C.B. as Aylestone C.P. in 1892. The remainder (pop. 27 in 1881) was transferred to Lubbesthorpe. The populations of the affected areas in 1891 are shown as altered both in the *Census Report* and in this table. Aylestone had already been diminished in 1885 by the transference of parts of it (pop. nil in 1891) to Glen Parva and Lubbesthorpe.
(k) Part of Bagworth (pop. nil in 1891) was transferred to Newbold Verdon in 1886.
(l) The whole of Thornton was transferred to Bagworth in 1935.
(m) The part of Hugglescote and Donington C.P. not in Coalville U.D. (pop. 287 in 1901) was transferred to Bardon in 1893.
(n) In 1935 part of Bardon (pop. 1 in 1931) was transferred to Markfield, and in 1936 another part (pop. 407 in 1931) was transferred to Coalville U.D. and C.P.
(o) Part of Barkby (pop. 17 in 1901) was transferred to Barkby Thorpe in 1897.
(p) Part of Thurmaston U.D. was transferred to Barkby in 1914.
(q) In 1935 part of Barkby (pop. 566 in 1931) was transferred to Thurcaston, and part of Syston (pop. 24 in 1931) was transferred to Barkby.
(r) The whole of Barkestone was transferred to Redmile in 1936.
(s) Part of Newbold Verdon (pop. nil in 1891) was transferred to Barkstone in 1882.
(t) Part of Newbold Verdon (pop. nil in 1931) was transferred to Barlestone in 1935.

POPULATION TABLE, 1801–1951 (*continued*)

	1801	*1811*	*1821*	*1831*	*1841*	*1851*	*1861*	*1871*	*1881*	*1891*	*1901*	*1911*	*1921*	*1931*	*1951*
BARRONS PARK ham.	See Desford A.P.			..	..	..	..	..	..	..	..	..	..	..	..
BARROW UPON SOAR R.D.	..	..	..	..	..	..	..	..	18,244	19,072	21,623	23,758	25,209	30,862	47,395
BARROW UPON SOAR A.P.[a]	..	..	..	..	5,782	5,728	5,633	5,870	..	..	..	..	..	..	..
BARROW UPON SOAR	1,090	1,303	1,568*	1,638*	1,841*	1,736	1,800	1,963*	See Barrow upon Soar C.P.				..	..	..
MOUNTSORREL, NORTH END chap.	1,233[a]	1,502[a]	1,422[a]	1,602[a]	821	802	857	1,046*	See Mountsorrel North End C.P.					..	..
QUORNDON chap.	1,237	1,281	1,503*	1,752	1,811	1,876	1,622*	1,516	See Quorndon U.D. and C.P.				..	..	..
BEAUMANOR lib.	See Beaumanor E.P.P.[b]					113	137	137							
WOODHOUSE chap.	668	893	1,067*	1,262	395	1,201	1,205	1,195	See Woodhouse C.P.			..	..	..	..
ALDERMAN'S HAW					25										
WOODHOUSE EAVES ham.					861										
MAPLEWELL LONGDALE ham.					28		12	13	See Maplewell Longdale C.P.				..	..	..
BARROW UPON SOAR C.P.	Part of Barrow upon Soar A.P., q.v.								2,024	2,245[c]	2,409[d]	2,481	2,575	2,661	2,788
BARSBY C.P.	Chapelry of Ashby Folville A.P., q.v.								254	188[e]	171	180	163	162	See Gaddesby C.P.[f]
BARTON IN THE BEANS C.P.	Township of Nailstone A.P., q.v.								136	146[g]	152	151	168	177	See Shackerstone C.P.[h]
BARWELL C.P.	Part of Barwell A.P., q.v.								1,506	2,022	2,721	2,998	3,098[i]	3,869*	See Hinckley U.D.[j]
BARWELL A.P.	995	1,162	1,371	1,505	1,607	1,613	1,613	1,523	..	..	..	..	..	..	..
BARWELL	787	928	1,095	1,245	1,351	1,362	1,358	1,303	See Barwell C.P.			..	..	..	..
MARSTON, POTTERS ham.	18	14	16	11	11	12	15	21	See Marston, Potters C.P.				..	..	..
STAPLETON ham.	190	220	260	249	245	239	240	199	See Stapleton C.P.			..	..	..	..
BASSETT HOUSE E.P.P.	See Knoll and Bassett House E.P.P. and C.P.						..	..	..	..	..	..	..	..	..
BEAUMANOR E.P.P.	61	73	96	98	87	See Barrow upon Soar A.P.[k]				..	..	..	..	..	..
BEAUMONT LEYS E.E.P. and C.P.	20	21	14	28	29	28	31	36	39	127[l]	167	174	170	169	..[m]
BEEBY A.P. and C.P.	128	121	120	120	115	139	119	114	108	106	93	95	98	97	109
BELGRAVE A.P.	1,481	1,607	1,904	2,329	2,609	2,870	2,808	3,515	..	..	..	..	..	..	..
BELGRAVE	601	631	735	989	1,193	1,398	1,510	2,049*	See Belgrave U.D. and C.P.				..	..	..
BIRSTALL chap.	285	302	371	393	438	491	405*	437	See Birstall C.P.			..	..	..	..
THURMASTON, SOUTH chap.	595	674	798	947	978	981	893*	1,029*	See Thurmaston U.D.			..	..	..	..
BELGRAVE U.D. and C.P.	Part of Belgrave A.P., q.v.								7,260	See Leicester C.B.[n]			..	..	..
BELTON A.P. and C.P.	586	544	664	735	718	751	781	684	645	571	542	607	588	554	653[o]
BELTON	..	..	..	..	..	719	..	..	..	..	..	..	..	..	..
GRACE DIEU	..	..	..	..	..	32	..	..	..	..	..	..	..	..	..
BELVOIR R.D.	..	..	..	..	..	..	..	..	..	..	3,459	3,255	3,239	3,035	..
BELVOIR E.P.P. and C.P.	80	96	88[p]*	105*	109*	178	171	211	141	144	94	111	77	80	445[q]
BESCABY E.P.P. and C.P.	See Croxton Kerrial A.P.[r]				7	17*	26	25	9	31	20	22	26	17	See Sproxton C.P.[s]

(a) Although Mountsorrel South End was in Rothley A.P. the population of the whole of Mountsorrel was returned together under Mountsorrel North End, 1801–31. It is therefore impossible to state the population of Barrow upon Soar A.P. for those years.

(b) Beaumanor was returned as an extra-parochial liberty 1801–41, but as part of Barrow upon Soar A.P. 1851–71.

(c) That part of Mountsorrel North End (pop. 28 in 1891) which was not joined to Mountsorrel South End to form the new C.P. of Mountsorrel was transferred to Barrow upon Soar in 1884.

(d) Part of Barrow upon Soar (pop. 29 in 1901) was transferred to Mountsorrel C.P. in 1896.

(e) In 1884 Ashby Newbould (pop. nil in 1891) was transferred from Ashby Folville to Barsby, part of South Croxton (pop. nil in 1891) was transferred to Barsby, and Barsby Lodge (pop. nil in 1891) was transferred from Barsby to South Croxton.

(f) The whole of Barsby was transferred to Gaddesby in 1936.

(g) Part of Market Bosworth (pop. 6 in 1891) was transferred to Barton in the Beans in 1882, and part of Nailstone (pop. nil in 1891) was transferred to Barton in the Beans in 1886.

(h) The whole of Barton in the Beans was transferred to Shackerstone in 1935.

(i) In 1920 part of Barwell (pop. nil in 1921) was transferred to Hinckley U.D. and part of Hinckley (pop. 9 in 1921) was transferred to Barwell.

(j) The whole of Barwell was transferred to Hinckley U.D. in 1936.

(k) Returned as a liberty in Barrow upon Soar A.P. 1851–71.

(l) Part of Belgrave U.D. (pop. 48 in 1891) and part of Leicester Abbey (pop. 11 in 1881) were transferred to Beaumont Leys in 1892 when the remainder of them became part of Leicester C.B. The affected areas are shown in 1891 as altered both in the *Census Report* and in this table.

(m) Beaumont Leys C.P. was dissolved in 1935. Part of it (pop. 169 in 1931) was transferred to Leicester C.B., part (pop. nil in 1931) to Anstey, and part (pop. nil in 1931) to Thurcaston.

(n) Belgrave U.D. was dissolved in 1892. Part of its constituent C.P. (pop. 11,405 in 1891) was transferred to Leicester C.B. as Belgrave C.P., and the remainder was transferred to Beaumont Leys C.P. The affected areas are shown in 1891 as altered both in the *Census Report* and in this table.

(o) Part of Thringstone (pop. 14 in 1931) was transferred to Belton in 1936.

(p) Belvoir was said in 1821 to extend into Lincs., but it was always returned in Leics., and there was no later mention of its being in two counties.

(q) The whole of Harston and Knipton C.P.s were transferred to Belvoir in 1936.

(r) Bescaby was returned as part of Croxton Kerrial until it was said to be extra-parochial in 1841.

(s) The whole of Bescaby was transferred to Sproxton in 1936.

POPULATION TABLE, 1801–1951 (*continued*)

	1801	*1811*	*1821*	*1831*	*1841*	*1851*	*1861*	*1871*	*1881*	*1891*	*1901*	*1911*	*1921*	*1931*	*1951*
BILLESDON R.D.	..	..	..	..	..	..	..	..	10,073	6,309	6,172	6,913	7,283	11,073	7,822
BILLESDON A.P.	695	665	751	908	878	948	1,085	968	..	..	..	..	..	..	..
BILLESDON	580	534	624	769	713	763*	909	802*	See Billesdon C.P.			..	..	..	..
GOADBY chap.	72	87	96	98	122	141	134	126	See Goadby C.P.			..	..	..	..
ROLLESTON chap.	43	44	31	41	43	44	42	40	See Rolleston C.P.			..	..	..	..
BILLESDON C.P.	Part of Billesdon A.P., q.v.								839	754	726	594	514	543	717
BILSTONE C.P.	Township of Norton juxta Twycross A.P., q.v.								102	91	80	79	79	68	See Shackerstone C.P.[a]
BIRSTALL C.P.	Chapelry of Belgrave A.P., q.v.								487	566	611	751	796	3,131*	6,667[b]
BITTESBY C.P.	Liberty of Claybrooke A.P., q.v.								37	44	35	38	48	40	32[c]
BITTESWELL A.P. and C.P.	398	352	427	439	495	474	438	400	364	330	324	308	351	293	346
BLABY R.D.	..	..	..	..	..	..	..	..	21,853	21,695	16,569	19,114	17,072	32,764	39,214
BLABY A.P.	1,258	1,422	1,730	1,840	1,896	1,952*	1,998	2,092	..	..	..	..	..	..	..
BLABY	718	829	989	1,001	1,081	1,003	1,023	1,066	See Blaby C.P.			..	..	..	..
COUNTESTHORPE chap.	540	593	741	839	815	949	975	1,026	See Countesthorpe C.P.			..	..	..	..
BLABY C.P.	Part of Blaby A.P., q.v.								1,303	1,646	1,842	1,959	2,012	2,329	2,991[d]
BLACKFORDBY C.P.	Chapelry, partly in Ashby de la Zouch A.P., q.v., and partly in Seal A.P., q.v.								1,047	1,040[e]	588[f]	517	525	705	..[g]
BLACKFRIARS E.P.P. and C.P.	See Leicester		..	..	..	..	..	..	..	..	..	..	..	..	..
BLASTON A.P. and C.P.	76	58	58	73	102	88	93	82	114	100	92	95	76	73	59
ST. GILES chap.	..	..	..	..	34	33	25	56	..	..	..	..	..	..	..
ST. MICHAEL chap.	..	..	..	..	68	55	68	26	..	..	..	..	..	..	..
BOSWORTH, HUSBANDS A.P. and C.P.	660	1,024	817	865	953	1,002	934	934	831	845	741	779	732	713	781
BOSWORTH, MARKET R.D.	..	..	..	..	..	..	..	..	14,611	15,640	18,549	21,858	23,196	23,544	26,370
BOSWORTH, MARKET A.P.[h]	1,949	2,166	2,500	2,367	2,539	2,449*	2,376	2,416	..	..	..	..	..	..	..
BOSWORTH, MARKET } COTON ham.	} 791	865	1,117[h]	1,049	1,068	} 1,058	997	949	See Bosworth, Market C.P.				..	..	..
COTON ham.					67										
BARLESTONE chap.	505	558	617	582	580	576	544	602	See Barlestone C.P.			..	..	..	..
CARLTON chap.	160	219	218	201	282	290	277	252	See Carlton C.P.			..	..	..	..
SHENTON chap.	177	185	194	200	190	185	206	273*	See Shenton C.P.			..	..	..	..
SUTTON CHENEY chap.	316	339	354	335	352	340	352	340	See Sutton Cheney C.P.			..	..	..	..
BOSWORTH, MARKET C.P.	Part of Bosworth, Market A.P., q.v.								881	836[i]	659	729	886	864	1,213
BOTCHESTON ham.	See Ratby A.P.			..	..	..	..	..	..	..	..	..	..	..	..
BOTTESFORD A.P. and C.P.	804	891	1,070	1,320	1,375	1,374	1,415	1,315	1,331	1,286	1,221	1,174	1,204	1,093	1,481[j]
BOTTESFORD	..	..	..	..	855	..	..	..	..	..	..	..	..	..	..
EASTHORPE ham.	..	..	..	..	417	..	..	..	..	..	..	..	..	..	..
NORMANTON ham.	..	..	..	..	103	..	..	..	..	..	..	..	..	..	..
BOWDEN, GREAT A.P.	2,499	2,530	2,834	3,346	3,698	3,624*	3,697	3,812	..	..	..	..	..	..	..
BOWDEN, GREAT	783	826	961	1,074	1,265	1,299	1,395	1,450	} See Harborough, Market U.D.				..	..	..
HARBOROUGH, MARKET chap.	1,716	1,704	1,873	2,272*	2,433*	2,325*	2,302	2,362*							
BOWDEN, LITTLE C.P.	See Harborough, Market U.D.				..	..	..	..	..	..	..	..	..	..	..
BRADGATE PARK E.P.P. and C.P.	8	8	10	10	7	7	9	12	6	..[k]	..	..	..	..	..
BRANSTON A.P. and C.P.	209	236	282	298	333	317	297	319	247	257	221	222	218	249	See Croxton Kerrial C.P.[l]
BRASCOTE ham.	See Newbold Verdon A.P.				..	..	..	..	..	..	..	..	..	..	..

(a) The whole of Bilstone was transferred to Shackerstone in 1935.

(b) In 1935 part of Birstall (pop. 741 in 1931) was transferred to Leicester C.B.

(c) In 1935 parts of Wibtoft and Willey C.P.s (Warws.) (pop. nil in 1931) were transferred to Leics. administrative county and to Bittesby C.P.

(d) In 1935 and 1936 part of Blaby (pop. 25 in 1931) was transferred to Countesthorpe and part (pop. nil in 1931) to Wigston Magna C.P. in Wigston U.D.

(e) Part of Over and Nether Seal (pop. 33 in 1891) was transferred to Blackfordby in 1884.

(f) Part of Blackfordby (pop. 441 in 1901) was transferred to Derbys. administrative county as part of the new C.P. of Woodville in 1897.

(g) In 1936 Blackfordby C.P. was dissolved. Its area was divided between Ashby de la Zouch U.D. and Ashby Woulds U.D. According to *Census, 1931: Leics. pt. II* (1937) the two parts had pops. in 1931 of 493 and 137 respectively.

(h) Barton in the Beans township was said from 1811 to 1861 to be partly in Market Bosworth A.P., Nailstone A.P., and Shackerstone A.P. From 1871 on it was assumed to be all in Nailstone and has been treated in this table as always having been entirely contained in that A.P. Osbaston township was similarly said to be partly in Market Bosworth and partly in Cadeby. It was all returned with Cadeby except in 1821 when part of it was said to have been included in the return for Market Bosworth. From 1871 it was assumed to be all in Cadeby and has been treated as if it had always been entirely contained in that A.P.

(i) Part of Market Bosworth (pop. 6 in 1891) was transferred to Barton in the Beans in 1882, and in 1884 Naneby House (pop. 4 in 1891) was transferred from Market Bosworth to Cadeby, and another part of Market Bosworth (pop. 18 in 1891) was transferred to Congerstone.

(j) The whole of Muston C.P. was transferred to Bottesford in 1936.

(k) In 1884 Bradgate C.P. was dissolved: part of it (pop. nil in 1891) was transferred to Anstey, part (pop. 4 in 1891) to Newtown Linford, and part, called Lea Wood (pop. nil in 1891), to Ulverscroft.

(l) The whole of Branston was transferred to Croxton Kerrial in 1936.

POPULATION TABLE, 1801–1951 (*continued*)

	1801	*1811*	*1821*	*1831*	*1841*	*1851*	*1861*	*1871*	*1881*	*1891*	*1901*	*1911*	*1921*	*1931*	*1951*
BRAUNSTONE C.P.	Chapelry of Glenfield A.P., q.v.								193	169[a]	143	125	238	6,997*	8,986[b]
BRAUNSTONE FRITH C.P.	Liberty of Glenfield A.P., q.v.								12	10	14	6	3	7	See Leicester C.B.[c]
BREEDON ON THE HILL A.P.	2,198	2,302	2,630	2,656	2,625*	2,553	2,417	2,246	..	..	..	..	..	..	..
BREEDON ON THE HILL	} 815 (Breedon on the Hill, Tonge and Wilson)	569	} 1,044 (Breedon on the Hill, Tonge and Wilson)	1,103	766	} 1,024 (Breedon on the Hill, Tonge and Wilson)	893*	824	See Breedon on the Hill C.P.				..	..	..
TONGE ham.		173			150								..	..	..
WILSON ham.		166			177										
STAUNTON HAROLD tnp.	287	281	329	342	389	326	352	288	See Staunton Harold C.P.				..	..	..
WORTHINGTON chap.	} 1,096 (Worthington and Newbold)	1,113	1,257	1,211	802	848	} 1,172 (Worthington and Newbold)	1,134	See Worthington C.P.			..	..	..	..
NEWBOLD lib.					341	355									
BREEDON ON THE HILL C.P.	Part of Breedon on the Hill A.P., q.v.								717	649	704	752	730	806	810[d]
BRENTINGBY AND WYFORDBY A.P. and C.P.	78	97	126	98	129	161	144	103	104	141	115	105	102	86	See Freeby C.P.[e]
BRENTINGBY	..	..	..	..	75	..	..	..	..	..	..	..	..	..	..
WYFORDBY	..	..	..	..	54	..	..	..	..	..	..	..	..	..	..
BRINGHURST A.P.	777	737	735	782	840	934	825	827	..	..	..	..	..	..	..
BRINGHURST	98	94	102	85	92	110	109	109	See Bringhurst C.P.			..	..	..	..
DRAYTON tnp.	136	129	104*	156	148	157	126	115	See Drayton C.P.			..	..	..	..
EASTON, GREAT chap.	543	514	529	541	600	667	590	603	See Easton, Great C.P.			..	..	..	..
BRINGHURST C.P.	Part of Bringhurst A.P., q.v.								73	33	49	45	40	42	55
BROOKSBY A.P. and C.P.	43	23	23	10	20	20	44	61	67	42	73	58	43	69	See Hoby with Rotherby C.P.[f]
BROUGHTON AND OLD DALBY C.P.[g]	..	..	..	..	..	..	..	..	..	..	..	..	..	..	1,145
BROUGHTON ASTLEY A.P. and C.P.	458	585	630	726	728	746	785	746	708	785[h]	1,172*	1,339	1,292	1,440	1,523[i]
BROUGHTON ASTLEY	..	..	210	..	306	323	354	311	..	..	..	..	..	..	..
PRIMETHORPE tnp.	..	..	270	..	286	284	} 431 (Primethorpe and Sutton in the Elms)	321	..	..	..	..	..	..	..
SUTTON IN THE ELMS tnp.	..	..	150	..	136	139		114	..	..	..	..	..	..	..
BROUGHTON, NETHER A.P. and C.P.	324	367	435	415	412	423	519*	405*	454	400	369	380	373	345	See Broughton and Old Dalby C.P.[j]
BRUNTINGTHORPE A.P. and C.P.	259	332	348	382	423	392	413	368	304	258	233	227	225	203	215
BUCKMINSTER A.P.	483	596	625	842	697	685	655	544	..	..	..	..	..	..	..
BUCKMINSTER	262	330	327	474*	405*	375	348	312	See Buckminster C.P.			..	..	..	..
SEWSTERN chap.	221	266	298	368	292	310	307	232	See Sewstern C.P.			..	..	..	..
BUCKMINSTER C.P.	Part of Buckminster A.P., q.v.								253	328[k]	274	246	287	265	520[l]
BURBAGE C.P.	Chapelry of Aston Flamville A.P., q.v.								1,691	1,876	2,196	2,412	2,589	3,570	See Hinckley U.D.[m]
BURROUGH ON THE HILL A.P. and C.P.	138	138	183	173	149	135	138	200*	149	139[n]	149	200	206	214	See Somerby C.P.[o]
BURTON AND DALBY C.P.[p]	..	..	..	..	..	..	..	..	..	..	..	..	..	..	635
BURTON LAZARS A.P. and C.P.	218	212	249	258	262	See Melton Mowbray A.P.[q]			244	311	240	238	192	197	..[r]

(a) Part of Braunstone C.P. (pop. 25 in 1891) was transferred to St. Mary C.P. in Leicester C.B. in 1892. The affected areas are shown in 1891 as altered, both in the *Census Report* and in this table.

(b) Part of Braunstone (pop. 4,753 in 1931) was transferred to Leicester C.B. in 1935 and part of Lubbesthorpe (pop. 22 in 1931) was transferred to Braunstone in 1936.

(c) The whole of Braunstone Frith was transferred to Leicester C.B. in 1935.

(d) In 1936 part of Breedon on the Hill (pop. 77 in 1931) was transferred to Worthington.

(e) The whole of Brentingby and Wyfordby was transferred to Freeby in 1936.

(f) The whole of Brooksby was transferred to Hoby with Rotherby C.P. on its formation in 1936.

(g) Broughton and Old Dalby C.P. was formed in 1936 out of the whole of Nether Broughton and Old Dalby C.P.s.

(h) Platt House, &c. (pop. 12 in 1891) was transferred from Croft to Broughton Astley in 1885.

(i) Part of Broughton Astley (pop. nil in 1931) was transferred to Cosby in 1935.

(j) The whole of Nether Broughton was transferred to Broughton and Old Dalby C.P. on its formation in 1936.

(k) Part of Sewstern (pop. nil in 1891) was transferred to Buckminster in 1884.

(l) The whole of Sewstern was transferred to Buckminster in 1936.

(m) The whole of Burbage was transferred to Hinckley U.D. in 1936.

(n) Ward's Farm. &c. (pop. 25 in 1891) was transferred from Somerby to Burrough on the Hill in 1887.

(o) The whole of Burrough on the Hill was transferred to Somerby in 1936.

(p) Burton and Dalby C.P. was formed in 1936 out of the whole of Great Dalby and Little Dalby C.P.s and part (pop. 191 in 1931) of Burton Lazars.

(q) Burton Lazars was returned as a separate parish 1801–41, but as a chapelry of Melton Mowbray A.P. 1851–71.

(r) Burton Lazars C.P. was dissolved in 1936. Part (pop. 191 in 1931) became part of Burton and Dalby C.P. and the remainder (pop. 6 in 1931) was transferred to Melton Mowbray U.D.

POPULATION TABLE, 1801–1951 (*continued*)

	1801	*1811*	*1821*	*1831*	*1841*	*1851*	*1861*	*1871*	*1881*	*1891*	*1901*	*1911*	*1921*	*1931*	*1951*
BURTON ON THE WOLDS C.P.	Township of Prestwold A.P., q.v.								356	309	309	293	262	297	938
BURTON OVERY A.P. and C.P.	399	386	383	418	449	484	465	469	424	348	292	304	311	311	259
BUSHBY C.P.	Hamlet of Thurnby A.P., q.v.								56	47	72	116	194*	336*	See Thurnby C.P.[a]
CADEBY A.P.[b]	304	302	343	361	387	406	422	391	..	..	..	..	..	..	..
CADEBY	152	123	167	175	178	179	194	170	See Cadeby C.P.			..	..	..	..
OSBASTON tnp.[b]	152	179	176[b]	186	209	227	228	221	See Osbaston C.P.			..	..	..	..
CADEBY C.P.	Part of Cadeby A.P., q.v.								149	166[c]	124	114	138	122	158
CARLTON C.P.	Chapelry of Bosworth, Market A.P., q.v.								274	267	199	178	170	192	193
CARLTON CURLIEU A.P.	224	162	174	182	208	235	308	349	..	..	..	..	..	..	..
CARLTON CURLIEU	47	44	49	51	57	41	73	59	See Carlton Curlieu C.P.				..	..	..
ILLSTON ON THE HILL chap.[d]	177	118	125	181	151	194	235	290	See Illston on the Hill C.P.				..	..	..
CARLTON CURLIEU C.P.	Part of Carlton Curlieu A.P., q.v.								69	90	66	93	74	72	61
CASTLE VIEW E.P.P.	52	167	149	127	120	See Leicester[e]		..	..	..	..	..	..	..	..
CATTHORPE A.P. and C.P.	159	167	164	199	167	132	146	154	137	160	166	176	130	135	128[f]
CHADWELL	See Rothley A.P., and Wycomb and Chadwell C.P.							..	..	..	..	..	..	..	..
CHARLEY E.P.P. and C.P.	59	49	42	41	53	35	34	38	43	151[g]	145	138	155	148	339[h]
CHILCOTE C.P.[i]	..	..	..	..	..	..	..	..	..	..	95	126	130	124	104
CLAWSON AND HARBY C.P.[j]	..	..	..	..	..	..	..	..	..	..	..	..	..	..	1,726
CLAWSON, LONG A.P. and C.P.	604	627	678	776	838	869	820	780	738	753	776	735	657	664	See Clawson and Harby C.P.[j]
CLAYBROOKE A.P., part of[k]	942[l]	1,047	1,200	1,242	1,319	1,280	1,195	1,053	..	..	..	..	..	..	..
CLAYBROOKE MAGNA chap.	331	442	458	481	519	512	424	404	See Claybrooke Magna C.P.				..	..	..
CLAYBROOKE PARVA tnp.	58	61	54	82	104	76	84	61	See Claybrooke Parva C.P.				..	..	..
BITTESBY lib.	..[l]	5	11	11	28	17	12	18	See Bittesby C.P.			..	..	..	..
ULLESTHORPE ham.	494	470	598	599	594	592	600	490	See Ullesthorpe C.P.			..	..	..	..
WIGSTON PARVA tnp.	59	69	79	69	74	83	75	80	See Wigston Parva C.P.			..	..	..	..
CLAYBROOKE MAGNA	Chapelry of Claybrooke A.P., q.v.								433	376[m]	323	321	330	382	469
CLAYBROOKE PARVA	Township of Claybrooke A.P., q.v.								64	84[m]	76	75	74	93	95[n]
COALVILLE U.D.; from 1936 U.D. and C.P.[o]	..	..	..	..	..	..	..	..	..	..	15,281	18,548	20,467[p]	21,880	25,744[q]
COALVILLE C.P.	..	..	..	..	..	..	..	..	..	..	7,157[o]	8,756*	9,476[p]	10,391	..[q]
HUGGLESCOTE AND DONINGTON C.P.	..	..	..	..	..	..	..	..	..	..	4,404[o]	5,659*	6,475	6,637	..[q]
WHITWICK C.P.	..	..	..	..	..	..	..	..	..	..	3,720[o]	4,133	4,516	4,852	..[q]

(a) The whole of Bushby was transferred to Thurnby in 1935.

(b) From 1811 to 1861 Osbaston was said to extend into Market Bosworth A.P. It was all returned with Cadeby except in 1821 when part was said to have been included in the return for Market Bosworth. From 1871 it was assumed to be entirely in Cadeby, and has been treated here as if it had always been in that parish.

(c) Naneby House (pop. 4 in 1891) was transferred from Market Bosworth to Cadeby in 1884.

(d) From 1811 to 1831 Illston on the Hill was said to extend into King's Norton A.P., though it was all returned with Carlton Curlieu. From 1841 it was all assumed to be in Carlton Curlieu and has been treated here as if it had always been in that parish.

(e) Castle View was returned in Guthlaxton Hundred from 1801 to 1841, but in 1851 it was said to be in the borough of Leicester, and it was thereafter returned in it.

(f) Part of Catthorpe (pop. 5 in 1931) was transferred to Warws. administrative county and Newton and Biggin C.P. in 1935.

(g) Part of Markfield (pop. 65 in 1891) and The Oaks (pop. 23 in 1891) in Newtown Linford were transferred to Charley in 1885.

(h) In 1936 part of Charley (pop. nil in 1931) was transferred to Coalville U.D. and parts of Whitwick (pop. 174 in 1931) and Woodhouse (pop. 54 in 1931) were transferred to Charley.

(i) Chilcote C.P. was transferred from Derbys. to Leics. administrative county in 1897.

(j) Clawson and Harby C.P. was formed in 1936 out of the whole of Long Clawson, Harby and Hose C.P.s.

(k) Claybrooke A.P. also included Wibtoft hamlet (Warws.) but the population of the A.P. shown here does not include Wibtoft, which became a separate C.P.

(l) No return was apparently made for Bittesby in 1801, so the population of the A.P. was probably slightly over 942.

(m) Part of Claybrooke Magna (pop. 13 in 1891) was transferred to Claybrooke Parva in 1885.

(n) In 1935 part of Wibtoft C.P. (Warws.) (pop. 26 in 1931) was transferred to Leics. administrative county and Claybrooke Parva C.P.

(o) In 1892 Whitwick U.D. was dissolved and Coalville U.D. was created out of Whitwick C.P. (i.e. the whole of the former U.D.), part of Hugglescote and Donington C.P. (pop. 6,594 in 1901), part of Ravenstone with Snibston C.P. (pop. 2,464 in 1901) and part of Swannington C.P. (pop. 299 in 1901). In 1893 the part of Hugglescote and Donington not in Coalville U.D. was transferred to Bardon C.P., so that the whole of the parish was now included in the U.D. In 1894 the whole of the urban parts of Ravenstone with Snibston and Swannington, part of Hugglescote and Donington (pop. 2,190 in 1901) and part of Whitwick (pop. 2,204 in 1901) were formed into the new C.P. of Coalville.

(p) Parts of Ravenstone with Snibston and Swannington (pop. respectively 142, 132 in 1921) were transferred to Coalville C.P. and Coalville U.D. in 1912.

(q) In 1936 parts of Coalville U.D., viz. part of Hugglescote and Donington C.P. (pop. 8 in 1931) and part of Whitwick C.P. (pop. 174 in 1931), were transferred respectively to Ibstock and Charley. The three constituent C.P.s of the U.D. were united as Coalville C.P., which thus became coextensive with the U.D., and parts of Bardon, Charley, Ibstock, Ravenstone with Snibston, Swannington, and Thringstone (pop. respectively 407, nil, 76, 614, 682, 997 in 1931) were added to Coalville U.D. and C.P.

POPULATION TABLE, 1801–1951 (*continued*)

	1801	1811	1821	1831	1841	1851	1861	1871	1881	1891	1901	1911	1921	1931	1951
COLEORTON A.P. and C.P.	1,069	910	883	848*	601*	549	626*	654	598	761[a]	783	735	726	764	1,112[b]
CONGERSTONE A.P. and C.P.	230	244	149	170	267	298	250	222	132	205[c]	216	195	223	209	See Shackerstone C.P.[d]
COSBY A.P. and C.P.	555	826	883	1,009	1,013	1,026	974	944	1,004	1,161[e]	1,351	1,560	1,577	1,701	1,533[f]
COSBY	..	..	..	..	779	..	..	..	..	..	..	..	..	..	..
THORPE, LITTLE ham., part of[g]	..	..	..	..	234[g]	..	..	..	..	..	..	..	..	..	..
COSSINGTON A.P. and C.P.	298	288	237	283	310	341	408*	462	403	371	446	388	496*	351*	419[h]
COSTON A.P. and C.P.	150	152	162	170	147	185	179	164	133	104	91	78	75	74	See Garthorpe C.P.[i]
COTES C.P.	Township of Prestwold A.P., q.v.								52	54	53	57	39	42	62
COTESBACH A.P. and C.P.	91	98	118	108	82	107	125	111	138	109	91	104	124	136	143[j]
COTES-DE-VAL ham.	See Kimcote A.P.			..	..	..	..	..	..	..	..	..	..	..	..
COTON ham.	See Bosworth, Market A.P.				..	..	..	..	..	..	..	..	..	..	..
COUNTESTHORPE C.P.	Chapelry of Blaby A.P., q.v.								1,103	1,344	1,429*	1,450	1,473	1,921*	2,109[k]
CRANOE A.P. and C.P.	91	97	101	100	137	128	107	121	106	66	98	89	67	61	41
CROFT A.P. and C.P.	255	248	297	284	321	338	319	299	576	661[l]	740	742	720	961*	984
CROPSTON C.P.	Township of Thurcaston A.P., q.v.								144	143	190	310	330	404	See Thurcaston C.P.[m]
CROXTON KERRIAL A.P. and C.P.	387[o]	471[o]	527	594	657	621	594	618	548	567	498	452	414	409	545[n]
CROXTON KERRIAL	..	..	518	585	..	..	..	..	..	..	..	..	..	..	..
BESCABY place	..[o]	..[o]	9	9	See Bescaby E.P.P. and C.P.[p]				..	..	..	..	..	..	..
CROXTON, SOUTH A.P. and C.P.	221	253	316	315	297	324	311	296	251	234[q]	222	211	200	221	153
DADLINGTON C.P.	Chapelry of Hinckley A.P., q.v.								170*	163	154	189	212	200	See Sutton Cheney C.P.[r]
DALBY, GREAT A.P. and C.P.	345	378	402	411	479	512	484	468	455	392	356	341	317	323	See Burton and Dalby C.P.[s]
DALBY, LITTLE A.P. and C.P.	162	155	185	194	184	199	183	210*	154	184	144	151	118	118	
DALBY, OLD[t] A.P. and C.P.	254	320	357	393	410	371*	359	320	335	345	353	368	330	315	See Broughton and Old Dalby C.P.[u]
DALBY ON THE WOLDS	See Old Dalby[t]		..	..	..	..	..	..	..	..	..	..	..	..	..
DESFORD A.P. and C.P.	661[v]	744	872	971	1,006	1,025	981	911	900	794	830	1,118*	1,167	1,163	1,983[w]
DESFORD	..	729	864	952	988	1,013	970	894	..	..	..	..	..	..	..
BARRONS PARK ham.	..[v]	15	8	19	18	12	11	17	..	..	..	..	..	..	..
DISEWORTH A.P. and C.P.	628	656	718	764	739	617*	567	493*	416	369	383	331	318	345	See Long Whatton C.P.[x]

(a) Rotten Row (pop. 194 in 1891) was transferred from Thringstone to Coleorton in 1884.

(b) In 1936 part of Coleorton (pop. nil in 1931) was transferred to Swannington, and parts of Swannington (pop. 46 in 1931), Thringstone (pop. 377 in 1931) and Worthington (pop. 22 in 1931) were transferred to Coleorton.

(c) In 1884 part of Market Bosworth (pop. 18 in 1891) and in 1886 part of Shackerstone (pop. 17 in 1891) and part of Nailstone (pop. 36 in 1891) were transferred to Congerstone.

(d) The whole of Congerstone was transferred to Shackerstone in 1935.

(e) Part of Narborough (pop. 88 in 1891) was transferred to Cosby in 1885.

(f) In 1935 part of Cosby (pop. 392 in 1931) was transferred to Narborough and part of Broughton Astley (pop. nil in 1931) was transferred to Cosby.

(g) Part of Little Thorpe was said to be in Cosby and part in Narborough in 1841 and 1851.

(h) In 1935 part of Cossington (pop. 2 in 1931) was transferred to Syston and part of Syston (pop. nil in 1931) was transferred to Cossington.

(i) The whole of Coston was transferred to Garthorpe in 1936.

(j) In 1935 part of Cotesbach (pop. nil in 1931) was transferred to Warws. administrative county and Churchover C.P.

(k) In 1935 and 1936 part of Countesthorpe (pop. nil in 1931) was transferred to Wigston U.D. and part of Blaby (pop. 25 in 1931) was transferred to Countesthorpe.

(l) Platt House, &c. (pop. 12 in 1891) was transferred from Croft to Broughton Astley in 1885.

(m) The whole of Cropston was transferred to Thurcaston in 1935.

(n) The whole of Branston was transferred to Croxton Kerrial in 1936.

(o) No return was apparently made for Bescaby in 1801 or 1811. If it was not included in the return for Croxton Kerrial then the population of the A.P. was probably slightly greater than is shown.

(p) Bescaby was returned as an extra-parochial place from 1841 to 1871.

(q) In 1884 Barsby Lodge (pop. 6 in 1891) was transferred from Barsby to South Croxton and part of South Croxton (pop. nil in 1891) was transferred to Barsby.

(r) The whole of Dadlington was transferred to Sutton Cheney in 1935.

(s) Both Great Dalby and Little Dalby became part of Burton and Dalby C.P. on its formation in 1936.

(t) Old Dalby was called Dalby on the Wolds in the *Census Reports* until 1911.

(u) Old Dalby became part of Broughton and Old Dalby C.P. on its formation in 1936.

(v) No return was apparently made for Barrons Park in 1801. If it was not included in the return for Desford, then the population of the A.P. was probably slightly greater than is shown.

(w) Part of Ratby (pop. 367 in 1931) was transferred to Desford in 1935.

(x) The whole of Diseworth was transferred to Long Whatton in 1936.

POPULATION

POPULATION TABLE, 1801–1951 (*continued*)

	1801	*1811*	*1821*	*1831*	*1841*	*1851*	*1861*	*1871*	*1881*	*1891*	*1901*	*1911*	*1921*	*1931*	*1951*
DISHLEY	See Thorpe Acre and Dishley A.P. and C.P.						..	..	..	..	..	..	..	..	..
DONINGTON	See Ibstock A.P., and Hugglescote with Donington C.P.								..	..	..	..	..	..	..
DONINGTON, CASTLE R.D.	..	..	..	..	..	..	..	..	..	..	6,223	6,416	6,459	3,164	9,273
DONINGTON, CASTLE A.P. and C.P.	1,959	2,308	2,560	3,182	3,508	3,028*	2,445*	2,512	2,662	2,591	2,514	2,529	2,736*	2,674	3,140[a]
DONISTHORPE	See Seal, Nether and Over A.P., and Oakthorpe with Donisthorpe C.P.									..	..	..	..	..	..
DRAYTON C.P.	Township of Bringhurst A.P., q.v.								137	105	93	101	97	121	99
DRAYTON, FENNY A.P. and C.P.	109	139	118	127	127	115	134	134	139	116	112	113	121	125	..[b]
DUNTON BASSETT A.P. and C.P.	407	432	460	514	553	528	524	496	409	368	385	482	523	506	568
EASTHORPE ham.	See Bottesford A.P.			..	..	..	..	..	..	..	..	..	..	..	..
EASTON, GREAT C.P.	Chapelry of Bringhurst A.P., q.v.								540	510	424	418	397	349	398
EASTWELL A.P. and C.P.	107	114	109	125	131	156	160	159	163	200	192	194	146	152	See Eaton C.P.[c]
EATON A.P. and C.P.	247	269	284	350	404	442	421	382	351	437	421	436	490	413	658[c]
EDMONDTHORPE A.P. and C.P.	129	158	148	211	261	256	233	238	209	251*	165	207	173	195	See Wymondham C.P.[d]
ELMESTHORPE A.P. and C.P.	35	38	46	34	36	45	45	44	34	38	70	84	77	134*	392
ENDERBY A.P. and C.P.	513	804	1,143	1,141	1,336	1,335	1,333	1,390	1,677	2,399	2,638	2,667	2,635	3,040*	3,378[e]
EVINGTON A.P. and C.P.	177	222	257	260	285	293	275	310	450	239[f]	248	958*	1,072	1,802*	..[g]
EVINGTON, NORTH C.P.	See Leicester C.B.[f]			..	..	..	..	..	..	..	..	..	..	..	..
EYE KETTLEBY	See Kettleby, Eye			..	..	..	..	..	..	..	..	..	..	..	..
FLECKNEY A.P. and C.P.	348	373	450	514	473	518	581	658	770	1,254	1,516	1,852	1,699	1,552	1,490
FOSTON A.P. and C.P.	24	28	24	32	41	34	27	38	43	56	45	51	40	36	See Kilby C.P.[h]
FOXTON A.P. and C.P.	420	365	383	346	385	413	388	336	348	284	313	324	348	321	352[i]
FRAMLAND HUNDRED	11,624	12,936	15,314	17,197	18,724	..	23,455	22,286	19,632	..	..	..	..	..	..
FREAKS GROUND E.P.P. and C.P.[j]	..	..	..	..	..	5	7	15	59	See Leicester C.B.[j]			..	..	..
FREEBY C.P.	Chapelry of Melton Mowbray A.P., q.v.								132	131	134	143	153	136	412[k]
FRISBY C.P. (1)	Chapelry of Galby A.P., q.v.								19	18	14	18	18	12	26
FRISBY C.P. (2)[l]	..	..	..	..	..	..	..	..	..	..	..	..	..	..	597
FRISBY ON THE WREAK A.P. and C.P.	386	344	376	442	429	455	424	366	396	381	341	385	370	360	See Frisby C.P. (2)[l]
FROLESWORTH A.P. and C.P.	297	265	301	278	318	296	291	258	214	201	216	243	220	245	210
GADDESBY A.P. and C.P.	263	230	282	276	331	325	341	280	241	240[m]	301	273	271	249	900[n]
GALBY A.P.	104	129	114	118	108	103	93	117	..	..	..	..	..	..	..
GALBY	81	108	96	97	93	80	74	90	See Galby C.P.		..	..	..	..	..
FRISBY chap.	23	21	18	21	15	23	19	27	See Frisby C.P. (1)	..	..	..	..	..	..
GALBY C.P.	Part of Galby A.P., q.v.								88	69	52	53	56	70	90
GARENDON E.P.P. and C.P.	43	23	43	51	71	44*	38	55	40	34[o]	39	46	32	30	..[p]
GARTHORPE A.P. and C.P.	134	107	115	117	135	132	113	128	120	125	85	71	106	92	138[q]
GARTREE HUNDRED	14,290	14,697	16,006	17,059	17,990	..	18,762	18,579	19,478	..	..	..	..	..	..

(a) Part of Castle Donington (pop. 11 in 1931) was transferred to Isley cum Langley in 1936.

(b) Fenny Drayton C.P. was dissolved in 1935. Part of it (pop. 107 in 1931) was transferred to Witherley and the rest (pop. 18 in 1931) to Caldecote, Hartshill, and Mancetter C.P.s in Warws. administrative county.

(c) The whole of Eastwell C.P. and Goadby Marwood C.P. were transferred to Eaton in 1936.

(d) The whole of Edmondthorpe was transferred to Wymondham in 1936.

(e) In 1935 part of Enderby (pop. 20 in 1931) was transferred to Lubbesthorpe.

(f) Part of Evington (pop. 4,173 in 1891) was transferred to Leicester C.B. as North Evington C.P. in 1892. The affected areas are shown in 1891 as altered, both in the *Census Report* and in this table.

(g) Evington C.P. was dissolved in 1936. Part of it (pop. 1,791 in 1931) was transferred to Leicester C.B., part (pop. 11 in 1931) to Oadby U.D., and part (pop. nil in 1931) to Stoughton.

(h) The whole of Foston was transferred to Kilby in 1935.

(i) In 1935 part of Foxton (pop. 5 in 1931) was transferred to Market Harborough U.D., and part of Market Harborough U.D. (pop. 3 in 1931) was transferred to Foxton.

(j) No return was apparently made for Freaks Ground until 1841, when it was returned as part of Augustine Friars in Leicester borough. In 1851 it was said to be outside the borough, and was returned as outside until it was transferred to Leicester C.B. in 1892, and became part of Leicester Abbey C.P. The areas affected by this change are shown in 1891 as altered both in the *Census Report* and in this table.

(k) The whole of Brentingby and Wyfordby, Saxby and Stapleford C.P.s were transferred to Freeby in 1936.

(l) Frisby C.P. (2) was formed in 1936 out of the whole of Frisby on the Wreak and Kirby Bellars C.P.s.

(m) The 'Cheney Arms', &c. (pop. 7 in 1891) was transferred from Ashby Folville to Gaddesby in 1882.

(n) The whole of Ashby Folville and Barsby C.P.s were transferred to Gaddesby in 1936.

(o) In 1891 parts of Garendon (pop. 2 and 4 respectively in 1901) were transferred to Shepshed and to Thorpe Acre and Dishley, and parts of Knight Thorpe and of Thorpe Acre and Dishley (pop. nil in 1901) were transferred to Garendon.

(p) Garendon C.P. was dissolved in 1936. Part of it (pop. 4 in 1931) was transferred to Shepshed U.D., part (pop. 26 in 1931) to Loughborough M.B.

(q) The whole of Coston was transferred to Garthorpe in 1936.

POPULATION TABLE, 1801–1951 (*continued*)

	1801	*1811*	*1821*	*1831*	*1841*	*1851*	*1861*	*1871*	*1881*	*1891*	*1901*	*1911*	*1921*	*1931*	*1951*
GILMORTON A.P. and C.P.	554	638	718	830	866	899	853	732*	644[a]	534	512	464	467	481	454
GILROES E.P.P. and C.P.	..	4	5	11	19	8	12	10	27	34	154*	158	341*	380	See Leicester C.B.[b]
GLENFIELD A.P.	..	..	932	1,166	1,032	1,064	1,041	1,117	..	..	..	..	..	..	..
GLENFIELD	302	347	430	653*	516	537	522	553	See Glenfield C.P.			..	..	..	..
BRAUNSTONE chap.	202	193	214	198	188	192	197	215	See Braunstone C.P.			..	..	..	..
BRAUNSTONE FRITH lib.	13	9	10	8	7		7	7	See Braunstone Frith C.P.				..	..	..
GLENFIELD FRITH lib.	..	4	4	Nil	See Glenfield Frith E.P.P. and C.P.[c]					..	..	..	..	..	..
KIRBY FRITH lib.	16	18	18	32	See Kirby Frith E.P.P. and C.P.[c]					..	..	..	..	..	..
KIRBY MUXLOE chap.	167	231	256	275	321	335	315	342	See Kirby Muxloe C.P.			..	..	..	..
GLENFIELD C.P.	Part of Glenfield A.P., q.v.								632	734	997	1,105	1,121	1,590	See Glenfields C.P.[d]
GLENFIELD FRITH E.P.P. and C.P.	See Glenfield A.P.[c]				10	7	9	11	10	8	9	17	22	527*	
GLENFIELDS C.P.[d]	..	..	..	..	..	..	..	..	..	..	..	..	..	..	3,470
GLEN, GREAT A.P.	571	675	714	770	833*	822*	827	800	..	..	..	..	..	..	..
GLEN, GREAT	549	651	697	743	795	782	785	767	See Glen, Great C.P.			..	..	..	..
STRETTON, GREAT chap.	22	24	17	27	38	40	42	33	See Stretton, Great C.P.				..	..	..
GLEN, GREAT C.P.	Part of Glen, Great A.P., q.v.								854	704	728	776	763	826	925[e]
GLEN PARVA C.P.	Township of Aylestone A.P., q.v.								742*	483[f]*	834*	620*	635	749[g]*	3,223[h]
GLOOSTON A.P. and C.P.	129	135	142	177	157	153	157	127	105	73	63	70	71	65	64
GOADBY C.P.	Chapelry of Billesdon A.P., q.v.								103	93	74	62	55	47	64
GOADBY MARWOOD A.P. and C.P.	181	168	171	161	202	248	195	173	155	155	188	176	157	144	See Eaton C.P.[i]
GOPSALL E.P.P. and C.P.	4	7	7	7	7	41*	63	76	24	25	22	35	14	13	See Twycross C.P.[j]
GOSCOTE, EAST HUNDRED	14,437	15,705	17,501	18,770	19,904	..	16,239	18,543	29,756	..	..	..	..	..	..
GOSCOTE, WEST HUNDRED	31,148	34,696	40,788	47,312	48,875	..	51,427	54,520	59,011	..	..	..	..	..	..
GRACE DIEU	See Belton A.P.		..	..	..	..	..	..	..	..	..	..	..	..	..
GRIMSTON A.P. and C.P.	183	167	200	185	175	182	190	164	153	175	137	176	198	145	259[k]
GROBY ham.	See Ratby A.P.		..	..	..	..	..	..	..	..	..	..	..	..	..
GROBY C.P.[l]	..	..	..	..	..	..	..	..	..	..	928	910	887	1,122	1,929[m]
GUMLEY A.P. and C.P.	224	261	289	272	240	210	214	265	232	169	201	172	133	148	183
GUTHLAXTON HUNDRED	15,282	17,622	20,528	22,591	24,502	..	21,894	21,411	26,817	..	..	..	..	..	..
HALLATON R.D.	..	..	..	..	..	..	..	..	..	..	1,925	1,867	1,746	1,554	..
HALLATON A.P. and C.P.	548	598	644	653	637	691	696	614	716	755	602	566	465	423	422
HALSTEAD C.P.	Township of Tilton A.P., q.v.								309	187	197	174	176	170	See Tilton C.P.[n]
HAMILTON ham.	See Barkby A.P.			..	..	..	..	..	..	..	..	..	..	..	..
HARBOROUGH, MARKET R.D.	..	..	..	..	..	..	..	..	10,845	10,522	7,250	7,770	7,508	7,523	9,835
HARBOROUGH, MARKET U.D.; from 1927 U.D. and C.P.[o]	..	..	..	..	..	..	..	..	5,351	5,876	7,735	8,853	8,578	9,312[p]	10,400[q]
HARBOROUGH, MARKET C.P.	Chapelry of Bowden, Great A.P., q.v.								2,418	2,131	1,755	1,542	1,487	..[o]	..
BOWDEN, GREAT C.P.	Part of Bowden, Great A.P., q.v.								1,985	2,259	3,749*	4,427*	4,323	..[p]	..
BOWDEN, LITTLE part of C.P.; from 1896 C.P.[r]	..	..	..	..	..	..	..	..	948	1,486	2,231	2,884*	2,768	..[o]	..

(a) A detached part of Kimcote (pop. 17 in 1881) was transferred to Gilmorton in 1877.

(b) The whole of Gilroes was transferred to Leicester C.B. in 1935.

(c) Glenfield Frith and Kirby Frith were returned as liberties of Glenfield A.P. from 1811 to 1831, but from 1841 they were returned as extra-parochial places.

(d) In 1936 Glenfield, Glenfield Frith, and Kirby Frith were united to form the new C.P. of Glenfields. Parts of Anstey, Anstey Pastures, Leicester Frith, and New Parks (pop. respectively 9, 17, 2, 4 in 1931) were added.

(e) Part of Great Glen (pop. 3 in 1931) was transferred to Oadby U.D. in 1936.

(f) Part of Aylestone (pop. nil in 1891) was transferred to Glen Parva in 1885.

(g) Part of Glen Parva (pop. 507 in 1921) was transferred to Wigston U.D. and Wigston Magna C.P. in 1928.

(h) Part of Lubbesthorpe (pop. 234 in 1931) was transferred to Glen Parva in 1935.

(i) The whole of Goadby Marwood was transferred to Eaton in 1936.

(j) The whole of Gopsall was transferred to Twycross in 1935.

(k) The whole of Saxelby and Shoby C.P.s were transferred to Grimston in 1936.

(l) Part of Ratby was created the new C.P. of Groby in 1896.

(m) Part of Markfield (pop. 55 in 1931) was transferred to Groby in 1935, and in 1936 part of Groby (pop. nil in 1931) was transferred to Newtown Linford, and part of Newtown Linford (pop. nil in 1931) to Groby.

(n) In 1935 the whole of Halstead was transferred to Tilton.

(o) In 1927 Great Bowden C.P. and Little Bowden C.P. were transferred to Market Harborough C.P., which thus became coextensive with the U.D.

(p) Part of Lubenham (pop. 19 in 1921) was transferred to Great Bowden C.P. and Market Harborough U.D. in 1924.

(q) In 1935 parts of Market Harborough U.D. (pop. respectively 3, nil in 1931) were transferred to Foxton and Lubenham, and parts of Foxton pop. 5 in 1931) and Lubenham (pop. 1 in 1931) were transferred to Market Harborough U.D.

(r) Little Bowden A.P. and C.P. was in Northants. Only part of it was included in Market Harborough U.D. This part became part of Leics. administrative county under the Local Government Act 1888. In 1896 the rural part of the C.P., which had remained in Northants., was transferred to Great Oxendon C.P. (Northants.), so that the whole of Little Bowden C.P. was now in Market Harborough U.D. and Leics. administrative county.

POPULATION

POPULATION TABLE, 1801–1951 (*continued*)

	1801	*1811*	*1821*	*1831*	*1841*	*1851*	*1861*	*1871*	*1881*	*1891*	*1901*	*1911*	*1921*	*1931*	*1951*
HARBY A.P. and C.P.	343	364	457	488	629	640	655	539	591	637	652	603	619	608	See Clawson and Harby C.P.[a]
HARSTON A.P. and C.P.	136	151	162	182	181	177	164	162	165	159	182	157	184	182	See Belvoir C.P.[b]
HATHERN. A.P. and C.P.	956	1,098	1,144	1,289	1,252	1,187*	1,112	1,120	1,312	1,133	1,114	1,209	1,124	1,225	..[c]
HEATHER A.P. and C.P.	314	334	411*	449*	368	384	371	429*	447	538	624	702	687	678	661[d]
HEMINGTON C.P.	Township of Lockington A.P., q.v.								380	358	332	383	330	298	See Lockington-Hemington C.P.[e]
HIGHAM ON THE HILL A.P. and C.P.	431	469	533	560	556	544	559	532	445	553	525	614	553	738	674[f]
HIGHAM ON THE HILL	..	..	..	..	469	..	..	..	..	..	..	..	..	..	..
LINDLEY ham.	..	..	..	..	76	..	..	..	..	..	..	..	..	..	..
ROWDEN ham.	..	..	..	..	11	..	..	..	..	..	..	..	..	..	..
HINCKLEY R.D.	..	..	..	..	..	..	..	..	9,729	11,061	12,636	13,825	14,296	16,916	..
HINCKLEY A.P., part of[g]	5,676	6,730	6,706*	7,180	7,291*	7,050	7,274	7,738	..	..	..	..	..	..	..
HINCKLEY[g]	5,070	6,058	1,619	6,468	6,356	6,111*	6,344	6,779*	See Hinckley U.D. and C.P.						
HINCKLEY BOND			4,216										..	..	..
WYKIN ham.	88		98		92	66	76	81							
DADLINGTON chap.	131	147	179	169	180	212	216	230	See Dadlington C.P.			..	..	..	..
STOKE GOLDING chap.	387	525	594	543	663	661	638	648	See Stoke Golding C.P.			..	..	..	..
HINCKLEY U.D. and C.P.[h]	Part of Hinckley A.P., q.v.								7,673	9,638	11,304	12,837	13,652[i]	16,030[j]	39,094[k]
HINCKLEY BOND	See Hinckley A.P.			..	..	..	..	..	..	..	..	..	..	..	..
HOBY A.P. and C.P.	294	303	352	357	392	405	369	327	311	290	285	294	249	229	See Hoby with Rotherby C.P.[l]
HOBY WITH ROTHERBY C.P.[l]	..	..	..	..	..	..	..	..	..	..	..	..	..	..	595
HOLT, NEVILL C.P.	Chapelry of Medbourne A.P., q.v.[m]								88	41	53	76	128*	66*	42
HOLWELL C.P.	Township of Kettleby, Ab A.P., q.v.								268	238[n]	272	249	199	191	See Ab Kettleby C.P.[o]
HOLYOAKS lib.	See Stoke Dry A.P.			..	..	..	..	..	..	..	..	..	..	..	..
HORNINGHOLD A.P. and C.P.	76	83	97	97	98	103	105	106	126	97	116	124	112	91	86
HOSE A.P. and C.P.	264	296	325	385	417	471	477	403	438	408	443	441	427	421	See Clawson and Harby C.P.[p]
HOTON C.P.	Chapelry of Prestwold A.P., q.v.								308	294	273	251	250	238	240
HOUGHTON ON THE HILL A.P. and C.P.	299	329	374	395	451	442	449	374*	415	332	278	271	317	392	662
HUGGLESCOTE AND DONINGTON C.P.	Chapelry of Ibstock A.P., q.v.								4,750	4,069	See Coalville U.D.[q]			..	..
HUMBERSTONE A.P. and C.P.	412	393	415	470	462	480	515	852*	2,638	365[r]	385	538	847	3,267*	See Leicester C.B.[s]

(a) Harby became part of Clawson and Harby C.P. on its formation in 1936. (b) The whole of Harston was transferred to Belvoir in 1935.

(c) Hathern C.P. was dissolved in 1936. Part of it (pop. 1,225 in 1931) was transferred to Loughborough M.B., and the remainder (pop. nil in 1931) to Shepshed U.D. and Long Whatton C.P.

(d) Part of Heather (pop. 40 in 1931) was transferred to Ibstock in 1936.

(e) The whole of Hemington was transferred to Lockington in 1936. The name of the parish was altered in 1938 to Lockington-Hemington.

(f) Parts of Higham on the Hill (pop. together 175 in 1931) were transferred to Nuneaton M.B. and Caldecote C.P. in Warws. administrative county in 1935. Part of Stoke Golding (pop. 18 in 1931) was transferred to Higham on the Hill in 1936.

(g) Hinckley A.P. was generally considered to include the hamlet of Hydes Pastures (Warws.) though Hydes Pastures was sometimes said to be in Hunningham A.P. (Warws.). The population of Hinckley township includes that of Hydes Pastures 1801–41. It was not included 1851–71.

(h) Hinckley U.D. and C.P. consisted of Hinckley township, Hinckley Bond, Wykin, and Hydes Pastures (Warws.), which had a pop. of 29 in 1881. Hydes Pastures became part of Leics. administrative county under the Local Government Act 1888.

(i) In 1920 part of Hinckley U.D. (pop. 9 in 1921) was transferred to Barwell and part of Barwell (pop. nil in 1921) was transferred to Hinckley.

(j) In 1928 part of Hinckley U.D. (pop. nil in 1931) was transferred to Burbage and part of Burbage (pop. nil in 1931) was transferred to Hinckley.

(k) In 1935 and 1936 parts of Hinckley U.D. (pop. nil in 1931) were transferred to Nuneaton M.B. and Stretton Baskerville C.P. in Warws. administrative county; parts of Nuneaton M.B., Stretton Baskerville C.P., and Wolvey C.P. (pop. respectively nil, nil, 24 in 1931) were transferred from Warws. to Leics. administrative county and Hinckley U.D.; and the whole of Barwell, Burbage, and Earl Shilton C.P.s and part of Stoke Golding (pop. 713 in 1931) were also transferred to Hinckley U.D.

(l) Hoby with Rotherby C.P. was formed in 1936 out of the whole of Brooksby, Hoby, Ragdale, and Rotherby C.P.s.

(m) Holt and Bradley (i.e. Nevill Holt) were returned independently of Medbourne 1801–31, though they were said to be sometimes considered as a chapelry of it. From 1841 they were treated as an ordinary chapelry.

(n) In 1884 Landike Lane (pop. 8 in 1891) was transferred from Wartnaby to Holwell and part of Ab Kettleby (pop. nil in 1891) was transferred to Holwell.

(o) The whole of Holwell was transferred to Ab Kettleby in 1936.

(p) The whole of Hose became part of Clawson and Harby C.P. on its formation in 1936.

(q) Part of Hugglescote and Donington (pop. 6,594 in 1901) was included in Coalville U.D. when it was formed in 1892. The rest of the parish was transferred to Bardon C.P. in 1893, so that from then on the whole of Hugglescote and Donington C.P. was within Coalville U.D.

(r) In 1892 part of Humberstone (pop. 3,284 in 1891) was transferred to Leicester C.B. as West Humberstone C.P. The affected areas are shown in 1891 as altered both in the *Census Report* and in this table.

(s) The whole of Humberstone was transferred to Leicester C.B. in 1935.

POPULATION TABLE, 1801–1951 (*continued*)

	1801	*1811*	*1821*	*1831*	*1841*	*1851*	*1861*	*1871*	*1881*	*1891*	*1901*	*1911*	*1921*	*1931*	*1951*
HUMBERSTONE, WEST C.P.	See Leicester C.B.			..	..	..	..	..	..	..	..	..	..	..	..
HUNCOTE C.P.	Hamlet of Narborough A.P., q.v.								462	489	539	610	612	587	536[a]
HUNGARTON A.P. and C.P.	203	218	292	260	267	289	302	238	439*	307	289	260	285	274	313
HUNGARTON	} 173	} 200	233	198	195	219	196	161	..	..	..	..	..	..	..
QUENBY ham.			30	17	19	11	26	10	..	..	..	..	..	..	..
INGARSBY ham.	28		14	29	26	35	54	34	..	..	..	..	..	..	..
BAGGRAVE lib.	2	18	15	16	27	24	26	33	..	..	..	..	..	..	..
IBSTOCK A.P.	..	..	1,741	1,830	2,002	2,202	2,334	3,983	..	..	..	..	..	..	..
IBSTOCK	763	836	1,058	1,044*	1,138	1,188	1,107	1,656*	See Ibstock C.P.			..	..	..	..
HUGGLESCOTE } DONINGTON } chap.	} 525	614	683	786	677 187	} 1,014	1,227	2,327*	See Hugglescote and Donington C.P.					..	..
IBSTOCK C.P.	Part of Ibstock A.P., q.v.								2,335	2,937	3,922	4,946*	5,211	5,365	5,406[b]
ILLSTON ON THE HILL C.P.	Chapelry of Carlton Curlieu A.P.								311	254	254	212	159	205	169
INGARSBY ham.	See Hungarton A.P.			..	..	..	..	..	..	..	..	..	..	..	..
ISLEY CUM LANGLEY C.P.[c]	..	..	..	..	..	..	..	..	..	..	..	..	..	..	149
KEGWORTH A.P.	1,416	1,605	1,672	1,821	1,945	1,854*	1,819	1,834	..	..	..	..	..	..	..
KEGWORTH	1,360	1,550	1,607	1,749	1,880	1,782	1,773	1,788	See Kegworth C.P.			..	..	..	..
WALTON, ISLEY chap.	56	55	65	72	65	72	46	46	See Walton, Isley C.P.			..	..	..	..
KEGWORTH C.P.	Part of Kegworth A.P., q.v.								2,142	2,149	2,078	2,220	2,139	2,107	2,508
KETTLEBY, AB A.P.	254	237	319	331	380	374	371	349	..	..	..	..	..	..	..
KETTLEBY, AB	169	142	187	200	224	221	224	202	See Kettleby, Ab C.P.			..	..	..	..
HOLWELL tnp.	85	95	132	131	156	153	147	147	See Holwell C.P.			..	..	..	..
KETTLEBY, AB C.P.	Part of Kettleby, Ab A.P., q.v.								230	242[d]	308	267	263	283	623[e]
KETTLEBY, EYE C.P.[f]	..	..	..	..	..	..	..	..	..	..	60	65	85	88	See Melton Mowbray U.D.[g]
KEYHAM C.P.	Chapelry of Rothley A.P., q.v.								301*	137	119	130	118	108	126
KEYTHORPE lib.	See Tugby A.P.			..	..	..	..	..	..	..	..	..	..	..	..
KIBWORTH BEAUCHAMP A.P.	1,232	1,313	1,372	1,500	1,740	1,752	1,867	1,975	..	..	..	..	..	..	..
KIBWORTH BEAUCHAMP	485	555	588	604	748	733	868	1,015	See Kibworth Beauchamp C.P.				..	..	..
KIBWORTH HARCOURT tnp.	382	385	396	421	425	466	466	474	See Kibworth Harcourt C.P.				..	..	..
SMEETON WESTERBY tnp.	365	373	388	475	567	553	533	486	See Smeeton Westerby C.P.				..	..	..
KIBWORTH BEAUCHAMP C.P.	Part of Kibworth Beauchamp A.P., q.v.								1,123	1,003	1,157	1,361	1,521	1,592	1,729
KIBWORTH HARCOURT C.P.	Township of Kibworth Beauchamp A.P., q.v.								450	460	508	446	435	520	578
KILBY A.P. and C.P.	242	331	409	434	408	387	362	334	291	242	282	253	249	242	264[h]
KILWORTH, NORTH A.P. and C.P.	298	327	391	390	422	414	409	434	443	428	413	405	375	363	416
KILWORTH, SOUTH A.P. and C.P.	397	431	450	437	478	509	421	402	423	365	294	275	376*	386	355
KIMCOTE A.P. and C.P.	645[i]	721[i]	505	490	552	603	501	476	393[j]	334	See Kimcote and Walton C.P.[k]				..
KIMCOTE	..	..	498	484	136	..	..	..	..	..	..	..	..	..	..
COTES-DE-VAL ham.	..	..	7	6	6	..	..	..	..	..	..	..	..	..	..
WALTON ham., part of[i]	..	..	..	..	410	..	..	..	..	..	..	..	..	..	..
KIMCOTE AND WALTON C.P.[j]	..	..	..	..	..	..	..	..	..	..	468	483	471	419	407
KIRBY BELLARS A.P. and C.P.	173	196	203	227	236	226	243	257	271	258	264	271	247	220	See Frisby C.P. (2)[l]

(a) Part of Huncote (pop. 31 in 1931) was transferred to Lubbesthorpe in 1935.

(b) In 1936 part of Ibstock (pop. 76 in 1931) was transferred to Coalville U.D. and C.P., and part of Coalville U.D., viz. part of Hugglescote and Donington C.P. (pop. 8 in 1931), and part of Heather C.P. (pop. 40 in 1931) were transferred to Ibstock.

(c) Isley cum Langley C.P. was created in 1936 out of the whole of Isley Walton and Langley Priory C.P.s and part (pop. 11 in 1931) of Castle Donington.

(d) Part of Ab Kettleby (pop. nil in 1891) was transferred to Holwell in 1884.

(e) The whole of Holwell and Wartnaby C.P.s were transferred to Ab Kettleby in 1936.

(f) In 1894 the part of Melton Mowbray C.P. not in Melton Mowbray U.D. was created Sysonby with Eye Kettleby C.P. The name was later changed to Eye Kettleby C.P.

(g) The whole of Eye Kettleby was transferred to Melton Mowbray U.D. and C.P. in 1935.

(h) The whole of Foston was transferred to Kilby in 1935.

(i) The returns for Kimcote in 1801 and 1811 included the whole of Walton hamlet which was said, however, to be in Knaptoft A.P. From 1841 only that part of Walton which was in Kimcote (called Walton in Kimcote) was included.

(j) In 1877 detached parts of Kimcote (pop. respectively 6, 17, nil in 1881) were transferred to Leire, Gilmorton, and Ashby Parva.

(k) Kimcote and Walton C.P. was formed in 1898 out of the whole of Kimcote and Walton in Knaptoft C.P.s.

(l) The whole of Kirby Bellars became part of the new C.P. of Frisby (distinguished in this table from another previously existing Frisby as Frisby C.P. (2)) on its formation in 1936.

POPULATION TABLE, 1801–1951 (*continued*)

	1801	1811	1821	1831	1841	1851	1861	1871	1881	1891	1901	1911	1921	1931	1951
KIRBY FRITH E.P.P. and C.P.	See Glenfield A.P.[a]				20	21	24	13	15	18	17	11	19	35	See Glenfields C.P.[b]
KIRBY MUXLOE C.P.	Chapelry of Glenfield A.P., q.v.								382	554[c]	820*	1,063[d]	1,145	1,598*	2,866[e]
KIRKBY MALLORY A.P.	..	..	2,067	2,261	2,479	2,625	2,392	2,275	..	..	..	..	..	..	..
KIRKBY MALLORY	243	248	296	244	259	261	216	222	See Kirkby Mallory C.P.				..	..	..
SHILTON, EARL chap.	1,287	1,533	1,771	2,017	2,220	2,364	2,176*	2,053	See Shilton, Earl C.P.			..	..	..	..
KIRKBY MALLORY C.P.	Part of Kirkby Mallory A.P., q.v.								190	179	169	219	230	231	..[f]
KNAPTOFT A.P.	..[g]	..[g]	864	924	936	913	841	810	..	..	..	..	..	..	..
KNAPTOFT	..[g]	52	60	53	53	55	54	53	See Knaptoft C.P.			..	..	..	..
MOWSLEY chap.	248	229	263	283	267	263	241	239	See Mowsley C.P.			..	..	..	..
SHEARSBY chap.	249	260	310	354	379	372	306	299	See Shearsby C.P.			..	..	..	..
WALTON ham., part of	..[g]	..[g]	231	234	237	223	240	219	See Walton in Knaptoft C.P.				..	..	..
KNAPTOFT C.P.	Part of Knaptoft A.P., q.v.								54	58	46	65	50	44	39
KNIGHTON C.P.	Chapelry of St. Margaret A.P., q.v.								1,827	See Leicester C.B.[h]			..	..	..
KNIPTON A.P. and C.P.	262	277	310	322	363	386	369	338	327	328	331	280	281	273	See Belvoir C.P.[i]
KNOLL AND BASSETT HOUSE E.P.P. and C.P.	17	16	15	23	30	19	14	11	18	12	23	See Thurlaston C.P.[j]			..
KNOSSINGTON A.P. and C.P.	126	150	193	240	252	230	251	319	291	323	297	247	230	252	335[k]
LANGLEY PRIORY E.P.P. and C.P.	15	10	13	16	16	4	11	26	22	16	14	22	14	16	See Isley cum Langley C.P.[l]
LANGTON, CHURCH A.P.	942	840	932	868	869	847	842	757	..	..	..	..	..	..	..
LANGTON, EAST tnp.	329	265	309	281	288	294	303	245	See Langton, East C.P.				..	..	..
LANGTON, THORPE chap.	186	180	215	177	160	147	120	127	See Langton, Thorpe C.P.				..	..	..
LANGTON, TUR chap.	345	317	318	338	350	329	337	323	See Langton, Tur C.P.				..	..	..
LANGTON, WEST chap.	82	78	90	72	71	77	82	62	See Langton, West C.P.				..	..	..
LANGTON, EAST C.P.	Township of Langton, Church A.P.								242	225[m]	252	244	230	208[n]	228
LANGTON, THORPE C.P.	Chapelry of Langton, Church A.P.								83	108[o]	106	103	83	90	99
LANGTON, TUR C.P.	Chapelry of Langton, Church A.P.								279	235	211	237	188	190	208
LANGTON, WEST C.P.	Chapelry of Langton, Church A.P.								60	71[p]	83	95	83	89[n]	70
LAUGHTON A.P. and C.P.	162	152	173	154	180	165	152	136	136	108	107	115	87	89	92
LAUNDE E.P.P. and C.P.	28	40	36	60	38	30	42	57	67	65	57	58	38	43	43
LEESTHORPE	See Pickwell with Leesthorpe A.P. and C.P.						..	..	..	..	..	..	..	..	..
LEICESTER	See beginning of table			..	..	..	..	..	..	..	..	..	..	..	..
LEICESTER ABBEY E.P.P. and C.P.	18	19	15	18	22	18	40	35	35	See Leicester C.B.[q]			..	..	..
LEICESTER FOREST EAST E.P.P. and C.P.	53	70	71	67	62	81	82	89	77	96[r]	107	100	116	487*	See Kirby Muxloe C.P.[s]
LEICESTER FOREST WEST E.P.P. and C.P.					44	50	51	34	48	45	41	41	59	54	42

(a) Kirby Frith was returned as a liberty in Glenfield A.P. until 1841, when it was said to be extra-parochial.

(b) Kirby Frith became part of Glenfields C.P. on its formation in 1936.

(c) Part of Leicester Forest East (pop. 16 in 1891) was transferred to Kirby Muxloe in 1885.

(d) Part of Kirby Muxloe (pop. 276 in 1911) was transferred to Ratby in 1904.

(e) In 1935 part of Kirby Muxloe (pop. nil in 1931) was transferred to Leicester C.B. and the whole of Leicester Forest East C.P. was transferred to Kirby Muxloe.

(f) Kirkby Mallory C.P. was dissolved in 1925. Part of it (pop. 13 in 1931) was transferred to Newbold Verdon and part (pop. 218 in 1931) to Peckleton.

(g) No return was apparently made for Knaptoft township in 1801, and the whole of Walton was returned with Kimcote A.P. 1801–11, so that no total can be given for the A.P. for these years. From 1841 Walton in Kimcote and Walton in Knaptoft were returned separately with their respective A.P.s.

(h) In 1892 part of Knighton (pop. 6,075 in 1891) was transferred to Leicester C.B. as Knighton C.P. The remainder (pop. 6, 8 respectively in 1891) was transferred to Lubbesthorpe and Oadby. The affected areas are shown in 1891 as altered both in the *Census Report* and in this table.

(i) The whole of Knipton was transferred to Belvoir in 1936.

(j) The whole of Knoll and Bassett House was transferred to Thurlaston in 1909.

(k) The whole of Cold Overton was transferred to Knossington in 1936.

(l) The whole of Langley Priory became part of Isley cum Langley C.P. on its formation in 1936.

(m) In 1885 parts of Thorpe Langton and West Langton (pop. nil in 1891) were transferred to East Langton, and Vendy's Lodge (pop. 2 in 1891) in East Langton was transferred to Thorpe Langton.

(n) The boundary between East and West Langton was defined in 1927, with the result that the population in 1921 for each parish as altered would have been: East Langton 233, West Langton 80.

(o) In 1885 Vendy's Lodge (pop. 2 in 1891) in East Langton, and part of West Langton (pop. nil in 1891) were transferred to Thorpe Langton, Caudwell (pop. nil in 1891) in Thorpe Langton was transferred to Welham and another part of Thorpe Langton (pop. nil in 1891) was transferred to East Langton.

(p) In 1885 parts of West Langton (pop. nil in 1891) were transferred to East Langton and Thorpe Langton.

(q) In 1892 part of Leicester Abbey (pop. 20 in 1891) was transferred to Leicester C.B. as Leicester Abbey C.P., and the remainder was transferred to Beaumont Leys C.P. The affected areas are shown in 1891 as altered, both in the *Census Report* and in this table.

(r) Part of Leicester Forest East (pop. 16 in 1891) was transferred to Kirby Muxloe in 1885.

(s) The whole of Leicester Forest East was transferred to Kirby Muxloe in 1935.

POPULATION TABLE, 1801–1951 (*continued*)

	1801	*1811*	*1821*	*1831*	*1841*	*1851*	*1861*	*1871*	*1881*	*1891*	*1901*	*1911*	*1921*	*1931*	*1951*
LEICESTER FRITH[a] E.P.P. and C.P.	..	7	19	23	25	33	24	47	35	49	36	50	119*	383*	..[b]
LEIRE A.P. and C.P.	347	418	435	485	406	433	433	354*	286[c]	283	239	279	298	305	303
LINDLEY ham.	See Higham on the Hill A.P.				..	..	..	..	..	..	..	..	..	..	..
LOCKINGTON A.P.	573	583	627	624	617	635	571	532[d]	..	..	..	..	..	..	..
LOCKINGTON	236	199	206	235	236	203	186	149	See Lockington C.P.			..	..	..	..
HEMINGTON tnp.	337	384	421	389	381	432	385	383[d]	See Hemington C.P.			..	..	..	..
LOCKINGTON C.P.	Part of Lockington A.P., q.v.				..	..	..	..	175	219[e]	155	143	151	186	See Lockington-Hemington C.P.[f]
LOCKINGTON-HEMINGTON C.P.[f]	..	..	..	..	..	..	..	..	..	..	..	..	..	..	538
LODDINGTON A.P. and C.P.[g]	130	137	148	145	137	112	142	166	147	123	118	128	99	64	88
LOUGHBOROUGH R.D.	..	..	..	..	..	..	..	..	13,080	8,321	4,387	4,579	4,526	4,822	..
LOUGHBOROUGH A.P. and U.D.	4,603	5,556	7,494	10,969	10,170	11,339	10,955	11,588	14,803	..	..	..	..	..	..
LOUGHBOROUGH tnp. and C.P.	4,546	5,400	7,365*	10,800*	10,025*	11,210*	10,830	11,456	14,681	See Loughborough C.P.			..	..	..
THORPE, KNIGHT tnp. and C.P.	7	86	52	79	60	44	58	71	65	See Loughborough M.B.			..	..	..
WOODTHORPE ham. and C.P.	50	70	77	90	85	85	67	61	57	See Woodthorpe C.P.			..	..	..
LOUGHBOROUGH C.P.[h]	..	..	..	..	..	..	..	..	..	18,357[i]	..	..	..	..	..
urban part: in Loughborough M.B., q.v.	..	..	..	..	..	..	..	..	..	18,123	See Loughborough M.B.[j]			..	..
rural part	..	..	..	..	..	..	..	..	..	234	See Nanpantan C.P.[j]			..	..
LOUGHBOROUGH M.B.;[h] from 1902 M.B. and C.P.[k]	..	..	..	..	..	..	..	..	..	18,196	21,508	22,990	25,857	26,945	34,731[l]
LOUGHBOROUGH C.P., part of;[h] from 1894 C.P.[j]	..	..	..	..	..	..	..	..	..	18,123[i]	21,382	..[k]	..	..	..
THORPE, KNIGHT C.P.	..	..	..	..	..	..	..	..	..	73[i]	126	..[k]	..	..	..
LOWESBY A.P.	147	190	217	231	220	243	259	248	..	..	..	..	..	..	..
LOWESBY	46	79	113	111	116	132	121	109	See Lowesby C.P.			..	..	..	..
NEWTON, COLD chap.	101	111	104	120	104	111	138	139	See Newton, Cold C.P.			..	..	..	..
LOWESBY C.P.	Part of Lowesby A.P., q.v.				..	..	..	..	142	136	107	147	118	135	133
LUBBESTHORPE C.P.	Chapelry of Aylestone A.P., q.v.					..	..	..	52	96[m]	75	81	118	4,891*	75[n]
LUBENHAM A.P. and C.P.	504	477	531[o]	542[o]	578	601	640	663	590	680	618	661	597	614[p]	1,167[q]
LUTTERWORTH R.D.	..	..	..	..	..	..	..	..	13,356	12,391	9,448	9,931	10,198	10,685	11,820
LUTTERWORTH A.P. and C.P.	1,652	1,845	2,102	2,262	2,531	2,446*	2,289	2,080*	1,965	1,800	1,734	1,896	2,092	2,395	3,197[r]

(a) Leicester Frith was called Shermans Grounds in the *Census Reports*, 1801–51.

(b) Leicester Frith C.P. was dissolved in 1936. Part (pop. 381 in 1931) was transferred to Leicester C.B., and the remainder (pop. 2 in 1931) became part of Glenfields C.P. on its formation in 1936.

(c) In 1877 detached parts of Kimcote (pop. 6 in 1881) were transferred to Leire and detached parts of Leire (pop. 27 in 1881) were transferred to Ashby Parva.

(d) In the *Census Report* of 1881 part of Sawley with Wilsthorpe parish (Derbys.) was said to be in Leics., and to have been returned in 1871 with Hemington.

(e) Cliff Farm (pop. 2 in 1891) was transferred from Sawley with Wilsthorpe (Derbys.) to Lockington in 1884. Presumably this was the part of Sawley with Wilsthorpe which was in Leics. See Sawley with Wilsthorpe A.P.

(f) The whole of Hemington C.P. was transferred to Lockington in 1936. The name of the parish was changed in 1938 to Lockington-Hemington.

(g) Part of Whatborough liberty was said to be in Loddington 1811–21, but from 1831 it was all said to be in Tilton A.P. and has been treated here as if it had always been there.

(h) Loughborough M.B. was incorporated in 1888. Its boundaries did not correspond to those of Loughborough U.D., which was then dissolved, since the whole of Woodthorpe C.P. and parts of Loughborough C.P. and Knight Thorpe C.P. (pop. 234, nil respectively in 1891) were excluded and part of Thorpe Acre and Dishley C.P. (pop. nil in 1891) was included: see also notes i and j.

(i) In 1891 the part of Thorpe Acre and Dishley inside Loughborough M.B. was transferred to Knight Thorpe and the part of Knight Thorpe outside it was divided between Thorpe Acre and Dishley and Garendon. As a result Loughborough M.B. now contained only Knight Thorpe C.P. and part of Loughborough C.P. Part of Knight Thorpe (pop. nil in 1891) was also transferred to Loughborough C.P. in 1891.

(j) In 1894 the part of Loughborough C.P. outside Loughborough M.B. was created Nanpantan C.P., so that the whole of Loughborough C.P. was now contained within the M.B.

(k) In 1902 Knight Thorpe C.P. (pop. 250 in 1911) was transferred to Loughborough C.P., so that Loughborough M.B. and C.P. became co-extensive.

(l) In 1935 and 1936 the whole of Nanpantan C.P. and Thorpe Acre and Dishley C.P. and parts of Garendon, Hathern, Quorndon U.D., Shepshed U.D., Woodhouse, and Woodthorpe (pop. respectively 26, 1,225, nil, 40, 79, 47 in 1931) were transferred to Loughborough M.B.

(m) Part of Aylestone (pop. nil in 1891) was transferred to Lubbesthorpe in 1885. In 1892 part of Aylestone (pop. 27 in 1881) and part of Knighton (pop. 6 in 1881) were transferred to Lubbesthorpe. The affected areas are shown in 1891 as altered.

(n) In 1935 and 1936 parts of Lubbesthorpe (pop. respectively 4,513, 45, 22, 234 in 1931) were transferred to Leicester C.B., Wigston U.D., Braunstone, and Enderby, and parts of Enderby, Huncote, and Narborough (pop. respectively 20, 31, 7 in 1931) were transferred to Lubbesthorpe.

(o) In 1821 and 1831 Lubenham was said to contain part of Thorpe Lubenham, which was chiefly in Marston Trussell A.P. (Northants.) and returned with it.

(p) Part of Lubenham (pop. 19 in 1921) was transferred to Great Bowden C.P. in Market Harborough U.D. in 1924.

(q) In 1935 part of Lubenham (pop. 1 in 1931) was transferred to Market Harborough U.D. and part of Market Harborough (pop. nil in 1931) was transferred to Lubenham.

(r) In 1935 parts of Lutterworth (pop. nil in 1931) were transferred to Monks Kirby C.P. and Churchover C.P. in Warws. administrative county, and parts of Monks Kirby C.P. and Willey C.P. (Warws.) (pop. respectively 7, 3 in 1931) were transferred to Leics. administrative county and Lutterworth C.P.

POPULATION

POPULATION TABLE, 1801–1951 (*continued*)

	1801	1811	1821	1831	1841	1851	1861	1871	1881	1891	1901	1911	1921	1931	1951
MAPLEWELL LONGDALE C.P.	Hamlet of Barrow upon Soar A.P., q.v.								20	See Woodhouse C.P.[a]			..	..	..
MAREFIELD C.P.	Township of Tilton A.P., q.v.								19	25	19	17	19	21	26
MARKFIELD A.P. and C.P.	591	907	1,078	1,088	1,203	1,261	1,391	1,406	1,605	1,439[b]	1,632	1,757	1,899	1,975	2,760[c]
MARSTON, POTTERS C.P.	Hamlet of Barwell A.P., q.v.								20	19	21	30	32	57	44
MEASHAM C.P.[d]	..	..	..	..	..	..	..	..	..	..	2,075	2,303	2,425	2,519	2,766[e]
MEDBOURNE A.P.	496	468	567	555	574	567	613	516	..	..	..	..	..	..	..
MEDBOURNE	441	420	514	513	534	523	580	488	See Medbourne C.P.			..	..	..	..
HOLT, NEVILL chap.[f]	55	48	53	42	40	44	33	28	See Holt, Nevill C.P.			..	..	..	..
MEDBOURNE C.P.	Part of Medbourne A.P., q.v.								556	428	427	393	380	352	398
MELTON AND BELVOIR R.D.	..	..	..	..	..	..	..	..	..	..	..	..	..	..	18,644
MELTON MOWBRAY R.D.	..	..	..	..	..	..	..	..	14,726	15,198	14,814	15,271	14,627	14,719	..
MELTON MOWBRAY A.P.	..	..	2,990	3,520	3,937*	4,956*	4,936	5,559	..	..	..	..	..	..	..
MELTON MOWBRAY	1,766	2,145	2,815*	3,356*	3,740	4,434	4,446	5,033*	See Melton Mowbray C.P.				..	..	..
FREEBY chap.	134	111	110	120	139	133	126	131	See Freeby C.P.			..	..	..	..
BURTON LAZARS chap.	See Burton Lazars A.P.[g]					239	233	260*	See Burton Lazars C.P.			..	..	..	..
SYSONBY chap.	See Sysonby A.P.[g]					84	67	73	See Sysonby C.P.			..	..	..	..
WELBY tnp.	57	76	65	44	58	66	64	62	See Welby C.P.			..	..	..	..
MELTON MOWBRAY C.P.	Part of Melton Mowbray A.P., q.v.								5,820	6,449	..	..	..	..	..
urban part: in Melton Mowbray U.D., q.v.	..	..	..	..	..	..	..	..	5,766	6,392	See Melton Mowbray U.D.[h]				..
rural part	..	..	..	..	..	..	..	..	54	57	See Kettleby, Eye C.P.[h]				..
MELTON MOWBRAY U.D.; from 1894 U.D. and C.P.[h]	..	..	..	..	..	..	..	..	5,766	6,392	7,454	9,202*	9,187	10,437[i]	14,053[j]
MELTON MOWBRAY C.P. part of	..	..	..	..	..	..	..	..	5,766	6,392	..	..	..	..	..
MEREVALE A.P. and C.P. (Warws. and Leics.)	201	189	208	246	208	212	212	185	189	..	..	..	..	..	..
the part in Leics.[k]	85	..	..	..	106	106	80	..[l]*	77[m]	..[n]	..	..	..	..	..
MISTERTON A.P. and C.P.	..[o]	429	539	587	589	589	554	536	486	449	441	435	507	541	459
MISTERTON	..[o]	56	..	..	39	..	..	..	..	..	..	..	..	..	..
WALCOTE ham.	341	373	..	..	521	..	..	..	..	..	..	..	..	..	..
POULTNEY ham.					29	..	..	..	..	..	..	..	..	..	..
MOUNTSORREL C.P.[p]	..	..	..	..	..	..	..	..	..	2,209	2,417[q]	2,491	2,596	2,622	3,877[r]
MOUNTSORREL NORTH END C.P.	Chapelry of Barrow upon Soar A.P., q.v.								1,272	See Mountsorrel C.P.[p]			..	..	..
MOUNTSORREL SOUTH END C.P.	Chapelry of Rothley A.P., q.v.								1,045	See Mountsorrel C.P.[p]			..	..	..
MOWSLEY C.P.	Chapelry of Knaptoft A.P., q.v.								208	168	168	169	243	239	157
MUSTON A.P. and C.P.	204	226	242	310	351	411	360	353	312	290	268	262	261	218	See Bottesford C.P.[s]
MYTHE E.P.P.[t]	..	15	14	..[t]	42	5	See Sheepy Magna A.P. and C.P.[t]					..	..	..	..

(a) The whole of Maplewell Longdale was transferred to Woodhouse in 1884.

(b) Part of Markfield (pop. 65 in 1891) was transferred to Charley in 1885, and Copt Oak (pop. 11 in 1891) was transferred from Newtown Linford to Markfield in 1884.

(c) In 1935 parts of Markfield (pop. 55, nil respectively in 1931) were transferred to Groby and Ratby, and part of Bardon (pop. 1 in 1931) and the whole of Stanton under Bardon were transferred to Markfield.

(d) Measham C.P. was transferred from Derbys. to Leics. administrative county in 1897.

(e) In 1935 part of Willesley (pop. nil in 1931) was transferred to Measham.

(f) Holt and Bradley (i.e. Nevill Holt) chapelry was generally said to be independent until 1841, when it was returned as an ordinary chapelry of Medbourne. It has been treated here as part of Medbourne A.P. throughout.

(g) Both Burton Lazars and Sysonby were returned as independent parishes until 1851, when they were said to be chapelries of Melton Mowbray A.P.

(h) In 1894 the part of Melton Mowbray C.P. not in the U.D. was created Sysonby with Eye Kettleby C.P., so that Melton Mowbray U.D. and C.P. became coextensive. Sysonby and Eye Kettleby was later renamed Eye Kettleby and is entered under that name.

(i) The whole of Sysonby was transferred to Melton Mowbray U.D. in 1930.

(j) In 1935 part of Melton Mowbray U.D. (pop. nil in 1931) was transferred to Asfordby, and the whole of Eye Kettleby and parts of Burton Lazars, Thorpe Arnold, and Welby (pop. respectively 6, nil, 9 in 1931) were transferred to Melton Mowbray.

(k) No separate return was made for the part of Merevale in Leics. 1811–31.

(l) Shown in different parts of the *Census Report* as 85 and 52. The population of the whole parish shown in both cases as 185.

(m) A detached part of Merevale in Leics. (pop. 2 in 1881) was transferred to Norton juxta Twycross in 1880.

(n) In 1885 part of Merevale (pop. 28 in 1891) was transferred to Orton on the Hill and part (pop. 43 in 1891) was transferred to Sheepy Magna. This comprised all the portion of Merevale in Leics.

(o) No return was apparently made for Misterton in 1801.

(p) Mountsorrel C.P. was formed in 1884 out of the whole of Mountsorrel South End, part of Mountsorrel North End (pop. 1,123 in 1891), and part of Rothley Temple (pop. 66 in 1891). The remainder of Mountsorrel North End (pop. 28 in 1891) was transferred to Barrow upon Soar.

(q) Part of Barrow upon Soar (pop. 29 in 1901) was transferred to Mountsorrel in 1896.

(r) Part of Rothley (pop. 383 in 1931) was transferred to Mountsorrel in 1935, and part of Quorndon (pop. 7 in 1931) was transferred to Mountsorrel in 1936.

(s) The whole of Muston was transferred to Bottesford in 1936.

(t) No return for the Mythe was apparently made in 1801. In 1831 it was included in Sheepy Magna, and from 1861 was apparently assumed to be part of Sheepy Magna.

POPULATION TABLE, 1801–1951 (*continued*)

	1801	1811	1821	1831	1841	1851	1861	1871	1881	1891	1901	1911	1921	1931	1951
NAILSTONE A.P.	..	664	751	800	710	668	639	691	..	..	..	..	..	..	..
NAILSTONE	492	293	359	421	314	341	302	367	See Nailstone C.P.			..	..	..	..
BARTON IN THE BEANS[a]	..	169	177	163	161	157	159	168	See Barton in the Beans C.P.				..	..	..
NORMANTON LE HEATH chap.	200	202	215	216	235*	170	178	156	See Normanton le Heath C.P.				..	..	..
NAILSTONE C.P.	Part of Nailstone A.P., q.v.								398	341[b]	333	346	375	349	525
NANPANTAN C.P.[c]	..	..	..	..	..	..	..	..	..	..	260	316	356	680*	See Loughborough U.D.[d]
NARBOROUGH A.P.	791	932	1,064	1,147	1,329*	1,283*	1,156	1,162	..	..	..	..	..	..	..
NARBOROUGH	541	635	775	792	804	842	716	753	See Narborough C.P.			..	..	..	..
THORPE, LITTLE ham., part of[e]					100										
HUNCOTE ham.	250	297	289	355	425	441	440	409	See Huncote C.P.			..	..	..	..
NARBOROUGH C.P.	Part of Narborough A.P., q.v.								884	873[f]	902	1,839*	1,847	2,245*	3,460[g]
NETHERSEAL	See Seal, Nether, and Over A.P. and C.P.						..	..	..	..	..	..	..	..	..
NEWARKE lib. and C.P.	See Leicester		..	..	..	..	..	..	..	..	..	..	..	..	..
NEWBOLD ham.	See Owston and Newbold A.P. and C.P.					..	..	..	..	..	..	..	..	..	..
NEWBOLD lib.	See Breedon on the Hill A.P.				..	..	..	..	..	..	..	..	..	..	..
NEWBOLD VERDON A.P. and C.P.	339	410	576	590	660	712	708	716	729	784[h]	851	1,064	1,280	1,251	1,217[i]
NEWBOLD VERDON	..	..	..	..	605	681	668	646	..	..	..	..	..	..	..
BRASCOTE	..	..	..	..	55	31	40	70	..	..	..	..	..	..	..
NEW FOUND POOL E.P.P. and C.P.[j]	..	..	..	..	..	7	75	60	56	See Leicester C.B.[k]			..	..	..
NEW HALL PARK lib.	See Thurlaston A.P.			..	..	..	..	..	..	..	..	..	..	..	..
NEW PARKS E.P.P. and C.P.[l]	..	..	..	..	..	46	52	69	72	71	69	161	373	704*	..[m]
NEWTON BURGOLAND ham.	See Swepstone A.P.			..	..	..	..	..	..	..	..	..	..	..	..
NEWTON, COLD C.P.	Chapelry of Lowesby A.P., q.v.								185	93	128	107	107	104	90
NEWTON HARCOURT C.P.	Township of Wistow A.P., q.v.								185	167	154	148	138	142	..[n]
NEWTON NETHERCOTE ham.	See Swepstone A.P.			..	..	..	..	..	..	..	..	..	..	..	..
NEWTOWN LINFORD A.P. and C.P.	377	403	549	449	495	483	500	450	479	357[o]	361	419	395	620*	901[p]
NEWTOWN UNTHANK ham.	See Ratby A.P.		..	..	..	..	..	..	..	..	..	..	..	..	..
NORMANTON ham.	See Bottesford A.P.			..	..	..	..	..	..	..	..	..	..	..	..
NORMANTON LE HEATH C.P.	Chapelry of Nailstone A.P., q.v.								162	166	134	143	156	143	113
NORMANTON TURVILLE tnp.	See Thurlaston A.P.			..	..	..	..	..	..	..	..	..	..	..	..
NORTON, EAST A.P. and C.P.	128	127	120	137	137	151	139	125	134	139	149	120	137	92	111
NORTON JUXTA TWYCROSS A.P.	399	434	502	497	526*	468	451	397	..	..	..	..	..	..	..
NORTON JUXTA TWYCROSS	283	289	326	361	400	344	335	299	See Norton juxta Twycross C.P.					..	..
BILSTONE tnp.	116	145	176	136	126	124	116	98	See Bilstone C.P.			..	..	..	..

(a) Barton in the Beans was said to extend into Market Bosworth A.P. and Shackerstone A.P. until 1871, when it was apparently assumed to be entirely in Nailstone. It has been treated here as if it had always been in this parish. No return for Barton in the Beans was apparently made in 1801, so that it has not been possible to show the total population of the whole A.P.

(b) Parts of Nailstone (pop. respectively 36, 2, nil in 1891) were transferred to Congerstone, Shackerstone, and Barton in the Beans in 1886, 1882, and 1886.

(c) Nanpantan C.P. was formed in 1894 out of that part of Loughborough C.P. which was not in Loughborough M.B.

(d) The whole of Nanpantan was transferred to Loughborough M.B. and C.P. in 1936.

(e) Little Thorpe hamlet was said in 1841 and 1851 to be partly in Narborough and partly in Cosby A.P.

(f) Part of Narborough (pop. 88 in 1891) was transferred to Cosby in 1885.

(g) In 1935 part of Narborough (pop. 7 in 1931) was transferred to Lubbesthorpe and part of Cosby (pop. 392 in 1931) was transferred to Narborough.

(h) Part of Bagworth (pop. nil in 1891) was transferred to Newbold Verdon in 1886 and part of Newbold Verdon (pop. nil in 1891) was transferred to Barlestone in 1882.

(i) In 1935 part of Newbold Verdon (pop. nil in 1931) was transferred to Barlestone and part of Kirkby Mallory (pop. 13 in 1931) was transferred to Newbold Verdon.

(j) No return was apparently made for New Found Pool until 1841, when it was included in the return for Augustine Friars E.P.P., in Leicester borough. From 1851 to 1881 it was said to be outside the borough.

(k) New Found Pool was transferred to Leicester C.B., as New Found Pool C.P. in 1892. It is shown there in 1891 both in the *Census Report* and in this table.

(l) No return was apparently made for New Parks until 1841, when it was returned as part of Augustine Friars E.P.P., in Leicester borough. From 1851 to 1881 it was said to be outside the borough.

(m) Most of New Parks (pop. 700 in 1931) was transferred to Leicester C.B. in 1936 and the remainder became part of Glenfields C.P.

(n) Newton Harcourt C.P. was dissolved in 1936. Part (pop. 142 in 1931) was transferred to Wistow and part (pop. nil in 1931) to Oadby U.D.

(o) In 1884 Rothley Plain, &c. (pop. 47 in 1891) was transferred from Newtown Linford to Rothley, Copt Oak (pop. 11 in 1891) was transferred from Newtown Linford to Markfield, another part of Newtown Linford (pop. nil in 1891) was transferred to Ulverscroft, and part of Bradgate Park C.P. (pop. nil in 1891) was transferred to Newtown Linford. In 1885 The Oaks (pop. 23 in 1891) was transferred from Newtown Linford to Charley.

(p) In 1935 part of Newtown Linford (pop. 132 in 1931) was transferred to Anstey, and in 1936 another part (pop. nil in 1931) was transferred to Groby and part of Groby (pop. nil in 1931) was transferred to Newtown Linford.

POPULATION TABLE, 1801–1951 (*continued*)

	1801	1811	1821	1831	1841	1851	1861	1871	1881	1891	1901	1911	1921	1931	1951
NORTON JUXTA TWYCROSS C.P.	Part of Norton juxta Twycross A.P., q.v.								293[a]	251	228	217	245	249	See Twycross C.P.[b]
NORTON, KING'S A.P.[c]	157	..	..	..	172	163	154	135	..	..	..	..	..	..	..
NORTON, KING'S	60	73	71	65	64	68	71	60	See Norton, King's C.P.			..	..	..	..
STRETTON, LITTLE chap.	97	96	128	96	108	95	83	75	See Stretton, Little C.P.			..	..	..	..
NORTON, KING'S C.P.	Part of Norton, King's A.P., q.v.								52	59	32	48	51	47	43
NOSELEY E.P.P. and C.P.	4	2	18	11	20	40	48	61	70	26	57	68	66	63	51
OADBY A.P., C.P., and from 1913 U.D. and C.P.[d]	624	766	856	1,023	1,085	1,196	1,254	1,250	1,731	1,865[e]	1,890	2,609*	3,229*	4,724	6,205[f]
OAKTHORPE AND DONISTHORPE C.P.[g]	..	..	..	..	..	..	..	..	1,494	1,678[g]	2,048	2,444	2,768	2,463	2,398[h]
the part in Leics.[g]	Hamlet of Seal, Nether and Over A.P., q.v.								370	..	..	..	..	..	..
ODSTONE C.P.	Hamlet of Shackerstone A.P., q.v.								192	170	154	142	165	142	See Shackerstone C.P.[i]
ORTON ON THE HILL A.P. and C.P.[j]	303	279	370	350	348	330	334	296	275	238[k]	215	183	208	191	See Twycross C.P.[l]
OSBASTON C.P.	Township of Cadeby A.P., q.v.								219	226	249	307	325	292	211
OSGATHORPE A.P. and C.P.	318	313	352	344	396*	346	351	350	304	306	312	298	298	357	404[m]
OVERSEAL	See Seal, Nether and Over A.P. and C.P.					..	..	..	..	..	..	..	..	..	..
OVERTON, COLD A.P. and C.P.	88	96	123	123	118	106	97	85	80	110	84	116	107	133	See Knossington C.P.[n]
OWSTON AND NEWBOLD A.P. and C.P.	176	216	212	197	213	178	169	181	189	136	127	121	142	125	110
OWSTON	..	..	..	..	189	..	..	..	..	..	..	..	..	..	..
NEWBOLD ham.	..	..	..	..	24	..	..	..	..	..	..	..	..	..	..
PACKINGTON A.P. and C.P. (Leics. and Derbys.; from 1884 all in Leics.)[o]	563	698	702	730	1,024	1,294	1,190	1,226	1,153	489[oq]	473	443	441	508	405[r]
the part in Leics.	439	455	446	476	407[p]*	1,017[p]	938*	978	872	..[o]	..	..	..	..	..
PACKINGTON	..	..	..	..	55	367	343	295	..	..	..	..	..	..	..
SNIBSTON chap.	..	..	..	..	352	650	595	683	..	..	..	..	..	..	..
PEATLING MAGNA A.P. and C.P.	170	186	228	267	308	301	272	228	194	160	147	183	172	194	159
PEATLING PARVA A.P. and C.P.	117	136	173	174	159	215	168	161	147	117	113	120	117	140	145
PECKLETON A.P. and C.P.	290	331	359	294	347	399	378	302	267	242	266	239	274	283	830[s]
PECKLETON	..	..	..	..	322	..	..	..	..	..	..	..	..	..	..
TOOLEY PARK ham.	..	..	..	..	25	..	..	..	..	..	..	..	..	..	..

(a) In 1880 a detached part of Merevale (pop. 4 in 1881) was transferred to Norton juxta Twycross.

(b) The whole of Norton juxta Twycross was transferred to Twycross in 1935.

(c) Illston on the Hill was said to be partly in Carlton Curlieu A.P. and partly in King's Norton A.P. until 1841 when it was apparently assumed to be entirely in Carlton Curlieu. It has been treated in this table as if it had always been in that parish.

(d) Oadby U.D. was created in 1913. It was coextensive with Oadby C.P.

(e) Part of Knighton (pop. 8 in 1881) was transferred to Oadby in 1891. The affected areas are shown in 1891 as altered both in the *Census Report* and in this table.

(f) In 1936 part of Oadby U.D. (pop. nil in 1931) was transferred to Leicester C.B., and parts of Leicester C.B., Wigston U.D., Evington, Great Glen, Newton Harcourt, Stoughton, and Great Stretton (pop. respectively 16, 11, 3, nil, 12, nil in 1931) were transferred to Oadby U.D.

(g) Part of the hamlet and C.P. of Oakthorpe and Donisthorpe was said to be in Derbys. and part in Leics. until 1891 when it was all said to be in Derbys. In 1884 parts of Measham and Stretton en le Field (Derbys.) (pop. respectively 158, 376 in 1891) were transferred to Oakthorpe and Donisthorpe and part of Over and Nether Seal (pop. 420 in 1891) was transferred to Oakthorpe and Donisthorpe and to Derbys. No order has been found transferring the part of Oakthorpe and Donisthorpe in Leics. to Derbys. The whole of Oakthorpe and Donisthorpe C.P. was transferred to Leics. administrative county in 1897.

(h) Part of Willesley (pop. nil in 1931) was transferred to Oakthorpe and Donisthorpe in 1936.

(i) The whole of Odstone was transferred to Shackerstone in 1935.

(j) Orton on the Hill was said to include Little Orton until 1851, when Little Orton was deemed to be part of Merevale.

(k) Part of Merevale (pop. 28 in 1891) was transferred to Orton on the Hill in 1885.

(l) The whole of Orton on the Hill was transferred to Twycross in 1935.

(m) In 1936 part of Thringstone (pop. 28 in 1931) was transferred to Osgathorpe.

(n) The whole of Cold Overton was transferred to Knossington in 1936.

(o) The part of Packington in Derbys. was transferred to Leics. in 1884.

(p) 'The proportion of the population of Packington in Derbys. and Leics. appears to have been erroneously stated in 1841': *Census Report*, 1851.

(q) The hamlet of Snibston (pop. 768 in 1891) was transferred from Packington to the new C.P. of Ravenstone with Snibston on its formation in 1884.

(r) Part of Packington (pop. 421 in 1931) was transferred to Ashby de la Zouch U.D. in 1936.

(s) Part of Kirkby Mallory (pop. 218 in 1931) and the whole of Stapleton were transferred to Peckleton in 1935.

POPULATION TABLE, 1801–1951 (*continued*)

	1801	1811	1821	1831	1841	1851	1861	1871	1881	1891	1901	1911	1921	1931	1951
PICKWELL WITH LEESTHORPE A.P. and C.P.	121	123	167	160	163	172	169	195	249	262	237	217	170	182	See Somerby C.P.[a]
PICKWELL	..	..	..	..	120	..	..	..	..	..	..	..	..	..	..
LEESTHORPE ham.	..	..	..	..	43	..	..	..	..	..	..	..	..	..	..
PLUNGAR A.P. and C.P.	157	191	203	244*	280	272	251	224	252	224	194	184	180	205	See Redmile C.P.[b]
POULTNEY ham.	See Misterton A.P.			..	..	..	..	..	..	..	..	..	..	..	..
PRESTWOLD A.P.	747	855	974	942	1,043	965	969	854	..	..	..	..	..	..	..
PRESTWOLD	62	52	72	62	60	58	72	65	See Prestwold C.P.			..	..	..	..
BURTON ON THE WOLDS tnp.	315	384	416	411	448	412	441	398	See Burton on the Wolds C.P.				..	..	..
COTES tnp	70	83	74	68	75	75	55	59	See Cotes C.P.		..	..	..	..	..
HOTON chap.	300	336	412	401	460	420	401	332	See Hoton C.P.		..	..	..	..	..
PRESTWOLD C.P.	Part of Prestwold A.P., q.v.								83	87	93	84	81	61	68
PRIMETHORPE tnp.	See Broughton Astley A.P.				..	..	..	..	..	..	..	..	..	..	..
QUENBY ham.	See Hungarton A.P.			..	..	..	..	..	..	..	..	..	..	..	..
QUENIBOROUGH A.P. and C.P.	429	446	469	518	530	536	511	489	549	510	532	557	648	946*	1,201
QUORNDON U.D. and C.P.	Chapelry of Barrow upon Soar A.P., q.v.								1,816	1,888	2,173	2,363	2,417	2,604	See Quorndon C.P.[c]
QUORNDON C.P.[c]	..	..	..	..	..	..	..	..	..	..	..	..	..	..	3,157
RAGDALE A.P. and C.P.	81	95	98	108	121	114	120	127	102	104	101	92	90	104	See Hoby with Rotherby C.P.[d]
RATBY A.P. and C.P.	873	962	1,025	996	1,274	1,241*	1,264	1,289	1,615	2,201	1,803[e]*	2,112[f]	2,205	2,181	2,093[g]
RATBY	480	541	614*	579	663	719	690	679	..	..	..	..	..	..	..
BOTCHESTON ham.	94	99	87	82	37	81	113	57	..	..	..	..	..	..	..
NEWTOWN UNTHANK ham.	..	..	..	..	532	..	..	38	..	..	..	..	..	..	..
GROBY ham.	299	322	324	335	42	441	461	515	..	..	..	..	..	..	..
RATCLIFFE CULEY C.P.	Chapelry of Sheepy Magna A.P., q.v.								228	220	212	205	220	184	See Witherley C.P.[h]
RATCLIFFE ON THE WREAKE A.P. and C.P.	107	117	124	144	142	128	126	96	106	131	109	101	126	180	179[i]
RAVENSTONE A.P. and C.P. (Leics. and Derbys.)	409	431	444	430	394	396	392	409	451	See Ravenstone with Snibston C.P.[k]					..
the part in Leics.	215	..[j]	255*	187	218	208	248	244	190	..	..	..	..	..	..
RAVENSTONE WITH SNIBSTON[k]	..	..	..	..	..	..	..	..	..	1,277	1,015[l]	1,820*	1,778[m]	1,777	1,215[n]
urban part: in Ashby de la Zouch U.D.	..	..	..	..	..	..	..	..	..	39	..	..	..	..	..
rural part	..	..	..	..	..	..	..	..	..	1,238	..	..	..	..	..
REARSBY A.P. and C.P.	445	426	451	503	471	500	468	458	477	400	427	409	424	538	692[o]
REDMILE A.P. and C.P.	301	328	411	461	518	527	521	503	489	417	401	382	383	337	755[p]
ROLLESTON C.P.	Chapelry of Billesdon A.P., q.v.								68	57	74	59	54	67	61

(a) The whole of Pickwell with Leesthorpe was transferred to Somerby in 1936.

(b) The whole of Plungar was transferred to Redmile in 1936.

(c) Quorndon U.D. was dissolved in 1935. The greater part of its constituent C.P. (pop. 2,597 in 1931) remained Quorndon C.P., while parts of it (pop. respectively nil, 7 in 1931) were transferred to Loughborough M.B. and C.P. and to Mountsorrel. Parts of Woodhouse (pop. nil in 1931) and Woodthorpe (pop. 6 in 1931) were transferred to Quorndon.

(d) The whole of Ragdale was transferred to Hoby with Rotherby C.P. on its formation in 1936.

(e) Part of Ratby (pop. 928 in 1901) was created Groby C.P. in 1896.

(f) Part of Kirby Muxloe (pop. 276 in 1911) was transferred to Ratby in 1904.

(g) Part of Markfield (pop. nil in 1931) was transferred to Ratby in 1935, and part of Ratby (pop. 367 in 1931) was transferred to Desford in 1936.

(h) The whole of Ratcliffe Culey was transferred to Witherley in 1935.

(i) In 1935 part of Ratcliffe on the Wreake (pop. nil in 1931) was transferred to Rearsby, and part of Rearsby (pop. nil in 1931) was transferred to Ratcliffe on the Wreake.

(j) No separate return was made in 1811 of the part of Ravenstone in Leics.

(k) Ravenstone with Snibston C.P. was formed in 1884 out of the whole of Ravenstone C.P. (pop. 470 in 1891), a detached part of Ashby de la Zouch C.P. called Alton Grange (pop. 39 in 1891), and Snibston hamlet (pop. 768 in 1891) from Packington C.P. The part of the parish formerly in Derbys. was transferred to Leics. at the same time. The part of Ravenstone with Snibston which had formerly been in Ashby de la Zouch C.P. was, and remained, in Ashby de la Zouch U.D.

(l) Part of Ravenstone with Snibston (pop. 2,464 in 1901) was included in Coalville U.D. on its formation in 1892. In 1894 all of this part of the parish became part of the new C.P. of Coalville, and the small part of Ravenstone with Snibston in Ashby de la Zouch U.D. was transferred to Ashby de la Zouch R.D., so that the whole parish became united in one R.D.

(m) Part of Ravenstone with Snibston (pop. 142 in 1921) was transferred to Coalville C.P. and Coalville U.D. in 1912.

(n) In 1936 part of Ravenstone with Snibston (pop. 614 in 1931) was transferred to Coalville U.D. and C.P.

(o) In 1935 part of Ratcliffe on the Wreake (pop. nil in 1931) was transferred to Rearsby, and part of Rearsby (pop. nil in 1931) was transferred to Ratcliffe on the Wreake.

(p) The whole of Barkestone and Plungar C.P.s were transferred to Redmile in 1936.

POPULATION

POPULATION TABLE, 1801–1951 (*continued*)

	1801	1811	1821	1831	1841	1851	1861	1871	1881	1891	1901	1911	1921	1931	1951
ROTHERBY A.P. and C.P.	95	110	143	152	142	130	134	132	153	138	111	156	128	133	See Hoby with Rotherby C.P.[a]
ROTHLEY A.P.[b]	..	..	..	..	2,179	2,047	2,213	2,362	..	..	..	..	..	..	..
ROTHLEY	775[c]	857[c]	948[c]	981[c]	1,055*	985*	939	1,040*	See Rothley C.P.			..	..	..	..
KEYHAM chap.	177	207	210	172*	184	144	122	147	See Keyham C.P.			..	..	..	..
MOUNTSORREL SOUTH END chap[b]	..	..	..	..	715	795	897	949	See Mountsorrel South End C.P.				..	..	..
WARTNABY chap.	77	80	90	86	107	123	116	129	See Wartnaby C.P.			..	..	..	..
WYCOMB and CHADWELL chap.	105	95	101	103	58 60	166	139	97*	See Wycomb and Chadwell C.P.				..	..	..
ROTHLEY C.P.	Part of Rothley A.P., q.v.								1,048	1,199[d]	1,463	2,006	2,264[e]	2,734	2,486[f]
ROTHLEY TEMPLE E.P.P. and C.P.[c]	..	..	..	..	42	67	80	85	91	..[g]	..	..	..	..	..
ROWDEN ham.	See Higham on the Hill A.P.				..	..	..	..	..	..	..	..	..	..	..
SADDINGTON A.P. and and C.P.	241	215	232	268	279	262	259	268	185	182	243	210	213	243	190
ST. LEONARD A.P. and C.P.	See Leicester		..	..	..	..	..	..	..	..	..	..	..	..	..
ST. MARGARET A.P.	..	..	..	..	..	..	..	..	..	..	..	..	..	..	..
part in Leicester, q.v.	..	..	..	..	..	..	..	..	..	..	..	..	..	..	..
KNIGHTON chap.	337	377	383	402	465	494	641*	928*	See Knighton C.P.			..	..	..	..
ST. MARTIN A.P. and C.P.	See Leicester		..	..	..	..	..	..	..	..	..	..	..	..	..
ST. MARY A.P. and C.P.	..	..	..	..	..	..	..	..	..	..	..	..	..	..	..
part in Leicester, q.v.	..	..	..	..	..	..	..	..	..	..	..	..	..	..	..
SOUTH FIELDS lib.	..[h]	..[h]	762*	1,608*	2,566	See Leicester, St. Mary A.P.[i]				..	..	..	..	..	..
ST. NICHOLAS A.P. and C.P.	See Leicester		..	..	..	..	..	..	..	..	..	..	..	..	..
SALTBY A.P. and C.P.	185	213	234	263	299	296	292	290	272	253	227	207	192	170	See Sproxton C.P.[j]
SAPCOTE A.P. and C.P.	555	692	797*	871*	773	724	668*	600*	693	732	845	872	877	862	794
SAWLEY WITH WILSTHORPE C.P. (Derbys. and Leics.)	..	..	..	..	..	..	..	..	..	..	..	..	..	..	..
part in Leics.[k]	..	..	..	..	..	..	..	..	2	See Lockington C.P.[l]			..	..	..
SAXBY A.P. and C.P.	127	131	153	206	163	140	117	126	120	182	134	116	95	89	See Freeby C.P.[m]
SAXELBY A.P.[o] and C.P.	97	123	134	120	112	118	120	91	84	98	94	109	71	75	See Grimston C.P.[n]
SAXELBY	82	100	103	105	..	..	..	..	..	..	..	..	..	..	..
SHOBY ham.	15	23	31	15	See Shoby E.P.P. and C.P.[o]				..	..	..	..	..	..	..
SCALFORD A.P. and C.P.	333	371	438	467	517	555	553	544	684	646	631	688	581	595	634[p]
SCRAPTOFT A.P. and C.P.	107	110	126	126	89	120	108	86	120*	90	116	113	153	424*	1,075
SEAGRAVE A.P. and C.P.	301	365	424	426	451	428*	443	412	360	325	311	396	386	351	329
SEAL, NETHER, AND OVER A.P.[q]	906	991	1,160	1,222*	1,281	1,330	1,576	1,695	..	..	..	..	..	..	..
SEAL, NETHER tnp.	..	..	..	..	535	1,085	1,246	1,240	See Seal, Nether, and Over C.P.				..	..	..
SEAL, OVER tnp.	..	..	..	..	513										

(a) Rotherby became part of Hoby with Rotherby C.P. on its formation in 1936.

(b) The population of Mountsorrel South End was included with that of Mountsorrel North End in Barrow upon Soar A.P. 1801–31. No total for Rothley A.P. can therefore be shown for these years.

(c) The population of Rothley Temple was included in that of Rothley township 1801–31.

(d) In 1884 Rothley Plain, &c. (pop. 47 in 1891) was transferred from Newtown Linford to Rothley, and part of Rothley Temple (pop. 14 in 1891) was transferred to Rothley.

(e) Parts of Swithland and Thurcaston (pop. respectively nil, 120 in 1921) were transferred to Rothley in 1912.

(f) Part of Rothley (pop. 383 in 1931) was transferred to Mountsorrel in 1935.

(g) Rothley Temple was dissolved in 1884. Part of it (pop. 66 in 1891) was transferred to Mountsorrel C.P. on its formation, the remainder (pop. 14 in 1891) was transferred to Rothley.

(h) No return was apparently made for South Fields in 1801 or 1811. In 1811 there were apparently only 6 houses there, while there were 182 occupied and 14 being built in 1821.

(i) South Fields liberty was said to be outside Leicester until 1851, when it was said to be inside the borough.

(j) The whole of Saltby was transferred to Sproxton in 1936.

(k) Part of Sawley with Wilsthorpe was said for the first time in 1881 to be in Leics. It was said to have been returned with Hemington township in Lockington A.P. in 1871.

(l) Cliff Farm (pop. 2 in 1891) was transferred from Sawley with Wilsthorpe to Lockington in 1884.

(m) The whole of Saxby was transferred to Freeby in 1936.

(n) The whole of Saxelby was transferred to Grimston in 1936.

(o) Shoby was returned as a hamlet of Saxelby until 1841, when it was said to be an extra-parochial place. It had already claimed to be extra-parochial in 1831.

(p) The whole of Wycomb and Chadwell C.P. was transferred to Scalford in 1936.

(q) The whole of Seal A.P. was in Leics. but the hamlets of Oakthorpe and Donisthorpe were partly in Nether Seal, partly in Measham (Derbys.) and partly in Church Gresley (Derbys.) where they were wholly entered 1801–31. Sometimes only Donisthorpe was said to extend into Seal, but the boundary between it and Oakthorpe seems never to have been defined.

POPULATION TABLE, 1801–1951 (*continued*)

	1801	1811	1821	1831	1841	1851	1861	1871	1881	1891	1901	1911	1921	1931	1951
BLACKFORDBY chap. part of[a]	..	..	..	..	34	34	24	5	See Blackfordby C.P.			..	..	..	..
OAKTHORPE AND DONISTHORPE ham.; part of[b]	..	..	..	..	199	211	306	450	See Oakthorpe and Donisthorpe C.P.					..	..
SEAL, NETHER AND OVER C.P.	Part of Seal, Nether and Over A.P., q.v.								1,338	1,513[c]	..[d]	..	..	..	..
SEWSTERN C.P.	Chapelry of Buckminster A.P., q.v.								201	203[e]	167	189	222	241	See Buckminster C.P.[f]
SHACKERSTONE A.P.[g]	431	426	486	432	424	466	462	489	..	..	..	..	..	..	..
SHACKERSTONE	250	255	270	267	344	299	278	315	See Shackerstone C.P.			..	..	..	..
ODSTONE ham.	181	171	216	165	180	167	184	174	See Odstone C.P.			..	..	..	..
SHACKERSTONE C.P.	Part of Shackerstone A.P., q.v.								288	252[h]	277	229	258	214	765[i]
SHANGTON A.P. and C.P.	34	36	44	39	39	55	82	101	74	77	51	42	58	43	46
SHARNFORD A.P. and C.P.	373	394	460	545	624	611	589	472	459	361	418	373	399	469	576[j]
SHAWELL A.P. and C.P.	195	196	209	216	203	207	205	205	205	172	138	173	181	158	154[k]
SHEARSBY C.P.	Chapelry of Knaptoft A.P., q.v.								261	225	207	180	160	172	144
SHEEPY C.P.[l]	..	..	..	..	..	..	..	..	..	..	..	..	..	..	881
SHEEPY MAGNA A.P.	583	564	638	627[m]	572	637	647[m]	656	..	..	..	..	..	..	..
SHEEPY MAGNA	385	363	427	415[m]	353	396	439[m]	446	See Sheepy Magna C.P.			..	..	..	..
RATCLIFFE CULEY chap.	198	201	211	212	219	241	208	210	See Ratcliffe Culey C.P.			..	..	..	..
SHEEPY MAGNA C.P.	Part of Sheepy Magna A.P., q.v.								415	470[n]	464	492	472	448	See Sheepy C.P.[o]
SHEEPY PARVA A.P. and C.P.	82	92	87	87	104	112	114	110	89	69	63	77	79	70	
SHENTON C.P.	Chapelry of Bosworth, Market A.P.								210	201	170	181	141	154	See Sutton Cheney C.P.[p]
SHEPSHED A.P. and C.P.	2,627	3,026	3,464*	3,714	3,872	3,759	3,626	3,784	4,437	4,416[q]	See Shepshed U.D.[q]			..	..
urban part: in Shepshed U.D., q.v.	..	..	..	..	..	..	..	..	..	4,414	..	..	..	..	..
rural part	..	..	..	..	..	..	..	..	..	2	..	..	..	..	..
SHEPSHED U.D.; from 1894 U.D. and C.P.[q]	..	..	..	..	..	..	..	..	..	4,414	5,293[q]	5,542	5,533	5,758	6,235[p]
SHEPSHED C.P., part of	..	..	..	..	..	..	..	..	..	4,414	..	..	..	..	..
SHERMANS GROUNDS	See Leicester Frith E.P.P. and C.P.					..	..	..	..	..	..	..	..	..	..
SHILTON, EARL C.P.	Chapelry of Kirkby Mallory A.P., q.v.								2,252	2,594[s]	3,595	4,190	4,434	4,838	See Hinckley U.D.[t]
SHOBY E.P.P. and C.P.	See Saxelby A.P.[u]				35	28*	39	29	35	26	36	23	53	49	See Grimston C.P.[v]

(a) Most of Blackfordby chapelry was in Ashby de la Zouch A.P. No mention of its extension into Seal was made until 1841.

(b) See note (q) on previous page.

(c) Parts of Over and Nether Seal C.P. (pop. respectively 33, 420 in 1891) were transferred to Blackfordby and to Oakthorpe and Donisthorpe in 1884.

(d) Nether and Over Seal was transferred to the administrative county of Derbys. in 1897. It was divided into two C.P.s later known as Netherseal and Overseal.

(e) Part of Sewstern (pop. nil in 1891) was transferred to Buckminster in 1884.

(f) The whole of Sewstern was transferred to Buckminster in 1936.

(g) Barton in the Beans township was said to extend into Nailstone A.P., Market Bosworth A.P., and Shackerstone A.P. until 1871 when it was assumed to be entirely in Nailstone. It has been treated here as if it had always been in that parish.

(h) Part of Nailstone (pop. 2 in 1891) was transferred to Shackerstone in 1882 and part of Shackerstone (pop. 17 in 1891) was transferred to Congerstone in 1886.

(i) The whole of Barton in the Beans, Bilstone, Congerstone, and Odstone C.P.s were transferred to Shackerstone in 1935.

(j) Part of Copston Magna C.P. (Warws.) (pop. 13 in 1931) was transferred in 1935 to Leics. administrative county and Sharnford C.P.

(k) Parts of Shawell (pop. together 12 in 1931) were transferred in 1935 to Churchover C.P. and Newton and Biggin C.P. in Warws. administrative county.

(l) Sheepy C.P. was formed in 1935 out of the whole of Sheepy Magna, Sheepy Parva, Sibson, and Upton C.P.s.

(m) The population of the Mythe E.P.P. was included in that of Sheepy Magna in 1831, and from 1861 onwards the place was apparently considered to be part of Sheepy Magna and its population included as a matter of course.

(n) Part of Merevale (pop. 43 in 1891) was transferred to Sheepy Magna in 1885.

(o) Sheepy Magna and Sheepy Parva both became part of Sheepy C.P. on its formation in 1935.

(p) The whole of Shenton was transferred to Sutton Cheney in 1935.

(q) Shepshed U.D. was created in 1886. It was coextensive with Shepshed C.P. until part of Garendon (pop. 2 in 1901) was transferred to Shepshed C.P. in 1891. Since this piece of land was not transferred to the U.D. as well, the U.D. and C.P. ceased to be coextensive. In 1894 the rural part of Shepshed C.P. was constituted Shepshed Parva C.P., so that Shepshed U.D. and C.P. once again became coextensive. In 1896 Shepshed Parva was transferred to Shepshed U.D. and C.P.

(r) In 1936 parts of Shepshed U.D. (pop. 40, 34 respectively in 1931) were transferred to Loughborough M.B. and the whole of Long Whatton and parts of Garendon (pop. 4 in 1931) and of Hathern (pop. nil in 1931) were transferred to Shepshed.

(s) Spinner's Meadow (pop. nil in 1891) was transferred from Stoney Stanton to Earl Shilton in 1885.

(t) The whole of Earl Shilton was transferred to Hinckley U.D. in 1936.

(u) Shoby was returned as a hamlet of Saxelby A.P. until 1841, when it was said to be an extra-parochial place. It had already claimed to be independent in 1831.

(v) The whole of Shoby was transferred to Grimston in 1936.

POPULATION TABLE, 1801–1951 (*continued*)

	1801	1811	1821	1831	1841	1851	1861	1871	1881	1891	1901	1911	1921	1931	1951
SIBSON A.P.	356	332	378	427	504	484	480	437	..	..	..	..	..	..	..
SIBSON	220	191	237	279	280	252	242	220	See Sibson C.P.			..	..	..	..
WELLSBOROUGH and	See Wellsborough and Temple Hall E.P.P.[a]				76	80	93	69							
TEMPLE HALL ham.								12							
UPTON tnp.	136	141	141	148	148	152	145	136	See Upton C.P.			..	..	..	..
SIBSON C.P.	Part of Sibson A.P., q.v.								278	272	248	258	258	264	See Sheepy C.P.[b]
SILEBY A.P. and C.P.	1,111	1,200	1,328	1,491	1,473	1,660	1,572	1,766*	2,033	2,380	2,752	3,082	3,202	3,598	4,236
SKEFFINGTON A.P. and C.P.	120	136	169	180	187	205	244	231	150	172	173	153	138	121	131
SKETCHLEY	See Aston Flamville A.P.				..	..	..	..	..	..	..	..	..	..	..
SLAWSTON A.P. and C.P.	266	203	228	243	250	281	246	202	184	152	145	134	126	121	124
SMEETON WESTERBY C.P.	Township of Kibworth Beauchamp A.P., q.v.								390	342	344	336	302	343	321
SNARESTONE A.P. and C.P.	324	309	356	353	404*	387	355	353	318	302	281	277	338	347	316
SNIBSTON	See Packington A.P. and Ravenstone with Snibston C.P.								..	..	..	..	..	..	..
SOMERBY A.P. and C.P.	350	333	384	377	480	503	506	523*	531	488[c]	503	507	480	474	864[d]
SOUTH FIELDS lib.	See St. Mary A.P.			..	..	..	..	..	..	..	..	..	..	..	..
SPARKENHOE HUNDRED	26,341	30,660	34,309	35,170	37,705	..	37,579	38,752	44,188	..	..	..	..	..	..
SPROXTON A.P. and C.P.	260	310	372	378	394	426	455	408	335	336	306	282	316	287	572[e]
STANTON, STONEY A.P. and C.P.	355	446	533	549	663	751	703*	681*	993	1,220[f]	1,515	1,539	1,507	1,560	1,430
STANTON UNDER BARDON C.P.	Township of Thornton A.P., q.v.								259	352	525	657*	710	690	See Markfield C.P.[g]
STAPLEFORD A.P. and C.P.	179	162	218	185	184*	98	109	114	114	125	142	170	133	145	See Freeby C.P.[h]
STAPLETON C.P.	Hamlet of Barwell A.P., q.v.								204	221	184	227	215	252	See Peckleton C.P.[i]
STARMORE	See Westrill and Starmore E.P.P. and C.P.						..	..	..	..	..	..	..	..	..
STATHERN A.P. and C.P.	404	372	456	481	549	620	524	495	539	608	594	578	531	528	574
STAUNTON HAROLD C.P.	Township of Breedon on the Hill A.P., q.v.								237	227	218	206	197	182	150
STOCKERSTON A.P. and C.P.	56	49	50	60	48	39	50	54	56	70[j]	69	49	51	37	50
STOKE DRY A.P. and C.P. (Rutl. and Leics.)	..	..	..	..	..	..	..	..	..	..	..	..	..	..	..
HOLYOAKS lib. (i.e. the part of Stoke Dry in Leics.)	..[k]	4	7	3	2	11	9	7	5	See Stockerston C.P.[j]			..	..	..
STOKE GOLDING C.P.	Chapelry of Hinckley A.P., q.v.								551	619	625	613	628	731	..[l]
STONESBY A.P. and C.P.	181	194	246	287	283	286	271	236	216	231	199	172	166	140	See Sproxton C.P.[m]
STONTON WYVILLE A.P. and C.P.	96	93	122	106	102	106	102	84	88	56	65	42	55	60	62
STOUGHTON C.P.	Chapelry of Thurnby A.P., q.v.								144	118	136	136	108	122	358[n]
STRETTON EN LE FIELD C.P.[o]	..	..	..	..	..	..	..	..	..	..	63	57	64	67	47
STRETTON, GREAT C.P.	Chapelry of Glen, Great A.P., q.v.								34	32	27	43	43	56	231[p]
STRETTON, LITTLE C.P.	Chapelry of Norton, Kings A.P., q.v.								84	72	83	73	93	86	105
SUTTON CHENEY C.P.	Chapelry of Bosworth, Market A.P., q.v.								300	239	205	182	215	207	590[q]
SUTTON IN THE ELMS tnp.	See Broughton Astley A.P.				..	..	..	..	..	..	..	..	..	..	..
SWANNINGTON C.P.	Township of Whitwick A.P., q.v.								1,417	1,711	1,737[r]	2,050	2,113[s]	2,239	1,509[t]

(a) Wellsborough and Temple Hall were returned as extra-parochial until 1841 when they were said to be a hamlet of Sibson.
(b) The whole of Sibson was transferred to Sheepy C.P. on its formation in 1935.
(c) Ward's Farm, &c. (pop. 25 in 1891) was transferred from Somerby to Burrough on the Hill in 1887.
(d) The whole of Burrough on the Hill, and Pickwell with Leesthorpe C.P.s were transferred to Somerby in 1936.
(e) The whole of Bescaby, Saltby, and Stonesby C.P.s were transferred to Sproxton in 1936.
(f) Spinner's Meadow (pop. nil in 1891) was transferred from Stoney Stanton to Earl Shilton in 1885.
(g) The whole of Stanton under Bardon was transferred to Markfield in 1935.
(h) The whole of Stapleford was transferred to Freeby in 1936.
(i) The whole of Stapleton was transferred to Peckleton in 1935.
(j) Holyoaks (i.e. the part of Stoke Dry C.P. in Leics.) (pop. 6 in 1891) was transferred to Stockerston in 1885.
(k) No return was apparently made for Holyoaks in 1801.
(l) Stoke Golding C.P. was dissolved in 1936. Part of it (pop. 713 in 1931) was transferred to Hinckley U.D. and the rest (pop. 18 in 1931) to Higham on the Hill.
(m) The whole of Stonesby was transferred to Sproxton in 1936.
(n) In 1936 part of Stoughton (pop. 12 in 1931) was transferred to Oadby U.D. and part of Evington (pop. nil in 1931) was transferred to Stoughton.
(o) Stretton en le Field was transferred from Derbys. to Leics. administrative county in 1897.
(p) Part of Great Stretton (pop. nil in 1931) was transferred to Oadby U.D. in 1936.
(q) The whole of Dadlington and Shenton C.P.s were transferred to Sutton Cheney in 1935.
(r) Part of Swannington (pop. 299 in 1901) was included in Coalville U.D. on its formation in 1892. In 1894 all this part of Swannington was transferred to the new C.P. of Coalville.
(s) Part of Swannington (pop. 132 in 1921) was transferred to Coalville U.D. and Coalville C.P. in 1912.
(t) In 1936 parts of Swannington (pop. respectively 682, 46 in 1931) were transferred to Coalville U.D. and C.P. and to Coleorton, and parts of Coleorton and Thringstone (pop. respectively nil, 142 in 1931) were transferred to Swannington.

POPULATION TABLE, 1801–1951 (*continued*)

	1801	1811	1821	1831	1841	1851	1861	1871	1881	1891	1901	1911	1921	1931	1951
SWEPSTONE A.P. and C.P.	412	520	625	627	614	585	566	556	526	509	525	570	630	629	501
SWEPSTONE	..	..	..	..	245	..	..	..	..	..	..	..	..	..	..
NEWTON BURGOLAND ham.	..	..	..	..	244	..	..	..	..	..	..	..	..	..	..
NEWTON NETHERCOTE ham.	..	..	..	..	125	..	..	..	..	..	..	..	..	..	..
SWINFORD A.P. and C.P.	358	410	450	438	444	420	402	375	403	392	306	311	339	313	368
SWITHLAND A.P. and C.P.	322	305	336	352	306	285	255	255	246	213	195	182	190[a]	168	167
SYSONBY A.P. and C.P.	65	48	67	81	68	See Melton Mowbray A.P.[b]			96	147	157	214	191	See Melton Mowbray U.D.[c]	
SYSONBY WITH EYE KETTLEBY C.P.	See Kettleby, Eye C.P.			..	..	..	..	..	..	..	..	..	..	..	..
SYSTON A.P. and C.P.	1,124	1,223	1,264	1,349	1,421	1,669*	1,656	1,877*	2,470	2,582	2,930	3,087	3,214	4,322*	5,508[d]
TEMPLE HALL	See Wellsborough and Temple Hall E.P.P. and Sibson A.P.								..	..	..	..	..	..	..
THEDDINGWORTH A.P. (Leics. and Northants.)[e]	..	..	..	..	..	..	..	..	..	..	..	..	..	..	..
THEDDINGWORTH (i.e. the part in Leics.)	162	196	202	257	254	267	269	268	See Theddingworth C.P.				..	..	..
THEDDINGWORTH C.P.	Part of Theddingworth A.P., q.v.								246	204	201	228	193	183	204
THORNTON A.P.	935	1,028	1,096	1,078	1,375	1,350	1,292	1,216	..	..	..	..	..	..	..
THORNTON	320	367	405	455*	491	460	446	436	See Thornton C.P.			..	..	..	..
BAGWORTH chap.	320	} 371	389	328	569	560	534	505	See Bagworth C.P.			..	..	..	..
BAGWORTH PARK lib.	8														
STANTON UNDER BARDON tnp.	287	290	302	295	315	330	312	275	See Stanton under Bardon C.P.				..	..	..
THORNTON C.P.	Part of Thornton A.P., q.v.								426	500	510	673*	666	711	See Bagworth C.P.[f]
THORPE ACRE AND DISHLEY A.P. and C.P.	225	287	351	366	298	260*	195*	153	212	194[g]	196	174	201	152	See Loughborough M.B.[h]
THORPE ACRE	..	..	..	..	265	..	..	..	..	..	..	..	..	..	..
DISHLEY chap.	..	..	..	..	33	..	..	..	..	..	..	..	..	..	..
THORPE ARNOLD A.P. and C.P.	73	88	109	117	134	122	124	147	147	133	117	119	133	128	..[i]
THORPE, KNIGHT	See Loughborough A.P., U.D., and M.B.					..	..	..	..	..	..	..	..	..	..
THORPE, LITTLE ham.	See Cosby A.P.	..	..	..	..	..	..	..	..	..	..	..	..	..	..
THORPE SATCHVILLE C.P.	Hamlet of Twyford A.P., q.v.								169	176	217	256	195	186	See Twyford and Thorpe C.P.[j]
THRINGSTONE C.P.	Township of Whitwick A.P., q.v.								1,238	911[k]	1,238	1,279	1,447	1,566	..[l]
THRUSSINGTON A.P. and C.P.	390	417	466	454	645*	544	574	624	604	489	456	445	494	522	469
THURCASTON A.P.	1,001[m]	1,106[m]	1,159	1,241	1,230	1,102	1,095	1,421	..	..	..	..	..	..	..
THURCASTON	215	259	277	276	281	230	248	249	See Thurcaston C.P.			..	..	..	..
ANSTEY chap.	660[m]	747[m]	784	850	838	760	734	1,012*	See Anstey C.P.			..	..	..	..
CROPSTON tnp.	126	100	98	115	111	112	113	160	See Cropston C.P.			..	..	..	..
THURCASTON C.P.	Part of Thurcaston A.P., q.v.								223	195	268	345	245[n]	336	1,126[o]

(a) Part of Swithland (pop. nil in 1921) was transferred to Rothley in 1912.

(b) Sysonby was returned as a separate parish 1801–41, but as a chapelry of Melton Mowbray 1851–71.

(c) The whole of Sysonby was transferred to Melton Mowbray U.D. in 1930.

(d) In 1935 parts of Syston (pop. respectively nil, 24 in 1931) were transferred to Barkby and Cossington and parts of Barkby and Cossington (pop. respectively 566, 2 in 1931) were transferred to Syston.

(e) The only part of Theddingworth A.P. in Northants. was Hothorpe hamlet. It became a separate C.P.

(f) The whole of Thornton was transferred to Bagworth in 1935.

(g) Part of Thorpe Acre and Dishley (pop. nil in 1891) was included in Loughborough M.B. in 1888, but in 1891 this piece of land was transferred to Knight Thorpe C.P., while part of Knight Thorpe outside Loughborough M.B. (pop. nil in 1891) was transferred to Thorpe Acre and Dishley. Part of Garendon (pop. 4 in 1901) was also transferred to Thorpe Acre and Dishley, and part of Thorpe Acre and Dishley (pop. nil in 1891) was transferred to Garendon.

(h) The whole of Thorpe Acre and Dishley was transferred to Loughborough M.B. in 1936.

(i) Thorpe Arnold C.P. was dissolved in 1936. Part of it (pop. nil in 1931) was transferred to Melton Mowbray U.D. and the remainder became part of the new C.P. of Waltham.

(j) Thorpe Satchville became part of Twyford and Thorpe C.P. on its formation in 1936.

(k) Rotten Row (pop. 194 in 1891) was transferred from Thringstone to Coleorton in 1884.

(l) Thringstone C.P. was dissolved in 1936. Part of it (pop. 997 in 1931) was transferred to Coalville U.D. and C.P., part (pop. 14 in 1931) to Belton, part (pop. 377 in 1931) to Coleorton, part (pop. 28 in 1931) to Osgathorpe, part (pop. 142 in 1931) to Swannington, and part (pop. 8 in 1931) to Worthington.

(m) The population of Anstey Pastures E.P.P. was included in that of Anstey in 1801 and 1811. The total for Anstey A.P. should therefore probably be slightly less than that shown.

(n) Part of Thurcaston (pop. 150 in 1921) was transferred to Rothley in 1912.

(o) Part of Beaumont Leys (pop. nil in 1931) and the whole of Cropston were transferred to Thurcaston in 1935.

POPULATION

POPULATION TABLE, 1801–1951 (*continued*)

	1801	1811	1821	1831	1841	1851	1861	1871	1881	1891	1901	1911	1921	1931	1951
THURLASTON A.P. and C.P.	364	487	549	636	694	796	698*	536*	533	514	526	541[a]	542	484	430
THURLASTON	320	469[b]	513	556	} 646	748	679	507	..	..	..	..	..	..	..
NEW HALL PARK lib.	3	18	17	25											
NORMANTON TURVILLE tnp.	41	..[b]	19	55	48	48	19	29	..	..	..	..	..	..	..
THURMASTON U.D.; from 1903 U.D. and C.P.[c]	..	..	..	..	..	..	..	..	1,545	1,681	1,732	1,824	2,206[d]	3,723*	See Thurmaston C.P.[e]
THURMASTON, NORTH C.P.	Chapelry of Barkby A.P., q.v.								420	489	513	..[c]	..	..	..
THURMASTON, SOUTH C.P.	Chapelry of Belgrave A.P., q.v.								1,125	1,192	1,219	..[c]	..	..	..
THURMASTON C.P.[e]	..	..	..	..	..	..	..	..	..	..	..	..	..	..	4,178
THURNBY A.P.	369	320	400	383	369	373	375	375	..	..	..	..	..	..	..
THURNBY	115	120	146	158	162	180	196	185	See Thurnby C.P.			..	..	..	..
BUSHBY ham.	96	71	87	86	86	63	60	51	See Bushby C.P.			..	..	..	..
STOUGHTON chap.	158	129	167	139	121	130	119	139	See Stoughton C.P.			..	..	..	..
THURNBY C.P.	Part of Thurnby A.P., q.v.								232	223	234	226	241	348	843[f]
TILTON A.P.	311	332	417	361	408*	410	432	460	..	..	..	..	..	..	..
TILTON	140	146	180	158	190	202	180	222	See Tilton C.P.		..	..	..	..	..
HALSTEAD tnp.	123	138	187	162	186	176	211	204	See Halstead C.P.			..	..	..	..
MAREFIELD tnp.	27	27	32	22	21	27	28	23	See Marefield C.P.			..	..	..	..
WHATBOROUGH lib.[g]	21	21	18	19	11	5	13	11	See Whatborough C.P.			..	..	..	..
TILTON C.P.	Part of Tilton A.P., q.v.								235	152	128	130	145	152	357[h]
TONGE ham.	See Breedon on the Hill A.P.				..	..	..	..	..	..	..	..	..	..	..
TOOLEY PARK ham.	See Peckleton A.P.			..	..	..	..	..	..	..	..	..	..	..	..
TUGBY A.P. and C.P.	..[i]	250	265	266	288	365	360	438	344	317	271	300	271	259	231
TUGBY	230	230	239	250	275	337	331	364	..	..	..	..	..	..	..
KEYTHORPE lib.	..[i]	20	26	16	13	28	29	74	..	..	..	..	..	..	..
TWYCROSS A.P. and C.P.	319	292	373	319	336	305	336	340	354	350	317	248	276	269	642[j]
TWYFORD A.P.	397	410	495	512	478	526	543	591	..	..	..	..	..	..	..
TWYFORD	256	279	313	349	325	367	372	373	See Twyford C.P.			..	..	..	..
THORPE SATCHVILLE ham.	141	131	182*	163	153	159	171	218*	See Thorpe Satchville C.P.				..	..	..
TWYFORD C.P.	Part of Twyford A.P., q.v.								426	330	312	332	333	282	See Twyford and Thorpe C.P.[k]
TWYFORD AND THORPE C.P.[k]	..	..	..	..	..	..	..	..	..	..	..	..	..	..	495
ULLESTHORPE C.P.	Hamlet of Claybrooke A.P., q.v.								523[l]	423	312	395	402	409	607[m]
ULVERSCROFT E.P.P. and C.P.	58	88	87	100	146	102	104	81	91	90[n]	100	89	121	131	124
UPTON C.P.	Township of Sibson A.P., q.v.								103	105	94	109	110	104	See Sheepy C.P.[o]
WALCOTE ham.	See Misterton A.P.			..	..	..	..	..	..	..	..	..	..	..	..
WALTHAM C.P.[p]	..	..	..	..	..	..	..	..	..	..	..	..	..	..	694
WALTHAM ON THE WOLDS A.P. and C.P.	440	512	622	653	768	732	672	623	595	547	538	543	484	510	See Waltham C.P.[p]
WALTON ham.	See Kimcote A.P. and Knaptoft A.P.					..	..	..	..	..	..	..	..	..	..
WALTON IN KNAPTOFT C.P.	Hamlet of Knaptoft A.P., q.v.								174	208	See Kimcote and Walton C.P.[q]				..
WALTON, ISLEY C.P.	Chapelry of Kegworth A.P., q.v.								26	42	43	36	41	57	See Isley cum Langley C.P.[r]
WALTON ON THE WOLDS A.P. and C.P.	249	222	289	289	285	260	221*	240	227	179	192	225	231	229	257

(a) The whole of Knoll and Bassett House C.P. was transferred to Thurlaston in 1909.
(b) The population of Normanton Turville was included in that of Thurlaston township in 1811.
(c) North Thurmaston and South Thurmaston C.P.s were united in 1903 to form Thurmaston C.P. which was thus coextensive with the U.D.
(d) Part of Thurmaston U.D. (pop. nil in 1921) was transferred to Barkby in 1914.
(e) Thurmaston U.D. was dissolved in 1935. Part of its constituent C.P. remained Thurmaston C.P., while the remainder (pop. 1,127 in 1931) was transferred to Leicester C.B.
(f) In 1935 part of Thurnby (pop. 88 in 1931) was transferred to Leicester C.B., and the whole of Bushby was transferred to Thurnby.
(g) Part of Whatborough liberty was said to be in Loddington A.P. 1811–21, but from 1831 it was all said to be in Tilton and has been treated here as if it had always been in this parish.
(h) The whole of Halstead C.P. was transferred to Tilton in 1935.
(i) No return was apparently made for Keythorpe in 1801, so that the population of the whole of Tugby A.P. cannot be shown.
(j) The whole of Gopsall, Norton juxta Twycross, and Orton on the Hill C.P.s were transferred to Twycross in 1935.
(k) Twyford and Thorpe C.P. was formed in 1936 out of the whole of Thorpe Satchville and Twyford C.P.s.
(l) In 1877 a detached part of Monks Kirby (Warws.) (pop. 4 in 1881), including the Manor House, was transferred to Ullesthorpe C.P. and became part of Leics.
(m) Part of Wibtoft (Warws.) (pop. nil in 1931) was transferred to Leics. administrative county and Ullesthorpe C.P. in 1935.
(n) In 1884 part of Newtown Linford (pop. nil in 1891) was transferred to Ulverscroft, and Lea Wood (pop. nil in 1891) was transferred from Bradgate Park to Ulverscroft.
(o) The whole of Upton was transferred to Sheepy C.P. on its formation in 1935.
(p) Waltham C.P. was formed in 1936 out of the whole of Waltham on the Wolds and part of Thorpe Arnold (pop. 128 in 1931).
(q) Walton in Knaptoft (pop. 152 in 1901) became part of Kimcote and Walton C.P. on its formation in 1898.
(r) Isley Walton became part of Isley cum Langley C.P. on its formation in 1936.

POPULATION TABLE, 1801–1951 (*continued*)

	1801	*1811*	*1821*	*1831*	*1841*	*1851*	*1861*	*1871*	*1881*	*1891*	*1901*	*1911*	*1921*	*1931*	*1951*
WANLIP A.P. and C.P.	103	126	128	91	122	137	117	123	108	91	110	96	104	103	88
WARTNABY C.P.	Chapelry of Rothley A.P., q.v.								165	103[a]	86	89	127	99	See Ab Kettleby C.P.[b]
WELBY C.P.	Township of Melton Mowbray A.P., q.v.								55	51	38	70	107	96	..[c]
WELHAM A.P. and C.P.	78	75	74	73	66	68	65	73	68	60[d]	59	61	44	39	40
WELLSBOROUGH AND TEMPLE HALL E.P.P.	68	70	105	28	See Sibson A.P.[e]		..	..	..	..	..	..	..	..	..
WELLSBOROUGH	45	..	..	..	..	..	..	..	..	..	..	..	..	..	..
TEMPLE HALL	23	..	..	..	..	..	..	..	..	..	..	..	..	..	..
WESTRILL AND STARMORE E.P.P. and C.P.	27	31	6	7	8	4	3	11	15	22	8	5	nil	nil	15
WHATBOROUGH C.P.	Liberty of Tilton A.P., q.v.								19	19	12	13	11	19	15
WHATTON, LONG A.P. and C.P.	612	782	820	855	842	838	779	756	702	638	537	571	604	587	1,136[f]
WHETSTONE A.P. and C.P.	598	732	883	903	956	986	1,077	1,088	1,186	1,117	1,113	1,386	1,388	1,403	1,466
WHITEFRIARS	See Leicester, Augustine Friars E.P.P. and C.P.						..	..	..	..	..	..	..	..	..
WHITWICK A.P.	2,206	2,270	2,858	3,368	4,286	4,956	6,439*	7,265	..	..	..	..	..	..	..
WHITWICK	817	895	1,146	1,552*	2,310	2,836	3,759	4,277*	See Whitwick U.D. and C.P.				..	..	..
SWANNINGTON tnp.	488	427	541	549	744	822	1,276	1,586*	See Swannington C.P.			..	..	..	..
THRINGSTONE tnp.	901	948	1,171	1,267	1,232	1,298	1,404	1,402	See Thringstone C.P.			..	..	..	..
WHITWICK U.D. and C.P.	Part of Whitwick A.P., q.v.								3,881	4,564	See Coalville U.D.[g]			..	..
WIGSTON U.D.[h]	..	..	..	..	..	..	..	..	..	..	8,404	8,650	8,595	11,389[i]	15,457[j]
WIGSTON MAGNA C.P.	..	..	..	..	..	..	..	..	..	..	8,404	8,650	8,595	11,389	15,457[j]
WIGSTON, EAST C.P.[h]	..	..	..	..	..	..	..	..	..	..	102	87	96	119	See Wigston U.D.[j]
WIGSTON MAGNA A.P. C.P.	1,658	1,901	2,089	2,174	2,189*	2,441	2,521	2,638	4,299	7,013	See Wigston U.D. and Wigston, East C.P.[h]				
WIGSTON MAGNA U.D.	See Wigston U.D.			..	..	..	..	..	..	..	..	..	..	..	..
WIGSTON PARVA C.P.	Township of Claybrooke A.P., q.v.								65	47	49	52	50	38	40[k]
WILLESLEY C.P.[l]	..	..	..	..	..	..	..	..	..	..	69	40	76	80	..[m]
WILLOUGHBY WATERLESS A.P. and C.P.	272	278	322	327	348	361	372	377	316	279	244	207	210	206	213
WILSON ham.	See Breedon on the Hill A.P.				..	..	..	..	..	..	..	..	..	..	..
WILSTHORPE	See Sawley with Wilsthorpe C.P.				..	..	..	..	..	..	..	..	..	..	..
WISTOW A.P.	201	225	307	298	296	261	247	251	..	..	..	..	..	..	..
WISTOW	15	11	9	19	18	17	40	46	See Wistow C.P.			..	..	..	..
NEWTON HARCOURT tnp.	186	214	298	279	278	244	207	205	See Newton Harcourt C.P.				..	..	..
WISTOW C.P.	Part of Wistow A.P., q.v.								49	36	61	54	49	50	211[n]
WITHCOTE A.P. and C.P.	52	50	51	32	30	40	45	62	41	44	49	46	47	53	39
WITHERLEY A.P.	..[o]	417	471	492	509	540	528	453	..	..	..	..	..	..	..
WITHERLEY	383	334	396	416	425	474	450	407	See Witherley C.P.			..	..	..	..
ATTERTON ham.	..[o]	83	75	76	84	66	78	46	See Atterton C.P.			..	..	..	..
WITHERLEY C.P.	Part of Witherley A.P., q.v.								457	455[p]	493	482	429	468	968[q]
WOODHOUSE C.P.[r]	Chapelry and liberty of Barrow upon Soar A.P., q.v.								1,288	1,370[s]	1,342	1,458	1,603	1,435	2,049[t]
WOODHOUSE EAVES ham.	See Barrow upon Soar A.P.				..	..	..	..	..	..	..	..	..	..	..

(a) Landike Lane (pop. 8 in 1891) was transferred from Wartnaby to Holwell in 1884.

(b) The whole of Wartnaby was transferred to Ab Kettleby in 1936.

(c) Welby C.P. was dissolved in 1935. Part of it (pop. 9 in 1931) was transferred to Melton Mowbray U.D. and part (pop. 87 in 1931) to Asfordby .

(d) Caudwell (pop. nil in 1891) was transferred from Thorpe Langton to Welham in 1885.

(e) Wellsborough and Temple Hall were returned as extra-parochial until 1841, when they were said to be a hamlet of Sibson.

(f) The whole of Diseworth and parts of Hathern (pop. nil in 1931) and of Shepshed U.D. (pop. 34 in 1931) were transferred to Long Whatton in 1936.

(g) In 1892 Whitwick U.D. was dissolved and its constituent C.P. was transferred to Coalville U.D., which was then formed, as Whitwick C.P.

(h) Part of Wigston Magna C.P. was constituted an U.D. in 1894. The remaining part of the parish was created East Wigston C.P. so that Wigston Magna C.P. was coextensive with the U.D., which was renamed Wigston U.D. in 1930.

(i) Part of Glen Parva (pop. 507 in 1921) was transferred to Wigston Magna U.D. and C.P. in 1928.

(j) In 1935 and 1936 parts of Wigston U.D. (pop. respectively 648, nil in 1931) were transferred to Leicester C.B. and Oadby U.D., and the whole of East Wigston and parts of Blaby, Countesthorpe, and Lubbesthorpe (pop. respectively nil, nil, 45 in 1931) were transferred to Wigston U.D. and Wigston Magna C.P. In 1939 part of Leicester C.B. (pop. nil in 1931) was transferred to Wigston U.D. and Wigston Magna C.P., and part of Wigston U.D. and Wigston Magna C.P. (pop. nil in 1931) was transferred to Leicester C.B.

(k) In 1935 part of Copston Magna (Warws.) (pop. 2 in 1931) was transferred to Leics. administrative county and Wigston Parva C.P.

(l) Willesley C.P. was transferred from Derbys. to Leics. administrative county in 1897.

(m) Willesley C.P. was dissolved in 1936. Part of it (pop. 80 in 1931) was transferred to Ashby de la Zouch U.D. and the remainder (pop. nil in 1931 was divided between Measham and Oakthorpe and Donisthorpe.

(n) Part of Newton Harcourt (pop. 142 in 1931) was transferred to Wistow in 1936.

(o) No return was apparently made for Atterton in 1801, but the return for Witherley may have included Atterton.

(p) Part of Atterton (pop. nil in 1891) was transferred to Witherley in 1885.

(q) In 1935 part of Witherley (pop. 78 in 1931) was transferred to Mancetter C.P. in Warws. administrative county, and the whole of Atterton and Ratcliffe Culey C.P.s and part of Fenny Drayton (pop. 107 in 1931) were transferred to Witherley.

(r) Woodhouse C.P. at first consisted of Beaumanor liberty and the chapelry of Woodhouse (including Woodhouse Eaves and Alderman's Haw), except for Maplewell Longdale, which formed a separate C.P.

(s) The whole of Maplewell Longdale (pop. 19 in 1891) was transferred to Woodhouse in 1884.

(t) In 1935 parts of Woodhouse (pop. nil, 79, 54 respectively in 1931) were transferred to Quorndon, Loughborough M.B., and Charley, and part of Woodthorpe (pop. nil in 1931) was transferred to Woodhouse.

POPULATION TABLE, 1801–1951 (*continued*)

	1801	1811	1821	1831	1841	1851	1861	1871	1881	1891	1901	1911	1921	1931	1951
WOODTHORPE C.P.[a]	..	..	..	..	..	..	..	..	..	58	56	56	57	53	..[b]
WORTHINGTON C.P.	Chapelry of Breedon on the Hill A.P., q.v.								970	928	953	1,016	1,002	1,088	1,213[c]
WYCOMB AND CHADWELL C.P.	Chapelry of Rothley A.P., q.v.								107	89	93	103	94	106	See Scalford C.P.[d]
WYFORDBY	See Brentingby and Wyfordby A.P. and C.P.						..	..	..	..	..	..	..	..	..
WYKIN ham.	See Hinckley A.P.			..	..	..	..	..	..	..	..	..	..	..	..
WYMESWOLD A.P. and C.P.	788	1,002	1,061	1,276*	1,270	1,235	1,209	1,113*	936	863	770	777	777	755	765
WYMONDHAM A.P. and C.P.	301	437	624	746	766*	800	851	776	655	905	620	626	610	565	710[e]

(a) Woodthorpe was formerly a hamlet of Loughborough A.P., and was included in Loughborough U.D. When Loughborough U.D. was replaced by Loughborough M.B. in 1888, Woodthorpe was not included in the new boundaries.
(b) Woodthorpe C.P. was dissolved in 1935. Part of it (pop. 47 in 1931) was transferred to Loughborough M.B., part (pop. 6 in 1931) to Quorndon, and part (pop. nil in 1931) to Woodhouse.
(c) In 1936 part of Worthington (pop. 22 in 1931) was transferred to Coleorton and parts of Breedon on the Hill and Thringstone (pop. respectively 77, 8 in 1931) were transferred to Worthington.
(d) The whole of Wycomb and Chadwell was transferred to Scalford in 1936.
(e) The whole of Edmondthorpe was transferred to Wymondham in 1936.

COMMENTARY

The *Census Reports* contain notes which either explain such substantial changes in population as could not be ascribed to alterations in boundaries or comment upon the occupations or condition of the population when these are unusual or of particular interest. The notes occur with varying frequency and seem to follow no particular plan—in 1881 and 1891, for instance, they were virtually discontinued, but where they occur they have been copied, with verbal alterations, in this list. The presence of a note of this nature relating to any return is indicated in the Population Table by an asterisk.

1811

LEICESTERSHIRE. The population of the whole county included the First Regiment of Local Militia (total, including officers: 957) which was assembled for 14 days' exercise on 15 May 1811. It was drawn from the borough of Leicester and its vicinity, extending into all the hundreds except Framland.

1821

APPLEBY. See note for 1831.

BARROW UPON SOAR. The House of Industry was supported by only 8 parishes in 1811, but by 26 in 1821.

BELVOIR. Except for an innkeeper and his family the inhabitants were chiefly servants with their families, and mechanics, employed by the Duke of Rutland and occupying the detached offices belonging to Belvoir Castle.

DRAYTON. Decrease attributed to an inclosure and to the putting out of many apprentices.

HEATHER. A coal-pit had been opened and several new houses were inhabited by colliers.

HINCKLEY. The population was said to have increased from 1811 to 1815 and to have declined afterwards, in consequence of the cessation of trade with America. For the same reason the number of paupers had increased and they were very burdensome to the rest of the inhabitants.

LEICESTER, ST. MARGARET. Increase partly attributed to the return of discharged soldiers together with a continuance of public tranquillity.

LEICESTER, NEWARKE. There was a decline in the number of females between 1811 and 1821, which was attributed to the removal of a large boarding school. There was also a large proportion of old persons, owing to the presence of a hospital containing an average of 40 aged men and women.

LOUGHBOROUGH. Increase attributed to the sale in lots of a considerable estate, to the inclosure of Charnwood Forest, and to the establishment of a lace manufactory about 12 years before.

LUTTERWORTH. Included one woman over 100 years old.

MELTON MOWBRAY. Increase attributed chiefly to a large hunting establishment being kept in the town and neighbourhood.

QUORNDON. Increase attributed to a lace manufactory recently established there.

RATBY. Increase attributed to the increase of framework-knitting.

RAVENSTONE. The hospital for Coleorton and Ravenstone parishes and Swannington township accounted for a considerable number of aged females.

SAPCOTE. Included 55 persons in a house of industry.

SOUTH FIELDS. There was an excess of females owing to the great number of servants among whom there were only 2 men. In 1811 there were apparently only 6 houses here, but in 1821 there were 182 occupied and 14 being built.

SHEPSHED. Increase attributed to the inclosure of Charnwood Forest and to the framework-knitting trade, which employed a large part of the population.

THORPE SATCHVILLE. Included one woman over 100 years old.

WOODHOUSE. The increase of 174 persons, and of 49 families employed in agriculture, was attributed to the inclosure of a considerable tract of waste land. The increase would have been still greater but for the decline of framework-knitting.

1831

APPLEBY. The apparent decrease attributed to an erroneous return in 1821.

BARKESTONE AND PLUNGAR. The families of the labouring classes in these parishes were greatly benefited by the employment of women and children in spotting and flowering lace.

BARROW UPON SOAR. 92 labourers were employed in stone quarries.

BELVOIR. See note for 1821, which was repeated.

BREEDON ON THE HILL. 59 labourers were employed in lime-works and 54 in coal-pits.

BUCKMINSTER. Increase attributed to the presence of a number of Irish labourers employed by Lord Huntingtower.

COLEORTON. Decrease attributed to the demolition of several houses. 41 labourers were employed in collieries.

GLENFIELD. 39 labourers were employed in excavating a tunnel and 41 in building a railway.

HARBOROUGH, MARKET. Included 84 travellers (principally vagrant tramps), 71 of whom were adult males.

HEATHER. 13 labourers were employed in coal-pits.

IBSTOCK. 12 labourers were employed in collieries.

KEYHAM. Decrease attributed to the removal of a ladies' school.

LEICESTER, BLACKFRIARS. Increase attributed to the increase in building and also to the erection of a lying-in hospital.

LEICESTER, ST. MARGARET. Increase attributed to the extension of factories. Railways were mentioned as employing a few labourers.

LOUGHBOROUGH. Increase attributed to the extension of the lace manufacture and the shoe trade.

MELTON MOWBRAY. Increase attributed to a large fox-hunting establishment in the town and neighbourhood, which caused the residence and settlement of a number of grooms and their families.

PLUNGAR. See Barkestone.

SAPCOTE. Included 70 persons in a poor-house belonging to 25 united parishes.

SEAL, NETHER AND OVER. 24 labourers were employed in collieries adjacent to Nether Seal and 5 in stone quarries.

SOUTH FIELDS. Increase attributed to the healthy situation of the place.

THORNTON. 6 men were employed on a railway.

WHITWICK. 72 labourers were employed in coal-pits and stone quarries.

WYMESWOLD. Increase attributed to the introduction of lace-making.

1841

APPLEBY. Included 11 persons in the endowed grammar school.

ASHBY DE LA ZOUCH. Included 140 persons in the union workhouse, 4 in the endowed Blue-coat School, 19 in the grammar school, and 15 in barns and tents.

BARROW UPON SOAR. Included 70 persons attending the annual feast. The 1851 *Report* also says that the population in 1841 included several persons employed on the works of the Midland Railway.

BELVOIR. All houses were detached offices attached to the castle, except that occupied by an innkeeper and his family.

BREEDON ON THE HILL. 8 persons had emigrated since 31 Dec. 1840.

BUCKMINSTER. Decrease attributed to removal of a number of Irish labourers employed here in 1831.

COLEORTON. Including 16 persons in the endowed school and hospital. Decrease attributed partly to the removal of the poor-house and partly to the demolition of about 35 cottages.

GLEN, GREAT. Included 34 persons in the Billesdon Union Workhouse.

HARBOROUGH, MARKET. Included 68 persons in the Market Harborough Union Workhouse.

HINCKLEY. Including 195 persons in the Hinckley Union Workhouse and 9 in barges.

Leicester, All Saints. Included 41 persons in the borough house of correction.

Leicester, Augustine Friars. Included 48 persons in boats on the Soar.

Leicester, St. Margaret. Included 319 persons in the Leicester Union Workhouse.

Leicester, St. Martin. Included 23 persons in the borough jail, which was partly in St. Martin's and partly in All Saints' parish.

Leicester, St. Mary. Included 100 persons in the county jail, 110 in the county house of correction, 122 in the Leicester Infirmary, and 118 in the county lunatic asylum.

Loughborough. Included 41 soldiers in the barracks, 163 persons in the union workhouse, 4 in the house of detention, and 12 in barns.

Melton Mowbray. Included 109 persons in the Melton Mowbray Union Workhouse and 14 in barges. Increase attributed chiefly to a large fox-hunting establishment.

Narborough. Increase attributed partly to the establishment of 2 boarding schools.

Normanton le Heath. Increase attributed to the visit of strangers to the annual feast.

Norton juxta Twycross. Included 7 persons in tents.

Osgathorpe. Included 11 persons in the Residence for Clergymen's Widows.

Packington. Increase attributed to the opening of a colliery.

Rothley. Included 108 persons in the Barrow upon Soar Union Workhouse.

Snarestone. Included 4 persons in the endowed school.

Stapleford. Included 40 persons at the annual feast.

Thrussington. Included 81 visitors at the annual feast.

Tilton: Included 8 persons in tents.

Wigston Magna. Included 12 persons in the lunatic asylum.

Wymondham. 36 persons were said to be temporarily absent.

1851

Market Harborough Registration District (see *Census Report* for constituent parishes). Decrease in some parishes attributed to the facts that fewer hands than formerly were employed in agriculture and that the unemployed had gone to the manufacturing towns.

Lutterworth and other parishes in Lutterworth Registration District (see *Census Report* for constituent parishes). Decrease attributed partly to employment afforded in 1841 to workmen on the Midland Railway and to building having ceased, and partly to emigration.

Waltham Registration Sub-District (see *Census Report* for constituent parishes). Decrease in some parishes attributed chiefly to emigration and to removals in search of employment.

Wigston Registration Sub-District (see *Census Report* for constituent parishes). The removal of framework-knitters and others in search of better employment had caused the population of several parishes to decrease.

Ashby de la Zouch. Included 188 persons in the union workhouse.

Aylestone. Several cottages had been pulled down and few rebuilt.

Bescaby. Since 1841 a barn had been converted into a dwelling-house, in which a large family resided.

Billesdon. A new union workhouse, containing 40 persons, had been built since 1841.

Blaby. Several large old houses had been pulled down and their places supplied by smaller ones. The population had slightly decreased through the ravages of smallpox in 1848.

Bosworth, Market. Several small tenements had been pulled down and not rebuilt: most of them were formerly inhabited by framework-knitters who had removed to other parts. The union workhouse contained 64 persons.

Bowden, Great. Including 84 persons in Market Harborough Union Workhouse.

Dalby, Old. Decrease attributed to emigration and to the fact that fewer indoor farm servants were kept than formerly.

Diseworth. Decrease attributed to the employment of fewer agricultural labourers and to emigration.

Donington, Castle. Decrease attributed mainly to the decline in lace manufacture which had caused many persons to seek employment elsewhere, and others to emigrate.

Enderby. The union workhouse contained 65 persons.

Garendon. The principal family usually resident at Garendon was absent when the census was taken.

Glen, Great. The Billesdon Union Workhouse had been pulled down since 1841 and a new one erected in Billesdon.

Gopsall. Gopsall Hall was occupied by a larger establishment than formerly.

Harborough, Market. The recent stoppage of a carpet factory had caused many families to remove to Yorkshire in search of employment.

Hathern. Many journeymen stocking-makers had left the parish since 1841.

HEATHER. Increase attributed to the opening of a coal-pit.

HINCKLEY. Decrease attributed to removals in search of employment and to emigration caused by depression in the stocking manufacture. The union workhouse contained 118 persons.

KEGWORTH. Decrease attributed to the temporary employment of labourers in 1841 and to emigration.

LEICESTER, ALL SAINTS. Included 56 persons in the borough house of correction, and 35 persons in a temporary workhouse.

LEICESTER, ST. MARGARET. Included 143 persons in the Leicester Union Workhouse.

LEICESTER, ST. MARY. Included 201 persons in the county jail and house of correction, 132 in the Leicester Infirmary, 268 in the county lunatic asylum, and 120 in a temporary workhouse.

LOUGHBOROUGH. Included 38 soldiers in barracks and 124 persons in the Loughborough Union Workhouse.

LUTTERWORTH. Included 74 persons in the union workhouse.

MELTON MOWBRAY. Included 151 persons in Melton Mowbray Union Workhouse.

NARBOROUGH. Several large families had left the parish.

RATBY. Increase attributed to the progress of framework-knitting.

ROTHLEY. The Barrow upon Soar Union Workhouse in Rothley contained 76 persons.

SEAGRAVE. The school at Seagrave Rectory had been given up since 1841.

SHOBY. Decrease attributed to the death of a principal occupier of the land, whose successor had a smaller family and establishment.

SYSTON. The Midland Counties Railway had a station in the vicinity of Syston and there was a great improvement in the parish, and consequent increase of population.

THORPE ACRE AND DISHLEY. Some houses had been pulled down and their late occupants had left the place.

1861

From 1861 the notes to the main population table seldom contain information about persons in workhouses and other public institutions. Separate tables supply these figures in the *Reports*, and no attempt has been made to include this information here, unless it is included in the notes to the parish tables.

APPLEBY. Decrease attributed to the closing of a large public school and to migration.

AYLESTONE. Decrease attributed to the want of sufficient cottage accommodation.

BIRSTALL. Decrease attributed partly to the Hall being unoccupied and to the removal of a school.

BREEDON ON THE HILL. Decrease attributed to the depressed state of trade in the adjoining town of Melbourne.

BROUGHTON, NETHER. Included 38 gipsies.

COLEORTON. Increase attributed to the opening of a coal-pit.

COSSINGTON. Increase attributed to an addition in the number of scholars at Ratcliffe College and at a ladies' seminary.

DONINGTON, CASTLE. Decrease attributed to migration.

KNIGHTON. Increase attributed to proximity to Leicester.

PACKINGTON. Decrease attributed to the closing of a school and to migration to the colliery districts.

QUORNDON. Decrease attributed to migration owing to want of employment.

SAPCOTE AND STONEY STANTON. Decrease attributed partly to migration to the manufacturing towns and partly to emigration.

SHILTON, EARL. Decrease attributed to migration owing to introduction of machinery in the stocking manufacture.

STANTON, STONEY. See Sapcote.

THORPE ACRE AND DISHLEY. Decrease attributed to migration.

THURLASTON. Decrease attributed to the removal of families to Leicester to work at a shoe manufactory.

THURMASTON, NORTH AND SOUTH. Decrease attributed to migration to the manufacturing towns.

WALTON ON THE WOLDS. Decrease attributed to migration.

WHITWICK. Increase attributed to the establishment of a reformatory and to the opening of a colliery in Swannington.

1871

ANSTEY. Increase attributed to the development of the shoe trade and stocking-framework-knitting and to the increased demand for labour at the granite quarries.

APPLEBY. Decrease attributed to the demolition of a number of cottages.

ARNESBY. Decrease attributed to removals to Leicester and other towns.

ASHBY DE LA ZOUCH. Increase attributed to the presence of a number of persons constructing a railway.

BARKESTONE. Decrease attributed to migration and emigration in consequence of want of employment.

BARROW UPON SOAR. Increase attributed to the opening of lime-works where high wages were obtained.

BELGRAVE AND SOUTH THURMASTON. Increase attributed to proximity to Leicester.

BILLESDON. Decrease attributed mainly to the migration of several large families.

BROUGHTON, NETHER. Decrease attributed to migration in search of employment and to the fact that a large number of gipsies were included in 1861.

BURBAGE. Decrease attributed to migration to the manufacturing towns.

BURROUGH ON THE HILL, BURTON LAZARS, LITTLE DALBY, MELTON MOWBRAY, SOMERBY, AND THORPE SATCHVILLE. Increase attributed partly to the presence of a large number of strangers attending the steeplechases.

BURTON LAZARS. See Burrough on the Hill.

DALBY, LITTLE. See Burrough on the Hill.

DISEWORTH. Decrease attributed to migration in search of employment.

GILMORTON. Decrease attributed to removals to Leicester and other towns.

HARBOROUGH, MARKET. There was said to be abundance of employment here, which had caused the population of Little Bowden (Northants.) to increase.

HEATHER. Increase attributed to the presence of a number of men constructing a railway.

HINCKLEY. Increase in population attributed to the improvement in the hosiery trade, and the increase of inhabited houses to the establishment of building societies.

HOUGHTON ON THE HILL. Decrease attributed mainly to migration.

HUGGLESCOTE AND DONINGTON, WHITWICK, AND SWANNINGTON. Increase attributed to the sale of large quantities of land in small building allotments and the erection thereon of dwellings for colliers and others.

HUMBERSTONE. The Leicester borough lunatic asylum containing 317 persons had been erected here since 1861.

IBSTOCK. Increase attributed to the working of collieries in the vicinity.

KNIGHTON. Increase attributed to proximity to Leicester.

LEICESTER. 'The old manufactures in Leicester have not increased, but have rather diminished during the last ten years. About the year 1861 the strike at Northampton caused the removal of a large portion of its shoe trade to Leicester, and the depression at Coventry a year or two later brought a large number of ribbon weavers from that city and neighbourhood who were absorbed by the elastic web trade. Prior to 1861 the principal manufacture was hosiery. Since that time new trades have been introduced. The shoe trade has brought sewing machine and nail makers, and others have arisen in connexion with the elastic web and other trades. There has been a large immigration from other places, and it is still going on. Houses are being rapidly built, and are no sooner finished than they are occupied. There is a small extension beyond the municipal limits, but this is mainly by the erection of villa residences, occupied by the employers of labour.' (*Census Report*, 1871).

LEIRE. Decrease attributed to the demolition of a number of houses and to the migration of young persons into the towns.

LUTTERWORTH. Decrease attributed to want of railway accommodation.

MELTON MOWBRAY. See Burrough on the Hill.

MEREVALE. Decrease attributed to diminished demand for manual labour on farms in consequence of the introduction of machinery.

MOUNTSORREL NORTH END. Increase attributed to the demand for labour at the granite quarries.

QUORNDON. Decrease attributed to the almost complete removal of the hosiery manufacture.

ROTHLEY. Increase attributed to the improved state of stocking-framework-knitting and to the demand for labour at the granite quarries.

SAPCOTE AND SHARNFORD. Decrease attributed to migration to the manufacturing towns.

SHARNFORD. See Sapcote.

SHENTON. Increase attributed to the presence of a large number of men constructing a railway.

SILEBY. Increase attributed to the opening of a small factory, and to the introduction of the shoe trade.

SOMERBY. See Burrough on the Hill.

STANTON, STONEY. Decrease attributed to migration to the manufacturing towns.

SWANNINGTON. See Hugglescote and Donington.

SYSTON. Increase attributed to the facilities for railway communication with Leicester.

THORPE SATCHVILLE. See Burrough on the Hill.

THURLASTON. Decrease attributed to removals of families to Leicester to work at a shoe manufactory.

THURMASTON, SOUTH. See Belgrave.

WHITWICK. See Hugglescote and Donington.

WYCOMB AND CHADWELL. Decrease attributed to migration in search of employment.

WYMESWOLD. Decrease attributed to migration to manufacturing towns.

1881

DADLINGTON. Decrease attributed to absence of a number of persons who were building a railway in 1871.
GLEN PARVA. Increase attributed to the establishment of a military centre here since 1871.
HUNGARTON, KEYHAM, AND SCRAPTOFT. Increase attributed to the presence of a number of labourers building a railway.
KEYHAM. See Hungarton.
SCRAPTOFT. See Hungarton.

1891

EDMONDTHORPE. Included a considerable number of men constructing a new line of railway.
GLEN PARVA. A considerable proportion of the population was in the Glen Parva barracks. Decrease mainly attributed to the decrease of the number in the barracks.
LEICESTER C.B.; HUMBERSTONE, WEST, AND LEICESTER ABBEY. A considerable proportion of the population was enumerated in institutions.

1901

ANSTEY. Increase attributed mainly to the establishment of shoe factories.
ASFORDBY. Increase attributed mainly to the erection of blast furnaces at which many workmen were employed.
BOWDEN, GREAT. Increase attributed mainly to the development of factories in the vicinity.
BROUGHTON ASTLEY. Increase attributed mainly to the establishment of a hosiery factory.
COUNTESTHORPE. A considerable proportion of the population was in the Leicester Parish Cottage Homes.
GILROES. Increase due to the opening since 1891 of the Borough of Leicester Hospital for Infectious Diseases, in which a considerable proportion of the population was enumerated.
GLEN PARVA. A considerable proportion of the population was enumerated in the barracks.
KIRBY MUXLOE. Increase attributed mainly to proximity to Leicester.
RATBY. A considerable proportion of the population was in the Leicester School Board Industrial School for Boys.

1911

ASFORDBY. Increase attributed mainly to the erection of a steel foundry and to the extension of iron-smelting furnaces.
BAGWORTH, DESFORD, IBSTOCK, NEWBOLD VERDON, STANTON UNDER BARDON, THORNTON. Increase attributed mainly to colliery development.
BOWDEN, GREAT AND LITTLE. Increase attributed mainly to industrial development.
COALVILLE. Increase attributed mainly to the extension of railway wagon works and to colliery development.
DESFORD. See Bagworth.
EVINGTON. Increase attributed mainly to the erection of the Leicester Parish Infirmary.
GLEN PARVA. Decrease attributed mainly to the decrease in the number of troops stationed at the military depot.
HUGGLESCOTE AND DONINGTON. Increase attributed mainly to colliery development.
IBSTOCK. See Bagworth.
MELTON MOWBRAY. Increase attributed mainly to the development of the woollen and shoe-manufacturing industries.
NARBOROUGH. Increase attributed mainly to the erection since 1901 of the Leicester and Rutland Counties Lunatic Asylum.
NEWBOLD VERDON. See Bagworth.
OADBY. Increase attributed mainly to proximity to Leicester.
RAVENSTONE WITH SNIBSTON. Increase attributed mainly to colliery development.
STANTON UNDER BARDON. See Bagworth.
THORNTON. See Bagworth.

1921

BUSHBY. Increase attributed mainly to residential development.
COSSINGTON. Increase attributed mainly to the occupation of Ratcliffe College (168 persons).
DONINGTON, CASTLE. Increase attributed to the temporary presence of soldiers in camp.
GILROES. Increase attributed mainly to the increased number of patients in the isolation hospital.

HOLT, NEVILL. Increase attributed mainly to the presence of pupils at a preparatory school established since 1911.

KILWORTH, SOUTH. Increase attributed mainly to the development of a garden village.

LEICESTER FRITH. Increase attributed mainly to the alteration of a large private house by the Ministry of Pensions for the occupation of ex-soldiers.

OADBY. Increase in St. Peter's Ward attributed mainly to the temporary presence of soldiers in camp.

1931

ASFORDBY. Increase attributed mainly to the building of houses for the purpose of accommodating workmen and to other residential developments.

BARWELL, BIRSTALL, BRAUNSTONE, BUSHBY. Increase attributed mainly to residential development.

COSSINGTON. Decrease attributed mainly to a college being on vacation at the time of the census.

COUNTESTHORPE, CROFT, ELMESTHORPE, ENDERBY, EVINGTON, GLENFIELD, GLENFIELD FRITH, GLEN PARVA. Increase attributed mainly to residential development.

HOLT, NEVILL. Decrease attributed to the fact that a school was on vacation at the time of the census.

HUMBERSTONE, KIRBY MUXLOE. Increase attributed mainly to residential development.

LEICESTER. Increase in Aylestone Ward attributed mainly to residential development.

LEICESTER FOREST EAST. Increase attributed mainly to residential development.

LEICESTER FRITH. Increase attributed to the conversion of a Ministry of Pensions Hospital into a mental hospital.

LUBBESTHORPE, NANPANTAN, NARBOROUGH, NEW PARKS, NEWTOWN LINFORD, QUENIBOROUGH, SCRAPTOFT, SYSTON, THURMASTON. Increase attributed mainly to residential development.

THE HUNDREDS AND THEIR CONSTITUENT PARISHES

These are taken from the *Census Reports* of 1831 and 1841. Extra-parochial places are included.

Framland

Barkestone
Belvoir
Bescaby
Bottesford
Branston
Brentingby and Wyfordby
Broughton, Nether
Buckminster
Burton Lazars
Clawson, Long
Coston
Croxton Kerrial
Dalby, Little
Eastwell
Eaton
Edmondthorpe
Garthorpe
Goadby Marwood
Harby
Harston
Hose
Kettleby, Ab
Kirby Bellars
Knipton
Melton Mowbray
Muston
Overton, Cold
Plungar
Redmile
Saltby
Saxby
Scalford
Somerby
Sproxton
Stapleford
Stathern
Stonesby
Sysonby
Thorpe Arnold
Waltham on the Wolds
Withcote
Wymondham

Gartree

Billesdon
Blaston
Bosworth, Husbands
Bowden, Great
Bringhurst
Burrough on the Hill
Burton Overy
Carlton Curlieu
Cranoe
Evington
Fleckney
Foxton
Galby
Glen, Great
Glooston
Gumley
Hallaton
Horninghold
Houghton on the Hill
Hungarton (part of—i.e. Baggrave and Ingarsby)
Kibworth Beauchamp

Knaptoft (part of—i.e. Mowsley)
Knossington
Langton, Church
Laughton
Lubenham
Medbourne
Norton, King's
Noseley
Owston and Newbold
Pickwell
Saddington
St. Margaret, Leicester (part of the parish, called Bishop's Fee, was said in 1831 to be 'locally situated in Gartree Hundred', but was never otherwise mentioned as being outside the borough)
Scraptoft
Shangton
Slawston
Stockerston
Stoke Dry (the part in Leics.—i.e. Holyoaks)
Stonton Wyville
Theddingworth (the part in Leics.)
Thurnby
Tilton (part of—i.e. Marefield)
Tugby (part of—i.e. Keythorpe)
Welham
Wistow

Goscote, East

Allexton
Asfordby
Ashby Folville
Barkby
Barrow upon Soar (part of—i.e. Barrow upon Soar itself)
Beeby
Belgrave (part of—i.e. Belgrave itself and South Thurmaston)
Brooksby
Cossington
Croxton, South
Dalby, Great
Dalby, Old (or Dalby on the Wolds)
Frisby on the Wreak
Gaddesby
Grimston
Hoby
Humberstone
Hungarton (part of—i.e. Hungarton itself and Quenby)
Launde
Loddington
Lowesby
Norton, East
Prestwold
Queniborough
Ragdale
Ratcliffe on the Wreake
Rearsby
Rotherby
Rothley (part of—i.e. Keyham, Wartnaby, Wycomb, and Chadwell)
Saxelby
Seagrave
Shoby
Sileby
Skeffington
Syston
Thrussington
Tilton (part of—i.e. Tilton itself, Halstead, and Whatborough)
Tugby
Twyford
Walton on the Wolds
Wymeswold

Goscote, West

Anstey Pastures
Ashby de la Zouch
Barrow upon Soar (part of—i.e. Mountsorrel North End, Quorndon, and Woodhouse)
Beaumanor
Beaumont Leys
Belgrave (part of—i.e. Birstall)
Belton
Bradgate Park
Breedon on the Hill
Charley
Coleorton
Diseworth
Donington, Castle
Garendon
Gilroes
Hathern
Kegworth
Langley Priory
Leicester Abbey
Leicester Frith (or Shermans Grounds)
Lockington
Loughborough
Newtown Linford
Osgathorpe
Packington (the part in Leics.)
Ravenstone (the part in Leics.)
Rothley (part of—i.e. Rothley itself and Mountsorrel South End)
Rothley Temple
Seal, Nether and Over
Shepshed
Swepstone
Swithland
Thorpe Acre and Dishley
Thurcaston
Ulverscroft
Wanlip
Whatton, Long
Whitwick

POPULATION

Guthlaxton

Arnesby
Ashby Magna
Ashby Parva
Aylestone (part of—i.e. Aylestone itself and Glen Parva)
Bitteswell
Blaby
Broughton Astley
Bruntingthorpe
Castle View (said to be in the borough of Leicester from 1851 onwards)
Catthorpe
Claybrooke
Cosby
Cotesbach
Dunton Bassett
Foston
Frolesworth
Gilmorton
Kilby
Kilworth, North
Kilworth, South
Kimcote
Knaptoft (part of—i.e. Knaptoft itself, Shearsby and Walton)
Leire
Lutterworth
Misterton
Oadby
Peatling Magna
Peatling Parva
St. Margaret (part of—i.e. Knighton)
St. Mary (part of—i.e. South Fields, which was said to be in the borough of Leicester from 1851 onwards)
Shawell
Swinford
Westrill and Starmore
Whetstone
Wigston Magna
Willoughby Waterless

Sparkenhoe

Appleby (the part in Leics.)
Aston Flamville
Aylestone
Bardon
Barwell
Bosworth, Market
Cadeby
Congerstone
Croft
Desford
Drayton, Fenny
Elmesthorpe
Enderby
Glenfield
Glenfield Frith
Gopsall
Heather
Higham on the Hill
Hinckley (the part in Leics.—i.e. all except Hydes Pastures)
Ibstock
Kirby Frith
Kirkby Mallory
Knoll and Bassett House
Leicester Forest East
Leicester Forest West
Markfield
Merevale (the part in Leics.)
Mythe
Nailstone
Narborough
Newbold Verdon
Norton juxta Twycross
Orton on the Hill
Peckleton
Ratby
Sapcote
Shackerstone
Sharnford
Sheepy Magna
Sheepy Parva
Sibson
Snarestone
Stanton, Stoney
Thornton
Thurlaston
Twycross
Wellsborough and Temple Hall
Witherley

RURAL DISTRICTS AND THEIR CONSTITUENT PARISHES

No attempt has been made in this list to trace changes in the composition of civil parishes, or to show what happened to any parish when it ceased to form part of a rural district, unless it became part of another rural district. For such information the main population table and its notes must be consulted. An asterisk after the name of a parish indicates that it was removed from the rural district concerned to one in another county, under the Local Government Act 1894.

Ashby de la Zouch R.D.

Formed under the Public Health Act 1872.

Appleby (Leics. and Derbys.) until 1898: see Appleby Magna
Appleby Magna—formed 1898
Bardon

Blackfordby—dissolved 1936
Boundary (Derbys.)*
Calke (Derbys.)*
Chilcote—transferred from Tamworth R.D. 1895.
Coleorton
Hartshorn (Derbys.)*
Heather
Hugglescote and Donington—part transferred to Coalville U.D. 1892: remainder transferred to Bardon 1893
Measham
Normanton le Heath
Oakthorpe and Donisthorpe
Osgathorpe
Packington
Ravenstone—until 1884: see Ravenstone with Snibston
Ravenstone with Snibston—created 1884. Part in Ashby de la Zouch U.D. 1884–92 and part in Coalville U.D. 1892–4, but all in this R.D. from 1894
Seal, Nether and Over—removed on transference to Derbys. 1897
Smisby (Derbys.)*
Snarestone
Staunton Harold
Stretton en le Field
Swannington
Swepstone
Thringstone—dissolved 1936
Ticknall (Derbys.)*
Willesley—dissolved 1936
Worthington

Atherstone R.D.

Atherstone R.D. lay chiefly in Warwickshire but included the following Leicestershire parishes. All except Merevale, q.v., were transferred to Market Bosworth R.D. under the Local Government Act 1894.

Atterton
Drayton, Fenny
Merevale—the part which lay in Leics. Transferred to Orton on the Hill C.P. and Sheepy Magna C.P. in 1885
Ratcliffe Culey
Sheepy Magna
Sheepy Parva
Witherley

Barrow upon Soar R.D.

Formed under the Public Health Act 1872.

Anstey
Anstey Pastures—dissolved 1936
Barkby
Barkby Thorpe
Barrow upon Soar
Beaumont Leys—dissolved 1935
Beeby
Birstall
Bradgate Park—dissolved 1884
Burton on the Wolds—transferred from Loughborough R.D. 1936
Cossington
Cotes—transferred from Loughborough R.D. 1936
Cropston—dissolved 1935
Croxton, South
Gilroes—dissolved 1935
Hoton—transferred from Loughborough R.D. 1936
Leicester Abbey—transferred to Leicester C.B. 1892
Leicester Frith—dissolved 1935
Maplewell Longdale—dissolved 1884
Mountsorrel—formed 1884
Mountsorrel North End } united as Mountsorrel
Mountsorrel South End } 1884
Newtown Linford
Prestwold—transferred from Loughborough R.D. 1936
Queniborough
Quorndon—transferred from Quorndon U.D., which was dissolved 1935
Ratcliffe on the Wreake
Rearsby
Rothley
Rothley Temple—dissolved 1884
Seagrave
Sileby
Swithland
Syston
Thrussington
Thurcaston
Thurmaston—transferred from Thurmaston U.D., which was dissolved 1935
Ulverscroft
Walton on the Wolds
Wanlip
Woodhouse
Wymeswold—transferred from Loughborough R.D. 1936

POPULATION

Belvoir R.D.

Formed under the Local Government Act 1894 out of parishes in Leicestershire which had formerly been in Bingham R.D. and Grantham R.D., the remainder of which lay in Nottinghamshire and Lincolnshire respectively. Belvoir R.D. was dissolved in 1935 and all its constituent parishes were transferred to Melton and Belvoir R.D.

Barkestone
Belvoir
Bottesford
Croxton Kerrial
Harston
Knipton
Muston
Plungar
Redmile

Billesdon R.D.

Formed under the Public Health Act 1872.

Allexton
Billesdon
Burton Overy
Bushby—dissolved 1935
Carlton Curlieu
Evington—dissolved 1936
Frisby
Galby
Glen, Great
Goadby
Halstead—dissolved 1935
Houghton on the Hill
Humberstone—dissolved 1935
Hungarton
Illston on the Hill
Keyham
Launde
Loddington
Lowesby
Marefield
Newton, Cold
Newton Harcourt—dissolved 1936
Norton, East
Norton, King's
Noseley
Owston and Newbold
Rolleston
Scraptoft
Skeffington
Stoughton
Stretton, Great
Stretton, Little
Thurnby
Tilton
Tugby
Whatborough
Wistow
Withcote

Bingham R.D.

Bingham R.D. lay chiefly in Nottinghamshire, but included the following Leicestershire parishes, which were transferred to Belvoir R.D. under the Local Government Act 1894.

Barkestone
Plungar

Blaby R.D.

Formed under the Public Health Act 1872.

Aston Flamville—transferred from Hinckley R.D. 1936
Aylestone—transferred to Leicester C.B. 1892
Blaby
Braunstone
Braunstone Frith—dissolved 1935
Cosby
Countesthorpe
Croft
Elmesthorpe—transferred from Hinckley R.D. 1936
Enderby
Foston—dissolved 1935
Freaks Ground—dissolved 1892
Glenfield—dissolved 1936
Glenfield Frith—dissolved 1936
Glenfields—formed 1936
Glen Parva
Huncote
Kilby
Kirby Frith—dissolved 1936
Kirby Muxloe
Knighton—transferred to Leicester C.B. 1892
Knoll and Bassett House—dissolved 1909
Leicester Forest East—dissolved 1935
Leicester Forest West
Lubbesthorpe
Marston, Potters
Narborough
New Found Pool—transferred to Leicester C.B. 1892
New Parks—dissolved 1936
Oadby—created an U.D. 1913
Sapcote—transferred from Hinckley R.D. 1936
Sharnford—transferred from Hinckley R.D. 1936
Stanton, Stoney—transferred from Hinckley R.D. 1936
Thurlaston
Whetstone
Wigston, East—formed 1894, dissolved 1936
Wigston Magna—created an U.D. 1894
Wigston Parva—transferred from Hinckley R.D. 1936

Bosworth, Market, R.D.

Formed under the Public Health Act 1872

Atterton—transferred from Atherstone R.D. under L.G.A. 1894
Bagworth
Barlestone
Barton in the Beans—dissolved 1935
Bilstone—dissolved 1935
Bosworth, Market
Cadeby
Carlton
Congerstone—dissolved 1935
Dadlington—dissolved 1935
Desford
Drayton, Fenny—transferred from Atherstone R.D. under L.G.A. 1894
Gopsall—dissolved 1935
Groby—formed 1896
Higham on the Hill—transferred from Hinckley R.D. 1936
Ibstock
Kirkby Mallory—dissolved 1935
Markfield
Nailstone
Newbold Verdon
Norton juxta Twycross—dissolved 1935
Odstone—dissolved 1935
Orton on the Hill—dissolved 1935
Osbaston
Peckleton
Ratby
Ratcliffe Culey—transferred from Atherstone R.D. under L.G.A. 1894
Shackerstone
Sheepy—formed 1935
Sheepy Magna, Sheepy Parva } transferred from Atherstone R.D. under L.G.A. 1894; dissolved 1935
Shenton—dissolved 1935
Sibson—dissolved 1935
Stanton under Bardon—dissolved 1935
Stapleton—dissolved 1935
Sutton Cheney
Thornton—dissolved 1935
Twycross
Upton—dissolved 1935
Witherley—transferred from Atherstone R.D under L.G.A. 1894

Donington, Castle, R.D.

Formed under the Local Government Act 1894 out of parishes in Leicestershire which had formerly been in Shardlow R.D., the remainder of which lay in Derbyshire.

Belton—transferred from Loughborough R.D. 1936
Breedon on the Hill
Charley—transferred from Loughborough R.D. 1936
Diseworth—dissolved 1936
Donington, Castle
Hemington—dissolved 1936
Isley cum Langley—created 1936
Kegworth
Langley Priory—dissolved 1936
Lockington—name changed 1938 to Lockington-Hemington, q.v.
Lockington-Hemington
Walton, Isley—dissolved 1936
Whatton, Long—transferred from Loughborough R.D. 1936

Grantham R.D.

Grantham R.D. lay chiefly in Lincolnshire, but included the following Leicestershire parishes, all of which were transferred to Belvoir R.D. under the Local Government Act 1894.

Belvoir
Bottesford
Croxton Kerrial
Harston
Knipton
Muston
Redmile

Hallaton R.D.

Formed under the Local Government Act 1894 out of all but one of the parishes in Leicestershire which had formerly been in Uppingham R.D., the remainder of which lay in Rutland. Hallaton R.D. was dissolved in 1935 and its constituent parishes were transferred to Market Harborough R.D.

Blaston
Bringhurst
Drayton
Easton, Great
Hallaton
Holt, Nevill
Horninghold
Medbourne
Stockerston

POPULATION

Harborough, Market, R.D.

Formed under the Public Health Act 1872.

Arthingworth (Northants.)*
Ashley (Northants.)*
Blaston—transferred from Hallaton R.D. 1935
Bosworth, Husbands
Bowden, Little (Northants.)—the part not included in Market Harborough U.D.*
Brampton Ash (Northants.)*
Braybrooke (Northants.)*
Bringhurst—transferred from Hallaton R.D. 1935
Clipston (Northants.)*
Cranoe
Dingley (Northants.)*
Drayton—transferred from Hallaton R.D. 1935
Easton, Great—transferred from Hallaton R.D. 1935
Farndon, East (Northants.)*
Fleckney
Foxton
Glooston
Gumley
Hallaton—transferred from Hallaton R.D. 1935
Holt, Nevill—transferred from Hallaton R.D. 1935
Horninghold—transferred from Hallaton R.D. 1935
Hothorpe (Northants.)*
Kelmarsh (Northants.)*
Kibworth Beauchamp
Kibworth Harcourt
Langton, East
Langton, Thorpe
Langton, Tur
Langton, West
Laughton
Lubenham
Marston Trussell (Northants.)*
Medbourne—transferred from Hallaton R.D. 1935
Mowsley
Oxendon, Great (Northants.)*
Saddington
Shangton
Sibbertoft (Northants.)*
Slawston—transferred from Uppingham R.D. 1895
Smeeton Westerby
Stockerston—transferred from Hallaton R.D. 1935
Stoke Albany (Northants.)*
Stonton Wyville
Sulby (Northants.)*
Sutton Bassett (Northants.)*
Theddingworth
Thorpe Lubenham (Northants.)*
Welham
Weston by Welland (Northants.)*
Wilbarston (Northants.) part of*

Hinckley R.D.

Formed under the Public Health Act 1872, and dissolved in 1936, when such of its constituent parishes as were not dissolved and transferred to Hinckley U.D. or transferred to Market Harborough R.D., were transferred to Blaby R.D.

Aston Flamville
Barwell—dissolved 1936
Burbage—dissolved 1936
Burton Hastings (Warws.)*
Elmesthorpe
Higham on the Hill—transferred to Market Bosworth R.D. 1936
Sapcote
Sharnford
Shilton, Earl—dissolved 1936
Stanton, Stoney
Stoke Golding—dissolved 1936
Stretton Baskerville (Warws.)*
Wigston Parva—transferred from Lutterworth R.D. 1895.
Wolvey (Warws.)*

Loughborough R.D.

Formed under the Public Health Act 1872. Dissolved in 1936, when such of its constituent parishes as were not dissolved were transferred to Barrow upon Soar R.D. and Castle Donington R.D.

Belton—transferred to Castle Donington R.D. 1936
Burton on the Wolds—transferred to Barrow upon Soar R.D. 1936
Charley—transferred to Castle Donington R.D. 1936
Costock (Notts.)*
Cotes—transferred to Barrow upon Soar R.D. 1936
Garendon—dissolved 1936
Hathern—dissolved 1936
Hoton—transferred to Barrow upon Soar R.D. 1936
Leake, East (Notts.)*
Leake, West (Notts.)*
Loughborough, part of, from 1894 to 1894
Nanpantan—formed 1894, dissolved 1936
Normanton upon Soar (Notts.)*
Prestwold—transferred to Barrow upon Soar R.D. 1936
Rempstone (Notts.)*

Shepshed—whole of parish until 1886; part of parish until 1896
Stanford upon Soar (Notts.)*
Sutton Bonnington (Notts.)*
Thorpe Acre and Dishley—dissolved 1936
Thorpe in the Glebe (Notts.)*
Whatton, Long—transferred to Castle Donington R.D. 1936
Willoughby on the Wolds (Notts.)*
Woodthorpe—from 1888; dissolved 1935
Wymeswold—transferred to Barrow upon Soar 1936
Wysall (Notts.)*

Lutterworth R.D.

Formed under the Public Health Act 1872.

Arnesby
Ashby Magna
Ashby Parva
Bittesby
Bitteswell
Broughton Astley
Bruntingthorpe
Catthorpe
Claybrooke, Great
Claybrooke, Little
Copston Magna (Warws.)*
Cotesbach
Dunton Bassett
Frolesworth
Gilmorton
Kilworth, North
Kilworth, South
Kimcote—until 1898
Kimcote and Walton—formed 1898
Kirby, Monks (Warws.)*
Knaptoft
Leire
Lutterworth
Misterton
Pailton (Warws.)*
Peatling Magna
Peatling Parva
Shawell
Shearsby
Stretton under Foss (Warws.)*
Swinford
Ullesthorpe
Walton in Knaptoft—until 1898
Welford (Northants.)*
Westrill and Starmore—transferred from Rugby R.D. 1895
Wibtoft (Warws.)*
Wigston Parva—transferred to Hinckley R.D. 1895
Willey (Warws.)*
Willoughby Waterless

Melton and Belvoir R.D.

Formed in 1935 out of part of Melton Mowbray R.D. and the whole of Belvoir R.D. In 1936 many of its constituent parishes were combined: they are shown here as altered.

Asfordby
Belvoir
Bottesford
Broughton and Old Dalby
Buckminster
Burton and Dalby
Clawson and Harby
Croxton Kerrial
Eaton
Freeby
Frisby
Gaddesby
Garthorpe
Grimston
Hoby with Rotherby
Kettleby, Ab
Knossington
Redmile
Scalford
Somerby
Sproxton
Stathern
Twyford and Thorpe
Waltham
Wymondham

Melton Mowbray R.D.

Formed under the Public Health Act 1872. It was dissolved in 1935, when all its constituent parishes except Eye Kettleby and parts of Burton Lazars, Thorpe Arnold, Waltham on the Wolds, and Welby were transferred to Melton and Belvoir R.D.

Asfordby
Ashby Folville
Barsby
Bescaby
Branston
Brentingby and Wyfordby
Brooksby
Broughton, Nether
Broughton, Upper (Notts.)*
Buckminster
Burrough on the Hill
Burton Lazars
Clawson, Long
Coston
Dalby, Great
Dalby, Little

Dalby, Old
Eastwell
Eaton
Edmondthorpe
Freeby
Frisby on the Wreak
Gaddesby
Garthorpe
Goadby Marwood
Grimston
Harby
Hoby
Holwell
Hose
Kettleby, Ab
Kettleby, Eye—dissolved 1935
Kirby Bellars
Knossington—transferred from Oakham R.D. under L.G.A. 1894
Melton Mowbray—part of parish until 1894
Overton, Cold—transferred from Oakham R.D. under L.G.A. 1894
Pickwell with Leesthorpe
Ragdale
Rotherby
Saltby
Saxby
Saxelby
Scalford
Sewstern
Shoby
Somerby
Sproxton
Stapleford
Stathern
Stonesby
Sysonby—dissolved 1930
Thorpe Arnold
Thorpe Satchville
Twyford
Wartnaby
Welby
Wycomb and Chadwell
Wymondham

Oakham R.D.

Oakham R.D. lay chiefly in Rutland, but contained the following parishes in Leicestershire, which were transferred to Market Harborough R.D. under the Local Government Act 1894.

Knossington
Overton, Cold

Rugby R.D.

Rugby R.D. lay chiefly in Warwickshire, but contained the following parish in Leicestershire, which was transferred to Lutterworth R.D. in 1895.

Westrill and Starmore

Shardlow R.D.

Shardlow R.D. lay chiefly in Derbyshire, but contained the following parishes in Leicestershire. All except Sawley with Wilsthorpe were formed into Castle Donington R.D. under the Local Government Act 1894.

Breedon
Diseworth
Donington, Castle
Hemington
Kegworth
Langley Priory
Lockington
Sawley with Wilsthorpe—the part in Leicestershire, until 1884
Walton, Isley

Uppingham R.D.

Uppingham R.D. lay chiefly in Rutland and Northamptonshire, but contained the following parishes in Leicestershire. All but Slawston and Stoke Dry were formed into Hallaton R.D. under the Local Government Act 1894.

Blaston
Bringhurst
Drayton
Easton, Great
Hallaton
Holt, Nevill
Horninghold
Medbourne
Slawston—transferred to Market Harborough R.D. 1895
Stockerston
Stoke Dry, the part in Leicestershire until 1885

LEICESTERSHIRE ARTISTS

FROM the point of view of the historian of art Leicestershire is not a specially notable county. No such distinctively local art as that of the Nottingham alabaster carvers, the Coventry glass-painters, or the Staffordshire potters has been centred there, unless we may regard the craft of the incised and engraved slate headstones, which are such a notable feature of many Leicestershire churchyards, and which, at their best, rise to a level of style genuinely distinguished, as a local art. It was an art not of course confined to this county, but one which had special connexions with Leicestershire, for the slate itself came from the Swithland quarries, and the craft was largely centred in and near Swithland. But in the arts usually designated 'fine', Leicestershire has little enough to boast of. None of the greatest of British painters or sculptors was born or bred, or worked mainly there; and only two art-collections of national importance, those of the dukes of Rutland at Belvoir Castle and of Sir George Beaumont at Coleorton Hall, were ever housed in the county. None the less, quite a few interesting artists have been connected with the county, and although it would be too much to claim that they constitute a distinctive local school, it has seemed worth while to collect together a skeleton account of the more important of the painters, and of one or two artists in other media.

The Leicestershire painters who have been selected for comment fall into two easily separable categories: first, the sporting painters from Loraine Smith and the Boultbees through Marshall and the Ferneleys down to the second half of the last century; and secondly, the landscape painters from Sir George Beaumont and John Glover, John Flower, Harry Ward, to Fulleylove, Davies, and Henton. Both groups begin with gentlemen amateurs. In portraiture there are only the two somewhat isolated figures of L. F. Abbott and Violet, Duchess of Rutland, and M. W. Peters, R.A., who was not of Leicestershire birth, and was not entirely a painter of portraits. This relative strength and continuity of the tradition of sporting painters is of course significant, and by comparison with the sporting painters the group of landscape artists is discontinuous and scrappy. It is also noticeable that apart from the sporting painters, and Ferneley in particular, any artist of real quality and ambition had to leave the county in order to achieve recognition and success. London was the Mecca of the artist, and inevitably drew Abbott, Marshall, Ferneley, Glover, even Harry Ward, Fulleylove, and Harry Morley, away from the provinces. Only the nature of their specialization permitted Marshall and Ferneley to return to the midlands, one to Newmarket, the other to Melton, centres of the cult of the horse.

No attempt has been made here to include every painter who ever worked in Leicestershire or for a Leicestershire patron. The artists selected for treatment are, in the first place, artists of distinction who were born in the county, and secondly, artists who although not born in the county were closely associated with it.

There are many others who have worked within the borders of the county and attained a respectable level of merit. The most important artist who might with some show of reason be claimed for the local school is Sir Francis Grant, P.R.A., who married a daughter of the Duke of Rutland, hunted in Leicestershire, and died at Melton. Almost all the specialist painters of hunting subjects who worked at some time in the neighbourhood of Melton Mowbray, especially Henry Alken and Sir John Dean Paul, might be claimed as regional artists. As there will be occasion to mention in connexion with Charles Loraine Smith, George Morland visited the county and possibly painted some of his best pictures in the neighbourhood of Enderby and in Charnwood Forest. A string of leading painters worked for the earls and dukes of Rutland at Belvoir Castle, including Lely and Kneller, Hudson, Reynolds, Hoppner, and Sir Francis Grant, and Reynolds acted as adviser to Charles, 4th Duke of Rutland in the formation of his magnificent art collection, still by far the richest in the county, despite recent dispersals of some sections of it under the hammer. To write about all these, however, and all the artists who enjoyed the patronage of Sir George Beaumont, would be to write a history of the English School of painting.

Among portrait painters of earlier periods, those with an appreciable practice within the county include Jacopo D'Agar, Enoch Seeman, John Baptist Closterman, a rather obscure person named Van der Eyden (much employed by the Duke of Rutland towards the end of the 17th century,[1] an even more obscure painter who signed his pictures *I. W. F.*,[2] Phillippe Mercier, Richard Collins,[3] and, around the turn of the 18th–19th centuries, Beechey, Northcote, and William Artaud. The practice of Joseph Wright of Derby also extended into Leicestershire. Among lesser artists, one may list G. Smeeton, portrait painter of Kibworth; a portrait painter named W. Walton, who exhibited portraits in London in 1814; Webb, a sporting painter of Melton Mowbray who exhibited one picture at the Royal Academy in 1844; G. Gillett, another sporting artist of Melton, who exhibited in London from 1862 to 1871; and C. J. Adams, J. M. Barber, Louisa Dudgeon (still-life painter), Alice Mary Hobson, R.I., Kate Mary Whitley, R.I.,[4] and George S. Elgood, R.I. (1851–1943), painter of gardens and author of *Some English Gardens* (1904) and *Italian Gardens* (1907).[5] It is unlikely, however, that any of these figures will be found to have added anything in quality to the work of the artists who will be discussed. A particular mention should, however, be made of F. L. Griggs, R.A. (1876–1938), the illustrator of J. B. Firth's *Highways and Byways in Leicestershire* (1926). The drawings reproduced in this book include some of his best work and the originals are preserved in the Leicester Museum and Art Gallery. Griggs was not a Leicestershire man but he deserves a distinguished position among Leicestershire topographers.

In order of time the gentlemen amateurs head the principal artists of the county. The first of these was Charles Loraine Smith, who has been called 'after Stubbs, the man who probably had most influence on sporting art'.[6] This claim would be a palpable exaggeration if applied to the influence of his own

[1] Hist. MSS. Comm., *Rutland*, iv, 552–3; I. Eller, *Hist. Belvoir Castle*, 228.

[2] A. C. Sewter, 'The Master I.W.F.', *Burlington Mag.* lxxvi, 20–25.

[3] A. C. Sewter, 'Richard Collins', *Apollo*, xxxvi, 71–73, 103–5.

[4] A. Graves, *Dict. of Artists* (1895).

[5] *Who's Who* (1944), 842.

[6] G. Paget, 'Sporting Pictures of England', *Aspects of Brit. Art*, ed. W. J. Turner, 270.

work as a painter; it must be understood as referring rather to the influence of his artistic interests among the hunting fraternity.

Charles Loraine Smith was born in 1751, the second son of Sir Charles Loraine, 3rd baronet, and his second wife. He assumed the additional surname of Smith on succeeding to the property of his grandmother Anne, second wife of Sir William Loraine, 2nd baronet, which included Enderby Hall, where Charles Loraine Smith took up residence. In 1781 he married Elizabeth Ann, daughter of William Skrine of Westminster.[7] He became separated from his wife in 1817, however, and eloped with Frances, Lady Tyrconnel, eldest daughter of the Marquess of Granby.[8] He was M.P. for Leicester 1784–90,[9] Sheriff of Leicestershire in 1783, and was made an honorary freeman of Leicester in 1815.[10] He died in 1823.

Such a bald account of his life, however, by no means conveys an adequate picture of the man, whose vivid and picturesque personality is better suggested by Major Paget's description of him as 'M.P., J.P., poet, deputy master of the Quorn, painter, fiddler, jack-of-all-trades'.[11] But here we are concerned with him only as a painter. Where and how he learned to paint is unknown, but it may be presumed he was self-taught. The first definite information we have about his artistic interests comes from J. Hassell's *Life of George Morland* (1806), which states, after a paragraph referring to the years 1790–2, that Morland received an invitation to Enderby from 'Claude Lorrain Smith, Esquire' (*sic*), who, according to Hassell, 'was renowned not only for his abilities as an artist, but for his liberal encouragement of the arts.' Hassell also tells us that Smith advised Morland in the choice of subjects for painting.[12] As late as 1797, however, two plates, entitled *A Litter of Foxes* and *Victory for the Brush*, were published, in which the animals were by Charles Loraine Smith and the landscape by George Morland. In the meantime, perhaps as a result of encouragement from Morland or progress made in his company, Smith had become an honorary exhibitor at the Royal Academy, where he showed six pictures between 1795 and 1806. Of these, five represented sporting subjects, and the sixth, shown in 1805, was *A View in Charnley Forest*.[13] A series of six coloured aquatints of *Dick Knight's Doings* was engraved after Smith's designs by H. T. Alken; and another set of coloured prints after his *Scenes from the Smoking Hunt* was engraved by J. Watson and published in 1826, 4 years after they had been painted. In these two series there is no trace of Morland's influence, but in certain plates of the second series, such as *A Leicestershire Burst* and *The Rendez-vous of the Quorn Hounds at Grooby Pool*, the influence of Alken is unmistakable. To claim, as W. S. Sparrow has done, that Smith 'may be regarded as one of Alken's understudies',[14] is certainly going too far, however, for these works belong only to the late phase of Smith's career. In his *Billesdon Coplow Day*, perhaps his best picture, the style is quite personal and individual. There was a rough vigour in his work, which often ignored anatomical accuracy

7 Burke, *Peerage* (1949), 1256, and *The Field*, Christmas 1920, 23.

8 G. Paget and Lionel Irvine, *The Flying Parson and Dick Christian*, 49.

9 R. Beatson, *Chronol. Reg. both Ho. of Parl.* ii, pp. vi, 139.

10 *Reg. Freemen of Leic. 1770–1930*, ed. H. Hartopp, 136.

11 *Aspects of Brit. Art*, ed. Turner, 270. For another excellent description of his character see *Nimrod's Hunting Reminiscences*, ed. W. S. Sparrow, 221.

12 J. Hassell, *Memoirs of the Life of George Morland*, 17–18. Major Paget maintained a later dating (1794–6) for Morland's visit (*Aspects of Brit. Art*, ed. Turner, 272) but gave no reasons for this opinion.

13 A. Graves, *R.A. Exhibitors*, vii, 171–2.

14 W. S. Sparrow, *Brit. Sporting Artists*, 151.

and gave a suggestion occasionally of amateurish crudity; but, on the other hand, coupled with his bluff sense of humour, this vigour gave life to everything he painted.

So far as is known, none of Loraine Smith's original works is to be found in any public collection. Major Guy Paget (d. 1952) owned the original of *Bagging the Fox*, by Smith and Morland, and the *Billesdon Coplow Day*.

With the second of these gentlemen amateurs, Sir George Howland Beaumont, 7th bt., a fully professional level of skill and accomplishment is reached. This distinguished collector, connoisseur, and landscape painter was born in 1753, the son of Sir George Beaumont, 6th baronet, and his wife Rachel. His father died while he was still a child, and he succeeded to the baronetcy in 1762. He was educated at Eton and New College, Oxford.[15] The drawing master at Eton from 1763 to 1768 was Alexander Cozens, and the effect of Cozens's teaching on the young Beaumont was permanent and profound. While at Oxford he had lessons from the drawing master, John Baptist Malchair.[16] In 1778 Beaumont married Margaret, daughter of John Willes of Astrop, Northants., and with her he made his first continental tour, in Switzerland and Italy, in 1782–3. From 1790 until 1796 he was M.P. for Bere Alston,[17] but never sought re-election. In 1800 he began, with George Dance, R.A., as architect, to rebuild Coleorton Hall near Ashby de la Zouch, a project which took 8 years to complete. There he installed his notable collection of pictures and sculpture, and entertained many notable figures in the worlds of art, letters, and science, including Wordsworth and Coleridge,[18] Wilkie, Haydon, John Jackson, and John Constable. Innumerable young poets, painters, and sculptors enjoyed the benefits of his patronage and friendship, including, besides those already mentioned, Thomas Girtin, Julius Caesar Ibbetson, Sir Francis Chantrey, George Arnald, Beechey, Hazlitt, and Robert Bloomfield, author of *The Farmer's Boy*. In 1819 and 1822 he made a further visit or visits to the continent, travelling through Holland, Germany, Switzerland, and Italy, and revisiting many of the places where he had sketched 40 years earlier. In 1824 he was largely instrumental in persuading the government to acquire the Angerstein collection, which with sixteen of the most important pictures from Beaumont's own collection which he presented to the nation in 1826, formed the foundation of the National Gallery. This group included Sebastian Bourdon's *Return of the Ark*, which had been bequeathed to Sir George by Sir Joshua Reynolds as a memorial of his esteem, as well as four Claudes, two Rembrandts, and Rubens's magnificent landscape *The Chateau de Steen*. He also presented his famous bas-relief by Michelangelo to the Royal Academy, of which he had been an honorary exhibitor since 1779.[19] For many years he was one of the directors and a chief moving spirit of the British Institution, and for a whole generation his position as the acknowledged doyen of artistic taste was virtually unchallenged. He became a Fellow of the Royal Society and of the Society of Antiquaries, and a trustee of the British Museum,[20]

15 Burke, *Peerage* (1949), 161, and *D.N.B.* iv, 56, are the most convenient authorities for Beaumont's biography. References to him abound in such works as *Farington Diary*, ed. J. Greig, and Haydon's *Autobiography and Jnls.* in the correspondence of Wordsworth, Coleridge, and others.

16 *Farington Diary*, ed. Greig, i, 290.

17 R. Beatson, *Chronol. Reg. both Ho. of Parl.* ii, pp. vii, 84.

18 For Beaumont's relations with Coleridge a convenient summary is given by A. C. Sewter, 'Coleridge, Beaumont and Coleorton', *Leics. and Rut. Mag.* i, 30–35.

19 Graves, *R.A. Exhibitors*, i, 154.

20 *Gent. Mag.* xcvii, 464–5.

and one of the first trustees of the National Gallery.[21] He died in 1827. A poem, *Elegiac Musings*, mourning his death was written by his friend Wordsworth, who had also inscribed to him the *Elegiac Stanzas, suggested by a picture of Peel Castle, in a storm, painted by Sir George Beaumont.* The picture which inspired these verses is now in the Leicester Art Gallery, to which it was presented by the trustees of Sir Francis Beaumont in 1938.

Sir George Beaumont was not only a distinguished artist, patron, and collector, but he knew and was on terms of intimacy with many of the most important figures of his times, from Dr. Johnson and Sir Joshua Reynolds to Sir Humphrey Davy, Scott, and Byron. His interests ranged over literature, the theatre, and the visual arts, and no account of the culture of the time would be complete without a reference to him.

As a patron, collector, and munificent benefactor of the National Gallery, Beaumont has received the honour and respect due to him;[22] but as an artist he has generally met with less than justice. This neglect is probably due mainly to the somewhat misleading references to him in two widely read books, C. R. Leslie's *Life of Constable* and B. R. Haydon's *Autobiography and Journals.* Leslie's intention was to emphasize the advances in landscape painting made by his idol Constable, and he used Beaumont as a foil for this purpose, especially in the much-quoted anecdote of the Cremona fiddle,[23] which it is unnecessary to repeat here. Any first-hand study of Beaumont's own paintings and drawings, however, is sufficient to show that he was by no means tied to the outworn conventions of the brown tree and the golden tone. He had a lively response to nature, constantly developing his style throughout his long life, and was never averse to learning from his younger friends.[24] Constable himself thought highly enough of his work to make careful copies of at least two of his drawings.[25] Haydon, on the other hand, fell out with Beaumont, as he did with almost everybody, over a commission for a picture of Macbeth, and wrote of him in anger as mean and unjust. But the eventual outcome of this unhappy dispute, and the terms in which Haydon later wrote of 'Dear Sir George', prove clearly enough on which side the fault lay.[26]

During his lifetime Beaumont seems never to have exhibited a drawing, though probably all his best work is in this medium; and since his death a high proportion of his large output, amounting to some 120 oils and over 2,000 drawings, remained until recently in the possession of his descendants. Allan Cunningham, who wrote a short life of Beaumont in 1833,[27] had never, apparently, seen the drawings, and no later critic took the trouble to investigate them until 1938, when an exhibition of his work was arranged at the Leicester Art Gallery.[28] The Tate Gallery, the Victoria and Albert Museum, and the British Museum[29] possess works by him which have seldom been exhibited, and the National Gallery of Scotland has a watercolour, catalogued under his name,

[21] *Year's Art*, ed. A. C. R. Carter (1947), 1.

[22] See, e.g. H. Furst, 'Two famous connoisseurs and collectors: Beaumont and Beckford', *Apollo*, xxv, 59–61.

[23] C. R. Leslie, *Life of Constable*, ed. A. Shirley, 155.

[24] It is certainly untrue to say that 'he disapproved of everything Constable did', as does Shirley, op. cit. 6.

[25] One of Constable's copies is repr. in Leslie, *Constable*, pl. 85*a*.

[26] B. R. Haydon, *Autobiography and Jnls.* ed. T. Taylor, i, 136–45, 175–7, 368, 401; ii, 148–9.

[27] A. Cunningham, *Lives of the Most Eminent Brit. Painters*, vi, 134–54.

[28] Leic. Art Gallery, *Exhibition of Paintings and Drawings by Sir George Beaumont*, 29 June–7 Aug. 1938. The cat. has an introduction analysing the development of his work, by the present writer, and several illustrations.

[29] *Tate Gallery, Cat. Brit. Sch.* (1947), 8, no. 119; *B.M. Cat. Drawings by Brit. Artists*, i, 93.

which is not by him.[30] The only public gallery where his work can be adequately studied is the Leicester Art Gallery, which in addition to the *Peel Castle in a Storm* has five other oils and eighty-three watercolours and drawings by him, representing all phases of his career.

Sir George Beaumont had a long working life, and it is scarcely surprising to find great diversity in his expression; nor is it surprising, in view of his connoisseurship and his activities as a collector, to find frequent echoes of other masters. The influence of Alexander Cozens runs throughout, but it is primarily technical and an aid to Beaumont's own personal expression; while traces of the influence of Claude and Wilson, Gainsborough, J. R. Cozens, John 'Warwick' Smith, Girtin, Hearne, Rembrandt, Magnasco, and of Constable may easily be found. Yet there is hardly a work from his hand which is not strongly personal and characteristic. He was not, of course, a painter of the highest rank, and could never be regarded as in the same class with Gainsborough, Wilson, or Constable. He never had a true flair for oil paint, and his feeling for colour was not strong. But as a landscape draughtsman he deserves high consideration, and the range and completeness of his expression entitle him to rank not far below those masters considered as draughtsmen. He occupies a position of vital importance in the history of English drawing; he might well be called the last of the old masters, and he provides the direct personal link between the 18th-century art of Alexander and John Cozens, Wilson, and Gainsborough on the one hand, and the younger generation of Girtin and Constable on the other. The dramatic and intense mood of certain of his pictures and drawings, such as the *Peel Castle* or the drawings of Borrowdale and Honister Crag represents the transition from the sublime and picturesque manner of the 18th century to early romanticism, which is nowhere else so clearly exemplified.

A man of great personal charm, he practised his art with the greatest seriousness and assiduity,[31] and earned the respect of many professional painters.[32] His reputation as an artist is likely to stand higher in the future than it does today.

From these two distinguished amateurs we pass to the twin brothers John and Thomas Boultbee, painters of sporting pictures, landscapes, and portraits. They were the sons of Thomas Boultbee and his wife Jane of Stordon Grange, and were baptized at Osgathorpe in 1753.[33] No information is available about their earliest artistic training, though a family tradition[34] maintains that both were pupils of Sir Joshua Reynolds. This is very improbable. They both, however, entered the Royal Academy schools in 1775,[35] and both made their debut in the same year, when they exhibited three pictures each at the Free Society in London, their address being given as 83 Oxford Street; so, presumably, they had received some earlier instruction. In the following year, they again showed three pictures each at the Society of Artists, while John had one and Thomas two landscapes hung at the Royal Academy. In 1777 only Thomas exhibited in London, showing at the Royal Academy a *View of Staunton*

[30] *Cat.* (1946), 74.

[31] Leslie, *Constable*, 151–3; Haydon, *Autobiography and Jnls.* i, 133–5.

[32] See, e.g. *Farington Diary*, ed. Greig, i, 45, where the diarist records Copley's opinion of a landscape by Beaumont in the 1794 exhibition of the R.A., which he said 'wd. have done credit to any artist of any country'.

[33] W. S. Sparrow, 'John Boultbee: sporting painter', *Connoisseur*, xci, 150.

[34] Recorded by Sir W. Gilbey, *Animal Painters of Engl.* i, 68, and Sparrow, op. cit. 154–5.

[35] Sparrow, ibid., noted that Thomas was entered at the R.A. schools in 1775, but was apparently unaware that John entered on the same day.

Harold, his address now being 347 Oxford St.[36] There is then a gap of several years before they again exhibited in London, so we are perhaps justified in assuming that about 1777 they left the capital to start their independent careers. All their works up to this point had been landscapes or portraits; but the tastes and interests of the country gentlemen on whom they were to depend for patronage are clearly reflected in the change which then took place. In 1783 Thomas reappeared at the Royal Academy with three pictures of horses, one of them representing a hunter and a shooting-horse, the property of T. W. Coke, of Loughborough. The painter's address was now given as Derby. The late W. S. Sparrow very plausibly suggested that an entry under the name of John Boultbee in the catalogue of the same exhibition, of another picture of *Penseroso, a stallion, the property of T. W. Coke, esq.* is a mistake, and that this item also properly belongs to Thomas.[37] John, however, reappeared in two further Royal Academy Exhibitions, in 1787 and 1788, on each occasion with two horse pictures, one of the animals in the latter year being described as 'a favourite horse of Mr. Bakewell'. The artist's address in these years is given as Loughborough.[38] Thomas had apparently married a young woman with money, and after his marriage painted as an amateur, generally at Great Chatwell, near Newport, Salop, where he lived with his family, and where he died in 1808.[39] This explains the rarity of Thomas's works, in contrast to the much more prolific John, who seems to have been well supported, largely by local patronage. Throsby, writing in or shortly before 1789, was able to record pictures by Boultbee at Bosworth Hall, Skeffington Hall, Beaumanor Park, Braunstone Hall, and Osbaston Hall. That these references belong to John is indicated by Throsby's twice calling him 'Mr. Boultbee of Loughborough'. His reputation already stood high, and he was 'deservedly patronized by the first families in the county'.[40] Among other local families which employed him were the Packes of Prestwold, the Pagets of Humberstone, and the Pochins of Barkby; farther afield, the Earl Spencer, the Duke of Bedford, and the Earl of Egremont were among his patrons. In 1798 he painted for Lord Egremont a picture of the mare *Gohanna, with a portrait of Mr. Thomas Bird*, which was engraved in 1808 by Jukes and Sargent. This picture, together with a series of eleven canvases representing cattle of various breeds, remains in the possession of Mr. John Wyndham at Petworth. Two of the cattle pictures contain views of Windsor Castle in the landscape backgrounds, so that they probably represent the royal livestock and confirm a family tradition that George III commissioned such a series from Boultbee and assigned to him a house near Cumberland Lodge, Windsor Great Park, while it was in course of execution.[41] Two of the Petworth pictures are dated 1797 and signed 'J. Bolteby', a form of his name which does not seem to occur elsewhere.[42] In 1812 John Boultbee moved from Chester to Liverpool, where he exhibited eight pictures at the Liverpool Academy before his death in the same year.[43] His second son, Thomas Joseph Boultbee,

[36] Graves, *R.A. Exhibitors*, i, 250.

[37] *Connoisseur*, xci, 155.

[38] Graves, *R.A. Exhibitors*, i, 250.

[39] *Connoisseur*, xci, 159. *Gent. Mag.* lxxvii, 276, records the death of 'Thomas Boultbee Esq., of Chetwynd End in Shropshire' on 4 Mar. 1808.

[40] J. Throsby, *Leics. Views*, i, 201, 212, 230, 257, 305.

[41] Gilbey, *Animal Painters*, i, 71–72; *Connoisseur*, xci, 158.

[42] One of the series is repr. in *Connoisseur*, xci, 159.

[43] Ibid.; *Gent. Mag.* lxxxviii, 37.

born at Loughborough in 1787, also showed three pictures at the same exhibition.

In John Boultbee's mature work the dominant influence, as W. S. Sparrow has observed, is that of Stubbs, so much so, indeed, that Boultbee's are often mistaken for Stubbs's, and Boultbee has been called a disciple of the older master.[44] Boultbee, however, lacked the exquisite precision and refinement of Stubbs, and his paint suffers from a certain thinness, especially in the landscape backgrounds. The reasons which Sparrow advanced in favour of believing that John Boultbee had studied with Sawrey Gilpin, R.A.,[45] whose influence is certainly perceptible in his work, can be given little weight now that we know him to have been a student at the Academy schools. In public collections his work appears to be unrepresented. A picture of a mare, *Rachel by Blank* (*Dam of Highflyer*), was in the so-called National Gallery of British Sports and Pastimes.[46] One of the best of his authenticated works is the *Charles James Packe the younger, with his servant Bonam, at Prestwold*, formerly in the collection of Lt.-Col. E. C. Packe. His reputation has been rising steadily during the last 20 years.

Matthew William Peters was actually born earlier than any of the artists hitherto considered, at Freshwater (I.W.) in or about 1741.[47] His association with Leicestershire, however, did not begin until about 1777, and only a very brief summary of his career is possible in this place. After some preliminary training in Dublin, where, from a date very soon after his birth, his father held a post connected with inland waterways, Peters was sent to Italy with a scholarship from the Dublin Society, and lived there for several years. Following an abortive attempt to set up as a painter in Dublin, he settled in London in 1766 and began exhibiting.[48] His success was rapid; when elected A.R.A. in 1771, he already numbered the Duchess of Ancaster among his patrons. In 1772 he made a second, and shorter, visit to Italy, whence he continued to send a few pictures, portraits in crayons, to the Royal Academy exhibitions.[49] In 1776 he was back in London, and among the five pictures which he exhibited at the Royal Academy in the following year was a *Portrait of a Gentleman in Masquerade Dress*, in which the sitter was Col. George Pochin of Barkby. This picture, which still hangs at Barkby Hall, was engraved in mezzotint by John Dean in the same year, and it has a companion piece in the portrait of Mrs. Pochin. A *St. John* exhibited in the same year, was evidently purchased by the Marquess of Granby, and was subsequently destroyed in the fire at Belvoir Castle in 1816.[50] By this time he had secured an extremely influential clientèle, including, beside the Marquess of Granby, Lord Courtenay, Lord Grosvenor, and Lord Melbourne, and had been elected to full membership of the Academy.[51] Peters's plans, however, now underwent a marked change of

[44] W. S. Sparrow, *Bk. of Sporting Painters*, 59.

[45] *Connoisseur*, xci, 154–5.

[46] *First 618 selected pictures, Nat. Gallery of Brit. Sports and Pastimes*, 15, no. 50. This collection, though called a 'National Gallery', was never in fact transferred to public ownership, and after the death of its owner, Walter Hutchinson, it was dispersed by auction at Christie's in July 1951.

[47] W. G. Strickland, *Dict. Irish Artists*, ii, 230; Thieme-Becker, *Künstlerlexikon*, xxvi, 481, says he was born in 1742; W. A. Sandby, *Hist. R.A.* i, 187, says he was born in Dublin, which is incorrect.

[48] *D.N.B.* xviii, 86–87; Lady V. Manners, *M. W. Peters, R.A.*

[49] Graves, *R.A. Exhibitors*, vi, 112.

[50] I. Eller, *Hist. Belvoir Castle*, 130. This fire also destroyed his copy of Le Brun's *Mme de la Valliere*: ibid. 131.

[51] Sandby, *Hist. R.A.* i, 188; Strickland, *Dict. Irish Artists*, ii, 230; Thieme-Becker, *Künstlerlexikon*, xxvi, 481, and others give the date of his election as 1777; Graves, *R.A. Exhibitors*, vi, 112, gives 1778.

course, and in 1779 he matriculated at Exeter College, Oxford, and prepared himself to take Orders, the calling for which his father had originally intended him. He was ordained deacon in 1781, and priest in 1782. From portraiture he now turned his attention partly to the painting of religious subjects, and in 1782, as the Revd. William Peters, R.A., of Exeter College, Oxford, he showed at the Royal Academy a picture of *An Angel carrying the spirit of a child to Paradise*, in which the angel was said to be a portrait of Mary Isabella, Marchioness of Granby. In the same year he was sent by the Marquess to Paris, to copy for him a picture by Le Brun, and he remained there for some time, associating closely with certain French painters, especially L. L. Boilly and A. Vestier.[52] In 1784 the Marquess, now 4th Duke of Rutland, presented him to the living of Scalford, and in the same year he became chaplain to the Royal Academy. About the same time he painted some ceilings at Carlton House for the Prince of Wales, to whom he was also appointed chaplain; and he became Grand Portrait-Painter to the Freemasons, and secretary of the newly-formed Prince of Wales's Lodge in 1787. In 1785 he exhibited at the Royal Academy two full-length portraits, painted for the Freemasons' Hall, of the Grand Masters, the Duke of Manchester and Lord Petre. He continued to pursue his career as a painter actively until 1790, contributing five pictures to Boydell's Shakespear Gallery, and two to Macklin's Gallery; and a number of his works were engraved by leading engravers.[53] In 1788 Mary Isabella, Duchess of Rutland presented him to the rectory of Knipton, near Belvoir Castle, and appointed him curator of the pictures at Belvoir, of which he wrote an account in Nichols's *History of Leicestershire*.[54] In the same year he accepted a third living, that of Woolsthorpe (Lincs.) under the shadow of Belvoir Castle, and only a couple of miles from his other parish of Knipton. In 1790 he appears to have been under the displeasure of the Church authorities for his paintings of Shakespearian subjects, and as he now enjoyed the income of three benefices, the objection had some force. He had not exhibited at the Academy since 1785, but he now resigned his membership; he had ceased to be chaplain in 1788. In 1790 he married Margaret Susannah Knowsley, daughter of the Revd. John Fleming,[55] and the couple went to live at Woolsthorpe Rectory, and in 1791–2 Peters rebuilt the church. He had not, however, altogether given up painting, and he continued as an amateur to paint occasional presentation portraits for Freemasons' Hall, and as late as 1799 he presented to Lincoln Cathedral an altarpiece of the Annunciation which he had painted.[56] He also took a very active part in masonic affairs, being appointed Provincial Grand Master of Lincolnshire and Deputy Grand Master of Nottinghamshire, Derbyshire, Leicestershire, and Rutland. Ecclesiastical preferment also came his way. In 1791 he became prebendary of St. Mary Crackpool, Lincoln; and 4 years later he exchanged this for the richer prebend of Langford Ecclesia. In 1795 the king presented him to the living of Eaton, near Knipton. He appears to have discharged his ecclesiastical duties in the neighbourhood of Knipton until about 1806, when he moved from Woolsthorpe to his prebend of Langford (Oxon.),[57] but about 1811 he moved again to Brasted Place (Kent), where he died in 1814.

In his earlier work Peters modelled his style on that of Sir Joshua Reynolds,

[52] R. See, *Gaz. des Beaux-Arts* (1911), ii, 394–404.

[53] Manners, *M. W. Peters, R.A.* lists 66 prints after his works.

[54] Eller, *Hist. Belvoir Castle*, 213.

[55] Manners, *M. W. Peters, R.A.* 25.

[56] Ibid.

[57] Ibid. 26–33.

as Horace Walpole tersely noticed in 1771,[58] and his *The Fortune Teller*, for example, exhibited at the Royal Academy in 1785 was directly based on Reynolds's example now in the Iveagh Bequest at Kenwood House. Such works as his *Woman in Bed* and *Lydia*, however, of the 1770's, had a lascivious intention which obviously owed a great deal to French influences, and which he afterwards regretted. The *Col. Pochin* at Barkby is certainly among his most powerful portraits. His best quality was a freshness and brilliance of colour, which he had learnt from his studies in Venice, but his lack of the highest qualities of imagination is only too evident in his weak and insipid Shakespearian illustrations.

Peters is hardly represented at all in public galleries: the National Portrait Gallery has a charcoal drawing of himself with his first teacher, Robert West, which is dated 1758: the Diploma Gallery of the Royal Academy, Nottingham Castle Museum, and Exeter College, Oxford, have specimens of his work. Several of his works, despite losses in the fire of 1816, still remain at Belvoir Castle. All but one of his works for Freemasons' Hall were destroyed in a fire of 1883.[59] Probably many of his portraits pass today dubiously under the name of Reynolds.

The first Leicestershire painter to achieve success in the metropolis as a professional artist was Lemuel Francis Abbott, the portrait painter. He was the son of the Revd. Lemuel Abbott, who became curate of Anstey in 1756, and vicar of Thornton in 1773.[60] His son, the artist, was born about 1760, presumably at Anstey. At the age of 14 he became the pupil of Francis Hayman, the painter, in London; but on Hayman's death in 1776, shortly afterwards,[61] he returned to his parents. About 1780 he settled in London, and between 1788 and 1800 he exhibited fifteen portraits at Royal Academy exhibitions.[62] He seems to have been much employed for portraits of diplomats, colonial governors, and senior naval officers, and Nelson sat to him after losing his right arm at Teneriffe, during his period of sick leave between 1 September 1797 and 29 March 1798. Abbott made what Sir Francis Grant, who knew him well, called a 'mere sketch', and from this he composed a full-length picture for Captain Locker, then Lieutenant-Governor of Greenwich Hospital, and a head and shoulders picture for Alexander Davison, Nelson's prize-agent and business man. The full-length was engraved by Barnard and published on 25 May 1798; and Davison's version was also engraved by Richard Earlom, and published on 7 December 1798. Three replicas of the full-length portrait, with modifications, were subsequently made by Abbott, and several replicas of the smaller picture.[63] These undertakings must mark the end of the artist's career, for in 1798 he became incurably insane.[64] He died in 1802.[65]

Abbott had retained some connexions with his native county after his removal to London, and two head and shoulders portraits by him of William

[58] Graves, *R.A. Exhibitors*, vi, 112. [59] *D.N.B.* xlv, 78. [60] *D.N.B.* i, 30.

[61] Thieme-Becker, *Künstlerlexikon*, xvi, 180.

[62] Graves, *R.A. Exhibitors*, i, 2. [63] *Nat. Maritime Mus. Cat.* 196.

[64] C 211/A 59. It nevertheless appears that for a time Abbott may have continued to paint, for his portraits of Sir Peter Parker and Sir Robert Calder at the Nat. Maritime Mus. seem to be datable to 1799 (*Cat.*, pp. 163, 211), and one of the two Nelson portraits by him in the same collection was not finished until June 1799 (*Cat.*, p. 196). The fact that a lunacy commission was not taken out until 1801 perhaps indicates that until that year his insanity was intermittent. See also Edw. Edwards, *Anecdotes of Painters etc.* 281–2, who seems inaccurate on some points.

[65] Though most reference books say 1803, the correct date of his death was 5 Dec. 1802. P.P.R., P.C.C. 1 Marriott.

Pochin, M.P., painted in 1793, still hang at Barkby Hall. A *Self-Portrait* by him was engraved in mezzotint by Valentine Green in 1805, and over fifty other portraits by him, including one of Green were also engraved.[66] Of these, only one represents a lady, and for some reason female portraits by him are virtually unknown. In style Abbott's work has a certain attractive softness of modelling and of colour, which suggests a possible influence of the pastellist John Russell; and a sensitivity of feeling for the personality of his sitter, in which he is superior to either Beechey or Hoppner. But, although a good draughtsman, he lacked the facility of those masters, and—fatal shortcoming—evidently failed to please the ladies. He does not appear to have possessed much originality, fire, or invention, and it is doubtful whether, had his working life been longer, he would have advanced in style much farther than in fact he did. His work is well represented in public galleries. The National Portrait Gallery has twelve of his pictures,[67] the National Maritime Museum eight,[68] and the Tate Gallery a single example.[69]

His son, Edward Francis Abbott, was studying, after his father's death, with the sculptor, Joseph Nollekens,[70] but nothing further is known of his career.

John Glover, landscape painter in watercolours and in oils, was born in 1767 at Houghton on the Hill.[71] He was the youngest of three children of a 'poor man engaged in agriculture'. A physical defect—he was club-footed—perhaps caused him to turn his attention to studies rather than to the normal rural pursuits. At the age of 19 he was appointed writing master at the Appleby Free School, and he began his professional practice as an artist by painting views of gentlemen's houses. In 1790 he married Sarah Young;[72] and about this time, on a visit to London, he took eight lessons from William Payne the watercolour painter, and also a single lesson from 'Smith', possibly John 'Warwick' Smith. In 1794 he moved to Lichfield, one of the most cultured of midland cities, and set up there as a drawing master, with immediate success. He resided at Lichfield for about eleven years, but during this period made a number of sketching tours to other parts of the country. He first exhibited in London at the Royal Academy of 1795,[73] and in addition to landscapes in oils and watercolour he made a number of etchings. In 1805 he moved to London, and joined the newly-formed Society of Painters in Watercolours, with whom he exhibited regularly. Again his success was immediate, and according to a note in Farington's diary, dated 1805, he had already 'sold drawings since he came to town to the amount of 700 guineas'. There may be an element of jealous exaggeration in this report, but Farington goes on to record that 'he is said to have 5 guineas a day for teaching'.[74] Moreover an anonymous writer (probably Richard Redgrave) recorded that Glover's *View of Durham Cathedral*, then at Lambton Hall, had realized 500 guineas.[75] Nearly 3 years later we learn from Farington

[66] *B.M. Cat. Engraved Brit. Portraits*, vi, 453.

[67] *Nat. Portrait Gallery Cat.* (1949), 291.

[68] *Nat. Maritime Mus. Cat.* (1931), 163, 168–9, 183, 195–6, 211–12, 220.

[69] *Tate Gallery, Cat. Brit. Sch.* (1947), 2, no. 1198.

[70] *Farington Diary*, ed. Greig, ii, 134.

[71] The principal sources for Glover are B. S. Long, 'John Glover', *Walker's Quarterly*, no. 15, Apr. 1924; J. L. Roget, *Hist. Old Watercolour Soc.*; R. and S. Redgrave, *Cent. Brit. Painters* (1947); and an anonymous article in *Art Jnl.* 1 July 1850.

[72] *Leics. Par. Rec.: Marriages*, ed. E. K. Elliott, x, 128.

[73] Graves, *R.A. Exhibitors*, iii, 251.

[74] *Farington Diary*, ed. Greig, 20 June 1805.

[75] *Art. Jnl.* 1 July 1850, 216.

that Glover was paid 2 guineas for a lesson of 3 hours.[76] He was, clearly, one of the most popular and sought-after drawing masters in the country. In 1807–8 he became President of the Watercolour Society; in 1814 he exhibited at the Paris Salon, and in Paris he painted imitations of Poussin and Claude. One of his Salon exhibits earned him a Gold Medal.[77] About 1817 or 1818 he bought a property at Ullswater, a house which had once been Wordsworth's, but sold it again 2 years later for £1,100 in order to buy a picture by Claude, and returned to London. In 1820 he opened his own annual exhibition at 16 Old Bond Street, where, in addition to his own works and those of his pupils, he exhibited two Claudes and some pictures by Poussin and Richard Wilson. He had by this time resigned from the Watercolour Society over a disagreement about the method of dividing profits from the exhibitions.[78] This was in 1817. In 1823 he became one of the founder members of the Society of British Artists. After making various further visits to the Continent, he sold his house in Montagu Square about 1830–1, auctioned his works and emigrated to Australia, taking with him, it is said, £60,000. In 1831 he settled in Tasmania, and died at Launceston in 1849. His wife survived him, and his estate was sold for £10,000. He had continued sending pictures for exhibition in London down to 1832, and altogether 445 of his works were shown in London exhibitions apart from his own exhibitions in Old Bond Street.[79]

Two of his sons, John and William, also became artists and drawing masters. The younger John Glover exhibited 26 works at the Royal Academy between 1808 and 1829; and William, between 1813 and 1833, exhibited a total of 42 works, at the Royal Academy (1), the British Institution (7), the Society of British Artists (10), and the Old Watercolour Society (24). His pupils also included James Holworthy of Bosworth (1781–1841),[80] who exhibited 3 works at the Royal Academy and 36 at the Old Watercolour Society between 1803 and 1813. William Glover is represented at the Victoria and Albert Museum by a large watercolour, and Holworthy by a watercolour and an indian-ink drawing.[81]

John Glover's work is well represented at the British Museum,[82] the Victoria and Albert Museum,[83] and at other galleries,[84] and the Leicester Art Gallery has a characteristic watercolour.[85] His brilliant success was perhaps due more to charm of personality and to commercial acumen than to strictly artistic merit. He was evidently an attractive man. Tall, powerful, heavy, and though club-footed a good walker, he possessed phenomenal energy and a great fondness for music, and he delighted in catching and taming small birds and animals. He rode on the crest of the wave of enthusiasm for watercolour sketching which affected polite society like an epidemic in the first decades of the 19th century. As the Redgraves wrote, 'the impression he made in his day was more that of

76 *Farington Diary*, ed. Greig, v, 53.

77 *Art Jnl.* 1 July 1850, 216.

78 Roget, *Hist. Old Watercolour Soc.* i, 398, 403.

79 A. Graves, *Dict. Artists* (1895), 112.

80 Ibid. 112, 142. According to *Farington Diary*, ed. Greig, ii, 242, Glover senior was in May 1804 lodging at Holworthy's address in Mount St. and both men were in practice as drawing masters.

81 *Vic. and Albert Mus. Cat. Watercolour Paintings* (1927), 236, 286.

82 *B.M. Cat. Drawings by Brit. Artists*, ii, 235–6.

83 *Vic. and Albert Mus. Cat. Watercolour Paintings* (1927), 234–6; *Abridged Cat. Oil Paintings* (1908), 47.

84 *Tate Gallery Cat. Brit. Sch.* (1947), 101.

85 The oil landscape recorded in the 1899 catalogue (p. 93) is no longer at the Leicester Art Gallery. The watercolour was purchased in 1936. One of Glover's sketch bks. is in the City of Birmingham Art Gallery: *Birmingham Art Gallery Cat.* (1930), 93.

successful novelty than of art-excellence, and art was little advanced by him'.[86] This severe verdict is undoubtedly justified. His early works follow the manner of William Payne, his mature ones nearly all ape Claude Lorraine, but with a finical trickery of finish and a poverty of colour which deprive his works of any real force. One of his favourite devices was the use of a brush, of which the hairs were divided into four small groups, so as to make four fine parallel strokes, for the depiction of foliage. In watercolour his feeling for light and atmosphere was often sweet and pleasing, but his colours have generally proved fugitive and his drawings are now generally pale and yellowish. It seems unlikely that his reputation will ever again reach the level attained during his own lifetime. The best that one can say of him as an artist is that his success, despite humble origins and lack of systematic instruction, is evidence of a remarkable degree of ability and application.

Ben Marshall, one of the three or four best sporting painters of the British School, was certainly a Leicestershire man, but the exact place of his birth remains unknown. He seems to have been born in 1768 or 1769; he died in 1835.[87] It seems to be commonly believed that he was born at Barkby, but there seems to be no evidence for this. Nothing is certainly known of his career until 1791, when he left Leicestershire for London, with a recommendation from Mr. Pochin of Barkby, and became a pupil of Lemuel Francis Abbott for about 3 years. He must, however, have been already a proficient painter, having been trained perhaps under one of the Boultbees, for in 1792 he painted a large picture of the Prince of Wales's horse Escape.[88] This appears to disprove the story told in the *Sporting Magazine*, that he was so impressed with Sawrey Gilpin's 1793 Academy picture, *The Death of a Fox*, that he turned from portraiture to the painting of sporting subjects,[89] though it does not disprove the influence of Gilpin on the formation of his style. In the early years of his independent career, however, his work was of mixed categories: the Marquess of Hartington employed him as a portrait painter, for the Duchess of Devonshire he painted a picture of Chiswick House, and for the duke a portrait of a favourite hunter. The first engraving after a picture by Marshall appeared in the *Sporting Magazine* for February 1796, and his position as a sporting artist seems then to have been established. Pictures by him first appeared at the Royal Academy in 1800, and he again exhibited there in 1801, 1806, 1807, 1808, 1810, 1812, 1818, and 1819.[90] By 1804 his reputation with leading painters was already very high. Sir Francis Bourgeois spoke of him to Farington as having extraordinary ability, and reported Gilpin as saying that 'in managing his backgrounds he had done that which Stubbs and himself could never venture upon.'[91] It is said that Marshall once went to Italy,[92] but this journey cannot be dated, though it probably belongs to the earlier part of his career. In 1812 he moved from London to Newmarket, in order to meet the sporting gentry the more easily, and he remained centred there for 13 years. In 1819 he was severely injured in a coach accident to the Leeds mail, while on his way to Rockingham Castle, where a fine series of his works still hangs. For many

[86] Redgrave, *Cent. Brit. Painters*, 211.

[87] W. S. Sparrow, *Geo. Stubbs and Ben Marshall*, 78. All facts in these paragraphs not specifically acknowledged are taken from this book.

[88] Sparrow, *Stubbs and Marshall*, 47–48.

[89] *Sporting Mag.* 1796, 254.

[90] A. Graves, *R.A. Exhibitors*, v, 190.

[91] *Farington Diary*, ed. Greig, ii, 216–17.

[92] W. S. Sparrow, 'Ben Marshall's Centenary', *Connoisseur*, xcv, 65.

months he was unable to work; indeed, he never entirely recovered, and all his best work was done before this date. In later years he seems to have devoted a good deal of his time to writing, and the late W. S. Sparrow held that Marshall was the writer 'Observator' of the *Sporting Magazine*. In his last years, when he was a widower, and very poor, he lived in London Terrace, Hackney Road, London. In 1826 Marshall attempted to force his son Lambert into popular fame as a sporting painter at the age of 16, but the attempt failed.[93] On his death, Ben Marshall's property was valued for probate at only £200.[94]

In spite of the rapid rise of his fame during the last 20 years or so, Marshall is still inadequately represented in public collections. The Tate Gallery has one portrait by him,[95] and the National Gallery of British Sports and Pastimes had three pictures: a self-portrait of 1799, a portrait of the pugilist John Jackson dated 1810, and a picture of *Sam Chifney on the Duke of Rutland's Sorcery*, dated 1812.[96] But the best collections of his works are still the private ones owned by the Duke of Rutland, Lord Woolavington, Mrs. Macdonald Buchanan at Cottesbrooke, and Sir Michael Culme-Seymour at Rockingham Castle. Perhaps his finest pictures are the *Lord Sondes and Hounds* of 1815 at Rockingham Castle,[97] and *Francis Dukinfield Astley and Hounds* of 1800 at Upton House.[98] Critics who are also hunting men, such as the late Major Guy Paget, have always criticized Marshall adversely from the point of view of his representation of the hunt. Paget even asserted that 'strictly speaking Ben Marshall remained a portrait painter and a very good one too. He is not essentially a sporting artist. The portrait comes first and the sport second. The arrangement of his hounds in his big hunting pictures gives away the fact that he was not a hunting man. . . . He never gets his hunt beyond the meet.'[99] No doubt there is some truth in these assertions, but to the critic who is not a hunting man Marshall is the prince of sporting painters. No better illustration of his power of composition could be found than is provided by a comparison between his study of F. D. Astley and the finished composition in which the group in the study is combined with three other figures.[1] The arrangement of the group represented in the study is repeated in the finished picture, but the total effect is utterly different. The angle of view, the level of the skyline, and the disposition of light and tone have been completely altered in the larger composition. Marshall's pictures have a bold, square, and masculine handling which recalls that of Géricault, and, indeed, of all the English sporting painters it must have been Marshall who most impressed and influenced the French painter on his visit to this country. His colour is strong, but always well controlled by an effect of tone, especially in the largest compositions. His art represents in many respects a combination of some of the best qualities of Stubbs with those of Sawrey Gilpin, the greatest sporting painters of the earlier generation. Good examples of his work already fetch high prices in the sale room,[2] and as the stock of them remaining in their original homes diminishes, these prices are likely to

[93] Lambert Marshall was represented in the *Nat. Gallery of Brit. Sports and Pastimes* by one picture, and the Nat. Portrait Gallery has his portrait of his father, *Cat.* (1949), 168.

[94] Sparrow, *Stubbs and Marshall*, 51–52, 64 ff., 78; *Connoisseur*, xcv, 67; Sparrow, *Bk. of Sporting Painters*, 95.

[95] *Tate Gallery Cat. Brit. School* (1947), p. xliii.

[96] *Nat. Gallery of Brit. Sports and Pastimes*, nos. 151 and 154. See note 46.

[97] Reproduced Sparrow, *Bk. of Sporting Painters*, opposite p. 104.

[98] Reproduced ibid. opposite p. 106; sold at Christie's 14 May 1926 for £2,730.

[99] G. Paget, *Aspects of Brit. Art*, 273.

[1] Reproduced *Connoisseur*, xcv, 66–67.

[2] *Year's Art*, ed. A. C. R. Carter (1947), 139, 141.

become higher still. His work is as representative of the English life of his time as that of any painter, and no valuation which places him on a level with the best portrait painters among his contemporaries can be said to be too high.

John Ferneley, by many esteemed the best of the Leicestershire sporting painters, was born at Thrussington in 1782,[3] the youngest of six children of a wheelwright, and baptized at St. Mary's Church, Melton Mowbray.[4] He was first apprenticed to his father's trade, but in 1801, at the age of 18, he went to London and entered into a further period of 3 years' apprenticeship under Ben Marshall.[5] It has been stated that he also entered the Royal Academy Schools,[6] but there is no record of his attendance in the academy registers. On the expiration of this apprenticeship he was employed at Dover by the Duke of Rutland and the officers of the Leicestershire Militia, who were then stationed at Dover Castle. From Dover he returned to London, and from there he went to Norwich where he painted some pictures for Mr. Gurney, the banker. During a tour in Lincolnshire he met Thomas Assheton Smith, later Master of the Quorn, whom he referred to as his first sitter in hunting pink. In July 1808, while staying at Staunton Harold, he was taken ill, and the following winter he spent in Ireland, in order to obtain the benefit of a milder climate, and there he enjoyed the patronage of Lord Rossmore, Lord Lismore, and others. Returning to Thrussington he married in 1809, as his first wife, Sarah Kettle,[7] who died in 1836. His successful tour in Ireland was repeated in the spring of 1810, 1811, and 1812, the painter being accompanied, except on the last occasion, by his wife. From 1813, however, he seems to have remained with his family, except for short trips to fulfil commissions in other parts of the country.[8] In 1814 he moved from Thrussington into Melton Mowbray, which was his home for the rest of his life.[9]

He first exhibited at the Royal Academy in 1806. Between that year and 1853 he showed there a total of twenty-two pictures. The exhibits were intermittent, and only on one occasion, in 1807, did he show more than two pictures.[10] Certainly from 1808, when his surviving account books begin,[11] he was kept pretty well occupied with commissions, and probably did not need the advertisement of pictures in the London exhibitions. A large number of prints were engraved after his work,[12] and he was in steady demand for portraits of horses and pictures of hunting scenes almost to the end of his life. His prices were not high, however, and on the basis of his own account books Paget has worked out that his average yearly income was only about £380, though in his best year, 1833, he made £1,254.[13] In 1823 his large picture of *The Meet of*

[3] *D.N.B.* xviii, 374–5.

[4] Sparrow, *Bk. of Sporting Painters*, 158.

[5] The *D.N.B.* dates his apprenticeship from 1803, and states that he remained with Marshall only a year, whereas it is now known that Ferneley was still with Marshall at Beaumont St. Marylebone in 1804, when he got Thomas Harrison to substitute for him in the Middlesex Militia: G. Paget, *Melton Mowbray of John Ferneley*, 15. Major Paget's date for the commencement of the apprenticeship is only conjectural, but seems logical.

[6] G. Paget, op. cit. 13–14.

[7] *Leics. Par. Reg. Marriages*, ed. W. P. W. Phillimore and T. M. Blagg, ii, 109. The certificate is repr. by W. S. Sparrow, *Bk. of Sporting Painters*, opposite p. 159.

[8] After one of these excursions, to Liverpool in 1839, he painted two important pictures of the Liverpool Races: Paget, *Melton Mowbray of John Ferneley*.

[9] *D.N.B.* xviii, 374–5. In one place, *Aspects of Brit. Art*, 274, Major Paget has given the date of Ferneley's settling at Melton as 1803; this is a mistake.

[10] A. Graves, *R.A. Exhibitors*, iii, 100.

[11] The account books have been fully published by G. Paget, *Melton Mowbray of John Ferneley*, 126–55.

[12] For list see Paget, op. cit. 157.

[13] Ibid. 159.

the Quorn at Quenby was raffled; the chances cost 5 guineas each, and the artist received £220. 10*s*. for the picture.[14] The Leicestershire gentry patronized him generously, but since he came into contact at Melton with hunting men from all parts of the country, and indeed from abroad also, his pictures were in wide demand and were well scattered in country houses all over England. The strength of his position as the leading hunting painter of his time, and something of his independence of character is well illustrated by an anecdote recounted by Dick Christian. Lord Brudenell, who was something of a tyrant, apparently

> 'tried his bully ways on Mr. Ferneley the painter, but he weren't taking any, and told his lordship he weren't his only customer, and if he didn't like his work he could go elsewhere an' welcome. He (Lord Brudenell) sweared he'd never go anear such a damned impertinent sign painter again, he did. He tries half a dozen, Brown o' Leicester, Barraud, and a Mr. Laporte; but when he come back from the War and wants a real nice picture done of his chargers, he goes back to Mr. Ferneley to paint it.'[15]

A nice story, which belongs, presumably, to Ferneley's earlier years, before 1820.

By his first wife Ferneley had seven children, of whom two followed his own profession; John Ferneley junior (1815–62) resided chiefly in Yorkshire, where he painted hunting and military subjects, and Claude Loraine Ferneley (1822–91), who assisted his father and continued his practice after his father's death.[16] A daughter, Sarah Ferneley (1812–1903), who married Henry Johnson in 1838,[17] engraved several of her father's pictures and painted water-colours. After Henry Johnson's death in 1850 she returned to her father's house in Melton, where she remained until her death.[18] John Ferneley's second wife, Ann, by whom he had one son, died in 1853.[19] Ferneley himself died in 1860, aged 78 years, in Scalford Road, Melton Mowbray.[20] Sales of his work were held at Melton in 1862 and 1903.[21] At these dispersals prices were very modest. Ferneley's auction reputation, however, has rapidly increased since the First World War, and good examples of his racing and hunting scenes now frequently fetch prices ranging well into four figures.[22] In public galleries his art is still inadequately represented; the Leicester Art Gallery has five of his pictures, and the Tate Gallery 1.[23]

John Ferneley's reputation as a painter depends mainly, but not entirely, upon his understanding of horses, which he rendered with a love and knowledge superior to that of any of his contemporaries, Herring not excepted. Nevertheless, as Paget has written, 'it would often be possible to take his animals out and still have a charming picture', for his feeling for landscape was genuine, and 'he invariably conveys a sense of space and fresh air . . . and his colouring is always soft and harmonious'.[24] His touch with the brush was light and delicate, and his pictures are seldom without grace and rhythm. In the composition of

[14] Major Paget's account of this raffle, op. cit. 54, corrects that given by Sparrow, *Brit. Sporting Artists*, 191.

[15] G. Paget and L. Irvine, *Flying Parson and Dick Christian*, 276.

[16] Paget, *Aspects of Brit. Art*, 278.

[17] A portrait of John Ferneley by Henry Johnson, dated 1838, is in the Nat. Portrait Gallery, *Cat.* (1949), 88.

[18] A *View of Melton Mowbray with Kite Flying*, in oils, by Sarah Ferneley, signed and dated 1836, was in the *Nat. Gallery of Brit. Sports and Pastimes*, no. 160.

[19] *D.N.B.* xviii, 374–5.

[20] Sparrow, *Bk. of Sporting Painters*, 160. His will is printed in the same work, 203–4.

[21] Paget, *Melton Mowbray of John Ferneley*, 158–9.

[22] *Year's Art*, ed. A. C. R. Carter (1938), 290; (1939), 271.

[23] *Tate Gallery Cat. Brit. School* (1947), p. xxv.

[24] Paget, *Melton Mowbray of John Ferneley*, 97.

hunting scenes he is unequalled. Both the landscape and the descriptive incident are rendered with a natural understanding. Unfortunately, his gifts were not as a rule equal to the organization of a large canvas, and his most elaborate compositions are seldom as attractive as his smaller sketches or hunt scurries. To some extent this may be due to his frequent reliance on tinted varnishes, subsequently removed during cleaning, to pull his compositions together in tone. But despite Ferneley's very real merits as a painter, it is rather misleading to call him, as the late W. S. Sparrow has done, 'the Gainsborough of English horse-painters',[25] for his work never achieved the expressive emotional power which alone could give such a comparison validity.

With the Ferneley children, the best period of the Leicestershire school of painters comes to an end. Of Leicestershire artists born since the 1820's none rises even into the second rank, and most of them can be regarded only as minor figures.

Of these minor figures the first, John Flower, came of a family which had for generations owned the old Castle Mill in Leicester, and he was born in the city in 1795. His father died while he was still a youth, but Flower's ability attracted the attention of Dr. Alexander of Danet's Hall, who encouraged him. Before he was 20 he had some employment as a drawing master, and was patronized by Miss Linwood. Through the interest of Miss Linwood, it was arranged that Flower should receive some lessons from Peter de Wint in London in 1816.[26] He then returned to Leicester, where he continued to practise as a drawing master, making periodical sketching tours, mostly in the midland and northern counties. Some engravings after his drawings were published in 1826,[27] and he was among the illustrators of a History of Staffordshire projected in 1832–3 by J. M. Mathew, F.S.A., which was never published. Some fifty of Flower's drawings made for this purpose have survived, and were purchased in 1934 for the William Salt Library, Stafford. They are small pencil drawings, with annotations by him, some of which show him to have been a man of a somewhat religious and moralizing turn of mind.[28] Flower is worthy of remembrance primarily as an illustrator of the former appearance of his native town and region. His drawings and watercolours are not uncommon in private houses in Leicester, and the Leicester Art Gallery possesses a wash drawing and a watercolour by him. He died at his house in Upper Regent Street, Leicester in 1861.[29]

After John Flower, and with the exception of the Ferneley children, almost 50 years elapsed before Leicestershire again produced a painter of any note, and then it was another minor figure, though one perhaps more interesting than Flower. Henry Ward, generally known as Harry Ward, was born at Kibworth in 1844, the eldest son of John Ward, a hosiery manufacturer and his wife Jane.[30] He attended Mr. Buzzard's school at Peatling, where he showed precocious skill with a pencil. He received encouragement in his drawing from

[25] Sparrow, *Bk. of Sporting Painters*, 157.

[26] Obituary in *Leic. Chron.* 7 Dec. 1861. Thieme-Becker, *Künstlerlexikon*, xii, 129, gives the date of these lessons as 'um 1815', but the obituary notice is definite that the year was 1816.

[27] Printed in J. Flower, *Views of Ancient Bldgs. in Town and City of Leic.*

[28] S.A.H.B., 'The John Flower Sketches', *Collect. for Hist. of Staffs.* 1947, 101–11. The cat. is unfortunately very badly compiled and it is impossible to tell from it even how many drawings there are.

[29] Leic. Registry, death cert. 29 Nov.

[30] S. H. Skillington, Introduction to *Cat. of an Exhibition of Watercolours and Sketches by Harry Ward*, Leic. Mus. and Art Gallery, May–June 1915. The birth, which appears to be omitted from Somerset Ho. rec., was registered at Market Harborough Registry.

his mother, but not from his father, who apprenticed him at the age of 15 to Mr. Kemp, a draper in the Market Place, Leicester.[31] When his family moved into Leicester in 1865, however, he left the drapery business and devoted himself to drawing. He took pupils, among whom was John Fulleylove,[32] and had rooms in Pocklington's Walk, from which he subsequently moved to the Stepped Houses, near Campbell Street, London Road. In 1871 he removed to London, and afterwards settled at Windsor, where he was befriended by A. Y. Nutt, Surveyor of the Castle. His work attracted the attention of the royal family, and he was employed to instruct the Princess Beatrice, who gave two drawings by him to her mother, Queen Victoria, at Christmas 1871. One of these, a watercolour of the entrance to the Prince Consort's mausoleum at Frogmore, signed 'H. Ward' and dated '1871', is in the Royal Library; and a companion drawing, of the Duchess of Kent's mausoleum at Frogmore, hangs at Osborne House.[33] Several members of the royal family are reported to have purchased his drawings. In 1871–2 he visited Belgium, and in 1873 he went to Switzerland and to Scotland. He had earlier made trips to Lincoln, York, and to Wales. He returned to Leicester in 1873, and died the same year at 49 Hinckley Road, Leicester.[34] His works, especially his pencil drawings, have a distinctly personal quality, sensitive and decorative. The influence which most determined his manner was probably that of Birket Foster, whose light touch with the brush he imitated, but his best watercolours, such as a view of Westminster in the possession of Mr. K. E. Houston, have a power of tone and a richness of colour seldom found in Foster's. That particular drawing, indeed, seems far nearer in style to Whistler or Monet than to any English watercolourist of his age, and represents a remarkable achievement for a young provincial drawing master who must have been almost entirely self-taught. If his career had not been prematurely cut short, his development might well have been spectacular. The Leicester Art Gallery has a collection of thirty-two watercolours and drawings by him, and a commemorative exhibition of his work was held there in May and June 1915.

Closely associated with Harry Ward was his contemporary and pupil, John Fulleylove, an architectural and topographical painter of considerable reputation in his own day. He was born at Leicester in 1845,[35] the son of John and Elizabeth Fulleylove. He was educated in Leicester at the private school of Dr. Highton, and was articled to Flint, Shenton, and Baker, a firm of architects.[36] After meeting and making friends with Harry Ward, from whom he received some instruction in watercolour painting, he turned his attention to painting, always retaining, however, a preference for architectural subjects. He began exhibiting in London in 1871, and showed frequently in subsequent years at the Royal Academy, the Royal Institute (of which he became an associate in 1878, member in 1879 and later a Vice-President), the Institute of

[31] Skillington, op. cit. *Reg. Freemen Leic. 1836–1930*, ed. H. Hartopp, 420, records that Hen. Ward, framework-knitter, eldest son of Wm., framework-knitter, was apprenticed 27 July 1859 to Flint. There is no record in this *Reg.* of the apprenticeship to Kemp. This Hen. Ward, however, was another person, as the name of the father proves.

[32] *D.N.B.* 2nd Supp. ii, 60–61; Thieme-Becker, *Künstlerlexikon*, xii, 582.

[33] Ex. inf. Sir Owen Morshead, Royal Librarian.

[34] Gen. Reg. Off., death cert. 2 Oct.

[35] Thieme-Becker, *Künstlerlexikon*, xii, 582; *D.N.B.* 2nd Supp. ii, 60–61; *Who Was Who, 1897–1916*, gives the date as 1847.

[36] *D.N.B.* 2nd Supp. ii, 60–61; *Who Was Who, 1897–1916*, 262.

Painters in Watercolours, and the Royal Society of British Artists.[37] In 1878 he married Elizabeth Sara, daughter of Samuel Elgood of Leicester,[38] and in 1883 he made his home in London. He travelled extensively, visiting Belgium, France, Italy, Greece, and Palestine. Many exhibitions of his works were held, at the Fine Art Society's galleries in Bond St., at the Goupil Gallery, London, in Oxford, and in Leicester. A series of his drawings of Oxford was published, with text by T. H. Ward in 1889. This was the first of a dozen or so volumes in which his illustrations were featured.[39] Through these publications he acquired an international reputation, and in 1891 he showed at the Berlin International Exhibition, and in 1900 at Paris. He died at 1 Denning Road, Hampstead, in 1908.[40]

Fulleylove is represented in the Leicester Art Gallery by 3 oil paintings and 26 watercolours and drawings; the Victoria and Albert Museum has 2 small oils by him, both views of Oxford, as well as 4 watercolours;[41] the British Museum has 12 drawings;[42] the Tate Gallery a pencil drawing;[43] and there are further examples in the galleries at Cardiff, Liverpool, and Norwich.

His watercolours, which are certainly his best works, show a variable style, at its best not unattractive, which conveys a genuine feeling for atmosphere, space, and colour. They tend to lack rhythm and emotional expression, however, and the colour is sometimes too strong for the tonal structure. In his oils these defects become still more noticeable, and his large pictures, such as *The Mosque of Omar at Jerusalem*, in the Leicester Art Gallery, are repulsively dead in surface. The high reputation which he enjoyed in the last two decades of his life has not been sustained since and is unlikely to be revived, though it is possibly true, as has been claimed, that he produced 'some of the most brilliant and accomplished watercolour work of his generation.'[44]

Edward Davies, though actually born before Ward and Fulleylove, turned to painting as a career comparatively late in life. He was not, strictly speaking, a Leicestershire man, but he spent over 50 years of his life in Leicester and the whole of his life as an artist centred there. He was born in 1841 at 6 St. James's Place, Aldgate, London, the son of Isaac Davies, hairdresser, and his wife Louisa.[45] He became a cigar-maker, and moved to Leicester at the age of 24. It has been stated that he attended the Royal Academy schools,[46] but this seems to be inaccurate; at any rate the registers there contain no entry that can be regarded as certainly belonging to him.[47] The date of his becoming a whole-time painter cannot be fixed with any certainty, but he began exhibit-

[37] Graves, *R.A. Exhibitors*, iii, 181; Graves, *Dict. Artists*, 105.

[38] *Who Was Who, 1897–1916*, 262.

[39] His other books included *The Picturesque Mediterranean Sea* (1889); *In the Footprints of Charles Lamb* (1891), with text by B. E. Martin; *Pictures of Classic Greek Landscape and Architecture* (1897), text by H. W. Nevinson; *The Holy Land* (1902), text by J. Kelman; *Oxford* (1903, reprinted 1922), text by P. E. Thomas; *Westminster Abbey* (1904), text by E. T. Bradley; *Edinburgh* (1904, reprinted 1931), text by R. O. Masson; *The Pageant of London* (1906), text by R. P. B. Davey; *Greece* (1906), text by J. A. MacClymont; *Middlesex* (1907), text by A. R. H. Moncrieff; *The Tower of London* (1908), text by A. Poyser; *The Scott Country* (1920).

[40] Death cert. 22 May; *D.N.B.* 2nd Supp. ii, 60–61, and other works incorrectly state that he died at 21 Church Row, Hampstead; *Who Was Who, 1897–1916*, incorrectly gives the date of death as 24 May 1908.

[41] *Vic. and Albert Mus. Abridged Cat. Oil Paintings* (1908), 44; *Cat. Watercolour Paintings* (1927), 217–18.

[42] *B.M. Cat. Drawings acquired bet. 1912 and 1914*, 32.

[43] *Tate Gallery Cat. Brit. School* (1947), 90.

[44] *D.N.B.* 2nd Supp. ii, 61.

[45] Birth Cert. Somerset Ho. 21 Mar.

[46] Obituary, *Leic. Daily Post*, 31 Aug. 1920.

[47] An Edward Davis entered the R.A. schools on 17 Jan. 1853, but was 20 years of age and therefore must have been another person.

ing at the Royal Academy in 1880,[48] and that can be taken as an approximate date. A great admirer of the work of David Cox and Constable, he modelled his style principally on the former, though he was also much influenced by his friends E. M. Wimperis and James Orrock (a dental surgeon who was also an enthusiastic collector and amateur painter), with the latter of whom he often painted in Bradgate Park, near Leicester. Edward Davies was exclusively a landscape painter, and his most typical works were painted in the mountains of Wales, Skye, and Iona. He exhibited frequently in London at the Royal Academy and the Royal Institute (of which he became a member in 1896), and at the Institute of British Painters in Watercolours.[49] His work was represented at the Rome International Exhibition of 1911, and he is reported to have sold many works to collections in the colonies. He is represented in the Leicester Art Gallery by nine oils and thirteen watercolours. He was a fine sportsman, a good runner and boxer, as well as a painter. He died in 1920 at 131 Narborough Road, Leicester.[50]

The romantic spirit and the dark tones of Davies's watercolours do not accord with the taste of the present day, but they are fine examples of the late tradition which began with Constable, and there can be no doubt of the artist's genuine feeling for the mists and storms and the deep sombre colouring of his favourite type of scenery. Though his draughtsmanship lacked delicacy and a sense of structure, his pictures seldom fail to convey a sense of weather and of dramatic effect.

An outstanding position among Leicestershire topographical artists belongs to the watercolourist George Moore Henton, who was born at 64 Regent Street, Leicester, in 1861, the son of George Henton, banker's clerk[51] and later manager of Paget's Bank. The Hentons were an old Leicestershire yeoman family, who had lived for some generations at Ragdale. George Moore Henton was educated at the Mill Hill House School, Leicester, and received his early artistic training from Wilmot Pilsbury, who was the first principal of the Leicester School of Art, 1870–81.[53] He began exhibiting at the Royal Academy in 1884, and in addition to his occasional exhibits there, he showed also at the Royal Watercolour Society.[53] He was for many years a member of the Leicester Society of Artists, and of the Leicestershire Archaeological Society, for which he took hundreds of excellent photographs. He was always most anxious to secure the preservation of buildings and places of artistic or antiquarian interest, and for years he had advocated the laying-out of the Castle Gardens, Leicester, which was finally done after his death. He died in 1924 at Charnwood House, Victoria Road, Leicester,[54] where he had lived for over 30 years. An exhibition of his work was held at the Leicester Art Gallery in 1934,[55] and the gallery possesses a collection of seventy-nine watercolours by him, mostly of local scenes. In his personal life Henton was completely dominated by his mother, with whom he lived until her death at an advanced age. It has been said that

48 Graves, *R.A. Exhibitors*, ii, 257.

49 Graves, *Dict. Artists*.

50 Death Cert. Somerset Ho. 29 Aug. The dates of his birth and death have been wrongly reported by Thieme-Becker, *Künstlerlexikon*, viii, 470 as 1843–1912, and by many other reference works, e.g. *Mallett's Index of Artists*, 102, Benezit, *Dict. des Peintres*, ii, 36.

51 Birth cert. Leic. Reg. 2 Jan.

52 Ex inf. the late S. H. Skillington of Leic.

53 Graves, *Dict. Artists*; Thieme-Becker, *Künstlerlexikon*, xvi, 435.

54 Death cert. Leic. Reg. 21 Apr. Short obit. notices appeared in *Leic. Mercury* and *Leic. Evening Mail*, 23 Apr. 1924.

55 *Leic. Mus., Art Gallery and Library Bull.* xl, Apr. 1934, 2.

'though he sold quite a lot of his work . . . he did not make high prices. He was immensely industrious, and his house was full to bursting with drawings, some unfinished'.[56] Many of these were dispersed in local sales at quite insignificant prices after his death. Despite its conservatism and deliberate cultivation of 'olde worlde' charm, his work at its best has real sensitivity to colour, light, and atmosphere, and he was particularly clever at rendering the colour effect of mellowed old brickwork, like that of Ragdale Hall. Any collection of his drawings provides a valuable and accurate record of the buildings and places which he frequented.

Though she was not born in the county it is impossible to omit from this account Marion Margaret Violet, Duchess of Rutland, who for many years lived at Belvoir Castle, and was a member of the Leicester Society of Artists. She was born in 1856, daughter of Col. the Hon. C. H. Lindsay, and granddaughter of the 24th Earl of Crawford. She married in 1882 Henry Manners, then private secretary to Lord Salisbury. He became Marquess of Granby when his father succeeded to the dukedom of Rutland, and himself succeeded to the title in 1906. He died in 1925 and was survived by his widow, who died in 1937.[57]

The duchess was a skilled amateur artist in pencil and watercolour, and also a sculptress. Her drawings, of which portrait heads form the largest proportion, are sensitive, and though structurally weak and lacking in decision of line and rhythm, they often convey a sympathetic understanding of personality. Almost invariably they have charm, and the fact that she often idealized the heads in the mode of the time will not seriously diminish their value as historical records. She exhibited frequently in London, at the Royal Academy, the Grosvenor, and New Galleries, in Leicester, Manchester, Paris, and elsewhere. Portrait drawings by her are to be found in many public collections, including the Louvre (*Henry Cust*, *Sir John Martin-Harvey*, *Princess Pierre Troubetzkoy*), and the Leicester Art Gallery (*John, 9th Duke of Rutland*, *Fridtjof Nansen*). Her volume of *Portraits of Men and Women*, containing fifty-one drawings, including a self-portrait, was published by Constable in 1900. Her best work in sculpture is the recumbent marble figure, in the chapel at Haddon, of her son Lord Manners of Haddon, who died in 1894 aged nine. It is a work of poignant quality.[58] Though perhaps no work which she left possesses the striking beauty which she herself had in her youth, she made a distinctive addition to the portraiture of her time.[59]

The last of the painters to be dealt with here is Harry Morley, who was born at Belgrave, Leicester, in 1881,[60] the second son of Thomas Morley, hosiery manufacturer. He was educated at Alderman Newton's School, Leicester, and at the age of nine joined a class in watercolour painting which was run by William Barrow in Belgrave. In 1897 he went to the Leicester School of Art with the intention of becoming an architect. He gained a scholarship to the Royal College of Art in 1900, and obtained there the travelling scholarship in architecture, which enabled him to travel in Italy in 1904. In competition for the Owen Jones Studentship of the R.I.B.A. he won the silver medal in 1905, and in the following year was awarded the studentship. In the meantime he

56 Ex inf. the late S. H. Skillington.

57 *The Times*, 28 Dec. 1937.

58 The plaster model was presented to the Tate Gallery in 1938 by members of the family; *Cat. Brit. School* (1947), p. liii.

59 An article on her work exists in *Russell Cotes Mus. Bull.* xii, 29–35.

60 Thieme-Becker, *Künstlerlexikon*, xxv, 160.

had been articled in 1905 to Beresford Pite, F.R.I.B.A. He travelled in Italy again in 1907, and while there decided to abandon architecture in favour of painting as a career. He went to Paris to study painting in 1908, and settled in London and began exhibiting in 1913. After the First World War he exhibited extensively in the U.S.A., France, and Italy. In 1924 his picture *Apollo and Marsyas* was bought under the terms of the Chantrey Bequest.[61] At the instigation of Robert Austin he began in 1928 to make engravings, and in the following year he won a silver medal at the Paris Salon. He was elected a member in 1931 and Vice-President in 1937 of the Royal Watercolour Society; a Fellow of the Royal Society of Painter-Etchers in 1931; a member of the Royal Society of Portrait Painters in 1936, and an Associate of the Royal Academy in the same year. In 1940 he was President of the Leicester Society of Artists.[62] In 1930–1 a group of his works was shown at the Leicester Art Gallery,[63] and many exhibitions were given at different dates in dealers' galleries in London. The Leicester Art Gallery possesses two oils and twelve watercolours by him; his work is also represented at the British Museum, the Victoria and Albert Museum,[64] in the galleries at Bath, Bradford, Leeds, Manchester (Whitworth Art Gallery), Reading, Boston (Mass.), and Durban (S. Africa). In 1939 he contributed an article 'In Praise of Watercolour' to the Old Watercolour Society's Annual Volume.[65] He died in 1943.[66]

Harry Morley's work is not easy to assess. His best work was probably done in the watercolour medium. In oils he never altogether avoided an academic stiffness and frigidity; in engraving he was too much influenced by Robert Austin.[67] Even in watercolour, in spite of his great ease and fluency of handling of both pen or pencil outline and colour wash, his work often looks like an imitation of the effects of Wilson Steer or D. S. MacColl. Towards the end of his life, however, in a series of watercolours made on the east coast, he found his natural expression. These drawings show the quality of his feeling for light and atmosphere, especially those which record transient effects of cold blue light under heavy clouds after rain; but they have insufficient variety of expression to retain interest in a large series.

It may not be out of place to conclude this chapter with notes on two artists who were not painters. An artist who fits into no ready-made categories, but belongs in her own little niche of the history of art, is Mary Linwood, maker of needlework pictures, author and musical composer, and school mistress. She came from a Northamptonshire family, and was born in Birmingham in 1755, but removed to Leicester, where she lived for most of her long life.[68] According to a source often quoted in accounts of her,

> 'in the year 1782 a friend sent her for inspection a large collection of prints, in various styles of engraving, with no other view than that of affording a casual amusement. Inspecting them with the eye of genius, Miss Linwood conceived that the force of an engraving might be united with the softness of a mezzotint, but being totally unacquainted with any process in that art, she had no instrument with

61 *Tate Gallery Cat. Brit. School* (1947), 184.

62 *Who's Who* (1943), 2214; obituary in *Mus. Jnl.* xliii, 140.

63 *Exhibition of Works by Three Leic.-born Artists, Harry Morley, Robert S. Austin, Frederick G. Austin,* Dec. 1930–Jan. 1931.

64 *Vic. and Albert Mus. Cat. Watercolour Paintings* (1927), 367.

65 *The Old Watercolour Society's 17th Annual Vol.* 41–43.

66 *Who's Who* (1944), 36.

67 For a detailed account of his engravings see: *Print Collector's Quarterly*, xviii, and *Apollo*, ix, 163–4.

68 *D.N.B.* xi, 1214 says she was still living in Birmingham in 1776, but the cat. of the Soc. of Artists in 1776 gives her address as 'of Leicester'; obituary in *Gent. Mag.* (N.S.), xxiii, 555–7, says she removed to Leic. aged 6.

which she could make the experiment, but her needle. With that she endeavoured to realise her first idea by copying such prints as most engaged her attention.'[69]

This romanticized account of the origin of her needlework pictures is certainly inaccurate, however, for she had already exhibited needlework pictures at the Society of Artists in 1776 and 1778, and in the former year a Mrs. Hannah Linwood (possibly Mary's mother) also exhibited needlework,[70] so that it appears probable that Mary was following in the footsteps of another. Needlework pictures were not, of course, any new invention, but already had a respectable history. There is no doubt, nevertheless, of Miss Linwood's exceptional ambition, skill, and diligence in this line, and her practice embodied certain significant innovations. Instead of using the normal petit-point or gros-point techniques, she varied the length of her stitches up to even several inches, in order to imitate the effect of brushwork; she worked on a specially woven canvas base, with wools specially dyed according to her instructions. The account quoted above may be taken, perhaps, as referring especially to her invention of these new technical devices.

At the request of the Russian Ambassador, General Landskoy, Miss Linwood presented a large picture to the empress in 1783; and in 1786 she addressed to the Society of Arts three imitations of pictures, a *St. Peter* after Guido Reni, a *Head of Lear* after Reynolds, and a *Hare* after a picture in the Houghton collection, for which the society rewarded her with a medal. In 1789 she copied in needlework Carlo Dolci's *Salvator Mundi* in the Earl of Exeter's collection, and was offered 3,000 guineas for the copy, which she refused,[71] and in her will she bequeathed 'unto the Reigning Sovereign of the United Kingdom of Great Britain and Ireland my picture of the "Salvator Mundi" as an heirloom to the Crown to be held and enjoyed accordingly'. It now hangs in the vestry of the Domestic Chapel, Windsor Castle.[72] Her needlework copy, the size of the original, from Gainsborough's *Woodman in a Storm*, formerly in the Earl of Gainsborough's collection and destroyed in the fire of 1810 at Exton, is certainly the best record of this important canvas which survives, and belongs now to the Leicester Art Gallery,[73] which owns also eight other works by her, including a *Nativity* after Carlo Maratti. In 1798 she opened a permanent exhibition of her work in Hanover Square, London, and in 1804 and the five subsequent years this exhibition was shown in Edinburgh, Glasgow, Belfast, Dublin, Limerick, and Cork. In March 1809 it was transferred to rooms in Leicester Square, where it remained until her death. This exhibition contained 100 copies of pictures by old and modern masters, and a portrait of herself after Russell, painted when she was 19. The exhibition was apparently a great success in its earlier years, but later she lost money over it. It was always her wish to preserve the collection entire, and with this end in view she offered it first to the British Museum and then to the House of Lords, but both offers were refused.[74] After her death, which took place at Leicester in 1845,[75] the collection was dispersed by auction at Christie's, and the whole realized less than

[69] *Connoisseur*, xlviii, 148, quoting from *Monthly Mirror* (no date given).

[70] A. Graves, *Soc. Artists*, 149.

[71] *D.N.B.* xi, 1214; *Gent. Mag.* (N.S.), xxiii, 555–7.

[72] Ex inf. Sir Owen Morshead, Royal Librarian.

[73] *Leic. Mus., Art Gallery and Libr. Bull.*, Oct. 1935, 1–2.

[74] *Gent. Mag.* (N.S.), xxiii, 555–7.

[75] C. P. Ingram in *Connoisseur*, xlviii, 148, transcribing the inscription from Miss Linwood's memorial tablet in St. Margaret's Church, Leic., gives the date of her death as 11 Mar. 1845. Her death cert., however, gives 2 Mar.

Mrs. George Pochin
From the oil-painting by M. W. Peters

William Pochin
From the oil-painting by L. F. Abbott

The Quorn at Quenby

From the oil-painting by John Ferneley

£1,000.[76] A Centenary Exhibition of her work was held at the Leicester Art Gallery in March 1945, to which, in addition to loans from private sources, the Victoria and Albert Museum contributed a needlework portrait of Napoleon I and a portrait of Miss Linwood herself by Hoppner. Miss Linwood's indefatigable industry was not exhausted by her labours in needlework, for she also ran a boarding school for girls in Belgrave Gate, Leicester; she wrote several books, *Leicestershire Tales* (1808) in 4 volumes, *The Anglo-Cambrian* (1818) a poem, and *The House of Camelot; a tale of the olden time* (1858) in 2 vols.; and she wrote a sacred oratorio *David's First Victory*, published in 1840, and an opera from which two ballads, *The Kellerin* and *The White Wreath* were published in 1853.[77]

She must have been a woman of remarkable personality. It has been recorded above how she encouraged and helped John Flower as a young artist, and an obituary notice speaks most highly of her character, especially of her benefactions to the local poor; she is reported on one occasion to have spent several days in the royal palace by invitation of Queen Charlotte; and when in Paris she had a long interview with Napoleon in the presence of Talleyrand and others.[78]

And finally, an artist who should certainly be included here is Ernest Gimson, architect, craftsman, and designer (1864–1919), who was born in Leicester, the son of Josiah Gimson, engineer.[79] He received his early training in an architect's office—he was articled in 1881 to Isaac Barradale, a Leicester architect, with whom he stayed about 3 years—and at the Leicester School of Art. When William Morris lectured in Leicester in 1884, young Gimson met him, and Morris exercised a powerful influence over him both personally and by his writings. In 1886 Gimson went to London and entered the office of the architect Sedding, which was at 447 Oxford Street, next door to Morris & Co.'s shop. There he found himself one of a group of young men, including the brothers Barnsley, Robert Weir, Alfred Powell, and W. R. Lethaby, all of whom worked in Sedding's or Norman Shaw's offices, and all of whom were subsequently to make their names by distinguished work in the crafts. In 1890 Gimson joined the Society for the Protection of Ancient Buildings, which Morris had founded, and on the committee he was in contact with another leader of the crafts movement, the architect Philip Webb. Perhaps following a suggestion of Webb's, Gimson learned the craft of chair-making from a country craftsman in Herefordshire; and in partnership with Mervyn Macartney, R. Blomfield, S. Barnsley, Col. Mallet, and Lethaby he formed the firm of Kenton & Co. Subsequently he made his home with the Barnsleys at Pinbury (Glos.) and at Sapperton where he lived and worked for 25 years. He married in 1900 Emily Ann, daughter of the Revd. Robert Thomson, vicar of Skipsea, Yorks.

Gimson's work in architecture was not extensive or ever on a large scale, but it was influential. His principal buildings were: a house in Leicester, built for himself, 1892; White House, Leicester, built for Arthur Gimson, 1897; two cottages at Markfield (Leics.) for James Bilson, 1897; Stoneywell Cottage,

[76] R. Chambers, *Bk. of Days*, i, 148–9.

[77] J. D. Brown and S. S. Stratton, *Brit. Musical Biog.* 249; and B.M. Cat.

[78] *Gent. Mag.* (N.S.), xxiii, 555–7.

[79] *Ernest Gimson, His Life and Work*, by W. R. Lethaby and others (1924). Most of the facts in the present account are summarized from this book.

Markfield, for Sydney Gimson, 1898; his own cottages at Pinbury and Sapperton; the Hall at Bedales School, Petersfield (Hants), 1910; a cottage at Budleigh Salterton (Devon), 1912; cottages at Kelmscott for Miss Mary Morris, 1915; Bedales School War Memorial Buildings, and Fairford War Memorial Cross. At his Daneway House workshops in Gloucestershire he designed and made the bishop's throne and the clergy seat for Khartoum Cathedral; the stalls for St. Andrew's Chapel, Westminster Cathedral, and the screen for Crockham Hill church (Kent), which are his principal achievements in woodwork. He worked also extensively in plaster, furniture, bookbinding, embroidery, and metals. The Leicester Museum and Art Gallery has a small collection of works by him.

EDUCATION

CHARITY SCHOOLS[1]

It is doubtful whether the dissolution of monasteries and other religious bodies in the reigns of Henry VIII and Edward VI made any serious alteration in the circumstances under which education was carried on in Leicestershire. Such education as had been provided by the monasteries of course came to an end, but it is unlikely that the number of pupils educated in the Leicestershire religious houses can ever have been very large. Of the Leicestershire chantries and religious guilds dissolved under Edward VI, the only ones known to have played any part in education are the chantry at Castle Donington, where one of the duties of the chantry priest was to teach in a grammar school, and the religious guilds at Melton Mowbray, which contributed to the support of the school there.[2] Both these schools were grammar schools, and therefore do not concern us here. It cannot be said that the religious changes of the 16th century involved any general destruction of schools in Leicestershire.

How many schools of the type later known as charity schools there were in Leicestershire in the period immediately after the Reformation it is impossible to decide with any accuracy. It is often difficult, for example, to distinguish between an endowment intended to support a new charity school, and one intended only to provide free education for a certain number of children at whatever school might be available. Again, the exact use to which an endowment was put can often not be ascertained, and indeed any given endowment might be used in different ways at different periods. Moreover there is little difference between an endowed charity school at which the master was allowed to take some paying scholars and a school, conducted by a master for profit, at which some charity school children were taught in return for the revenue from an endowment.[3]

Despite these difficulties, however, some attempt to assess charity school teaching from the materials available may be made. In the records of the visitation of Leicestershire by the Bishop of Lincoln in 1576, it is noted that thirteen incumbents were giving instruction in their own parishes, but it is not clear what the character of this teaching was.[4] When Leicestershire was visited by Bishop Neile in 1614, twenty-five schoolmasters were noted in the county. At Twyford, Higham,[5] Kilby, Fleckney, Goadby,[6] Illston, Bottesford, Waltham, and Kegworth the curates acted as schoolmasters;[7] the other places where there were masters were Croxton,[8] Catthorpe, Lutterworth, Narborough, Sapcote, Tilton, Orton on the Hill, Bringhurst, Carlton,[9] Foxton, Goadby Marwood, Hose, Muston, Scalford, Stapleford, and Thurcaston.[10] Of these twenty-five schools, the only one about which anything is known from other sources is that at Kegworth; in 1575 it was found that certain sums which had once provided money for religious purposes, but had later been used to maintain a schoolmaster at Kegworth, had been concealed from the queen, and it was ordered that they should be again paid to a schoolmaster. The Court of Exchequer confirmed this order in 1604.[11] Some of the schools listed in 1614 were no doubt very unimportant; at Higham, for example, it was said that the master taught only half a dozen small boys.[12] It is possible that a number of schools which were existing in the county in 1614 were not recorded at the visitation. At Wymeswold there was in 1575 already in existence a school, which lasted into the 19th century,[13] and there may have been other schools which passed unnoticed at the same time.

So far as is known the school at Kegworth was the earliest endowed school (other than a grammar school) to exist in the county. The school at

[1] This article is based upon extensive notes supplied by Mr. W. H. G. Armytage, M.A.

[2] Assoc. Arch. Soc. *Rep. and Papers*, xxx (2), 505; A. F. Leach, *Engl. Sch. at Reformation*, 505; Melton Mowbray Town Estate Order Bk. i, f.2 (in care of Melton Town Estate).

[3] The distinction between endowed charity schools and unattached educational endowments which has sometimes been made (M. G. Jones, *Charity Sch. Movement in 18th century*) tends to break down when cases are examined in detail.

[4] *State of the Church*, ed. C. W. Foster, i, 34–38, 41–43.

[5] Mentioned as 'Heighton'.

[6] In Gartree hundred; not Goadby Marwood.

[7] See Jones, *Char. Sch. Movement*, 66.

[8] Probably Croxton Kerrial.

[9] Near Market Bosworth; not Carlton Curlieu.

[10] Assoc. Arch. Soc. *Rep. and Papers*, xxix, 161–70; grammar school masters and masters of schools in the borough of Leicester have been omitted.

[11] *32nd Rep. Com. Char. Pt. 5* [163], p. 380, H.C. (1839), xv; E 134/20 Eliz./East. 5.

[12] Assoc. Arch. Soc. *Rep. and Papers*, xxix, 163.

[13] B.M. Add. MS. 10457; S. P. Potter, *Hist. of Wymeswold*, 64–67.

Wymeswold does not seem to have been endowed originally. During the 17th century charity schools, or endowments for providing gratuitous elementary education, are known to have been founded in Leicestershire at Thrussington in 1628,[14] Lutterworth in 1630,[15] Hemington in 1640,[16] Billesdon in 1650,[17] Prestwold in 1657,[18] Ashby de la Zouch about 1669,[19] Bagworth in or after 1675,[20] Claybrooke in 1680,[21] Barrow upon Soar, also in 1680,[22] Croxton Kerrial, Loughborough, and Rothley, all in 1683,[23] Cossington in 1684,[24] East Langton in 1685,[25] and at Diseworth and Ashby de la Zouch in 1695.[26] These sixteen schools, together with the two at Kegworth and Wymeswold, are the only endowed charity schools known to have existed in Leicestershire before 1700.

In the early 18th century a greater interest in charity schools was brought about by the activities of the Society for the Promotion of Christian Knowledge (founded in 1699), which stimulated the parish clergy to support charity schools as agencies for improving the morals of the poor, and of preventing the spread of subversive views. The society's encouragement of the new method of maintaining schools by subscription assisted men of moderate means to contribute to the founding of new schools. In Leicestershire the society's local secretary was the active and influential Samuel Carte, vicar of St. Martins, Leicester, and the county, being in Lincoln Diocese, benefited from the support given to the society by two successive bishops of Lincoln, William Wake (1705–16) and Edmund Gibson (1716–20).[27] The activities of the society, combined with other, more general, factors to produce in the early 18th century a rapid increase in the numbers of charity schools existing in the country as a whole.[28] In Leicestershire, endowments for charity schools were established at fourteen places between 1700 and 1724.[29] In a few cases these endowments were granted to provide additional support for schools which already existed and were being maintained by other means.[30] The new endowments, though thus not necessarily implying the establishment of a corresponding number of new schools, represented a considerable increase in the resources available to the charity schools in Leicestershire.

Endowed schools had a good chance of continuous existence, and of leaving behind them some record of their activities. Unendowed schools led a precarious life, and their history is more difficult to trace. The *Speculum* of Lincoln Diocese, compiled from returns made between 1706 and 1723, lists 15 charity schools,[31] apart from those known to have been endowed by 1724.[32] A work published in 1720 gives a list of 27 charity schools in all,[33] including 6[34] which are not otherwise known to have existed at that date, and which were not, so far as is known, endowed. The information given in the *Speculum* and in the list of 1720 is certainly incomplete, for both fail to include certain endowed schools which are known to have

[14] *32nd Rep. Com. Char. Pt.* 5, 493.

[15] Ibid. 127; *Educ. Enquiry Abstract*, H.C. 62, pp. 491–2 (1835), xlii; *Schools Enquiry Com.* [3966-xv], pp. 198–9, H.C. (1867–8), xviii (13).

[16] Nichols, *Leics.* iii, 876; *32nd Rep. Com. Char. Pt.* 5, 385.

[17] *32nd Rep. Com. Char. Pt.* 5, 219–20; Geo. Villiers, 1st Duke of Buckingham, went to school at Billesdon in 1602, but nothing is known of this earlier school: *D.N.B.*

[18] *32nd Rep. Com. Char. Pt.* 5, 483–4.

[19] Nichols, *Leics.* iii, 617.

[20] Ibid. iv, 987; *32nd Rep. Com. Char. Pt.* 5, 217.

[21] *32nd Rep. Com. Char. Pt.* 5, 299–300.

[22] Ibid. 471.

[23] Ibid. 393, 412, 437; [Thomas Cox], *Magna Britannia* (1720–31), ii, 1393; Nichols, *Leics.* iii, 960.

[24] *32nd Rep. Com. Char. Pt.* 5, 476.

[25] Ibid. 274; Nichols, *Leics.* ii, 664.

[26] *32nd Rep. Com. Char. Pt.* 5, 345, 378; Ashby had thus two charity schools in the late 17th cent.

[27] R. W. Greaves, 'An 18th cent. High Churchman', *Theology*, xxix, 272–86; Jones, *Char. Sch. Movement*, 40, 64–65.

[28] Jones, op. cit. 34.

[29]

1702	Coleorton	*32nd Rep. Com. Char. Pt.* 5, 375.
1704	Sileby	„ „ „ 490–1; Nichols, *Leics.* iii, 52.
1708	Hinckley	*32nd Rep. Com. Char. Pt.* 5, 171.
1711	Bottesford	„ „ „ 433.
1713	Blaby	„ „ „ 231–2.
1713	Hallaton	S.P.C.K. *Account of Char. Schools* (1713).
1714	Ibstock	*32nd Rep. Com. Char. Pt.* 5, 178.
1718	Grimston	„ „ „ 480.
1718	Saxelby (*with* Shoby)	„ „ „ 488.
1719	Kimcote	„ „ „ 315.
1719	Great Easton	„ „ „ 226; [Cox], *Magna Brit.* ii, 1394.
1720	Long Whatton	*32nd Rep. Com. Char. Pt.* 5, 377.
1721	Newbold Verdon	„ „ „ 200; *23rd Rep. Com. Char.* H.C. 462, p. 130 (1830), xii (2).
1724	Husbands Bosworth	*32nd Rep. Com. Char. Pt.* 5, 238; Nichols, *Leics.* ii, 469; the charity school existing there in 1720 does not seem to have been endowed: [Cox], *Magna Brit.* ii, 1393.

[30] e.g. a school existed at Hallaton in 1706 although it was not endowed until 1713: *32nd Rep. Com. Char. Pt.* 5, 231–2; S.P.C.K. *Account of Char. Schools* (1706).

[31] i.e. in the county excluding Leicester.

[32] Aylestone, Bringhurst, Congerstone, Garthorpe, Hathern, North Kilworth, Kirkby Mallory, Loddington, Medbourne, Shawell, Stoney Stanton, Stathern, Stoke Golding, Thurcaston, Waltham on the Wolds: Assoc. Arch. Soc. *Rep. and Papers*, xxii, 235–354; schools are mentioned at Enderby and Queniborough but their nature is uncertain; funds for educating the poor were available at Burton Overy.

[33] This figure excludes two grammar schools and the schools of Leicester: [Cox], *Magna Brit.* ii, 1392–4.

[34] Ashby Parva, Cotesbach, Swinford, Withcote, South Kilworth, and a boys' school at Loughborough.

existed from the 17th century to the 19th. A fairly comprehensive list of Leicestershire charity schools, drawn up in 1724, gives the names of 35 schools, including one[35] whose existence is not known from any other source.[36] Two of these schools, however, were the grammar schools at Appleby Magna and Wymondham,[37] so that the number of charity schools recorded was in fact only 33. The 1724 list, though fuller than any other, is not complete, as it does not mention several endowed charity schools[38] which were founded before 1724 and which had a continuous existence until the 19th century. In all, only 53 Leicestershire villages (out of some 250) are known to have possessed either charity schools or endowments for elementary education in or before 1724,[39] and it is uncertain how many charity schools were actually in existence at any one time.

After about 1725 the S.P.C.K. became less active in supporting charity schools, and directed its chief energies into other fields.[40] At the same time, the general enthusiasm for charity schools was lessening.[41] Between 1724 and 1800 endowments for charity schools were established in only nineteen places in Leicestershire where such endowments had not previously existed.[42] In addition, three further places obtained funds during the 18th century from the important endowment established by Alderman Gabriel Newton of Leicester in 1760 to maintain schools of a strictly Anglican character.[43] By 1800 the foundation of charity schools was almost at an end, and those who wished to promote elementary education were tending increasingly to give their support to schools of other types. Nevertheless in the 19th century charity schools were founded in six places in Leicestershire,[44] and the scope of Newton's charity was extended by assigning funds from its endowments for the support of charity schools at a further three places.[45] A mere list of the numbers of new charity schools founded gives a rather incomplete view of the support which the schools received, for in many cases the endowments given by founders were supplemented by later gifts. At Bagworth, for example, a small endowment for education was established in 1675, but in 1761 Lord Maynard provided a school house, and greatly augmented the endowment;[46] at Waltham on the Wolds, the school, which early in the 18th century was being maintained at the rector's expense, was first endowed soon after 1731, but by 1837 the endowment had been increased by six substantial gifts.[47]

In all, 58 places in Leicestershire are known to have possessed endowed charity schools, and a further eighteen places to have possessed unendowed ones. The information about endowed schools is probably fairly complete, but there may well have been a considerable number of unendowed schools which have left no record of their existence.

The value of schools' endowments, where they existed, varied greatly. The school at Breedon, for instance, was originally endowed with £300, but this was soon increased by a donation of £500, and by various lesser contributions in money, and about 1830 the Earl of Stamford provided the school with new buildings.[48] Many schools, however, were not so well provided for, and at the other end of the scale were places where the endowment consisted of only the schoolroom and its site, or of a few acres of land.[49] In some cases the endowments were too small to support a school even of the most modest size, and seem to have been intended to pay for the education of a few children at any school that might be available,

35 At Freeby.

36 Jones, *Char. Sch. Movement*, 367–8.

37 Wymondham was virtually a charity school at this date.

38 e.g. Lutterworth, Kegworth.

39 Excluding grammar schools and schools in Leicester.

40 Jones, *Char. Sch. Movement*, 24.

41 Ibid. 23.

42

1727	Rotherby	*32nd Rep. Com. Char. Pt.* 5, 486; Nichols, *Leics.* iii, 398.
1727	Hoby	*32nd Rep. Com. Char. Pt.* 5, 480–1; Nichols, *Leics.* iii, 265–7.
c. 1729	Ratcliffe on the Wreake	*32nd Rep. Com. Char. Pt.* 5, 485.
1731	Waltham on the Wolds	„ „ „ 453–4.
c. 1734	Stathern	„ „ „ 452.
1734	Breedon	Nichols, *Leics.* iii, 681–2; *32nd Rep. Com. Char. Pt.* 5, 371, gives a slightly different account.
ante 1741	Long Clawson	*32nd Rep. Com. Char. Pt.* 5, 436.
1742	Mountsorrel	„ „ „ 355.
1753	Countesthorpe	„ „ „ 305.
in or after 1759	Enderby	„ „ „ 157.
in or after 1761	Medbourne	„ „ „ 284.
1763	Tugby	*32nd Rep. Com. Char. Pt.* 5, 495–6.
1765	Twycross	„ „ „ 219.
in or after 1769	Asfordby	„ „ „ 459.
1774	Gilmorton	„ „ „ 308–9; Nichols, *Leics.* iv, 193.
1775	Old Dalby	*32nd Rep. Com. Char. Pt.* 5, 477.
1778	Wigston Magna	„ „ „ 324.
1790	Bitteswell	„ „ „ 296.
1799	Seagrave	„ „ „ 488–9.

Some places already possessed charity schools supported by subscription.

43 Ashby de la Zouch, Barwell, Earl Shilton: *32nd Rep. Com. Char. Pt.* 5, 152–3, 180–1, 344–5.

44 1804 Thurlaston 1820 Sapcote
1806 Broughton Astley 1830 Barkestone
1815 Lutterworth 1832 Ashby Parva
The information is drawn from the *32nd Rep. Com. Char. Pt.* 5.

45 1809, Hinckley; 1813, Claybrooke; 1815, Lubbenham: *32nd Rep. Com. Char. Pt.* 5.

46 Ibid. 216–17.

47 Ibid. 454–5; [Cox], *Magna Brit.* ii, 1393–4.

48 *32nd Rep. Com. Char. Pt.* 5, 371; Nichols, *Leics.* iii, 681–2.

49 *32nd Rep. Com. Char. Pt.* 5, 296, 477, 486.

rather than to establish new schools.[50] It is, however, very difficult to distinguish between endowments intended by the grantors to form the support of new charity schools, and those which were intended merely to provide children with gratuitous education at existing schools.[51] The fortunes even of the endowed schools, though less precarious than those of schools which depended entirely upon subscriptions, were in fact often fluctuating. The revenue from their initial endowments was not necessarily constant, and might be reduced or lost altogether by mismanagement,[52] while on the other hand a school's resources might be much increased by further gifts.[53] Schools maintained by subscriptions often owed their existence to a single individual, who was frequently the incumbent of the parish. The *Speculum* of Lincoln Diocese shows that early in the 18th century five charity schools were being maintained by incumbents alone, and two more by incumbents in conjunction with other people.[54] Other charity schools depended on the support of a more or less numerous body of subscribers, like that at Swinford, which was being maintained in 1720 by 'some neighbouring gentlemen'.[55] The revenues of charity schools, whether derived from endowments or subscriptions, were often inadequate, and it is not surprising that schoolmasters commonly supplemented their salaries by accepting paying pupils, in addition to those who were taught free. At Kimcote, for instance, in 1837 the school contained 25 paying pupils, in addition to 30 free scholars,[56] while at Gilmorton, at the same date, there were 16 paying pupils, and only 14 who were instructed free.[57] Very little can be discovered about the subjects taught, or about methods of teaching, but such information as there is indicates that in such matters charity schools in Leicestershire were very similar to those elsewhere. The children were taught reading, writing, and some arithmetic,[58] and at a few schools girls were also taught needlework or spinning.[59] At Enderby the children were taught to seam and knit stockings,[60] and at Gilmorton children were, early in the 19th century, allowed to seam stockings in school.[61]

The charity schools were in general closely connected with the Established Church. For a long period after the Reformation teachers were obliged to obtain a licence from their diocesans before they could teach, and strenuous efforts were made to track down those who taught without licences. In Leicestershire, the bishops of Lincoln and the archdeacons of Leicester were active in enforcing the Church's control. Robert Johnson, Archdeacon of Leicester from 1591 to 1625,[62] made vigorous attempts to deal with unlicensed teachers, besides trying to prevent the conversion of educational endowments to other uses.[63] At his visitation of the archdeaconry in 1607, two teachers not known to have licences were detected, while misconduct on the part of two other schoolmasters was also noted.[64] In the late 16th and early 17th centuries the bishops of Lincoln made repeated inquiries about schoolmasters in Leicestershire, and required them to produce their licences.[65] At the metropolitical visitation of Archbishop Laud in 1634, three unlicensed schoolmasters were presented in the county.[66] Ecclesiastical supervision of education continued into the 18th century, and the *Speculum* of Lincoln Diocese, drawn up from returns made between 1705 and 1723, lists details of the schools in the various parishes of Leicestershire.[67] From 1770 onwards, Protestant dissenters were allowed to teach. How far it was necessary in practice for teachers in elementary schools to possess episcopal licenses during the 18th century is uncertain.[68] Until well into the 19th century, charity schools were often held in parish churches.[69]

There is no evidence of any opposition to charity schools in Leicestershire, though in England generally they tended to be disliked in rural districts, especially by farmers.[70] On the other hand there are signs, apart from the provision of subscriptions and endowments, that in some parishes at least charity schools were highly valued. In some places the schools' resources were supplemented by grants from parish funds,[71] or by the diversion to the schools of charities originally intended for other purposes.[72] Even the fact that at times parishioners hotly disputed the

50 Assoc. Arch. Soc. *Rep. and Papers*, xxii, 257.

51 See above, note 3.

52 See the case of Barkby, below, p. 247.

53 See examples of Waltham and Bagworth, above, p. 245.

54 Assoc. Arch. Soc. *Rep. and Papers*, xxii, 234, 256, 289, 290, 293, 334, 350; and see *32nd Rep. Com. Char. Pt.* 5, 477, and [Cox], *Magna Brit.* ii, 1392–4.

55 [Cox], *Magna Brit.* ii, 1393.

56 *32nd Rep. Com. Char. Pt.* 5, 315.

57 Ibid. 309.

58 Ibid. 157, 170, 309, 355, 377, 454, 489, *et passim*.

59 Ibid. 294, 371; [Cox], *Magna Brit.* ii, 1393; White, *Dir. Leics.* (1877), 143.

60 *32nd Rep. Com. Char. Pt.* 5, 157.

61 Ibid. 309.

62 *D.N.B.*

63 *Certaine Advertisements Given by Robert Johnson* (London, 1613); *Articles to be Enquired of* (London, 1622), (pamphlets in B.M.).

64 Assoc. Arch. Soc. *Rep. and Papers*, xxii, 121, 124, 127, 128.

65 Ibid. xxix, 168–70; *State of the Church*, ed. C. W. Foster, i, p. xxxiii.

66 Assoc. Arch. Soc. *Rep. and Papers*, xxix, 490, 501, 509.

67 Ibid. xxii, 228–361.

68 H. C. Barnard, *Short Hist. Engl. Educ.* 16–17.

69 *32nd Rep. Com. Char. Pt.* 5, 285 *et passim*; White, *Dir. Leics.* (1877), 188; Assoc. Arch. Soc. *Rep. and Papers*, xxix, 143, 499.

70 Jones, *Char. Sch. Movement*, 67–68.

71 S. P. Potter, *Hist. of Wymeswold*, 64–67.

72 *32nd Rep. Com. Char. Pt.* 5, 452, 498.

use which was being made of charity school endowments[73] shows that the manner in which the schools were conducted was a matter which sometimes aroused public interest. It is true that several parishes refused offers from Alderman Newton's charity of assistance in maintaining schools,[74] but the refusals were probably due to a dislike of the High Church principles with which Newton's charity was associated, rather than to apathy about education, or to hostility to charity schools.

The charity schools suffered from certain defects. In the absence of any effective system of supervision the efficiency of the schools depended on the conscientiousness and honesty of those who were in control locally. In particular, much depended on the trustees who had charge of the endowments. In some cases endowments were allowed to disappear, as at Barkby,[75] or, as at Hinckley,[76] to be diverted to other purposes. In other places the revenue from endowments was cut off because of local disputes; at Hemington, for example, differences about the conduct of the school led to the suspension of income from the endowment in 1778, and in 1837 payment of the sums due was still being withheld.[77] Like other types of charity, the schools at times became involved in prolonged legal actions; in one case, at Knossington, the school's revenue was for some years unpaid owing to a long suit in Chancery, lasting from 1802 to 1815.[78]

Despite these dangers, most of the endowed charity schools survived into the 19th century. Their history after 1800 will be considered in another chapter.[79]

ELEMENTARY EDUCATION IN THE NINETEENTH AND TWENTIETH CENTURIES[1]

When the 19th century began, elementary education in Leicestershire was already being provided by the charity schools and the Sunday schools. The charity schools had a long history by 1800. There were rather more than 50 of them in the county at that date, and a further 6 were founded during the 19th century.[2] The character of the charity schools has already been discussed.[3] The Sunday schools had largely grown up during the later years of the 18th century. In Leicestershire they were given strong support by Andrew Burnaby, Archdeacon of Leicester, who in his charge to the clergy of the archdeaconry in 1786 declared 'the institution of Sunday schools . . . is so evidently replete with utility, that I should think myself deficient in my duty were I not to recommend them . . . as a likely means of repressing the growth of wickedness; and of establishing religion, piety, and good morals again in this kingdom'.[4] The first Sunday school in Leicestershire seems to have been that established by the Revd. Thomas Ford at Melton Mowbray.[5] When the Sunday School Union was set up in 1803, a local association within it was formed at Loughborough. By 1824 there were 43 schools, with 783 teachers and 4,671 pupils, connected with the Loughborough association.[6] By 1833 the number of Sunday schools in Leicestershire was 399, and they were attended by 31,200 children; of these, 149 schools, attended by 14,926 children, were being conducted by dissenters.[7] An institute was set up in Leicester in 1842 to train Sunday school teachers.[8] The teaching in the Sunday schools varied greatly in quality. The records of the Sunday school conducted at Market Harborough in the opening years of the 19th century, for example, show that an attempt was made to maintain a reasonable standard of discipline (while dispensing with corporal punishment) and to provide the essential rudiments of education.[9] At Great Easton, by contrast, the master of the endowed Sunday school was said, in 1837, to have been appointed rather for the sake of keeping him off the poor rates, than for carrying out the purposes of the endowment.[10] The charity and Sunday schools together, though their efforts were not negligible, were quite unable to teach more than a small proportion of the children of school age in Leicestershire. A census of children in the Archdeaconry

73 *32nd Rep. Com. Char. Pt.* 5, 385.
74 Ibid. 11.
75 *Educ. Enquiry Abstract* (1835), 497.
76 *32nd Rep. Com. Char. Pt.* 5, 171.
77 Ibid. 385.
78 Ibid. 457–9.
79 See below, pp. 247 sqq.
1 This article is based upon extensive notes supplied by Mr. W. H. G. Armytage, M.A.
2 These figures exclude the borough of Leicester, which will not be dealt with in this article.
3 See above, pp. 243 sqq.
4 A. Burnaby, *Charge to the Clergy of the Archdeaconry of Leic.* (1786): a copy is in the B.M.
5 B. Wing, *Reminiscences of Revd. Thomas Ford*, 17. The date of Ford's foundation of the Melton Mowbray Sunday school is unknown, but it seems to have been soon after Robert Raikes established his Sunday school at Gloucester in 1780.
6 *Annual Rep. of the Sunday School Union* (1824), 17, 43.
7 *Educ. Enquiry Abstract*, H.C. 62, pp. 502–3 (1835), xxviii; on Sunday schools for adults, see below, pp. 252, 256.
8 White, *Dir. Leics.* (1846), 100.
9 Recs. of Market Harborough Sunday school, now in custody of Youth Employment Bureau, Market Harborough.
10 *32nd Rep. Com. Char. Pt.* 5 [163], p. 226, H.C. (1839), xv.

of Leicester,[11] made privately in 1812, showed that of 15,000 children between the ages of 7 and 14, only 1,500 were obtaining education of any kind on week-days, and only a further 4,300 were attending Sunday schools.[12]

The provision for elementary education was thus in many ways inadequate. The early years of the 19th century, however, in Leicestershire as in the rest of Britain, saw a great expansion in the numbers of elementary schools, stimulated by the new techniques of teaching advocated by Andrew Bell and Joseph Lancaster. After the formation in 1811 of the National Society, with the object of establishing schools where Bell's monitorial system could be practised under the auspices of the Established Church, a district society was set up for the Leicester archdeaconry in 1812 to carry on the National Society's work locally.[13] The district society offered to supply books to all schools, and made grants of money to both Sunday and day schools.[14] By 1815 19 schools had been aided by grants; these were all day schools, but 14 of them gave instruction on Sundays also.[15] Two inspectors, the Revd. C. Pilkington and the Revd. R. Davies, were appointed to stimulate exertion on behalf of the National Society.[16] The scope of the society's activities in Leicestershire rapidly expanded. In 1817 it was found necessary to set up separate bodies to control the society's work in each of the rural deaneries of Leicester archdeaconry.[17] Many of the existing charity schools, attracted by the prospect of financial aid, became united with the National Society. In 1830 there were 64 schools in the Leicester archdeaconry affiliated to the society, and three years later the number had risen to 76.[18] In 1839 the Archdeaconry of Leicester was transferred from the Diocese of Lincoln to that of Peterborough, and at the same time the district society was replaced, as the controlling body of the National Society's work in Leicestershire, by a new Archidiaconal Board of Education. The first president of the new board was George Davys, Bishop of Peterborough, who was much interested in the progress of education, and himself wrote a number of manuals for use in schools.[19] A general inquiry made by the National Society in 1846 showed that only 16 of the 276 parishes in Leicestershire had no church school, and that, of the 396 schools in the county, 147 were in union with the National Society.[20]

The National Society, closely linked as it was with the Church of England, was much more active in Leicestershire than were the educational bodies connected with other religious denominations. In 1851 the Roman Catholics had 7 schools in the county,[21] the Independents 3, the Baptists 2, the Wesleyan Methodists 3, the Friends 1, and Lady Huntingdon's Connexion 1. There were also 6 schools maintained by the British and Foreign Schools Society, which were classed as undenominational, though closely linked with Protestant dissent.[22] There does not seem to have been any strong sectarian feeling about elementary education in Leicestershire during the 19th century. A report published in 1835 states that 'no school in the county of Leicester appears to be confined to the children of parents of the established church, or of any religious denomination, such exclusion being disclaimed in almost every instance, especially in schools established by Dissenters'.[23]

Meanwhile the state had begun to interest itself in elementary education. From 1833 onwards Parliament annually voted grants in aid of the building of schools.[24] In the first 5 years during which such grants were made £1,211 were given to Leicestershire schools. The 14 schools amongst which this sum was divided were Ashby de la Zouch, Belgrave, Great Bowden, Coalville, Market Harborough, Higham on the Hill, Hugglescote, South Kilworth, Quorndon, Rothley, Shepshed, Thurlaston, Whitwick, and Woodhouse.[25] From 1839 onwards building grants were made only on condition that the schools aided by such grants should be open to state inspection. Subsequently the scope of the state's financial assistance was gradually extended to include other things besides school buildings. The number of schools receiving government

[11] The archdeaconry as it existed in 1812 covered the same area as the county, but it included the borough of Leic., which is outside the scope of this article.

[12] *2nd Annual Rep. of the Nat. Soc.* (1812), 126–30. These figures include the borough of Leic. Presumably they also include children being educated in private schools. It is impossible to say how accurate these figures are.

[13] Ibid.; it was the district society which carried out the census mentioned above. See also *Rep. on Popular Education* [2794–I], p. 576, H.C. (1861), xxi (1).

[14] *2nd Annual Rep. of the Nat. Soc.* (1812), 126–30.

[15] *5th Annual Rep. of the Nat. Soc.* (1815). These figures do not include schools in the borough of Leic.

[16] Ibid.; Davies was headmaster of the Wyggeston Grammar School at Leic., 1816–41; Anon., *Wyggeston Grammar School for Boys* (1927), 95.

[17] *7th Annual Rep. of the Nat. Soc.* (1817).

[18] *19th* and *22nd Reps. of the Nat. Soc.*

[19] *D.N.B.*; *Leic. Jnl.* 4 Aug. 1843; *29th Annual Rep. of the Nat. Soc.* (1840).

[20] National Soc. *Ret. of Schools* (1846, priv. print.).

[21] Including Ratcliffe Coll., at Ratcliffe on the Wreake, founded in 1843, and the first college in the country to be conducted by the Order of Char.; White, *Dir. Leics.* (1846), 431.

[22] *Census*, 1851; these figures do not include Leicester.

[23] *Educ. Enquiry Abstract* (1835), 502; see also *Rep. of Educ. Cttee. of Council, 1876* [C. 1780–I], p. 429, H.C. (1877), xxix.

[24] See H. C. Barnard, *Short Hist. of Engl. Education*, 82, on the amounts of these grants, and the circumstances under which they were made.

[25] *Min. of Educ. Cttee. of Council, 1849* [1215], pp. ccix–ccxi, H.C. (1850), xliii.

grants increased fairly rapidly. In 1860–1 grants were made to 43 schools in Leicestershire;[26] by 1870, when fundamental changes were made in elementary education, the number of grant-aided schools had risen to 122.[27] The considerable efforts made by voluntary bodies produced a more adequate provision for elementary education in Leicestershire than was the case in many other parts of the country,[28] but the quality of the teaching was not always satisfactory. In 1864, for example, an inspector remarked that the Leicestershire children, though quiet and obedient, were careworn and depressed, and had been trained to rely too much on learning by rote.[29] No doubt this situation was chiefly due to the well-known system of 'payment by results', introduced by the Education Department in 1862.[30] In the late 1860's there was much dispute generally about the advisability of introducing a system of compulsory education. William Connor Magee, Bishop of Peterborough[31] 1869–90, strongly upheld the principle of voluntary education. He realized that once compulsory schools maintained from the rates were established, the great influence in education which the Church of England possessed would be endangered.[32] Lord John Manners, for many years an M.P. for one of the Leicestershire constituencies, was also against compulsory education.[33] At the time of the Foster Act in 1870 Leicestershire was relatively well provided with voluntary schools. There were at that date 115 schools in the county receiving government grants, excluding grammar schools and schools in the borough of Leicester.[34] Of these, 75 were in the hands of the National Society, and 20 others, though not connected with the society, were Church schools, so that a large majority of Leicestershire schools was controlled by the Established Church. There were 6 schools owned by the British and Foreign Schools Society,[35] and a further 6 managed by Protestant dissenters of several denominations; there were 3 Roman Catholic schools.[36] Four schools were listed as 'parish schools' in 1870, and one as 'Lancasterian'.[37] Because fairly adequate schooling was already provided in many parts of Leicestershire, the formation of school boards proceeded slowly, and for many years much of the county remained outside the control of any board. By June 1872 only 6 boards had been set up in Leicestershire.[38] Two years later there were only 10, and of these only 2 (Hinckley and Ratby) had as yet enacted by-laws requiring attendance at school.[39] It was not until 1876, when school attendance was made obligatory throughout the whole country by statute, that compulsory schooling was introduced to most areas in Leicestershire. By 1888 only 33 school boards had been established.[40] The Leicestershire school boards were small, with 5 or 7 members only;[41] some boards included manual workers, such as shoe clickers, among their members, especially after the legislation of 1880 which made it easier for men to become members of locally elected bodies without possessing a large property guarantee.[42] In a few instances the boards took over existing school buildings, as at Nailstone, Dunton Basset, Gaddesby, and Ashby Folville, but in most cases they found it necessary to erect new schools.[43]

In the years after 1870 the Anglican Church was by no means willing to abandon its influence on education.[44] Led by Bishop Magee, the Leicestershire clergy faced the new situation with a determined attitude, and sought both to maintain the existing Church schools, and to gain a footing on the new school boards. At Coston, for instance, a clergyman became chairman of the board, while at Dunton Basset a clergyman

[26] *Rep. of Educ. Cttee. of Council, 1861* [3007], pp. 53–54, H.C. (1862), xlii; these figures do not include schools in the borough of Leic.

[27] *Rep. of Educ. Cttee. of Council, 1870* [C. 406], pp. 489–91, H.C. (1871), xxii; these figures do not include schools in the borough of Leic.

[28] See below.

[29] *Rep. of Educ. Cttee. of Council, 1864* [3533], pp. 41–45, H.C. (1865), xlii.

[30] On the influence of this system generally, see F. Smith, *Hist. of Engl. Elementary Education*, 262–9.

[31] His dioc. included Leicestershire.

[32] W. C. Magee, *Speeches and Addresses*, ed. C. S. Magee, 60; J. C. Macdonnell, *Life and Correspondence of W. C. Magee*, i, 243.

[33] See his speech about the Loughborough schools, in 200 *Parl. Deb.* 3rd ser. 240.

[34] *Rep. of Educ. Cttee. of Council, 1870*, pp. 489–91. In addition there were 7 schools which had earlier received grants, but which had ceased to do so by 1870.

[35] One other school, at Appleby, was extinct by 1870.

[36] One other Roman Catholic school, at Sileby, had been withdrawn from government inspection by 1870. The Roman Catholic schools were all in the north and west of Leics.

[37] *Rep. of Educ. Cttee. of Council, 1870*, pp. 489–91.

[38] At Anstey, Gaddesby, Hinckley, Oadby, Ratby, Wigston Magna; *Rep. of Educ. Cttee. of Council, 1871* [C. 601], pp. xxii–xxiii, H.C. (1872), xxii.

[39] *Rep. of Educ. Cttee. of Council, 1873* [C. 1019–I], p. xlvi, H.C. (1874), xviii. Beside the areas under the 10 school boards, Welham, on the south-east border of Leics., was under the school board of Sutton Basset (Northants.).

[40] *Comm. for Enquiry into Elem. Educ. Acts, Stat. Rep.* [C. 5485–II], p. 104, H.C. (1888), xxxvi. The area controlled by a board was often only a single civil par., and there were over 250 pars. in Leics.

[41] The members of school boards, in areas outside London and the boroughs, could vary in number from 5 to 15; *Rep. of Educ. Cttee. of Council, 1870*, p. lxxxii.

[42] *Comm. for Enquiry into Elem. Educ. Acts, Stat. Rep.* p. 103; L.R.O. Min. of Leics. Sch. Bds. *passim*.

[43] L.R.O. Min. of Leics. Sch. Bds.

[44] See W. C. Magee, *Charge Delivered to the Clergy* (1872), 20–27.

became secretary.[45] The antagonism that existed between the Anglican clergy and the boards is shown by events at Anstey, where the vicar refused to allow the board to take over his school.[46] Strenuous efforts were made to bring the Church and National schools up to the standard required by the Education Department's inspectors. In the years 1870–1, for instance, a day and Sunday school was built at Bitteswell, and a teacher's house was given by the vicar and his daughter; Burbage and Hoby National schools were built on sites given by the incumbents; and the school at Netherseal was enlarged.[47] In 1875 Magee was able to say that 'with but few exceptions, our schools have been able to stand the strict, and in some cases perhaps the severe, requirements of the Education Department, and have become what many of them were not before, efficient and sufficient'.[48] By 1900, when further important changes in the educational system of the country were impending, there were 36 board schools in Leicestershire, controlled by 33 school boards; the number of other schools receiving grants (excluding grammar schools) was 223, of which 198 were Anglican.[49] At the end of the 19th century the Established Church thus still maintained its predominant position.

In Leicestershire, as elsewhere, considerable difficulty was experienced in securing regular attendance at school in the years after 1870, when compulsory education was being gradually introduced. In particular it was found that in the district around Leicester children were often kept away from school several half days a week to seam stockings.[50] Leicestershire was under a certain disadvantage because it contained many small, purely agricultural villages, where the schools were necessarily small, though often very efficient. In 1900, out of 33 school boards in the county, only 3 controlled areas with populations of more than 3,000.[51] In 1888 it was reported that most Leicestershire schools were charging fees. Only 5 of the voluntary schools, and none of the board schools, were providing completely free education, and the remainder charged small fees, usually with a maximum of 2*d.* to 4*d.* a week. Few parents in Leicestershire objected to such charges.[52] The payment of fees was abolished in most elementary schools in 1891,[53] but in 1903 fees were still being charged in 6 Leicestershire elementary schools.[54]

Under the Technical Education Act of 1889 the Leicestershire County Council was authorized to provide technical and manual instruction, and under an Act of 1890 the council received from the proceeds of certain excises an annual sum[55] (amounting at first to £5,000)[56] to be used for technical and secondary education. In order to carry out its functions under these acts the county council set up a Technical Education Committee, which made its first report in July 1891.[57] By 1900 the committee had come to control a variety of activities in connexion with education, including the bestowal of scholarships upon pupils at elementary schools to enable them to proceed to grammar schools, and the provision of financial aid for classes in art and science.[58] Consequently when, by the Education Act of 1902, county councils took over the management of board schools, and acquired a large measure of control over those voluntary elementary schools which were receiving state grants, the Leicestershire County Council had already gained much experience in education, and was already known as an exceptionally active body in that sphere.[59] The heavy task of organizing the new administrative system fell very largely on the Technical Education Committee, which was obliged to deal with a great number of practical details.[60] Under a scheme drawn up by the Technical Education Committee and the Finance and General Purposes Committee of the county council, in April 1903, it was provided that an Education Committee should be set up, consisting of 46 members, of whom 34 were to be members of the county council.[61] A Director of Education and a

[45] Clergy also sat on the school boards at Nailstone, Peckleton, Somerby, Loughborough, Walton on the Wolds, Dishley with Thorpe Acre, and Seagrave; L.R.O. Min. of Sch. Bds.

[46] L.R.O. Min. of Anstey Sch. Bd. A similar situation developed at Hinckley; H. J. Francis, *Hist. of Hinckley*, 144.

[47] White, *Dir. Leics.* (1877), 163, 177, 240, 558.

[48] W. C. Magee, *Charge Delivered to the Clergy* (1875), 8–15; and see *Rep. of Educ. Cttee. of Council, 1876*, p. 427.

[49] *Rep. Board of Education, 1900–1*, Vol. II [Cd. 757], pp. 360, 500, H.C. (1901), xix. These figures do not include the borough of Leic.

[50] *Comm. for Enquiry into Elem. Educ. Acts, Stat. Rep.* pp. 102–3; *Rep. of Educ. Cttee. of Council, 1895* [C. 8249], p. 62, H.C. (1896), xxi; Smith, *Hist. Engl. Elementary Educ.* 298.

[51] *Rep. Board of Education, 1899–1900*, Vol. III [Cd. 330], p. 249, H.C. (1900), xix; *1900–1*, Vol. II, pp. 380, 500.

[52] *Comm. for Enquiry into Elem. Educ. Acts, Stat. Rep.* pp. 104–5.

[53] Smith, *Hist. Engl. Elementary Educ.* 333, for details.

[54] *Leics. Cty. Council Minutes and Orders, 1903–4*, f. 105.

[55] Commonly known as 'whisky money'.

[56] L.R.O. Leics. Cty. Council Minute Bk. 1889–94, pp. 122, 252–9.

[57] Ibid. 197.

[58] See, e.g. rep. on the cttee.'s activities for 1900, in *Leics. Cty. Council Minutes and Orders, 1900–1*, pp. 38–41; and ibid. *1901–2*, ff. 147*b*, 148*a*; and see below, pp. 261–2.

[59] *Rep. Board of Educ. 1899–1900*, Vol. II [Cd. 329], pp. 24–25, H.C. (1900), xix.

[60] *Leics. Cty. Council Minutes and Orders, 1903–4*, ff. 103–4, *et passim.*

[61] *Leics. Cty. Council Minutes and Orders, 1902–3*, f. 204.

permanent secretary to the Education Committee were appointed.[62] They were assisted at first by a staff of only four clerks, a number which soon had to be increased.[63]

On 1 July 1903 the new Education Committee assumed control of the public elementary schools in Leicestershire,[64] and at the same time the Technical Education Committee ceased to exist.[65] Education in the municipal borough of Loughborough remained outside the control of the county council, and under the terms of the 1902 Act was controlled by the borough independently from May 1903 onwards.[66] A survey made by the Director of Education revealed that in many places the accommodation available in schools was insufficient.[67] The situation was especially critical in the mining areas of north-west Leicestershire, where the population was rapidly increasing, and where the school boards had for some time delayed taking action because they knew that control was about to pass to the county authorities.[68] Although the voluntary schools were expected to meet the needs of some areas,[69] the director considered that 3,600 additional school places would have to be provided by the county council, at an estimated cost of about £45,000.[70] The Education Committee at once began to remedy these deficiencies, and in August 1904 it reported that since the county council assumed control new council schools, or extensions to existing ones, had been made in 17 places, including some in the mining area; new voluntary schools, too, had been built at 3 places.[71] Despite these measures the schools in the mining districts remained inadequate for some years.[72] The number of teachers, also, had to be increased, and between the end of June 1903 and April 1904 the number of certificated assistant teachers in the county's elementary schools rose from 108 to 156, and the number of uncertificated assistants from 241 to 296.[73] The proportion of certificated teachers was considered too small.[74] Between 1903 and 1912 the number of certificated teachers almost doubled, and child and supplementary teachers were very largely replaced by the more satisfactory uncertificated teachers.[75] In July 1913 the total number of teachers in Leicestershire elementary schools was 1,162.[76] Some difficulty was experienced in staffing small rural schools,[77] and up to the start of the First World War the number of elementary teachers in Leicestershire remained a little low in relation to the number of pupils.[78]

The outbreak of war in 1914 had of course serious effects upon the county's schools. The construction of new buildings had to be deferred,[79] and the departure of both teachers and administrative officials to join the armed services gave rise to many difficulties.[80] At the end of the war the county council was faced with the urgent need for the construction of new schools at a number of places,[81] and at the same time it had to deal with the additional responsibilities laid on it by the Education Act of 1918.

In the period between the two wars elementary education remained under the control of the county council.[82] In accordance with the ideas put forward in the report on *The Education of the Adolescent* (issued in 1926),[83] the Leicestershire County Council undertook during this period to reorganize its schools, dividing them into primary schools, which were to educate children until they had attained the age of 11, and modern schools which (with the existing grammar and technical schools) were to provide for children above that age. The task of reorganization was a heavy one, and had necessarily to be spread over some years. Under a scheme drawn up for the county council in 1929, Leicestershire was divided into 33 modern school districts, which were to be reorganized in turn.[84] The number of districts was reduced to 28 in 1931 by uniting some of the smaller ones, and by 1938 the number had fallen to 24.[85] A good deal of building, and much rearrangement of classes and school staffs, was needed to bring the new system into effect.[86] A succession of

62 *Leics. Cty. Council Minutes and Orders, 1902–3*, f. 237; the first director was W. A. Brockington, previously principal of Victoria Coll. Worc. On his qualifications and past career, see ibid. 240.

63 Ibid. *1903–4*, ff. 103–4, 212.

64 Ibid. *1902–3*, f. 204.

65 Ibid. *1903–4*, ff. 103–4.

66 Loughborough borough council assumed control of elementary education in the borough on 1 May 1903; *Rep. Board of Education, 1903–4* [Cd. 2271], p. 75, H.C. (1905), xxv.

67 *Leics. Cty. Council Minutes and Orders, 1903–4*, ff. 155, 212 et seq.

68 Ibid. *1904–5*, f. 38; Ashby Woulds, Ellistown, and Coalville are mentioned as places where conditions were very acute.

69 16 areas where voluntary schools could meet the requirements are listed, ibid. f. 38*b*.

70 Ibid. f. 39.

71 Ibid. ff. 107 et seq.

72 *Leics. Cty. Council Minutes and Orders, 1910–13*, pp. 35, 36, 97, 137.

73 Ibid. *1904–5*, f. 38.

74 Ibid. f. 210.

75 Ibid. *1913–16*, p. 139.

76 Ibid.

77 Ibid. 140.

78 Ibid. 183.

79 Ibid. 464.

80 Ibid. 333, 414, 463, 501–4; for a full list of the teaching and administrative staff who served in the forces, see *Meeting of Leics. Cty. Council, 14 May 1919, Reps. of Cttees.* p. 16.

81 Ibid. pp. 21–22.

82 Except in Loughborough.

83 Commonly called the Hadow Rep.

84 *Leics. Cty. Council Minutes and Reps. 1934–5*, p. 275.

85 Ibid.; *Meeting of Leics. Cty. Council, 13 May 1931, Reps. of Cttees.* 30; *Leics. Cty. Council Minutes and Reps. 1938–9*, pp. 169 et seq.

86 See reps. of the Education Cttee. of the Leics. Cty. Council, in the council's *Minutes and Reps.* 1929–39, and especially *Minutes and Reps. 1938–9*, 169–71, and *1934–5*, 267–84.

conferences was held between the Director of Education and the managers of the voluntary schools, to secure agreement about the proposed changes.[87] The fact that Leicestershire contained many rural areas with rather sparse populations made the establishment of the new system difficult, and plans had to be revised because some areas did not possess enough senior pupils to fill a two-stream modern school.[88] Despite this, much was achieved. By 1935, out of 10,800 senior pupils in the Leicestershire elementary schools, just over 60 per cent. were being educated in modern schools, and a further 27 per cent. were in special senior divisions, each of at least two classes, where they could obtain instruction roughly comparable with that given in modern schools.[89] By 1938 16 out of 24 modern school districts had been reorganized; 74 per cent. of senior pupils were being taught in modern schools, and a further 17 per cent. in separate senior divisions.[90]

From the first the cost of elementary education imposed a heavy financial burden on the county council. For the financial year 1904–5 it was estimated that the council's total expenditure on elementary education would be over £93,000 (excluding capital expenditure on buildings),[91] and the county had to take over responsibility for the school boards' capital liabilities, which in July 1903 amounted to over £60,000.[92] In the financial year 1913–14 the total expenditure on elementary education in the county[93] was over £130,000; of this, rather more than £70,000 was provided by grants from the Exchequer.[94] These considerable sums were subsequently much exceeded; for the financial year 1938–9 it was estimated that the total expenditure on elementary education would be over £440,000.[95]

Under the Education Act of 1944 further major changes in elementary education were introduced, but it is yet too soon to discuss historically the situation thus created.

ADULT AND FURTHER EDUCATION

This chapter is concerned with education, full-time and part-time, given to pupils upwards of 18 years of age in both the county and the city of Leicester. It includes elementary education at the one extreme and university education at the other. In the earlier period the former predominates, whilst in the later period, as the public provision of elementary education for the country's children becomes general, it disappears from the scene.

The earliest examples in Leicester and Leicestershire of education provided for young people and adults are furnished by voluntary organizations whose primary object was to make good deficiencies in the elementary education of those who had received little or no schooling. Provision was made by the educationally privileged for the unprivileged in most cases out of a sense of Christian charity, in some, from prudential motives. Those who were moved to educational philanthropy by concern for the physical and spiritual wretchedness of the working-classes were clearly in a majority. They were the active workers in the early adult schools and other ventures, but among their financial supporters must have been many who (to judge by remarks they are reported to have made) saw in elementary education, provided for young people and adults, a kind of insurance against social revolution.

Between 1819 and 1845 there were founded many ventures of different kinds. Of Sunday-school classes for adults, of which there must have been at least a few in the early years of the 19th century, there is no evidence, but from the accounts of the Congregational Church at Hinckley we learn that in 1819 money was expended on copy-books, alphabets, quill pens, and the salary of a master, in connexion with an evening school.[1] According to Joseph Dare,[2] who taught in the writing department of this school, it had, in 1845, from 200 to 300 pupils on the roll, mostly factory children. The chief aim of the early Sunday schools and of 'night' schools everywhere was to teach their pupils to read, using the Bible as a primer, and to write. The pupils having mastered these arts were then expected to depart and make way for others. Some who had acquired a taste for learning wished to go on to arithmetic, geography, history, various branches of science, 'the mechanic arts', and political economy. For these, after 1824, mechanics' institutes came into being. Leicester Mechanics' Institute was founded in 1834, and others were established in the county at a later date—Wigston

[87] *Meeting of the Leics. Cty. Council, 13 May 1931*, 21; ibid. *29 July 1931*, 24–26.

[88] *Leics. Cty. Council Minutes and Reps. 1935–6*, 277–9.

[89] Ibid. Such senior divisions had been mentioned in the 1926 rep. as a substitute for modern schools where the latter could not be provided; Barnard, *Short Hist. Engl. Educ.* 276.

[90] *Leics. Cty. Council Minutes and Reps. 1938–9*, 169–71, where a list of reorganized schools is given.

[91] *Leics. Cty. Council Minutes and Orders, 1904–5*, f. 41.

[92] Ibid. f. 165.

[93] Excluding Leic. and Loughborough.

[94] *Leics. Cty. Council Minutes and Orders, 1913–16*, pp. 241, 261.

[95] *Leics. Cty. Council Minutes and Reps. 1938–9*, 167.

[1] H. J. Francis, *Hist. Hinckley*, 135.

[2] *1st Appendix to Rep. on Cond. of Framework Knitters* [618], Q. 4671, H.C. (1845), xv.

Magna (1839), Hinckley (1840), Lutterworth (1841), Melton Mowbray (1845), and Loughborough, Mountsorrel, and Ashby de la Zouch at dates unknown.

Information about most of the institutes is scanty. Though elsewhere, even in quite small towns, the mechanics' institutes were housed in imposing buildings, erected by public subscription, in Leicestershire towns they were accommodated in existing public buildings—the Assembly Rooms, the Corn Exchange, or a Sherrier's School. The one exception is the institute at Wigston Magna which was 'erected . . . by four spirited individuals at a cost of £600'.[3] Unfortunately, it was short-lived. In the early 1840's it was converted into a British School and later into two dwelling-houses, which still stand. Most of the institutes, rather exceptionally, numbered the local gentry and the Anglican clergy among their patrons and committee-men. All of them provided reading-rooms and a library, promoted lectures and attempted to organize classes. White's *Directory* for 1846, recorded that the Hinckley Mechanics' Institute had a reading-room well supplied with periodical literature. It had an increasing library, and its classes met in the infant school for instruction in reading, writing, arithmetic, grammar, and other subjects.[4]

Membership of mechanics' institutes in the county is not easy to determine: there is little information, and such published figures as there are do not always distinguish between quarterly and annual members. Numbers varied from 75 to 150. It must be remembered, of course, that in the 1840's the population of the country's urban centres was probably less than one-quarter of what it is today. Membership fees appear to have been less than in most mechanics' institutes elsewhere, doubtless because there were no large buildings requiring upkeep. Between 8*s.* and 12*s.* a year, or 2*s.* and 3*s.* a quarter, seems to have been the usual subscription. This entitled members to the use of the library and reading-room, and attendance at public lectures and the institute classes free or at a reduced rate. Lectures and classes were nowhere an outstanding success and in time were abandoned. Most of the institutes became in fact lower-middle-class clubs with reading-rooms and libraries. Where their membership had originally included mechanics these were soon lost and, in the hope of attracting clerks and tradesmen to membership, some institutes even changed their names. Thus in 1864, the Melton Mowbray Mechanics' Institute became the Literary Institute[5] and, at an unknown date, the institute at Ashby de la Zouch changed its name to The Library, News Room, and Literary and Scientific Institution.[6]

The Leicester Mechanics' Institute[7] deserves special mention, not only because it was the largest and longest-lived of the institutes in Leicestershire, but because it differed in some notable respects from other Leicestershire institutes. The initiative in starting it came, not from the well-to-do radicals of the town, but from a number of working men and little masters. Moreover, the founders set out to create an institute which should be what its name implied, that is, one largely supported and controlled by wage earners and small tradesmen. The backing of well-known public figures was sought, apparently rather as a guarantee that the venture was not a revolutionary club in disguise, than for financial or other reasons. Nevertheless, this did not save it from attack as a hotbed of subversive opinions. Early in its history the institute was attacked by the Revd. George Holt, who had been one of its patrons and committee-men. The citizens of Leicester were informed in a series of letters published by Holt in 1835[8], that from the democratic nature of its constitution the institute could easily be captured by atheists and levellers. Already, he said, the evil influence of such people was beginning to be felt in the decision of the committee to have a single price for seats at lectures and concerts: this he regarded as 'the introduction of the offensive Jacobin principle of an equality of ranks'.[9] He further distrusted the committee's refusal to prohibit the gift of such dangerous journals as the weekly *Gauntlet*, though the papers they had actually decided to buy were, even in his opinion, innocent enough.

The institute was stoutly defended by its leading members and by prominent middle-class radicals and dissenting ministers, and seems not to have lost anything by Holt's defection and opposition. Its membership in the early years was about 500. The library, which contained about 900 volumes at the end of the first year, was steadily enlarged and had increased, by 1856, to 3,500 volumes. By this time, however, the institute was little more than a reading-room and library. Its scheme of lectures had flourished for a season, but attendances fell off, especially in periods of bad trade. As time went on, the more serious subjects of the early years, electricity, chemistry, domestic and social economy, astronomy and mechanics, gave way to lecture-demonstrations on such topics as ventriloquism, phrenology, and mesmerism, but the decline in numbers could not be arrested, and the lecture scheme had to be abandoned. Concerts and penny readings were successful for a while but they, too, had to be given up when they became a source of loss to the institute. Classes were never very well supported. Four or five were run each year in

[3] White, *Dir. Leics.* (1846), 420.
[4] Ibid. 557.
[5] Ibid. (1877), 545.
[6] Ibid. 133.
[7] The following account is based on F. B. Lott, *Story of Leic. Mechanics' Inst. 1833–71.*
[8] G. Holt, *A Complete Exposure of the Abuses of the Leicester Mechanics' Institute*, Leic. Ref. Libr. Pamphlets, xi.
[9] Ibid. 6.

such subjects as astronomy, grammar, mathematics, and mutual instruction (see below), but the average size of a class seems to have been about twelve. The teaching was voluntary and the class fee nominal. The Annual Report for 1857–8 laments that 'there appeared to be no disposition on the part of the members to enter upon courses of study'. Thereafter, no more is heard of classes, lectures, concerts, or penny readings in the institute.

By 1857–8 the membership had declined to about 200, and the many efforts made thereafter to raise it above this figure were only temporarily successful. The financial position of the institute, never very satisfactory, became more and more difficult, so that in 1863 the winding up of its affairs was seriously considered, though it struggled on for another 7 years. The institute was closed in 1870. Its assets and liabilities were taken over by Leicester Corporation, and the 5,000 volumes in the library became the foundation stock of the Free Library and Reading Room, which was opened to the public on 9 January 1871. At no time in its 36 years' existence was the Leicester Mechanics' Institute dominated by any determined or colourful personality. It was a modest, retiring institution, quietly governed by a committee which faithfully represented its working-class and small-tradesman membership: and at no time did it come anywhere near to fulfilling Holt's alarmist prophecies.

It has already been noted that the Leicester Mechanics' Institute had a mutual instruction class. Throughout the 19th century this type of class was a popular educational device for adults. Just how many mutual classes and societies existed in Leicester and Leicestershire is uncertain, since the documents relating to most of them have long since perished, but there is every reason for believing that they were very numerous. The first of which there is any documentary evidence is a mutual instruction society at Hinckley, founded in 1834 by John Gent Brooks, a self-educated framework-knitter, who later became a prominent local Chartist of the non-militant party.[10] Of its activities we know little. Much more is known of a mutual discussion class started in 1845 by the Revd. Joseph Dare, under the aegis of the Leicester Domestic Mission.[11] There existed, in 1854, a Loughborough Working Men's Improvement Society,[12] and also a mutual improvement class at the Gallowtree Gate Congregational Sunday school.[13] In 1864 there was formed a St. Andrew's Mutual Improvement Society, and some time later a St. Stephen's Mutual Improvement Society, both in Leicester;[14] in 1877 Ashby de la Zouch is reported as having a Young Men's Improvement Society, which had science classes connected with it.[15]

In the mutual class, the better educated and more confident members took turns at reading papers and leading discussions. The methods used were variants upon the monitorial systems of Andrew Bell and Joseph Lancaster. Joseph Dare, in his Annual Report as head of the Domestic Mission,[16] tells us of the class he started that it 'affords an opportunity for becoming acquainted with the real sentiments and opinions of the operatives. Unbelief and socialistic opinions prevail amongst them. . . . Discussion classes, if managed with care, might be the means of spreading sounder views upon the various subjects on which the operatives *feel* strongly without much correct information. They act as a kind of safety valve to let off exasperated feelings and to modify erroneous opinions.' Large numbers of working men and small tradesmen must have profited by membership of mutual improvement classes, especially where they were under the guidance of such people as Joseph Dare, David James Vaughan, or Mary Royce. According to Dare, the widening of knowledge and the broadening of outlook they brought about, the improvement they effected in the capacity of their members to express themselves in speech and writing, and the confidence they engendered in those who ventured to take part in them were truly remarkable. Allowing for Dare's pardonable enthusiasm for one of the most successful and enduring of the Domestic Mission's ventures, it would still be true to say that the mutual improvement classes and societies were, in the years 1825 to 1875, a valuable instrument in adult education. It is to be regretted that we know so little of their history.

No history of adult and further education in Leicester and Leicestershire can omit a reference to Thomas Cooper's adult classes, which were held in connexion with his Shakespearian Association of Leicester Chartists during the winter of 1840–1, but it is doubtful whether they had much permanent influence. We owe to Cooper himself such information as we have about them. At the time he wrote his *Life*,[17] Cooper was not the most modest of men, and even he admits that at the end of the winter months the classes broke up never to assemble again.

A far more significant venture about this time was that of the Leicester Domestic Mission Society, to which reference has already been made. The society was founded and financed by some of the leading members of the congregation of Great Meeting, with the object of civilizing the life of one of the poorest and most degraded parts of Leicester. The preaching of the Gospel

[10] Francis, *Hist. Hinckley*, 129.

[11] Leic. Ref. Libr., *Annual Reps. Leic. Dom. Mission 1845–77*.

[12] Melville, *Dir. Leics.* (1854), 113.

[13] *Leics. Sunday School Union Jnl.* iv, no. 37.

[14] White, *Dir. Leics.* (1877), 314.

[15] Ibid. 133.

[16] Leic. Dom. Mission, *5th Annual Rep.* (1850), 12.

[17] T. Cooper, *Life of Thomas Cooper, written by Himself* (1872).

was to be only one aspect of the work of the mission: charity and education were to be not less important. The work of the mission was conducted in a hall in All Saints Open and in its missioner, the Revd. Joseph Dare, Great Meeting and the people in the then densely populated area around All Saints Open were fortunate. Dare united within himself the enlightenment of the 18th century and the evangelicalism of the 19th in the form of a well-developed nonconformist conscience. Dare's annual reports (there are thirty-two of them) are important social documents, exposing the fearful conditions under which his people existed, and urging remedies—decent housing, a drainage system, pure water, bath and wash houses, allotments, and, most of all, compulsory education. In one, he briefly sums up the situation as follows: 'they live in filthy and confined courts . . . their inmates clothed in the same dress all the year through . . . thronged with unhappy beings, who from early and continued neglect, never arrive either physically or intellectually at their proper station.'[18]

On assuming his mission in 1845, Dare, in addition to undertaking a social survey of his area, set about organizing sick and benefit and other mutual help societies and educational activities. These last he embarked upon because he saw that 'one of the evil influences at work among the industrial classes is a total want of education; ignorance of almost everything calculated to make them rational, intelligent beings'.[19] Men's classes, including the mutual class already alluded to, and, a little later, classes for women, were soon established, with Dare and leading members of the congregation of Great Meeting as teachers. Reading, writing, arithmetic, history, and geography were the main subjects taught, and the pupils numbered annually in the early years about seventy men and forty women. With the women's class, apparently the first of its kind in Leicester, Dare was especially pleased. He reports of the 1850 class that 'several who could scarcely write a line when admitted, copied as a dictation on the slate a verse or two of "How doth the little busy bee", &c., in a tolerable manner'.[20]

The Leicester Domestic Mission is an example of Christian philanthropy at its best. It was concerned primarily with the poor as men and women, and not with conditioning them to an existing social order. It was directed towards raising their mental, moral, and material welfare, and one of the chief means it used was education. The mission was, it is true, provided and administered for its members and not by them. It was governed by an aristocracy consisting for the most part of upper-middle-class Unitarians, but it was, on the whole, an enlightened and benevolent despotism.

After 1870 the educational work of the mission steadily declined and in 1877, when Dare retired from his position as missioner, and the work was transferred to the Great Meeting schools, the great days of the mission were virtually at an end. Lack of support for the classes was attributed by Dare to two causes: first, the growth of day-school provision since 1870, due to the activities of the Leicester School Board, and secondly, the formation, with the blessing of the mission, of Leicester's first working-men's club.[21] Public houses in the poorer working-class districts were then, for the most part, places of squalor and iniquity. Working-men's clubs were conceived of as sweeter and cleaner alternatives, where the sale of intoxicating drinks in preference to others would not be any-one's special interest, and where, through strict control over membership, undesirable patrons of the bar could be excluded. Dare, like others who were interested in promoting such clubs, rather naïvely believed that they would become what we now term community centres, in which there is a combination of recreation and education. A large proportion of the male members of the mission joined the new club, but the hopes in which it had been founded were disappointed. The club did not provide the educational service that was expected of it.

Within a stone's throw of the Domestic Mission, on the corner of what is now Great Central Street and Soar Lane, stood the meeting house of the Leicester Quakers. In 1861, following a visit by two Bristol Friends, who described to their fellow Quakers the work of the adult school movement in their own city, a school for men was opened in a small room in Sanvey Gate.[22] Membership soon outgrew the available accommodation, and, in 1864, the Friends built a new schoolroom in the grounds of their Soar Lane meeting house. Numbers continued to grow, so that a waiting-list had to be drawn up. In the hope of eliminating it the schoolroom was extended in 1868, but the list remained until 1886, when a branch school was opened in the adjoining Pike Street Board School. The combined membership of the two schools in 1886 was 302, with an average attendance of 198. A few years later the Friends' meeting house and the adult schoolroom were demolished to make way for the Manchester, Sheffield, and Lincolnshire Railway Company's new main line to London. The school met for a while in the Elbow Lane Board School, but in 1899, together with its offspring in Pike Street, and a women's school started in 1896 by the Friends in their new meeting house in Prebend Street, it moved into the present Churchgate adult school buildings, which were erected with the purchase money of the old Soar Lane school building.[23] The Churchgate adult schools were still in existence in 1954.

18 Leic. Dom. Mission, *1st Annual Rep.* (1846), 5.

19 Ibid. 9.

20 Leic. Dom. Mission, *5th Annual Rep.* (1850), 9.

21 Leic. Dom. Mission, *21st Annual Rep.* (1866), 6.

22 *Fifty Years of Adult School Work*, ed. A. F. Cholerton, 7.

23 Ibid. 8.

It was not until 1870 that the next adult school was opened. Then others followed in fairly rapid succession—Belgrave (1874), Paradise Mission (1877), Dover Street (1881), Emmanuel Church (1883), Clarendon Park (1887), and Victoria Park (1890).[24] As elsewhere in the country, the great majority of Leicester schools met on Sunday mornings. Belgrave and Paradise Mission began at 8.30 a.m., Soar Lane and Pike Street at 8.45 a.m., Dover Street at 9.15 a.m., and Clarendon Park at 9.30 a.m. These early hours were chosen in order to give the members a chance of going to church or chapel after school. The meetings opened with the singing of a hymn, a Bible reading, and a short prayer, and thereafter the pupils separated into their respective classes, to learn their letters, to read out of their Bibles, or to write. Sawbridge, in his article in *Fifty Years of Adult School Work*, remarks[25] that 'It is difficult nowadays to realize that vast numbers of adults had either forgotten how to read and write or had received no instruction whatever. Instruction in reading, writing, history, etc., was thus regarded as an indispensable feature in every school. . . . There were not wanting "unco guid" folk who severely condemned secular teaching on the Sabbath Day, forgetting that for those who toiled early and late, it was the only day free for this purpose.' When lessons were ended the school met again as a whole, sang a hymn, and, after benediction, dispersed.

The schools were generally led by men and women of some education and social standing, and much of the early teaching was done by philanthropically-minded members of the middle class. Government was formally democratic, but in the committees of management the few with social standing and means exerted a decisive influence. Most schools established night classes at a charge of 1*d.* a meeting, and evening discussion classes, school libraries, and sick and benevolent societies were common in the earlier days. How many men and women were touched by the beneficent influence of the Leicester schools in the years before the full effects of the Education Act of 1870 began to be felt it is impossible to say with any certainty, but the number must have run into many thousands. 'Those who were actually engaged in the schools', says John Sawbridge,[26] '. . . recognised the value of their work and saw tangible results in the changed lives and homes of the members. Habitual drunkards gave up drink and set about winning others to a temperate life. Gamblers burned their betting books and became comrades and co-workers. Idlers and wastrels were inspired to industry, thrift and integrity . . . [and] men were led to rational modes of thought and habit, resulting in greatly increased home happiness and family comfort.'

Until 1889 the various adult schools were not formally associated in any way, but in that year they united to form The Leicester and Leicestershire Working Men's Educational Union. The three county adult schools, namely, Hinckley, founded in 1888, Earl Shilton and Stoney Stanton, both founded in 1893,[27] were admitted to the Leicestershire Union in the latter year, and formed the nucleus of what was a little later to become the Hinckley sub-district of the union. In 1894 an Extension Committee was set up which actively undertook the formation of new schools, and within 3 years the number of schools was doubled. A new Loughborough sub-district was set up to draw together the many new schools in the northern part of the county. Altogether there were now thirty schools with a membership of 3,600. Although expansion since the formation of the union, which was now renamed the Leicestershire Adult School Union, had been steady and continuous, a decline now set in, and some prophesied that the days of the adult school movement were numbered.

They were mistaken; the movement had yet a period of exceptional growth before it, but in 1897 the future certainly looked unpromising, since, as Edwin Gilbert saw,

'with the general spread of elementary education . . . we had arrived at a time when everyone reaching manhood had at least the opportunity of knowing something of the art of reading, writing and arithmetic, and our adult school curriculum had not yet soared far beyond these elementary subjects. With the need for these things gradually diminishing the movement ran the serious risk of becoming simply a series of Bible classes, and oftentimes of a very stereotyped kind. With every denomination providing adult Bible classes for its own members and their friends, there seemed a possibility of the Adult School Movement either giving way to more modern institutions, or becoming an appanage of . . . the Society of Friends.'[28]

Gilbert became the secretary of the union in 1899. Under his energetic and far-sighted leadership successful efforts were made to escape the possibilities he foresaw. He induced the schools to widen their educational provision and he encouraged many non-Quakers, both from within and without the movement, to assume the responsibilities of leadership.[29]

Discussion classes, dealing with social and moral issues, gradually took the place of classes in the ordinary elementary school subjects. Lesson handbooks were prepared by the union and supplied to class leaders. These provided outline lessons arranged in series, and enabled classes to undertake courses of systematic study. The result was that interest in the existing schools revived and enthusiasm for the movement was rekindled. Fresh missionary efforts were under-

[24] *Fifty Years of Adult School Work*, 11.

[25] Ibid. 11–12.

[26] Ibid. 12.

[27] Ibid. 27.

[28] Ibid. 23.

[29] *Pioneering in Educ.* (Leics. Adult School Union), 6.

taken and to such good effect that in 1905 the union was able to report that in city and county together there were 119 schools, with a combined membership of 10,117.[30] This represents the high-water mark of the adult school movement. Numbers declined a little up to 1914 and after the war they were well down. In the years between the First and Second World Wars a steady fall occurred, so that in the year 1938–9 the number of schools and pupils was 81 and 2,374, respectively.[31]

The adult schools still retain their religious basis and the teaching they give still has an ethical character. Few of them, however, now follow the lesson handbook; most preferring to have weekly talks on different and usually unrelated topics. The education they give is thus, in most cases, far from systematic. Though the movement has thrown up some first-class leaders from its own ranks, these do not appear to have altogether made up for the aristocratic element which has steadily been lost as the years have gone by. Moreover, since the early years of this century, the movement has had to face increasing competition from other adult educational organizations with bigger financial resources and with a stronger sense of mission than the adult schools of today appear to possess. Whether the movement will be able to adapt itself to present-day educational needs, whilst retaining its informal character, is open to question. There is no reason, however, for doubting that since their foundation the adult schools of Leicester and Leicestershire have done much to raise the cultural level of many thousands of working-class men and women, and to bring to them Christian teaching in a form that they could understand and appreciate.

The founding, in 1862, of a reading-room and library in Union Street, Leicester, is a further example of Christian philanthropy expressed through the medium of adult education. The library and reading-room began very modestly, but its founder, the Revd. (later Canon) David James Vaughan, vicar of St. Martin's, and his associates, expected great things of it. They aimed at building up a Working Men's College[32] on the lines of that established in London in 1854 by the Revd. Frederick Denison Maurice. Government of the Working Men's Institute, as it was renamed in 1863, was of the mixed type. One-half of the committee of management consisted of representatives of the middle-class promoters of the venture, the other half of representatives of the working-class members. Vaughan was the institute's president and chairman of its management committee. A man of wide culture and impressive dignity, he was highly respected by all sections of the community, and not least by the working-class members of the institute, many of whom, as sympathizers with Chartism and Owenite Socialism, differed profoundly from him in politics. The great esteem in which he was held enabled him to put the stamp of his own personality on the organization, and throughout the first half of its history the institute was very largely his creature.

The library and reading-room, admission to which cost 2*d.* a week, or 6*d.* a month, soon attracted a satisfactory membership, but the earliest attempts to establish formal classes for instruction in reading, writing, and arithmetic were a failure. In 1864 a discussion class was formed. This seems to have been successful, since at the annual meeting, held on 6 April 1866, it was resolved that the thanks of the meeting be given to the Revd. J. A. Bonser and Messrs. Jones and Collin, for their work in connexion with the Bible class and a class in writing; to Vaughan, as teacher of the English grammar class; and to Messrs. Bland, Vernon, and Collin for taking a class in phonography. This last was, apparently, a class in Pitman's shorthand. Thereafter the institute was able in its annual reports to show increasing numbers of classes. What the students were required to pay in class fees is not very clear, but a payment of 4*d.* a week or 1*s.* a month seems to have entitled anyone to membership of the reading-room and library and of as many classes as he chose to attend. The class fee charged to non-members of the library seems to have been 2*d.* a week or 6*d.* a month for each class attended. At this time, and for many years to come, the teaching was given gratuitously.

In 1868 the name of the institute was changed to the Working Men's College, and at the annual meeting held in that year, the president gave the reasons for this change. He said that, the committee

'thought it important to mark in this way the characteristic features of the Institute, as an Institute for self-improvement, for mutual improvement, and for co-operation in a humble yet earnest endeavour to improve and elevate the working-classes of the town, intellectually and morally. The Committee see no reason to regret the change thus made . . . They believe that it has tended materially to help forward the spirit of human fellowship and Christian philanthropy, which it is one great object of the Institute to quicken and extend. . . . The success of the past half year has been mainly due to this spirit of zeal awakened in the members. They look forward confidently to the future, believing that the same spirit of real fellowship will achieve yet larger results in the time to come.'[33]

These sanguine hopes of the committee were realized. The number of classes and students and the range of studies increased year by year, and so

[30] *Pioneering in Educ.* (Leics. Adult School Union), 8.

[31] Ex inf. Miss Dorothy Wykes, Hon. Sec. Leics. Adult School Union.

[32] The following account is based chiefly upon *Vaughan Working Men's Coll. Leic. 1862–1912*, ed. Revd. E. Atkins.

[33] Rep. of Cttee. to Annual Meeting, 6 Apr. 1869.

did the successes in the annual examinations of the Society of Arts.

The college was not, however, merely a reading-room and library with classes. It had lectures, including one of the earliest of the Cambridge University Extension Lecture Courses, penny readings of passages from Shakespeare, Goldsmith, Dickens, and other great writers, and smoking concerts. An annual college service was held in St. Martin's Church, and there were student societies of various kinds—horticultural, photographic, and so forth—and sports clubs, among them one for the new sport of cycling.[34] There were also societies for self-help and mutual help—the Sick Benefit Society, the Provident Society, and the Christmas Club. All these activities knitted bonds of interest and fellowship between the members, and resulted in the college becoming what Canon Vaughan (as he became in 1872) had dreamed of when he started the venture in 1862. It remained, however, a male affair. Wives and daughters discovered the need of similar provision for themselves, and in 1880–1 classes were opened for them in the Friar Lane schools. The intention of Canon and Mrs. Vaughan was that ultimately there should be established a working women's college, parallel to the men's. The notion of a mixed college and of mixed classes, though favoured in some quarters, was, however, too advanced an idea to win general acceptance at the time. The women's classes were an immediate success, and from this time onward they formed an important part of the work of the college.

Like several of the adult educational organizations already noted, the Working Men's College found itself confronted by the challenge of the Education Act of 1870. By 1879–80 the effects of that great measure were beginning to be felt. In the annual report for that year, Canon Vaughan said: 'As the number of members increases and as the standard of education advances year by year under the presence of the Elementary Education Act of 1870; so the need of engaging the services of experienced teachers increases also, and with this the working expenses of the College.' Fortunately by this time government grants could be earned on many of the college classes and these helped to pay the fees of the increasing number of paid teachers employed. Elementary classes gradually disappeared from the programme, and their place was taken by recreative and commercial classes, and preparatory classes for the new Borough Technical and Art Schools. By the turn of the century, when this adaptation to the new circumstances was fairly complete, the enrolments had reached a figure well above 2,000, the various sections contributing to the total as follows: women's section 750, youths' section 325, men's section 1,150. How many individual students these numbers represent it is impossible to say with any certainty, but they would be not less than 1,500.

Scarcely had the college successfully met the challenge of the 1870 Act, however, than it had to face an even greater one in the Education Act of 1902, which empowered county and county borough authorities to provide a wide range of further and adult educational facilities. Fortunately for the college the Leicester Education Committee was at first so much occupied with founding a system of secondary education that it was not able to pay much attention to the development of evening-class work. Nevertheless, evening classes were established in various parts of the town in science, technology, and commerce, first for young people and later for adults. In 1906 the college transferred to the local education authority those of its classes held in the Mantle Road school and discontinued its Youth Department.[35] It still endeavoured to provide in its central building preparatory classes for the Schools of Technology and Art, but as time went on the better provision made by the education authority affected enrolments and had the college not been willing once again to adapt its programme to changing conditions its total enrolments must have suffered. An expansion, however, in the number and variety of recreative classes and classes in what the reports call 'civics' prevented this. Until the outbreak of the First World War numbers were kept up to 2,000. Class fees remained virtually unchanged from the earliest days, being now 1*s.* a session of twelve meetings instead of 1*d.* a meeting.

Canon Vaughan died in 1905, having completed 43 years' service as president of the college. Throughout this long period he had been its guiding spirit, and but for him it might long before have perished, like so many others which had been inspired by the London Working Men's College. As a tribute to his memory a new college building was erected by public subscription and named the Vaughan Working Men's College. It was opened in 1908, and the old institution, in its handsome new building, seemed to have before it a most promising future. With the opening of Vaughan College the physical separation of the provision for men and women came to an end. During the First World War numbers dwindled and fewer and fewer classes could be organized. Hopes of recovery after the war were disappointed, since the local authority had by this time entered the field of recreative further and adult education, and liberal studies were being provided by the University College of Nottingham and the Workers' Educational Association. In the report for 1922–4 it is stated that 'Your Committee . . . cannot be insensible to the yearly increasing difficulty of maintaining a numerical standard side by side with the efficient classes established by the Local Education Authority, not only for youths

[34] *Vaughan Working Men's Coll.* 140–2.

[35] *Leic. Daily Post*, 4 Jan. 1907.

and girls, but also at each centre for men and women without limit of age. There is now a centre close by, especially for adults.' In 1929 the college was handed over to University College, Leicester, to serve as a centre for university-provided adult education. Its subsequent history forms part of the history of University College.

The Leicester Working Men's College, to use the name by which it was known for so long, was the most successful and enduring of all the voluntary efforts made in 19th-century Leicester and Leicestershire to provide education for the adult population. It survived, partly through Canon Vaughan's leadership, partly because it proved itself so adaptable to changing needs and circumstances, and partly because, from the seventies onwards, it received government grants in aid of its classes. Had these grants been available to earlier ventures, such as the mechanics' institutes, they too might still survive. Since the foundation of the college, many thousands of men and women have passed through its classes and participated in its warm and friendly social life. The majority of these were and remained operatives, warehousemen, and clerks. Some of its students, however, made their way in the world and rendered valued service to their city and country. Thomas Adcock, who when little more than a boy was, as the annual report of 1919–20 puts it, 'smuggled into the College', became successively a part-time teacher in the college, one of the earliest board school teachers and first headmaster of the Desford Industrial School. He was actively associated with the college for 55 years. A railway clerk, who attended classes in the college more than half a century ago, was raised to the peerage in 1945, after a distinguished career as a trade-union leader and Member of Parliament. Lord Walkden always readily acknowledged the debt he owed to the old Working Men's College.

A final example of adult educational provision made in Leicester from motives of Christian charity is that of Mary Royce and her boys' class.[36] This began in 1868 in a Sunday school, held in an old stockinger's shop in Sanvey Gate. To the religious teaching she gave to her boys on Sundays, Miss Royce soon added instruction in reading, writing, and arithmetic at night classes that she arranged for them.[37] The teacher had a great capacity for winning and retaining the interest and loyalty of her pupils, so that they remained with her year after year in spite of frequent removals of the class. As the time went by, and the boys grew up, the scope of the class widened: it was a Sunday class, a night school, and a social club for all who cared to take advantage of it. The members were drawn from some of the poorest homes in Leicester, and to their intellectual and moral welfare, Mary Royce devoted the greater part of her immense energy and will-power. Speaking years later about her work, Mr. S. Palmer, then president of the Royce Institute, said, 'It was to me a puzzle why a lady of her social standing and education should condescend to come up those courts and into those vile dens to look after young fellows like me, to try to lift us up above our sordid surroundings, and help us to lead upright, manly lives; but it is no longer strange to me, for now I understand what it all meant—her heart, her soul, her life, was given over to the work.'[38]

Some time in the 1880's, Miss Royce bought and adapted two houses in Lower Churchgate and, numbers still continuing to grow, she purchased land adjoining the houses, and erected at her own expense the present Royce Institute buildings. Miss Royce was temperamentally something of an autocrat, but by conviction a devout Christian and a sincere liberal. Her temperament must often have been at war with her convictions, but on the whole the latter appear to have triumphed. Although her rule in the early years of the class was authoritarian, its vigour was progressively lessened with the object of preparing her boys for the exercise of what she might have termed Christian responsibility. Thus, shortly after the Lower Churchgate Institute was opened, she appointed stewards to assist her in its control, and, while in the beginning she was the leader of the mutual improvement class, in the course of time we find her encouraging and assisting the members to give papers, and gradually taking her place as an ordinary member of the class.[39] Miss Royce died in 1892. She left the institute, renamed the Royce Institute, to its members, by whom it has since been carried on in the spirit of its founder. The Sunday class is still its central feature, and though instruction in the elements is no longer provided, informal discussion classes on social and moral questions are included in the programme of activities.[40]

Hitherto, attention has been given to adult and further education provided by voluntary bodies. Provision by statutory bodies began shortly after the setting up of the school boards, but neither in Leicester nor in Leicestershire were the school boards able to make a beginning with classes for adults until 1893. In that year the Education Department issued a new set of evening-school regulations permitting the school boards greatly to widen the scope of their provision and lifting the virtual prohibition on adult attendance at evening schools. These changes were brought about largely by the efforts of the Recreative Evening Schools Association, founded by Dr. J. B. Paton of Nottingham.[41] A Leicester branch of

[36] The following account is based chiefly on E. Smith, *Short Hist. of Royce Inst.* (1916).

[37] Smith, op. cit. 4.

[38] Ibid. 30.

[39] Ibid. 49.

[40] Ex inf. Royce Inst.

[41] M. E. Sadler, *Continuation Schools in Engl. and Elsewhere*, 91–96.

this association was formed about 1891, and in 1893 the school board enlisted its support in the promotion of evening classes of a recreative character.[42] The more varied and interesting programme offered to the public brought a ready response. Within 5 years the number of schools and students was doubled—12 schools with a combined membership of about 1,500, of which perhaps 500 would be over 18 years of age.[43] In 1898 the first classes intended specially for adults were established.[44] Thereafter, though the total evening-school population declined, the number of adult classes increased. It is estimated that in 1903 when the education committee took over the work of the school board there were still 500 students over 18 years of age in evening schools, though the total enrolments had fallen to 1,200.

The education committee also took over in 1903 the work of the technical education committee of the borough council. This committee, which had been established in 1892 as a result of the passing of the Technical Instruction Act of 1889, owned and controlled an art school and a technical school, which were housed in buildings in The Newarke, erected by the corporation in 1897. At the time of transfer the numbers on the rolls of these two institutions were 31 full-time and approximately 500 part-time, mostly evening, students of 18 years of age and over. Thus slightly more than 1,000 men and women over 18 years of age were being provided for by statutory authority when the education committee came into being.

The School of Art, originally a voluntary enterprise, was founded in 1870, mainly by a group of Leicester business men, who were chiefly interested in raising the standard of industrial and commercial design. The school, in its earlier years, was housed in a converted warehouse in Pocklington's Walk, and had an enrolment in 1870 of 269, all of them part-time evening students.[46] The Technical School grew out of a series of evening classes held, from 1884 onwards, in the Wyggeston School, then situated in Highcross Street. These classes had been started by the headmaster, the Revd. James Went, at the request of the Chamber of Commerce, whose secretary, W. T. Rowlett, was a great admirer of Germany's system of technical education.[47] The art school and technical classes were made possible by South Kensington grants in aid of recognized science and art classes. Without them it is improbable that the School of Art or the Wyggeston science, technological, and trade classes could have been established in days when neither the school boards nor the corporation were authorized to spend public money on higher education.

Before the building in The Newarke was erected by the corporation in 1897, the art and technical classes of the town had poor and scattered accommodation. The new building enabled the evening classes to be brought together under one roof and made possible the provision of day-time courses. Under the education committee both schools made very good progress. New departments were added and advisory committees of employers and work-people were set up for all the main branches of the work carried on. These latter brought the schools into close and intimate touch with industry and commerce. In addition to ensuring that the instruction given should be realistic and closely related to modern conditions, the existence of these committees secured valuable gifts to the schools. One annual report of the education committee mentions the gift, from the Leicester Association of Master Printers, of equipment for a course in typography; another records the gift of several of the latest of their knitting-machines by a famous local firm of textile engineers, and others tell of a scholarship, a prize, or a challenge cup given by some firm or trade association. Thus, though voluntary gave way to statutory provision, the interest and support of the city's business leaders was retained.

Between 1903 and 1912 there was competition and overlapping in the provision of evening classes in art, technology, and commerce, but in the latter year, on the advice of H.M. Inspector for Higher Education, this was stopped.[48] The Working Men's College withdrew from the field, evening schools were made responsible for elementary work, and provision for more advanced studies, leading to national awards of various kinds, became the main concern of the schools of art and technology. In the session 1911–12 a virtually full-time organizer of evening schools was appointed[49] and between that date and 1913–14 the numbers of students attending evening continuation schools increased from 2,013 to 3,375. This increase was brought about by the introduction of grouped technological and trade courses for young people; by improved publicity; and by the establishment of closer contact with employers. Amongst the students in 1913–14 were 315 between the ages of 18 and 21, and 529 over 21 years of age: a total of 844 young persons and adults.[50] In the same year the numbers of students of 18 years of age and

[42] Leic. Sch. Bd. Minute Bks. viii, 102.

[43] Leic. Sch. Bd. *8th Triennial Rep. 1894–7*, 11.

[44] Ibid. 11.

[45] *Rep. Leic. Educ. Cttee. 1903–1912*, 33. The number of part-time students is an estimate based on the number of classes reported.

[46] *1st Annual Rep. of Leic. Sch. of Art: 1871* (Leic. Ref. Libr. Pamphlet iv-o-3).

[47] R. G. Waddington, *Leic.: Making of a Mod. City*, 56–57.

[48] *Rep. Leic. Educ. Cttee. 1903–1912*, 33.

[49] Ibid. 34.

[50] Ibid. *1913–14*, 16.

over in the Schools of Art and Technology were:[51]

	Full-time students	*Part-time students*	*Total*
School of Art	41	262	303
Technical School	51	941	992
	92	1,203	1,295

There was thus, on the eve of the First World War, a total of just under 2,200 men and women over 18 years of age in attendance at classes and courses provided by the Leicester Education Committee.

The war adversely affected both the evening schools and the schools of art and technology, but recovery afterwards was rapid, and in subsequent years an unprecedented expansion occurred in the scope of provision and in the numbers taking advantage of it. In 1924 the School of Art became the College of Art and Crafts, the Technical School the College of Technology; an Adult Evening Institute was established in the Alderman Newton's Girls' School, and the evening continuation schools adopted recreational adult education on a large scale.[52] In 1930–1, when Vaughan College ceased to provide classes of its own, the Vaughan Adult Institute was brought into being.[53] Shortly afterwards, under the direction of a newly appointed controller of evening institutes, considerable reorganization of evening schools took place.[54] Meanwhile the colleges of art and technology had found their accommodation quite inadequate. Temporary relief was gained by adding a new wing in 1928, and in 1938 it became necessary to add another, thus filling the whole Newarke site. In these years the two colleges began to draw their full-time students from wider areas, and to show promise of development into national institutions. They also embarked upon the provision of advanced studies by preparing students for the final examinations in the associateships of the Royal College of Art and the Royal Institute of British Architects, and in degrees in engineering, pharmacy, and commerce of the University of London.

On the eve of the Second World War the number of evening institutes, as they were known from about 1928, had risen to 21, including the City Literary Institute, held in the City Boys' School, and intended primarily for adults. The number of students had risen to 10,683, of which it is estimated that not less than 1,500 were from 18 to 21 years of age, and rather more than 3,500 were over 21 years of age, making a total of 5,000 of over 18 years of age.[55] The numbers of students of 18 years and over at the colleges of art and technology were in that year (1938–9) as follows:[56]

	Full-time students	*Part-time students*	*Total*
Colleges of Arts and Crafts	188	875	1,063
College of Technology and Commerce	62	1,718	1,780
	250	2,593	2,843

making a grand total of rather more than 7,800 young people and adults participating in statutorily-provided further and adult education in Leicester. During the years that followed there was some set-back to the work of the colleges and the evening institutes, but after the war a rapid recovery took place.

There is little information about the evening school provision outside Leicester under the school boards. More is known about that made by the county council, which in 1891 decided to adopt the Technical Instruction Act of 1889.[57] It appointed Andrew John Baker to be a full-time organizing secretary for technical education, and shortly afterwards a County Technical Instruction Committee was set up to supervise the organizing secretary's work.[58] Baker entered upon his duties with energy and enthusiasm. His first task was to ensure an adequate supply of trained teachers, and arrangements were made with the Leicester Technical School and the North Midland Training School for Cookery, whereby elementary school teachers should be trained for evening school work in science and technology in the former, and in domestic science in the latter. His second task was to organize local technical instruction centres. After a few months' strenuous work, Baker succeeded in establishing forty-eight local committees. Some of these, like that at Hinckley, were essentially sub-committees of school boards, while others, like that at Coalville, were independent of existing bodies. He also entered into a close working arrangement with the education committee of the Leicester Agricultural Society, to which the county council made a grant of £300 in aid of the society's work among the farming community.[59]

Though the available statistics for the first few years after the setting up of the County Technical Instruction Committee are inadequate, it seems clear that the people of Leicestershire responded well to the opportunities which technical education, widely interpreted by the council, offered to them. Classes in cookery, in mining, in hosiery, in boot and shoe manufacture, and in manual

[51] *Rep. Leic. Educ. Cttee. 1913–14*, 18. The number of part-time students is an estimate based on the number of classes reported.

[52] Ibid. *1923–4*, 24.

[53] Ibid. *1930–1*, 39–40.

[54] Ibid. *1932–3*, 45–47.

[55] Ibid. *1938–9*, 31–33.

[56] Ex inf. Registrar of Colleges of Art and Technology, Leic.

[57] L.R.O., Leics. C.C. Minute Bks. Aug. 1891, sect. 5.

[58] Ibid. Nov. 1891, sect. 5.

[59] Ibid. Feb. 1892, sect. 5.

work proved especially popular, and in 1892 the council decided that the possibilities in mining and manual work seemed so promising as to justify the appointment of full-time chief instructors in these subjects.[60] At the end of that year the technical instruction committee was able to report to the council that 200 teachers had now been trained for evening school work and would be available for the session 1893–4. A good idea of the provision being made in the county at this time is given in the organizing secretary's report for the session 1892–3, in which he says,

'These schools as a rule are taught by the Headmaster of the Day School held in the same building. Each School with few exceptions meets for two evenings weekly. A majority of the scholars are taught Reading, Writing and Arithmetic, while a few are taught technical subjects only. It is upon these scholars alone that the grant of the Council can be paid. One of the most popular subjects is Agriculture; this and Drawing are the best taught subjects. The other common subjects of instruction are Hygiene, Theoretical Mechanics, Physiology, Elementary Science, Book-keeping and Shorthand.... In a majority of cases it will be found that these Schools have succeeded in direct proportion to the enthusiasm of the teachers and the active and kindly interest of Members of the Local Committee.'[61]

In 1893–4 the number of local centres was raised to 83, with a combined student membership of 2,300 boys. 1,400 girls, and 650 adults. No doubt the novelty of evening schools was at least partly the attraction, since after 1893–4 there was some falling off. By 1902–3 there were again 83 centres in being, with more classes and students than ever: 650 science and art classes, 100 technical and trade classes, and 26 agricultural lecture and manual training classes, making 775 in all, with a student membership of 2,632 boys, 1,625 girls, 744 men and 548 women, making a total of 1,292 adults. In 1902–3 the newly created education committee of the county council took over the work of the technical education committee, as it had been called since 1896. General supervision of evening schools was made a responsibility of the higher education sub-committee; and Baker, who became secretary of the education committee, under the director, Mr. (now Sir William) Brockington, ceased to be specifically concerned with evening-school provision. The higher education committee decided to discontinue elementary education in evening schools, and for the next 9 years it steadily tightened up the conditions under which evening classes could be provided and reduced the financial allocations for evening-school work. As a result the number of centres and students fell to 27 and 1,000 respectively, until in 1912–13, after criticism of the committee's evening-school policy by H.M. Inspector for Higher Education, Baker returned to his former duties, and the limitations, financial and other, imposed in recent years were lifted.[62] The number of local centres rose sharply to 48, with an estimated student membership of 5,000, of which about 1,150 would be adults.[63]

The neglect of part-time evening-school education in the years before the First World War was due in part at least to the preoccupation of the education committee with secondary, including full-time technical, education, and to the heavy expenditure involved in providing the county with an adequate number of efficient secondary schools. Throughout this period many complaints were made against the increasing burden of the education rate.[64] Something had to be forgone, and that something was, apparently, part-time evening-school education. Against the policy of limiting part-time evening schools must be set that of establishing technical schools in which full-time as well as part-time studies could be undertaken. As early as 1895 the county council had joined with several other authorities in the establishment and maintenance of the Midland Farm Institute at Kegworth, where short-term residential courses in dairying, poultry-keeping and so forth were provided. The education committee continued to support this venture as it developed into the Sutton Bonington Agricultural College. Since it is outside the county no further consideration will be given to it. Some attention must, however, be given to the technical colleges established by the county council at Loughborough (1905), Coalville (1924), Hinckley (1931), and Melton Mowbray (1937).

The Loughborough venture began as a technical institute and pupil teachers' centre.[65] From the beginning it was well supported by the corporation which, from time to time, made gifts of land and buildings for the use of the institute and for many years annually rate-aided its work. The history of the institute as a centre of technical instruction really began in 1909, when the new buildings came into use and a principal for the technical and art sections was appointed. At that time the students numbered 481, most of them being part-time evening students.[66] A vigorous campaign to develop outside classes as feeders to the institute raised the number of students to 1,900 in 1911–12. There was then a steady development up to the outbreak of war, and it looked as though Loughborough would soon possess a local technical institution appropriate to the size of the town. In 1915, however, a new principal, Mr. Herbert Schofield, was appointed, and this made the institute into something wholly unexpected. Mr. Schofield persuaded the education committee to co-operate with the Ministry of Munitions in the training of war-workers at

[60] L.R.O., Leics. C.C. Minute Bks. Aug. 1892, sect. 5.
[61] Ibid. May 1893, sect. 3.
[62] Ibid. Aug. 1911, sect. 9.
[63] Ibid. Nov. 1913, Rep. Dir. Educ.
[64] Ibid. Nov. 1908, sect. 7.
[65] Ibid. Feb. 1905, sect. 10.
[66] Ibid. May 1910, sect. 8.

the lathe, the milling machine, and the bench, rather than in the classroom.[67] Additional buildings were rented and hastily adapted to training needs, and large amounts of machinery were installed. Canteen facilities and even hostel accommodation were brought into existence. Thousands of clerks, shop assistants, and other non-manual workers were trained in Loughborough on munitions work, and the greater part of the cost of this training, capital as well as maintenance, was met by the central government.

At the close of the war, when the munitions training scheme came to an end, the institute consisted of a great variety of buildings and equipment scattered all over the town, and a staff very different from that of the modest pre-war venture. Other technical institutions had done war-work similar to that at Loughborough, but, whereas they returned to normal as soon as circumstances would permit, Loughborough did not. Mr. Schofield had seen in the war-time developments several important opportunities, and he was able to persuade the county council to take some of them. Much of the equipment was purchased at a very low price from the government, the hostel was taken over, and, with the full support of seventy engineering firms, the war-time method of training on production was adapted to peace-time needs, so that practice and theory were kept in intimate relationship, whereas in most technical institutions they are separated.[68] Ever since that time Loughborough has deservedly been famous for its realistic methods of training. The county council declined to buy the canteen, but Mr. Schofield was unwilling to lose so vital a feature of collegiate life. So, with the tacit approval of the education committee, he purchased it himself and established the college refectory as a private enterprise. It proved a most successful and rewarding venture.

This was not the only case in which Dr. Schofield, as he became in 1920, ventured further than the county council. In its unwillingness to embark upon the provision of a refectory, additional halls of residence and so forth, the council was certainly not more cautious than most bodies of its kind. Indeed, the surprising thing is that it supported Dr. Schofield's schemes to the extent that it did. Loughborough is, after all, only a relatively small town, where the development of a great technical college with a national reputation could scarcely have been expected by the most sanguine educationists before the First World War. Whenever, and by whomsoever, money was made available for any development, in university adult education, in the training of teachers in arts and crafts, in the training of librarians, in physical education, and in numerous other directions, Dr. Schofield was among the first to take advantage of it. The result was a large and imposing college, which, however, lacked unity of function or purpose.

This fact must not be allowed to obscure the truth that the college had a solid core of technological departments. On its technical and trade side, with engineering as its main feature, Loughborough College had by 1938–9 become a national institution, doing an increasing amount of work at the highest academic levels and bearing comparison with the greatest technical institutions in the country. Students from all over the world were to be found in its numerous departments. By comparison the Mining and Technical College at Coalville and the Hinckley and Melton Mowbray Technical Colleges were modest affairs. The first was established partly through generous financial assistance from the Miners' Welfare Fund,[69] and has served the developing Leicestershire coalfield well. All the colleges have been able to command the support of local industry, from which they have received gifts of plant and machinery and monetary contributions in the form of scholarships and prizes. Loughborough College has even an endowment income derived from a capital fund raised from among firms, trade associations, and individuals. In this it is exceptional, as in so many other respects, among publicly provided technical institutions.

The Leicestershire County Council accomplished much in the inter-war years in the provision of technical education. Its achievements in this sphere bear comparison with the largest and most progressive authorities in the country. In terms of the number of students upwards of 18 years of age the provision made at different dates was as follows:[70]

	1922–3			*1930–1*			*1938–9*		
	Full time	*Part time*	*Total*	*Full time*	*Part time*	*Total*	*Full time*	*Part time*	*Total*
Loughborough College	675*	235	910	220	239	459	262	471	733
Mining and Technical College, Coalville	..	126	126	..	258	258	..	426	426
Technical College, Hinckley	..	..	..	..	601	601	1	497	498
Technical College, Melton Mowbray	..	..	..	..	..	..	1	490	491
Total	675	361	1,036	220	1,098	1,318	264	1,884	2,148

* This figure includes 450 ex-servicemen receiving vocational training under a Ministry of Labour scheme.

[67] L.R.O., Leics. C.C. Minute Bks. Feb. 1916, sect. 7.

[68] Ibid. May 1919, sect. 6.

[69] Ibid. Apr. 1922, p. 36; and Feb. 1924, sect. 12.

[70] Ex inf. Mr. W. E. Westhead, Leics. Co. Educ. Authy.

During the First World War Leicestershire's evening schools were, apparently, allowed to go out of existence altogether. They were restarted in 1920–1, but only in 15 centres, and in the next 2 years 5 of these collapsed. There was an increase to 17 in 1923–4, but during these years there were complaints that the fees charged were too high and the conditions imposed upon the students too onerous.[71] Only in the Loughborough and Coalville districts, where they were in the one case linked with a technical institute, and in the other with a projected institute, did evening classes flourish, and these were, for the most part, technical classes. No serious efforts seem to have been made until shortly before the Second World War to provide a wide range of studies or to promote recreational activities. Then, as the result of a changed outlook on the part of the education committee, a marked increase in provision took place. The number of evening institutes was raised to 72, with a total membership of 4,307, of which it is estimated that about 1,300 would be over 18 years of age.[72] These figures, it will be noted, are no greater than those for 1912–13.

In 1872 the Mayor of Leicester called two meetings of representative citizens to hear James Stuart, Fellow of Trinity College, Cambridge, expound his ideas on 'a sort of peripatetic university, the professors of which would circulate among the big towns'.[73] His ideas were warmly welcomed and a decision was taken to support a memorial, which had the backing of Nottingham and Derby, asking the Senate of the University of Cambridge to adopt a scheme of university extension, as it was called. Cambridge established a University Extension Syndicate and Leicester was among the first three towns in the kingdom to organize an extension lecture course. The course, for ladies only, was held in the town museum during the spring of 1873, and Professor Henry Morley, of the University of London, lectured on an historical subject.[74] By the autumn of 1873 an Extension Lecture Society had been formed, which advertised three ten-meeting courses—a further ladies' course on Friday mornings with Professor Morley on 'Literature in the Reign of James the First', a course on 'Force and Motion', with T. O. Hardy, Senior Wrangler, as lecturer, and a course by V. H. Stanton, Fellow of Trinity College, Cambridge, on 'Political Economy'.

At this time no grants from public funds were made towards the cost of providing university extension, the whole of which had to be borne locally. Fees were apt to be rather high. For the ladies' course the charge made was 10*s.* 6*d.* or 2*s.* a meeting and the members were therefore of the middle class; whilst for the course on Political Economy, intended for working men (ladies being excluded) a charge of 2*s.* 6*d.* was made for membership of the lecture course and class, and 1*s.* 6*d.* for the lecture course only or 3*d.* a meeting. For the science course the charge made lay between the other two.[75] The lecture was given on one evening and the class, intended for those who wished to discuss the lecture and do the written work set by the lecturer, held its meeting on another evening. The class members were entitled to sit for an examination at the end of the course, and the successful ones received a certificate from the University Syndicate. The courses and classes were well supported, but the fear of financial loss haunted the local committee, which decided to raise a guarantee fund by public subscription.[76] It is not known how successful they were in their efforts. Cambridge courses continued to be provided in Leicester with scarcely a break for more than half a century, and ceased only when the local university college became responsible for provision. Other Cambridge extension courses were held in several centres in the county, including Hinckley and Loughborough, and at some time towards the close of the century the local committees formed a county federation of extension societies, of which little is known. From time to time after 1903 the education committees of Leicester and Leicestershire assisted local committees in meeting the costs of provision.

Extension lectures everywhere were patronized chiefly by those who were able to pay the relatively high fees demanded and who had a fairly good educational background. It was from among the small minority of working-class members of extension societies that the Workers' Educational Association developed. These desired more systematic courses, provided for smaller and more compact groups than was usual in university extension, and at fees within the means of members of their own class. They also desired that the worker-students should have some measure of control over the kind of courses provided, to ensure that the teaching should take account of working-class interests and aspirations. The Workers' Educational Association was founded in 1903, but it was not until 5 years later that its Leicester branch was established. Those most actively concerned with its formation were members of various adult schools in the city. It is not unlikely that some of these were also members of the extension society, since that organization was one of the first to become affiliated to the branch. From the beginning financial assistance was given by the local education authority towards the provision of classes, and, though the branch

[71] L.R.O., Leics. C.C. Minute Bks. Nov. 1921, p. 28, and Nov. 1924, sect. 12.

[72] Ex inf. Mr. Westhead.

[73] Newspaper cutting in Leic. Working Men's Coll. Minute Bk.

[74] *Leics. Chron.* 1 Feb. 1873.

[75] Ibid. 4 Oct. 1873.

[76] Ibid. 27 Sept. 1873.

had to meet part of the cost of teaching itself, it was found possible to admit students to a session's course of 24 meetings on payment of a fee of 1*s*.[77]

The first really systematic class organized by the branch was one variously described in the annual reports as on industrial history and political economy. Presumably industrial history was taught in the first year (1909) as an introduction to a course on political economy in the second and third years, since this was a tutorial class. The class, provided by Cambridge University, had as its tutor Mr. W. T. (now Lord) Layton.[78] In the same year a preparatory class on 'Social Teachers in Literature' was organized with Mr. (now Sir Henry) Clay, as tutor.[79] Both classes appear to have been successful, the former, like most of its successors in the early days of the branch, being extended to a fourth year. Demand for entry into classes at this time must have been heavy since, when the organization of a second tutorial class was under consideration, the branch committee seriously entertained the notion of requiring intending students to submit essays in advance as an earnest of their willingness to undertake written work during the course.[80] At the conclusion of the first tutorial class the branch committee was able to report:

'Now that the first Tutorial Class has finished its course, your Committee feel the need for further developments in this direction. Throughout the four years during which the class has met, the students have exhibited marked determination and sacrifice, and the spirit of fellowship which has grown up among the pupils themselves and also between them and the teacher has been most noticeable. The amount of information gained has been great, but this does not constitute the main value of the course. The discipline of systematic study, the development of the power of self-expression, the gaining of a wider and more sympathetic outlook on life, the widening of the mental horizon, the learning to respect the opinions of others, have been the most important results, and these are the things the W.E.A. exists to help people to achieve.[81]

In the first decade of the existence of the branch three or four classes a year were organized, with a total membership of about 100. From 1911–12, University College, Nottingham, replaced Cambridge University as the provider of tutorial classes, and in 1913–14, the former set up a joint committee for tutorial classes on which the W.E.A. was given equal representation with the college. Until 1918–19 Leicester formed part of the Midland District of the W.E.A., whose headquarters were in Birmingham, but in that year an East Midland District was established with its head office in Nottingham. Then followed a considerable development both in Leicester and in the county. The branch raised the number of its classes to five, with outliers at Desford, Wigston, Dunton Basset, and Barwell, while new branches and class centres at Loughborough (1919), Woodhouse, Hinckley, Melton Mowbray, and Upper Broughton (all 1920), and Bagworth, Coalville, Shepshed, and Hathern (all 1921), were established by Mr. Frank Salter, the district secretary. It was a time of considerable expansion in adult education everywhere, and Leicester and Leicestershire fully shared in it. The eagerness among adults for liberal non-vocational education must have been considerable. Dr. R. F. Rattray stated in 1920 that in his Leicester tutorial class on 'The History of Civilisation' there was the maximum number of 32 students, many having been turned away, and that he had received during the first year of the class 250 pieces of written work.[82]

Development in Leicestershire was furthered by an arrangement, made in 1921–2 between University College, Nottingham, and the East Midland District of the W.E.A. on the one hand and Loughborough College on the other, under which Loughborough College became responsible for organizing and providing adult classes in liberal studies within Leicestershire.[83] At that time no sharp distinction was drawn in the east midlands between the functions of organizing and providing classes and courses, or between what were properly university classes and courses and what were not. The result was that, in co-operation with Nottingham University College and the W.E.A., Loughborough College, through its department of adult education, organized classes and courses from the terminal type at the one extreme to the tutorial type at the other, and also provided the tutors for them. Until 1929–30 the work of the Loughborough College Department of Adult Education was under the general supervision of a Leicestershire sub-committee of the University College, Nottingham, joint committee, but in that year a virtually autonomous Leicestershire joint committee for adult education was established. The setting up of a joint committee in association with a technical college was a novel experiment, justified, it seemed, by the past record of the college in promoting liberal adult education in the county.

When Loughborough College began to provide classes and courses in Leicestershire there were in existence about ten centres including those attached to the Leicester branch of the W.E.A. The total number of classes and students in these centres is unknown. By 1924–5 there were 14 centres in being, with 20 classes attended by 350 students.[84] This development was only a

[77] W.E.A. Leic. and Dist. Branch Minute Bk. Oct. 1908.
[78] Ibid. July 1909.
[79] Ibid. Aug. 1909.
[80] Ibid. Jan. 1910.
[81] W.E.A. Leic. and Dist. Branch Annual Rep. 1912–13, 9.
[82] Ibid. 1919–20, 41.
[83] W. A. Brockington, *Short Rev. of Educ. in Leics. since the War* (1925), 20.
[84] Leics. Joint Cttee. For Adult Education, Statement on 'Admin. of Adult Educ. in Leics.' (1947), 1.

beginning. Within the next 5 years the number of centres was raised to 23, the number of classes to 45, and the number of students to 877. It is, therefore, not surprising that the college should have been considered a suitable base from which to conduct liberal adult education in the county, in spite of the fact that its bias was of a technical nature and its location well away from the centre of the county's communications. From 1929–30 until the outbreak of the war there was a steady increase in the number of centres, classes, and students to 28, 99, and 1,679 respectively,[85] but much of this increase was in the less-advanced types of work. In provision made at the university level, practically no advance took place, due in part no doubt, to the limited teaching resources for university work at the disposal of the department of adult education and in part to the geographical situation of Loughborough College.

Meanwhile a university college had come into being in Leicester. The idea of a local university seems first to have been put forward in 1880 by the Revd. Joseph Wood in his presidential address to the Literary and Philosophical Society.[86] In this address he urged the society to take the initiative in starting a movement for the promotion of a local university, and he expressed the hope that the time would come when universities would be as common in England as they were in Germany. Five years later, in his presidential address to the same society, the Revd. James Went advocated the provision of courses of lectures which might, he thought, prepare the way for the founding of a university college, the object of which should be to give advanced instruction in every branch of human knowledge.[87] J. D. Paul, President in 1889–90, also spoke in his address on the subject of a university for Leicester, saying:

'May we not hope that some day we may have five or six men, every one of whom shall have had a brilliant career at one or other of our great universities who shall be a teaching body among us. . . . Depend upon it that such a body of men teaching in our midst . . . would do more to lift up the tone of the life of our town than any other agency which it is possible to invent . . . I know too well the objections which can be brought against my proposal. It is visionary, it is impossible. There are no students in Leicester. If a University were set up they would not go to it. I deny them all.'[88]

Finally, in 1912, Dr. Astley V. Clarke, in another presidential address to members of the society, outlined a plan for the establishment of a Leicester university college.[89]

The founding of the college took place in 1921, and this was chiefly due to Dr. Astley Clarke, Dr. J. W. Bennett and Sir Jonathan North, but especially to the first. Between 1912 and the date of the opening, Dr. Clarke gave much of his time and energy to convincing leading citizens of the need for a college, and to enlisting their active support for the venture.[90] At the close of the First World War Mr. T. Fielding Johnson purchased a large property, set in ample grounds, which had recently been used as a base hospital. His intention was to make a gift of it for public purposes. Those interested in the idea of a university institution for Leicester persuaded him to give the main buildings and half the site as a home for their proposed college. About the same time Dr. J. E. M. Finch, a medical practitioner with a keen interest in science, bequeathed £5,000 towards a fund for establishing a university institution, provided that the bequest were accepted by a responsible body within a few months.[91] Such a body, with Alderman Sir Jonathan North as chairman, and Mr. F. P. Armitage, Director of Education for Leicester, as honorary secretary, was duly created and urgent efforts were made to obtain funds to bring the college into being. The sum of £135,000 was collected, the college was incorporated under the Companies Acts, and Dr. R. F. Rattray was appointed principal. In its first year (1921–2) the college was able to boast that it had four departments, namely, English, French, Latin, and Geography, one full-time member of staff—the principal himself—and 6 part-time lecturers. There were 11 students, apparently not all full-time, in the autumn term, rising to 15 by the summer term.[92]

From the first the new college received generous financial support from the Corporation of Leicester, but like the other university colleges in the country it was denied the benefit of treasury grants, such as the full universities received on the advice of the University Grants Committee. The college—originally named the Leicester, Leicestershire, and Rutland College, but subsequently renamed University College, Leicester—had, therefore, to depend very largely on the generosity of local authorities, firms, and private persons. Unlike most cities of its size Leicester has never produced any great captains of industry to whose munificence it might confidently look for a library building, a hall of residence, or the endowment of professorial chairs. The college had, therefore, to spread its net wide for donations. This meant hard work, but in the years before the college was placed on the treasury grant list, the generosity of Leicester and Leicestershire firms and private persons enabled much to be done. Full-time lecturers were appointed in History, Geography, and Mathematics in 1922–3, in Botany, Zoology, Classics, French, and German

[85] Leics. Joint Cttee. For Adult Education, Statement on 'Admin. of Adult Educ. in Leics.' (1947), 2.

[86] F. B. Lott, *Centenary Bk. of Leic. Literary and Philosophical Soc.* 76.

[87] Ibid. 166.

[88] Ibid. 168.

[89] Ibid. 177–8.

[90] R. F. Rattray, 'Univ. Coll.' in *Leic., its Civic, Industrial Inst. and Social Life*, ed. C. Howes, 159.

[91] Ibid.

[92] Univ. Coll. Leic. *2nd Annual Rep. 1921–2.*

in 1923–4, in Chemistry and Physics in 1924–5, in Extra-Mural Adult Education in 1929–30 and in Education in 1930–1. In addition part-time lecturers were appointed in Music in 1922–3 and in Law in 1923–4. In this last year arrangements were also made, in co-operation with the Leicester College of Technology, for the provision of courses leading to the University of London degree in commerce. A college library was opened, also in 1923, by Viscount Haldane, the then Visitor. At the time of Dr. Rattray's resignation in 1931, the college had 2 faculties, 5 departments, a full-time staff of 15 and a part-time staff of 5, and 111 day and 83 evening students.[93]

The setting up of a department of Extra-Mural Adult Education in 1929–30 was encouraged by an offer, from the governors of Vaughan College, of the Vaughan College building as the headquarters of a department, and the home of its Leicester classes.[94] For the young university college, with its slender financial resources, to take over the responsibility of Vaughan College was a considerable undertaking. At the time it was hoped that by agreement with University College, Nottingham, the area of provision of the new department of extra-Mural Adult Education might include Leicestershire and Rutland. Thus Vaughan College would have become the base for work carried on over a wide area. The hope was only partially realized. University College, Leicester, obtained powers of provision for tutorial classes within Leicester city and Rutland only; and powers of provision for extension lecture courses in the city, in the southern half of Leicestershire and in Rutland. In addition, by an agreement with the W.E.A., it secured powers of provision for terminal and one-year classes within the city. Apart from the University of Reading, which has never had a department of adult education, Leicester University College found itself with easily the smallest territory of any university institution in the country. If the setting up of a department were to be justified, its head would, therefore, have to achieve exceptional results within Leicester city itself, since the scope for development in southern Leicestershire and Rutland was very narrow.

The appointment of Mr. H. A. Silverman as the head of the department of Extra-Mural Adult Education was a fortunate one. He was able to win the support of the local Branch of the W.E.A. for a bold policy of expansion, and to secure from the education authority, in a time of serious industrial depression, increasing financial assistance towards that policy. The results, in terms of increased numbers of courses, classes, and students were immediate, and the progress made in the first year continued up to the outbreak of the last war, as the following figures show:[95]

Classes

Year	*Extension courses*	*Tutorial*	*One-year or sessional*	*Terminal*	*Total classes*	*Total enrolments**
1928–9	1	3	5	4	13	260†
1929–30	6	5	6	..	17	310
1934–5	32	9	8	13	62	1,301
1938–9	2	9	14	46	71	1,387

* The number of individual students (or student entries) was about two-thirds of the total enrolments, i.e. approximately 174 in 1928–9, and 924 in 1938–9.

† The total enrolment for 1928–9 is an estimate.

The geographical distribution of courses and classes was as follows:

Year	*City of Leicester*	*South Leicestershire*	*Rutland*	*Total*
1928–9	11	2	..	13
1929–30	16	1	..	17
1934–5	51	11	..	62
1938–9	61	3	7	71

Before the department came into existence classes were provided only in the autumn and spring terms. Shortly afterwards, following the practice of the old Vaughan College, a summer term was added, and it was found possible to provide a programme of about a half the size of that in the winter terms. In addition to the greatly increased number of courses and classes there were brought into being within the college student clubs and societies of various kinds—a students' union, sports clubs, and literary, folk-dancing, drama, and rambling societies. As far as Leicester was concerned its provision for liberal adult education was raised to a height exceeded only by the largest cities in the kingdom. For the amount, variety, and quality of its provision Vaughan College was by 1938 deservedly well known in the world of adult education. Throughout these years of expansion the W.E.A. co-operated with the department, both within the college and in the outlying extension centres, but, increasingly in the case of the former, the planning and organization of classes passed into the hands of the department's staff. As a consequence the character of the courses and classes and of the students underwent a change. The proportion of social science courses and classes with a social purpose declined, whilst that of literature and the arts increased. The age-level of the students fell by about a decade, and men and women with a higher education who were engaged in middle-class employments became numerically predominant. Vaughan College ceased to be a working-man's college in the narrow sense of the

[93] Univ. Coll. Leic. *Annual Reps.* *1922–3—1929–30*.

[94] Vaughan Working Men's Coll. *Annual Rep.* *1925–6*, 4.

[95] Compiled from W.E.A. Leic. and Dist. Branch, *Annual Reps.* for years given in the tables.

term, though it remained essentially a college of the sons and daughters of weekly wage-earners who, through the growth of educational opportunity, had found their way into the lower and middle ranks of the many professional, administrative, and technical posts which the 20th century has created.

Under the principalship of Mr. F. L. Attenborough,[96] modest progress took place in almost all the internal departments of the university college. Numbers remained small, never rising above 122 in the day-time classes and 113 in the evening classes.[97] Thus the students had the benefit of what amounted in practice to a tutorial system of instruction, and this probably accounts for the relatively high proportion of successes obtained in the external degree examinations of the University of London in the years preceding the Second World War. During this period many of the benefactors and friends of the college must at times have wondered whether the founding of a university institution in Leicester had not after all been a mistake. From time to time there was talk in Nottingham, Derby, and Leicester, of establishing an east midlands university on federal lines, and several conferences of local authorities and university bodies were held on the subject, though nothing came of them.[98] The early hopes that Leicester might eventually have its own university, or even that its college might become an integral, yet self-governing, part of a wider regional university, seemed doomed to disappointment. Yet those who believed in the college struggled hard to keep it going, and succeeded. Even if, in the long run, they had been compelled to admit failure, they would have deserved praise for their loyalty to a great ideal.

This history of adult and further education in Leicester and Leicestershire has to end just before the beginning of a new era. Already in the few years that have passed since the end of the Second World War remarkable developments have taken place in adult and further education, not the least being those at University College, which can now look forward to becoming a full university.[99]

96 Appointed 1932.

97 Univ. Coll. Leic. *13th Annual Rep. 1931–2* and *19th Annual Rep. 1938–9*.

98 L.R.O., Leics. C.C. Minute Bks. Nov. 1918, sect. 7.

99 The granting of a royal charter to Univ. Coll. Leic. in 1950 foreshadows the attainment of full univ. status in a few years.

SPORT

HUNTING[1]

In the Middle Ages the beast that was chiefly hunted by the nobility was the deer. It is said to have been the sight of some hinds that led Henry I to establish a royal forest in south-east Leicestershire,[2] and Leicester Forest contained deer until its final inclosure in 1628.[3] About 1795, there were still free roaming deer around Belvoir, though their number was less than in earlier times.[4] The fox was originally considered as vermin, and only gradually became the chief object of the chase. As early as 1539 foxes were being hunted in east Leicestershire,[5] but in the 16th century fox-hunting was not a sport with any formal rules. In 1542 it was noted, in terms which suggest that the occurrence was exceptional, that foxes were being hunted with hounds at Croxton Kerrial because they ate lambs,[6] and in the 16th and early 17th centuries foxes were being snared or trapped in Leicestershire.[7] During the 17th century, however, fox-hunting seems to have become well established in Leicestershire.[8]

The great practical advantage of fox-hunting over deer hunting was that there was no need to preserve a large uncultivated area of 'forest'. If some small coverts and the breeding-earths were kept safe the fox could look after himself. If the earths were stopped the night before hunting, he would give a run over the open fields—and these were far more suitable than a rough forest for a mounted chase.

The right to hunt a particular country consisted in the ownership of coverts, or permission from the owners to draw them. It was not until after the inclosures that the right of a hunt to cross anyone's land was questioned—and then not usually by a landlord but by a tenant farmer.

About the year 1730 the Duke of Rutland and Lords Gainsborough, Cardigan, Gower and Howe agreed to subscribe £300 each to a United Hunt. This was the first pack in the midland counties that was set up under a formal agreement of which a record survives—one cannot say more. The establishment went for a part of each season to the estate of each contributor. An incidental mention of 'the stopping of earths' in the agreement makes it certain that it was a fox-hunt. A few years later it split into two establishments, one under the Duke of Rutland and the other under the Earl of Gainsborough. From these the Belvoir and the Cottesmore hunts are descended.[9] Both these hunts include pieces of the best hunting territory in Leicestershire; both draw coverts on the outskirts of Melton Mowbray. At the other end of the county the Pytchley also claims a small tract of country, though a much less important one, touching Market Harborough. All these three hunts, however, mainly belong to other counties—to Lincolnshire, Rutland, and Northamptonshire. They are therefore not dealt with in this account of Leicestershire hunting. The social history of Melton and Market Harborough as hunting centres has also been excluded. This will, it is hoped, be dealt with in other volumes under the towns themselves. It has seemed best to present the history of Leicestershire hunting as the history of the hunting countries that cover the two very different sides of the county. The Quorn and its offshoot the Fernie include most of the grass country which has made Leicestershire the resort of visiting fox-hunters. The Atherstone covers the mixed farming country on the west where no physical feature separates Leicestershire from Warwickshire. The hunting 'country' straddles the Roman road that marks the county boundary. If this hunt is dealt with in greater detail, it is out of no disrespect for the Quorn and Fernie but because so much less has been printed elsewhere about the Atherstone hunt and country.

THE QUORN HUNT

If a man rode from Market Harborough to the outskirts of Nottingham, leaving Leicester on the left, he would be almost all the while in a grass country and all the while in the original Quorn country. If he crossed the Soar at Leicester or

[1] It was originally arranged that the account of the Quorn Hunt should be written by Mr. C. D. B. Ellis, and that the rest of this article should be written by the late Major Guy Paget. Major Paget had largely completed his part of the article before his death in the hunting-field in March 1952. After Major Paget's death, Mr. Ellis revised and completed the whole article.

[2] *V.C.H. Leics.* ii, 265.

[3] L. Fox and P. Russell, *Leic. Forest.* 112–13.

[4] Nichols, *Leics.* i, p. cxci.

[5] Hist. MSS. Com. *Rutland,* iv, 294.

[6] Ibid. 323.

[7] Ibid. 324, 455.

[8] Ibid. 513, 522; T. F. Dale, *Hist. Belvoir Hunt,* 22, 33.

[9] Dale, op. cit. 32, 33.

a few miles south of it, and rode through Whitwick to Ashby de la Zouch and from there to Castle Donington, he would pass by hills and rocks and woods and quarries and coal-mines but he would still be in the Quorn country. The country east of the Soar has been for 200 years the chosen playground of wealthy visitors; local people have had the other side to themselves.

Thomas Boothby (1681–1752) of Tooley Park, near Desford, did not found the Quorn Hunt but he prepared the way for it. When he died, the *Gentleman's Magazine* described him as 'one of the greatest sportsmen in England'. An inscription on his hunting-horn, which is still in existence,[10] states that 'he hunted the first pack of fox-hounds then in England, 55 years'. Many details have been discovered about Thomas Boothby and his family, but as regards the Quorn Hunt the most significant is the fact that he owned the manor of Broadlow Ash in Derbyshire.[11] It was next door to the home of the Meynells.

Eight months after Thomas Boothby's death, Hugo Meynell, who is usually regarded as the founder of the Quorn, settled in Leicestershire.[12] In 1758 he married, as his second wife, Boothby's granddaughter, and about 1762 her brother, known as 'Prince' Boothby, seems to have become a sort of partner with him in his hunting establishment, Lord Richard Cavendish making a third.[13] It is fair to assume that Hugo Meynell succeeded to Thomas Boothby's permissive rights of hunting a large part of Leicestershire. His reason for renting (and afterwards buying) Quorn Hall rather than Tooley Hall was probably that the latter lay on a very bad cross-road whilst the former was on the good turnpike road between Loughborough and Market Harborough. This road commanded the whole length of the upland grass country on which he had set his heart. It was also the main road linking his family seat at Bradley (Derbys.) with London where both he and 'Prince' Boothby were members of the fashionable set.

Meynell did most of his hunting at the northern end,[14] within reach of Quorn Hall, but for a time he also rented Langton Hall[15] which was a good headquarters for the southern end. Meynell was the first to popularize fox-hunting in a grass country. He bred an improved type of foxhound for the purpose and it is more than likely that he exchanged ideas with Robert Bakewell, who was improving the breeds of agricultural animals at the same time, half a dozen miles away at Dishley. The friends who came to share his sport found that they must also improve the breed of horses to obtain hunters that could live with Meynell's pack.

In the meantime, Meynell was carefully establishing 'rights' for his hunt over a defined area of country. He negotiated agreements with the families of Manners, Noel, and Lowther on the east and with Earl Spencer in the south.[16] He might have been short of woodlands if the Earl of Stamford, who kept a pack at Bradgate, had not lived mainly in Staffordshire, and if Laurence, Earl Ferrers, the other principal landowner on that side, had not made everybody shun his society long before he became actually homicidal.[17] As it was, Meynell was able to hunt the forest in spring and autumn and he had a clear field to the north of it. By the 1780's the Quorn Hunt had become a fashionable subscription pack. Its followers filled Quorn Hall, the neighbouring houses and the inns of Loughborough. Later the majority of them migrated to Melton Mowbray,[18] probably when the Wreak Navigation brought coal there in 1794, where they could hunt with three packs and always hunt on grass. The son who might have succeeded Meynell died from a hunting accident in 1800 and the old man gave up the hounds, but not before they had achieved the classic run from Billesdon Coplow to Enderby.

In Meynell's time most of the parishes on the Melton side of the Quorn country were being inclosed. Inclosure, in this part of Leicestershire, meant more grass, better drainage and the division of fields by new fences that could be jumped. Meynell had showed how to hunt this country; the next generation learned how to ride it. They also improved it, from the fox-hunting point of view, by planting new coverts. Many of these have retained their names as the 'Gorses' of departed owners, though they have long since changed hands and though the gorse has been replaced by thorns and timber trees.[19]

Between 1800 and 1841 the Quorn Hunt had

[10] In the possession of Mrs. Edmond Browne of Adderley, Cheshire. The inscription gives the date of T. Boothby's birth as 1677 but the Peckleton Parish Reg. baptismal entry is Mar. 1680/81: Leic. City Mun. Room, Leic. Archd. Transcripts, Peckleton Par. Reg.

[11] P.C.C., will of Thomas Boothby, d. 1752.

[12] Thomas Boothby died Aug. 1752. Hugo Meynell rented Quorn Hall from Lady Day 1753: Nichols, *Leics.* iii, 553.

[13] Delmé Radcliffe, *The Noble Science.* 'Prince' Boothby cannot have joined him before about 1762 or Lord Richard Cavendish before about 1770.

[14] *The Diary of Thomas Jones* (1816), gives details of Meynell's meets and runs between 1790 and 1800. Jones was his whipper-in.

[15] Nichols describes Langton Hall as 'lately rented as a hunting-seat by Hugo Meynell Esq.'. Against the index reference is the date 1762: Nichols, *Leics.* i, 58; ii, 664.

[16] See T. F. Dale, *Hist. of the Belvoir Hunt* and Joseph Cradock, *Literary and Miscellaneous Memoirs.*

[17] See *Trial of Laurence, Earl of Ferrers, of Breedon (1760)*, evidence of the Revd. Walter Shirley.

[18] One of the first to go there was Mr. Lambton 'the father of the late Lord Durham'. He died in 1797: C. D. B. Ellis, *Hist. Quorn Hunt,* 18, citing 'The Druid', *Scott and Sebright.*

[19] For example, Ella's Gorse named after James Ella, lord of the manor of Wymeswold, who died in 1834.

eleven masters.[20] None of them was a Leicestershire man and only two held office for more than a few seasons. Lord Sefton (1800–1 to 1804–5) set a fast pace which Lord Foley (1805–6) was not willing or not able to keep up. Then came Thomas Assheton Smith (1806–7 to 1816–17), the greatest of the early masters. He hunted his own hounds, rode to them better than anyone of his day and ruled his field with a hand of iron. Napoleon once addressed him as 'le premier chasseur d'Angleterre':[21] he confirmed the reputation of the Quorn Hunt as the first in England. George Osbaldeston (1817–18 to 1820–1 and 1823–4 to 1826–7) may be said to have maintained that reputation, though his own renown as a huntsman and as a master in the field fell a little below what he thought were his deserts.[22] He was certainly more notable as an all-round sportsman than as a Quorn master, but he was a great hound-breeder and he showed a tenacity of purpose that was lacking in most of his successors. For two seasons (1821–2 and 1822–3), after he had broken his leg too badly to be able to ride the Quorn country, Osbaldeston exchanged masterships with Sir Bellingham Graham of the Hambledon who was as well liked and as well supported by the subscribers as any master. When Osbaldeston finally left, young Lord Southampton (1827–8 to 1830–1) succeeded. He began full of enthusiasm, made the unsuccessful experiment of moving the kennels to Leicester, and finished as a disillusioned absentee.

Sir Harry Goodricke (1831–2 and 1832–3) built new kennels at Thrussington, dispensed with a subscription and called the hunt 'Sir Harry Goodricke's Hounds'. He stood no nonsense from the Meltonians but took great pains to make himself acceptable to the local landowners and the local farmers.[23] He was hailed as another Meynell and was long remembered as a great sportsman, but he died before the promise of a new era could be fulfilled. The successor to his wealth and to his mastership was his friend Francis Holyoake, later Holyoake-Goodricke (1833–4 and 1834–5). He was a brilliant rider but he cared nothing for hounds and gave up the mastership as soon as he decently could—some thought sooner. In 1834, he lent the country north of the Charnwood Forest to the 2nd Marquis of Hastings who established the 'Donington' Hunt there. After the Marquis's health had broken down in 1842 Mr. J. B. Story of Lockington and other local gentlemen carried this hunt on for some years. As for the Quorn mastership, Mr. Rowland Errington (1835–6 to 1837–8) was good-natured enough to take it on when Holyoake left it vacant and had good sense enough to resign it before he was ruined by it. Lord Suffield (1838–9) was half ruined at the beginning of his only season and almost quite ruined at the end of it. Finally Mr. Hodgson (1839–40 and 1840–1), a very plain Yorkshireman, tried to hunt the country without spending more money, or jumping more fences, than he could help. In his second season he reluctantly allowed that great little huntsman, Tom Day, to adopt quicker tactics and Captain Percy Williams, who took charge of the subsidiary kennels at Oadby, rode the Harborough country as well as any in his field.

So ended the great aristocratic age of the Quorn Hunt, the age celebrated by 'Nimrod' and illustrated by Alken and Ferneley. The landowners, who had invented fox-hunting, were the dominant class in England between the age of inclosures and the age of railways and the richest of them came to Melton to enjoy fox-hunting at its best. They were joined in the field by the other class that had profited greatly from inclosures and from the Napoleonic wars, the yeoman graziers of Leicestershire, 'the Bluecoats'.[24] In Melton, the visitors found a select, gay, and mainly bachelor society. In High Leicestershire visitors and natives found an ideal galloping country with enough obstacles to test their nerve and hardihood. They went through, rather than over, many of the fences: it was the day of heavyweights who could bore a hole through a 'bullfinch' or smash an ox-rail without a fall.

For the next 30 years money was being made by new men. Only when they in turn provided a second generation of leisured gentlemen did Melton revive its glories and the Quorn Hunt enjoy a second great age.

When Mr. Hodgson left, the hunt had its first local master, though a group of Meltonians still governed its policy and provided its funds. Mr. Henry Greene of Rolleston (1841–2 to 1846–7) hunted the country, using the kennels which Lord Suffield had built at Billesdon. A fine horseman and universally liked, he gave general satisfaction, though the northern end of the country was probably rather neglected.

Sir Richard Sutton, who followed him (1847–8 to 1855), was a great master in the old tradition, a very rich man who lived for fox-hunting. During the latter part of his term he dispensed with a subscription and when the Donington Hunt came to an end he assumed responsibility for the whole of Meynell's original country. He had two separate establishments, one at Quorn and the

[20] Particulars of all the 19th-cent. masters are given in W. C. A. Blew, *The Quorn Hunt and its Masters*.

[21] Sir J. Eardley Wilmot, *A Famous Foxhunter* (biography of Assheton Smith).

[22] *Squire Osbaldeston, his Autobiography*, ed. E. D. Cuming.

[23] Sir Guy Fleetwood Wilson, *Green Peas at Christmas* (reminiscences of 'Gumley' Wilson, a contemporary).

[24] See 'The Druid's' books, particularly Dick Christian's reminiscences. The wealthy graziers were replaced, in the northern part of the Quorn country, by smaller dairy farmers in the latter part of the century.

other at Billesdon; the latter he handed over to his sons Richard and Frank, telling them (it was said) to go and break their necks over the ox-fences and leave him and his hounds alone.[25]

Sir Richard Sutton died suddenly in the autumn of 1855. No one was found willing to take over his immense responsibilities, but his sons carried on somehow for the rest of the season and eventually the Earl of Stamford agreed to hunt the northern part of the country. At the last moment Mr. Tailby of Skeffington got together a pack to hunt the Harborough or Billesdon country independently, the boundary being fixed at the Uppingham road.

Lord Stamford was allowed to include some coverts on his own estates which had formerly been drawn by the Atherstone. For the rest of the century there was a difference of opinion between the Quorn and that Hunt as to whether these coverts had been permanently ceded or merely lent during the earl's mastership.[26] There soon arose something more than a difference of opinion as to whether Mr. Tailby's country had or had not been permanently severed from that of the Quorn.

Lord Stamford (1856–7 to 1862–3) was good-natured and popular but he was not a strong master and he could not get the support he needed from the committee or from the country generally. Mr. S. W. Clowes (1863–4 to 1865–6) was ultimately obliged to resign for the same reason. The hounds were put up for sale and the Hunt seemed to have come to an end, but the 4th Marquis of Hastings, a wild and rather mad young man, bought the nucleus of a pack at the auction and hunted the country at his own expense and in his own way for the two seasons 1866–7 and 1867–8, after which he crashed financially and died.

The old Quorn Hunt was in a sad plight. Mr. J. C. Musters (1868–9 and 1869–70) brought his pack from the South Nottinghamshire country and retrieved its fortunes. Everyone rallied round Squire Musters. When his health gave way he lent his pack for a season to a new kind of master, Mr. Coupland, a business man—and a very business-like man—from Liverpool. Mr. Coupland's mastership (1870–1 to 1883–4) proved to be the longest since Meynell's and it inaugurated a new great age for the Quorn Hunt. Mr. Coupland was an organizer. His establishment ran smoothly and by paying well for damage and arranging puppy shows and earth-stoppers' dinners he gained the support of farmers and keepers. He was thus able to take full advantage of the great piece of luck that came his way. In 1870 he allowed that fine huntsman, Frank Gillard, to leave for the Belvoir, but two seasons later, in 1872, he secured that superb huntsman, Tom Firr. In Tom Firr's time—which lasted until 1898[27]—people came from all over the fox-hunting world to ride with the finest huntsman in the world over the finest country in the world. If they were not, now, all aristocrats and land-owners, they were all ladies and gentlemen acceptable to London society, a large contingent from which spent the winter in the hunting-field and for preference in Leicestershire. The country was at its best. Land ploughed before 1870 was reverting to grass. Drainage had improved the going. Hairy 'bullfinches' were giving place to neat cut-and-laid fences. Wire, at some expense, was kept under control. Railways did not check runs as badly as had been expected and they made it very much easier to get to, and about, the country.

There was one very unfortunate episode during Mr. Coupland's mastership. Since Lord Stamford's time the committee, led by Lord Wilton, had wanted to divide Meynell's original territory in a different way. In 1876 they lent most of the Donington country to the 10th Earl Ferrers who set up an agreeable local hunt there. When Mr. Tailby resigned in 1878 they proposed to reunite his country with the Quorn. The history of the dispute that followed belongs to the Fernie Hunt: it is enough to say here that the scheme failed and that the attempt caused much bitterness.[28]

Mr. Coupland, who had suffered some financial losses, resigned in 1884 and offered his pack to the country for £3,300. The committee thought the price too high, but the Duke of Portland, Julius Behrens, and the 3rd Earl of Wilton bought a third share each. When Behrens died in 1889 his share was bought by subscription and at the same time the Duke of Portland presented his own share. Lord Wilton's share had been taken over on his death in 1885 by Colonel Curzon (for Mrs. Herrick of Beaumanor) and in 1901 this share was also purchased for the country.[29] The pack which Coupland bought from the Craven in 1871 was therefore the foundation of the present Quorn pack, though many fresh strains have since been introduced.

The result of the 'Billesdon Hunt' dispute had been essentially a victory for local interests over the Melton clique. Its sequel, after some years, was a greater measure of local control in the Quorn Hunt itself. After a short mastership by

[25] The story is traditional. Sir Richard Sutton was in the fifties, no longer a very hard rider and notoriously severe on those who over-rode his hounds.

[26] Minutes of the Atherstone Hunt. The Quorn minutes merely record approval of negotiations about boundaries conducted by the masters.

[27] He injured his head through a fall during cub-hunting and never took the field again. He died from cancer in 1902.

[28] Some of the documents are printed in F. P. De Costobadie's *Annals of the Billesdon Hunt* but the full details of the controversy can be found in the *Leic. Advertiser* for 1878 and 1879.

[29] Quorn Committee minutes in custody of the Quorn Hunt. The account by the Duke of Portland in *Memories of Racing and Hunting* is inaccurate in several respects.

Lord Manners (1884–5 and 1885–6) Captain W. P. Warner, son of Mr. Warner of Quorn Hall, became master (1886–7 to 1892–3) with the backing of Mr. W. B. Paget of Loughborough who was in effect joint-master. Sir Frederick Fowke of Lowesby had for some years been chairman of the committee in which, after 1886, representative farmers were included. The secretary, from 1885, was that notable figure, J. D. Cradock, of Quorn, whose forebears had managed the coverts from Meynell's time until the sixties.[30] From this time on, the Quorn Hunt decided to make the best use of the country it had got. The Donington area was reclaimed from Earl Ferrers in 1887 and all attempts to recover the Billesdon country were abandoned. At last, in 1920, the Quorn's claim to any measure of suzerainty over the Fernie Hunt was formally and finally waived.

In Captain Warner's time, everything was done quietly and without friction. In Lord Lonsdale's (1893–4 to 1897–8) everything was done brilliantly—but not without friction. His magnificent establishment, his superb horsemanship, and his lavish generosity on the one hand, his capricious sternness, his egotism, and his insistent demands for subscriptions on the other, made up a mixed memory.[31] The free and easy ways of Captain Burns Hartopp (1898–9 to 1904–5) were a comfortable change. His cheerfulness overcame all difficulties and calamities—the Boer War, the loss of Tom Firr's services, a very bad accident to himself and the necessity of raising large sums to buy the last share in the hounds and to build new kennels. He was greatly helped by a strong committee and by Tempest Wade, secretary from July 1897 until his death in 1919.

The new kennels in Paudy Lane were completed, at a cost of £14,000, in the first year of the mastership of Captain Forester (1905–6 to 1917–18). Special expenses like this could be met by special appeals and by borrowing; but they forced the pace of a change in the matter of subscriptions that had been bound to come sooner or later. In the old days a whip round amongst a few rich men at Melton had been enough to make up a deficit and in Mr. Coupland's time subscriptions were still voluntary.[32] After 1903, rules were tightened up and 'capping' (which had been tried before and dropped again) was reintroduced. A good deal of the house-party atmosphere and social intimacy of the old days was necessarily lost in consequence. Captain Forester cared little for the social side of hunting but he was quite exceptionally keen in the field. He preferred the grass country and lent the Forest to the 8th Earl of Harrington who hunted it 2 days a week from 1906 until his death in February 1917. During the war seasons Captain Forester hunted hounds himself and in 1917–18 hunted the whole country with his daughter whipping in for him.

For the season 1918–19 the hunt was in the hands of a committee who were fortunate in securing Walter Wilson as huntsman. The next season Mr. Edmund Paget (1919–20 to 1927–8) and Major A. E. Burnaby (1919–20 to 1931–2) began a famous partnership which was ended by Mr. Paget's death in the hunting-field. Major Burnaby then had two seasons alone and two more as joint-master with Sir Harold Nutting, who then became sole master.

The nineteen-twenties were one of the Quorn's most brilliant periods. Mr. Paget managed the kennels and looked after the country west of the Soar. Major Burnaby's command of the Melton field became a legend. Sport was good and society on the Melton side can hardly ever have been gayer or smarter than in those days when the Prince of Wales kept his horses at Craven Lodge Club and motor-cars and motor-horse-boxes brought the field from all distances to the best Quorn meets. After 1930 economies were necessary but Sir Harold Nutting never lowered the standard of the establishment or failed to hunt the country faithfully and fairly. George Barker, after being second and first whip in turn, became huntsman in 1929 and at once proved a success in the post which he still (1954) holds.

In 1933 Captain J. B. Robinson, secretary since 1919, was killed in a motor accident. Major W. P. Cantrell-Hubbersty then became honorary secretary.[33] When Sir Harold Nutting resigned at the end of 1939–40 Major Cantrell-Hubbersty also became acting-master for the committee and held that post until he died hunting in March 1947.

During the war, the nucleus of an establishment was kept together and hounds met 3 days a week. In 1948–9 the normal pattern of fixtures was resumed—Mondays, north of the Wreak, Tuesdays, the Charnwood Forest, Fridays, between the Wreak and the Uppingham road, Saturdays, north and north-west of Loughborough. For the season 1947–8 Mrs. Cantrell-Hubbersty and Mr. Fred Mee were appointed joint-masters. They were joined in the following season by Major the Hon. Ronald Strutt. Mrs. Cantrell-Hubbersty and Mr. Mee resigned at the end of the season 1950–51

[30] For the Cradock family see G. D. Fletcher, *Leicestershire Pedigrees*. John Cradock (1766–1833) and his sons John (1792–1838) and Thomas (1795–1863), father of J. D. Cradock, all in turn managed the business of the hunt. In the interval between the death of Thomas and the appointment of J. D. Cradock, the secretaryship was held by Ernest Chaplin of Brooksby, Gen. E. S. Burnaby of Baggrave, and R. W. Johnson of Melton.

[31] See Lady Augusta Fane's *Chit Chat, passim*.

[32] Remarks by Lord Belper and Lord Lonsdale at general meeting 6 Feb. 1909.

[33] Capt. Higgins, appointed to succeed Capt. Robinson, died from a hunting accident before he had fully taken up his duties. Capt. R. Farquhar acted as Asst. Sec. and Capper until his death in 1937; Mrs. Farquhar then took over the same duties until 1945.

and Major Strutt became sole master. He resigned in 1954 and Major G. A. Murray Smith has been appointed to succeed him. The present chairman of the committee is Sir Harold Nutting[34] and Mr. Denis Aldridge is secretary.

There is more ploughed land in the Quorn country than before the war and there is more wire, but there is not enough of either to make good hunts impossible. A good many people still come from a distance to hunt in High Leicestershire but as very few have the time and the money to spend whole seasons doing nothing else, the future of the Quorn Hunt depends largely on the ability and the will of local people to maintain it. The will is certainly there.

THE FERNIE HUNT

The country hunted by the Fernie is bounded on the south by the Welland river from Husbands Bosworth to Rockingham. (The small triangle between the Welland, Husbands Bosworth, and Sibbertoft is in friendly dispute with the Pytchley, but as it is now part of an aerodrome it is of no possible importance.) The Hothorpe Hills on the Pytchley side of the river and the Laughton Hills on the Fernie side are neutral. The western boundary is the Walton–Gilmorton road and the Leicester–Lutterworth road and the northern one is the Leicester–Uppingham road. The eastern boundary runs roughly northwards from Rockingham to this road.

All this country originally belonged to the Quorn. In 1853 Sir Richard Sutton, in a moment of anger at the persistent over-riding of hounds by his sons, handed it over to them.[35] Sir Richard Sutton died in 1855 and his sons could not be persuaded to carry on after the end of the season. The Earl of Stamford was approached and he agreed to hunt all the Quorn country except the Harborough side. Negotiations were opened with Mr. Henry Greene of Rolleston, a former Quorn master, for hunting the southern portion, but they broke down at the last moment on the question of the boundary between the two parts of the country. On this, Mr. W. W. Tailby got a pack together and prepared to hunt the country as far north as the Uppingham road. In addition he borrowed from the Cottesmore the part of their country which lies north of that road and west of a line from Little Dalby to the Ayston turn. He gave an undertaking that he would return it if any member of the Lowther family ever wished to hunt it.[36]

As huntsman, Mr. Tailby engaged the veteran Tom Day who had been Quorn huntsman in Mr. Greene's time and kennel huntsman to Sir Richard Sutton. He had a bye day on 17 November 1856 and held his opening meet on 24 November at Nevill Holt. After the first season, Tom Day retired and Jack Goddard hunted hounds until 1863 when he was succeeded by Frank Goodall.[37] In 1859 Lord Stamford offered to hunt the Harborough country for the Quorn but Mr. Tailby was not willing to give it up and as he was strongly supported the claim was not pressed at that time.[38]

It seemed, however, that the end was coming a few years later. In October 1871 Colonel Henry Lowther (afterwards Earl of Lonsdale), master of the Cottesmore, requested the return of the Cottesmore land. Mr. Tailby surrendered it as he had agreed to do and announced that he would retire at the end of the season. The Earl of Cork took the opportunity to request the services of Frank Goodall as huntsman to the Royal Buck Hounds, the most coveted post in the hunting world.[39] Lastly, the Quorn Hunt, through Mr. Coupland, renewed their claim for the rest of the country. At a meeting at the Bell Hotel, Leicester, Sir Arthur Hazlerigg opposed this claim, stating that Lord Stamford had abandoned the Harborough country and that it was open to anyone to hunt it with the consent of the landowners. Lord Grey de Wilton proposed and Colonel Burnaby of Baggrave seconded a resolution that the matter be referred to the Foxhunting Committee of Boodle's Club, that body having been set up to deal with all disputes between hunts. This was carried, but Mr. Tailby subsequently withdrew his resignation and the dispute was again shelved.[40]

Deprived of his woodland country and of his huntsman, Mr. Tailby cut down his establishment and hunted hounds himself. He accounted for 104 foxes in his first season and 108 in his second. After a time, however, he found he could not hunt hounds and control his field as well, so he handed over the huntsman's functions to his whipper-in, Dick Christian, and then to a regular huntsman, Richard Summers. Neither was particularly successful and in 1878, after 22 seasons, Mr. Tailby finally resigned.[41]

Mr. Tailby's success and his great personal

[34] Chairmen of the committee have been: 2nd Earl of Wilton 1866 to about 1878, Sir Frederick Fowke, about 1878 to 1897, 2nd Lord Belper, 1897 to 1914, J. D. Cradock (acting), 1914 to 1920, 2nd Lord Crawshaw, 1920 to 1929, C. J. Phillips 1929 to 1930, Major A. E. Burnaby, 1930 to 1939, 3rd Lord Belper 1939 to 1951, Sir H. Nutting from 1951.

[35] C. D. B. Ellis, *Hist. Quorn Hunt*, 79–80; F. P. De Costobadie, *Annals of the Billesdon Hunt*, 9; W. C. A. Blew, *Quorn Hunt*, 238.

[36] Blew, op. cit. 249–50; Ellis, op. cit. 84; De Costobadie, op. cit. 9–12.

[37] Cecil, *Billesdon Hunt*, 14; De Costobadie, op. cit. 12–14, 29–30.

[38] Ellis, *Hist. Quorn Hunt*, 135.

[39] De Costobadie, *Annals of the Billesdon Hunt*, 41, 43.

[40] De Costobadie, op. cit. 42; Ellis, *Hist. Quorn Hunt*, 136.

[41] De Costobadie, op. cit. 42, 46–48.

prestige made everyone in the country anxious to keep the hunt going, but doubtful whether a worthy successor could be found. It was a beautiful but difficult hunting country, largely grass, but small, lacking in good coverts and very strongly fenced. It abounded in ox-fences and there were occasional 'double-oxers' with the two guard rails as much as 12 ft. apart. Mr. Tailby, a tiny man, rode big weight-carrying hunters. He took everything as it came and was quite undaunted by a number of damaging falls.[42]

During Mr. Tailby's last few seasons the popularity of Leicestershire fox hunting was at its zenith, and both he and the farmers in his country were much harassed by the crowds of visitors who took up their quarters at Melton and Market Harborough. Mr. Coupland's country was even more overcrowded and this was one reason for his eagerness to acquire the additional territory. Fear of the crowds that he would bring was, on the other hand, the reason why the farmers in Mr. Tailby's country were determined not to let him have it.[43]

When Mr. Tailby announced his intention of retiring, Mr. Coupland at once offered to hunt the country and wrote to the landowners for permission to draw their coverts. Within a few days, however, a counter-offer came from Sir Bache Cunard of Nevill Holt, to carry on a separate hunt. Being assured of support from the majority of local landowners and farmers, he bought Mr. Tailby's pack and set about building kennels at Medbourne.

A dispute of unexampled bitterness followed which went on for more than a year, Sir Bache Cunard meanwhile hunting the country 'under difficulties'. Boodle's Foxhunting Committee ultimately gave judgement on 'legal' grounds in favour of the Quorn; but the farmers in the country asked, 'Who is Boodle?', and threatened to lock their gates, wire up their fields and prosecute Mr. Coupland for trespass. Finally, in June 1879, 'The Red' Earl Spencer sent Mr. Coupland a round robin, signed by forty M.F.H.'s, suggesting that, having established his right, he should let Sir Bache Cunard hunt the country. The Quorn could not hold out against this. They gave Sir Bache Cunard permission to hunt the country as long as he liked, and as he was a rich man he was able to do so in a style that fully satisfied both the natives and the visitors.[44]

In 1888 Sir Bache Cunard was, with the consent of the Quorn, succeeded by a young Scot, Charles Fernie. Mr. Fernie had been told that he had tuberculosis and could only expect to live 3 years, but he remained master for 30. With the skilled assistance of his first huntsman, 'Charles' Isaac, he made a number of new coverts and improved old ones. In 1907 he engaged Arthur Thatcher as huntsman and for the next 7 years Market Harborough rivalled Melton as a hunting centre. When Mr. Fernie died in 1919 he left his hounds to the country on condition that the Quorn finally relinquished their claim to it.[45] By this time they retained, in practice, only a nominal right to confirm the appointment of a new master and they made no difficulties about renouncing this.

Mrs. Fernie carried on for three seasons after her husband's death, with Mr. Faber as joint-master for two of them. Mr. Fernie had spent £10,000 a year on his hounds and the committee raised about £6,000 a year to spend on the country. When, on Mrs. Fernie's retirement, it was faced with building new kennels at Great Bowden, the committee willingly accepted Lord Stalbridge's offer to hunt hounds himself at his own expense.[46]

Lord Stalbridge was perhaps too much of a hound man to suit a Leicestershire field. When he retired, Sir Harold Wernher, who had joined him in 1924, carried on with a succession of partners, Mr. Edmonstone (1928–34), Commander Alexander, and Captain Hignett. With Bert Peaker as huntsman they were very successful.[47]

In 1939 the Hunt found itself masterless. The committee asked the chairman, Major Gillilan, Mr. Forsell, and Major Guy Paget to carry on as best they could. Bert Peaker did four men's work for one man's pay, with very few of the tips that, in the old days, were the greater part of a huntsman's remuneration, and on about £1,000 a year they managed to hunt 2 days a week. The farmers were very helpful and quite half the subscriptions came from non-hunting landowners and residents. Lt.-Col. D. Hignett and Lt.-Col. Penn Lloyd, the present (1953) masters, took over in 1946.

A few words must be said about the name of the country. In the old Quorn days it was known as the 'Harborough', 'South Quorn' or 'Billesdon' side—the last from the kennels at Billesdon, built in 1838 by Lord Suffield from designs by Thomas Smith, which were the home of the Quorn hounds throughout Mr. Greene's mastership. Mr. Tailby did not use these kennels but he used the stables and made Billesdon the headquarters of his establishment so that the title of 'The Billesdon Hunt' came into general, though never into official, use. The correct style was 'Mr. Tailby's Hounds' and later 'Sir Bache Cunard's Hounds'.

[42] De Costobadie, op. cit. 4, 6; C. Simpson, *Harboro' Country*, 56.

[43] Simpson, op. cit. 99.

[44] On the dispute with the Quorn Hunt, see De Costobadie, *Annals of the Billesdon Hunt*, 153–67; Ellis, *Hist. Quorn Hunt*, 133–45.

[45] De Costobadie, op. cit. 179, 186–7; C. Simpson, *Harboro' Country*, 111, 119.

[46] Simpson, op. cit. 111, 230–1.

[47] The remaining part of the account of the Fernie Hunt is based on the late Major Paget's personal knowledge, and on the MS. Minutes of the Fernie Hunt.

When Mr. Fernie bought the pack, the Quorn committee formally approved his mastership but wanted the country to be called 'The South Quorn'. Mr. Fernie's committee suggested 'The South Leicestershire' but this was not acceptable and it was finally agreed that he also should use his own name. In 1920 the title of 'The Fernie Hunt' was officially assumed.

THE ATHERSTONE HUNT

The Atherstone country is mostly in the north-west of Leicestershire, and partly in Derbyshire, Staffordshire, and Warwickshire. It is roughly bounded by the roads joining Rugby, Leicester, Ashby de la Zouch, Lichfield, and Birmingham. It contains many great mansions lying inside walled parks, with woods laid out primarily for pheasant shooting, but nearly all are now empty or put to base uses. Much of the best country has been covered by the buildings of Leicester, Birmingham, Lichfield, Coventry, and Nuneaton, or ruined for hunting by coal-mining.

The origin of this hunt is uncertain. It has been stated that the country was hunted by Mr. Noel of Exton, who founded the Cottesmore in 1732.[48] On the other hand it has been said that Lord Lonsdale[49] hunted part of the Atherstone country.[50] This seems most unlikely. The first Lowther certainly known to have been a master of foxhounds was William, 1st Earl of Lonsdale (d. 1844) who was M.F.H. of the Cottesmore 1788–1802 and 1806–42.[51] He certainly did not hunt the Atherstone country. It is possible that about 1730 the United Pack may have come there.[52] There can be no doubt that Thomas Boothby hunted the Leicestershire side of the Atherstone country since his home, Tooley Park, is now part of it.[53] Hugo Meynell's hounds certainly met at Market Bosworth and Kirkby Mallory, but only very occasionally.[54] This side was probably neglected, one might say abandoned, by Lord Sefton and succeeding 'Meltonian' masters of the Quorn after 1801.

In 1804, the 2nd Lord Vernon, who hunted the present Meynell country and also used kennels at Gopsall,[55] allowed Richard (afterwards Sir Richard) Puleston, to hunt the country round Burbage, Kingsbury, and Clifton as far as Gopsall. Puleston was a famous master of hounds, who started his pack in 1786 and hunted a country 60 miles long, stretching from Flint to Leicestershire, for nearly 50 years. He had kennels at Shifnal, and must have used those at Gopsall, as well as those at Ivestsey Bank near Weston under Lizard.[56]

The next master is said to have been Colonel John Cook (1812–15).[57] He had hunted the Thurlow and Essex, and was the author of *Observations on Foxhunting*. Robert Vyner, in his *Notitia Venatica*,[58] however, says that 'Colonel Cook only hunted a small country round Birmingham'. Colonel Cook gave up or ceased to hunt the Atherstone country in 1815.[59]

At this time that curious character 'The Squire', George Osbaldeston, had left the Burton country and had moved his hounds into the South Nottinghamshire and Meynell countries. Owing to lack of foxes and support, 'The Squire' was very willing to abandon the South Nottinghamshire and hunt the country round Atherstone, where he established his headquarters, built the present kennels at Witherley and established an Atherstone Hunt Club on the same lines as its neighbour the Pytchley Hunt Club. The whereabouts of the records of this club before 1841 are unknown. 'The Squire' set about establishing recognized boundaries of which the general outline still remains though many small alterations have been made.[60]

It was while hunting the Atherstone that he called out Sir Henry Every of Eggington to a duel, because the latter preferred to beat a fox out of his willow bed for the Squire instead of having it drawn for by hounds in the ordinary way. Naturally, Sir Henry's friends refused to allow him to risk his life over so trivial a matter. Shortly afterwards Osbaldeston left the Atherstone,[61] and in 1817 gave way to his friend Sir Bellingham Graham, who in his time hunted more countries than anyone except perhaps John Warde of Squerries. Sir Bellingham Graham brought his own hounds to Witherley and, according to his diary, showed excellent sport in spite of the earth-stopping being anything but good. He did not, however, seem to mind digging, an occupation in more general favour with huntsmen than with the field. He was otherwise very popular, and obtained a piece of country from 'the Squire', then master of the Quorn, who ceded the salient bounded by the Lutterworth–Leicester and Ratby–Leicester roads, including Whetstone and part of Leicester Forest, now much built over.[62]

For some reason not given in his diary, Sir Bellingham gave up suddenly to go to Hampshire, and contracted to hunt the Hambledon for 3 years

48 See pamphlet by R. Greaves, *South Atherstone*.

49 It is not made clear which of the earls of Lonsdale is meant.

50 *Official Handbook of the Atherstone Hunt*.

51 *Complete Peerage*, viii, 136; *V.C.H. Rut.* i, 301.

52 T. F. Dale, *Hist. Belvoir Hunt*, 32–33.

53 Blew, *Quorn Hunt*, 39.

54 Joseph Jones, *Diary of the Quorndon Hunt*, 19, 24, 26, 37, 39, 43, 44, and *passim*.

55 T. F. Dale, *Fox-Hunting in the Shires* (1903), 173.

56 Baily, *Authentic Handbook of the Atherstone Hunt*.

57 Ibid. 58 R. Vyner, *Notitia Venatica*.

59 Dale, *Fox-Hunting in the Shires*, 173.

60 Ibid.; *Squire Osbaldeston, His Autobiography*, ed. E. D. Cuming, 36.

61 Cuming, op. cit. 37.

62 Ibid. 38–43; C. D. B. Ellis, *Hist. Quorn Hunt*, 37, 39; on Sir Bellingham Graham's career, see Sir Reginald Graham, *Fox Hunting Recollections*, *passim*.

for £700 a year—not enough to keep him in spur leathers, it was said.[63]

Lord Anson, son of the Earl of Lichfield, who lived in Cannock Chase (Staffs.) on the far north edge of the country, succeeded him. He collected a pack of hounds, including John Mytton's from Salop, steadied by drafts from Sir Thomas Mostyn and Mr. Musters of South Nottinghamshire. Lord Anson was not afraid of distances, and added a part of the Warwickshire country that lies round Dunchurch, which Lord Middleton had abandoned when he took over from Mr. Corbet in 1822. Lord Anson built kennels at his house at Shugborough (Staffs.), where the hounds were kept from April to November. He also built kennels at Dunchurch, which apparently he allowed Mr. Osbaldeston to use when he became master of the Pytchley (1827–34). He had two big pictures of the hunt painted by Webb, a Tamworth artist of some talent. They show the leading members of the hunt and the servants all with red collars, but some gentlemen are wearing blue stocks.[64]

In 1830 Lord Anson gave way to Sir John Gerrard who proved a great failure, so great that the members of the Atherstone field were induced to assist in meeting the hunt's expenses for the first time. In 1831 they agreed with Mr. Applethwaite to promote Thurlow, who had been kennel huntsman at Witherley since 1820, and hunt the country with a guarantee of £1,500. Mr. Applethwaite held office for 11 years, and showed average sport. He was followed by Charles (commonly called Peter) Colvile, who gave equal satisfaction to his field with Thurlow as his huntsman.[65]

From now on the ground is more certain, for the Minute Books of 1845–1949 contain the proceedings both of the hunt club and the general meetings between those dates.[66] The hunt club, founded in 1815, still exists. The members wear slate-blue facings on their hunt coats in the evening with gilt buttons with the letter A and a running fox. Their ladies were given the slate-coloured collar by Mr. Oakeley in the 90's when Lord Lonsdale gave an Eton blue collar to the Quorn ladies. The white collar which the servants wore could not be adopted, as, though not at that time worn in the hunting-field, it was very much worn at night by the Pytchley Hunt. The Atherstone Hunt Club is, or was, quite separate from the Hunt, which was managed by an annual meeting of landowners, subscribers, and members of the hunt club, summoned by the honorary secretary of the club. This was generally held at the 'Red Lion', Atherstone.

The general meeting appointed the masters and arranged how much they would receive to hunt the country, out of which they had to pay rent to the club for the kennels which the club leased, first from Mr. Osbaldeston and later from two or three landowners who guaranteed the overdraft or mortgage at the bank. The club had a 'Secret Service Fund', but the minutes do not disclose its purpose. The club paid the outside repair of the kennels and generally shared with the master any major improvements, such as the hospital in 1879, gas, and redraining. It also voted sums to the hunt funds, when there was a deficit of the master's guarantee and any loss on the annual hunt dance. About twelve members usually attended both the general meeting and the meeting of the club; the two meetings took place one after the other, and the proceedings of both are recorded on the same pages of the Minute Book. There seems to have been no regular chairman. The election of new members of the club is recorded but not their resignations or deaths. There is no mention of a committee until 1908.

The first record in the 1845 Minute Book instructs Mr. George Gisborne, the Secretary, to inform Thomas Smith of Hill House, Hambledon (Hants), that his offer to hunt the hounds in succession to C. R. Colvile, M.P., could not be agreed to. This was the well-known Gentleman Smith who had hunted the Pytchley for two seasons. Smith resented this refusal, as he had received the offer from several big landowners, including the retiring master. He states in a letter to the committee: 'When I had the Pytchley Hounds . . . there remained only between £1,100 and £1,000, yet I hunted the country four days a week though only bound to hunt it three. I did this, as I believed that the men would prefer four days with three horses than three days with four horses out, but I now think that I ought to have studied effect. . . . I killed four times as many foxes each season as Chesterfield did with five or six red coats to assist, with the worst crew of hounds ever collected in a pack. . . .'

John Anstruther Thomson was, however, appointed, with a subscription of £1,500 a year, guaranteed 'by G. Moore, Esq., and C. R. Colvile', the Atherstone Hunt Club paying earth-stopping and providing stables and kennels. No reason is given for preferring this young soldier boy to the best huntsman in England.

Several meetings which took place in the following years throw some light on the conduct of the hunt's affairs. Gisborne does not make it clear whether it was the members of the club or the supporters, landowners, and subscribers who were summoned by Sir John Chetwode, Sir John Berney, and George Moore, to attend the meeting at the Clarendon Hotel, Bond Street, London, on 22 May 1849. Gisborne also records a meeting

63 Graham, op. cit.

64 Dale, *Fox-Hunting in the Shires*, 174–5.

65 Baily, *Authentic Handbook of the Atherstone Hunt.*

66 Where no other reference is given, the remainder of the account of the Atherstone is based on the Hunt's Minute Bks., to which access has been granted by Sir William Dugdale and the Hunt Secretary.

of the Atherstone Hunt Club at the Albany, at the same time and date, attended by these three convenors and sixteen others, Earl Howe in the chair.

Gisborne summoned the Atherstone Hunt Club and Friends of Fox Hunting to support Mr. Wilson as master at the Clarendon on 16 June 1849. In 1850 'the Gentlemen of the A.H. met' at Curzon House, Lord Howe's town residence. About 1850 Sir Hanson Berney became honorary secretary, but there is no minute to that effect. The Minute Book records a long succession of complaints of lack of funds, but when properly approached the country could produce £2,500 a year, though the sum available soon fell to £1,300. This lack of financial support caused the loss of several masters.

John Anstruther Thomson, of Charlton (Fife), tells us in two well-written volumes the story of his life.[67] Between 1847 and 1871, he was thrice master, 1847–9, 1850–5, and 1870–1, the last time jointly with Mr. Oakeley. In 1847, in consequence of a fall, he nearly died of haemorrhage of the lungs, and was, like Charles Fernie, ordered to winter in Italy. He said, however, that he would rather hunt, and he did so to a good old age. On arrival at Witherley, Thomson found the hounds suffering from kennel lameness caused by the flooding of the drains by the river in wet weather. With his usual energy he set about remedying this by altering the drains and raising the floors above flood level.

During Colonel Thomson's masterships of the Atherstone there were several alterations in boundaries. In 1850, the North Warwick Hunt being in abeyance, the Atherstone drew Packington, Birchley Hayes, Castle Bromwich, Chelmsley Wood, York Wood, Park Hall to Minworthbrook and Coleshill. This arrangement lasted until 1871 when, after certain disputes, the matter was referred by Mr. Oakeley and Mr. Lant to the Hunting Committee of Boodle's Club which decided in favour of the North Warwick. Colonel Thomson was involved in other alterations of territory besides this one. In March 1848 he had a dispute with Sir Richard Sutton over the Bradgate coverts on the road between Leicester and Ashby de la Zouch. The matter was discussed at a formal meeting of the Atherstone Hunt Club in April, with Lord Curzon (son of Lord Howe of Gopsall) in the chair. It was settled amicably by the two masters and the owner, Lord Stamford. Colonel Thomson was thanked by the committee 'for the firm and gentlemanly way in which he had acted'.

Mr. 'Gumley' Wilson's year (1849–50) separated Colonel Thomson's first and second masterships. Thomson's resignation in 1849 left the Atherstone in a difficulty. No one came forward, but Thomson offered to lend his hounds 'to the Shareholders' (presumably the kennel-debt guarantors). Mr. Wilson was only secured on 24 July 1849, on Lord Curzon, Sir Charles Newdegate and Sir Grey Skipwith guaranteeing £1,800.[68] There were no changes either in the hounds or servants.

The gentlemen of the hunt, under the direction of Mr. Moore of Appleby, seem to have made some efforts to provide a pack for the country before Thomson's first mastership. Mr. Greene of Rolleston gave up the Quorn the same year, and the new master, Sir Richard Sutton, had his own pack. Moore drove Thomson to the sale of Greene's hounds at Quorn, where he bought several couples, which he gave to the country.

When Thomson first came he lived in a little house close to the kennels at Witherley, but on his return from the Fife in 1850 C. H. Bracebridge, a staunch supporter of the hunt, lent him his house in Atherstone rent free. The Fife hounds had been sold to Sir Richard Sutton in 1847 on the recommendation of Thomson, whose home was there, so when he gave up the Atherstone in 1849 to serve that hunt he had to form a new pack. He bought part of the Donington (North Quorn) pack from Mr. Story and Sir Seymour Blane for £200. These hounds he brought with him, when he returned to Atherstone in 1850 and the country's hounds were sold at Tattersall's with Mr. Wilson's horses on 6 June. Owing to the lung haemorrhage Thomson wintered in Rome for the season of 1851–2 and Lord Curzon acted for him.

Colonel Anstruther Thomson's masterships were a great success. He brought many people into the country, and made himself very popular with the landowners and farmers. He managed in 1850 to persuade them to subscribe £2,200, less £225 kennel rent, but it soon sank to less than £1,600 in 1853. The general standard of sport was good, and he did much to establish the hunt on a firm basis. The sale of the country's hounds in 1850 was no doubt a mistake, but it was far easier then than now to get a pack of foxhounds together, since quite three-quarters of the packs were owned by the master, and in this way there were generally two or three for sale at the end of each season. Thomson, in his *Reminiscences*, gives no reason for quitting the Atherstone for the Bicester, neither did the committee in thanking him for his services make any effort to retain him.

He was succeeded by another wanderer, Mr. Selby Lowndes of Whaddon Chase. When in 1853 Lord Southampton, master of the Grafton, reclaimed the country in Buckinghamshire which had been lent to Mr. Lowndes, he had found a country in Warwickshire, but on Thomson's retirement he offered to hunt the country and pay rent for the kennels without a guarantee. This offer was readily accepted, but at the end of five

[67] J. Anstruther Thomson, *Eighty Years' Reminiscences*.

[68] W. Wilson, *Green Peas at Christmas* (ed. Sir Guy F. Wilson), 85–89.

seasons Lowndes was offered his old home country and resigned, so that the Atherstone was again left without a master or a pack.

The most important period of this hunt's history began in 1859. William Edward Oakeley, of Cliff House, Twycross, then took over the secretaryship from Sir Hanson Berney and at the same time Berney's old friend and near neighbour Lord Curzon of Gopsall agreed to get a pack of hounds together to hunt the country. So started a connexion with the Atherstone Hunt which still (1950) persists. For almost a century Mr. Oakeley, his daughter and son-in-law, Mr. W. Inge of Thorpe, and their daughters have controlled the destiny of the Atherstone, and despite many difficulties they have conducted the hunt's affairs with great success.[69]

William Oakeley, born in 1828, was descended from a long line of Shropshire squires. From his grandmother he inherited Plas Tanybwlch and the richest slate quarries in Wales. For 11 years he remained second in command, but on Lord Curzon standing down in 1870 he undertook to hunt the country either by himself or in partnership with Anstruther Thomson. Thomson agreed to return but the partnership lasted only a year, owing to a breakdown in health of Thomson's eldest son, and for the next 20 years Mr. Oakeley carried on alone. He became the most popular and successful master the Atherstone ever had. Strong, good-looking, a magnificent horseman, he enjoyed hunting and his one wish was that all who came out with him should do the same.[70]

At the end of his twelfth season Mr. Oakeley stated that he could not carry on; the guarantee was always in arrears, whilst the cost of everything was going up. The country rose in protest. A petition signed by 1,100 farmers and landowners was presented to him within 10 days of his announcement, and he agreed to go on, subject to a guarantee of £2,500 and other concessions. The increasing use of wire fencing was the chief cause of Mr. Oakeley's eventual resignation. In 1891 he called a meeting of the country and announced his resignation. He thanked all who had given him support for 20 years, during which he had had hardly a wry word, but the country, he said, was not the same happy hunting ground as in 1870. Expenses and trouble in management were increasing, and many coverts were now closed to hounds before Christmas by shooting tenants. The danger and anxiety caused by the introduction of barbed wire became a new tax on an M.F.H. In spite of the co-operation of many of the farmers to get it down, it kept appearing in new places and the danger to man and horse went on increasing year by year. He was determined not to let 20 bright years be marred by adding a few of doubtful pleasure.

Mr. Oakeley seldom received his guarantee and the country only paid when he produced his books to prove that he was spending £2,000 a year apart from his own hunting. He constantly paid for the repairs to the kennels which properly belonged to the club. Real improvement only came when Mr. Townshend began his 40 years' term of office as secretary in 1888 and Mr. Inge personally guaranteed the £2,500 agreed in 1883. Printed meet cards were sent out for the first time in 1883, when a Vigilance Committee was also instituted to control damage. From then on wire took the place of lack of money in the minutes. When asked by the farmers what his daughter would like best for a wedding present, Mr. Oakeley replied, 'a bundle of all the wire in the country'. Even in 1870 plain wire, in the form of old cables from coal pits, was beginning to be a menace. Barbed wire is supposed to have come about 10 years later, first introduced from America by the 'Red Earl'[71] to fence fox coverts. Little do men realize the results of their best-meant actions.

Mr. Oakeley was called 'the most fortunate Master in England', for he was loved and welcomed by all his farmers without exception. He was also one of those masters of foxhounds whose counsel had most weight with their colleagues.

Oakeley's obvious successor was his son-in-law W. Inge of Thorpe Constantine, Tamworth. Mr. Inge carried on the hunt with the same courtesy and correctness as Mr. Oakeley and was ably assisted by his wife, but after four seasons he found the burden of wire and great distances from his home too much, and retired, but not before both he and Mrs. Inge had received substantial marks of appreciation for their services to the Atherstone Hunt.[72]

The period of the masterships of Oakeley and Inge was also the time when the more fashionable hunts which adjoined the Atherstone were flourishing greatly. Oakeley may have reigned in the age of large estates, peace and little wire, but he had to weather the agricultural depression of the eighties. The lot of his daughter and granddaughter fell in times of great difficulties caused by war, barbed wire, and economic changes. In both periods the hunt's affairs have been conducted in the best possible manner. The predominant note of their régime was courtesy and avoidance of both ostentation and shabbiness, every detail correct without extravagance. It can be said that better sport has never been known in this country.

Mr. Gerald Hardy (1895–1903) was a worthy successor to Mr. Inge. Though not an actual resident, he lived only just beyond the border, in the Meynell country, where he owned Foston Hall (Derbys.). His huntsman, George Whitemore, was an excellent man, both in the field and in kennels. Mr. Hardy was responsible for turning the 'Secret Service Fund' into the Poultry Fund.

[69] Dale, *Fox-Hunting in the Shires*, 175.
[70] Ibid.
[71] The 5th Earl Spencer.
[72] Dale, op. cit. 176.

Mr. J. C. Munro (1903–8), who succeeded, came from the Albrighton, of which he had been master since 1899.[73] He kept on Whitemore, contributed £2,000 towards the purchase of the hounds, and agreed, for a subscription of £2,500, to meet 5 days a week, hunting hounds himself on the fifth day. Both Hardy and Munro threw themselves wholeheartedly into the business of getting down wire.

Mr. Munro was succeeded by Warner Plantagenet Hastings, 15th Earl of Huntingdon (1908–13). Lord Huntingdon was a brilliant huntsman, unrivalled at catching foxes in that difficult, closely fenced country and he was very popular with everybody. He hunted hounds himself 2 days a week and Whitemore hunted them on the other days. After 3 years, however, Whitemore retired and Lord Huntingdon was joined by Captain Thomas Bouch who shared the duty for one season before going to the Belvoir. Lord Huntingdon carried on alone for one more season, 1912–13.

In October 1908 the first hunt committee was formed. It consisted originally of the earls of Huntingdon and Denbigh, Sir Francis Newdigate-Newdegate, and Messrs. Munro and Townshend, but in March 1909 Messrs. G. Moore, Wollaston, Pierpoint, Tollemache-Scott, and Chamberlayne were added, Munro dropping out. No powers or duties were specified, and the only rule was that three retired annually. It is curious that George Moore of Appleby was not one of the original committee, as it appears he was not only the most constant attendant at the hunt meetings, but a leader in all their discussions.

Mr. Norman Loder only held the mastership for one season (1913–14), but that season will always be famous for the account of it, and of the personalities of the country, given in Siegfried Sassoon's *Memoirs of a Foxhunting Man*.[74] Loder went to the FitzWilliam at the end of the season, after showing excellent sport and establishing, or rather confirming, the reputation he had brought with him from the Southdown which he had hunted for the two previous seasons.

The hounds were undoubtedly suffering from the effect of these quick-changing huntsmen, none of whom, even if brilliant, had given themselves time to get to know their hounds really well, less still the country. There seemed only one person who could put things right. Women masters of hounds before 1914 were very rare, especially of foxhounds. Mrs. Inge, after some persuasion, consented to become master to save the pack her father had founded. She set about it in a true masterly fashion. She engaged Sam Morgan from the Linlithgow and Stirlingshire Hunt. He came of a fine old hunting family and had served a long apprenticeship with some of the best kennels, including the Brocklesby, Bramham and Quorn. Jack Molyneux was first whipper-in. He too had served with the Quorn and Bramham. Jim Bowler became second whipper-in. Molyneux wrote of Mrs. Inge as 'the best sportsman and straightest lady to hounds' that he had ever seen, and described the excellency of the Atherstone Hunt during the five seasons he spent with it. Indeed the sport shown by Mrs. Inge and the hunt servants who worked under her was far above the average.[75] Miss Margaret Inge joined her mother in 1915, but died in 1919.

A remarkable point in the history of the Atherstone is the number of first-class amateur huntsmen the country has produced or attracted, since 'The Squire' set the example in 1815. This was particularly the case in the inter-war period—with the unfortunate corollary that most masterships were short ones, for hunting one's own hounds is generally a young man's game.

Major Harry Hawkins (1920–2) of Everdon Hall, near Daventry, although serving with the Forces, had carried the Grafton through the war. He showed excellent sport with the Atherstone during his first season and into the second, but gave up suddenly for personal reasons, leaving Mrs. Inge to carry on once more, with the first whipper-in hunting hounds. Major W. E. Lyon (1922–4) was another good and popular amateur, joined by another first-class man, Major B. Hardy, nephew of a former master, in his second season. Captain Ramsden (1924–33) had, for an amateur, a long mastership. He was a good hound man and liked to see hounds work out the line for themselves. In 1930 the hunt was divided into two countries, the north and the south, Ramsden keeping the north. He was followed as Master of THE NORTH ATHERSTONE HUNT[76] by Mr. Luke Lillingston (1933–7), who came with a reputation as a brilliant horseman and proceeded to make one as a brilliant huntsman. A farmer who had wired all his fields and saw him following his hounds wherever they went, took the wire down again; he said it was no good trying to stop Mr. Luke. Mr. Ansell joined Mr. Lillingston for his last two seasons.

When Mr. Peter Paget, whose father and grandfather had been Masters of the Quorn, became master of the North Atherstone in 1937, it seemed that the hunt was going to enjoy a long period of prosperity. Mr. Paget spared no pains and was a first-class huntsman and a charming master: his first two seasons were as good as any the hunt had enjoyed.

When the war came Paget was a major in the Yeomanry. In 1940 he rejoined his old regiment,

[73] Dale, op. cit. 176.

[74] S. Sassoon, *Memoirs of a Foxhunting Man* (1943), 182–97. The account is partly fictitious, but most of the characters are easily recognizable.

[75] J. Molyneux, *Thirty Years a Hunt Servant*, 92.

[76] On the history of the N. Atherstone as a separate hunt, see R. Greaves, *The N. Atherstone*, *passim*.

the Scots Greys, in Palestine and sent in his resignation, but was induced to withdraw it on Miss Hilda Inge agreeing to come in with him and run everything during his absence. In 1943 both masters tendered their resignations, but were induced to carry on with a guarantee of £500. Before the next annual meeting on 1 February 1945, Major Paget had been killed in action in Normandy. Miss Inge tendered her resignation at this meeting, but was again induced to withdraw it. In 1946 Miss Inge again withdrew her resignation under great pressure and a guarantee of £1,300. In 1947 she instituted a Farmers' Hunt Button, and hunted 5 days a fortnight for £1,500. A well-deserved testimonial of a gold watch and £234 was presented to H. Parish, the huntsman, after 19 years' service.

When Miss Inge finally resigned in 1949 her place was hard to fill. No master ever carried on through difficult times with more success. She knew the hounds and the traditions of the country. Her mother was at her side throughout.

The South Atherstone Hunt had kennels at Cotesbach just inside the Pytchley country. Mr. R. Wright (1930–5), the first master, engaged Arthur Thatcher as huntsman. When Thatcher died at the end of the second season Nimrod Capell was engaged. Both huntsmen showed excellent sport. Mr. Wright did wonders in 'panelling' the country and making it rideable. He is remembered as a quite exceptionally bold horseman with a great fondness for jumping high timber and gates. The Earl of Inchcape was joint master in 1934 and Captain G. Shaw in 1935.

Captain Shaw carried on after Mr. Wright resigned and with two more partners, Captain Kingscote (1936) and Major Townshend (1937–9), kept things going until the War, when he and Major Townshend both joined the forces. Mrs. John Atkins then agreed to act as field master, hon. secretary and whipper-in. Then she decided to take the hounds and throughout the War she succeeded not only in keeping the country going but in showing good sport. In 1948 she was joined by Captain Bryn Parry.

After Miss Inge's retirement the North Atherstone found it very difficult to find a really suitable master, so at the end of the season 1949–50 Captain Bryn Parry offered to hunt the whole country 4 days a week from Witherley as of old. After some debate the offer was cordially accepted by both sides at a general meeting in April 1950, and the two areas are now rejoined as the Atherstone Hunt.[77] Captain Parry was joined in 1953 by Colonel E. F. S. Morrison.

The Hounds of the Atherstone Hunt. The creation of the Atherstone Pack may be said to have sprung from Lord Curzon's courage and willingness to experiment. When Selby Lowndes took his hounds back to the Whaddon Hunt in 1859, he left a draft behind. To these Lord Curzon added Mr. Baker's hounds from north Warwickshire. These were originally bred from a Shropshire trencher-fed pack to which bloodhound strains had been freely added. Sir Richard Acton had added a draft of Belvoir bitches before giving them to Baker. We are told that they were great line hunters with handsome black and tan coats and a powerful cry. Lord Curzon added drafts from the South Wiltshire, Meynell, Pytchley, Oakley, and Badminton Hunts.

Whether Oakeley helped Lord Curzon in his experiments is not recorded, but the first thing Oakeley did was to buy a pack of 25 couple of pure Welsh hounds from Colonel Pryse of Gogerddan (Cardigan.), and he added drafts from the Bramham, Col. Wyndham's, Belvoir, Cotswold, FitzWilliam, Fife, Grove, Oakley, Pytchley, Quorn, Tailby's, Rufford, Southwold, and Portman; a 150 couple from 15 packs. As there is no notice of Lord Curzon's hounds being sold, presumably they too remained. 'After a lot of dog dealing' wrote Anstruther Thomson, his joint-master, 'we reduced them to eighty couples.'

As Thomson retired the same year, Oakeley and his huntsman, George Castleman, were left to deal with the problem of breeding. No one could say that they had not plenty of lines to choose from. Oakeley spared no expense and, in spite of the variety in his own kennels, he sent his bitches to the best sires in England—Belvoir Senator, and Weathergage and his son Gamester appear in the stud book beside the well-known Quorn Alfred. Whatever Oakeley's method was, it was successful, for his hounds hunted and stayed and were all up at the end of some famous hunts. When he retired he passed his pack on to his successor and his own interest did not lapse.

On Mr. Inge's resignation the hounds were sold to Gerald Hardy and when he gave up in 1905, Oakeley and a few friends joined Mr. J. C. Munro in paying Tattersall's valuation price of £3,500 for them. On Munro's retirement the Hunt Club raised enough to enable them to acquire the pack (on very generous terms) from the proprietor.

It will thus be seen that although the Hunt has owned the pack for less than 50 years, there has been continuity since 1870 and probably since 1860.

In 1938 Mrs. Inge, who owned the kennels at Witherley which were built by George Osbaldeston, gave them to the Hunt.

[77] The closing paragraphs of this account are based on the late Major Paget's personal knowledge.

CRICKET

The early years of the 18th century must have seen cricket firmly established in Leicestershire for in 1744 a reference was made to the game at Barrow on Soar.[1] This is the earliest mention of cricket in England north of Northampton. A further 30 years elapsed before any space in the local press was devoted to the pastime.

Cricket probably began as a recreation for rural and town craftsmen. In Leicester itself the first known ground was situated in St. Margaret's Pasture and until 1825 the chief contests were held there. During this first recorded period in the history of Leicestershire cricket there were many places in the county such as Loughborough, Melton Mowbray, Mountsorrel, and Quorndon, where the pastime was pursued with great enthusiasm; it is interesting to note that all these places are in the famous hunting country. It is very probable that the game was fostered by those hunting men who came from the south of England. Many years later south Leicestershire came to the fore and has been prominent ever since as a nursery of county cricketers.

As may be expected, much early Leicester cricket was closely connected with the neighbouring town of Nottingham. The first trial of strength took place near Loughborough in 1781[2] but the game was abandoned as a draw following a dispute which initiated verbal hostilities that lasted for about 50 years, although games were played at intervals during that period. Two games were played at Loughborough in 1789[3] and they are considered to be the first Leicestershire inter-county contests. Nottinghamshire won the first, but Leicestershire won the return by 1 run and the game has been referred to ever since as the 'Odd Notch Match'.

Leicestershire met the M.C.C. for the first time in 1791 when, at Burley on the Hill near Oakham, a strong M.C.C. eleven won by an innings and 41 runs.[4] In 1803 a combined Leicestershire–Nottinghamshire team paid a visit to Lord's where it sustained a severe defeat at the hands of Hampshire.[5]

It is surprising to read that women were playing cricket as far back as 1792, but in that year eleven girls of Rotherby beat eleven girls of Hoby during Rotherby's feast week.[6]

During the early years of the 19th century the county town became increasingly the chief centre of population in a mainly agricultural county, and it is only natural to find Leicester monopolizing the cricket scene. In 1824 Leicester met Sheffield for the first time and triumphed over the home side by 1 run.[7] Prominent local players of this period included Peter Heward, the well-known wicket-keeper, G. W. Owston, the brothers W. and G. Gamble, Sam Dakin of Sileby (a noted all-round player) and Capt. R. Cheslyn. Dick Cheslyn was a member of the M.C.C. and a national figure in the game; in 1827 he captained Sussex in three of the trial games arranged to investigate the advisability of legalizing the new form of round-arm bowling.[8]

As the game grew in popularity the provision of a new ground became a necessity, so, in 1825, the famous Wharf Street ground was opened. This ground extended from Wharf Street parallel with Humberstone Road at the rear of the Spa cottages and included a bowling green, quoit ground, and cricket ground which covered about 10 acres.[9] For the next 35 years some of the principal matches in England were staged on this ground and it obtained the reputation of being the finest ground in the country.

Following several important club matches, the first and most famous representative match took place in 1836 when the South beat the North by 218 runs.[10] This game was made memorable by the performance of Alfred Mynn, a well-known cricketer, who scored 21 and 125 undefeated in both innings, but was so badly battered by the fast bowling of Redgate that he was unable to play again for 2 years. The wicket was excellent, the ground shorn and perfectly flat—very unusual conditions for that time—but the absence of pads aggravated injuries Mynn had sustained at practice. A curious sidelight of the management of this historic encounter is noted by the Revd. James Pycroft in his *Oxford Memories*: 'The first I ever heard of the gate money interfering with the management of a match was, much to my surprise, at the famous North v. South match, when Mr. Mynn was so distinguished at Leicester. The publican (Barker) told me that he had the privilege of putting the men in and dividing the great batsmen between the two days: Very infradig. for Lord Frederick (Beauclerk) and the Marylebone club, by whom it was sanctioned.' In 1843 the Midland Counties, with Alfred Mynn in the side, lost to the M.C.C. at Wharf Street by 10 wickets,[11] but in the following year at the same ground a weakened M.C.C. team was defeated by the Northern Counties by an innings.[12]

Inter-county cricket fixtures were resumed with Nottinghamshire in 1845;[13] the away match was lost by 2 wickets but full revenge to the extent of an innings victory was obtained in the

[1] P. F. Thomas, *Cricket's Prime* (1923), 15.
[2] *Leic. Jnl.* 22 Sept. 1781.
[3] *Scores and Biographies*, i, 99, 100.
[4] Ibid. 117.
[5] Ibid. 307.
[6] *Sporting Mag.* (1792).
[7] *Scores and Biographies*, i, 505.
[8] Ibid. ii, 6, 8, 25.
[9] E. E. Snow, *Hist. Leics. Cricket*, 37–39.
[10] *Scores and Biographies*, ii, 389.
[11] Ibid. iii, 190.
[12] Ibid. 277.
[13] Ibid. 314, 322.

home game. In August of the following year the M.C.C. once again met the Northern Counties and won.[14]

The 1847 season was notable for the appearance of a powerful All England eleven at Wharf Street when twenty of Leicestershire were beaten by an innings.[15] A similar match took place in 1849 but Leicestershire fared better scoring 137 to England's 188.[16] The following year, 1850, Derbyshire was beaten at Derby by 8 wickets[17] and that game is ranked as the first full county match between the two counties. The M.C.C. was met twice in 1851 and the home game was won by 10 wickets.[18] All England drew with twenty-two of Leicestershire in 1855 at Wharf Street.[19] In 1856 the All England eleven visited Melton Mowbray[20] and Loughborough[21] while in the same year the United All England eleven was soundly beaten by twenty-two of Leicestershire at Wharf Street.[22] All England visited Loughborough in 1857[23] and Eastwell in the following year. In 1859 the United All England side beat twenty-two of Loughborough and district.[24] A strong England side, including R. Daft, Caesar, Hayward, and George Parr, was defeated at Wharf Street in 1860 by twenty-two of Leicestershire with a margin of an innings and 49 runs.[25] This proved to be the last game played at the old ground for, on 7 November 1860, the ground with some adjoining property was sold by auction and soon was lost for ever under scores of houses and streets.

This era was the first of importance in the annals of Leicestershire cricket, for, in addition to possessing the finest ground in England, the county was fortunate in having the services of some of the country's leading amateurs. Among names that must be mentioned we find T. C. Goodrich, a wonderfully good slow bowler, the Revd. R. T. King, the greatest of all 'points' and a first-class bat, the Revd. E. Elmhirst, the best amateur wicket-keeper of his day, the Revd. A. Payne and the Revd. J. Bradshaw. The number of clergy is large but not surprising in a county famous for its sporting parsons. Whether or not the individual continued playing after taking Holy Orders depended upon the opinion of his bishop, but in the case of most of the Leicestershire men considerable freedom was allowed. The end of this period, in 1860, was notable for the first appearance for Leicestershire of R. A. H. Mitchell who captained Oxford University for 3 years and was the greatest amateur batsman in England until W. G. Grace came to power. Unfortunately for cricket Mitchell became a master at Eton in 1866 and subsequently made but few appearances in first-class cricket.

Following the closure of the Wharf Street ground in 1860 there was a sad decline, all the more regrettable as this period was a critical one in the development of county cricket. Such matches as were arranged took place on private grounds in the county and at Victoria Park in Leicester. The chief interest was aroused when the various touring England elevens gave demonstrations against odds. Thus in 1862 All England defeated twenty-two of Leicestershire at Lindridge House near Desford.[26] Hinckley was visited by the United All England eleven in 1866 who drew with twenty-two of South Leicestershire.[27] In 1867 at Enderby Hall,[28] All England defeated twenty-two of the county; while at Narborough in the following year All England overcame twenty-two of Narborough and District.[29] Among other representative matches were All England and twenty-two of Loughborough at Loughborough in 1870,[30] the United South of England and Loughborough in 1871[31] and All England and twenty-two of Melton in 1872.[32] On Victoria Park W. G. Grace assisted the United South of England eleven against twenty-two of Leicestershire in 1872.[33]

In spite of the lack of proper headquarters the Leicestershire Cricket Association was formed in 1873, mainly through the efforts of Charles Marriott and Edward Holmes (late Chief Constable of Leicestershire). Following a 'Colts'' trial match, held for the first time by Leicestershire, the Association arranged home and away fixtures with the M.C.C. in 1873, and in both matches Leicestershire were victorious.[34] During the same season the United South of England eleven was beaten by twenty-two of Leicestershire.[35]

In 1874 twenty-two of the district easily beat All England at Victoria Park,[36] but by this time the importance of these touring sides was declining. Two county matches were arranged with Lancashire in 1875 but both games were lost.[37] The principal bowlers at this time were the left-handers, A. Rylott and J. Parnham, while G. Panter was a useful all-rounder. Rylott, Parnham, and J. H. Wheeler, a useful bat and wicket-keeper, were members of the M.C.C. ground staff at Lord's.

The Grace Road ground was opened in 1878 and new life given to the game in the district. In July the Australians attracted large crowds to the new ground and Leicestershire was rewarded for its enterprise in being the first county to make

14 Ibid. 452.
15 Ibid. 549.
16 Ibid. iv, 63.
17 *Lillywhite's Guide to Cricketers for 1851*, 40.
18 *Scores and Biographies*, iv, 283, 307.
19 Ibid. v, 110.
20 Ibid. 210.
21 Ibid. 258.
22 Ibid. 235.
23 Ibid. 349.
24 Ibid. vi, 298.
25 Ibid. 504.
26 Ibid. vii. 422.
27 Ibid. ix, 600.
28 Ibid. x, 146.
29 Ibid. 418.
30 Ibid. xi, 439.
31 Ibid. xii, 239.
32 Ibid. 385.
33 Ibid. 470.
34 Ibid. 853, 896.
35 Ibid. 792.
36 Ibid. xiii, 130.
37 Ibid. 517, 688.

arrangements with the Australians and guarantee them a lump sum for playing.

In 1879 the County Club was reformed on the lines we know today and several inter-county matches were arranged. As a matter of course famous players appeared on the scene and the side figured prominently in the second-class counties. A. D. Pougher and A. Woodcock were a particularly devastating pair of bowlers. The former was a medium-pace bowler who performed many great feats and gained renown when, for the M.C.C. at Lord's in 1896, he took 5 wickets for no runs against the Australians, who were dismissed for a total of 18. Woodcock was one of the fastest bowlers of his day and on many occasions he played for the M.C.C. in representative matches.

The season of 1888 was outstanding for three reasons; the Australians were beaten for the first and only time in the history of the club, the side finished at the top of the second-class counties, and C. E. de Trafford made his début.

Mainly owing to the efforts of C. E. de Trafford, captain from 1890 until 1906 inclusive, Leicestershire was admitted to the ranks of the first-class counties in 1895, though the previous year's matches also ranked as first-class. The first few years brought only moderate support and success, but the bold move of laying out a new ground nearer the centre of the town was undertaken and the Aylestone Road ground was opened in 1901. By a happy coincidence the new enterprise coincided with improved performances, which encouraged better attendances at the new headquarters. The attractive displays of the side during the next few years—the Golden Age of Leicestershire cricket—have never since been equalled. C. E. de Trafford, V. F. S. Crawford, Jayes, and Gill were hitters of character and quality; Albert Knight and John King were first-class batsmen with pleasing styles; and C. J. B. Wood was always difficult to remove. He carried his bat through the innings on seventeen occasions and, in 1911, against Yorkshire carried his bat through the two innings for 107 and 117, a feat without parallel in first-class cricket.

There were other very useful batsmen such as H. Whitehead and S. Coe. Whitehead shares with C. J. B. Wood the honour of participating in Leicestershire's highest stand for any wicket: 380 for the first wicket against Worcestershire in 1906. Sam Coe, one of the staunchest players the club has ever had, was a left-hand all-rounder who made the county's highest individual score—252 not out against Northamptonshire in 1914. He became the official scorer in 1931 and continued until the early matches of the 1950 season.

In 1907 Sir Arthur (later Lord) Hazlerigg took over the captaincy, and Leicestershire cricket, as well as so much else, owed much to his kind-hearted devotion and leadership. Even if the bowlers of this period did not equal the excellence of the batsmen, some were very useful and must be mentioned. W. W. Odell, an amateur medium-pace right-hander, took 649 wickets for Leicestershire, and made several appearances for the Gentlemen against the Players. G. C. Gill and T. Jayes apart from being big hitters were good fast bowlers and Jayes would undoubtedly have made a name for himself if he had not suffered from ill health. As it was he was chosen to play for England against Australia in 1909, but for some unaccountable reason was omitted at the last minute and England took the field on a hard wicket without a pace bowler.

The years before the outbreak of the First World War saw the development of Ewart Astill and George Geary who later became two of the outstanding figures in the game. W. E. Astill was one of the greatest players never to be chosen to play against Australia, though he played for England against South Africa and the West Indies, and altogether in first-class games scored 22,740 runs and took 2,433 wickets. George Geary appeared for England on many occasions against Australia and South Africa and his totals in first-class cricket were 13,697 runs and 2,063 wickets.

When play was resumed in 1919 new blood was sadly needed. Under the leadership of A. T. Sharp, Major G. H. S. Fowke, and E. W. Dawson, new players developed and in the late twenties the county possessed one of the best attacking sides in England. The batting was, unfortunately, comparatively undistinguished, although Armstrong, Berry, Dawson, Alan Shipman, and Astill obtained their thousand runs each season with some consistency. During this peak period in the county's modern history, the bowling was varied and suitable for every state of the wicket. Skelding, the fastest English bowler of his time, Alan Shipman, and Haydon Smith, a lion-hearted bowler if ever there was one, who captured 1,076 wickets during his first-class career, supplied the speed; Geary with his pace off the wicket was always dangerous, and Astill provided subtle spin and flight. Further variety was added by Snary, one of the most accurate bowlers of his generation, and by the left-handed Bale.

The 1935 season was brilliant: Leicestershire reached a high position (sixth) in the championship table. Not a little of the credit was due to the captaincy of Ewart Astill who was the first professional to be appointed to the regular captaincy of a county side. The highest number of runs scored in a season by a Leicestershire player stands to the credit of L. G. Berry, who scored 2,446 runs, with an average of 52·04, in 1937. Scoring over a thousand runs in each season from 1928 onwards, Berry has been one of the most consistent members of the side. He captained the team in 1946 and the two following seasons.

C. S. Dempster, a New Zealander and the best batsman ever to play for the county, captained the side in 1936, 1937, and 1938, and his brilliant batting and fielding were an inspiration to the team. Just when a most promising set of young players had been produced, the Second World War began and serious cricket had to be abandoned.

Almost at a moment's notice the ground and buildings were taken over by the National Fire Service and were later occupied by the fighting forces. The club's archives were hastily packed up and, unfortunately, may have been lost for ever. For many years the Freeman's Meadow generating station had overshadowed the ground and smuts from the huge chimneys had many times stopped play. When the Second World War was over, extensions to this plant were continued, and two new cooling towers were erected on the former practice end of the club ground. Fortunately the Leicester Education Committee came to the rescue of the club when play was resumed in 1946, and first-class cricket was once again seen on the old Grace Road ground.

The Leicestershire County Club has figured prominently in many cricket innovations. The guarantee to the Australians in 1878 has already been mentioned. At Lord's in 1900, when Leicestershire played the M.C.C., a 3 ft. high net was placed all round the boundary so that hits which did not go over the net should be run out. Nothing came of this innovation. When the season of 1908 opened with a match against Warwickshire at Leicester, the experiment was made of starting play on the Saturday, a step which was generally adopted in county cricket in later years. On several occasions the county was given the honour of being the first team to play on a newly opened ground. At Aylestone Road in 1930 Leicestershire Ladies met Nottinghamshire Ladies. This was the first inter-county ladies' match arranged for over a hundred years. Wicket covers, now a familiar sight on every first-class ground, were originally designed by a Leicestershire secretary, S. C. Packer.

Many remote corners of the British Isles and the Continent owe their initiation into the mysteries of cricket to a Leicestershire team. The first touring side was Sparkenhoe Rovers (later called the Incapables), and other prominent names are the Ivanhoe and Gentlemen of Leicestershire clubs. In addition a team of Leicester club cricketers went to Berlin in 1911, and Denmark in 1921, 1923, and 1928.

Cricketing ability often runs in families. Leicestershire has seen several who have figured prominently in local and county cricket. These include the Randons, Marriotts, Arnall-Thompsons, Lorrimers, Kings, Joyces, Crawfords, Shipmans, and Packes. There were many Randons at Hathern, all good cricketers, and three of them, C. Randon, F. J. Randon, and F. Randon, played for the county. Quite unrelated to the Marriotts of Kibworth, the Marriotts of Cotesbach played a great part in the development of county cricket in Leicestershire. Charles was captain from 1873 to 1885 and it is doubtful whether any one man gave as much support to the county club in its infancy; the other brothers were J. M. and the Revd. G. S. Marriott. They, too, played for Leicestershire. H. H. Marriott was the most prominent of the Kibworth family, where the five sons of Sir Charles Hayes Marriott, a noted Leicestershire surgeon, lived. A good bat, he was games master at Marlborough College for 3 years and is reputed to have invented the fielding position of short third man—the 'gully'. Although the other four brothers did not play for Leicestershire they were very useful players in club and college cricket. H. T. Arnall-Thompson captained the county from 1886 until 1889 and two more brothers, P. J. and W. E. Arnall-Thompson, played at infrequent intervals. A., B., and D. Lorrimer played, but, owing to business and military careers, not as much as their skill warranted.

A well-known player, J. H. King, came from Lutterworth and was the best left-hand all-round player the county has had. He played for England against Australia, and at Lord's in 1904 scored a century in each innings for the Players against the Gentlemen. His brother James and nephew J. W. also played a little first-class cricket, the former for Leicestershire while J. W. appeared for Worcestershire and Leicestershire. J. H., R., and F. M. Joyce came from Ashby de la Zouch and were all useful players.

The Revd. J. C. Crawford first played for Leicestershire in 1878 and his famous sons V. F. S. and R. T. Crawford played a prominent part in the early years of the 20th century. V. F. S. Crawford was one of the most attractive hitters ever seen and generally scored quickly. He had already made a name with Surrey before playing for his native county.

Of the six Shipman brothers of Ratby, only two, William and Alan, played first-class cricket and both were fast bowlers; Alan developed also into a steady opening batsman, but William was a hitter. The other four brothers, however, were very good players and Albert would probably have made a big name for himself had he not been killed in the First World War.

Lt.-Col. E. C. Packe, of Great Glen Hall, has been a prominent figure in Leicestershire cricket for a great many years and each of his three sons, C. W. C. Packe, R. J. Packe, and M. St. J. Packe, assisted the county with success, Charles and Michael captaining the side in 1932 and 1939 respectively.

In the hey-day of country-house cricket most of the big houses could boast their cricket grounds. Amongst these should be mentioned East Langton Grange, the home of J. W. Logan, who was M.P. for the Harborough division for many years. Major H. H. Robertson-Aikman entertained many teams on his splendid ground at

Dunton Basset. Gopsall Hall, in the great days of the Earls Howe was unsurpassed, while T. Fielding Johnson also provided great hospitality at Goscote Hall. There were, of course, many others, including the homes of three Leicestershire captains: Lowesby Hall, the home of Sir Frederick Fowke; Noseley Hall, where Sir Arthur Hazlerigg laid out a good wicket and on which the present Lord Hazlerigg learnt the game; and Launde Abbey, where the Dawsons entertained many strong elevens in past seasons.

Village-green cricket, in its literal sense, is rare in Leicestershire, but the village games are played in the true spirit which characterizes the pastime throughout the country. Most of the grounds are situated in rough fields with a comparatively smooth square surrounded by long grass, but there are some notable exceptions, such as the excellent run-getting ground at Kibworth. In the towns and villages in the county the interest for the game has usually continued over the years and there is often a definite connexion between the type of player produced and the type of ground available. County cricket has been staged at the Bath grounds at Ashby de la Zouch, Egerton Park at Melton Mowbray, Park Road and the college ground at Loughborough and also at Barwell, Coalville, and Hinckley. The two latter places have opened new grounds since the Second World War to enable first-class cricket to return after a lapse of many years. The Ashby and Melton grounds are two of the most picturesque in England but lack modern accommodation.

Egerton Park, the home of the leading Melton side, was formerly the seat of the earls of Wilton and was used as a circuit ground as far back as the 1880's. There is, however, an even better known ground at Melton Mowbray, Saxby Road, where an All England eleven met Melton in 1855. This ground is still known as the All England ground.

Few counties in England can show such a long history for their cricket clubs: Loughborough, Hinckley, and Melton teams have appeared almost continuously since the earliest recorded days. Barwell can claim the oldest continuous cricket fixture in England, for in 1807 they began their annual fixture with Coventry and North Warwickshire. This match has been played every succeeding year although occasionally the name of the Coventry team has been altered. Other strong and old-established clubs in the county include Lutterworth, Market Harborough, and Kibworth, the history of each of which goes back into the early years of the 19th century. The Ashby Hastings club was formed about 1860 although an Ashby team had played for many years before that date.

In Leicester itself there are a few survivors of the early clubs. The Leicester club was originally formed in 1866 and was first known as the Evington Lane Club; later the name was changed to the Victoria Park Club as the home matches were played there; and finally the name was changed to the Leicester Cricket Club in 1878. The Ivanhoe Club was formed in 1873 and has been prominent ever since; a tour to Holland was organized as early as 1895.

Leicester Banks and Temperance Clubs were formed about the same time as the Evington Lane Club, and are still active today. Other prominent Leicester clubs which were in existence during the latter half of the 19th century were the Arundel, South End, St. Mary's, Lansdowne, Dan Garner's, Oxford, and Roslyn clubs. These and others were quite often strong and many county players appeared in their ranks.

The leading amateur club in the county is the Gentlemen of Leicestershire Club, whose first recorded scores date back to 1820. This club has entertained some of the strongest amateur clubs in England, mainly during its annual cricket week.

Games have always formed a prominent part in army life and the Royal Leicestershire Regiment is no exception to this rule. The regiment is fortunate in having a delightful ground at Glen Parva and a strong fixture list usually includes an annual cricket week when well-known clubs test the strength of the regiment. Prominent names occur also in the home side's score book and three officers, E. L. Challenor, B. F. Clarke, and W. W. Jelf occasionally assisted Leicestershire in first-class cricket.

RUGBY FOOTBALL[1]

Leicestershire, like the rest of the midlands, was slow to take an interest in the new development in the game of football that originated at Rugby School in 1823, but this is not surprising as even at the school the game was at first little played. Once a start was made, however, steady progress was maintained throughout the county and for a great many years Leicester has been an honoured name in English rugby football.

The first clubs were formed in Leicester in 1869. They were the Leicester Athletic Society with such well-known players as J. Collier, A. T. Porter, and A. Wale, and St. Margaret's Club, whose members played at the Pasture. The game grew in popularity during the 1870's and other clubs, including Leicester Alert and Leicester Amateurs, were founded. Occasionally a few stalwarts from these clubs combined to form a team to play other towns, but a truly representative Leicester club was not yet in existence.

In the county, the honour of possessing the oldest club appears to belong to Lutterworth, where a club was formed in 1873, mainly through the efforts of T. P. Monnington. Born at

[1] This article is based on Brian Thompson, *Leic. Tigers*, and H. Grierson, *Ramblings of a Rabbit*.

Bitteswell in 1846, Monnington probably became interested in the game at Marlborough College. Lutterworth amalgamated with the Leicester club in 1890. An Ashby de la Zouch club, founded in 1876, was also flourishing in the 1870's under the leadership of N. J. Hughes-Hallett, whilst Market Harborough, Hinckley, and Ravenstone were established on sure foundations by 1880 and Loughborough was formed in 1891. Coalville and Belgrave were also prominent by the later part of the 19th century.

Of the county clubs Hinckley has generally been the strongest with considerably more than a local fixture list. The peak period in its history coincided with the appearance of the Palmers, S. H. Moore, and many others, some of whom represented Leicestershire.

Three local clubs—Leicester Societies Association Football Club, Leicester Amateur Football Club, and Leicester Alert—combined in 1880 to form the Leicester Football Club, but as there were only a few local rugby clubs, rugby and association were played more or less alternately. For three seasons the home matches were played on the Belgrave cricket and cycle ground which was situated on the Belgrave Road. Part of the site is now covered by the British United Co.'s buildings.

In the season 1883–4 the club moved to Victoria Park where it remained for five seasons and gained more public support, partly because the club entered for the Midland Counties Cup. Before they left the park after the 1887–8 season the club changed its colours to the present combination of green, scarlet, and white stripes which quickly earned for the wearers the nickname of 'Tigers'. Previously the players had worn black jerseys and were known as the 'Death or Glory Boys'. In these early days many well-known local sportsmen were connected with the club including J. Collier, Dr. H. Mason, J. G. S. Coleman, W. R. Porter, K. McAlpin, and J. Parsons.

So in 1888–9 the 'Tigers' returned to Belgrave Road confident of a considerable following of spectators who were willing to pay to watch. Season tickets were issued at 2*s*. 6*d*. and 5*s*. and non-ticket holders were charged 3*d*. for admission to the ground alone and 6*d*. a place in the stand.

The story of the second spell at Belgrave Road is one of continued progress and during the ensuing six seasons the fixture list was extended to include clubs from Lancashire, London, South Wales, and more from Yorkshire. By 1891 the financial position was so good that the 'Tigers' were able to take some ground between the Aylestone and Welford roads on a 10-year lease from the corporation and lay it out at an initial cost of £1,100. The ground was opened on 10 September 1892, the clubhouse was built in 1909, the members' stand reconstructed in 1914 and the Crumbie stand opened in 1920. For many years the Welford Road ground has been recognized as the best in England after Twickenham, with accommodation for 35,000 spectators who are able to leave the ground quickly and in comfort. International matches have been held there and many international trials, county finals, and other representative games.

There is little doubt that Leicester owes its present prominent position in the rugby world to the efforts of the late Tom Crumbie, who for 33 years (1895–1928) was honorary secretary of the club. Crumbie, a former Leicester Swifts player, played on a few occasions for the club. By the turn of the century the club's fixture list was as strong as any in the country; three teams were put into the field, and in 1898 the Midland Counties Cup was won for the first time. This cup was held for the next 7 years and again won in 1909, 1910, 1912, and 1913.

In 1901 the first England trial, North *v.* South, was played at Welford Road and in 1902 the first international, England *v.* Ireland. In 1905 a Dominion team—the All Blacks—visited Welford Road for the first time; the 'Tigers' lost 28–0. Included in the Leicester side on this occasion were A. O. Jones, the Nottinghamshire cricketer, Percy Oscroft, S. Penny, Matthews, Russell, Hind, Billy Foreman, J. Braithwaite, and Tom Goodrich. The latter, an international trialist, later gave great service to the club as bagman and trainer.

Except for the first few years, Leicester has always been an invitation club; there is no entrance subscription and the 'Tigers'' jersey is only worn at the invitation of the selection committee. This policy of attracting 'stars' from all over the country helped to cause trouble in 1908 when the Rugby Union had before them a resolution that Leicester be expelled from the union on the ground of professionalism. A full inquiry, however, held in Leicester on 16 January 1909, completely cleared the club of this charge.

In 1909 Leicester arranged a match with the Barbarians touring team, a fixture that has now become a traditional part of Leicester's Christmas festivities. From 1909 until the present day the 'Tigers' have been the only club in England to have a regular fixture with the Barbarians.

The outbreak of the First World War brought about the complete cancellation of all rugby football fixtures and the Welford Road ground was used for military training. As soon as the war ended T. H. Crumbie set about the task of reforming the side and by Christmas 1918 he had succeeded. The captain of this new side was P. W. Lawrie and he was assisted by F. M. (Tim) Taylor, G. W. Wood, Norman Coates, H. L. V. Day, E. E. Haslemere, and Frank Taylor. The early 1920's were great days for the club; in eight seasons Harold Day, a fine place-kicker, scored over a thousand points, exceeding the century seven times. But there were many other notable players, some of whom helped the county side. Between 1921 and 1927 Leicestershire reached the semi-final of the county championship six times and the final on four occasions, although the title was only gained once—in 1925.

The 'Tigers' usually played eight backs and seven forwards in those days and this formation was very successful. Support for rugby football in Leicester reached its peak during this period and 'gates' of 14,000 or so were common. Other well-known players came forward to replace their predecessors: F. D. Prentice, who eventually became secretary of the Rugby Union, the Collopys and the Beamishes, J. C. R. Buchanan and W. W. Wakefield often played in the same team. There were also D. J. Norman, R. A. Buckingham, and H. D. Greenlees, all of whom received international honours. George Beamish must also be mentioned; he was one of four brothers, all of whom played for Leicester.

Tom Crumbie was an enthusiastic supporter until his death in April 1928, for he never missed a match in which the 'Tigers' played until his last season. His successor was Eric Thorneloe, then secretary of the Leicestershire Rugby Union and a former 'Tiger', and he was soon faced with the universal problem of dwindling support, but he tackled all problems in a manner worthy of his predecessor. The 'Tigers' continued to attract first-class players, such as B. C. Gadney, D. A. Kendrew, R. J. Barr, M. Crowe, P. B. Coote, and J. T. W. Berry.

In 1931 was played what was probably the greatest game of any kind seen in Leicester when Leicestershire and East Midlands inflicted the season's only defeat on the South African 'Springboks'. To commemorate this solitary defeat, the South Africans presented their conquerors with a Springbok's head, which ever since has been awarded annually to the winners of the Leicestershire *v.* East Midlands match.

Fewer notable players were seen in the 'Tigers'' ranks in the late 1930's as an effort was made to concentrate on a regular, although not necessarily a local, side. Outstanding men, however, such as J. McD. Hodgson, Prince Obolensky, and Graham Meikle made frequent appearances in the fifteen.

Gradually many promising young players were found among the local clubs, and it seemed that the 1939–40 season would see an all-conquering Leicester side; but war came and once again first-class rugby was adjourned.

ASSOCIATION FOOTBALL

In April 1592 Mathewe Puchin of Barkby was summoned with eleven others for playing football on a Sunday at Oadby,[1] but the case was dismissed. This is by far the earliest reference to football in Leicestershire, although unorganized games must have been frequent even in those early days. Unlike cricket, football did not become a fashionable game, neither was it played apparently for high stakes, but the artisan class slowly developed the various junior local sides.

In 1884 came the enthusiasm necessary to form a truly representative town club.[2] Two old established clubs, Victoria and Hill Street, had closed down, but the club then known as Leicester Town and two schools, Wyggeston and Mill Hill House, were flourishing in a minor way. From these sources was formed, in the spring of 1884, the Leicester Fosse Club with Frank Gardner as treasurer and secretary; W. Johnson, captain; and A. West, F. S. Ashby, and F. Bromwich formed the committee.

The first game, twelve a-side, against Syston Fosse, was played in a field off Fosse Road South and was won 5–0. The first colours of the club were white and black jerseys with diagonal blue sashes. For the next season, 1885–6, a move was made to Victoria Park but support was still poor and fixtures were with such local sides as Coalville, Shepshed, Melton, and Loughborough.

More ambitious plans were made in the following season when the club moved to the Belgrave Road ground, and admission charges were first introduced on 5 November 1887. Burton Swifts, (Notts.) County Rovers, and Kettering Town were opponents of some reputation although the Fosse players were still amateurs. 'The Tigers' having outbid them for Belgrave Road, the season 1888–9 saw the Fosse return to Victoria Park. Their first professional, Harry Webb was signed from Stafford Rangers at 2*s.* 6*d.* a week. The newly formed Leicestershire Challenge Cup was entered but Loughborough knocked out the Fosse in the third round.

Mill Lane was the headquarters in 1889–90 with Sir Thomas Wright, president, and this year, the Leicestershire Challenge Cup was won, Coalville being beaten in the final. The County Cup was again won in the following year, but more important was the début in the Football Association Cup competition, although the Fosse suffered a defeat at Mill Lane to Burton Wanderers before a £15 gate. The players were not all professionals and in the whole of Leicestershire, only the Loughborough side was completely professional. The Midland League was entered in May 1891, but as Mill Lane was lost for Corporation building, the opening matches were played at the Grace Road cricket ground. The present ground at Filbert Street was opened on 7 November 1891 with a 1–1 draw against Notts. Forest. Joseph Johnson guaranteed the rent, and four of Johnson's sons eventually played for the

[1] Leic. City Mun. Room, Archd. Rec., 1 D41/13/18.

[2] This article is largely based on N. Tarbotton, *From Fosse to City* (1948).

club. A disastrous first season was experienced and the bottom place was shared with Derby Junction.

In 1892, the colours were changed to white shirts and navy shorts.

The Fosse were admitted to the second division of the Football League in 1894 and finished fourth from the top. The next season brought them into competition with their old rivals, Loughborough Town, who had also secured admission into the league, a position they held until 1899–1900.

Promotion to the first division just eluded the Fosse in 1898–90 by 1 point but the third place was very encouraging to the limited company which had been formed in the previous season. After another season of good performances came six less successful ones in spite of strenuous endeavours to improve the side. Billy Bannister, an international centre half, was signed from Woolwich Arsenal in 1904 and A. E. Lewis, a goal-keeper, who was also a Somerset cricketer, was signed from Luton. Lewis replaced Walter Smith who had gone to Manchester City at a fee of £600.

Success in the great fight for promotion was achieved in 1907–8, mainly due to steady defence which included H. P. Bailey, a brilliant Welsh international amateur goal-keeper who also played cricket for Leicestershire. Unfortunately, the first division found the weak spots in the side and despite the efforts of good men, like R. T. Turner, also a county cricketer, and Blacett, the team finished bottom. The next period, until the beginning of the First World War, was quite undistinguished. Tom Clay, the first Leicester-born man to gain international honours, was transferred to Tottenham Hotspur in 1913 to relieve the financial position.

On 16 May 1919 the Fosse became Leicester City, and another important step was taken when Peter Hodge was appointed manager in September of the same year and started a Scottish influx which was to influence the side's style for the next 20 years. Jock Paterson, a fine centre forward, and Adam Black who was to perform as left back with great distinction for the next 15 years, were two of Hodge's most important early captures.

The new grandstand was opened in 1921, when the season started in very moderate style. M. T. O'Brien was signed in 1922 and for three seasons was one of the finest centre halves in the game, but the most important move of all took place in the late summer of 1922 when John Duncan joined the club. Duncan was a brilliant inside forward who later played at right half and proved a great inspiration to the side.

The season 1922–3 was exciting and promotion was only missed on goal average; two men who later became internationals joined during the season. R. Osborne was a full back who was born in South Africa, but Hugh Adcock was a local man, born at Coalville, who played for Loughborough Corinthians, a club formed in 1921 and disbanded in 1938. Gradually Hodge knit together his ideal team and Chandler and Carr came to Filbert Street in 1923. Next season, a fine team inspired by Duncan's captaincy, gained promotion, Chandler scoring 32 goals and Duncan 30. Against stiff opposition, success did not come too easily; further additions being necessary, two more famous forwards arrived, Hine and Lochhead.

At the end of the 1925–6 season Hodge resigned his managership. This caused something of a stir, but his successor, William Orr, was very efficient and seventh place was reached. Next season was even better and third place was occupied in spite of unfortunate injuries. The double-deck stand was opened in November 1926 and formed part of a £40,000 development plan.

The 1928–9 season saw the city finish runners-up for the first division championship, only one point behind the leaders, Sheffield Wednesday. By this time they had the reputation of playing the finest football in the country with a forward line consisting of Adcock, Hine, Chandler, Lochhead, and Barry, second to none. This type of football was never very successful in the F.A. cup and that season, Tottenham Hotspur won at Filbert Street in the third round before a record crowd of 47,298. John Duncan left the club at the end of the next season and his departure saw the end of Leicester City's golden age. The inspiration and influence of this great player was never quite recaptured.

For the next five seasons, the side finished towards the bottom of the table and eventually were relegated to the second division in 1935. Hodge returned as manager in 1932 but the great players of the past could not easily be replaced. For the first time, the semi-final of the F.A. cup was reached in 1934 but Portsmouth won at Birmingham, 4–1. The club suffered a great loss in August 1934, when Peter Hodge died.

F. Womack was appointed manager after the start of the 1936 season which ended in promotion, Bowers scoring 33 goals in 26 league matches. S. Smith who had played since 1929 was another outstanding player with a touch of genius.

Following a very moderate season in the first division, the city finished sixteenth and it was obvious that the side was not good enough. The 1938–9 season was even worse, and once again the city suffered relegation. After only three games had been played at the beginning of the 1939 season, war was declared and serious football was at an end.

INDEX TO VOLUMES I—III

This is a comprehensive index to every part of these three volumes; there is no separate index to the translation of the Leicestershire section of Domesday Book or of the Leicestershire Survey. Persons named in natural history articles as having observed or recorded natural phenomena and the places at which they observed them have not normally been indexed. The index presupposes that the corrections printed on p. 338 have already been made.

The following abbreviations are used: abp., archbishop; And., Andrew; Ant., Anthony; Bart., Bartholomew; Ben., Benjamin; b., born; bp., bishop; bro., brother; cast., castle; Cath., Catherine; chant., chantry; chap., chapel; Chas., Charles; Chris., Christopher; ch., church; coll., college; ctss., countess; Dan., Daniel; dau., daughter; d., died; D.B., Domesday Book; dchss., duchess; Edw., Edward; Eliz., Elizabeth; fam., family; f., father; f.w.k., framework-knitter; Fred., Frederick; Geo., George; Geof., Geoffrey; Gil., Gilbert; grds., grandson; Hen., Henry; hosp., hospital; Humph., Humphrey; hund., hundred; inc., inclosure; ind., industry; Jas., James; Jos., Joseph; Kath., Katherine; Lawr., Lawrence; Ld., Lord; man., manor; mfg./mfr., manufacturing/manufacturer; Marg., Margaret; m., married; Mat., Matthew; Mic., Michael; Nat., Nathaniel; par., parish; pk., park; Phil., Philip; pop., population; rly., railway; Reg., Reginald; Revd., Reverend; Ric., Richard; riv., river; Rob., Robert; Rog., Roger; Rom., Roman; Sam., Samuel; sch., school; Sim., Simon; sis., sister; s., son; Steph., Stephen; T.R.E., Tempore Regis Edwardi; Thos., Thomas; Vct., Viscount; Vsctss., Viscountess; Wal., Walter; wid., widow; w., wife; Wm., William.

INDEX TO VOLUMES I—III

INDEX TO VOLUMES I—III

INDEX TO VOLUMES I—III

INDEX TO VOLUMES I—III

INDEX TO VOLUME I—III

INDEX TO VOLUMES I—III

INDEX TO VOLUMES I—III

CORRIGENDA TO VOLUME II

page 6*a*, lines 15–16	*delete* 'of the abbots, Geoffrey, seems to have been a married man, and one'
page 6, note 25	*delete whole note*
page 7*a*, line 3	*for* 'Geoffrey' *read* 'Godfrey'
page 58, line 19	*for* 'Braunston' *read* 'Braunstone'
page 64, line 8	*for* '(d. 1569)' *read* '(d. 1571)'
page 64, line 9	*for* '(d. 1593)' *read* '(d. 1592)'
page 127, line 7	*for* 'Bodenz' *read* 'Boden'
page 188, line 12 from end	*for* 'Humphrey Markham' *read* 'John Markham'
page 218, line 5	*for* 'Horsham (Surr.)' *read* 'Horsham (Suss.)'

35.00

PATHOLOGY ILLUSTRATED

For Churchill Livingstone:
Commissioning Editor: Timothy Horne
Project Editor: Dilys Jones
Indexer: Helen McKillop
Project Controller: Nancy Arnott
Sales Promotion Executive: Maria O'Connor